STUDIES IN THE TRANSMISSION OF TEXTS & IDEAS

15

EDITOR IN CHIEF

Pieter d'Hoine

EDITORIAL BOARD

Anthony Dupont
Michèle Goyens
Marleen Reynders
Stefan Schorn

SUBMISSIONS
SHOULD BE SENT TO

Marleen Reynders
marleen.reynders@kuleuven.be

True Warriors?
Negotiating Dissent
in the Intellectual Debate
(*c.* 1100–1700)

Edited by
Guy CLAESSENS
Fabio DELLA SCHIAVA
Wouter DRUWÉ
Wim FRANÇOIS

BREPOLS

© 2023, Brepols Publishers n.v., Turnhout, Belgium.

All rights reserved.
No part of this publication may be reproduced,
stored in a retrieval system, or transmitted,
in any form or by any means, electronic, mechanical,
photocopying, recording, or otherwise
without the prior permission of the publisher.

D/2023/0095/252

DOI 10.1484/M.LECTIO-EB.5.135093

ISBN 978-2-503-60763-4

e-ISBN 978-2-503-60764-1

ISSN 2565-8506

e-ISSN 2565-9626

Printed in the EU on acid-free paper.

TABLE OF CONTENTS

Wouter Druwé – Wim François
Introduction   9

Anita Traninger
Jousting Schoolmen: Managing Dissent in Scholastic Culture   25

Part 1
MIDDLE AGES (12TH – 15TH CENTURIES)

Dinah Wouters
Preposterous Debates: Parodies of Debate in Latin Literature before 1200   57

Siria De Francesco
Sulle tracce della Querelle du Roman de la Rose. *Alcune osservazioni su un anonimo* explicit *del MS Ludwig XV 7 (83.MR.177), J. Paul Getty Museum, Los Angeles*   91

Jacob Langeloh
A Fair Fight or a Rigged Jury? The Council of Basel (1431–1449) and the Structure of its Debate about the Immaculate Conception   117

Yelena Mazour-Matusevich
An Intellectual Warrior and his Hero: Johannes Wessel Gansfort (1420–1489) and Jean Gerson (1363–1429)   151

Marta Celati
Condemning Political Dissent and Anti-Princely Views in Fifteenth-Century Milanese Literature   177

TABLE OF CONTENTS

Part 2
EARLY MODERN PERIOD
(16ᵀᴴ – 18ᵀᴴ CENTURIES)

Antonio Gerace
Thomas Stapleton ed Elisabetta I: una relazione impossibile — 217

Giovanni Minnucci
Sileant theologi: nec alienam temnant temere disciplinam. La controversia fra giuristi e teologi nel I libro del De nuptiis *di Alberico Gentili: nuove indagini* — 245

Leen Spruit
Strategies and Agency in the Censorship of Modern Science and Natural Philosophy: Some Case Studies — 273

Mathilde Albisson
L'Inquisition espagnole, arbitre des controverses entre les ordres religieux (XVIIe siècle) — 303

Magdalena Ryszka-Kurczab
Vernacular Religious Disputes in the Polish-Lithuanian Commonwealth during the Later Sixteenth and Early Seventeenth Centuries — 311

Elena Dahlberg
Latin versus the Vernacular in Seventeenth-Century Uppsala. Johannes Schefferus' Latin Attack on Olof Rudbeck's Swedish Dissection Programme — 367

Laura Beck Varela
Historia litteraria iuris. Mapping Controversies in Eighteenth-Century Jurisprudence — 393

Name Index — 437

WOUTER DRUWÉ – WIM FRANÇOIS
KU Leuven

INTRODUCTION

The Roman third-century jurist Ulpian remarked that men have a natural inclination towards dissent (*naturalis ad dissentiendum facultas*; cf. Digest 4.8.17.6). History seems to have proven him right. Dissent, polemics and rivalry have always been at the centre of intellectual development. The scholarly *Streitkultur* was given a fresh impetus by the newly founded universities in the High Middle Ages and later turned into a quintessential part of early modern intellectual life, with the emergence of the Protestant Reformation creating a new momentum. It was not only mirrored in various well-known intellectual debates and controversies, but also embodied in numerous literary genres and non-literary modes of expression, as well as discursive or political strategies. Moreover, the harsh debates notwithstanding, consensus was also actively searched for, both with particular disciplines and within society as a whole.

This volume collects thirteen contributions by scholars from fields as diverse as history of literature, political history, history of philosophy, ecclesiastical history and legal history. All chapters reflect papers given at the 9th LECTIO International Conference, entitled *True Warriors? Negotiating Dissent in the Intellectual Debate (c. 1100–1700)*, held in Leuven on 11–13 December 2019. The contributions largely speak for themselves. The purpose of this introduction is primarily to point at a few general threads across the different chapters. This volume's contributions, thus, reflect *inter alia* upon the rules and conventions of the intellectual debate, upon the media used to negotiate disagreements, as well as upon the role of formal institutions created to judge and decide in cases of dissent.

Rules and Conventions of the Intellectual Debate

Establishing and Re-thinking the Framework for the Intellectual Debate

From the twelfth century onwards, rules and conventions that allowed for a 'serious play' within the intellectual debate have been developed. Thus, at the medieval universities, a culture of *disputationes* was established. Often, terms related to war and conflict are used to describe the *disputatio*, which functioned as a frame to channel the young academics' agression. Temporal and procedural boundaries within which to discuss, or — metaphorically — to 'fight', have been imposed, as **Anita Traninger** sets out in the opening contribution to this volume. As 'true warriors', and following specified rules that were institutionalized, the students and scholars went into the debating arena. It was a game, but not without real-life consequences. Winning the game could make a career, as — so Traninger — cardinal Cajetan (Tommaso de Vio, 1469–1534) experienced after having beaten Giovanni Pico della Mirandola (1463–1494) in a *disputatio* in 1494. Nonetheless, the consequences of losing this institutionalized debate were not so dramatic as they would have been without the boundaries offered by the university's debating framework. Traninger explains how managing dissent and creating spaces for freedom of speech thus went together. In the *disputationes de quolibet*, for instance, any topic could be discussed, albeit only through a particular set of 'speech acts'. Traninger's contribution interestingly discerns three different speech acts. A first typical speech act was that of *distinguere*, making distinctions and thus opening up a debate whilst remaining within a wider framework. Another speech act was that of *disputative loqui*, a way of speaking and arguing that is peculiar to the context of disputations, and that does not necessarily equal one's own opinion. A final speech act mentioned by Traninger, is that of *philosophice loqui*, giving the opportunity to reason in terms of probability.

Nonetheless, the traditional framework of *disputationes*, with those three speech acts, was not the only and definitive framework for channeling intellectual debate. Even before the first universities had been founded and the method of *disputatio* had been formally established, some rules for intellectual debates already existed, and were even the object of mockery and humour; they were laughed with and ridiculed. Thus, **Dinah Wouters**, in her contribution, discusses medieval Latin debate poetry before 1200, which often had a parodic character. And many years later, in the seventeenth century, once the societal and religious situation had profoundly changed, a renegotiation and a rethinking of the traditional rules of the intellectual debate became necessary, as **Magdalena Ryszka-Kurczab** explains in her contribution on (vernacular) religious disputations in multi-confessional Poland and Lithuania in the sixteenth and early seventeenth centuries. The Warsaw Confederation (1573) had ensured religious peace and tolerance in the Polish-Lithuanian Commonwealth. This also allowed for a more open and public participation to disputations by representatives of different Christian denominations. The precise framework of the *disputatio* did no longer have to comply with all traditional requirements for academic *disputationes*, but could now be agreed upon between the parties to the debate themselves. They had to agree in advance upon the exact topic, the duration, the venue, the positioning of the disputants in the venue, and even the adherence (or not) to a particular argumentative style, etc. Ryszka-Kurczab discusses how this often required negotiations, which were not free from strategic choices. Thus, she describes the different stances taken by Calvinists and Jesuits respectively with regard to disputations with the Polish Brethren, a radical anti-Trinitarian Protestant group. Whereas Ryszka-Kurczab still describes a case-by-case renegotiation of the *disputatio* framework in a religious context, **Traninger** explains how by the end of the seventeenth century the *disputatio* practice as a whole was called into question, even in academia itself, for instance by the jurist and philosopher Christian Thomasius (1655–1725) in 1691. Academics should henceforth only defend the theses which they could personally adhere to, so Thomasius.

The Evidence Used during an Intellectual Debate

As aforementioned, between approximately 1200 and 1650, the *disputatio* practice was well established in academia. Also outside of academia, frameworks for the intellectual debate were present. Thus, Church councils were held, where the debate had to follow very precise rules of procedure. Nonetheless, even within such a formal framework, discussion as to the kinds of arguments that could be used and the evidence that could be invoked, remained important, as **Jakob Langeloh** discusses in his contribution on the Council of Basel (1436) and its debate on the Immaculate Conception of Mary. In the opening sermon to that debate, the Franciscan preacher Jean de Rouvroy used three types of sources to defend the truth of Mary's Immaculate Conception: *auctoritates*, *rationes*, and *miracula*. De Rouvroy's approach led to a major discussion with the Dominican opponents, most notably on the admissibility of rational arguments and miracles. Langeloh sets out how the Dominican Giovanni di Montenero considered arguments based on reason (*ratio*) as less effective than those based on *auctoritates* like Holy Scripture or Church Fathers. Di Montenero also argued that miracles, as they could never go against the Church's teachings, could not be used to defend a particular doctrine which had not yet been formulated by the Church. In his opinion, one could only discern a true miracle after having defined Christian doctrine.

Auctoritates were undoubtedly the most used evidence, in Church councils, but also in academia. The way in which those authorities were adduced, differed often from author to author. Some authors had a particular 'devotion' for a specific 'intellectual hero'. A very good example hereof is given by **Yelena Mazour-Matusevich** in her contribution on Johannes Wessel Gansfort (1429–1489) and his reliance on the works and personality of Jean Gerson (1363–1429). Wessel Gansfort drew on Gerson in many ways, that included — but were not limited to — his academic writings on fundamental theology. He was also inspired by Gerson for personal reasons. Mazour-Matusevich shows how Wessel Gansfort drew on Gerson for his own spiritual and social life too. Wessel Gansfort also learned from Gerson how to manage dissent; both understood that when dealing with complex theological questions, it was essential not to scandalize the less educated faithful, 'those who were of slower apprehension' (*populus non capax veritatis*), an insight which determined their attitude to theological intellectual debate.

Other authors loved — in an intellectual debate — to refer to historical examples, both in political and in religious disputes.

Thus, **Marta Celati** explains how, in fifteenth-century Milan, political opponents to the duke, like the humanist Cola Montano (*c.* 1440–1482) associated the Milanese duke Galeazzo Maria Sforza, who would get murdered in 1476, with the Roman king Tarquinius Superbus. The same Montano had also praised Brutus and Cassius for their killing of the 'tyrant' Julius Caesar. Several other Milanese humanist authors, however, praised their dukes, and used historical examples in order to stress the importance of political unity over and above a misunderstood freedom (*libertas*). Thus, Francesco Filelfo (1398–1481), for instance, referred to how rebellions had often been suppressed by rulers before, and how that had consistently served as a guarantee to the *bonum commune*, the common good. **Antonio Gerace** also deals with the use of historical examples in negotiating dissent. His contribution focuses on the theologian Thomas Stapleton (1535–1598), who was an Elizabethan exile having taken refuge in the Southern Low Countries. Stapleton used several historical analogies taken from the history of Christianity as a retorical tool in order to attack the policies of the English Queen Elizabeth I. Thus, Gerace shows how Stapleton compared Elizabeth to the Arian emperor Valens and to Huneric, King of the Vandals, often, however, by twisting historical reality to a rather important extent in order to fit his purpose. Stapleton's *Promptuaria* — which were primarily meant to help priests with their preaching activities — thus indeed also constitute invective literature.

Disciplinary Boundaries

In medieval and early modern intellectual debate, also the boundaries between the disciplines mattered. In the present volume, two contributions deal with the role of those disciplinary boundaries. Thus, in his contribution, **Giovanni Minnucci** refers to a debate on the legitimacy of theatre plays that had arisen in England around 1593 between the jurist Alberico Gentili (1552–1602), regius professor of civil law in Oxford, and the Puritan theologian John Rainolds (1549–1607). Gentili used his own disciplinary formation as a jurist to set it out against and — by doing so — to disqualify his opponent. *Sileant theologi; nec alienam temnant temere disciplinam*, as Minnucci quotes a passage from Gentili's

Disputationes de nuptiis. According to Gentili, theologians should only occupy themselves with matters religious, i.e. with the so-called *ius religionis*, which regulates the relation between men and God, the forum of conscience. In matters political, however, and — more broadly — with regard to *ius humanum*, which regulates all relations between men, theologians were not qualified, so Gentili. He added that *ius religionis* roughly corresponded to the first table of the Decalogue, whereas *ius humanum* was related to the second table. Unsurprisingly, the theologian Rainolds did not agree with this division of competence. To the contrary, theology was — Rainolds argued — the sole competent discipline to interpret the whole of the Sacred Scripture, including the second table of the Decalogue.

The relation between legal studies and other disciplines remained a difficult one. Still in the eighteenth century, jurists struggled with their position within the 'Republic of Letters'. In her contribution, **Laura Beck Varela** introduces a literary genre, known as *historia litteraria iuris*, which was used by jurists to self-fashion and emphasize the role of jurisprudence within that *respublica litterarum*. It is a specific subgenre of the *historia litteraria* movement, which had been common in the Holy Roman Empire in several academic disciplines, such as theology, medicine and philosophy, from the mid-seventeenth century onwards. Jurists who dedicated themselves to this literary genre, wished to portray themselves as *polyhistores*, true academics knowledgeable and interested in many fields. Whereas most juridical literature was self-referential and only meant for a readership of those trained in law, *historia litteraria iuris* was meant for a wider public. Simultaneously, this genre was also used to emphasize the academic character of the study of law, in a time when this was sometimes questioned. With that aim in mind, authors like Carl Ferdinand Hommel (1722–1781) referred to the debates on the authenticity of juridical documents like the *Authenticum* (with imperial constitutions) and the *Littera florentina* (which contains Justinian's Digest).

Language in the Intellectual Debate

The choice of language, and especially the choice between Latin and the vernacular, played an important role in the academic and extra-academic intellectual debate as well. Thus, **Magdalena Ryszka-Kurczab** explains that there was a lot of discussion as to the language to be used in religious disputations in Poland and Lithuania after the Confederation of Warsaw. Thus, Calvinist disputants often wished to hold the disputations in the vernacular, as this would allow them to reach a wider public. Their Catholic opponents, and especially the Jesuits, were more reluctant to dispute in the vernacular. In their experience, disputations in the vernacular too often led to mockery and violence, when the public mood was getting heated. Calvinists, however, ascribed the reluctance to the Jesuits' fear that they would not be able to convince the public of their own arguments. Around 1677, the choice of language became also a controversial topic at the Swedish university of Uppsala, as **Elena Dahlberg** reveals in her contribution on a debate between the polymath Olef Rudbeck the Elder (1630–1702) and the philologist Johannes Schefferus (1621–1679). Rudbeck had published an announcement of a dissection of a human body; and he did so in Swedish. When Schefferus criticized Rudbeck for choosing Swedish as the language for this dissection and its announcement, the latter defended his choice with reference to Swedish's ancient Scythian origins, and to the possibility of thus informing a larger student public about human anatomy. Rudbeck realized that many students were no longer fluent in Latin. Although Schefferus was also aware of that fact, he found it a disgrace to the Uppsala university that Rudbeck gave in to those students. Schefferus stressed that Uppsala university, by doing so, would set itself apart from all other academies. When all universities across Europe would do so, every scholar would have to learn many languages, leaving less time for the actual scientific reflection. Moreover, students would be discouraged to learn Latin, and thus be deprived of the opportunity to form part of a Europe-wide scholarly community.

Nonetheless, sometimes research seems to have stressed the tensions between Latin and vernacular too much. Thus, **Dinah Wouters** challenges the discourse that parodic debate poetry was almost always written in the vernacular in order to contrast it with serious intellectual debate in Latin. Wouters falsifies that theory by discussing a sample of Latin debate poems, which date from the late ninth till the twelfth centuries. These poems cover mock debates, both in a classroom situation and in the (fictional) context of ecclesiastical and secular councils. These poems mainly parody the seriousness of many intellectual debates as such, rather than focusing on particular arguments used during such debates. Thus, Wouters shows that parody could very well be written in Latin too.

A Multiplicity of Media and Genres to Negotiate Dissent

A second recurring theme in this volume is the multiplicity of media and genres used to negotiate dissent. Several contributions refer to that aspect. Often, in one and the same dispute, several media and genres were combined.

One of the most popular ways of negotiating disagreements was undoubtedly the organization of academic disputations, live oral debates, as discussed in the opening contribution by **Anita Traninger**. Also in ecclesiastical councils, such as the Council of Basel, debates were held orally, even if the debaters — as **Jakob Langeloh** stressed — often decided to draft a more complete version of their arguments in writing. These writings were usually submitted after the oral defence. Also in case of public religious disputations, oral debates were held, often with a large audience. As aforementioned, that audience could have an important role in the debate, as the discussions on the choice of language in Poland and Lithuania — described by **Magdalena Ryszka-Kurczab** — show. Self-evidently, orality and trying to influence a public are also crucial to the preaching practice. Preaching could indeed be used as a way to negotiate dissent too. In order to equip priests with information for their predication, the 'controversialist' Catholic theologian Thomas Stapleton wrote a *Promptuarium catholicum* and a *Promptuarium morale*. In both sermon books, based on our author's academic biblical work and discussed in this volume by **Antonio Gerace**, Stapleton actively criticized the Calvinist theses, 'heresies' in the eyes of the Roman Church. However, the question remains along what lines the content of these Latin-language sermon books found a way into (vernacular) sermons to the faithful flock.

Often, dissent was also negotiated through writing, and that in many different forms. We have already discussed how poetry was a means to reflect in a humouristic way on the forms and structures that were used to debate, a kind of meta-reflection, as discussed by **Dinah Wouters**. Medieval parodic debate literature's main aim was, however, to entertain by drawing analogies to more formal ways of debate, and thereby reversing the roles. Whereas this particular genre of entertaining parodic poetry should not be understood as a criticism of the forms of intellectual debate, it is certain that in other situations poetry was used as a medium to negotiate one's dissent on a particular topic. Thus, **Marta Celati** discusses an Italian poem from 1477 (*Capitolo sulla morte di Galeazzo Maria Sforza*) by the Milanese humanist Antonio Cornazzano (1430–1484). In that poem, Cornazzano portrays duke Francesco Sforza as an ideal ruler, and reacts against rebellious movements, especially against the conspirator Giovanni Andrea Lampugnani (*c.* 1430–1476). Poetry itself could at its turn also lead to new dissent, as is shown by the very tense dispute regarding the thirteenth-century *Roman de la Rose*, discussed by **Siria De Francesco**. Interestingly, when it concerned the dispute itself, Christine de Pisan (1364–1430) chose for prose rather than poetry to negotiate her dissent, in order to follow the style of her adversaries: *comme la matiere ne le requiere, autressi est droit que je suive le stile de mes assaillans* (as quoted and analyzed in De Francesco's contribution).

Another traditional medium to negotiate dissent in writing were letters. Thus, **Giovanni Minnucci** describes the epistolary controversies between Gentili and Rainolds. Some of these letters were private ones, others have even been printed and thus made public. These letters were often used, either explicitly or implicitly, in other types of writings too, such as *disputationes* and treatises, written by Gentili and Rainolds in their fierce debate on the respective disciplinary boundaries of theology and legal studies. A similar multiplicity of media and genres to negotiate disagreements — where letters were an important part of — is also attested for several political controversies in fifteenth-century Milan, as **Marta Celati** shows in her contribution. She refers, for instance, to the fact that the Milanese humanist Francesco Filelfo kept a collection of his *epistolae*, which implied that they were probably not exclusively meant as private correspondence.

In her chapter on the controversy surrounding the *Roman de la Rose*, **Siria De Francesco** also deals with another art form, namely that of visual arts, especially miniatures, and with how they were used to take a stance. She focuses especially on manuscript Ludwig XV 7. The miniatures in that manuscript were used to strengthen a particular reading of certain controversial passages of the *Roman de la Rose*. Thus, De Francesco explains how the miniaturist wished to re-establish the close link between creature and Creator which — according to critics like Jean Gerson — had been neglected by the author of the *Roman de la Rose*, Jean de Meun.

A particular type of writing, primarily used to map dissent rather than to engage in it, is presented by **Laura Beck Varela** in the form of the aforementioned *historia litteraria iuris*. In her contribution, Beck Varela pays special attention to the *Litteratura iuris* by Carl Ferdinand Hommel (1722–1781), first published in 1761. Despite its primary aim to map dissent, sometimes the author couldn't resist to also take a position. Thus, Beck Varela states how the Protestant jurist Hommel, when discussing the debates between specialists of civil and canon law, was critical of the canon lawyers' opinions. Also, when Hommel had been engaged in a dispute himself, and mapped that dispute, he repeated his own position and used the opportunity to refer to his own work. Sometimes, when referring to recent events where jurists were belittling and insulting each other, the *historia litteraria iuris* in Hommel's *Litteratura* even gets a parodic character, aimed to communicate — in a humouristic way — some basic rules for academic disputes.

The Role of Formal Institutions in Judging Cases of Dissent in the Intellectual Debate

A final connecting thread between several contributions in this volume concerns the role formal institutions played in judging and deciding upon cases of disagreements in the intellectual debate. **Jakob Langeloh** briefly touches on the role of an ecclesiastical council, especially the Council of Basel, to decide on the question of Mary's Immaculate Conception, though the doctrinal decree in this regard was not accepted there, since the council ended in being considered schismatic. This volume, however, mainly pays attention to the role of several institutions of censorship.

Thus, in his contribution, **Leen Spruit** deals with the Roman Congregations of the Holy Office and of the Index. He especially discusses the agency and the defense strategies of authors whose books on science and natural philosophy have been subject to censorship by those Roman congregations. Thus, Spruit delves into the 1592–1594 proceedings with regard to the censoring of works by the Neoplatonic philosopher Francesco Patrizi (1529–1597). He shows how Patrizi had access to the censor's assessment. This access to the documentation allowed Patrizi to react to the criticism and to try to negotiate on the requested corrections, albeit with only very limited success. Spruit explains how, 160 years later, in 1752, when the *Lettera apologetica* by Raimondo di Sangro (1710–1771) was put on the Index, the latter was also given access to the assessment of his work. With the support of the Neapolitan plenipotentiary to the Holy See, Geronimo Sersale, di Sangro submitted a petition to Pope Benedict XIV. Spruit shows how the Pope actively considered the request (even if the final decision was to keep the book on the Index). Finally, Spruit deals with the 1688–1697 atheism trials in Naples, where several proponents of the scientific theory of atomism were among the accused. Here, too, the judicial proceedings allowed the accused for a certain degree of agency, bringing witnesses in their defence. Despite this agency, however, time and again, it seems that the manoeuvres by the authors themselves (whilst noteworthy) only had minimal results, definitely when compared to the system of reading permits, i.e. the permission to individual scientists to read books otherwise included in the Index. These reading permits — so Spruit — were granted regularly.

Whereas Spruit focused on the Roman Congregations, **Mathilde Albisson** studies the Spanish Inquisition. That institution had originally been founded to deal with converted Jews and converted Muslims who secretly adhered to their original faith and its practices. After the Council of Trent, however, the Spanish Inquisition also tried to contain dissent within Catholic theology and between different theological strands, in order to preserve the doctrinal unity of the Church. Albisson shows how difficult this often was, as the Spanish Inquisition itself was divided. Internal struggles between members of different religious orders, for instance, endangered the neutrality of the censorship proceedings. A censor's belonging to a particular religious order often impacted his decision. Albisson illustrates this by elaborating two examples. First, she discusses the famous (or ill-famed) controversy from the late sixteenth century between Dominicans and Jesuits on grace and free will, known as the *de auxiliis gratiae* debates. She shows how the Spanish Inquisition was so internally divided that it decided to pass on the matter to Rome, and thus gave up some of its own censorial prerogative. Secondly, Albisson deals with a dispute between Carmelites and (mainly) Jesuits on the prophetic origins of the Carmelite order, starting in the 1630s and revived in the 1690s. Also in this case, Albisson points out how long the Spanish Inquisition took to come to its conclusions, and how it tried to take a mediating position, sanctioning the excesses on either side, but without taking a stance as to the core of the dispute.

Structure of the Volume

In this introduction, a few overarching themes have been presented. Undoubtedly, many more aspects could have been highlighted, as the contributions consider a very rich variety of topics with regard to the negotiation of dissent from the twelfth till the eighteenth centuries. Apart from the opening contribution by **Anita Traninger**, we chose to structure the different contributions in a more or less chronological order. A first part concerns the period until the end of the fifteenth century, with the contributions by **Dinah Wouters** on Latin debate poetry, **Siria De Francesco** on the controversy around the *Roman de la Rose*, **Jakob Langeloh** on the debate over Mary's Immaculate Conception at the Council of Basel, **Yelena Mazour-Matusevich** on Wessel Gansfort, and **Marta Celati** on political controversies in fifteenth-century Milan. A second and final part concerns the early modern period, from the sixteenth till the eighteenth centuries. This part contains the contributions by **Antonio Gerace** on Thomas Stapleton's *Promptuaria*, by **Giovanni Minnucci** on the debate between Rainolds and Gentili, by **Leen Spruit** on censorship by the Roman Congregations of the Holy Office and the Index, by **Mathilde Albisson** on the Spanish Inquisition, by **Magdalena Ryszka-Kurczab** on vernacular religious disputations in Poland and Lithuania, by **Elena Dahlberg** on Swedish and Latin at the university of Uppsala, and by **Laura Beck Varela** on the *historia litteraria iuris*.

Acknowledgements

The editors wish to express their gratitude to all the authors who contributed to the conference and were willing to rework their papers into scholarly articles. The quality of their essays has also profited from the thorough but positive feedback offered by a group of reviewers. The editors' warmest thanks extend further to *Lectio: KU Leuven Institute for the Study of the Transmission of Texts, Ideas and Images in Antiquity, the Middle Ages and the Renaissance*, its director Prof. Pieter D'Hoine, former director Prof. Wim Decock, and the managing director Ms. Marleen Reynders, as well as to the editorial board of the book series *Lectio: Studies in the Transmission of Texts & Ideas* and Brepols Publishers in Turnhout. They are also grateful to Ms. Linde Van den Eede for her invaluable help in making the index of this volume.

Some Further Readings

Anderson, D. K. (2014), *Martyrs and Players in Early Modern England. Tragedy, Religion and Violence on Stage*, Farnham: Ashgate.

Baumann, U., Becker, A., & Laureys, M. (eds) (2015), *Polemik im Dialog des Renaissance-Humanismus: Formen, Entwicklungen und Funktionen*, Göttingen: V&R unipress, Bonn University Press (Super Alta Perennis, 19).

Bazàn, B. C. et al. (eds) (1985), *Les questions disputées et les questions quodlibétiques dans les facultés de théologie, de droit et de médecine*, Turnhout: Brepols (Typologie des sources du Moyen Âge occidental, 44–45).

Bremer, K. & Spoerhase, C. (eds) (2011), *Gelehrte Polemik: Intellektuelle Konfliktverschärfungen um 1700*, Frankfurt am Main: Vittorio Klostermann.

Broggio, P. (2009), *La teologia e la politica: controversie dottrinali, Curia romana e Monarchia spagnola tra Cinque e Seicento*, Firenze: Leo S. Olschki Editore.

Bouchard, C. B. (2003), *'Every Valley Shall Be Exalted': The Discourse of Opposites in Twelfth-Century Thought*, Ithaca, NY: Cornell University Press.

Celati, M. (2021), *Conspiracy Literature in Early Renaissance Italy: Historiography and Princely Ideology*, Oxford: Oxford University Press.

Chang, K. (2004), 'From Oral Disputation to Written Text: The Transformation of the Dissertation in Early Modern Europe', in *History of Universities*, 19/2, p. 129–187.

Conley, T. (2010), *Toward a Rhetoric of Insult*, Chicago, IL: The University of Chicago Press.

Dietl, C., Schmidt, B., & Stauffer, I. (eds) (2023), Special issue 'Words at War: "Invectivity" in Transformative Processes of the Sixteenth Century', in *The Journal of Early Modern Christianity*, 10/1.

Ellerbrock, D. et al. (2017), 'Invektivität – Perspektiven eines neuen Forschungsprogramms in den Kultur-und Sozialwissenschaften', in *Kulturwissenschaftliche Zeitschrift* 2/1, p. 2–24.

Fichte, J. G. et al. (eds) (2019), *Das Streitgedicht im Mittelalter*, Stuttgart: Hirzel (Relectiones, 6).

François, W. (2023), 'Augustinus und die Löwener Kontroversen über Prädestination, Gnade und freien Willen', in *„Totus noster?" Augustinus zwischen den Konfessionen*, ed. Günter Frank et al., Göttingen: Vandenhoeck & Ruprecht (Refo500 Academic Studies, 93), p. 189–215.

Fuchs, Th. (1995), *Konfession und Gespräch: Typologie und Funktion der Religionsgespräche in der Reformationszeit*, Köln: Böhlau Verlag (Norm und Struktur, 4).

Garavelli, B. (2006), *Il Dibattito sul Romanzo della Rosa di Christine de Pizan, Jean Gerson, Jean de Montreuil*, Milano: Medusa.

Goldgar, A. (1995), *Impolite Learning: Conduct and Community in the Republic of Letters, 1680–1750*, New Haven, CT: Yale University Press.

Grunert, F. & Vollhardt, F. (eds) (2007), *Historia literaria: Neuordnungen des Wissens im 17. und 18. Jahrhundert*, Berlin: Akademie Verlag.

Hempfer, K. (ed.) (2002), *Möglichkeiten des Dialogs: Struktur und Funktion einer literarischen Gattung zwischen Mittelalter und Renaissance in Italien*, Stuttgart: Franz Steiner (Text und Kontext, 15).

Horst, U. (1987), *Die Diskussion um die immaculata conceptio im Dominikanerorden: Ein Beitrag zur Geschichte der theologischen Methode*, Paderborn et al.: Schöningh (Veröffentlichungen des Grabmann-Institutes zur Erforschung der mittelalterlichen Theologie und Philosophie N.F., 34).

Hundt, M. (2022), *Sprachliche Aggression bei Martin Luther: Argumentationsformen und -funktionen am Beispiel der Streitschrift "Wider das Papsttum zu Rom vom Teufel gestiftet" (1545)*, Berlin: De Gruyter.

Kraye, J., Laureys, M., & Lines, D.A. (eds) (2023), *Management and Resolution of Conflict and Rivalries in Renaissance Europe*, Göttingen: V&R unipress, Bonn University Press (Super Alta Perennis, 25).

Laureys, M. & Simons, R. (eds) (2010), *Die Kunst des Streitens: Inszenierung, Formen und Funktionen öffentlichen Streits in historischer Perspektive*, Göttingen: V&R unipress, Bonn University Press (Super Alta Perennis, 10).

Lawn, B. (1993), *The Rise and Decline of the Scholastic 'Quaestio Disputata', with Special Emphasis on its Use in the Teaching of Medicine and Science*, Leiden: Brill (Education and Society in the Middle Ages and Renaissance, 2).

Lines, D.A., Laureys, M., & Kraye J. (eds) (2015), *Forms of Conflict and Rivalries in Renaissance Europe*, Göttingen: V&R unipress, Bonn University Press (Super Alta Perennis, 17).

Maierù, A. (1994), *University Training in Medieval Europe*, Leiden: Brill (Education and Society in the Middle Ages and Renaissance, 3).

Marcus, H. (2020), *Forbidden Knowledge: Medicine, Science, and Censorship in Early Modern Italy*, Chicago, IL & London: University of Chicago Press.

McWebb, C. (ed.) (2007), *Debating the Roman de la Rose: A Critical Anthology*, New York: Routledge (Routledge Medieval Texts).

Meyer, C. H. F. (2000), *Die Distinktionstechnik der Kanonistik des 12. Jahrhunderts: Ein Beitrag zur Wissenschaftsgeschichte des Hochmittelalters*, Leuven: Leuven University Press (Mediaevalia Lovaniensia. Series I, Studia, 29).

Novikoff, A. (2013), *The Medieval Culture of Disputation: Pedagogy, Practice, and Performance*, Philadelphia, PA: University of Pennsylvania Press.

Ong, W. J. (1983), *Ramus, Method, and the Decay of Dialogue: From the Art of Discourse to the Art of Reason*, Cambridge, MA: Harvard University Press.

Panou, N., & Schadee, H. (eds) (2018), *Evil Lords: Theories and Representations of Tyranny from Antiquity to the Renaissance*, Oxford: Oxford University Press.

Pettegree, A. (2005), *Reformation and the Culture of Persuasion*, Cambridge: Cambridge University Press.

Sablotny, A., Münkler, M. & Dröse, A. (eds) (2021), Special issue 'Invektive Gattungen', in *Kulturwissenschaftliche Zeitschrift,* 6/1.

Scharloth, J. (2017), 'Hassrede und Invektivität als Gegenstand der Sprachwissenschaft und Sprachphilosophie: Bausteine zu einer Theorie des Metainvektiven', in *Aptum,* 2, p. 116–132.

Schwerhoff, G. (2020), 'Invektivität und Geschichtswissenschaft: Konstellationen der Herabsetzung in historischer Perspektive – ein Forschungskonzept', in *Historische Zeitschrift* 311/1, p. 1–36.

Sère, B. (2018), *Les régimes de polémicité au Moyen Âge,* Rennes: PUR.

Weijers, O. (2013), *In Search of the Truth: A History of Disputation Techniques from Antiquity to Early Modern Times,* Turnhout: Brepols (Studies on the Faculty of Arts: History and Influence, 1).

Wijffels, A. (2019), '*Audiuntur theologi.* Legal Scholarship's Claim on the "Second Table" in Alberico Gentili's *De nuptiis* (1601)', in *De rebus divinis et humanis: Essays in Honour of Jan Hallebeek,* ed. H. Dondorp, M. Schermaier, & B. Sirks, Göttingen: Vandenhoeck & Ruprecht, p. 497–512.

ANITA TRANINGER
Freie Universität Berlin

JOUSTING SCHOOLMEN: MANAGING DISSENT IN SCHOLASTIC CULTURE

In December 1486, while in Rome, the young nobleman Giovanni Pico della Mirandola received a package from the printer's workshop. Pico was a temporary resident in the city; he originally came from the north of the Italian peninsula, from Concordia near Modena, where his family had dwelt at the castle of Mirandola for generations. Being many years younger than his brothers, Giovanni had been able to focus on his studies and invest his considerable fortune in the pursuit of scholarship. So by the time he arrived in Rome, he had already established a considerable reputation. What he received from Eucario Silber's workshop was a printing of 900 theses, fresh off the presses on December 7. They were meant to serve as the basis for a disputation before the collegium of cardinals; the disputation was to be chaired by the pope himself and was scheduled for the sixth of January, the feast day of Epiphany, in the following year.[1] Pico, the convenor of this event, was twenty-four years old at the time, and the disputation would have secured his academic fame, but his efforts ultimately came to nothing. The disputation had to be cancelled,[2] leaving posterity with the long list of theses and the introductory speech he prepared for the occasion. Later editors titled this speech

---

[1] For an edition based on the *editio princeps* and a modern English translation of the theses, see Farmer 1998.

[2] See di Napoli 1965, esp. ch. 2 'La disputa romana: I fatti', p. 81–137 and ch. 3 'La disputa romana: L'ortodossia delle tredici tesi', p. 139–194.

Oratio de dignitate hominis, and it would come to be regarded as the manifesto of the Renaissance philosophy of man.[3]

Despite this elevated status, the text remains very much tied to its original purpose. Pico described his enterprise in the terms of a scholastic disputation, a fact that has puzzled generations of Renaissance scholars, who struggled to reconcile Pico's humanist credentials with his reliance on humanism's abhorred Other, scholasticism.[4] What Pico hoped to achieve was not only the reconciliation of humanism and scholasticism, but of pagan wisdom and Christian belief. Pico aimed at demonstrating that the teachings of Zoroastrianism, Pythagoreanism, and the Kabbala coincide and converge with Christian doctrine. He also boasted that he could have added another 600 theses about the concordance between Platonism and Aristotelianism.[5] Despite its intellectual ambition, however, the *oratio* resembles not so much a philosophical treatise as the opening remarks for the ensuing debate. In the subsequent editions, neither the contextual information nor the hortatory tone has been edited out. Consequently, the *oratio* ends with a call to arms clearly intended to inaugurate the disputation:

> *Quod ut vobis re ipsa, patres colendissimi, iam palam fiat, ut desiderium vestrum, doctores excellentissimi, quos paratos accintosque exspectare pugnam non sine magna voluptate conspicio, mea longius oratio non remoretur, quod felix faustumque sit, quasi citante classico iam conseramus manus.*

> And now, most esteemed Fathers, in order that this claim [to syncretism] may be vindicated by the fact, and in order that my address may no longer delay the satisfaction of your desire — for I see, reverend doctors, with the greatest pleasure that you are armed and ready for the fight — let us now, with the

---

[3] Burckhardt 1955, p. 241; Cassirer 2002, p. 100; Garin 1973, p. 93; cf. also Craven's and Copenhaver's critical assessments in Craven 1981; Copenhaver 2019.

[4] On the importance of scholastic philosophy for Pico's thought, see Dulles 1941, esp. p. 25–45. Dulles differentiates between Paduan and Parisian scholasticism, with Pico categorised as a representative of Paduan scholasticism, which Dulles paints in brighter colours than its Parisian counterpart. The Paris faculty of theology, however, did indeed appreciate Pico and refused to condemn him as a heretic; see Farge 1985, p. 221; Renaudet, *Préréforme et humanisme*, p. 127–129. For Pico's extensive use of scholastic sources, see e.g. Caroti 2008; Edelheit 2011.

[5] Pico 1997, p. 76.

prayer that the outcome may be fortunate and favorable, as to the sound of a trumpet, join battle.[6]

This bellicose call to arms comes as a surprise and appears to be in stark contrast to the reconciliation project Pico had just described. The reason for this contrast resides in his methods. Although conceived as an exercise in reconciliation, the project was firmly anchored in the agonistic debating style created by and cultivated in the medieval universities.

It has long been observed that medieval philosophers and theologians often chose to speak of their activity in military terms, 'as clashes of arms, conflicts, or battles, often developing the metaphor at length.'[7] This tendency goes back to the very beginnings of the medieval university: Abelard, for example, described debates with William Campeaux as 'a full-fledged siege'. The medievalist Andrew Taylor interpreted the metaphor thus:

> Abelard's depiction of dialectic as a kind of war is no casual trope but reflects an actual transference of social energy, whereby ambitious young men channeled their aggression into the disputation of the schools, just as they might otherwise have channeled it into the regulated warfare of the early tournament, a social mechanism that was expanding at this time. In many ways the groups of students resembled the contemporary war bands of *juvenes* described by Georges Duby. The *juvenes*, the original knights errant, were young warriors who had no land and no immediate prospects and set out to make a name for themselves and win what booty they could. In this quest they wandered freely; indeed, wandering was considered a necessary part of their professional formation, a kind of *studium militiae*. [...] Much the same could be said of the students who moved from one cathedral school to another in the pursuit of logic. They too were young, ambitious, rowdy, and highly mobile, and they were often united by their loyalty to a charismatic leader who could best all comers in individual combat.[8]

---

[6] Pico 1997, p. 76; Pico 1956, p. 69.
[7] Taylor 1998, p. 16.
[8] Taylor 1998, p. 17–18; Duby 1977, p. 114–118. Taylor does not distinguish between clerics and laypeople, which may be neglected here as he is quoted for his broader argument about the channelling of aggression.

Among students, fights were not uncommon, emerging at times around disputations, and at other times involving local citizens. That students were subject to the universities' jurisdiction, and thus exempt from secular rule and able to escape punishment, was a constant source of disgruntlement.[9] Like the princely courts, however, the universities did not put up with the unruliness of these bands of young men. Both created institutionalised frames of practice in the hope that they would serve as training arenas for the respective social pursuits: namely, tournaments or jousts for knights, and disputation for scholars. Tournaments, in the sense of military games and exercises, had been around since antiquity as staged fights, apparently organised in preparation for real-life battles. Scholars agree that it is impossible to determine when the first 'medieval' tournament took place, but chronicles show a sudden surge of references to tournaments between 1125 and 1130, and in different parts of Europe (which is around the time the first universities emerged).[10] The term 'joust' specifically refers to contests conducted on horseback and with heavy lances, while 'tournament' includes all forms of staged fights, including on foot, with clubs, stone-throwing, and fist-fights. In the late Middle Ages and the Renaissance, the practice took two major paths of development:

> full-scale jousts became extremely expensive, surrounded by elaborate scenery and dramatic programmes, so that only the wealthiest princes could afford to mount them, while at the other extreme the individual challenge grew in popularity, as one of the few ways in which an up-and-coming knight could make his mark. The actual general *mêlée* or tournament proper, became increasingly rare, and the distinctive form of the sport was the *pas d'armes*, in which individuals or teams proclaimed their intention to defend a given place against all comers.[11]

Training for doing battle, however, was not really at the heart of the exercise, as Ruth Mazo Karras observed:

---

[9] See e.g. Maisel 1993; Krug-Richter 2004.
[10] Barber & Barker 1989, p. 16.
[11] Barber & Barker 1989, p. 107.

> The experiences of tournament and joust, with their focus on individual glory, taught the young knight a very different lesson from the discipline needed for an actual campaign, and in practice, except for certain periods of the Hundred Years War, it was tournaments rather than wars that tended to bring a young knight his reputation.[12]

Equally, a successful disputation could make or break a career. Cardinal Cajetan, for instance, who played a decisive role in the Luther Affair, was fast-tracked in the Church after he had beaten the by then universally admired Giovanni Pico della Mirandola in disputation in 1494.[13]

Importantly, neither phenomenon was limited to the Middle Ages. Jousting continued to occupy the imagination of early modern princes. Literary texts, in particular the *Amadís de Gaula* and the cycles of chivalric novels that emerged in its wake, supplied the plotlines for ever-more-extravagant tournaments, including those hosted by Emperor Charles V and his son Philipp II.[14] When Charles V staged a series of tournaments in celebration of the birth of his son Philipp in 1527, the imperial ambassador remarked that they surpassed even the adventures of Amadís.[15] The universities, on the other hand, upheld disputation as their core intellectual activity until well into the seventeenth century and, in some parts of Europe, even the eighteenth.[16]

Serious Play

Both frameworks, the culture of tournaments and the practice of scholastic disputation, drew on youthful male aggression and developed, over time, sets of rules that managed and tamed the tempers that inevitably flared up in antagonistic confrontation.[17]

---

[12] Karras 2003, p. 41.

[13] Dulles 1941, p. 34–35; Wicks 1983, p. 13–14. For a biographical sketch of Cajetan in English, see Wicks 1978.

[14] Parker 2014, n. 7.

[15] Frieder 2008, p. 37. Fallows 2010, p. 21, quoting Megías 2000. See also Édouard 2005, p. 38–39.

[16] Weijers 2002, p. 25.

[17] Cf. Ong 1983, p. 139–140, on how medieval and early modern logic was informed by its juvenile practitioners; and Feingold 2001, p. 147–156 for exam-

In my contribution to this volume about managing dissent in the learned world of the Middle Ages and the Renaissance, the point I will make is more far-reaching than just interpreting the two practices as instances of the framing and taming of juvenile male agonality. Rather, I would like to propose that tournaments and disputations share one important trait: they offered institutional frameworks which allowed for action with real-world consequences — compare the making or breaking of a reputation and the forging of careers just mentioned — while suspending, at the same time, other aspects by imposing frames, marking the beginning and the end of an encounter, and implementing complex rules and customs. Tournaments and disputations were, to use the words of Gregory Bateson, instances of serious play, where 'the playful nip denotes the bite, but does not denote that which would be denoted by the bite.'[18]

How was dissent managed within the university? The university made provisions not only to frame disputations by pragmatic arrangements, as would equally happen for tournaments, but also by connecting disputations with particular speech acts that modern theory would locate somewhere between fact and fiction — though this characterisation does not at all do justice to the sophistication of scholastic argumentation. What I offer is an apologia of the early modern university's fine-grained conventions of discourse, which, on the one hand, served the ultimate purpose of managing dissent, but which, on the other, created spaces for freedom of speech that have yet to be sufficiently acknowledged.

The chapter proceeds in three steps: First I look at attempts to manage dissent by delimiting the range of topics that could be debated and at the notion of *exercitatio*, which does not simply refer to propaedeutic exercises. I then discuss the significance of the roles adopted in disputation; and finally I turn to three characteristic speech acts: *distinguere*, *disputative loqui*, and *philosophice loqui*.

---

ples of the continued physical disputes. With a view to commonalities between rhetorical and dialectical education, see the chapter on 'disputatiousness' in Sloane, p. 80–130.

[18] Bateson 2000, p. 183.

Delimiting Issues

Thanks to the research of Olga Weijers and others, it is well known today that disputation, as it took shape in the medieval university, differed from ancient dialectical practice and also cannot be explained in its entirety as deriving from the Aristotelian *Organon*.[19] Nonetheless medieval disputation did, of course, take up syllogistic reasoning as expounded in the *Prior* and *Posterior Analytics*, and it also imported some aspects of the pragmatics of dispute as set out in the *Topics*. The constellation of 'questioner' and 'answerer' that informs Aristotle's *Topics* was transformed into a three-part arrangement: a presiding master, a respondent, who is supposed to defend the master's position, and an opponent, who attacks that position.[20] In particular, the role of opponent must be understood as a function that could be adopted by a group of scholars in one particular disputation. Yet while scholastic disputation involved more than two discussants, it was nevertheless concerned with contrasting just two sides. The primary objective of dialectical teaching, which was at the core of the beginners' curriculum in the arts faculties, was to inculcate the ability to argue for or against any proposed thesis. This objective was not only a precept of medieval dialecticians, it was equally stressed by those works that were pushed by humanists as replacements for the old textbooks, such as Petrus Hispanus' *Summulae logicales*. George of Trebizond, the Byzantine scholar whose manual on dialectics was written before 1440 and then seen into print for the first time in Paris by Jacques Lefèvre d'Étaples in 1506, held forth on this very aim of dialectics: 'Est autem fructus totius artis dialecticae, huiusmodo de re aliqua in utramque partem disputare.' 'It is thus the fruit of the whole art of dialectics to dispute in this way about any topic on either side.'[21]

Teaching at the medieval university revolved around the *quaestio*, which, in line with the antagonistic format, typically took the form 'whether ... or' (*utrum ... an*) and informed engagement with

---

[19] For a brief account, see Weijers 2013, ch. 3.

[20] On the history of *opponens* and *respondens* as roles in disputation, cf. Bazàn 1985, p. 39–42; and Moraux 1968.

[21] George of Trebizond 1539, p. 193. On Trebizond's *Dialectica*, see Monfasani 1976, p. 294–337.

texts, magisterial teaching, and learned debate, that is, the *disputatio*.[22] A question could be the starting point or, in a different sense, the result of a disputation. The *quaestio disputata* appears to have emerged as an edited compilation of the arguments pro and contra forwarded in a debate; nevertheless the *quaestio disputata* was not a transcript of the debate, and apparently the genre soon became quite independent of actual disputations.[23] When it served as the starting point for a disputation, the *quaestio* was answered either in the negative or in the positive in a series of theses. These theses were propounded one after another by the *respondens* and duly attacked, one after the other, by the *opponens*. This could be described as the academic equivalent of the *pas d'armes*, a tournament technique popular in the Renaissance, which placed a single knight in the middle of the arena who would then take on all comers. A disputation is thus not a dialogue but a contest in which one of two possible answers to a question is tested in a collaborative effort. Consequently it does not come as a surprise that the schoolmen began to leave out the question altogether and turned straight to writing theses as the starting point for debate.[24]

In the earliest stages of its development, Gilbert de la Porrée, also known as Gilbert of Poitiers or Gilbertus Porretta (*c.* 1075–1154), laid down the conditions under which a question would qualify as a scholastic *quaestio*. Not all disagreements give rise to a *quaestio*, he says in his commentary on Boethius' *De trinitate*; if one of the sides cannot be substantiated with probable arguments or if it is impossible to argue for the truth of the one and the falseness of the other side, there is no *quaestio* to be disputed. Only if there is a question in which both sides are equally probable (*cujus vero utraque pars argumenta veritatis habere videtur*), thus only if there is justified doubt, does a *quaestio* emerge.[25]

---

[22] Even if the pattern of *utrum ... an* was not spelled out in each case, open questions were not typically debated at a disputation. Cf. Schulthess and Imbach's pun on *Zweifel*, meant to conjoin the characteristic epistemic stance of doubt with the two (*zwei*) options pondered in each *quaestio*. See Schulthess & Imbach 2002, p. 148.

[23] See Marenbon 1991, p. 28–31.

[24] Chang 2004, p. 135.

[25] Gilbert of Poitiers, *Commentaria*, in *Patrologia Latina* 64, 1258A. On this definition, see Grabmann 1911, vol. 2, p. 424–430.

This definition clearly set a standard to which, however, the schoolmen did not adhere in practice (just as the jousters were not impressed by the Church's stark warnings against their tournaments). As Brian Lawn has commented, '[...] we find the *quaestio*, especially in Paris, escaping from the narrow bounds of this definition and embracing every kind of enunciation, even statements about which no doubt at all seemed to exist.'[26] Managing dissent by limiting the issues that can or should be debated was a noble and reasonable idea. It was quickly superseded, however, by the ongoing practice of disputation, which was omnivorous in the sense that anything and everything could be debated. The medieval university even invented a dedicated format, the *disputatio de quolibet*, held on feast days throughout the year, which allowed for anyone present (*a quolibet*) to bring up any topic for debate (*de quolibet*).[27] With disputation being in fact omnivorous, it was all the more important to safeguard it by other means that would convey the idea of serious play.

exercitatio

In the setting of the university, one could be asked to act as a respondent or opponent at any time. This circumstance required the ability to separate the task of producing the strongest possible argument from any desire to make a case for personal convictions. A premium was placed on an equal facility in defending or opposing a particular thesis. While this requirement may be taken as a call for an encyclopaedic education, it was also a safeguard against prolonged dissent. This is exactly the theme to which Heinrich Bebel, a professor of rhetoric in Tübingen who was crowned *poeta laureatus* in 1501, turned in his *Comoedia de optimo studio iuvenum*. He wrote the play specifically for the occasion of the celebration of his promotion, and it was quite fittingly staged in the very setting in which the action takes place: the university. In a classicising form, Bebel addresses contemporary concerns, namely, the ongoing battles between Scotists and Ockhamists. His main goal of promoting the new *studia humanitatis* should not overshadow

---

[26] Lawn 1993, p. 12.
[27] See Maierù 1994, p. 66; Glorieux 1935, p. 33; Wippel 1985, p. 165–175.

the fact that the *poeta* — introduced as an impartial observer — is also given the task of reminding the quarrelsome crowd of the old rationale for university debates:

> *Diversitas enim opinionum non introducta est ad odium atque invidiam, sed ad nudam exercitationem, ut in scholis contrarii, in foro amici et fratres, quemadmodum illi, qui certant pila, lucta, ceterisque gymnasiis, id est exercitationibus.*
>
> The diversity of opinions is not introduced to create hate or envy, but only for the purpose of exercise (*exercitatio*). This is why those who are pitted against each other in disputation in the schools can be friends and brothers outside, just like those who compete in ball games, wrestling, or gymnastics, i.e. in sports (*exercitatio*).[28]

The key word is *exercitatio*, which is not to be confused with propedeutics or pedagogical trifles. Rather, it points to serious debate that sets clear temporal and procedural boundaries for the confrontation and thus lets the contestants return to friendly socialising afterwards. Such boundaries were all the more important as the contestants shared dormitories in the *collegia*, where a continuation of the verbal fight by physical means would have been detrimental. What is more, this type of exercise inculcated a habit that was regarded as tremendously important in professional life. Contrary to humanist polemics, which liked to portray the universities as home to quixotic sophists who squandered their lives on empty quibbles, the universities were actually tasked with producing officials for all sorts of administrative positions. In the play's peroration, the poet presents his audience with the example of scholars at Paris who moved on to be counsellors to the same prince, offering him at times contrary advice (*diversas et contrarias* [...] *sententias*). But their education had prepared them for just this situation: *Nihilominus non altercantur mutuo, non invident. Cum senatum exeunt, salutem sibi impertiunt, brachiis cohaerent, simul pransitant et inter se gratificantur.* ('Nevertheless, there were no altercations and no envy. When they left the senate,

---

[28] Bebel, 1982, p. 68, my translation. On neo-humanist drama in Germany, see the overview in Dietl 2013; on the humanist concern with quarrelling sects, cf. Kivistö 2014, esp. ch. 4, 'Logomachia and Futile Quarrelling'.

they greeted and hugged each other; they had breakfast together and helped each other.')[29]

Thus *exercitatio* on the one hand refers to the specific frames that were introduced during university training, but also to the mindset that such training imparted. That training aimed at separating man and argument, personal conviction and defended position, as the default mode of debate — within and outside the university. The highly regulated framework of disputation that made serious play possible in the first place helped to form a habit that, ideally, persisted when real life demanded leaving roleplaying behind while at the same time upholding the civilised manner such play had (hopefully) imparted.

Before moving on to the next point, let us consider for a minute the utter paradox that the medieval university, which built on and defended a revealed religion and thus an unshakeable truth, chose a method of doubt as its core practice. In order to appreciate this paradox fully, however, we need to take account of the mindset of the sworn *magistri*. Generally speaking, of course, they were not opposed to revelation, or even critical of it. What they had to do was make sense of a body of texts from the Church Fathers and scholastic commentators which contained positions that appeared partly irreconcilable. It is not revealed truth itself that is at stake in disputations but competing interpretations of that truth. The competing interpretations are compared by identifying semantic imprecisions or different choices of wording in the hope that it was only a superficial difference that concealed the actual convergence of these opinions. With the help of dialectics, which guided the careful exploration of semantics and offered tools for logical inference, the *magistri* hoped to reconcile divergent positions. This was the essence of their profession — managing dissent. The method of scholasticism is thus, as Mary McLaughlin put it, '[the pursuit of] truth in the clash of ideas'.[30] The format of disputation was invented to provide a framework precisely for these explorations and, eventually, for the reconciliation of received wisdom with revelation — and not for challenging one or the other.

---

[29] Bebel 1982, p. 70, my translation.
[30] McLaughlin 1977, p. 36; see also de Rijk 1962–1967, vol. 1, p. 269.

In disputation, the need to be flexible in the assumption of roles enforced a kind of disinterested partiality and a focus on procedure. This flexibility was fostered by a heavily shielded institutional arrangement. When, in the High Middle Ages, privileges began to be defined for the communities of scholars in the nascent universities, intellectual liberties were not at the forefront of the concerns. *Libertas scholastica* referred to the sum of the prerogatives and privileges members of the university could count on, from the *licentia ubique docendi*, which was the right to teach anywhere, to the right to study without disruption by excessive noise.[31] These concessions turned the highly precarious minority of masters and scholars into a privileged group with wide-ranging immunities. The group not only obtained extensive rights in regulating the conduct of university members, but would also hold sway over scholarship in general for centuries to come. Internally, the masters awarded themselves intellectual liberties that were unheard of outside the universities. These liberties were safeguarded by the privileges awarded to the universities, but they were also tied to specific speech acts. Of course the university recognised a whole range of speech acts that informed its everyday operations, such as presiding over a disputation, arguing in the role of a respondent or an opponent, or lecturing from the *cathedra*. But the university also cultivated specific modes of speech that were meant to diminish or even eliminate the real-world consequences of what was said within university walls. The modes of speech are specific to medieval scholastic culture and do not have exact modern counterparts, which poses a challenge to their description.

distinguere

The first speech act is that of *distinguere*, which is customary in disputation, where it is one of the three main types of reaction to which a respondent may resort when countering the attacks of the opponent. These are: *concedere*, i.e. accepting an objection, thereby admitting that it is true; *negare*, i.e. to declare that the

---

[31] Classen 1983, p. 246–248; Schwinges 2008, p. 4–6; Boehm 1970. On academic jurisdictional privileges, see also Alenfelder 2002.

objection is false or unacceptable; and *distinguere*, i.e. to draw a distinction.[32] *Distinctio* is the operation of choice if a proposition could be understood in more than one way; it is, thus, an exercise in teasing out these competing or contradictory semantics.

The instrument of *distinguere* must not be underestimated as a means of managing dissent. Within the antagonistic framework of disputation, *distinguere* allows for nuance and differentiation, yet is not limited to disputation. Rather, *distinctio* refers to the overarching technique that was used to resolve contradictions in the authoritative, received corpus of texts. *Distinctio* was common in the faculties of theology and law, which were committed to safeguarding dogmatic frameworks. Faced with a growing body of authoritative texts, these disciplines were in were in need of a method for reconciling teachings that appeared to contradict each other, in order to integrate them into a coherent whole. As shown by Christoph H. F. Meyer, who called the procedure of drawing distinctions (*Distinktionsverfahren*) one of the most important devices of scholasticism, *distinctio* can be traced back to antiquity but achieved its specific role in the schools of the Middle Ages.[33] *Distinguere* originated from the *trivium* (and in particular from dialectics), but gained particular importance in theological and legal contexts. The term referred to the partitioning and structuring of texts, but more importantly, to drawing distinctions, which became a foundational technique in the interpretation of texts. While the precise procedure could vary considerably, it consisted in dissecting notions found in the sources into two, three, or more subordinate terms, including contrary and contradictory ones.[34]

I do not have to stress that the Reformation had its origin in the announcement of a disputation with the posting of the theses to be debated, most probably by the beadle of the University of Wittenberg (and most certainly not by the convening mas-

---

[32] *Omnis propositio ab opponente proposita, cum peculiari suæ denominationis, vt antecedentis, consequentis, maioris aut minoris expressione, a respondente est concedenda, neganda, aut distinguenda.* Lefèvre & Clichtove 1535, f. 14v–15r. On Lefèvre's and Clichtove's collaboration on the *Introductiones*, see Massaut 1968, p. 226–231. *Distinguere* appears to have been an option only since the fourteenth century, and not everyone was convinced of its usefulness; cf. Ashworth 1986, p. 26–27.

[33] See Meyer 2000, the quotation at p. 64.

[34] Meyer 2000, p. 74.

ter, Martin Luther himself). Closely following the unfolding the events, the Nuremberg diplomat and humanist, Christoph Scheurl, reported to the scholar Johannes Eck in November 1518 that Rome demanded from Luther that he recant two of the ninety-five theses. The rest, according to Cardinal Cajetan — the same Cajetan who had made his name beating Pico della Mirandola in disputation — could be resolved by way of *distinctiones*.[35] That things did not go quite as Cajetan had hoped is well known. Still, *distinctiones* must not be underestimated as a powerful tool for managing dissent. Within the university, they helped to nuance the debate and get to the bottom of disagreements; outside the university, they allowed for mitigating propositions of, to put it mildly, dubious accordance with doctrine. That Cajetan proposed to apply *distinctiones* as a way to mitigate the incendiary character of Luther's theses and what would soon become the *causa Lutheri*, leads directly to the next speech act, that of 'speaking in disputation'.

disputative loqui

Speech acts were categorised with a view to whether they are uttered within or outside the university. The medieval university's gravest concern, heresy, was defined not only with a view to content, but also — and equally — with regard to the manner in which it was brought forward. In the thirteenth century, Robert Grosseteste defined heresy as an opinion that is at odds with Scripture *and* that is propounded publicly and obstinately. Stubbornly adhering to such a position and propounding it publicly, either in teaching, writing, or — worst of all — preaching in the vernacular, are the elements of heresy.[36] The university sought to prevent this situation by introducing an important distinction, in particular where theological issues were concerned: what was brought forward — either defended or attacked — in disputation

---

[35] Eck 2011, ep. 67, Scheurl to Eck, 24 November, 1518: *Hucusque Roma tacet neque mihi etsi Martini familiarissimo constat nisi duos articulos abiectos. Hos revocato, ait Caietanus, reliqua per distinctiones solvamus.*

[36] Larsen 2011, p. 6–7. Koch 1973, vol. 2, p. 445–448. See also Thomas Aquinas, *Summa theologica*, I. q. 32 a. 4: *Et circa haec opinari falsum, hoc ipso inducit haeresim, maxime si pertinacia adiungatur.*

was to be considered as propounded only *disputative*, for the sake of argument. This is a consequence of the arbitrary distribution of roles and the necessity for scholars to act as respondents or opponents in disputation regardless of personal convictions.[37] In disputation, propositions were or could be treated as a kind of thought experiment, unless they were, in a separate speech act, asserted. Speaking *assertive* meant accepting responsibility for an utterance and being prepared to be held accountable for it. The disputative mode of explorative or tentative statements knew a set of synonyms and related terms, as Mary McLaughlin has put it:

> A master might venture almost any idea or opinion *narrando, dubitando, inquirendo* or *querendo*. In presenting the arguments or doctrines of his philosophical authorities, he customarily used the terms *recitare, disserere, declarare*. Only when a personal and formal solution was reached did masters use the words *asserere* and *determinare*.[38]

This fundamental distinction between utterances made either *disputative* (often called *scholastice*) or *assertive* thus attributes different meaning — or rather, different consequences — to identical propositions, depending on where and how they are articulated. Again it is Cardinal Cajetan who supplies an example. In his letter to the elector Frederick III of Saxony on 25 October 1518, he argues that Luther's theses had been brought forward *disputative*, but what was worrisome was that Luther had published them in different formats as well, including in sermons preached in the German language.[39] It was these public speech acts that turned theses into heresies, by giving them the weight of assertions.

In general, as soon as utterances were issued in print or transferred to the vernacular, the option of speaking *disputative* ceased

---

[37] On the development of these roles, see Bazàn 1985, p. 39–42.

[38] McLaughlin 1977, p. 67.

[39] Cajetan to Elector Friedrich of Saxony, 25 October 1518, WABr 1, no. 110, p. 233–235, here p. 234, 70–74: *In causa vero tria affirmo. Primo, dicta Fratris Martini, licet in Conclusionibus sint disputative, in sermonibus tamen ab eo scriptis affirmative et assertive esse posita, et confirmata in vulgari Germanico, ut aiunt. Ea autem sunt partim contra doctrinam Apostolicae Sedis, partim vero damnabilia.*

to exist. Thus it is all the more surprising that Marsilio Ficino, when publishing his *Theologia platonica* in 1482, prefixed the printed version with a disclaimer: 'In whatever subject I discuss, here or elsewhere, I wish to assert only what is approved by the Church' (*In omnibus quae aut hic aut alibi a me tractantur, tantum assertum esse volo quantum ab ecclesia comprobatur*).[40] It is doubtful, however, that it was this disclaimer which spared Ficino trouble with the authorities. In general, the peculiar type of as-if that underwrites the suspension of assertion in disputation did not suffer a transfer into print. And neither as an oral practice nor as a (never realised) licence in print did such a suspension of assertion survive into modernity.

philosophice loqui

The statutes of the University of Paris from 1255 declared a pragmatic autonomy of 'philosophy' — referring of course to the arts faculty — from theological discourse and entrusted philosophy with a particular speech act: *philosophice loqui*, speaking philosophically. That this discursive distinction did not, however, result, in two kinds of truth, one theological, the other philosophical, was made blatantly clear when the Bishop of Paris, Étienne Tempier, condemned 219 theses that were debated in the arts faculty in 1277.[41] This condemnation has long been described as being at the root of what has been become the trope *philosophia ancilla theologiae*, philosophy as the handmaid of theology.[42] It would appear that philosophy was subjected to the rule of theology, thus hampering inquiry and inhibiting insight. Yet the separation of the two realms, theology and philosophy, conceived as a device that would fortify theology and the inviolability of its doctrine, opened up liberties of inquiry within philosophy. Limited as these liberties may have been, *philosophice loqui* became the

[40] Ficino 2001–2006, vol. 1, p. 1. Allen's translation renders *assertum esse* as 'state'. I have substituted 'assert' in keeping with the historical terminology.

[41] *Chartularium Universitatis Parisiensis*, vol. 1, p. 543–558; on the condemned theses, see Wippel 1977, p. 169–201; on the historical context, Libera 2003, p. 191–220; Bianchi 1999; Bianchi 2008.

[42] For a comprehensive critical review of the interpretations of this formula, see Mowbray 2004; Seckler 1991.

code word for both restriction and leeway in thinking about the natural and social world.

Where no questions of faith and doctrine were concerned, *magistri* could proceed according to the principle of *probabilitas*: the validity of an argument depended on its probability, on its being philosophically demonstrable (*probabilis*) according to the rules of natural reason (*naturaliter loquendo*). Thinking philosophically meant operating in a mode of as-if: thinking as if Catholic doctrine did not exist and as if only natural reason were the basis for judgement. To quote just one example: Johannes Buridan, a fourteenth-century Parisian philosopher and author of *Quaestiones super octo physicorum libros Aristotelis* (and notoriously, yet quite inexplicably, associated with an ass he never had anything to do with),[43] who was convinced that his work on the cosmos must not touch upon revelation, nevertheless thought it probable, under the premise of *philosophice loqui*, that the world is eternal but that the soul is not.[44] To employ the terminology of Robert Merton, the separation of theological and philosophical argumentation had the 'unanticipated consequence' of opening up a space for the exploration of unorthodox thought while preserving the untouchability of revelation.[45] Of course, these distinctions continued to be precarious and were hotly debated throughout the early modern period. Nevertheless, this was where the idea of *libertas philosophandi* originated. The idea gained particular momentum in early modern debates about Aristotle's cosmology and, consequently, his status as an untouchable authority. Over time, the idea became synonymous with demands for freedom of thought beyond the university,[46] though its early propagators such as Giordano Bruno were acutely aware that it was a specific privilege granted to members of the faculty of philosophy. When Bruno wrote to King Henri III after a disputation that he had organised in Paris in 1586 ended in tumult, Bruno stipulated that everyone should be able to discuss new ideas — not,

---

[43] 'Buridan's ass', the donkey which dies from not being able to decide which pile of hay to feed off of first, does not figure in Buridan's writings; see Rescher 1960.
[44] Maier 1955, p. 27.
[45] Cf. Merton 1936.
[46] For an overview, see Traninger 2016.

however, without qualifying his demand. Free reasoning (*libere opinari*) should be allowed *philosophice in philosophia*, that is, as a particular speech act in the faculty of philosophy: 'if a (or a new) theory excites us and grips us, everyone should be at liberty to reason freely, philosophically in philosophy, and to express his own opinion' (*si qua (vel nova) ratio nos excitet atque cogat, cuicumque liceat philosophice in philosophia libere opinari, suamque promere sententiam*).[47]

Erasmus of Rotterdam, despite the contempt in which he held the schoolmen, variously drew on their discursive conventions. Throughout his life he shied away from the arena of disputation, a fact for which he was openly ridiculed by Maarten van Dorp in the controversy about the *Praise of Folly*.[48] But as he sought to forge formats that would allow him to become a published author, Erasmus clearly took the measure of scholastic practice and sought to establish genres that would echo central tenets of scholastic argumentation. The choice of one genre is counterintuitive at first sight, at least it was to his contemporaries: his favourite genre for expressing current ideas and for addressing topical issues was declamation. If philology was the method of the new Erasmian theology, declamation was to be its mode of controversy. The fictitious orations uttered by *personae* adopted by the declaimers of the Second Sophistic — collected by Seneca the Elder in the *controversiae* and *suasoriae*[49] — spoke to Erasmus, who, throughout his career, liked to stage arguments by having fictitious characters propound them, be it in the dialogues of the *Colloquies*, or in the letters he wrote 'as' someone else.[50] But for Erasmus declamation carried even more weight; he hoped to establish declamation as the written equivalent of oral scholastic debate, not least with a view to the liberties awarded to philosophy in comparison with theology.

---

[47] Bruno 1879–1891, vol. 1, 1, p. 57, my translation. Sutton 1953 does not place Bruno's claim in the context of the university; cf., on the contrary, Peters 2001, p. 95, who somewhat overrates Bruno's claim by asserting that it was Bruno's letter which 'finally put [a name] to a practice developed in the twelfth and thirteenth-century schools.'

[48] Erasmus, *Opus epistolarum*, Allen, ep. 347, lines 238–243, 298–302, 311–313.

[49] See Bloomer 1997; Bonner 1969.

[50] See Traninger 2017. On the revival of declamation in the early modern period, see the magisterial study by van der Poel 1987.

Even if he was not a seasoned practitioner, Erasmus was very much aware of the workings of a university and the privileges enjoyed by faculty members. He knew well that *philosophice loqui* was the formula that opened up the possibility of discussing questions independently from doctrinal rigidity and deciding them according to the principle of probability. But that declamation could be an apt genre for negotiating serious philosophical and even theological matters was hotly contested. In 1526, when the Paris theologian Josse Clichtove denounced Erasmus' *Encomium matrimonii* (written in the 1490s, printed in 1518) in his *Propugnaculum Ecclesie aduersus Lutheranos* as of a piece with Luther's erroneous doctrine, Erasmus defended himself by invoking the generic conventions of declamation and by likening them to the scholastic practice of disputation.[51] In the first of his replies to Clichtove, the *Appendix de scriptis Clithovei*, of 1526, he complained: 'Those who put forward before theologians tenets of Aristotle that are diametrically opposed to the teaching of Christ only have to say: "I speak as a philosopher."' (*Qui inter Theologos proferunt Aristotelis placita ex diametro pugnantia cum doctrinam Christi, sat habent dicere, loquor ut Philosophus*).[52]

In his second refutation of Clichtove's attacks, the *Dilutio eorum quae Iodocus Clithoveus scripsit adversus declamationem suasoriam matrimonii*, published in 1532, Erasmus takes his protest further and demands that the philosophers' prerogative be extended to rhetoricians:

> *In concertationibus scholasticis etiamsi quid dicitur repugnans catholicae ueritati, satis est dicere, Nunc loquor ut philosophus: et mihi nihil proderit uociferanti, Loquor ut rhetor, nec formo / mores, sed instruo linguam.*[53]

> In scholastic disputations, even if something is said that is contradictory to the Catholic faith, it is sufficient to say, 'I speak now as a philosopher.' But it did me no good to shout at the top of my voice, 'I am speaking as a rhetorician; I am not fashioning morals, but I am teaching language.'[54]

---

[51] Clichtove 1526, ch. 34.
[52] LB 9, 812F; CWE 83, p. 113 (Appendix).
[53] Erasmus 1968, p. 71.
[54] CWE 83, p. 118 (*Dilutio*).

It is not, however, simply rhetoric to which Erasmus resorts in his defence, but more specifically declamation. Like disputation, with its assignment of the roles of respondent and opponent, declamation allows for assuming a role in arguing a fictitious case. It is important to Erasmus that declamation not be confused with a sermon. In the *Encomium matrimonii*, he appears to advocate marriage for priests, whence Clichtove's allegation that Erasmus is propounding Lutheran ideas. Yet in fact, Erasmus counters, he was adopting the *persona* of a layman counselling another layman. It is thus not only the prerogative of *philosophice loqui* that Erasmus claims for the orator but also the liberties of *disputative loqui*, which in his view should extend to declamation. The keyword for marking his discourse as framed is *fides*: *totum hoc argumentum tanquam rhetorum more declamatum, prorsus careret omni fide*. The English translation of *fides* offered in the *Collected Works* is 'credibility': 'this whole argument was a rhetorical declamation and was totally lacking in any credibility.'[55] While 'credibility' is of course a possible translation of *fides*,[56] Erasmus does not mean to say here that the argument would not be credible in the sense of 'convincing'; rather, *fides* is used to signal the framing of the discourse that is analogous to a speech act made *disputative*. It is the claim to this speech act, which separates the man from the argument, that allows Erasmus to argue for marriage, just as a theologian would if tasked to defend this position for the sake of argument:

> *Sed utor aliquot rationibus falsis. Mirum uero, si id fit in ficto themate, quum idem faciant Theologi in serijs diatribis. Si nulla essent argumenta inualida, quid haberet alterius partis tractatio quod adferret?*[57]
>
> It is true that I do use some false arguments. That is not surprising, certainly, if we are dealing with a fictitious theme, when theologians do the same in serious discussions. If there were no invalid arguments, what would the other side have to present?[58]

---

[55] CWE 83, p. 123 (*Dilutio*).

[56] Cf. Marc van der Poel's discussion of the meaning of *fides* in this context, in van der Poel 2005.

[57] Erasmus 1968, p. 81.

[58] CWE 83, p. 128 (*Dilutio*).

Doubtlessly sensing how audacious his defence was, Erasmus at the same time seeks to prove that his arguments were in line with Christian orthodoxy. Despite the supposed liberties granted by the format, he had not really strayed from Christian doctrine: 'Now consider how even in a fictitious argument I was not totally oblivious of Christian orthodoxy' (*Nunc uide quam in ficto etiam themate non fuerim prorsus Christianae synceritatis immemor*).[59]

Still, the *Dilutio* is all about drawing parallels between disputation and declamation. The work's very title signals that Erasmus hoped to present himself as well-versed in the jargon of the schoolmen. It is not by chance that he chose an expression stemming directly from the realm of disputation as his title: *dilutio* does not refer to a general brushing off or, literally, to washing away the accusations. Rather, *dilutio* is a specialised term that refers to a particular dialectical move. *Diluere* is at the heart of the task of acting as a respondent in disputation, refuting and resolving arguments brought forward by the *opponens*, a definition Clichtove himself had offered in the introductory manual he had co-authored with Lefèvre d'Étaples.[60]

Unfollowing Amadís

To conclude, let us jump to the end of the seventeenth century and back to the analogy with jousting. In 1691, the Leipzig professor of law and philosophy, Christian Thomasius, could still characterise disputation as a kind of war: *Disputationes ad instar bellorum esse.*[61] Yet he felt that important qualifications needed to be added:

> Derowegen sind die gemeine Disputirenden nicht einmahl würdig/ daß man sie so zu reden mit raisonablen Kriegs=Leuten vergleiche/ sondern es hat sie albereit ein scharffsinniger Kopff nicht unbillig mit denen thörrichten Amadis Rittern verglichen/ die sich an die öffentlichen Stras-

---

[59] CWE 83, p. 128 (*Dilutio*); Erasmus 1968, p. 81.
[60] Lefèvre & Clichtove 1534, f. 15r: *Respondens, est qui argumentationem ab altero propositam diluit & dissoluit.*
[61] Thomasius 1998, V, 11, p. 271.

sen lagerten/ daselbst das portrait einer Liebsten/ die sie nach ihrer Phantasie sich erkieset/ auffhiengen/ und die vorüber ziehenden Ritter zwungen/ daß sie entweder bekennen musten/ es wäre dieselbige die schöneste in der gantzen Welt/ oder musten mit ihnen fechten/ und allerhand Verdrusses/ auch wohl gar des Halsbrechens gewärtig seyn.[62]

Ordinary disputers are not worthy of being compared with sensible warriors. A sharp-witted mind compared them quite rightly with the foolhardy Amadís knights who set up camp next to public roads and hung the portrait of their beloved whom they had chosen in their imagination. Then they forced passing knights to admit that she was the most beautiful woman in the world. If they did not conform, they had to fight them and expect all sorts of trouble, including even breaking their necks.

By evoking the deluded imitators of Amadís, Thomasius seeks to underscore his demand for a general reform of academic practice: that only such theses be treated at university which are brought forward as the respondent's own position. The portrait of the lady is of course a metaphor for the thesis in the old sense, which was typically not in accordance with the defender's own ideas. In Giovanni Pico della Mirandola's 900 theses, one has to read well beyond number 400 before one encounters *conclusiones ... secundum opinionem propriam*.[63] Thomasius now denounces this age-old practice as a quixotic fiction that has no place in what would begin to transform itself, in the course of the following century, into the modern research university. This transformation also involves a serious loss: it does away with the discursive spaces for negotiating dissent. And while our modern academic culture may describe itself in less bellicose terms, it has also narrowed the spaces, and above all the techniques, for nuanced if agonistic debate.

---

[62] Thomasius 1998, V, 14, p. 272–273. My translation. On Thomasius' plans for reforming university disputations, see Marti 2005, p. 328.
[63] Farmer 1998; Dougherty 2002, p. 225.

Bibliography

Primary Sources

Bebel, H., *Comoedia de optimo studio iuvenum. Über die beste Art des Studiums für junge Leute*, ed. and trans. W. Barner, Stuttgart: Reclam, 1982.

Bruno, G. (1879–1891), *Opera latine conscripta*, ed. F. Fiorentino, 3 vols, Naples: Dom. Morano (repr. Stuttgart-Bad Cannstatt: Frommann-Holzboog, 1962).

Chartularium Universitatis Parisiensis, ed. H. Denifle & E. Chatelain, 4 vols, Paris: Delalain, 1889–1897.

Clichtove, J. (1526), *Propugnaculum ecclesiae aduersus Lutheranos*, Cologne: Hittorpius.

Eck, J. (2011), *Briefwechsel*, ed. Vinzenz Pfnür et al., trans. Peter Fabisch, University of Muenster (online edition); http://ivv7srv15.uni-muenster.de/mnkg/pfnuer/Eck-Briefe.html (accessed 09.09.2023).

Erasmus of Rotterdam, Desiderius, *Dilutio eorum quae Iodocus Clithoveus scripsit adversus declamationem Des. Erasmi Roterodami suasoriam matrimonii*, ed. É. V. Telle, Paris: Vrin, 1968 (De Pétrarque à Descartes, 15).

Erasmus of Rotterdam, Desiderius, *Desiderii Erasmi Roterodami opera omnia*, ed. J. LeClerc, 10 vols, Leiden: Petrus van der Aa, 1703–1706 (repr. Hildesheim: Olms, 1961) [= LB].

Erasmus of Rotterdam, Desiderius, *Opera omnia Desiderii Erasmi Roterodami*, Amsterdam, 1969– [= ASD].

Erasmus of Rotterdam, Desiderius, *Collected Works of Erasmus*, Toronto: Toronto University Press, 1974– [= CWE].

Erasmus of Rotterdam, Desiderius, *Opus epistolarum Desiderii Erasmi Roterodami*, eds P. S. Allen et al., 12 vols, Oxford: Oxford University Press, 1906–1958.

Farmer, S. A. (1998), *Syncretism in the West: Pico's 900 Theses (1486). The Evolution of Traditional Religious and Philosophical Systems. With Text, Translation and Commentary*, Tempe, AZ: Arizona State University (Medieval & Renaissance Texts & Studies, 167).

Ficino, Marsilio, *Platonic Theology*, ed. J. Hankins, trans. M. J. B. Allen, 6 vols, Cambridge, MA: Harvard University Press, 2001–2006 (I Tatti Renaissance Library, 2, 4, 7, 13, 17, 23).

George of Trebizond (1539), *Utilissimus de re dialectica libellus, diligentius multo quam antehac unquam recognitus & emendatus, cum scholijs Iohan. Nouiomagi,* Cologne: Eucharius (repr. Frankfurt a. M.: Minerva, 1966).

Lefèvre d'Étaples, J. & Clichtove, J. (1534), *In hoc opusculo contentae introductiones. In atrium diuisionem. In suppositiones. In prædicabilia. In diuisiones. In præedicamenta. In librum de enuntiatione. In primum priorum. In secundum priorum. In libros posteriorum. In locos dialecticos. In fallacias. In obligationes. In insolubilia*, Paris: Petrus Gaudoul.

Pico della Mirandola, Giovanni, *Oratio de hominis dignitate. Rede über die Würde des Menschen*, ed. and trans. G. von der Gönna, Stuttgart: Reclam, 1997.

Pico della Mirandola, Giovanni, *Oration on the Dignity of Man*, trans. A. R. Camponigri, Washington, DC: Regenery Publishing, 1956.

Thomasius, Christian, *Ausgewählte Werke*, ed. W. Schneiders, Hildesheim et al.: Olms, 1993–2015, vol. 9: *Ausübung der Vernunftlehre* (1998).

Secondary Sources

Alenfelder, K. M. (2002), *Akademische Gerichtsbarkeit*, Baden-Baden: Nomos (Bonner Schriften zum Wissenschaftsrecht, 7).

Ashworth, E. J. (1986), 'Renaissance Man as Logician: Josse Clichtove (1472–1543) on Disputations', in *History and Philosophy of Logic*, 7, p. 15–29.

Barber, R. & Barker, J. (1989), *Tournaments: Jousts, Chivalry and Pageants in the Middle Ages*, Woodbridge, NY: The Boydell Press.

Bateson, G. (2000), *Steps to an Ecology of Mind: Collected Essays in Anthropology, Psychiatry, Evolution, and Epistemology*, Chicago, IL: The University of Chicago Press.

Bazàn, B. C. (1985), 'Les questions disputées, principalement dans les facultés de théologie', in B. C. Bazàn et al. (eds), *Les questions disputées et les questions quodlibétiques dans les facultés de théologie, de droit et de médecine*, Turnhout: Brepols (Typologie des sources du Moyen Âge occidental, 44–45), p. 21–147.

Bianchi, L., *Censure et liberté intellectuelle à l'université de Paris (XIIIe–XIVe siècles)*, Paris: Les Belles Lettres, 1999 (Âne d'or, 9).

Bianchi, L., *Pour une histoire de la 'double vérité'*, Paris: Vrin, 2008.

Bloomer, W. M. (1997), 'Schooling in *persona*: Imagination and Subordination in Roman Education', in *Classical Antiquity*, 16/1, p. 57–78.

Boehm, L. (1970), '*Libertas scholastica und negotium scholare*. Entstehung und Sozialprestige des akademischen Standes im Mittelalter', in H. Rössler & G. Franz (eds), *Universität und Gelehrtenstand 1400–1800. Büdinger Vorträge 1966*, Limburg: Starke (Deutsche Führungsschichten in der Neuzeit, 4), p. 15–61.

Bonner, S. F. (1969), *Roman Declamation in the Late Republic and Early Empire*, Liverpool: Liverpool University Press.

Burckhardt, J. (1955), *Die Kultur der Renaissance in Italien. Ein Versuch*, Berlin: Rütten & Loening (Gesammelte Werke 3).

Caroti, S. (2008), 'Le fonti medievali delle "Disputationes adversus astrologiam divinatricem"', in Bertozzi, M. (ed.), *Nello specchio del cielo. Giovanni Pico della Mirandola e le 'Disputationes contro l'astrologia divinatoria'. Atti del convegno di studi, Mirandola, 16 aprile 2004, Ferrara, 17 aprile 2004* (Studi pichiani, 12), p. 67–94.

Cassirer, E. (2002), *Individuum und Kosmos in der Philosophie der Renaissance. Die Platonische Renaissance in England und die Schule von Cambridge*, ed. F. Plaga & C. Rosenkranz, Darmstadt: Wissenschaftliche Buchgesellschaft (Gesammelte Werke. Hamburger Ausgabe, ed. Birgit Recki 14).

Chang, K. (2004), 'From Oral Disputation to Written Text: The Transformation of the Dissertation in Early Modern Europe', in *History of Universities*, 19/2, p. 129–187.

Classen, P. (1983), *'Libertas scolastica* – Scholarenprivilegien – Akademische Freiheit im Mittelalter', in P. Classen, *Studium und Gesellschaft im Mittelalter*, J. Fried (ed.), Stuttgart: Hiersemann (Schriften der Monumenta Germaniae Historica, 29), p. 238–284.

Copenhaver, B. P. (2019), *Magic and the Dignity of Man: Pico della Mirandola and His Oration in Modern Memory*, Cambridge, MA: Harvard University Press.

Craven, W. G. (1981), *Giovanni Pico della Mirandola – Symbol of His Age. Modern Interpretations of a Renaissance Philosopher*, Geneva: Droz (Travaux d'humanisme et Renaissance, 185).

di Napoli, G. (1965), *Giovanni Pico della Mirandola e la problematica dottrinale del suo tempo*, Roma: Desclée et al. (Collectio philosophica Lateranensis, 8).

Dietl, C. (2013), 'Neo-Latin Humanist and Protestant Drama in Germany', in J. Bloemendal & H. B. Norland (eds), *Neo-Latin Drama in Early Modern Europe*, Leiden: Brill (Drama and Theatre in Early Modern Europe, 3), p. 103–183.

Dougherty, M. V. (2002), 'Two Possible Sources for Pico's *Oratio*', in *Vivarium*, 40/2, p. 220–241.

Duby, G. (1977), *The Chivalrous Society*, trans. C. Postan, London: Arnold.

Dulles, A. (1941), *Princeps Concordiae: Pico della Mirandola and the Scholastic Tradition*, Cambridge, MA: Harvard University Press.

Edelheit, A. (2011), 'Henry of Ghent and Giovanni Pico della Mirandola: A Chapter on the Reception and Influence of Scholasticism in the Renaissance', in G. A. Wilson (ed.), *A Companion to Henry of Ghent*, Leiden: Brill (Brill's Companions to the Christian Tradition, 23), p. 369–397.

Édouard, S. (2005), *L'empire imaginaire de Philippe II. Pouvoir des images et discours du pouvoir sous les Habsbourg d'Espagne au XVIe siècle*, Paris: Honoré Champion (Bibliothèque d'histoire moderne et contemporaine, 17).

Fallows, N. (2010), *Jousting in Medieval and Renaissance Iberia*, Woodbridge, NY: The Boydell Press.

Farge, J. K. (1985), *Orthodoxy and Reform in Early Reformation France. The Faculty of Theology of Paris, 1500–1543*, Leiden: Brill (Studies in Medieval and Reformation Thought, 32).

Feingold, M. (2001), 'English Ramism: A Reinterpretation', in M. Feingold, J. S. Freedman, & W. Rother (eds), *The Influence of Petrus Ramus. Studies in the Sixteenth and Seventeenth Century Philosophy and Sciences*, Basel: Schwabe (Schwabe philosophica, 1), p. 127–176.

Frieder, B. K. (2008), *Chivalry and the Perfect Prince. Tournaments, Art, and Armor at the Spanish Habsburg Court*, Kirksville, MO: Truman State University Press (Sixteenth Century Essays & Studies, 81).

Garin, E. (1973), *Medioevo e Rinascimento. Studi e ricerche*, Roma: Laterza (Economica Laterza, 363).

Glorieux, P. (1935), *La littérature quodlibétique*, 2 vols, Paris: Vrin (Bibliothèque thomiste, 21).

Grabmann, M. (1911), *Die Geschichte der scholastischen Methode*, 2 vols, Freiburg: Herdersche Verlagshandlung (repr. Berlin: Akademie Verlag, 1956).

Imbach, R. (1989), *Laien in der Philosophie des Mittelalters: Hinweise und Anregungen zu einem vernachlässigten Thema*, Amsterdam: John Benjamins (Bochumer Studien zur Philosophie, 14).

Karras, R. M. (2003), *From Boys to Men: Formations of Masculinity in Late Medieval Europe*, Philadelphia, PA: University of Pennsylvania Press.

Kivistö, S. (2014), *The Vices of Learning: Morality and Knowledge at Early Modern Universities*, Leiden: Brill (Education and Society in the Middle Ages and Renaissance, 48).

Koch, J. (1973), 'Philosophische und theologische Irrtumslisten von 1270–1329. Ein Beitrag zur Entwicklung der theologischen Zensuren', in J. Koch, *Kleine Schriften*, 2 vols, Rome: Ed. di Storia e Letteratura (Storia e letteratura, 127–128), p. 423–450.

Krug-Richter, B. (2004), 'Von Messern, Mänteln und Männlichkeit. Aspekte studentischer Konfliktkultur im frühneuzeitlichen Freiburg im Breisgau', in *Wiener Zeitschrift zur Geschichte der Neuzeit*, 4/1, p. 26–52.

Larsen, A. E. (2011), *The School of Heretics: Academic Condemnation at the University of Oxford 1277–1409*, Leiden: Brill (Education and Society in the Middle Ages and Renaissance, 40).

Lawn, B. (1993), *The Rise and Decline of the Scholastic 'Quaestio Disputata', with Special Emphasis on its Use in the Teaching of Medicine and Science*, Leiden: Brill (Education and Society in the Middle Ages and Renaissance, 2).

Libera, A. de (2003), *Raison et foi. Archéologie d'une crise d'Albert le Grand à Jean Paul II*, Paris: Seuil.

Maier, A. (1955), 'Das Prinzip der doppelten Wahrheit', in A. Maier, *Metaphysische Hintergründe der spätscholastischen Naturphilosophie*, Rome: Ed. di Storia e Letteratura (Storia e letteratura, 52; Studien zur Naturphilosophie der Spätscholastik, 4), p. 1–44.

Maierù, A. (1994), *University Training in Medieval Europe*, Leiden: Brill (Education and Society in the Middle Ages and Renaissance, 3).

Maisel, T. (1993), '*Bellum Latinum*. Eine studentische Rebellion des frühen 16. Jahrhunderts in Wien', in K. Mühlberger & T. Maisel (eds), *Aspekte der Bildungs- und Universitätsgeschichte. 16. bis 19. Jahrhundert*, Wien: WUV-Universitätsverlag (Schriftenreihe des Universitätsarchivs, 7), p. 191–231.

Marenbon, J. (1991), *Later Medieval Philosophy (1150–1350)*, London: Routledge.

Marti, H. (2005), 'Kommunikationsnormen der Disputation. Die Universität Halle und Christian Thomasius als Paradigmen des Wandels', in U. J. Schneider (ed.), *Kultur der Kommunikation. Die europäische Gelehrtenrepublik im Zeitalter von Leibniz und Lessing*, Wiesbaden: Harrassowitz (Wolfenbütteler Forschungen, 109), p. 317–344.

Massaut, J.-P. (1968), *Josse Clichtove, l'humanisme et la réforme du clergé*, 2 vols, Paris: Les Belles Lettres (Bibliothèque de la Faculté de Philosophie et Lettres de l'Université de Liège, 183).

McLaughlin, M. M. (1977), *Intellectual Freedom and its Limitations in the University of Paris in the Thirteenth and Fourteenth Centuries*, New York: Arno Press.

Megías, J. M. L. (2000), *Imprenta y libros de caballerías*, Madrid: Ollero & Ramos.

Merton, R. K. (1936), 'The Unanticipated Consequences of Purposive Social Action', in *American Sociological Review*, 1/6, p. 894–904.

Meyer, C. H. F. (2000), *Die Distinktionstechnik der Kanonistik des 12. Jahrhunderts. Ein Beitrag zur Wissenschaftsgeschichte des Hochmittelalters*, Leuven: Leuven University Press (Mediaevalia Lovaniensia. Series I, Studia, 29).

Monfasani, J. (1976), *George of Trebizond: A Biography and a Study of his Rhetoric and Logic*, Leiden: Brill (Columbia Studies in the Classical Tradition, 1).

Moraux, P. (1968), 'La joute dialectique d'après le huitième livre des *Topiques*', in G. E. L. Owen (ed.), *Aristotle on Dialectic: The Topics. Proceedings of the Third Symposium Aristotelicum*, Oxford: Clarendon, p. 277–311.

Mowbray, M. de (2004), 'Philosophy as Handmaid of Theology: Biblical Exegesis in the Service of Scholarship', in *Traditio*, 59, p. 1–37.

Ong, W. J. (1983), *Ramus, Method, and the Decay of Dialogue. From the Art of Discourse to the Art of Reason*, Cambridge, MA: Harvard University Press.

Parker, G. (2014), *Imprudent King: A New Life of Philip II*, New Haven, CT: Yale University Press.

Peters, E. (2001), '*Libertas Inquirendi* and the *Vitium Curiositatis* in Medieval Thought', in E. Peters, *Limits of Thought and Power in Medieval Europe*. Aldershot: Ashgate (Variorum Collected Studies Series, 721), p. 89–98.

Poel, M. G. M. van der (1987), *De Declamatio bij de Humanisten. Bijdrage tot de studie van de functies van de Rhetorica in de Renaissance*, Nieuwkoop: de Graaf (Bibliotheca humanistica & reformatorica, 39).

Poel, M. G. M. van der (2005), 'For Freedom of Opinion: Erasmus' Defense of the *Encomium matrimonii*', in *Erasmus of Rotterdam Society Yearbook*, 25, p. 1–17.

Renaudet, A. (1953), *Préréforme et humanisme à Paris pendant les premières guerres d'Italie (1494–1517)*. Second edition. Paris: Argences.

Rescher, N. (1960), 'Choice without Preference. A Study of the History and the Logic of the Problem of "Buridans's Ass"', in *Kant-Studien*, 51, p. 142–175.

Rijk, L. M. de (1962–1967), *Logica Modernorum: a Contribution to the History of Early Terminist Logic*, 3 vols, Assen: Van Gorcum et al. (Wijsgerige teksten en studies, 6,16).

Schulthess, P. & Imbach R. (2002), *Die Philosophie im lateinischen Mittelalter. Ein Handbuch mit einem bio-bibliographischen Repertorium*. Second edition. Düsseldorf: Artemis & Winkler.

Schwinges, R. C. (2008), 'Libertas scholastica im Mittelalter', in R. A. Müller & R. C. Schwinges (eds), *Wissenschaftsfreiheit in Vergangenheit und Gegenwart*, Basel: Schwabe (Veröffentlichungen der Gesellschaft für Universitäts- und Wissenschaftsgeschichte, 9), p. 1–16.

Seckler, M. (1991), '"Philosophia ancilla theologiae". Über die Ursprünge und den Sinn einer anstößig gewordenen Formel', in *Theologische Quartalschrift*, 171, p. 161–187.

Sloane, T. O. (1997), *On the Contrary: The Protocol of Traditional Rhetoric*, Washington, DC: The Catholic University of America Press.

Sutton, R. B. (1953), 'The Phrase *Libertas Philosophandi*', in *Journal of the History of Ideas*, 14/2, p. 310–316.

Taylor, A. (1998), 'A Second Ajax. Peter Abelard and the Violence of Dialectic', in D. Townsend & A. Taylor (eds), *The Tongue of the Fathers: Gender and Ideology in Twelfth-Century Latin*, Philadelphia (PA): University of Pennsylvania Press, p. 14–34.

Traninger, A. (2016), 'Libertas philosophandi', in H. Jaumann & G. Stiening (eds), *Neue Diskurse der Gelehrsamkeit in der frühen Neuzeit*, Berlin: de Gruyter, p. 269–318.

Traninger, A. (2017), "'Erasmus' *personae* between Rhetoric and Dialectics', in *ERSY*, 37/1, p. 5–22.

Weijers, O. (2013), *In Search of the Truth. A History of Disputation Techniques from Antiquity to Early Modern Times*, Turnhout: Brepols (Studies on the Faculty of Arts: History and Influence, 1).

Wicks, J. (1978), 'Introduction', in J. Wicks (ed.), *Cajetan Responds: A Reader in Reformation Controversy*, Washington, DC: The Catholic University of America Press, p. 1–46.

Wicks, J. (1983), *Cajetan und die Anfänge der Reformation*, Münster: Aschendorff (Katholisches Leben und Kirchenreform im Zeitalter der Glaubensspaltung, 43).

Wippel, J. F. (1977), 'The Condemnations of 1270 and 1277 at Paris', in *The Journal of Medieval and Renaissance Studies*, 7, p. 169–201.

Wippel, J. F. (1985), 'Quodlibetal Questions Chiefly in Theology Faculties', in B. C. Bazàn et al., *Les questions disputées et les questions quodlibétiques dans les facultés de théologie, de droit et de médecine*, Turnhout: Brepols (Typologie des sources du Moyen Âge occidental, 44–45), p. 157–222.

Abstract

Scholastic culture was built on dissent. By employing disputation as its core format, scholastic culture subjected everything, from beginner's questions in dialectics to reconciling authorities who differed in their reading of revelation, to antagonistic debate. Yet just as with the tournaments that appear to have emerged around the same time as the universities, rules and conventions were introduced that allowed for 'serious play.' By means of these rules and conventions, the universities awarded their sworn members intellectual liberties unknown in the outside world, but the universities also stipulated specific frames and speech acts to which these liberties were tied. In this chapter, several of these stipulations will be discussed: the notion of *exercitatio*; the methods of delimiting the issues to be debated; and some of the speech acts that informed disputation and thus were at the heart of the culture of disputation yet have no counterpart in modern academia: *distinguere*, *philosophice loqui*, and *disputative loqui*.

PART 1
MIDDLE AGES (12TH – 15TH CENTURIES)

DINAH WOUTERS
Huygens Institute, Amsterdam

PREPOSTEROUS DEBATES: PARODIES OF DEBATE IN LATIN LITERATURE BEFORE 1200

Literary debate texts often parody the structures and arguments of non-literary debates.[1] The more regulated and systematised a certain form of debate, so it seems, the more that form becomes the target of parody. Debate poems of the High and Later Middle Ages play with the discursive norms of the scholastic disputation, civil law, and parliamentary debate. For instance, the troubadour *tensos* and *partimens* adopt some structures from scholastic disputation, thereby creating a parodic tension between formal philosophical debate and the themes of love and sex. But traditions of parodic debate predate the popularity of vernacular debate poetry. This continuity has been somewhat obscured by the tendency of scholarship to focus on vernacular poems and to contrast these with official debate practices in Latin. In this article, I explore some Latin debate texts from before the year 1200 in order to diffuse this contrast and highlight the continuity of parodic debate.

Latin Literary Dialogue and Debate

Debate literature, which is a subgenre of the literary dialogue,[2] distinguishes itself from other forms of dialogue by the marked opposition between speakers. Even in Antiquity, dialogue literature always contained formats in which speakers argue against

---

[1] I would like to thank the editor, the anonymous reviewers, and the proofreader for their valuable feedback.

[2] Cardelle de Hartmann 2007; Fichte et al. 2019; Hempfer 2002; Jacobi 1999; Jantzen 1977; Kasten 1973; Schmidt 1993; Stotz 1999; Walther 1920.

each other rather than speaking to each other. The two major dialogic genres from Antiquity illustrate the difference.[3] The first is the philosophical dialogue, such as the ones written by Plato and Cicero. In these dialogues, the participants come together to share knowledge, with the goal of reaching an agreement about a philosophical question. The second genre is the pastoral dialogue or eclogue; these texts often represent a singing contest between shepherds and declare a winner at the end. Next to these two genres, there developed a form in which the speakers are not equals but master and student. These are didactic dialogues, which obviously have more in common with the deliberative mode of philosophical dialogue than with the contentious sphere of the eclogue. The difference between philosophical and didactic dialogues is that in the latter one speaker already knows the answers to the questions, and sharing knowledge is a one-way street.

During the period of Late Antiquity, philosophical dialogue gained a polemical variant, as it was called upon to represent debates between a speaker defending Christian doctrines against the arguments of a pagan, Jew, or Christian heretic. As the need to defend Christian orthodoxy grew, so did the magisterial dialogue, for instance in the work of Augustine. The eclogue, in turn, was reinvented by Carolingian writers looking for classical models of dialogue. Still set in a bucolic setting, these debates took on allegorical proportions, as speakers became stand-ins for abstractions. For instance, in Alcuin's debate between Spring and Winter, the two personifications enter a shepherds' singing contest to find out who of them is superior to the other. Another example is the textbook favourite *Ecloga Theoduli*, in which a pagan shepherd named *Pseustis* ('Falsehood') comes up with mythical stories, and the Christian shepherdess *Alithia* ('Truth') answers him with biblical stories.[4]

Later on, the genre expanded beyond the bucolic setting and developed its allegorical aspect. From the late eleventh century onward, (allegorical) debate poetry flourished. Some pairings were especially beloved and produced numerous variants in many languages: the debate between the body and the soul, for instance,

---

[3] Binkley 1996, p. 677.
[4] Green 1982; Henkel 1991.

or that between the cleric and the knight.[5] Prose debates, such as those between adherents of different religions or representatives of different religious orders or political factions, also enjoyed renewed popularity.

Carmen Cardelle de Hartmann has proposed the following classification for Latin dialogue literature from the High and Later Middle Ages.[6] Her first category includes didactic dialogues, characterised by the question-and-answer format. She points out that the border between didactic dialogue and debate is fluid. Didactic dialogues often acquire a polemical tone, thereby turning into debates. Debates, conversely, tend to represent one speaker as morally superior from the outset; as a result, it can happen that this speaker adopts a dominant role and thus becomes a teacher.[7]

The second category includes debates (in German: *Streitgespräche*) about concrete contemporary issues, often religious conflicts, which are argued from opposing points of view. This category may be subdivided into debates against Jews and heretics, debates about religious controversies within Christianity, debates between a master and a student, and Raymond Lull's own innovative brand of literary debate.

The third category, soliloquies (in German: *selbstbetrachtende Dialoge*), includes dialogues in which a person searches for knowledge of the self in interaction with an aspect of the mind or the soul. An example is Hugh of St Victor's *Soliloquium de arrha animae*, in which *homo* converts *anima* from love for the world to love for God.

The fourth category is the philosophical dialogue, which is the most difficult category to define. In contrast to didactic dialogues and debates, in philosophical dialogues partners work together on an equal footing to tackle a problem. The problem or question arises out of a narration or in the course of the discussion itself. The issue that is raised is philosophical in nature but not polemical, and the speakers do not argue from theses proposed at the outset but propose their own solutions.

---

[5] Batiouchkof 1891; Bossy 1976; Faral 1912; Oulmont 1911.

[6] Cardelle de Hartmann 2007. I only discuss the major types within this classification and leave out mixed forms as well as the minor category of debates about salvation history.

[7] Cardelle de Hartmann 2007, p. 93.

The final category is that of dramatic allegory. Cardelle de Hartmann includes in this category dialogues with an elaborate fictional context and multiple allegorical characters, which associate this type of text closely with drama.

Note that this classification has no place for Latin debates of the kind I discuss in this article, namely, debates between two fictional or allegorical characters. This kind of debate, often written as poetry, flourished during the long twelfth century. Because Cardelle de Hartmann treats the period between 1200 and 1400 and excludes poetry, she did not encounter enough representatives of this type to include it in her classification.

Whereas Cardelle de Hartmann records almost no instances of fictional or allegorical debate, Peter Stotz's list of forty-six *Streitgedichte* includes debate poetry from the entire period of the Middle Ages but with a majority of texts from the eleventh and twelfth centuries.[8] Limiting the corpus to poetry means that the share of debates with fictional or allegorical speakers is large. Most of these debates are set in a narrative context, and in many cases, this narrative context includes the presence of a judge who pronounces a judgment at the end. Such a judgment, however, does not always proclaim one party as the winner of the debate. Often, the judge refuses to decide or grants a shared victory to both speakers.

Literary Debate in Interaction with Other Forms of Debate

The remarkable popularity of debate literature in various European languages, starting in the twelfth century, coincides with new uses of debate in judicial inquest and in scholastic disputation. Thomas Reed, writing about Middle English debate poetry, has claimed that scholastic, legal, and parliamentary disputation became institutionalised so quickly that 'debate poetry could probably have evolved directly from these institutional practices, even had there been no strictly literary precedent for such a genre.'[9] Ingrid Kasten has pointed out that analogous debating techniques are at work both in scholastic disputations and in

---

[8] Stotz 1999.
[9] Bloch 1977, p. 97.

(Middle High German) debate texts.[10] She notes the following elements: a strong appeal to authority; the practice of distinguishing between the different uses of terms for the sake of clarity; the discursive situation, which reminds one of public disputations, where it was more important to impress rhetorically than to argue convincingly; the confrontation of two ideas that seem mutually exclusive; the tripartite structure of thesis, antithesis, and solution; and, lastly, the aim to overcome situations in which two truths seem equally supported by logic.

Howard Bloch argued that both literary and non-literary forms of disputation went through a parallel evolution, from (the description of) actual and physical combat to mediated and verbal debate, from actual violence to symbolic violence.[11] He posited the parallel development of the system of civil judicial procedure, the growing corpus of vernacular debate literature, and the dialectical method in philosophy:

> The rise of an inquisitor court system, in which argumentation was practiced in the place of battle, along with the increasingly dialectical patterns of Latin and vernacular poetry, attest to the tremendous importance in all areas of cultural life — legal, intellectual, and literary — of what remains the verbal form of violence par excellence: the debate.[12]

Bloch names, for example, the *tenso*, a genre of troubadour song in which two poets defend opposite points of view, mostly in questions of love.[13] This kind of text became fully formalised as the *jeu-parti*. In a *jeu-parti*, the first speaker proposes a question together with two possible theses and gives the opponent the choice of which thesis to defend. Bloch also cites the example of Andreas Capellanus' treatise about courtly love, *De Amore*, in which amorous and sexual questions are debated in a way that is 'substantially the same as that of the inquisitor court, that is to say, a system of advocacy, negotiation, and arbitration.'[14]

---

[10] Kasten 1973, p. 228–232.
[11] Bloch 1977, p. 11, p. 163.
[12] Bloch 1977, p. 165.
[13] See also Bec 2000; Harvey & Paterson 2010.
[14] Bloch 1977, p. 212.

These two examples show that, although debate literature developed in parallel with judicial and scholastic forms of disputation and was not merely an imitation of these practices, the genre of debate literature does include imitation and parody of the forms of debate institutionalised by courts and universities. In fact, one could argue that this parodic stance is how the genre of literary debate becomes institutionalised itself, since its enormous appeal seems to derive largely from its constant interaction with the role of debate in society.

Apart from parody, scholars have mostly emphasised the marked preference of medieval literary debates for an unresolved ending: many debates end without a judgment, or with a judge declaring that neither or both of the speakers are right, or with the speakers debating who should be the judge. Some see this lack of resolution as a subversion of the principles of debate itself, namely opposition and resolution. One example of a debate poem without a decisive ending is the Middle English text titled *The Owl and the Nightingale*, which may be dated to the end of the twelfth or the beginning of the thirteenth century. Whereas early critics sought to provide the debate with a resolution that the text lacks, by declaring one of the birds the winner, later critics have concluded that the lack of resolution is exactly the point.[15] By refusing to satisfy the reader's desire for an ending with a clear winner, they argue, the debate offers a commentary on the rigidities and norms of non-literary debate.[16] Karen Gasser adds that this meta-function of *The Owl and the Nightingale* is not just a matter of literary play or pedagogical pragmatics. As she observes, 'there is a debate but the birds do not debate each other.'[17] Rather, they work together to overcome their apparent disagreement. Without a disagreement, there can be no winner. Resolution is achieved not in the manner of a debate but in the manner of a philosophical dialogue. Gasser concludes that this debate poem demonstrates the inadequacy of debate as an exercise in logic grounded upon dogma: 'The effect of the debate in *The Owl and*

---

[15] Gasser 1999.
[16] Gasser 1999.
[17] Gasser 1999, p. 92.

the Nightingale is to undermine the world of black and white distinctions which support traditional debate.'[18]

Gasser thus opposes literary debate to scholastic debate, which she calls traditional despite its novelty around 1200 in comparison with the long tradition of literary debate. Instead of subversion and undermining, however, one might also see shared goals and a common philosophy. Edmund Reiss, for instance, connected *The Owl and the Nightingale* to Abelard's *Sic et non*, which Reiss regards as setting the trend for a new kind of debate.[19] By confronting contradictory arguments from different authorities, *Sic et non* reflects a change from the debate as a rhetorical mode of representing a truth that one already knows to the debate as a dialectical mode of inquiry for finding the truth.[20] In its attempt to focus on the arguments rather than the resolution, the debate between the birds reveals an affinity with this new trend.

Ingrid Kasten makes a similar point in her study of Middle German debate poetry.[21] The irresolution that we find at the end of many debate poems, she says, is akin to the scholastic method of concordances, in which contradictory phrases are placed together in anticipation of, but temporarily without, a resolution.[22] She points out the similarity between the ways in which many debate poems and scholastic disputations deal with contradiction. The aim in both is to overcome conflict; the dissonance of an apparent contradiction is shown to be relative and connected to the limitations of human knowledge. In this way, temporary contradiction is turned into essential agreement.[23]

In sum, a number of scholars read the lack of resolution in debate poems as undermining the principles of debate established by non-literary forms of debate, namely, the opposition of two mutually exclusive points of view and a resolution of this situation by declaring one viewpoint to be true and the other false. Other scholars, however, hold that these principles do not in fact underlie non-literary debate as such and state that irresolu-

---

[18] Gasser 1999, p. 92.
[19] Reiss 1969, p. 870.
[20] Reiss 1969, p. 870.
[21] Kasten 1973.
[22] Kasten 1973, p. 229.
[23] Kasten 1973, p. 232–233.

tion and an attempt at reconciliation are features of all forms of medieval debate. Furthermore, the lack of a clear winner need not imply irresolution: resolution can be found in a reconciliation of opinions that only seemed contradictory at the outset of the disagreement.

It is not only the continuity between literary and non-literary debates that we need to stress in this regard, but also the continuity between literary debates before and after the twelfth century. In 1940, Friedrich Ranke still thought that irresolution was a development of the later Middle Ages, positing that the unresolved debate was an innovation of the fourteenth century.[24] The unresolved debate, however, seems to be as old as medieval debate literature itself. For example, in the Carolingian *Conflictus Veris et Hiemis*, a widely beloved text on one of the most popular debate themes, Spring is declared the winner, but the debate ends with two arguments in which the opponents admit that each is tied to the other: Winter argues that all of the activity in Spring is just a preparation for the wintertime, but Spring counters that this demonstrates Winter's dependence on Spring. In the end, one could argue that Spring wins the debate because the narrative is set in springtime, and that the course of the seasons will determine another winner in a few months. At the end of his discussion of this poem, Jon Whitman declares that 'one of the salient features of the poetic debate is its effort to show contraries complementing, rather than simply opposing, each other.'[25]

Latin Parody as a Scholarly Blind Spot

The twelfth century is the crucial time for medieval debate. A flowering of Latin debate poetry at monastic and cathedral schools takes place, building on a tradition that started in the Carolingian period. At universities, the scholastic disputation takes shape, and the judicial debate emerges in law courts. Lastly, the genres of the *tenso* and the *partimen*, written in Old Occitan, signal the start of vernacular debate poetry. A problem with the study of this formative period, however, is that it is often viewed

---

[24] Ranke 1940, p. 316.
[25] Whitman 1987, p. 142.

from the perspective of later times, when the scholastic disputation was a ubiquitous and institutionalised presence. As a result, contrasts that are more appropriate to a later period, such as that between Latin scholastic disputation as a cultural norm and vernacular debate poetry as a playful undermining of that norm, are projected onto the period before 1200.

The tension between discourses with serious and with parodic intent is often equated with the tension between Latin, as the language of intellectual debate, and the vernaculars. For the period after 1200, this assumption seems justifiable. Although even less research has been done on Latin debate texts after the twelfth century than before that time, the repertory and explorative study by Carmen Cardelle de Hartmann seem to indicate that this corpus contains both less parody and fewer fictional elements than before 1200. She notes a sharp decrease of fictional and allegorical debate partners starting in the thirteenth century.[26]

Regarding the period before 1200, however, it is often overlooked that the opposition between serious Latin debate texts and fictional vernacular parody does not hold. The reason for this blind spot is that Latin debate and dialogue literature is pushed to the background in two ways. First, the corpus is studied as the background against which vernacular debates profile themselves, as the 'literary tradition' which vernacular parody imitates and parodies. In this way, the Latin literature becomes disconnected from its historical context. For instance, Howard Bloch acknowledges the twelfth century, when the majority of debates are written in Latin, as the '[t]erminus a quo of a fundamental formal shift' and 'the beginning of the institutionalization of literary debate'.[27] Yet he studies this formal shift only in the vernacular texts; or rather, he studies the vernacular debates as shifting *away from* the Latin tradition.

Another example is Thomas Reed, who speculates that debate literature waned between the ninth and the twelfth centuries and that the supposed resurgence in the second half of the twelfth century, attested by the writing of vernacular debate literature,

---

[26] Cardelle de Hartmann 2007, p. 157.
[27] Bloch 1977, p. 167.

was 'a by-product of Aristotelian scholasticism'.[28] In reality, the debate had never gone away: the Carolingian debate culture, itself a revival of the Greco-Roman tradition, was continued in the following centuries without any lag in popularity. Reed takes this tradition into account only as a background to vernacular literature, and not even a necessary background. I have already quoted him as saying that 'the natures of medieval scholastic, legal, and parliamentary disputation were such that debate poetry could probably have evolved directly from these institutional practices, even had there been no strictly literary precedent for such a genre.'[29] At the most, he concedes that '[w]hile probably bred and fostered in the environments we have just examined, [debate poems] undoubtedly owe much of their vitality to long-established literary traditions as well.'[30]

Second, the studies that we do have on Latin debate and dialogue literature reinforce this association between Latin literary dialogue and normative tradition by focusing on didactic dialogue and scholastic disputation.[31] For instance, the part of Latin debate literature that has been analysed most profoundly are the interfaith debates between Christians, Jews, and, occasionally, Muslims about true religion.[32] Such texts are studied as belonging to a process of rationalisation: their Christian interlocutors cannot appeal to doctrine as a common ground and so must prove the superiority of their faith by argument alone.

We find this same focus on rationalisation in Alex Novikoff's work on Latin dialogues. Novikoff has argued that the scholastic debate came about through a rationalising tendency in didactic monastic dialogue during the eleventh and twelfth centuries.[33] He describes how didactic dialogue became more formalised and polemical, and thus developed into scholastic debate, in reaction to which literary debate poems emerged in vernacular languages. Novikoff's innovative research, however, disregards the role of Latin debate literature, even though this literature seems espe-

---

[28] Reed 1990, p. 111.
[29] Reed 1990, p. 97.
[30] Reed 1990, p. 97.
[31] Breitenstein 2011; Ronquist 1990.
[32] Abulafia 1998; Funkenstein 1971.
[33] Novikoff 2013.

cially pertinent to his model of development, since it already possesses the qualities of opposition and polemical argumentation characteristic of the scholastic disputation.

In sum, the scholarship on vernacular and Latin debate texts hardly overlaps. Although in both cases debate literature is associated with scholastic disputation and rationalisation, scholarship on vernacular debates after 1200 disregards the Latin corpus and focuses on parody and subversion, whereas scholarship on Latin dialogues before 1200 disregards exactly this aspect of parody and play in Latin texts.

Parody in Latin Debates

I want to show that Latin debate literature before 1200 already contained the kind of reactions to other forms of debate that are so characteristic of the genre after the twelfth century. I shall limit myself to an interaction that is both quite explicit and exclusive to literary debate, namely, parody. Simon Dentith defines parody as 'any cultural practice which provides a relatively polemical allusive imitation of another cultural production or practice.'[34] Martha Bayless, however, has downplayed the polemical character of medieval parody, arguing that even social parody in the Middle Ages is not necessarily critical of the subject it satirizes. The aim of medieval parody, she says, is more often to entertain than to criticise.[35] In contrast to modern parody, which is often critically directed at exceptional or novel phenomena, medieval parody concerns itself almost exclusively with norms and conventions, and not in a critical but in a playful way. In the words of Bayless, medieval parody is levelled against 'the classical and the conventional rather than the idiosyncratic and the avant-garde'.[36]

Bayless thus defines parody as follows, including the standard distinction between textual and social parody:

> [...] an intentionally humorous literary (written) text that achieves its effect by (1) imitating and distorting the distinguishing characteristics of literary genres, styles, authors, or specific texts (textual parody); or (2) imitating, with or with-

[34] Dentith 2000, p. 9.
[35] Bayless 1996, p. 7.
[36] Bayless 1996, p. 6.

out distortion, literary genres, styles, authors, or texts while in addition satirizing or focusing on non-literary customs, events, or persons (social parody).[37]

Most Latin parodic debates are classified as Goliardic poetry, which Marian Weiß defines according to six criteria: (1) a poem dated to the High Middle Ages, (2) with secular content, (3) written mainly in Latin, (4) rhymed, (5) with a comical intention that manifests itself not only through theme or narrative, (6) but primarily through language, intertext, and semantics.[38] I will first give an overview of the twelfth- and thirteenth-century Goliardic debates that Weiß lists,[39] although the rest of this article will focus on debate poems that fall outside these criteria, either because the poems were written before the year 1000 or because they do not use rhyme.

The first of the Goliardic debate poems is also the most famous, namely, the *Concilium Romarici Montis*, a poem which describes a debate in the monastery of Remiremont on the subject of whether knights or monks are the best lovers for nuns.[40] In the end, the abbess, who for the occasion is called *Cardinalis domina*, declares that from now on nuns will only be allowed to take monks as lovers and that anyone who offends against this rule will be excommunicated.

Two other erotic debates are the equally famous *Altercatio Ganimedes et Helene* and a lesser-known debate between Ganymede and Hebe.[41] These poems evidently inspired two debates between Summer and Winter that show many similarities to the debate between Ganymede and Helen.[42] A further love debate between mythological characters is the one between Acis and Polyphemus about who is worthier of Galathea's love.[43]

---

[37] Bayless 1996, p. 3.

[38] Weiß 2018, p. 9–10.

[39] The following references are all to Weiß 2018, p. 188–189.

[40] Anonymous, *Concilium Romarici Montis* (*Concilium*); Schulz 2014; Weiß 2018; nr. 21 in Stotz 1999.

[41] Weiß 2018, p. 177.

[42] Both are called *Conflictus hiemis et estatis*. Nr. 31 in Stotz 1999 begins with *Taurum sol intraverat, ivi spaciatum/ urebat me nimius*; see Walther 1920, p. 203–206. Nr. 32 in Stotz begins with *Taurum sol intraverat, ivi spaciatum / parens florum ver erat*; see Walther 1920, p. 206–209.

[43] Walther 1920, p. 224–227. This one is not in Stotz's list.

In the debate *De presbitero et logico*, also known as the *Causa pauperis scolaris cum presbytero*, dating to either the twelfth or the thirteenth century, the protagonists are a logician and a priest. The priest tricks the logician, who is then beaten by the parishioners.[44] Another debate in which the participants almost come to blows is *De Clarevallensibus et Cluniacensibus*. This debate parodies similar didactic or philosophical dialogues between members of different monastic orders. In these serious dialogues, the debaters are not drunk and do not resort to violence, as they do in the parody.[45] A second debate between a poor Cistercian and a rich Benedictine monk is the one between two monks called Maurus and Zoilus.[46] Lastly, Weiß lists a debate between the body and the spirit, one of the most beloved themes in debate literature.[47]

Although restrictions of space here forbid an overview and analysis of the content and forms of these debates, the kinds of debaters indicated above make clear that parodic debates model themselves on various genres of debate and dialogue, both non-literary, such as church councils (*Concilium Romarici Montis*), and literary, such as pastoral debates between Summer and Winter, interreligious or intermonastic debates, and spiritual debates. In the remainder of the article, I examine five lesser-known debate poems that fall outside the criteria of Goliardic poetry. I will discuss their methods of parody and the genre of debate or dialogue that becomes the object of their ridicule.

Parody of the Teacher and the School

First, I look at to two early debates situated in a school context. In these debates, the authority of the teacher or the curriculum is under attack. The similarities between the two debates are striking and led Michael Lapidge to suggest that we are dealing 'with a distinct genre of medieval Latin school poetry which has left very few descendants.'[48]

---

[44] Nr. 36 in Stotz 1999, p. 21.
[45] Nr. 41 in Stotz 1999, p. 21.
[46] This one is not in Stotz's list.
[47] Nr. 37 in Stotz 1999.
[48] Lapidge 1972, p. 102.

The first text, which has been called *Terentius et Delusor*, is a short fragment from the late ninth or tenth century and is found in a manuscript together with texts by classical school authors such as Martial, Lucan, and Vergil (but not Terence).[49] The debate is conceived as a play and accompanied by stage directions. A first speaker, presumably a pupil, complains that the canonical school author Terence is boring and difficult to read: *Vade, poeta uetus, quia non tua carmina curo; / Iam retice fabulas, dico, uetus ueteres*.[50] He says there is nothing useful in Terence's plays, except that they teach how to fart (*Quae nil, credo, iuvant, pedere ni doceant*).[51] Not only are the plays of Terence boring, it is not even clear if they are written in prose or in poetic metre. Therefore the pupil's challenge to Terence is: *Dic, vetus auctor, in hoc quae iacet utilitas?*[52]

Prompted by these words, the character of Terence enters the stage (*Nunc Terentius exit foras audiens haec*) and demands to know who is slandering his muse.[53] In the remainder of the fragment, the first speaker, identified by the rubrics as *persona delusoris*,[54] pesters Terence about his old age. Terence reacts by threatening physical violence yet does not dare to execute his threats. In this way, the duo enacts a reversal and parody of a classroom situation. The pupil even adopts the didactic form of question and answer in a mocking way:

> *Si rogitas, quis sum, respondeo: te melior sum:*
> *Tu uetus atque senex, ego tyro ualens adulescens;*
> *Tu sterilis truncus, ego fertilis arbor, opimus.*
> *Si taceas, uetule, lucrum tibi quaeris enorme.*[55]

---

[49] Paris, Bibliothèque nationale de France, MS Latin 8069, f. 127v–128r. Anonymous, *Terentius et Delusor*, p. 1088–1090.

[50] *Terentius et Delusor*, p. 1088, l. 3–4. 'Go away, old poet, because I don't care about your poems; / you are old and should keep your old stories to yourself, I tell you.' Translations are my own.

[51] *Terentius et Delusor*, p. 1088, l. 6.

[52] *Terentius et Delusor*, p. 1089, l. 12. 'Tell me, old writer, what is the use of it?'.

[53] *Terentius et Delusor*, p. 1089, l. 13. 'Now Terence steps outside and hears these words [...]'.

[54] On the ambiguous meaning of the phrase *persona delusoris*, see Symes 2003, p. 37–38.

[55] *Terentius et Delusor*, p. 1089, l. 29–32. 'If you ask who I am, I will answer you: I am better than you: / You are old and grey, I am young, healthy, and strong; / You are a fruitless trunk, I am a fertile tree in bloom. / If you would remain silent, little old man, you would do yourself a huge favour.'

The pupil questions the author's authority by opposing his own youth to the irrelevance of old age. The author, in turn, resorts to threats of corporal punishment but is too afraid to lift his hand against the physically stronger pupil.

Because he posited an association between this fragment and Hrotsvitha's imitation of Terence, Winterfeld published the fragment in his edition of Hrotsvitha's plays.[56] The suggestion has also been made that the fragment served as an introduction to a recitation of Terence's plays by an actor impersonating the playwright and possibly accompanied by mime.[57] By supposing that Terence gains the upper hand and humbles the pupil, these suggestions put forward a rather different reading of the fragment than mine. For instance, Carol Symes reads the humour of the piece as a case of subtle irony: 'In fact, the prose stage directions not only help to explain the versified action, they assist in playing a theatrical joke on the Deludor [Symes' translation of *Delusor*]. Anonymous and alone when he begins his complaint, he is suddenly "revealed" or unmasked as a character like those in the very plays he despises, when he is surprised by the entrance of the playwright himself.'[58] I find it difficult to follow this line of thought; Terence is clearly a victim of ridicule and has his back against the wall, at least for the duration of the fragment. I find it more illuminating to read the poem in the context of parodic school debates and to compare it, for instance, to the following text, which is a clear example of the genre.

The *Altercatio magistri et discipuli* is a school debate that Michael Lapidge dates to the end of the tenth century and situates in the circle of Bishop Aethelwold at Winchester.[59] In the manuscript, this poem is found together with such texts as the *Aetna*, a didactic poem on volcanoes; the *Culex*, a mock pastoral epyllion; the *Carmen de ponderibus*, a didactic poem on units of measurement; and poems by Ausonius.[60] In the debate, a disgruntled pupil attacks his foreign teacher by exposing the latter's

---

[56] Winterfeld 1902.
[57] Stotz 1999, p. 6. Tydeman 1979, p. 27.
[58] Symes 2003, p. 38.
[59] Anonymous, *Altercatio magistri et discipuli*.
[60] Cambridge, Cambridge University Library, MS Kk.5.34.

arrogance and incompetence. The pupil opens his remarks with an elaborate series of similes from nature to show that the magister is a kind of monster and a perversion of nature for thinking of himself as a true scholar when he is only an amateur. Then the pupil launches into a tirade of invectives: *uafer atque furcifer insipidus, monstrum, sicophanta baburus, cerritus balatro, spurcus si non silicernus*, and so on.[61] The pupil poses his teacher a pedagogical challenge: if the teacher really is as good a poet and philosopher as he alleges, then he ought to teach his pupils the skills he possesses instead of chiding them for writing bad poetry.

> [...] *summum profiterier audit*
> *se fore philosophum cunctoque sophismate comptum,*
> *dum minime sciat hoc quid philosophus sit (et unde est*
> *hoc nomen tractum? Cuius generis siet, ede).*[62]

The teacher replies with matching eloquence and similes, likening the pupil to someone who is foolish enough to brave the ocean in a rickety vessel. The pupil responds that the teacher would do better to prove his authority by teaching the class about *genus*, *species*, harmonies, and the like. Only then will he have the right to use the rod on them. The teacher indignantly demonstrates his knowledge by discoursing about the measurement of time; then he orders the pupil to stop writing slanderous poems. The pupil finally relents on the condition that there will be less scolding and more teaching in the future.

The poem parodies the pedagogical methods of presumptuous teachers: instead of sharing the little knowledge they have, they aggrandise their own qualities by degrading those of their pupils. The poem parodies not only bad teachers but also the genre of the didactic dialogue, in which an admiring and obedient student asks questions of an authoritative teacher-philosopher. Here the roles

---

[61] *Altercatio magistri et discipuli*, p. 110, l. 15–16. 'The cunning and unsavoury rascal [...], the monster, the foolish slanderer, the crazy buffoon if not foul bag of bones [...]' Translations of this and the following excerpts from this work are also by Lapidge.

[62] *Altercatio magistri et discipuli*, p. 112, l. 27–30. '[...] he dares to profess himself the greatest philosopher, accomplished in all learning, while at the same time he hardly knows what a philosopher is. (And from whence is this noun derived? Tell what gender it is!)'.

are reversed, with the student having to blackmail and threaten his teacher to get him to teach. Lapidge considers this debate a combination of two kinds of dialogue literature: the Latin didactic dialogue and the vernacular flyting, a verbal contest by means of personal insults.[63]

Parody of Church and State Councils

In the twelfth century, instead of parodies of the classroom situation, we find many debates that imitate and parody the discussions held at ecclesiastical and state councils. The most famous among these is the *Concilium Romarici Montis*, which I have already mentioned. The text imitates the formal language and procedures of church councils and combines this language with a debate about questions of love and sex. This work belongs to the genre of the love courts, or courtly councils that pass judgment in love matters, of which Andreas Capellanus' treatise *De Amore* is a prime example. The parody of the *Concilium* is both textual, subverting the protocols and idiom of church councils, and social, making fun of both the high seriousness of such councils and the failure of monastics to live up to their vows of chastity. That being said, the text is not so much a critique as an exploration of the amusing combination of a highly formal debate with an inappropriate subject and unlikely participants.

As to parodies of state councils, two examples are of particular note. They are both by Petrus Riga (*c*. 1140–1209), who was a canon at Reims and assembled his early poetry, including these two debate poems, in a collection entitled *Floridus Aspectus*. The book has survived in various manuscripts.[64]

The first of these debates, the *Causa duorum apostolicorum*, refers to the papal election of 1159 following the death of Adrian IV. After a majority of the cardinals elected Alexander III as the new pope, a minority rejected this decision and elected their own candidate, Victor IV. The debate opens with

---

[63] *Altercatio magistri et discipuli*, p. 99. In this regard, the debate resembles the *magister-discipulus* flytings of the *Hisperica Famina*.

[64] http://www.mirabileweb.it/title/floridus-aspectus-petrus-riga-m-1209-title/15427 (accessed 11.02.2021).

an address by both parties to the council. Both advocates express their wish for unity and justice in the Church. They then try to establish a legal basis for the debate.

Alexander's representative, who will eventually be declared the winner of the debate, makes a plea for considering the case in its logical order: *Si bene metitur rem recti linea, Victor, / quem melius Victum nomino, causa mali.*[65] Since Alexander was declared pope first, this is a logical argument for the representative to make. But Victor's advocate also declares himself willing to look at the order of events: *Me iuvat ordo rei, rem prosequar ordine certo; / res discussa dabit, quae mala, quisve malus.*[66] At that, Alexander's representative accuses his opponent of using rhetorical tricks and pleads for *simplicitas*: *Iste suam causam polit, utar simplice vero, / veri simplicitas verba polita fugit.*[67]

After establishing these principles for the debate, it is time for the two opponents to breach them. First, they fight about the papal mantle, the *mantum*, which Victor apparently wore first. And here we have the explanation for why Victor's advocate declared himself in favour of considering the logical order of events. Alexander's representative objects that Rome had given him the mantle, and Victor stole it. Victor's advocate refutes this accusation: *Non dedit, ille sibi manti mentitur honorem, / pagina mantatos non habet ulla duos.*[68] Alexander's advocate responds with rhetorical flair: *Non habet, unus erat, nec habens mantum neque mentem / qui rapuit mantum, mente monente manum.*[69] The debate then turns into a rhetorical game. Alexander's advocate refutes his opponent by subverting his

---

[65] Petrus Riga, *Causa duorum apostolicorum* (Riga, *Causa duorum apostolicorum*), l. 11–12, p. 549. 'If the case is considered in its logical order, Victor, / whom I should rather call Victum [i.e., in Latin, "the loser, the vanquished"], is the cause of this wrongdoing.' Translations of this text are my own.

[66] Riga, *Causa duorum apostolicorum*, l. 13–14, p. 549. 'The order of events pleases me, I will describe the case in the right order; / an examination of the case will establish what is wrong, or who is wrong.'

[67] Riga, *Causa duorum apostolicorum*, l. 15–16, p. 549. 'He polishes his case, I simply make use of the truth, / the simplicity of the truth flees from polished words.'

[68] Riga, *Causa duorum apostolicorum*, l. 33–34, p. 550. 'Rome did not give him the mantle, he is falsely claiming the honour of the mantle, / there is not one document that attests to two mantled popes.'

[69] Riga, *Causa duorum apostolicorum*, l. 35–36, p. 550. 'Indeed he does not

words with rhyme. When Victor's representative says: *Laudibus assurgit obvia Roma patri*,[70] Alexander's advocate answers: *Non laudes, sed erant fraudes, non palma, sed arma*.[71] When Victor's representative mentions that people are singing and making music in honour of Victor, the other answers: *Non cantus, sed erant plantus, lira nulla, sed ira*.[72]

A major bone of contention is not the *res* in its *ordine certo*, but rather Victor's name. Right at the beginning, Alexander's representative had already remarked that Victor should rather be called *Victum* (the vanquished instead of the victor). Later in the discussion, Victor's advocate brings up the name as an argument: *Victor, victoris nomen et omen habes*.[73] His opponent answers that, in this case, the name stands for its opposite: *Ludit et eludit suus illum nominis error, / Nomen ab opposito, non quia vincat, habet*.[74] At the end, the judges declare: *Victor – res nova – victus erit. Vicit Alexander*.[75] Whereas the debate starts out with legal principles, its arguments ultimately revolve around rhetorical tricks. Victor's advocate bases his plea on two 'facts': the mantle and the name. The judges, however, overthrow his rhetoric.

The second debate from the *Floridus Aspectus* takes up a conflict between the king of France and the king of England and is titled *Causa regis Francorum contra regem Anglorum*.[76] The title refers to a historical conflict between Louis VII of France and Henry Plantagenet of England about the marriage of their children. The

---

have it, there was only one, and who stole the mantle has neither the mantle nor his mind, because his mind was guiding his hand.'

[70] Riga, *Causa duorum apostolicorum*, l. 42, p. 550. 'Rome rises up to praise her father.'

[71] Riga, *Causa duorum apostolicorum*, l. 43–44, p. 550. 'It was not praise [*laudes*] but delusion [*fraudes*], no palms but arms.'

[72] Riga, *Causa duorum apostolicorum*, l. 47, p. 550. 'It was not songs [*cantus*] but complaints [*plantus*], no lyre, but ire.'

[73] Riga, *Causa duorum apostolicorum*, l. 38, p. 550. 'Victor, you carry your name as the sign of a victor.'

[74] Riga, *Causa duorum apostolicorum*, l. 39–40, p. 550. 'His mistake about his name tricks and mocks him, / He has his name not because he is a winner but because he is the opposite.'

[75] Riga, *Causa duorum apostolicorum*, l. 106–107, p. 551. 'Victor — here is something new — will be defeated. Alexander has won.'

[76] Petrus Riga, *Causa regis Francorum contra regem Anglorum* (Riga, *Causa regis*).

marriage contract stipulated that the dowry would include two fortified castles, which would only be transferred to Henry once the marriage between the children, who were still too young at the time, was officially celebrated. Henry, however, seized the two fortifications before the marriage had taken place. The text represents a debate about this question between the advocates of the kings.

The advocate of the French king begins by praising the moral qualities of his king, whom he calls, among other things, *flos rerum, generis fulgor, honoris apex*.[77] He describes how the kingdom of France enjoyed a period of perfect peace until England brought war upon it. He then foresees and tries to pre-empt the use of a certain argument by his opponent, namely, allegorical etymology.[78]

> *Nec bene respondent nomen opusque sibi.*
> *Nominis augurium scrutare: uel angelus Anglus*
> *Ille, uel angelicus Anglicus ille sonat.*
> *Facta notes: Anglus, non angelus est, neque coelo*
> *Dignus, sed sceleris angulus, imo scelus.*[79]

The association between *anglus* and *angelus* goes back to a tale told about Gregory the Great, who visits a slave market in Rome and asks about the origin of some young men. When told that they are *Angli*, he says that is a fitting name because they look like *angeli*.[80] It is ironic that although the speaker rejects the truth of allegorical etymology in the case of the English, he himself then offers an alternative etymology, appealing to the word *angulus*.

---

[77] Riga, *Causa regis*, p. 7. 'the flower of the country, the glory of his house, the crown of honour.' Translations are my own.

[78] Del Bello 2007, p. 45–46: 'To conclude, we may say that allegorical etymology (*etymegoreia*) is present when a linguistic form, a signifier, is created or is read as an allegory [...] of its possible meaning(s), or signified(s).'

[79] Riga, *Causa regis*, p. 8. 'Nor is there a good match between his name and his deeds. / You look at what his name tells you, and think that either this Englishman (*Anglus*) sounds like an angel (*angelus*), / or that Englander (*Anglicus*) sounds angelic (*angelicus*). / But if you look at his deeds, you see he is an Englishman, not an angel, and not worthy of heaven, / but the angle (*angulus*) of evil, yes evil itself.'

[80] Anonymous Monk of Whitby, *The earliest life of Gregory the Great*. Bede, *Bede's ecclesiastical history of the English people*. Harris 2002.

The advocate of the English king responds to the pun on *anglus*, *angelus*, and *angulus* not with a further pun but with an argument hinting at the discipline of logic:

> *Obiicis, o linguae uenalis caupo, quod Anglus*
> *Iste nec est nec erit angelus; ad quod ego:*
> *Laus est esse bonum si non sis optimus, actu*
> *Si non angelus est, nomen inhaeret ei.*[81]

The Englishman here casts the etymological argument in the form of a logical dispute, with a thesis (*Objicis [...] nec est nec erit angelus*), an antithesis (*ad quod ego*), and the use of philosophical terminology (*actu* and *nomen inhaeret*). He reaffirms that the etymological allegory of the name is valid. Even though the association between *anglus* and *angelus* does not mean that the Englishman is actually an angel (*actu*, commonly used in opposition to *potentia*), the name still indicates a property that is inherent in him (*inhaeret*).

The first argument of the Englishman is that the advocate of the French king speaks with too much rhetorical flourish to be trustworthy. The Englishman draws a contrast between the grandiloquent French and the English, who actually get things done, with weapons and not with words. Ironically, the words with which he makes this argument are themselves an exercise in rhetoric:

> *Qualiter haec linguam pictura coloris inauret*
> *Rhetorici certum, sancta senatus, habes;*
> *Sed sub flore rubus, sed fel sub melle, sed anguis*
> *Sub foliis, sed pix sub niue saepe latet.*[82]

He then proceeds to describe the course of events in chronological order. In his version, the French king had been the one to urge the signing of the marriage contract and who broke his promises.

---

[81] Riga, *Causa regis*, p. 9. 'You argue, you seller of your tongue, that the Englishman / Neither is nor will be an angel. To which I say: / Being good is a virtue even though you are not the best; / Even if he is not actually an angel, the name still inheres in him.'

[82] Riga, *Causa regis*, p. 9. 'Revered council, you surely see how / he gilds his tongue with rhetorical paint; / But beneath the flower often hide thorns, gal beneath the honey, a snake / beneath the leaves, pitch beneath the snow.'

Consequently, the English use of violence was a justified reaction. The English advocate's plea ends with a proud challenge to look at the cracks in the shields of the English and the blood on their weapons, followed by an insulting pun on the name of the French:

> *Non mihi sed clypeis aut armis credite, rimas*
> *Ostendunt clypei, purpurat arma cruor.*
> *Talis laus Anglis blanditur saepe, sed illa*
> *Vobis, o Galii, semper avara manet.*
> *Vos etenim crista gallorum, non galearum*
> *Vertice cristari, nomine teste, decet.*[83]

At the end of the debate, the judges base their decision in favour of the French king on rhetorical grounds as well. They employ their own play on words: *Singula rimamur: tu plenus es, Anglice, rimis; / Integra, Galle, tuo uernat in ore fides.*[84] The word *rimare* can mean 'to examine' or 'to make verses.' But the word also alludes to the Englishman's request that the judges look at the cracks (*rimae*) in his shield. The judges now respond that he too is full of cracks. Furthermore, the phrase *plenus rimis* could also be read as referring to that beloved author Terence, who writes in his *Eunuchus* about a slave who will not gossip about things that are true but will only repeat lies: *sin falsum aut uanum aut finctumst, continuo palamst:/ plenus rimarum sum, hac atque illac perfluo.*[85] Thus, the *rimis* in question could have a material as well as a rhetorical nature.[86] In contrast to the rhetorically compromised Englishman, the Frenchman is declared the winner because the judges find that his honesty is proven by his rhetoric.

By equating the rhetorical with the argumentative value of the debate, the text appears to parody the idea of the debate as a way

---

[83] Riga, *Causa regis*, p. 11. 'Do not believe me but our shields and weapons, cracks / are shown by our shields, and blood turns our weapons purple. / The English are often flattered with such praise, but / from you, Frenchmen, it is always withheld. / It is more fitting for you to wear on your head (*vertice cristari*) the cockscomb (*crista gallorum*) than the plume of a helmet ([*crista*] *galearum*), going by your name [i.e., *Galli*, French, and *galli*, cocks].'

[84] Riga, *Causa regis*, p. 11. 'Let us examine these arguments: you, Englishman, are too full of cracks; Frenchman, your good faith flourishes in your speech.'

[85] Terentius 2001, p. 325. 'But if anything's false or fanciful or fictional, it's out at once: I'm full of cracks, I leak all over.' Translation by Barsby.

[86] And, not to forget, often of a sexual nature, which could also play a role in insulting the Englishman.

to determine who has the strongest arguments. Both speakers present their own twisted truth and are more concerned with insulting the opponent and with scoring rhetorical points than with the argument itself; the Englishman resorts to showing off his weapons and threatening violence, and the judges give the victory to the most flowery speech. The text makes fun of state councils by representing a diplomatic meeting as a rhetoric class. The parody makes use of rhetorical exercises as well as disputations in logic. With this text as well, however, the aim of the parody is probably not to express any fundamental critique of debate but rather to poke intertextual fun at a serious matter.

Parody of Theological Debate

In the previous cases, the parody included the combination of an official debate setting and silly argumentation. A last type of parody I want to discuss does the opposite; it places serious theological argumentation in the mouth of unusual debate partners. This type of debate often features animals or objects as speakers, as in the debates between water and wine or the debate between the spider and the fly.[87] The debate that interests us here is between a sheep and a flax plant.[88] The debate was probably composed between 1068 and 1075 by a certain Winrich, a teacher and librarian at the cathedral in Trier, and it has survived in a number of manuscripts.[89]

The text opens with a flock of sheep grazing in a field of flax. Suddenly, a flax plant speaks up to protest being trampled and defecated upon by the sheep. The argument quickly develops from basic facts about utility to evidence from the Bible, and then turns into a theological discussion. Each phase of the debate elevates the subject.

In the first phase, the animal and the plant insult each other. The sheep cruelly taunts the plant by describing the whole process

---

[87] *Dialogus inter aquam et vinum*, nr. 18 in Stotz 1999. *Pulicis et musce iurgia*, nr. 23 in Stotz 1999.

[88] Winrich of Trier, *Conflictus ovis et lini* (Winrich, *Conflictus*). Due to restricted access to library resources, I refer to the older edition by Haupt instead of the newer edition by Dräger. Stotz 2002.

[89] Stotz 2002.

of converting flax into linen, during which the plant will be left to rot in order to remove the inner stalk, after which what remains of the plant will be broken and scraped. The flax plant responds by describing how a sheep's skin is made into leather.

In the second phase, the sheep argues that it is more useful to people than the plant. The sheep begins by stating that humans need two things in life: clothing against the cold and food to take away hunger. Both of these are provided by sheep in the form of wool and milk. The flax plant agrees that clothing and food are most important to humans but argues that they can be had without the help of sheep. In fact, many people never consume the meat, cheese, or milk of sheep and never wear clothing made of sheepskin or wool, either because they find it too cheap or too heavy. No one, however, dresses without linen, if only because it is the fabric of undergarments.

> *applicat interius, nudos adstringit ad artus.*
>   *tamquam dicat 'amo quod mihi sic socio.'*
> *si nix aut imber aut turbidus irruit aer,*
>   *cautus ovem nostrum tradit ad obsequium;*
> *te tradit ventis obicitlque furentibus auris.*[90]

The sheep objects that, whereas many animals provide skins, only sheep provide wool. The sheep continues by singing the praises of wool, not least its receptivity to dye of every possible colour. A panegyric follows about the different kinds of dyes and where they come from. The flax plant, however, protests:

> *Ut laudetur ovis, species numerare coloris*
>   *quae poscat ratio non penitus video.*
> *splendor enim caeli suus est, suus est viror agri;*
>   *quod nix albescit, id decor eius erit.*
> *sic diversorum sua laus est forma colorum:*
>   *non sit ovis, numquid non color ullus erit?*[91]

---

[90] Winrich, *Conflictus*, p. 219. 'They place [these garments] on the inside, / they bind them around their naked limbs, / as if to say: "I love what I keep so close to me." / When snow or rain or storm besets them, / cautious people put sheep into our service; / they surrender you to the winds and place you between me and the howling storms.' Translations of this text are my own.

[91] Winrich, *Conflictus*, p. 221. 'I do not quite understand which kind of logic demands / that you enumerate all the different colours in order to praise sheep. /

By contrast, there are many uses to which linen is put that accrue to the plant's own merit: it can be made, for instance, into towels, tablecloths, pillowcases, tents, and so on.

Whereas phase two was concerned with basic utilities, the talk now turns, in phase three, to more exclusive and holy uses of both wool and linen. The sheep smartly counters the temporary prevalence of the plant by pointing out that wool is the preferred garment of holy people when they flee from the world and its luxuries. Moreover, sheepskin provides parchment, without which no books would be copied, and the whole of Christianity would fall apart. All of the prose and poetry of the world would not have existed:

> *omnes postremo res gestas a patre primo,*
> *quod fuit ante chaos, seria sive iocos,*
> *quod Phoebus Musas, Musae docuere poetas,*
> *quae ratio Stellas, quaeve polos moveat,*
> *quae metuenda malis, quae sint speranda beatis,*
> *quid sit qui rebus praesidet ipse deus,*
> *omnia novit ovis, per oves haec percipit orbis,*
> *ipsa dei patris mystica novit ovis.*[92]

The plant scoffs that this honour could more fittingly be claimed by calves and young goats, as they provide softer vellum. Concerning the clothing of holy people, it is obvious that they want to punish their bodies by wearing woollen garments. Next, the flax plant enumerates various references to the use of linen in Leviticus and challenges the sheep to do the same. The sheep, in referring to the Passover ritual, clearly dominates on this front, so the plant proposes to talk about the Church, recalling the use of linen for liturgical vestments. The sheep of course exploits this oppor-

---

The splendor of the sky is its own, the greenness of the field its own; / that snow is white will contribute to the beauty of the snow. / Likewise the form of all the colours is their own praise: / if there would be no sheep, surely there would still be colours?'.

[92] Winrich, *Conflictus*, p. 224. 'In short, all the things that happened since the first father, / what existed before the chaos, both the serious and the playful texts, / which Phoebus taught the Muses and the Muses to the poets, / which order moves the stars and which the poles, / what is to be feared by evil persons and what to be hoped for by good persons; / what is the nature of God himself who rules everything, / the sheep knows everything, through sheep the world perceives this knowledge, / even the mysteries of God the Father the sheep knows.'

tunity to speak about the symbol of the lamb, and again gets carried away:

> *agne, tibi tellus, tibi subdita servit abyssus;*
> *tu regis, agne, polos inferiusque chaos;*
> *agne, tui iuris haec sunt et quicquid in illis:*
> *talia gratuitae praemia mortis habe.*[93]

At this the flax plant falls silent and has no answer, but then it recollects itself and gives the sheep a lesson in semiotics: to say that Christ is a lamb is only a way of speaking and has no importance for the worth of actual sheep.

> *est aliquid porro cur se similaverit agno:*
> *nec tamen ipse tulit vellera factus ovis:*
> *significativam speciem vidisse prophetam*
> *ius erat: id typicis convenit eloquiis.*[94]

Something exists, however, which is not only a symbol but also real presence, namely, the Eucharist. The flax plant now delivers a final blow by reminding its opponent that the chalice and the paten which hold the wine and bread during Mass are wrapped in linen (i.e., the corporal).

At this point, the sheep decides to call in the help of a judge. Both discussion partners then spend a lot of time deliberating about who would make a good judge. The sheep suggests an abbot, the flax plant prefers a king, and eventually they decide on a council of archbishops. The text ends with this preliminary agreement.

This final exchange about who has the right to declare a winner is typical for the tendency of the text to focus on the terms of the debate. It happens multiple times, for instance, that the sheep in its arrogance declares itself the winner without giving the plant

---

[93] Winrich, *Conflictus*, p. 233. 'Lamb, it is you the world serves, and the abyss obeys you; / lamb, you rule the poles and the chaos underneath; / lamb, under your jurisdiction is all of this and what is in them: / such a reward you get for your voluntary death.'

[94] Winrich, *Conflictus*, p. 234. 'There is a deeper reason why Christ likens himself to a lamb: / and it is not because he himself turned into a sheep and wore a sheepskin: / as a rule, the prophet saw things in symbolical appearance: / this is proper to allegorical speech.'

a chance to respond. In one such case, the plant sharply retorts: *In causa recipi pro iudice non solet hostis, / nec lis ista tuo constat in arbitrio.*[95] As the terminology here used by the plant indicates (*causa, iudex, hostis, lis, arbitrium*), theological argument is not the only kind of debate to which the text refers. The sheep's infringement on the plant's territory and the subsequent debate between the two are drawn into the judicial sphere and treated with no less fervour than the act of war perpetrated by the king of England in France. In neither case, though, would the arguments be of much use in a court of law.

In the course of their discussion, the animal and the plant progress from ordinary insults and threats, as in the tradition of flyting, to reminding each other of the legal rights of each opponent, as in a judicial debate, and then to quoting biblical evidence for their case and not even shying away from (ab)using the most central theological dogmas of Christianity to win an argument about their own superiority over the other. All the while, the sheep is so intent on rhetorically crushing the plant that it makes the most absurd and illogical inferences, for instance, that parchment carries all the knowledge of the world and therefore sheep do as well, or that the symbol of something is the same as the thing itself. But although the plant gains the argumentative upper hand every time, the plant is no less arrogant than its opponent and equally blind for not seeing that the question of superiority has become irrelevant and irreverent once the argument enters the domain of theology. So once again, a mock debate is first of all a parody of the different forms and practices of debating.

Conclusion

In conclusion, parodying normative forms of dialogue and debate is a practice common to debate as a literary genre throughout the Middle Ages (and later times, for that matter). New norms, such as the judicial and scholastic forms of debate, evoke new forms of parody, but earlier genres come with their own parodic imitations.

---

[95] Winrich, *Conflictus*, p. 229. 'It is not the custom in a debate to let one's opponent become the judge, / nor do you have the authority to judge this lawsuit.'

I have focused on parody, although the interaction between literary debate and other forms of debate is of course much broader. But parody as a form of interaction is both the most explicit kind of interaction and something that exclusively belongs to literary debate. My aim has been to draw attention to the continuity between Latin and vernacular mock debates. It is true that Latin mock debates are less abundantly attested after 1200 and that vernacular debate poetry becomes immensely popular around the same time, bringing new subgenres in its wake. But I would argue that these new genres are not the beginning of parodic debate but rather a reaction to the institutionalisation of new forms and norms of debate. Parodic debates written before the completion of this institutionalisation process are directed at many different debate genres, such as the school dialogue, the church council, the diplomatic debate, or the theological discussion. Most of all, however, these literary forms play with and parody the discipline of rhetoric.

The texts that I have analysed parody specific forms of serious debate. The debates between impertinent pupils and terrible teachers parody the didactic dialogue, in which model students ask questions of wise teachers. The parody reverses the roles between pupils and teachers: either the pupil does not care about learning and threatens the teacher (or the author, in the case of *Terentius et Delusor*) with corporal punishment, or the pupil yearns for learning and forces the teacher to finally deliver some good teaching, as in the case of the *Altercatio magistri et discipuli*. Moreover, these texts parody rhetorical school exercises by putting this specific method of teaching in the service of insulting the teacher.

Parody of school exercises in rhetoric is an element not only of the debates set in a school context. Many literary debates parody official and public ways of debating matters of state, such as the proceedings of church councils, by replacing serious argumentation with over-the-top rhetorical fireworks and nonsense arguments. What is noteworthy is that literary debates do not seem to parody specific ways of argumentation and reasoning. Rather, by substituting silly wordplay for serious argument, the literary debates parody the seriousness of such occasions. Where we do find such a parody of argumentation itself is in literary debates in which animals or objects hold theological discussions. In such cases, however, the cause and stakes of the debate are so ridiculous that the arguments can no longer be taken seriously. A constant element in all of these debates is that the opponents discuss the terms of the debate itself, such as which arguments are allowed and who has the authority to pass judgment. Despite this reflection on the norms and rules of the debate, however, the purpose of parody seems to lie more in diversion than in a commentary on or critique of the hermeneutical value of debate.

To conclude, Latin literary debates before 1200 are not only the background against which scholastic debate and vernacular parody develop; genres of serious argumentative debate had been producing their own mock debates for a much longer time and in various ways.

Bibliography

Primary Sources

Anonymous, *Altercatio magistri et discipuli*, ed. M. Lapidge, in *Anglo-Saxon England*, 1, ed. P. Clemoes et al., Cambridge: Cambridge University Press, 1972, p. 85–137.

Anonymous, *Causa duorum apostolicorum*, ed. H. Boehmer, Berlin: MGH, 1896 (Monumenta Germaniae Historica, III: Libelli de Lite Imperatorum et Pontificum), p. 547–554.

Anonymous, *Concilium Romarici Montis*, ed. P. Pascal, Bryn Mawr, PA: Hackett Publishing Company, 1993.

Anonymous, *Terentius et Delusor*, ed. K. Strecker, Berlin: MGH, 1891 (Monumenta Germaniae Historica, IV.3: Poetae latini aevi Carolini), p. 1088–1090.

Anonymous Monk of Whitby, *The Earliest Life of Gregory the Great*, ed. Bertram Colgrave, Cambridge: Cambridge University Press, 1986.

Bede, *Bede's ecclesiastical history of the English people*, ed. Bertram Colgrave and R. A. B. Mynors, Oxford: Clarendon Press, 1969.

Petrus Riga, *Causa regis Francorum contra regem Anglorum*, ed. B. Hauréau (1883), 'Un poème inédit de Pierre Riga', in *Bibliothèque de l'École des chartes*, 44, p. 5–11.

Publius Terentius Afer, *Eunuchus*, ed. and trans. John Barsby, Cambridge, MA: Harvard University Press, 2001 (Loeb Classical Library, 22–23).

Winrich of Trier, *Conflictus ovis et lini*, ed. and trans. P. Dräger, Trier: Kliomedia, 2010.

Winrich of Trier, *Conflictus ovis et lini*, ed. M. Haupt (1859), '*Hermanni Contracti. Conflictus ovis et lini*', in *Zeitschrift für deutsches Alterthum*, 11, p. 215–238.

Secondary Sources

Abulafia, A. S. (1998), *Christians and Jews in Dispute: Disputational Literature and the Rise of Anti-Judaism in the West (1000–1150)*, Aldershot: Ashgate (Collected Studies, 621).

Batiouchkof, T. (1891), 'Le débat de l'âme et du corps', in *Romania*, 22, p. 513–578.

Bayless, M. (1996), *Parody in the Middle Ages: The Latin Tradition*, Ann Arbor, MI: University of Michigan Press.

Bec, P. (2000), *La joute poétique: De la tenson médiévale aux débats chantés traditionnels*, Paris: Belles Lettres (Architecture du verbe, 14).

Binkley, P. (1996), 'Debates and Dialogues', in F. A. C. Mantuello & A. G. Rigg (eds), *Medieval Latin: An Introduction and Bibliographical Guide*, Washington, DC: Catholic University of America Press, p. 677–681.

Bloch, H. R. (1977), *Medieval French Literature and Law*, Berkeley, CA: University of California Press.

M.-A. Bossy (1976), 'Medieval Debates of Body and Soul', in *Comparative Literature*, 28/2, p. 144–163.

Bouchard, C. B. (2003), *'Every Valley Shall Be Exalted': The Discourse of Opposites in Twelfth-Century Thought*, Ithaca, NY: Cornell University Press.

Breitenstein, M. (2011), '"Ins Gespräch Gebracht": Der Dialog als Prinzip monastischer Unterweisung', in S. Vanderputten (ed.), *Understanding Monastic Practices of Oral Communication*, Turnhout: Brepols (Utrecht Studies in Medieval Literacy, 21), p. 205–229.

Cardelle de Hartmann, C. (2007), *Lateinische Dialoge 1200–1400: Literaturhistorische Studie und Repertorium*, Leiden: Brill (Mittellateinische Studien und Texte, 37).

Del Bello, D. (2007), *Forgotten Paths: Etymology and the Allegorical Mindset*, Washington, DC: Catholic University of America Press.

Dentith, S. (2000), *Parody*, London: Routledge.

Faral, E. (1912), 'Les débats du clerc et du chevalier dans la littérature des XIIe et XIIIe siècle', in *Romania*, 41, p. 473–517.

Fichte, J. G. et al. (eds) (2019), *Das Streitgedicht im Mittelalter*, Stuttgart: Hirzel (Relectiones, 6).

Funkenstein, A. (1971), 'Basic Types of Christian Anti-Jewish Polemics in the Later Middle Ages', in *Viator*, 2, p. 373–382.

Gasser, K. (1999), *Resolution of the Debate in the Medieval Poem, 'The Owl and the Nightingale'*, Lewiston, NY: E. Mellen Press (Studies in Mediaeval Literature, 18).

Green, R. P. H. (1982), 'The Genesis of a Medieval Textbook. The Model and Sources of the "Ecloga Theodoli"', in *Viator*, 13, p. 49–106.

Harris, Stephen J. (2002), 'Bede and Gregory's Allusive Angles', in *Criticism* 44/3, p. 271–289.

Harvey, R. & L. Paterson (2010), *The Troubadour 'Tensos' and 'Partimens': A Critical Edition*, Cambridge: Brewer (Gallica, 14).

Hempfer, K. (ed.) (2002), *Möglichkeiten des Dialogs. Struktur und Funktion einer literarischen Gattung zwischen Mittelalter und Renaissance in Italien*, Stuttgart: Franz Steiner (Text und Kontext, 15).

Henkel, N. (1991), 'Die Ecloga Theodoli Und Ihre Literarischen Gegenkonzeptionen', in W. Berschin (ed.), *Lateinische Kultur im X. Jahrhundert: Akten des 1. Internationalen Mittellateinerkongresses*, Stuttgart: Hiersemann (Mittellateinisches Jahrbuch, 24–25), p. 151–162.

Hunt, T. (1979), 'Aristotle, Dialectic, and Courtly Literature', in *Viator*, 10, p. 95–130.

Jacobi, K. (1999), *Gespräche Lesen: Philosophische Dialoge im Mittelalter*, Tübingen: Gunther Narr (ScriptOralia, 115).

Jantzen, H. (1896), *Geschichte des deutschen Streitgedichtes im Mittelalter: Mit Berücksichtigung ähnlicher Erscheinungen in anderen Literaturen*, Breslau: Marcus (Germanistische Abhandlungen, 13; repr. Hildesheim: Olms Verlag, 1977).

Kasten, I. 'Studien zu Thematik und Form des mittelhochdeutschen Streitgedichts' (unpublished doctoral thesis, Hamburg University, 1973).

Kay, S. (2001), *Courtly Contradictions: The Emergence of the Literary Object in the Twelfth Century*, Stanford, CA: Stanford University Press.

Novikoff, A. (2013), *The Medieval Culture of Disputation: Pedagogy, Practice, and Performance*, Philadelphia, PA: University of Pennsylvania Press.

Oulmont, C. (1911), *Les débats du clerc et du chevalier dans la littérature poétique du Moyen-Âge: étude historique et littéraire suivie de l'édition critique des textes*, Paris: Champion.

Ranke, F. (1940), 'Zum Formwillen und Lebensgefühl in der deutschen Dichtung des späten Mittelalters', in *Deutsche Vierteljahrsschrift für Literaturwissenschaft und Geistesgeschichte*, 18, p. 307–327.

Reed, T. (1990), *Middle English Debate Poetry and the Aesthetics of Irresolution*, Columbia, MO: University of Missouri Press.

E. Reiss (1969), 'Conflict and its Resolution in Medieval Dialogues', in *Arts Libéraux et Philosophie Au Moyen Âge*, Paris: J. Vrin, p. 863–872.

Ronquist, E. C. (1990), 'Learning and Teaching in Twelfth-Century Dialogues', in *Res Publica Litterarum*, 13, p. 239–256.

Schmidt, P. G. (1993), 'I Conflictus', in G. Cavallo, C. Leonardi, & E. Menestò (eds), *Lo Spazio Letterario Del Medioevo*, vol. 1, Rome: Salerno, p. 157–169.

Schulz, A. (2014), *Das Konzil der fröhlichen Fräulein von Remiremont: Concilium in monte Romarici*, Butjadingen: MMO-Verlag (Nemus. Series latina medii aevi, 1).

Stotz, P. (1999), 'Beobachtungen zu lateinischen Streitgedichten des Mittelalters: Themen – Strukturen – Funktionen', original German version of 'Conflictus. Il contrasto poetico nella letteratura latina medievale', in M. Pedroni & A. Stäuble (eds), *Il genere 'tenzone' nelle letterature romanze delle origini*, Ravenna: A. Longo, German version: https://www.sglp.uzh.ch/static/MLS/files/Stotz-Streitgedichte.pdf (accessed 11.05.2020).

Stotz, P. (2002), 'Der "Conflictus ovis et lini": eine Bestandsaufnahme', in M. W. Herren, C. J. McDonough & R. G. Ross (eds), *Latin Culture in the Eleventh Century*, 2 vols, Turnhout: Brepols (Publications of the Journal of Medieval Latin, 5).

Symes, C. (2003), 'The Performance and Preservation of Medieval Latin Comedy', *European Medieval Drama*, 7, p. 29–50.

Tydeman, W. (1978), *The Theatre in the Middle Ages: Western European Stage Conditions, c. 800–1576*, Cambridge: Cambridge University Press.

Walther, H. (1920), *Das Streitgedicht in der lateinischen Literatur des Mittelalters*, München: Beck (Quellen und Untersuchungen zur lateinischen Philologie des Mittelalters, 5, 2).

Weiß, M. 'Die mittellateinische Goliardendichtung und ihr historischer Kontext: Komik im Kosmos der Kathedralschulen

Nordfrankreichs' (unpublished doctoral thesis, Justus-Liebig-Universität, 2018).

Winterfeld, P. K. R. von (ed.) (1902), *Hrotsvithae Opera*, Berlin: Weidmannos (Monumenta Germaniae Historica: Scriptores rerum Germanicarum in usum scholarum separatim editi, 34).

Abstract

This article explores a corpus of Latin debate poetry in which the rules and norms of other forms of dialogue and debate become the target of parody. The article's goal is to show that Latin literature already embraced the practice of poking fun at normative forms of debate prior to the institutionalisation of the scholastic disputation and the corresponding parodies in a variety of vernacular European literatures. The article first surveys the history of Latin literary dialogue and debate from Antiquity to the early Middle Ages and discusses the central focus of scholarship: vernacular debate poetry and its parodic and subversive stance in relation to scholastic disputation and legal debate. Then we turn to Latin debate parodies from before 1200 to see whether they exhibit the same dynamics. The article discusses three kinds of parodies: parody of the teacher and the school (*Terentius et Delusor, Altercatio magistri et discipuli*), parody of church and state councils (*Causa duorum apostolicorum, Causa regis Francorum contra regem Anglorum*), and parody of theological debate (*Conflictus ovis et lini*).

SIRIA DE FRANCESCO
Freie Universität Berlin

SULLE TRACCE DELLA *QUERELLE DU ROMAN DE LA ROSE*
ALCUNE OSSERVAZIONI SU UN ANONIMO *EXPLICIT* DEL MS LUDWIG XV 7 (83.MR.177), J. PAUL GETTY MUSEUM, LOS ANGELES*

La *Querelle du Roman de la Rose* si svolse in forma epistolare fra il 1401 e il 1403,[1] ma è figlia di un più ampio dibattito morale che coinvolse gli intellettuali italiani e francesi già dal 1340, anno dell'epistola di Petrarca a Guido Gonzaga,[2] e che termina solo con l'opera di Christine de Pizan (*c.* 1365 – *c.* 1431), il *Livre des fais d'armes et de chevalerie*, nel 1410.[3] Il terreno di scontro è il

---

* Si ringrazia Nancy Turner, conservatrice della sezione manoscritti del Getty Museum di Los Angeles, per aver condotto un'analisi a raggi ultravioletti delle carte 135v e 136r e per aver provveduto ad inviarmi una riproduzione digitale delle suddette carte. Si ringraziano inoltre i revisori anonimi per le ipotesi di traduzione del settimo e dell'ultimo verso del componimento che qui si esamina.

[1] Per una ricostruzione della cronologia dello scambio epistolare dal 1401, anno in cui Jean de Montreuil legge il romanzo e compone il trattatello in lode della *Rose*, al 1403-1404, anno dell'invio delle lettere 118 e 154 di Montreuil ad un *prélat de haut rang*, cf. la *Chronologie* curata da Eric Hicks in Christine de Pizan & al., *Le débat*, p. li–liv. Per le lettere che compongono il dossier di Christine de Pizan cf. anche l'*Appendice* di Andrea Valentini in Christine de Pizan, *Le Livre des epistres*, p. 139–140. In questo contributo si citano i testi delle epistole del dossier dalla più recente edizione curata da Andrea Valentini, mentre per le lettere che non sono comprese nel dossier l'edizione di riferimento è quella curata da Eric Hicks. Le traduzioni dei documenti del dibattito sono tratte da Garavelli 2006.

[2] La lettera in questione è l'epistola metrica inviata da Francesco Petrarca intorno al 1340 (*Epyst.* III, 30) a Guido Gonzaga, signore di Mantova, che accompagnava il dono di un esemplare del *Roman de la Rose*. Nell'epistola il poeta dichiara la superiorità dell'eloquenza italiana ed esprime il suo giudizio negativo sul libello francese, il *Roman de la Rose*. Per il testo dell'epistola cf. Francesco Petrarca, *Epistulae metricae*, p. 314–315 (p. 384–385 per la questione della datazione).

[3] McWebb 2007, p. xiii–xiv. L'antologia critica della studiosa presenta la *Querelle* come parte di una polemica più ampia, il *débat* secolare sul romanzo che

sedizioso *Roman de la Rose* e in particolare la seconda e più voluminosa parte del romanzo, vergata tra la fine degli anni Sessanta e la metà degli anni Ottanta del Duecento[4] dalla penna del 'claudicante' Jean de Meun. Un testo mostruoso,[5] quello del *Roman*, lungo oltre ventiduemila versi, il cui carattere teratologico,[6] per motivi diversi da quelli avanzati dalla critica, doveva aver turbato Christine de Pizan e Jean Gerson (1363–1429) che ne riconobbero la dubbia statura morale.

La storia della ricezione della *Querelle*, la cui fortuna è stata sicuramente minata dai tragici eventi che coinvolsero i partecipanti al dibattito,[7] è stata analizzata per lo più nella letteratura secolare e religiosa che subito seguì la disputa e in particolare nelle opere di Christine de Pizan, in cui forte è l'impronta della polemica. Sebbene gli esiti non siano quelli sperati dalla scrittrice e dal teologo, il dibattito deve aver avuto una certa risonanza negli ambienti di corte dove il *Roman de la Rose* continuava ad essere letto, copiato e miniato. In quest'atmosfera di rinnovato interesse per le fonti della seconda *Rose*, più volte oggetto di censura da parte di Gerson e Christine, è da collocare l'allestimento di alcuni codici miniati del romanzo, testimoni di un vero e proprio processo di cristianizzazione degli *exempla* di Jean.

Questo contributo si propone di analizzare un piccolo componimento in calce al manoscritto Ludwig XV 7 (83.MR.177), conservato presso il J. P. Getty Museum di Los Angeles, alla luce delle sue possibili relazioni con la *Querelle*. Il codice fa parte di uno sparuto gruppo di manoscritti del primo quarto del XV secolo le cui miniature fanno eco alla disputa e in cui le lascive parti del

---

inizia con l'epistola petrarchesca datata al 1340. Per questo la suddetta antologia raccoglie, oltre alle epistole del dossier compilato da Christine, le epistole dello scambio edite da Hicks, i sermoni della serie *Poenitemini* di Gerson che fanno riferimento al romanzo, il *Jardin amoureux* di Pierre d'Ailly, i riferimenti alla questione presenti nelle opere di Christine de Pizan e i commenti sul *Roman* di Laurent de Premierfait nel *De casibus virorum illustrium* del 1409.

[4] Sul problema della datazione della *Rose* cf. l'introduzione di Pietro Beltrami in Beltrami 2014, p. 29–35.

[5] Secondo la celebre definizione di Joseph Bédier in Bédier 1925, p. 370.

[6] Pasero 2003, p. 48.

[7] Jean de Montreuil e Gontier Col muoiono nel 1418 per mano borgognona nel periodo delle rappresaglie ordite da Giovanni senza Paura subito precedenti la presa di Parigi.

romanzo di Jean sono emendate in senso religioso. Un'analisi di questo tipo permette da un lato di gettare nuova luce sulla fortuna della controversia letteraria, dall'altro di individuare 'spazi' di circolazione del testo sinora poco noti.

Lo scambio epistolare inizia in sordina nella primavera del 1401 quando Jean de Montreuil (1354-1418) compone un *petit traité* in francese, l'*Opusculum Gallicum*, in lode del *Roman*[8] e lo invia ad un *notable clerc* che rimane anonimo nello scambio.[9] Il 'trattatello' non passa inosservato: alla fine del maggio dello stesso anno Christine de Pizan scrive al preposto di Lille, 'Jehan Johannéz', criticando il *Roman* per la sua natura misogina. La prima fase della disputa si consuma fra Christine e Gontier Col (*c.* 1350/52-1418), amico fraterno di Jean de Montreuil e strenuo difensore della *Rose*; al fianco di Christine, come si accennava, interviene il teologo e predicatore Jean Gerson,[10] canonico del capitolo di Notre Dame di Parigi, che continuerà la sua opera di censore del *Roman* nelle sue prediche in francese[11] presso la chiesa di St. Jean-en-Grève a Parigi. Le *couple fraternel* di Jean de Montreuil e Gontier Col spinge un altro personaggio di diversa levatura ad entrare nella disputa: si tratta di Pierre Col, fratello di Gontier, segretario del re e canonico del capitolo di Notre Dame, a cui si deve un compendio dei contenuti ideologici del partito 'rodofilo'.

In un articolo di poco precedente la sua edizione delle lettere della *Querelle*, Eric Hicks si interroga sul ruolo assunto dalla pole-

---

[8] Sono rintracciabili diversi rimandi al trattato ormai perduto di Jean de Montreuil nelle epistole di Christine de Pizan (cf. Christine de Pizan, *Le Livre des epistres*, p. 283-284, § 8a), nel trattato-visione di Jean Gerson (Christine de Pizan, *Le Livre des epistres*, p. 303, § 14b; p. 304, § 14p) e nella stessa epistola 154, *Ut sunt mores*, di Jean de Montreuil che doveva accompagnare l'invio di un esemplare del trattatello ad un poeta, forse Deschamps o Honoré Bouvet (?), nell'estate 1402 (cf. Christine de Pizan et al., *Le débat*, p. 44, 36-42).

[9] L'*ami notable clerc* è stato identificato da Pierre-Yves Badel (cf. Badel 1980, p. 412) con Nicolas de Clamanges (*c.* 1355-1437) membro di un circolo di intellettuali, fra i quali lo stesso Montreuil e i fratelli Col. L'epiteto tuttavia, ricorda Hicks, doveva essere abbastanza comune, cf. L'introduzione di Hicks in Christine de Pizan et al., *Le débat*, p. xxvi, n. 9.

[10] Sulla complicità ideologica fra Christine de Pizan e Jean Gerson la critica non è unanime, sui contatti letterari fra le opere dei due intellettuali cf. Richards 2000, p. 197-228 e relativa bibliografia.

[11] Per l'uso del francese da parte del predicatore come lingua veicolare per un pubblico eterogeneo cf. Iribarren 2014, p. 223-251.

mica a corte e sull'accoglienza che la corrispondenza doveva aver avuto presso gli intellettuali del tempo, soprattutto fra quelle personalità che *plus humbles ou du moins plus obscures*[12] non videro la loro opinione immortalata nella dimensione scritta della questione. Come ricorda lo studioso, il circolo di intellettuali coinvolti nella disputa è probabilmente più ampio di quanto il dossier compilato da Christine lasci intravedere: già la poetessa nella sua prima 'invettiva' allude alla pluralità dei suoi nemici,[13] una turba di seguaci senza nome, come li definisce Gerson, partigiani di Jean de Meun. Una folta schiera, ribadisce Pierre Col, pronta a difendere la *Rose* dai suoi censori: *et sachent tuit cil qui le reprannent qu'il reste encore VII mille, [...], qui sont tous prests de le deffendre* (E sappiano tutti quelli che lo criticano che ne restan ancora settemila [...] pronti a difenderlo).[14]

La corrispondenza di Montreuil rivela l'esistenza di altri due destinatari del libello gallico, il già citato *notable clerc*, e il vescovo di Cambrai, Pierre d'Ailly (1351–1420),[15] che non condivide l'entusiasmo di Montreuil per il romanzo e che infatti, in risposta alla missiva *Cum ut dant*[16] di Montreuil, compone il sermone *Ille vos docebit omnia* (del 22 maggio del 1401) e più tardi il poemetto devozionale *Le jardin amoureux de l'âme devote* — spesso attribuito a Gerson — in cui il giardino di Piacere di Guillaume si popola di elementi cristiani e l'*ars amandi* di ascendenza ovidiana è corretta in senso religioso.[17]

---

[12] Hicks 1976, p. 519.

[13] Cf. Christine de Pizan, *Le Livre des epistres*, p. 155, § 3a. Il riferimento può essere variamente interpretato: se da un lato la folla di innominati può indicare un numero indefinito di intellettuali laici e religiosi coinvolti nella polemica, dall'altro potrebbe riferirsi per mezzo di iperbole allo stesso Montreuil che rimarrà fuori dallo scambio epistolare.

[14] Christine de Pizan, *Le Livre des epistres*, p. 345, § 22c, per la trad: Garavelli 2006, p. 95.

[15] Jean de Montreuil scrive a Pierre d'Ailly nel maggio 1401 (cf. Hicks & Ornato 1977, p. 34–64, per la datazione dell'epistola cf. p. 51–62).

[16] Nell'epistola 103, *Cum ut dant*, a Pierre d'Ailly Montreuil chiede al vescovo la sua opinione sul trattato in lode del *Roman* che accompagna l'epistola: *Vestrum ergo fuerit, domine mi, an nimium aut minus debito seu cum temperamento actorem laudauerim decernere, ac nichilominus uestro huic adoptivo [...]* (Spetta a te, mio Maestro, determinare se ho lodato questo autore troppo o meno di quanto gli sia dovuto, o con misura, e a te spetta guidare il tuo figlio adottivo in questa materia), cf. Jean de Montreuil, *Opera*, I, p. 145.

[17] Per l'attribuzione del breve poemetto in prosa al vescovo di Cambrai

Le parole di Christine e Gerson fanno pensare ad un avversario plurale, una *cabale rhodophobe*, che esercita una censura *à rebours* sul trattato della poetessa,[18] censura che presuppone quindi una certa circolazione della disputa, sia nella dimensione orale che in quella della corrispondenza privata, almeno fra gli intellettuali di corte.[19]

Alcune riflessioni sull'influsso del dibattito sulla confezione dei manoscritti parigini del *Roman* sono state avanzate dagli studiosi della tradizione iconografica del testo, una lunga storia che interessa una tradizione di circa 200 manoscritti. Fra questi uno dei più finemente miniati, con le sue 101 miniature in *semi-grisaille*, è il nostro Ludwig XV 7 che tramanda il testo del solo poema. Il codice, databile al 1405 circa, presenta una serie di interpolazioni e aggiunte che lo legano al secondo gruppo di testimoni individuato dal Langlois nel suo monumentale spoglio dei codici della tradizione manoscritta del romanzo.[20] Il *destinataire* e/o committente[21] del codice è purtroppo sconosciuto, il primo possessore noto è Jean du Rueil (1474–1537), come si legge sul *recto* del foglio di guardia del manoscritto ('J Duryeil'), traduttore di opere mediche dal greco e dal latino, medico di Francesco I e canonico di Notre Dame.[22] Dalla descrizione del codice offerta da Anton von Euw e Joachim Plotzek apprendiamo che il copista, unico per l'intero manoscritto (f. 1r–135v), potrebbe essere lo stesso delle carte 1r–66r del MS Paris, BnF, fr. 12201,[23] codice che nel marzo del 1403 arriva nelle mani del colto colle-

---

cf. Badel 1976, p. 369–438. Lo studioso offre due ipotesi di datazione: il 14 maggio 1402 e l'estate, fra luglio e agosto, del 1401.

[18] Cf. L'introduzione di Hicks in Christine de Pizan et al., *Le débat*, p. xvii.

[19] Pierre Col afferma nella sua seconda epistola (giuntaci incompleta) di non conoscere nessun altro che abbia criticato il *Roman* prima o dopo Christine, fatta eccezione per Gerson che partecipa alla polemica letteraria in prima persona. Qui Pierre Col pare però contraddire non solo la scrittrice, ma anche le parole di Montreuil, Gontier Col, Jean Gerson e le proprie (cf. Combes 1973, p. 95–98).

[20] Cf. von Euw & Plotzek 1985, IV, p. 234.

[21] Los Angeles, J. P. Getty Museum, Ludwig XV 7 (83.MR.177). La lista dei possessori del manoscritto è consultabile al sito: http://www.getty.edu/art/collection/objects/1439/unknown-guillaume-de-lorris-and-jean-de-meun-roman-de-la-rose-french-about-1405/.

[22] Reulos & Bietenholz 1985, p. 415.

[23] Anton von Euw e Joachim M. Plotzek riportano l'ipotesi di Christopher de Hamel (che si legge nel Catalogo Sotheby del 1977, p. 47).

zionista e patrono delle arti Jean de Berry (1340–1416).[24] Nello stesso circolo, quello della corte francese del primo Quattrocento, è da ricercare il committente o il primo proprietario del nostro manoscritto. La *textualis* dall'elaborata grafia, più elegante della bastarda solitamente adoperata per i codici del *Roman de la Rose* del periodo,[25] era indubbiamente destinata a soddisfare le esigenze del committente di questa prestigiosa copia miniata del romanzo. Il ciclo di miniature, anch'esse opera di un solo autore, è da ricondurre alla corrente artistica parigina definita nel 1967 da Millard Meiss 'Bedford Trend', dalla quale più tardi sarebbe emersa la personalissima mano del Maestro delle Ore del duca di Bedford. Non mancano inoltre coincidenze e somiglianze con i codici BnF, fr. 12420 e BnF, fr. 290,[26] il primo acquisito dal fratello del duca di Berry nel 1403 e il secondo in possesso del duca già dal 1401. Il codice è stato in più modi collegato a botteghe e biblioteche frequentate da Christine de Pizan che, ricordiamo, aveva trovato in Jean de Berry un patrono reale.[27]

Marie-Hélène Tesnière, che ha condotto uno studio su quattro codici dell'inizio del XV secolo, colloca il manoscritto nel milieu *des grandes officiers royaux proches de la cour*, come dimostrano le somiglianze con i codici manoscritti BnF, fr. 1570 e BnF, fr. 1563, copia di una raccolta del rodofilo Pierre Col.[28] Più avanti la studiosa descrive così l'operato del miniatore del Ludwig XV 7: *une véritable éducation sentimentale de l'Amant inscrite dans une philosophie chrétienne de la Création* (un'educazione sentimentale

---

[24] Meiss 1967, p. 252, fig. 438.

[25] von Euw & Plotzek 1985, IV, p. 234.

[26] von Euw & Plotzek 1985, IV, p. 234–236.

[27] Desmond & Sheingorn 2003, p. 277 n. 56. Si ricordi inoltre che l'apparato iconografico del codice presenta alcune somiglianze con le miniature del manoscritto Oxford, Bodleian Library, MS Bodley 421 (in part. f. 69v) contenente l'*Epistre d'Othea* (*c.* 1400) di Christine de Pizan, cf. Braet 1994, p. 115.

[28] La studiosa conclude il contributo asserendo che il manoscritto è la copia di una raccolta illustrata costituita da Pierre Col: *Nous avons ainsi tout lieu de penser que le manuscrit français 1563 est la copie d'un recueil illustré, constitué sans doute par Pierre Col, chanoine de Notre-Dame de Paris, à la suite de la Querelle du Roman de la Rose* (Abbiamo quindi tutte le ragioni di pensare che il MS fr. 1563 sia la copia di una raccolta illustrata, costituita senza dubbio da Pierre Col, canonico di Notre-Dame, a seguito della *Querelle du Roman de la Rose*); cf. Tesnière 2017, p. 334.

dell'Amante inscritta in una filosofia cristiana della Creazione),[29] collocando il codice in quella cerchia di manoscritti parigini quattrocenteschi che presentano una forte cristianizzazione dell'apparato iconografico e di cui ci occuperemo, per quanto concerne il nostro manoscritto, più avanti.

Il codice qui presentato acquista particolare rilievo per un elaborato *explicit*, di mano più tarda di quella del copista,[30] che fregia la carta 135v.[31] Riportiamo di seguito il testo del componimento di *octosyllabes* in rima:

> Cy gist le Romant de la Rose,   1
> ou tout l'Art d'Amours se repose,
> la fleur des beaulx bien dire l'ose,
> qui bien y entend texte et glose.
> Aucuns blasment qu'il n'est en prose,   5
> mais le moyne castel s'oppose
> qu'autrement soit pour nulle chose,
> car tout grant clerc qui se dispose
> d'entendre la substance enclose
> dedens, et les vers pointe et pose,   10
> savoure et gouste en longue pose
> tout ainsi que l'acteur propose
> en ryme et sense et le compose.
> Est bien digne qu'on le despose
> et que silence on luy impose   15
> qui rien y contredit ou glose.

[Qui giace il Romanzo della Rosa, dove tutta l'arte d'Amore riposa, chi ben comprende il testo e la glossa può ben osare chiamarlo il più bel fiore. Alcuni lamentano che il *Roman de la Rose* non sia in prosa, tuttavia il monaco Castel si oppone

---

[29] Tesnière 2012, p. 11.

[30] I sedici versi del componimento occupano le righe 23–38 delle 44 della carta. L'autore, o il copista, pare si preoccupi di adeguare il testo al foglio, come pure dimostrano le punte di giallo che decorano le iniziali di ogni *octosyllabe*, la precisa collocazione del testo sulla carta e l'elegante grafia con la quale il testo è vergato.

[31] L'intero manoscritto e l'*explicit* in esame sono consultabili al sito della Digital Library of Medieval Manuscripts che raccoglie le riproduzioni digitali dei manoscritti del *Roman de la Rose* e dello *Scriptorium* di Christine de Pizan, cf. https://dlmm.library.jhu.edu/en/digital-library-of-medieval-manuscripts/. Per il codice in esame è disponibile una trascrizione parziale del testo e di alcune rubriche.

a qualsiasi cambiamento. Poiché ogni dotto teologo che si appresti a comprendere la sostanza che vi è racchiusa (nel *Roman de la Rose*), e che legga e analizzi i versi, lo assapora e gusta lungamente, proprio così come l'autore lo propone e lo compone in rima e senso. E chi ne contraddice o critica qualsivoglia aspetto è degno di essere allontanato e (merita) che il silenzio si imponga su di lui].

Nel suo censimento dei codici manoscritti della *Rose*, il Langlois[32] ricorda il Ludwig XV 7 fra i codici dalla collocazione ignota proprio per la bellissima fattura dell'*explicit*.[33] Lo studioso cita il testo dal catalogo dei manoscritti pergamenacei della collezione Hamilton[34] nel quale si accenna ad una rasura dell'*explicit* originale che sarebbe stato poi sostituito dal componimento qui trascritto.[35] Il codice oggi conservato presso il Getty Museum non riporta tracce della rasura, la cui menzione potrebbe essere dunque un semplice errore di catalogo.[36]

I primi quattro versi del componimento ricompaiono circa sessant'anni dopo il lavoro del Langlois nello studio monografico di Fleming sull'iconografia del *Roman*:[37] lo studioso pone l'accento sulla rima *glose*: *rose* per sottolineare il significato della *glossa* e della pratica della *glossatio* come metafora istruttiva nel romanzo. Nel nostro componimento la voce *glose*, con il significato di 'senso del testo' piuttosto che di 'commento al testo', entra in dialogo

---

[32] Langlois 1910, p. 211.

[33] L'alto grado di elaborazione dell'*explicit* fa pensare che l'autore fosse un abile versificatore: si pensi alla trama di rime femminili in -*ose*, alle strutture chiastiche del testo, all'uso di dittologie sinonimiche, di strutture di inversione e di figure eleganti come quella iniziale che sovrappone la *quête* dell'amante verso il bocciolo più bello all'opera stessa, definita 'il più bel fiore'.

[34] Sotheby's 1889, 23 May, lot 10, ill, p. 14–15.

[35] La rasura non viene menzionata neppure nei cataloghi: Debure 1763, p. 468–471 e Wattenbach 1883, p. 329–346. Il Debure, che descrive brevemente il manoscritto (n. 2983), parla di un altro codice di pari bellezza conservato presso il Cabinet M. Gaignat. Non sappiamo quale relazione intercorresse fra i due codici e se nel secondo, quello di cui parla il Debure, ci fosse un'analoga rasura.

[36] Il pellegrinaggio di questo manoscritto è stato ricostruito nel dettaglio da Seymour de Ricci, il cui studio ha permesso di gettare nuova luce su uno dei primi possessori, il suddetto Jean du Rueil, e sul luogo di stesura e prima circolazione del codice: probabilmente una bottega parigina vicina a quelle di corte, cf. de Ricci 1910, p. 81–82.

[37] Fleming 1969, p. 7–9.

con il rimante dell'ultimo verso, *glose* (da *gloser*), voce verbale con il significato di criticare, controbattere, in rapporto parasinonimico con il *contredit* che lo precede (*qui rien y contredit ou glose*).[38] Dunque, chi legge la *Rose* deve assaporare il testo così come l'autore l'ha composto, chiunque provi a criticare il romanzo in qualsiasi sua parte merita di essere emarginato e dimenticato. Il breve testo, insomma, può essere ascritto nel novero degli *explicit* che celebrano la forma e il contenuto della *Rose*, seppur con un grado di elaborazione retorica insolito rispetto agli esempi che affollano i testimoni manoscritti del romanzo.[39] I versi si presentano come un *divertissement* letterario il cui carattere canzonatorio può essere compreso proprio alla luce della *Querelle* e del ruolo giocato da Christine nel dibattito.

A collegare il componimento alla disputa è il nome del monaco Castel che campeggia nel sesto verso della chiusa in qualità di difensore del romanzo.[40] Un Jean (de) Castel (*c.* 1383 – *c.* 1425), figlio di Christine de Pizan, risulta fra gli adepti dell'ordine benedettino; il monaco, vissuto fra gli anni Ottanta del Trecento e il primo trentennio del Quattrocento, fu segretario reale di Carlo VI.[41] Il figlio di Christine aveva fama di essere un grande retore e compositore di versi,[42] tanto che alcuni oppositori della scrittrice avevano attribuito le opere della donna al figlio.[43]

---

[38] Le voci *glose* e *gloser* fanno eco ad una serie di termini appartenenti al lessico scolastico della seconda parte del romanzo. L'uso del lessico scolastico nella *Rose* è oggetto di uno studio monografico da parte di Gérard Paré (1947). Un intero capitolo è dedicato al discorso di *Raison* e al continuo ricorso delle voci *glose, gloser, expondre, entendre*, etc. (cf. Paré 1947, p. 81–135, in part. p. 133–135).

[39] Cf. gli esempi in Huot 1993 p. 27–34.

[40] L'ipotesi che qui si propone è che la menzione del monaco sostituisca quella del nome di Christine de Pizan come attacco indiretto alla scrittrice. Ci riserviamo di indagare in altra sede l'ipotesi che l'antroponimo possa essere *senhal* per un gruppo di intellettuali, ad esempio i detrattori del *Roman*, oppure che il nome abbia un significato metaforico giocoso non ben decifrabile. Come riscontro per quest'ultima ipotesi cf. la nota 46 di questo contributo.

[41] Sulla figura di Jean Castel *père* cf. Delsaux 2011 e relativa bibliografia.

[42] Christine nella sua *Advision* del 1405 descrive il figlio (alla tenera età di dodici anni) come abile rimatore: *assez abille et bien chantant enfant* (III, § 11, 24) e più avanti narra che, a non più di vent'anni, Jean è già grande conoscitore delle arti (grammatica, retorica, poesia) e giovane morigerato e giudizioso (III, § 17, 73–81); cf. Christine de Pizan, *Le livre de l'advision Cristine*, p. 112 e 122.

[43] Sull'argomento cf. Christine de Pizan, *Le livre de l'advision Cristine*, p. 174, n. XXII/23–28. Nell'opera Christine fa pronunciare queste parole a

L'unica opera ascrivibile con certezza alla mano del benedettino è un poema allegorico di 626 versi, *Le Pin*,[44] una finzione amorosa costruita sulla *Rose* di Guillaume de Lorris, con intenti di propaganda politica. Più famoso, e spesso confuso nelle cronache con il padre, è il figlio Jean Castel (prima del 1425–1476), anch'egli monaco benedettino, che fu segretario reale e *chroniqueur de France*,[45] destinatario di una lettera in versi del più brillante fra i cronisti della corte di Borgogna, Georges Chastellain (*c.* 1405–1475).[46] Il nipote di Christine, lodato per la sua attività di storico da Jean Molinet (1435–1507), è autore di una serie di opere di carattere morale in latino e francese. L'incertezza della datazione del componimento non ci permette di identificare con precisione il monaco col figlio o col nipote di Christine, ma, come vedremo, il riferimento a Castel potrebbe essere una strategia retorica per tenzonare la scrittrice che aveva preso parte alla *Querelle*.

Il monaco in questione si oppone al fatto che la *Rose* possa essere scritta in prosa o alterata in qualsiasi altro modo. Se la

Dama Opinione: *les aucuns dient que clercs ou religieux les te forgent* (alcuni dicono che religiosi e chierici le scrissero per te), cf. II, § 22, 27–28, p. 88. In una traduzione fiamminga del XV secolo dell'opera *Le Livre de la Cité des Dames* (1405) il volgarizzatore fa riferimento alla diceria secondo la quale l'opera di Christine sarebbe stata scritta da un monaco che, per sfuggire alla fama, avrebbe utilizzato il nome di Christine come pseudonimo (Christine de Pizan, *Le Livre de la Cité des Dames*, p. 313–314, n. 23). Molte delle sue opere venivano alterate in modo che il suo nome non fosse riconducibile ai testi. Il nome di Christine è stato omesso nella traduzione inglese dell'*Epistre d'Othéa* (*c.* 1400), in alcune copie del *Le Livre des fais d'armes et de chevalerie* (cf. Willard 1984, p. 186) e nel MS fr. 1563 della Bibliothèque nationale de France, ricondotto al rodofilo Pierre Col (cf. Tesnière 2017, p. 317–318).

[44] Nell'opera *Le Pin* si fa continuo riferimento alla prima parte del *Roman*, quella cortese di Guillaume. Questo si deve forse al messaggio politico di cui il testo è portatore, meglio decifrabile nella veste di metafora cortese che di allegoria teologica. Interessanti sono i continui riferimenti dell'io lirico, alter ego di Jean Castel, alla difesa dello statuto delle donne nella società, che riecheggiano gli insegnamenti di Christine raccolti nel suo *Charles V* e nel *Corps de Policie*. Cf. Delsaux 2011, p. 335–375, in part. p. 341, n. 24.

[45] Sulla figura di Jean Castel *fils* (*petit-fils* di Christine de Pizan) cf. Quicherat 1841; Thomas 1892; Droz 1921; Brunelli 1956; Bossuat 1958.

[46] La lettera a Jean de Castel è imperniata su una metafora onomastica che identifica il monaco con un magnifico castello celeste di cui il *chroniqueur* è umile castellano. La risposta di Castel non equivale in pregio retorico quella del suo corrispondente, ma il monaco dimostra di essere rimatore esperto ed ironico nella sua lettera del 1465 a Charles de Gaucourt in cui si autodefinisce *petit moine* (cf. LeBlanc 1995, p. 87–90).

dichiarazione di dignità dell'opera è in linea con il tipo di componimento elogiativo che di solito conclude il testo del romanzo, piuttosto inconsueto è il rifiuto della prosa. Nella sua lettera del (primo febbraio?) 1402 a Guillaume de Tignonville, Christine de Pizan afferma di scrivere in prosa per necessità, perché la questione lo richiede, anche se non è al pari dei suoi interlocutori:[47]

> Aussi, chier seigneur, ne vous soit merveille, pour ce que mes autres dittiés ay acoustumé a rimoyer, cestui estre en prose, car, comme la matiere ne le requiere, autressi est droit que je suive le stile de mes assaillans, combien que mon petit savoir soit pou respondent a leur belle loquence.[48]

> Inoltre, caro signore, non meravigliatevi del fatto che mentre di solito i miei altri scritti sono in rima, questo sia in prosa. Dato che il contenuto non impone diversamente, è giusto che io segua lo stile dei miei avversari, per quanto il mio limitato sapere sia poco corrispondente alla loro bella eloquenza.[49]

La scrittrice rivendica quindi l'uso della prosa per il tenore della materia trattata, di cui Christine parla non per opinione ma per *certaine science*.[50] Gli insegnamenti del *Roman* di Jean, che avevano spinto Montreuil a scrivere il trattato gallico, non potevano essere certo oggetto di trattazione seria per Christine che avrebbe preferito vedere il romanzo avvolto nel fuoco, piuttosto che incoronato d'alloro.[51] Infatti, pur riconoscendo il pregio letterario di alcuni luoghi dell'opera — *il y a de bonnes choses et bien dittes sans faille*[52] (che contiene senza dubbio buone cose e ben scritte)[53] — la scrittrice considera il romanzo pericoloso, poiché incita le anime incerte al vizio della lussuria.

---

[47] Sulle formule di modestia come strategia di una particolare *Selbstinzenierung* nelle opere di Christine de Pizan cf. Brownlee 1992, p. 234–261.
[48] Christine de Pizan, *Le Livre des epistres*, p. 265, § 3e.
[49] Garavelli 2006, p. 25.
[50] Christine de Pizan, *Le Livre des epistres*, p. 150, § 4c.
[51] Ricordiamo che nella disputa non è solo Christine a voler bruciare il romanzo (cf. Christine de Pizan, *Le Livre des epistres*, p. 166, § 8a, p. 196–197, § 25a), il motivo ricorre anche negli scritti di Gerson: sia nell'epistola *Talia de me* (dicembre 1402), risposta al trattato di Pierre Col, sia nei sermoni contro la lussuria (dicembre 1402) della serie *Poenitemini* (cf. Christine de Pizan et al., *Le débat*, p. 172, 194–198; p. 182, 67–69).
[52] Christine de Pizan, *Le Livre des epistres*, 165, § 7.
[53] Garavelli 2006, p. 37.

> Je dis que c'est [il *Roman*] exortacion de vice confortant vie dissolue, doctrine plaine de decevance, voye de dampnacion, diffameur publique, cause de souspeçon et mescreandise, honte de plusieurs personnes, et peut estre d'erreur. [...] nature humaine, qui de soy est encline a mal, n'a nul besoing que on lui ramentoive le pié dont elles cloche pour plus droit aler.[54]
>
> Io dico che è un'esortazione al vizio che incoraggia la vita dissoluta, una dottrina piena di inganno, via di dannazione, diffamazione pubblica, causa di dubbio e diffidenza, di vergogna per molti, e forse di errore. [...] il genere umano, che di per sé è incline al male, non ha nessun bisogno che gli si rammenti il peccato per cui zoppica invece di camminare bene.[55]

La preoccupazione di Christine, che la spingerà a mettere in guardia il figlio Jean dalle insidie della lettura del romanzo, è l'idea che il sostrato morale della *Rose*, così adornato di belle rime leonine dall'autore,[56] possa fuorviare le menti più deboli, insicure nel cammino religioso. La pretesa *pruderie* della scrittrice[57] nasconde dunque il timore che l'opera possa essere letta e intesa come un testo didattico, modello di ammaestramenti in materia amorosa,[58] in cui — secondo la Ragione di Jean — è meglio ingannare che essere ingannati.

---

[54] Christine de Pizan, *Le Livre des epistres*, p. 165, § 8a.

[55] Garavelli 2006, p. 36.

[56] Christine de Pizan, *Le Livre des epistres*, p. 157, § 3f. Il fatto che l'opera sia scritta in versi non fa che rendere il romanzo più pericoloso, la forma e le rime distraggono il lettore meno attento e lo conducono a seguire l'esempio dei personaggi del romanzo.

[57] La scrittrice critica aspramente il discorso di Ragione in cui la dama, per descrivere la castrazione di Saturno, nomina i genitali maschili con il loro nome. Nell'*Epistre d'Othea* il discorso in questione, in cui compare la voce *coilles*, è tradotto in prosa dalla scrittrice (che traduce il termine con *genitaires*). La riscrittura dei versi di Jean dimostra che la posizione assunta da Christine nel dibattito non è riconducibile a semplice *pruderie*, per la scrittrice è una questione di *decorum* poetico (cf. Desmond & Sheingorn 2003, p. 65), oltre che di correttezza morale.

[58] Ricordiamo che nell'*Epistre d'Othea* (considerata dall'autrice un'opera in versi), proprio per guidare l'interpretazione del testo, ogni passaggio mitologico delle sezioni in cui l'opera è divisa è accompagnato da una chiosa, che interpreta il testo in versi e offre una lettura morale dell'*exemplum*, e da una *pièce* allegorica in prosa che spiega attraverso la 'voce' di *auctoritates* secolari e religiose i versi dell'epistola.

Come già sottolineato da Fleming, madonna *Raison*, ipostasi del controllo razionale dei sensi, è l'esegeta per eccellenza del romanzo. La personificazione si presenta come una divinità antropomorfa che condivide allo stesso tempo gli attributi iconografici della Filosofia boeziana e quelli della Divina Sapienza.[59] Inascoltata maestra, Ragione, dopo essere discesa dalla torre del castello, dichiara di essere stata creata da Dio, fatta a sua immagine e somiglianza e per questo superiore a qualsiasi cosa che la Natura possa generare. Christine si esprime a più riprese sullo statuto ambiguo di Ragione, indignata per i precetti che la dama impartisce all'Amante:

> Et encor ne me puis taire de ce dont trop suis mal contempt, que l'office de Raison, la quelle il meismes dit fille de Dieu, doye mettre avant tele parole et par maniere de proverbe comme je ay notté en ycellui chapitre, la ou elle dit a l'amant que en la guerre amoureuse vault mieulx decevoir que deceus estre.[60]

> Ancora non posso passare sotto silenzio questo, di cui sono troppo indignata: che in quel libro il dovere di Ragione, la quale l'autore stesso dice figlia di Dio, sia fare una tale affermazione e in forma di proverbio comune, come ho notato nel capitolo in cui dice all'Amante che 'nella guerra d'amore è meglio ingannare che essere ingannati'.[61]

La scrittrice torna sulla funzione pedagogica e didattica dei discorsi di Ragione in diversi luoghi della disputa: la personificazione del raziocinio si comporta in maniera tutt'altro che razionale ai suoi occhi; le parole della dama — ricorda Christine – non sono rivolte ad un *clerc*, in grado quindi di discernere fra bene e male, ma ad Amante, folle d'amore, che rischia di essere infiammato dai discorsi della donna.

Nel suo trattato in difesa della *Rose*[62] Pierre Col tenta di riabilitare la persona di Jean de Meun affermando che le intenzioni

---

[59] In questa prospettiva, Ragione è assimilabile alla donna del *Convivio* dantesco, cf. Fenzi 2016, p. 61.
[60] Christine de Pizan, *Le Livre des epistres*, p. 158, § 31.
[61] Garavelli 2006, p. 30-31.
[62] Si tratta del trattato in forma di epistola che Pierre Col scrive per controbattere le critiche mosse al romanzo da Christine de Pizan nella sua lettera a Jean

del *maistre* sono diverse da quelle dei suoi personaggi, le cui parole sono conformi alle figure allegoriche che rappresentano e non al pensiero e alle intenzioni dell'autore. La sua difesa del romanzo assume presto toni accesi e si sposta dall'elogio dell'opera alla critica dei suoi censori: il segretario accusa la scrittrice prima di non aver letto il *Roman*, poi di averlo letto solo superficialmente[63] e quindi di non averne compreso il messaggio morale.[64] Christine non lascia l'accusa impunita e nella sua replica del 2 ottobre 1402[65] rimprovera Pierre Col di aver commesso lo stesso errore di cui lui la accusa, quello di interpretare il testo del romanzo di Jean alla lettera:

> Tu (Pierre Col) dis oultre que qui lit et entent le dit rommant, que il entendra que maistre Jehan de Meung ne devoit autrement parler qu'il parle [...]. Scez tu comme il va de celle lecture? Ainsi comme des livres des arquemistes:[66] les uns les lisent et entendent d'une maniere, les autres qui les lisent, les entendent tout au rebours, et chacun cuide trop bien entendre [...] Et tu mesmes n'as pas tenue la rigle en toutes tes solucions, dont tu me veulx reprendre, et merveilles interpretes ce qui est dit clerement et a la lettre — 'il vault trop mieulx, beau maistre, decevoir que estre deceu' [...].[67]
>
> Dici in seguito che chi legge e comprende il *Romanzo della Rosa* 'capirà che Jean de Meun non doveva parlare diversamente da come ha parlato' [...]. Sai come va con una tale

---

de Montreuil e da Jean Gerson nel suo trattato-visione. L'epistola, scritta probabilmente alla fine dell'estate del 1402, è l'unico documento che possediamo del partito rodofilo.

[63] Nella sua *responsio* ai due trattati di Christine e Gerson, Pierre Col in tono beffardo afferma: *L'en ne doit pas prendre ainssy les mos a la lettre, mais selonc les mos precedans et l'entendement de l'aucter* (Non si deve prendere le parole così alla lettera, ma nel loro contesto, e tenendo presenti le intenzioni dell'autore): Christine de Pizan, *Le Livre des epistres*, p. 336, § 4c; per la trad: Garavelli 2006, p. 87.

[64] *Je ne doubte point que, c'il eust veu et releu par fois souvent recordees, que de tant come son entendement passe tant autres que je ne say les quelz non, de tant plus le louast, prisast, amast et honnourast* (Non dubito affatto che se l'avesse letto e riletto e spesso ricordato, come altri libri, dato che la sua intelligenza supera quella di molti altri, tanto più lo loderebbe, lo apprezzerebbe, lo amerebbe e lo onorerebbe): Christine de Pizan, *Le Livre des epistres*, p. 333, § 19b; per la trad.: Garavelli 2006, p. 83.

[65] Pierre Col la riceve solo il 30 ottobre.

[66] Sul duplice significato della voce cf. Mcwebb 2007, p. xxiv–xxv.

[67] Christine de Pizan, *Le Livre des epistres*, p. 185–186, § 12j, 12l, 14b.

lettura? Come per i libri degli alchimisti: c'è chi li legge e li capisce in un modo, c'è chi li legge e li interpreta in un altro. E ciascuno è convinto di capirli perfettamente. [...] E neanche tu hai rispettato la regola in tutte le tue argomentazioni con cui mi critichi, e, in modo sbalorditivo, interpreti quanto è detto alla lettera 'è molto meglio, mio buon maestro, ingannare che essere ingannati'.[68]

Più avanti, Christine mette in guardia suo figlio dagli insegnamenti del romanzo, riportando la questione su un piano personale, quello attaccato dai suoi avversari:[69]

> Je ay un seul filz — que Dieu me vueille conserver, se il lui plaist —, mais je aimeroie mieulx qu'il feust parfaictement amoureux (avec le sens que je espere que Dieux lui donra, comme ont hommes raisonnables) d'une femme bien condicionnee et sage qui amast honneur — et lui en avenist ce que avenir lui en pourroit — que je ne feroie que a son pouoir feust deceveur de toutes ou de plusieurs, car je cuideroie que a plusieurs decevoir il peust plus tost perdre sens, temps, ame, corps et loz, que de bien amer une seule.[70]
>
> Io ho un solo figlio — che Dio voglia conservarmelo, per sua bontà — ma io preferirei che fosse totalmente innamorato, con il senno che spero Dio gli darà, come hanno gli uomini ragionevoli, di una sola donna ben educata e saggia che amasse l'onore — e gliene venisse quel che ne può venire — piuttosto di sapere che a suo piacimento possa ingannarle tutte e molte. Perché sarei convinta che ingannandone molte lui possa perdere senno, tempo, anima, corpo e lode molto più che amandone una.[71]

La scrittrice non condanna quindi il sentimento amoroso, ma il vizio della carne a cui i comandamenti di Ragione istigano. Chri-

---

[68] Garavelli 2006, p. 108-109.
[69] Nel corso della disputa i sostenitori della *Rose* attaccano la scrittrice in maniera diretta e personale. Si pensi ad esempio all'epistola 154, *Ut sunt mores* (1402), di Jean de Montreuil in cui il teologo paragona Christine alla cortigiana greca Leonzio che, secondo Cicerone, ebbe l'ardire di contraddire il filosofo Teofrasto. Christine de Pizan riabilita prontamente il nome della cortigiana nella sua opera *Le Livre de la Cité des Dames* (1405) come donna di grande erudizione.
[70] Christine de Pizán, *Le Livre des epistres*, p. 187-188, § 15i.
[71] Garavelli 2006, p. 111.

stine torna sull'importanza dell'amore coniugale e del vincolo del matrimonio, svilito da Pierre Col nella sua epistola, nella quale egli, peraltro, era incorso in diverse inesattezze teologiche, già avvertite da Christine e che verranno più tardi confutate da Gerson.

Nella sua lettera a Gontier Col (fine settembre 1401) la scrittrice aveva fatto appello *au jugement de tous justes preudes hommes theologiens et vrays catholiques*[72] (al giudizio di tutti i giusti saggi teologi e veri cattolici),[73] mostrando così una certa complicità ideologica con il cancelliere Gerson[74] e circoscrivendo il pubblico della polemica a quel ceto promiscuo di corte di cui i suoi interlocutori facevano parte. Ad un pubblico di *clercs* si rivolge anche il piccolo *divertissement* di sedici versi, in cui *grant clerc* sta appunto per intellettuale, teologo che si rispetti, in grado di comprendere la sostanza morale del *Roman* sotto il velo dei versi (*car tout grant clerc qui se dispose/ d'entendre la substance enclose/ dedens* [...]). La chiusa sembra quasi richeggiare le parole di Pierre Col che intima alla *femme* della polemica di leggere bene il romanzo, anzi di leggerlo tre volte (secondo una simbologia che richiama la Santa Trinità), poiché se Christine lo avesse letto attentamente, avrebbe avuto modo di capire le intenzioni di Jean e la grandezza della sua opera.[75]

L'atto di rifiutare qualsiasi cambiamento del testo, così come è esplicitato nel nostro componimento di 16 versi (*Aucuns blasment qu'il n'est en prose,/ mais le moyne castel s'oppose/ qu'autrement soit pour nulle chose*), assume, alla luce delle considerazioni della scrittrice sul romanzo e sulla sua accattivante, e per questo pericolosa, forma poetica, un rinnovato valore satirico e derisorio. I versi acquistano il carattere di una critica trasposta che, attraverso il nome di un familiare di Christine, il monaco della chiusa, colpisce la scrittrice per via indiretta. La menzione del monaco da un lato rievoca i temi della *Querelle*, dall'altro nega la dignità di Christine come partecipante al dibattito. L'autrice si trova quindi ad essere oggetto di un attacco teso a delegittimare la sua persona e non a confutare i suoi argomenti, come già era accaduto nello

---

[72] Christine de Pizan, *Le Livre des epistres*, p. 173, § 3i.
[73] Garavelli 2006, p. 41.
[74] Richards 2000, p. 197–208.
[75] Christine de Pizan, *Le Livre des epistres*, p. 347, § 22m.

scambio epistolare. La professata scelta della prosa e i tentativi della scrittrice di mettere in luce i pericoli nascosti nella *Rose* sono rifunzionalizzati nel testo dell'*explicit* in modo da diventare argomenti del monaco contro chiunque osi criticare il *Roman*. Il componimento individua così un pubblico specifico, quello di colti teologi e intellettuali in grado di bucare il velo allegorico del testo e di comprendere gli ammaestramenti dell'opera. Un gruppo dal quale la scrittrice è dunque esclusa.

Nella sua epistola responsiva al trattato di Pierre Col,[76] Gerson difende la 'virile'[77] Christine e gli argomenti della donna contro il romanzo. Accusato insieme alla scrittrice di non aver compreso il testo di Jean, il teologo rimprovera aspramente Pierre e contraddice in più punti il suo trattato. Gerson si concentra non tanto sulla problematica cara a Christine della deriva dei valori cortesi, ma sull'uso di fonti moralmente discutibili (come l'*ars amatoria* di Ovidio) e sull'alterazione di fonti dal grande valore morale (le opere di Alain de Lille o di Guillaume de Saint-Amour) che secondo il teologo erano state mal tradotte dall'autore della *Rose*.[78]

La sua condanna non si ferma al solo testo del romanzo, ad essere stigmatizzate sono anche le illustrazioni dei codici della *Rose* che, al pari delle parole di Jean, inducono la fragile natura dell'uomo alla lussuria. Secondo il predicatore, le realistiche immagini dei manoscritti non facevano altro che istigare le anime dei peccatori, inclini a seguire i comportamenti illustrati, piuttosto che a evitarli. Nel suo ultimo intervento diretto nello scambio epistolare, Gerson, quasi a voler concludere la questione, torna sull'argomento:[79]

> Illic peroratum satis arbitror scripta, verba et picturas provocatrices libidinose lascivie penitus execrandas esse et a re

---

[76] Si tratta dell'epistola latina *Talia de me* (inverno 1402–1403) indirizzata a Pierre Col e composta nello stesso periodo dei sermoni della serie *Poenitemini* (cf. Christine de Pizan et al., *Le débat*, p. 163–175).

[77] L'appellativo di 'donna virile' è dato da Gerson alla scrittrice proprio per sottolineare l'impegno della donna nella nobile causa di criticare il romanzo di Jean, cf. Christine de Pizan et al., *Le débat*, p. 168, 105.

[78] Cf. Christine de Pizan et al., *Le débat*, p. 172, 201–211.

[79] La critica delle miniature dei codici del *Roman* è già presente nel primo trattato contro il romanzo del 18 maggio 1402 (cf. Christine de Pizan, *Le Livre des epistres*, p. 324, § 27f).

> publica christiane religionis exulandas, — et hoc quidem apud omnem intellectum, qui et catholica fide illustratus est, et nequaquam viciosa passione corruptus.[80]
>
> Ritengo di aver dimostrato abbastanza che gli scritti, le parole e i dipinti che provocano una sfrenata lussuria devono essere esposti all'esecrazione di tutti e banditi da uno stato di religione cristiana — e certo questo sarà chiaro ad ogni mente illuminata dalla fede cattolica e non corrotta da una passione viziosa.[81]

Nella sua *responsio* a Pierre Col, Gerson ripropone alcuni dei temi sviluppati nei suoi sermoni sui vizi capitali tenuti presso la chiesa di St. Jean-en-Grève. La serie dei *Poenitemini* è strettamente legata alla *Querelle* e ne diventa cassa di risonanza, tanto che nella sua lettera dell'estate del 1402 Pierre Col fa esplicito riferimento al sermone predicato nel giorno della Trinità. Non è improbabile che Pierre e Christine avessero ascoltato i sermoni[82] di Gerson, 'visto che i sermoni di Gerson erano molto frequentati e spesso persino copiati parola per parola e fatti circolare'.[83]

L'ipotesi che il nostro *explicit* dialoghi con il sottotesto polemico della *Querelle* è avvalorata dalla sua collocazione nel contesto del Ludwig XV 7. Se infatti gli indizi testuali del componimento lasciano pensare che il testo sia una critica obliqua a Christine, è vero anche che il codice che ospita i 16 novenari presenta diverse relazioni con un gruppo di manoscritti influenzati dalla disputa.

Fra la fine del XIV secolo e l'inizio del XV si assiste ad una diversificazione dei cicli d'illustrazione del *Roman de la Rose* che fa eco agli interrogativi morali sollevati dal dibattito. L'allestimento e la decorazione dei codici del romanzo risentono dei cambiamenti sociali e culturali che attraversano il mondo parigino nei primi anni del Quattrocento,[84] ossia gli anni delle contese universitarie cittadine, delle intransigenti crociate gersoniane contro le

---

[80] Christine de Pizan et al., *Le débat*, p. 352, 15–19.

[81] Garavelli 2006, p. 139.

[82] I sermoni contro la lussuria trattano in più punti della censura del romanzo e delle miniature dei testimoni della *Rose* (cf. Christine de Pizan et al., *Le débat*, p. 183, 75–76).

[83] Walters 2012, p. 122: *Since Gerson's sermons were widely attended, and frequently copied uerbatim and circulated afterwards.*

[84] Cf. Tesnière 2012, p. 6–7.

false credenze e del conciliarismo, ma sono anche, come abbiamo visto, anni di prezioso fermento culturale e di produzione letteraria. Il Ludwig XV 7 risale ai primi anni del XV secolo, quando lo scambio epistolare si era ormai concluso e il dibattito sul romanzo aveva intrapreso sentieri di espressione letteraria differenti. Il ciclo di miniature del codice risente di quell'atmosfera di *paganisme retrouvé* tanto avversato da Gerson e rintracciabile nei molteplici esempi antichi di cui il testo è fregiato. Accanto ai miti di Didone (f. 84v) e Medea (f. 85r), ritroviamo la rappresentazione delle vicende esemplari di Virginia, la cui testa è fra le mani del padre (f. 36v), di Creso di Lidia, immortalato sulla pira mentre la pioggia spegne le fiamme del rogo (f. 42r), della povera Filide che giace impiccata accanto a Medea intenta ad uccidere i propri figli (f. 85r), l'autocastrazione di Origene ed Empedocle fra le fiamme (f. 107v). I personaggi della mitologia antica non sono i soli a popolare le miniature del codice, in cui trova spazio anche il celebre amore di Eloisa ed Abelardo (f. 56r) illustrato nel suo divenire, dall'incontro al matrimonio.

Come già notava Marie-Hélène Tesnière, alcune di queste storie esemplari erano state *remis[es] à l'honneur* dalle traduzioni in francese delle opere boccacciane, il *De mulieribus claris* e il *De casis virorum illustrium*, che diventano modello testuale e iconografico anche per altri codici dell'inizio del secolo.[85] Si pensi ad esempio al manoscritto valenciano della *Rose* (Valencia, Biblioteca Histórica de la Universitat, MS 387), che da un lato riprende modelli pittorici e testuali boccacciani e dall'altro quelli delle versioni moralizzate dei racconti ovidiani in lingua francese.[86] Heidrun Ost, che si è occupata dell'analisi delle miniature della *Rose* di Valencia, ha messo in luce la relazione fra l'apparato iconografico del codice, il committente del manoscritto e la *Querelle* di cui trattiamo:[87] l'interesse per il richiamo erudito, probabilmente rivitalizzato dalla controversia morale, doveva aver spinto il committente a collaborare con i miniatori in modo che anche la seconda parte del romanzo potesse essere ben rappresentata nel codice. Nel mano-

---

[85] Tesnière 2012, p. 11.
[86] Ost 2006, p. 405–435.
[87] La studiosa ipotizza che il committente del codice possa essere il Duca di Berry, cf. Ost 2006, p. 434–435; ma anche Tesnière 2012, p. 7.

scritto valenciano (che contiene anche il *Testament*, il *Codicille* e il *Trésor*),[88] oltre ad una certa attenzione per i modelli classici, assistiamo, soprattutto per le sequenze finali, ad un più audace e realistico modo di rappresentare gli avvenimenti della presa del castello.[89] Questo duplice approccio manca nel Ludwig, il cui ciclo iconografico si conclude con la miniatura rappresentante Venere intenta a dar fuoco al castello, mentre i suoi abitanti in fuga, *Dangier*, *Paor* e *Honte*, ne gettano le chiavi abbandonando le mura (f. 132v) e il bocciolo al proprio destino. La presa del bocciolo e la *defloratio* finale non sono rappresentate, lasciando all'*explicit* il compito di concludere il testo del *Roman*.[90] Il maestro del Ludwig pone la sua attenzione sulle virtù protettrici della rosa, *Franchise* (f. 8v), *Chasteté*, *Danger* e *Malebouche* (f. 19r): le personificazioni sono rappresentate come dame dall'eleganza aristocratica intente a mettere in guardia il bocciolo dalle insidie di *Richesse*.[91] Allo stesso tempo, gli ammaestramenti della Vecchia a *Bel Acueil*[92] non si esplicitano in realistiche descrizioni (f. 80v)[93] e l'educazione sentimentale dell'Amante è inserita nella cornice di una *philosophie de la nature voulue par Dieu*.[94] La Natura come personaggio è rappresentata in quattro miniature: dedita a creare uomini e animali nella sua fucina (f. 101r; f. 121v); vestita di un abito decorato da immagini di animali mentre consegna a Genio un messaggio (f. 121r); e di fronte a Dio, circondata dalle sue crea-

---

[88] Il *Roman de la Rose*, il *Codicille* e il *Testament* sono spesso riuniti nei codici della seconda metà del XIV secolo che offrono un'immagine cristianizzata dell'autore, cf. Tesnière 2017, p. 332. Per i codici destinati all'ambiente di corte cf. Walters 2012, p. 110-138; Walters 2017, p. 15-66.

[89] Cf. Tesnière 2012, p. 13.

[90] Anche nel valenciano la presa del bocciolo è rappresentata in modo più pudico, l'atto sessuale tra il bocciolo-donna e l'Amante, seppur non eraso, è sostituito dall'immagine di questi intento a scuotere la rosa, illustrazione che si attiene, diremmo, ad una interpretazione più letterale dell'ultima sequenza del *Roman*.

[91] Tesnière 2012, p. 11.

[92] Il violento sostrato erotico e misogino degli insegnamenti della *Vielle* è a più riprese oggetto di precise critiche da parte di Christine, cf. ad esempio la prima epistola della scrittrice in risposta al trattatello di Montreuil in Christine de Pizan, *Le Livre des epistres*, p. 158-159.

[93] Nel codice l'atto sessuale adulterino è rappresentato nella miniatura del f. 62v Col.a subito seguito dall'immagine di Amante che si occupa della sua amata malata, costretta a letto (f. 62v Col.b).

[94] Cf. Tesnière 2012, p. 11.

zioni, con il viso rivolto al Creatore. Quest'ultima miniatura offre un'immagine emendata, corretta in senso religioso del lavoro di Natura, quasi a ristabilire quel legame fra creature e Creatore che Gerson[95] riteneva esser stato messo in ombra dalle parole di Jean.[96] In questo modo anche la conclusione del romanzo è posta sotto l'egida di Natura che, come *procreatrix* dell'officina di Venere, è messa al servizio della creazione divina.[97]

In conclusione, il ciclo di illustrazioni del manoscritto Ludwig XV 7 è interessante sia per l'attenzione ai rimandi eruditi delle sequenze digressive della seconda parte del *Roman*, sia per la tendenza a correggere le parti più licenziose del poema. Un manoscritto di questa fattura, la cui copia e decorazione sono state ricondotte al circolo delle botteghe commerciali di corte, doveva incontrare il favore di un pubblico di intellettuali bibliofili che avessero una certa familiarità con le problematiche morali sollevate dalla *Querelle*. Si pensi alla censura gersoniana del romanzo e delle sue miniature, alla critica delle fonti avanzata dal teologo nell'epistola a Pierre Col o alle 'invettive' di Christine contro i discorsi dei personaggi di Jean. Il Ludwig XV 7 offre un'interpretazione moralizzata del poema, quella che un vero credente e un dotto teologo avrebbero potuto offrire.

La presenza del nostro *explicit* in un testimone di questo tipo avvalora l'ipotesi che il testo sia legato alle tematiche della *Querelle* e a Christine, tacita protagonista della chiusa monorima. In dialogo da un lato con la disputa, dall'altro con la seconda *Rose*, il componimento di *octosyllabes* risente di quel taglio dissacrante e

---

[95] Walters 2012, p. 123.

[96] In apparente disaccordo con il ciclo decorativo del codice è la miniatura che decora la sequenza della presa del castello da parte di Venere (f. 129v). La dea, che aveva intimato a *Honte* di farsi da parte (nel MS vv. 20745–54), è rappresentata nel momento che precede lo scocco del suo tizzone, quando, con l'arco teso fino all'orecchio, si appresta a colpire la piccola feritoia, nascosta nella facciata della torre, che Natura aveva posto con maestria tra due pilastri d'argento. La statua d'argento sostenuta dai due pilastri rappresenta un corpo di donna nudo, visibile solo dal ventre ai piedi. Nella sua 'grafica' rappresentazione la miniatura solleva il velo allegorico della scena, diventando glossa figurale dei versi che seguono, in cui si narra della storia di Pigmalione. Anche se la miniatura rende esplicito il significato della sequenza, la rappresentazione della battaglia di Venere non assume i tratti 'realistici' che ha per esempio nei testimoni della *Rose* analizzati da Tesnière in Tesnière 2012.

[97] Tesnière 2012, p. 12.

ironico che informa il romanzo di Jean, della sua duplicità di senso e sostanza satirica, sostanza ancor più stridente perché veicolata dal registro allegorico.

Nel breve ed enigmatico *explicit* l'allusione al monaco Castel, padre o figlio, permetterebbe quindi di leggere il testo come il *divertissement* canzonatorio di un accolito di Jean, conoscitore della tenzone epistolare e dunque vicino ai circoli di corte dove la polemica aveva avuto certa circolazione. Il 'rodofilo' rimatore, allora, deriderebbe Christine de Pizan per ribadire la bellezza del *Roman*, un testo che qualsiasi *clerc* che si rispetti assapora, gusta e legge fino alla fine, così come l'autore l'ha composto, poiché è in grado di carpirne l'essenza e la sostanza morale senza esserne ingannato.

Bibliografia

Fonti primarie

Christine de Pizan, *The Livre de la Cité des Dames*, ed. M. Cheney Curnow, Nashville, TN: Vanderbilt University, 1975.

Christine de Pizan, Jean Gerson, Jean de Montreuil, Gontier & Pierre Col, *Le débat sur le 'Roman de la Rose'*, éd. Eric Hicks, Paris: Champion, 1977 (Bibliothèque du XVe siècle, 43).

Christine de Pizan, *Le livre de l'advision Cristine*, éd. C. Reno & L. Dulac, Paris: Champion, 2001.

Christine de Pizan, *Le Livre des epistres du debat sus le 'Rommant de la Rose'*, éd. A. Valentini, Paris: Garnier, 2016² (Textes littéraires du Moyen Âge, 29).

Francesco Petrarca, *Epistulae metricae. Briefe in Versen*, hg., übers. und komm. von Otto und Eva Schönberger, Würzburg: Königshausen & Neumann, 2004.

Jean de Montreuil, *Opera*, 4 vols, ed. E. Ornato, Torino: Giappichelli, I, 1963.

Fonti secondarie

Badel, P.-Y. (1976), 'Pierre d'Ailly, auteur du *Jardin amoureux*', in *Romania*, 97, p. 369–381.

Badel, P.-Y. (1980), *Le 'Roman de la Rose' au XIVe siècle: étude de la réception de l'œuvre*, Genève: Droz.

Bédier, J. (1925), *Les fabliaux. Études de littérature populaire et d'histoire littéraire du Moyen Âge*, Paris: Champion.

Beltrami, P. G., Jean de Meun (2014), *Ragione, Amore, Fortuna (Roman de la Rose, vv. 4059-7230)*, Alessandria: Edizioni dell'Orso (Gli Orsatti, 38).

Bossuat, A. (1958), 'Jean Castel, chroniqueur de France', in *Le Moyen Âge*, 64, p. 285-304, 499-538.

Braet, H. (1994), 'Aux Sources du *Roman de la Rose*', in P. Rolfe Monks & D. D. R. Owen (eds), *Medieval Codicology, Iconography, Literature, and Translation: Studies for Keith Val Sinclair*, Leiden: Brill, p. 110-119.

Brownlee, K. (1992), 'Discourses of the self: Christine de Pizan and the *Romance of the Rose*', in K. Brownlee & S. Hout (eds), *Rethinking the Romance of the Rose. Text, Image, Reception*, Philadelphia, PA: University of Pennsylvania Press, p. 234-261.

Brunelli, G. A. (1956), 'Jean Castel et le *Mirouer des dames*', in *Le Moyen Âge*, 62, p. 93-117.

Combes, A. (1973²), *Jean de Montreuil et le chancelier Gerson: contribution à l'histoire des rapports de l'humanisme et de la théologie en France au début du XVe siècle*, Paris: Vrin.

Debure, G. F. (1763), *Bibliographie instructive: ou traité de la connoissance des livres rares et singuliers*, Paris: De Bure le Jeune.

Delsaux, O. (2011), '*Le Pin* de Jean Castel, fils d'Étienne Castel et de Christine de Pizan', in *Archives d'histoire doctrinale et littéraire du Moyen Âge*, 78/1, p. 335-375; 10.3917/ahdlm.078.0335 (22.2.2021).

de Ricci, S. (1910), *Les Pérégrinations d'un Manuscrit du Roman de la Rose*, Paris: Revue des Bibliothèques.

Desmond, M. & P. Sheingorn (2003), *Myth, Montage, and Visuality in Late Medieval Manuscript Culture: Christine De Pizan's Epistre Othea*, Ann Arbor, MI: University of Michigan Press.

Droz, E. (1921), 'Jean Castel, chroniqueur de France', in *Bulletin philologique et historique (jusqu'à 1715) du Comité des travaux historiques et scientifiques. Année 1919*, 1, Paris: Imprimerie nationale, p. 95-113.

Fenzi, E. (2016), 'Dal *Roman de la Rose* al *Fiore* alle rime allegoriche di Dante: sconfitte e vittorie di Ragione', in N. Tonelli (ed.), *Sulle tracce del Fiore*, Firenze: Le Lettere, p. 55-86.

Fleming, J. V. (1969), *The Roman de la Rose: A Study in Allegory and Iconography*, Princeton, NJ: Princeton University Press.

Garavelli, B. (2006), *Il Dibattito sul Romanzo della Rosa di Christine de Pizan, Jean Gerson, Jean de Montreuil*, Milano: Medusa.

Hicks, E. (1976), 'De l'histoire littéraire comme cosmogonie: la querelle du *Roman de la Rose*', in *Critique*, 348, p. 510–519.

Hicks, E. & E. Ornato (1977), 'Jean de Montreuil et le débat sur le *Roman de la Rose*', in *Romania*, 98, p. 34–64.

Huot, S. (1993), *The Romance of the Rose and its Medieval Readers: Interpretation, Reception, Manuscript Transmission*, Cambridge, UK: Cambridge University Press (Cambridge Studies in Medieval Literature, 16).

Iribarren, I. (2014), 'Le Paradis retrouvé: l'utopie linguistique de Jean Gerson', in *Revue de l'histoire des religions*, 2/2, p. 223–251; 10.4000/rhr.8247 (22.2.2021).

Langlois, E. (1910), *Les manuscrits du Roman de la Rose, description et classement*, Paris: Champion (Droit-Lettres, 7).

LeBlanc, Y. (1995), *Va Lettre Va. The French Verse Epistle (1400–1550)*, Birmingham: Summa.

McWebb, C. (ed.) (2007), *Debating the Roman de la Rose. A Critical Anthology*, New York: Routledge (Routledge Medieval Texts).

Meiss, M. (1967), *French Painting in the Time of Jean de Berry: The Late Fourteenth Century and the Patronage of the Duke*, 2 vols, London: Phaidon.

Ost, H. (2006), 'Illuminating the *Roman de la Rose* in the time of the debate. The Manuscript of Valencia', in G. Croenen & P. Ainsworth (eds), *Patrons, Authors and Workshops. Books and Book Production in Paris around 1400*, Leuven: Peeters, p. 405–435.

Paré, G. (1947), *Les idées et les lettres au XIIIe siècle. Le Roman de la Rose*, Montréal: Centre de psychologie et de pédagogie (Bibliothèque de philosophie, 1).

Pasero, N. (2003), 'Un testo mostruoso. *Roman de la Rose*', in F. Moretti (ed.), *Il romanzo*, 5 vols, Torino: Einaudi, V, p. 47–63.

Quicherat, J. (1841), 'Recherches sur le chroniqueur Jean Castel', in *Bibliothèque de l'École des Chartes*, 2, p. 461–477.

Reulos, M. & P. G. Bietenholz (1985), 'Jean du Ruel of Soissons', in P. G. Bietenholz & T. B. Deutscher (eds), *Contemporaries of Erasmus: A Biographical Register of the Renaissance and Reformation*, I, Toronto: University of Toronto Press.

Richards, E. J. (2000), 'Christine de Pizan and Jean Gerson: an intellectual friendship', in J. Cambell & N. Margolis (eds), *Christine de Pizan 2000. Studies on Christine de Pizan in Honour of Angus J. Kennedy*, Amsterdam-Atlanta: Rodopi, p. 197–208, 328–330.

Sotheby's (1889), *Catalogue of Manuscripts on Vellum Chiefly from the Famous Hamilton Collection*, London, p. 46–51.

Tesnière, M.-H. (2012), 'Manuscrits enluminés du *Roman de la Rose* au début du XVe siècle', in *Art de l'enluminure*, 42, p. 2–57.

Tesnière, M.-H. (2017), 'Le *Roman de la Rose* d'un rhodophile: le manuscrit français 1563 de la Bibliothèque nationale de France', in J. Boudet (ed.), *Jean de Meun et la culture médiévale: littérature, art, sciences et droit aux derniers siècles du Moyen Âge*, Rennes: Presses universitaires de Rennes, p. 317–340.

Thomas, A. (1892), 'Jean Castel', in *Romania*, 21, p. 271–274.

von Euw, A. & J. M. Plotzek (1985), *Die Handschriften der Sammlung Ludwig*, 4 Bd, Köln: Schnütgen-Museum, IV, p. 228–239.

Walters, L. J. (2012), 'The Foot on Which He Limps: Jean Gerson and the Rehabilitation of Jean de Meun in Arsenal 3339', in *Digital Philology*, 1/1, p. 110–138.

Walters, L. J. (2017), 'Remembering Christine de Pizan in Paris, BnF, MS fr. 24392, a Manuscript owned by Anne de France, Duchess of Bourbon', in *Digital Philology*, 6/1, p. 15–66.

Wattenbach, W. (1883), *Die Handschriften der Hamiltonschen Sammlung*, 8 Bd, Hannover: Hahn, VII, p. 329–346.

Willard, C. C. (1984), *Christine de Pizan: Her Life and Works*, New York: Persea Books.

Abstract

The moral controversy known as *Querelle du Roman de la Rose* owes its critical success to Christine de Pizan, who made it public by bringing the question to the Parisian court in 1402. From that moment on, the controversy reached areas belonging to different traditions, from the naturalistic movement of the Universities to the philogynist defense of female *honor* and expressed itself in moral as well as in pedagogical texts.

In order to shed new light on the *Querelle*'s fortune, my case study will be a rare example of poetic writing: an anonymous *explicit* of 16 *octosyllabes* preserved in the manuscript Ludwig XV 7 (Los Angeles, J. P. Getty Museum), which is a precious codex attributable to the commercial shops close to the court's milieu. In this paper I will show how the short poem depends on and at the same time conveys the moral controversy, on the basis of some textual clues and on the renewed value that they assume in the context of the codex to which they belong.

On the one hand, the investigation will allow to give onomastic depth to the character of the monk Castel, mentioned in the composition, who could be identified with the son or grandson of Christine de Pizan; on the other hand, it will help place the author of this poem among the hosts of Jean's partisans, probably more numerous than the epistolary exchanges suggest.

Riassunto

La controversia morale conosciuta come *Querelle du Roman de la Rose* deve la sua fortuna critica a Christine de Pizan, che ebbe il merito di portare la questione a corte nel 1402: da qui la polemica toccò ambiti appartenenti a diverse tradizioni, dalla corrente naturalistico-universitaria alla difesa filogina dell'*honor* femminile, e si espresse in testi tanto di stampo morale quanto di matrice didattico-didascalica.

Il caso di studio che qui si propone è un raro esempio di scrittura poetica: un anonimo *explicit* di 16 *octosyllabes* conservato in calce al manoscritto Ludwig XV 7 (Los Angeles, J. P. Getty Museum), un codice pregiato riconducibile alle botteghe commerciali vicine alla corte parigina. In questo lavoro si vuole dimostrare in che modo il componimento dipenda da e allo stesso tempo veicoli il sottotesto polemico della *Querelle*, sulla base di alcuni indizi testuali e del rinnovato valore che questi assumono nel contesto del codice al quale appartengono.

L'indagine permette da un lato di dare profondità onomastica alla menzione nel componimento del monaco Castel, identificabile con il figlio o con il nipote di Christine de Pizan, dall'altro di collocare l'autore del componimento fra i partigiani di Jean, probabilmente più numerosi di quanto le epistole dello scambio lascino pensare.

JACOB LANGELOH
University of Copenhagen

A FAIR FIGHT OR A RIGGED JURY? THE COUNCIL OF BASEL (1431–1449) AND THE STRUCTURE OF ITS DEBATE ABOUT THE IMMACULATE CONCEPTION

1. *Introduction*

'Both sides fought fiercely, and finally the pious opinion carried away the noble palm of victory from this singular battle.'[1] Such was the conclusion of the Franciscan historian Hyacinthus Ameri, who wrote the classic account of how the doctrine of the Immaculate Conception was debated and decided at the Council of Basel.[2] The present contribution sheds light on the shape that this intellectual battle took and on its structural components. In short, my goal is more to describe *how* the engagement was fought than *what* was said.[3]

To describe this debate, I proceed in five steps. In the first, I introduce, in general terms, the question of Mary's Immaculate Conception. In the second, I describe how the Council of Basel came to focus on this topic. In the third, I detail how the debate itself proceeded, introduce the speakers, and lay out the order and interaction of their presentations, in so far as these can be known. In the fourth, I focus on the aspects of this debate

---

[1] [...] *ex una et altera parte acriter pugnatum est, et pia sententia singulari ex hoc certamine illustrem palmam reportavit*, Ameri 1954, p. 9–10. Unless otherwise noted, the translations in this article are mine.

[2] For his historical sketch, see Ameri 1954, p. 1–29, which Johannes Helmrath still deemed 'fundamental'; see Helmrath 1987, p. 384.

[3] For overviews, see Ameri 1954; Helmrath 1987, p. 383–394; Lamy 2000; Izbicki 2005, as well as the studies focusing on individual participants: Binder 1955, Emmen 1956, Emmen 1957, Horst 1994. Some studies have focused on the *officium* that John of Segovia composed, e.g. Ricossa 1994. In terms of describing Segovia's theological point of view, though, Ricossa falls short.

that made it special. I highlight the large amount of attention given to the question of permissible arguments, and explain how bringing them forward was navigated in the two teams of debaters. I show that these teams divided the task of presenting their arguments. It will also be evident that there was a clear hierarchy within each team. In the fifth and final step, I examine one specific exchange in which the strategies and viewpoints of the two parties materialized in a particularly clear way. It was at this point that the gloves came off, and the fight was joined in earnest. In the conclusion, I summarize my findings and suggest new directions for research.

2. *Mary's Status at her Conception: The Issue and the Earlier Debates*

Since misconceptions abound, one should first clarify what the Immaculate Conception refers to. While Scripture clearly states that Jesus Christ was conceived and born without sin, the same cannot be said of his mother. Thus, one might assume that she, like all other humans, was conceived and born with the stain of original sin and thus required redemption in some shape and form at some point in time.[4] This assumption is consistent with Christ's privilege as the one Mediator, the only one who frees and saves from sin.[5] Nevertheless, as devotion to Mary grew in the Western Church, it became inconceivable, particularly amongst laypeople, that Mary was affected by original sin.[6] As early as the period stretching from the tenth to twelfth centu-

---

[4] From the early Church Fathers onwards, there were diverse positions concerning Mary's relation to sin. See Reynolds 2012, 332–333: 'Broadly speaking, three separate positions may be identified concerning the sinfulness or lack thereof of the Virgin. Some held that the Virgin, although of exceptional purity, was not entirely lacking in minor faults. Others, beginning with Irenaeus († *c.* 202), held that she underwent a purification at the time of the Incarnation. [...] Still others asserted that she was purified either at the time of her conception or at least while still in the womb, though the exact mechanism whereby this took place was not made clear, and that she received a second infusion of grace prior to the Incarnation.'

[5] This view was clearly articulated by Augustine and remained very influential in the West; see Reynolds 2012, p. 344–348.

[6] On the *dissensiones* among the believers, see Ameri 1954, p. 5.

ries, theologians began to argue for the doctrine of the Immaculate Conception.[7] As the name implies, this doctrine asserts that Mary was unaffected by original sin; she was preserved from it and was therefore immaculate from the moment of her conception.[8] Since her birth is celebrated on the 8th of September, her conception was assumed to be exactly nine months earlier, and the feast in honor of her conception was therefore celebrated on the 8th of December.[9]

Perhaps the first to argue this point explicitly in the West were Anselm of Canterbury and even more so his biographer Eadmer.[10] From the thirteenth century on, battle lines were drawn between the two great mendicant orders, the Franciscans and the Dominicans, who were on opposite sides of the issue.[11] While the Franciscans made Mary's conception a feast of the order as early as 1263, the Dominicans were still arguing against it in the nineteenth century.[12] Among the opponents of the doctrine were famous theologians such as Bernard of Clairvaux, Albert the Great, Thomas Aquinas, and, in a more cautious manner, Bonaventure, though he was, of course, a Franciscan. It should be noted that, as far as time-spent-in-sin is concerned, the proponents and adversaries of the doctrine did not disagree about much. In the view of Thomas Aquinas, to cite a famous example, Mary was purified when her body was animated by her soul, which was thought to happen during the growth of the embryo in the womb. Therefore,

---

[7] Kappes 2014 argues that it might have been prefigured by the Greek Church Fathers' use of the term 'prepurification' (προκαθαρθεῖσα). They also effusively praised her as 'immaculate', but this should not necessarily be understood in the sense of being preserved from original sin; cf. Reynolds 2012, p. 333–334 and 337–342.

[8] See the definition in MC III/1, 364 sq. Volumes 2 and 3 of this collection contain John of Segovia's history of the council.

[9] For a summary of the history, cf. Boss 2000, p. 123–155; Lamy 2000, passim; and Reynolds 2012, p. 330–369. The latter also stresses the multifaceted role Mary has played in Church history (ibid., p. 1–8).

[10] See Ingham 2019, p. 176–177; Izbicki 2005, p. 147; and Boss 2000, p. 126–128.

[11] See Izbicki 2005, p. 151–152.

[12] See Horst 1987 and Horst 2009 for a diachronic overview of the Dominican opposition.

according to him, she was purified after her conception but before her birth.[13]

The immaculist point of view is often summarized in the classic formula *potuit, decuit, ergo fecit* ('He could do it, it was fitting, therefore he did it'), which can be traced back to Eadmer of Canterbury.[14] The doctrine's most striking defense, though, came from John Duns Scotus in his *Quaestiones disputatae de immaculata conceptione beatae Mariae virginis*.[15] As mentioned above, the debate about the Immaculate Conception was generally framed as a conflict between the honor of Mary and the function of Christ as the one Mediator, the argument *ex excellentia Filii sui*, as Scotus calls it.[16] Scotus turned this argument on its head. As the most perfect mediator, Christ would offer the best mediation to all creatures.[17] And with regard to his mother, such mediation would consist precisely in preserving her from original sin. Furthermore, if Christ was unable to preserve someone from sin entirely and before the sin occured, then he might not appear to be the best mediator at all.[18] In that sense, Christ's excellence

---

[13] STh III q. 27 a. 1 co: *Respondeo dicendum quod de sanctificatione beatae Mariae, quod scilicet fuerit sanctificata in utero, nihil in Scriptura canonica traditur, quae etiam nec de eius nativitate mentionem facit. Sed sicut Augustinus, de assumptione ipsius virginis, rationabiliter argumentatur quod cum corpore sit assumpta in caelum, quod tamen Scriptura non tradit; ita etiam rationabiliter argumentari possumus quod fuerit sanctificata in utero.* ('Concerning the sanctification of the blessed Mary, namely, that she was sanctified *in utero*, I respond that it must be acknowledged that nothing is transmitted in the canon of Scripture, which also does not mention her birth. But, as Augustine says about the Assumption of the Virgin, it should be argued from reason that she was bodily taken up into heaven, which, however, is not reported by Scripture. In the same way we can conclude from reason that she was sanctified *in utero*.') STh III q. 27 a. 1 ad 4 clarifies that the sanctification happened instantly when the embryo was animated by the soul.

[14] Eadmer, *Tractatus de conceptione beatae virginae*, PL 159, 305D: *potuit plane, et voluit; si igitur voluit, fecit.* ('He clearly could, and he wanted to; but if he wanted to, he did it.') There is a new edition by Thurston, 1904. Eadmer compares Mary, who is untouched by the stain of sin, to a chestnut that is protected by its spines on the outside and grows untouched inside. Cf. Reynolds 2012, p. 353.

[15] Published separately in Scotus et al. 1904, but originally taken from his final commentary on the *Sentences*: Ordinatio III, d. 3, q. 1, which was edited as Scotus 2006, p. 169–196. Cf. the lucid reconstruction by Ingham 2019, p. 180–192. Scotus dealt with this issue in all three of his commentaries on the *Sentences*; see Ingham 2019, p. 180.

[16] Scotus et al. 1904, p. 13.

[17] Scotus et al. 1904, p. 14.

[18] Scotus et al. 1904, p. 14–15.

and his mother's Immaculate Conception would not only be compatible, they would be connected by necessity.[19] But even if 'all the pieces of the theological puzzle were now available [...] [it] would take centuries of heated debate and sometimes bitter enmities before a consensus emerged.'[20] The University of Paris proved to be one of the battlegrounds. Generally speaking, Paris backed the Immaculate Conception; in 1387 the university condemned John of Monzón who had argued that affirming the Immaculate Conception was heretical.[21]

3. *The Doctrine at the Council of Basel (1431–1449)*

At the Council of Basel (1431–1449), many parties tried to push the council towards accepting the Immaculate Conception as a dogma of the Church. Apart from the Franciscans and the University of Paris, worldly rulers such as Alfonso V of Aragon made their endorsement of the doctrine abundantly clear.[22] The council itself hardly behaved in a neutral manner when, in 1431, 1432, and 1435, it celebrated the feast of Mary's conception,[23] and it would appear plausible that the council did so as well in 1433 and 1434.[24]

It was apparently the festal sermon on 8 December 1435 that pushed the council to take a definitive stance.[25] The preacher on that day, Jean de Rouvroy (*c.* 1371–1461),[26] who represented the

---

[19] Reynolds 2012, p. 368.

[20] Reynolds 2012, p. 368.

[21] CUP III, p. 490–491. That Monzón not only rejected the doctrine but also thought it heretical may have been the primary reason for his condemnation. See Moule 2016, p. 177.

[22] See Helmrath 1987, p. 385. Alfonso V of Aragon had already pressured the Council of Constance to make this move (see Ameri 1954, p. 5), and he had recruited a theologian to write a series of letters to Emperor Sigismund to convince him to intervene. Ameri 1954, p. 6, identifies the writer with John of Palomar, but Lamy 2000, p. 592, points out that this is unlikely.

[23] Ameri 1954, p. 8.

[24] Lamy 2000, p. 594 n. 119.

[25] See Emmen 1956 for an edition and a German translation.

[26] For a summary of his life, see Santoni 1979, p. 21–46. At that time, he was a canon of Bourges and St Étienne. Frequent misspellings of his name in official documents or their editions have made it difficult to reconstruct his entire range of activities (see ibid., 20–22). The maximum amount of confusion was probably

French king, Charles VII, preached on the theme *Mater pulchrae dilectionis*. In addition, Rouvroy named a large number of arguments in favor of the Immaculate Conception, consisting of *auctoritates*, viz. authoritative statements from Church Fathers, as well as arguments based on reason (called *rationes*), and miracles. He concluded that the council should prescribe celebrating the Feast of the Conception for all Christians:

> Rejoice, therefore, and be glad (Mt 5.12) on this day, most distinguished fathers, and honor the mother of fair love (Eccl 24.24) by celebrating the feast of her conception; and take care that from now on such will happen in every part of the earth.[27]

As we shall see soon, the council reacted quickly to this exhortation. The final result of the process is well known. Jean's wish was granted, albeit with some delay. In its thirty-sixth session, on 17 September 1439, the council concluded that Mary had never been affected by original sin, and it prescribed celebration of the feast.[28] Yet the council was considered to be schismatic at that time. After the resolution of the schism, the Church only adopted the first twenty-two sessions, thereby excluding the declaration on the Immaculate Conception. In the following centuries, the doctrine remained a difficult, unresolved topic[29] until the Immaculate Conception was finally given dogmatic definition in the bull *Ineffabilis deus* by Pius IX on 8 December 1854.[30]

In the following section, the debates at the Council of Basel that followed Jean de Rouvroy's sermon are reconstructed. Instead of reiterating the views expressed at the council, the emphasis here is on the way the debate unfolded, the dynamics of the debate, and how this intellectual warfare was conducted at the council.

---

reached when the *Dictionnaire de théologie catholique* cited three different theologians as supporters of the doctrine of the Immaculate Conception, all of which were distorted versions of Rouvroy's name and thus referred to just one person. See Santoni 1979, p. 31, n. 1, and Emmen 1957, p. 345.

[27] Emmen 1956, p. 98–99: *Gaudete ergo et exultate hac die, patres percelebres, et honorate matrem pulchrae dilectionis, celebrando festum suae Conceptionis; curateque ut sic ammodo fiat per omnia climata orbis.*

[28] See MC III/1, p. 364–365.

[29] See Izbicki 2005, p. 154–170.

[30] See Seifert 2013 for the chronology of events.

In order to approach these issues, I first set out the basic facts. Which speakers were selected for the debate and what was their task? When did they present their points of view? When did the opposition learn about these points of view, and did it even have access to the texts? Then I examine several features of the debate itself. First, what kind of arguments, or intellectual weapons, were accepted by each side? Second, how did the theologians divide up their work, and how did they build on each other's arguments? Third, how did the opposing sides refer to each other? Ameri wrote that the decision at the council was made 'with the greatest possible fairness, justice, diligence, maturity, and prudence'.[31] But was this really the case?

4. *Terms of Engagement: Who, What, and When?*

On 23 March 1436,[32] the council decided to address the question of the Immaculate Conception. This decision was not a given, since the main tasks of the council were to fight heresy, to create peace in Europe, and to reform the Church.[33] The Delegation of Peace (*delegatio pacis*) had therefore proposed to hold a simple vote on whether or not to adopt the feast as a feast of the Church, but the majority opted to hold a proper debate. In less than a week, on 29 March 1436, four theologians were appointed to argue for and against the thesis. Jean de Rouvoy and the general of the Aquitanian Franciscans, Pierre Porcher, were nominated to speak in favor of the doctrine[34] while Gio-

---

[31] Ameri 1954, p. 22–23: *Exinde apparet quanta cum aequitate et iustitia processerint, quantamque diligentiam adhibuerint Patres, ut ad decisionem huius controversiae ea maturitate et prudentia, qua par erat procedetur.* ('From this it becomes clear with how much equity and justice they would proceed, how much diligence the Fathers would employ, so that they might advance towards a decision about this controversy with the maturity and prudence that was required.')

[32] MC II, p. 896.

[33] John of Segovia offers the explanation that Mary's favor would help them to do all three; see John of Segovia 1664, p. 389, and Lamy 2000, p. 595.

[34] On Porcher, Ameri 1954, p. 10, writes: *Primus in certamen descendit pro defensione mariani privilegii Petrus Porqueri vel Perqueri, Ordinis Minorum, patria tolosanus, sacrae theologiae magister, ac minister franciscanae provinciae Aquitaniae.* ('The first to enter the battle in defense of the Marian privilege was Peter Porcher or Percher, from the order of the Friars Minor, a native of Tou-

vanni di Montenero[35] and Juan de Torquemada were chosen as their opponents. Soon after his appointment, Pierre Porcher had to leave the council in order to prepare the general chapter of his order; he was replaced by John of Segovia, who went on to play a central role in the whole process. The question they had to answer was couched in rather careful terms: 'Whether it is more pious to believe that the soul of the most holy mother of God was preserved from original sin right from the moment it was poured into the body than to believe that the virgin was conceived in original sin.'[36] The hearings were to take place in the refectory of the Franciscan monastery at Basel, which could hardly be considered neutral ground.

The contestants were officially nominated by Cardinal Louis d'Aleman, who presided over the proceedings. The contestants could profit from a collection of materials on this topic that Louis had ordered to be gathered in the summer of the previous year.[37]

Let us consider the sources and who had access to them. We have an edition of Rouvroy's sermon which initiated this process, viz. the aforementioned sermon, pronounced on 8 December 1435.[38] The sermon itself was based on a treatise called *Sapientia aperuit* that was later used to compose the *Relatio Tota pulchra es*,[39] which was supposed to be presented to the council fathers. We lack the original text of Porcher's address from 20 April 1436. What we know about his statement is contained in John of Segovia's *historia* of the council, which also constitutes the most valuable source concerning the proceedings of the debate. Segovia reports that Porcher brought up, in a summary fashion (*summarie*), thirty authorities of Holy Scripture and thirty doctors of the

louse, master of sacred theology, and minister of the Aquitanian province of the Franciscans.')

[35] Ameri 1954, p. 12, again, uses military language: *privilegia Mendicantium acriter tutatus est*. For general information on Giovanni de Montenero, see Ameri 1954, p. 11-15.

[36] MC II, p. 846: *magis pium est credere animam beatissime Dei genitricis fuisse in instanti sue infusionis in corpore preservatam a peccato originali, quam credere ipsam virginem in originali peccato fuisse conceptam.*

[37] Ameri 1954, p. 8-9. See also Helmrath 1987, p. 387, who cites the *Septem Allegationes* 1 and the text of the declaration from MC III/1, p. 364.

[38] Emmen 1956.

[39] Edited as Jean de Rouvroy 1664.

Church who were convinced of the Immaculate Conception, 'reciting their names'. Porcher also claimed to have thirty-one ways of refuting the opposing side. On the following day, his testimony was expanded by a colleague, who added miracles as further evidence. Another miracle was spontaneously mentioned by a member of the audience, the bishop of Montauban.[40]

When the available documents and Segovia's report are examined, it is clear that it was Jean de Rouvroy who supplemented Porcher's testimony with miracles. Although Rouvroy's *Tota pulchra es* covers all available sources of arguments and is addressed directly to the fathers of the council, it is unclear whether this treatise was even presented to them at full length.[41] Perhaps Rouvroy was content with his colleague's treatment and just added what was still missing.

When Giovanni di Montenero answered over the course of three days (2, 6, 10) in May of 1436, he mentioned that he had not received Porcher's written statement.[42] The next in line,

---

[40] MC II, p. 896: [...] *frater Petrus Porquerii Aprilis die xxa. coram patribus in refectorio fratrum minorum, ubi omnes allegaciones audite fuere, mane et sero scripto recitans legit in parvo sexterno, summarie referens triginta esse auctoritates scripture sacre, ex quibus magis pium erat credere concepcionem beatissime virginis fuisse absque originali peccato; dicebat eciam xxx. esse doctores id tenentes, eorum nominibus recitatis; attestabatur item generaliter referens triginta et unum esse modos solvendi allegandas in contrarium auctoritates et raciones. Collega item eius scripto recitavit nonnulla miracula circa dictam materiam. Episcopus eciam Montis Albani miraculum narravit in eius personam desuper contigisse, multa referens de disputactione (habita) Parisius super ea materia et determinacionibus doctorum.* ('[...] On the 20th, friar Pierre Porcher read in front of the fathers at the refectory of the Franciscans, where all the statements were heard, from a small sextern, bringing forward in condensed form that there were thirty authorities from Holy Scripture proving that it is more pious to believe that Mary was conceived without original sin. He said that there were thirty doctors of the Church who maintained this. Having recited their names, he further stated that there were generally thirty-one ways to resolve the authorities and rational arguments that the opposing side could bring forth. His colleague then recounted from his script some miracles regarding this matter. The bishop of Montauban recounted a miracle that had happened to him personally, and reported many things from a disputation that was held at Paris about this topic, and about the conclusions of the doctors.')

[41] Emmen 1957, p. 349 and Santoni 1979, p. 35.

[42] Basel UB, A I 33, 312r and Horst 1994, p. 173 n. 22: *auctoritates scripturae quae in sensu mistico adducuntur pro altera partium in praesenti materia et quae iam adductae sunt ex veteri testamento per venerabilem magistrum quod perlocutus est, in robur sue opinionis numero fere 24 aut 26, si bene tenui cum dictorum copia non tradiderit, fidem non faciunt evidentem seu efficacem probationem cum ipsarum*

John of Segovia, also received the opposing view too late to incorporate it into his remarks. In his *Allegationes*, Segovia says that he was only given Montenero's *Relacio* after he had concluded his presentation to the council. In the full written version that he obviously finished after he had given his presentation, Segovia addresses Montenero's arguments and apologizes for that fact that his responses have made numbers five, six, and seven of the *Allegationes* much longer than the first four.[43] From this statement, we can also infer that the debaters' work was not done once they had completed their presentation to the council. As Rouvroy's complete treatise, which was not even used for oral argument, and Segovia's expanded version of his statements indicate, additional energy was expended to compose a written, more complete version of the arguments.

In his history of the council, which was written after 1450, Segovia repeats the claim that he received Montenero's statements late, but he asserts that at least he himself did better by handing his own work to Juan de Torquemada in a timely fashion.[44]

---

rectitudo ex litteralis scriptis certitudine dependet ut ex dictis bene colligitur ('The scriptural authorities that have been brought up in a mystical sense for the other side in the present matter, and which have already been brought up from the Old Testament by the venerable Master who spoke before, in the core of his statement, numbering perhaps 24 or 26, if I remember correctly, since he did not give me a copy of his statement, do not constitute evident or effective proof, since their correctness depends on the certainty of literal Scripture, which clearly follows from the aforesaid.')

[43] John of Segovia 1664, p. 381a: *Item cum propter convenientiam nostram universa relatio haec distincta sit in septem Allegationes, quarum tres ultimae in magna quantitate excedunt priores quatuor: causa disparitatis fuit, quia completa relatione coram Sacro Concilio venit ad manus referentis scriptura Allegationum ex adverso, et quoniam primae quatuor vix, aut nullis paucis additis, vel mutatis sicut verbo pronunciatae, ita in scriptis redactae fuerunt.* ('For our convenience, we have divided our statement into seven allegations, of which the last three exceed the previous four by a lot. The reason for this disparity was that the written statement of the opposition only came into the hands of this speaker after he had completed his statement before the Sacred Council, and since hardly anything has been added to the first four, or changed compared to the spoken word, they have been rendered into writing as such.')

[44] MC II, p. 896: *post dictas septem allegaciones per eum factas a dicto Johanne de Monte nigro receperit trium suarum allegacionum continenciam in tribus sexternis, porrexit ipse Johannes de Segobia magistro Johanni de Turrecremata in oppositum, quod nunquam fecit, allegaturo, de per eum allegatis librum continentem viginti sexternos et amplius.* ('Having presented his seven allegations, he received from the aforesaid Giovanni of Montenero a volume containing three of his alle-

Torquemada's work clearly shows that he had access to a copy of Segovia's text. Juan de Torquemada was typically combative as a debater, a characterization that holds true in this case. He engages the opposing arguments head-on and tries to refute them in a definitive fashion. After his initial declarations regarding the method of his inquiry, Torquemada states that he will follow the order of his opponent and in so doing will reinforce some points his *collega* (Montenero) had already made.[45] The downside of this approach was that it took him until March 1437 to finish his statement.[46] As we learn from both Segovia's account and Torquemada's *post scriptum* to his work, Torquemada was unable to step before the congregation and defend his position orally. At that time, the council was busy trying to bring the Hussites, who were considered heretical, back into the fold, as well as attempting to reunite the Western Church with the Eastern Church.

---

gations in three sexterns, and John of Segovia himself gave to Master Juan de Torquemada of the opposition — something that he [Torquemada] never did, when he was ready to give his statement — a book of what he had presented, which contained more than twenty sexterns.')

[45] Torquemada 1869, I.8, p. 22a: *Harum autem regularum doctrinam ego complexus, talem in generali ordinem in meae relationis processu tenere disposui, conformans me ordini observato in relatione ex adverso facta per venerabilem sacrae theologiae professorem et magistrum Joannem de Sagobia [sic] compatriotam meum, ut primo terminis expositis quaestionis, testimonia Sacrae Scripturae et sanctorum doctorum, quae ad propositum facere videbuntur, confutando solutiones datas ex adverso et dari consuetas, in medium conferam: inter quae scripturarum testimonia aliqua repetam, eorum quae adducta sunt per venerabilem patrem collegam meum in relatione sua, ostensurus quod eis per relatorem ex adverso non sit satisfactum. Secundo rationes doctorum partem hanc quaestionis tenentium roborabo. Tertio respondebo auctoritatibus omnibus et rationibus ex adverso in duabus relationibus adductis. Quarto concludam relationem meam per unum correlarium responsivum.* ('Sticking to the guidance of these rules, I have decided to structure my statement in the following way, thereby conforming to the order observed in the statement of the opposition made by the venerable professor and Master of Sacred Theology John of Segovia, my compatriot. So, after having laid out the terms of the debate, I will first focus on the testimonies of Sacred Scripture and of the Holy Doctors, which are relevant to this issue, refuting the explanations given by the opposition and giving the accepted ones. During that I will repeat some of the scriptural testimonies that my venerable colleague brought up in his statement. I intend to show that they are not treated properly by the speaker of the opposition. Second, I will strengthen the reasoning of the doctors who defend this side of the doubtful question. Third I will respond to all authorities and rational reasoning presented in the two opposing statements. Fourth, I want to finish my statement with one corollary in response.')

[46] See Lamy 2000, p. 597.

Since it appeared likely that a Greek delegation would join the council soon to discuss the latter matter, Torquemada was told to wait. A union council with the Eastern Church would necessitate solving many questions of the faith anyway, and thus the question of Mary's Immaculate Conception would also have to be discussed at the joint ecumenical council. Torquemada acceded to this request and stayed ready to present his point of view. When the Greeks spurned Basel and decided to join Pope Eugene IV for the Council of Ferrara-Florence, Torquemada followed.[47] Therefore, he was never able to present his view to the Council of Basel. Given the length of the work, we can only speculate about how many sessions it would have taken to read.

After its defeat in the Greek question, the council resumed its deliberations about the Immaculate Conception. Another committee was formed on 20 May 1438.[48] John of Segovia was asked to write a summary of the proceedings that could be the basis for a final decision. This was done in his *Septem Avisamenta*.[49]

---

[47] The main source is the *post scriptum* in Torquemada 1869, p. 780. In the published version, which was obviously written after May 1439, he added that the any decision by the Council of Basel would be void, since it lacked the participation of important churchmen. Since the official council (in Torquemada's view) had been transferred to Bologna by Pope Eugene IV, the meeting at Basel had become an instrument of the devil. See Torquemada 1869, p. 780–781: *Invalida etiam est praefata determinatio et vacua omni auctoritate. Tum primo, quia facta est post recessum reverendissimorum patrum dominorum cardinalium, legatorum, et dominorum praesidentium; et ita per quosdam Acephalos. Tum secundo, quia facta est post translationem concilii factam de Basilea in Bononiam, et ita non est facta per Universalis Ecclesiae synodum, sicut quidam mentiuntur, sed per quandam congregationem Sathanae sive ecclesiam malignantem. Tum tertio, quia facta fuit per eos qui pro suis erroribus et diabolicis temeritatibus, excommunicati et tanquam schismatici et haeretici per Apostolicam sedem et Sanctae Universalis Ecclesiae synodum fuerunt justissime condemnati. Sicut apparet ex processibus factis Bononiae et Florentiae contra eos.* ('The decision mentioned is invalid and lacks authority. First, because it was made after the departure of the most venerable cardinals, legates, and presidents, and therefore by a headless group. Second, since it was made after the council was transferred from Basel to Bologna, and therefore it was not performed by a universal synod of the Church, as some wrongly claim, but through some congregation of Satan or malignant church. Third, because it was decided by those, who, for their errors and diabolical temerities, have been excommunicated and justly condemned as schismatics and heretics by the apostolic see and the synod of the Holy Catholic Church. This is apparent from the processes at Bologna and Florence against them.') See also Izbicki 2005, p. 153.

[48] MC III/1, p. 362.

[49] John of Segovia 1664, p. 391–534.

Although he engages with the opposing position throughout, the main work is done in numbers four and five of the series. In the fifth *Avisamentum* it becomes clear that Segovia was still using Giovanni di Montenero's work as the main source for the opposing point of view. Segovia declares that he will refute a 'fundamental premise' of the opposing side, which had supported that premise with nine arguments from Scripture and nine rational arguments.[50] This basic proposition is identical with the one that Giovanni di Montenero put forward;[51] Montenero had also used exactly the nine authorities that Segovia now lists.[52] Given that Segovia still treated Montenero as his primary opponent, it is unlikely that Torquemada had done anything to communicate his views to the opposition before he was allowed to present. So while Segovia was writing his *Septem Avisamenta*, he did not know what Torquemada would have said.

To summarize, we are lucky that most of the materials from the debate about the Immaculate Conception have survived. We know the chronological order in which the materials were presented and also have some clues as to who knew what at what time. A full recapitulation of the debate might start with a reconstruction of these available source materials, including unedited sources.[53] Then it would proceed to an analysis of the seven pri-

---

[50] John of Segovia 1664, p. 483: *Quintum Avisamentum est specifica responsio ad novem auctoritates Sacrae Scripturae, et totidem rationes principales assertionis adversae. Quae in principio Allegationum suarum posuit hanc conclusionem, quam dixit fundamentalem propositionem: Beata et Gloriosa Virgo Maria in peccato originali concepta fuit, quemadmodum et coeteri, qui ex Adam carnali origine propagantur.* ('The fifth declaration is a specific response to the nine authorities from Sacred Scripture and to the same number of main arguments by the opposing side, which has put at the beginning of their statements the following conclusion that has been called a fundamental premise: The blessed and glorious Virgin Mary was caught in original sin, just like the others who descended from Adam through carnal means.')

[51] See Horst 1994, p. 172, n. 15: *Hiis premissis sit totius relationis iuxta intentionem sanctorum doctorum propositio fundamentalis: Beata et gloriosa Virgo Maria in peccato originali concepta fuit quemadmodum et ceteri, qui ex Adam carnali origine propagantur.*

[52] John of Segovia 1664, p. 383a–384b. Cf. Basel, E I 33, f. 312v–313r, where Montenero lists and interprets these authorities in precisely this order, and where some scribe has conveniently numbered the first seven of them in the margin.

[53] Among these, the principal ones are Rouvroy's treatise *Sapientia aperuit*, which is contained in Brussels, Bibliothèque royale 3446–3484, f. 241vo–258vo, and Giovanni di Montenero's *Relacio*. Some excerpts of the latter are edited in the notes of Horst 1994, and the manuscripts used are also listed there (p. 172, n. 13).

mary works; three by Rouvroy, two by Segovia, and one each from Montenero and Torquemada. One would trace the argumentative interactions between the works and their chronological order and the distribution of tasks between the proponents of the same viewpoint would also be considered. It would be necessary, for example, to detail both how John of Segovia tried to merge the previous presentations into the *Septem Avisamenta* and in what way he modified his old view, which is contained in the *Allegationes*. Presenting this complete picture, however, is beyond the scope of the present article. In order, rather, to highlight some of the most defining traits of this debate, I would now like to focus on two central aspects. First is the question of which arguments were permissible, and how considerations of permissability allowed the theologians to divide and thus share the burden of argumentation. Second, I would like to examine one specific exchange in which the interaction between the two parties is especially pronounced and in which the fault lines between the positions become particularly visible.

5. *Permissible Arguments and Sharing the Load*

A large part of the debate about Mary's Immaculate Conception was concerned with the question of which polemical weapons were permissible. Rouvroy prepared the field in his sermon. He used *auctoritates*, *rationes*, and *miracula*. His enumeration of authorities mainly consists of the names of those who argued in favor of the doctrine and some choice quotes by Church Fathers that were meant to convey the same point. He then adds ten rational arguments and eight miracles. It seems that the first statements by Pierre Porcher and Jean de Rouvroy took a similar shape. As we know from Segovia's characterization,[54] Porcher used thirty *rationes* and thirty *auctoritates* and tried to refute thirty-one counter arguments. The day afterwards, miracles were added by Jean de Rouvroy, and the account of another miracle was related by a member of the council, as previously mentioned.[55]

---

[54] See above n. 39.

[55] The miracle is reported in John of Segovia 1664, p. 539–540. A bishop is riding over a bridge with a large hole in the middle. His horse steps into the hole. The rider, the bishop himself, pledges to celebrate Mary's conception every year

For the affirmative side, three things become apparent. First, the canon of available arguments appears to be quite fixed, since all are using the trifecta of *rationes, auctoritates,* and *miracula*. Second, the two disputants obviously shared the load. Porcher presented one part and Rouvroy covered the next. Third, there was also a difference in detail. As the expression *summarie* indicates, Porcher only named the arguments and did not fully develop them. Segovia picked up the slack at the beginning of his fifth *allegatio*, where he states that he will revisit sixteen arguments that Pierre Porcher had presented, 'naming the authors that advocate them', but 'without deduction'.[56]

Turning to the other side, the Dominicans generally tried to limit the scope of the debate. Giovanni di Montenero argued that one should focus on four things: first, the authorities from Holy Scripture; second, expositions of Scripture by *sancti doctores*; third, testimony by those saintly doctors whose lives and doctrines are approved by the Church; and fourth and final, rational arguments. He regards rational argument as less effective (*minus efficax*) and leaves most of it to his colleague: 'The fourth way, although less effective, will be through rational argument, as long as the lengthiness of the current proceeding, namely, the allegations of the doctors, does not prevent it. In that case, it will be passed on to my colleague, so that he will deal with them at

---

from that point on and then finds himself miraculously on the other side of the hole. As mentioned above, the bishop was most likely Bernard de la Roche Fontenilles, the Franciscan bishop of Montauban.

[56] John of Segovia 1664, p. 124: *ut plenior certitudinis firmitas ex omni parte assistat, nunc opus est intendere ad declarandum illas sexdecim propositiones, quae ab insigni S. Theologiae Professore Reverendo Patre Petro Porqueri ordinis Minorum Aquitaniae Ministro in prima actione hujus materiae generaliter absque deductione alia, sed nominando ipsarum auctorem, fuerunt recitatae. Equidem perceptum est, multis ex Patribus Sacri Concilii gratam esse illorum specificam declarationem.* ('so that there be more firm certainty on all sides, it is now necessary to explain those sixteen propositions that have been recited in a general manner and without deduction by the famous professor of sacred theology, the revered father Pierre Porcher, minister of the Aquitanian Franciscans, in the first proceedings of this matter, where he just named their authors. However, it has been observed that many fathers of this Sacred Council would appreciate a specific declaration of them.') Aquilin Emmen also pointed out common ground between Rouvroy's *sermo* and Segovia's arguments (Emmen 1956, p. 81–83).

the time and in the space that will be assigned to him to speak.'[57] In his response, John of Segovia picked up on this disregard for rationality. He accused the authors of the opposing side of completely neglecting one of the necessary modes of argumentation, as they seemed to shy away from *rationes*.[58]

Montenero's colleague, Juan de Torquemada, takes up this very point in his preface. He admits that reaching conclusions and gauging the weight of an argumentation cannot be done without rational judgement. Rational reasoning could indeed be used to support faith by making the truth manifest and by showing that the objects of faith are not impossible.[59] Yet if the question is what

---

[57] See Horst 1994, p. 174, especially n. 23: *Nunc ad principale propositum decendens quadruplici via probabo, quod beata Virgo concepta fuit in peccato originali, prout dicit propositio fundamentalis. Prima erit per auctoritates sacre scripture. Secunda per expositiones dictarum auctoritatum, quas faciunt sancti doctores, quorum vita et doctrina est per ecclesiam approbata. Tertia erit per dicta eorundem sanctorum doctorum vel eorum, quorum vita per ecclesiam est approbata et doctrina non reprobata, sive etiam quorundam aliorum scholasticorum et potissimorum doctorum in iure divino et humano, quorum vita, etsi per ecclesiam approbata non sit, doctrina tamen non est per ecclesiam hucusque reprobata. Quarta, licet minus efficax, erit per rationes, si prolixitas actus presentis relationis quoad allegationes doctorum non impediat. Quo in casu reservabitur college dato, ut illam aperiat tempore et loco, qui sibi ad referendum assignabitur.* ('Proceeding towards the first matter, I will prove in four ways that, as the fundamental proposition states, the blessed Virgin was conceived in original sin. The first way will be through the authorities of Sacred Scripture. The second, through the explanations of these authorities which were made by holy doctors whose life and doctrine is approved by the Church. The third way will be through the statements of these very same holy doctors or of those whose life has been approved by the Church and their doctrine not reproved, or also of some of these other Scholastic and most prominent doctors in divine and human law, whose doctrine, even if their life has not been approved by the Church, has so far not been reproved by the Church. The fourth way, although less effective, will be through rational argument, as long as the lengthiness of the current proceeding, namely, the allegations of the doctors, does not prevent it. In that case, it will be passed on to my colleague, so that he will deal with them at the time and in the space that will be assigned to him to speak.')

[58] John of Segovia 1664, p. 376b: *Duodecima differentia inter has duas doctrinas est in modo probandi quantum ad duo. Primo: quia haec in modo probationis suae dicit utendum esse rationum evidentia, et auctoritatum testimoniis: illa vera primum refugisse videtur.* ('The twelfth difference between these two doctrines consists in the mode of proof, and this in two ways. First, while this [Segovia's] position states that one ought to use rational evidence and the testimonies of authorities as means of proof, that position seems to shy away from the first one.')

[59] Torquemada 1869, p. 8b: *Ubi notandum propter argumenta quae in relatione ex adverso dicta sunt, quod per illam regulam non excluditur a judicio fidei,*

the faithful should believe, then the main source should always be Holy Scripture. In that sense, the presupposition of his colleague should be upheld.[60]

It appears that the especially thorny issues were handed to the more renowned theologians, just as in a relay race the weaker person starts and the heavier load is left to the strongest runner, who takes the anchor leg. In the first instance, this duty fell to Juan de Torquemada, in the second, to John of Segovia. Juan de Torquemada also points out that Segovia used more time than Montenero, and he then seeks to rectify this issue.[61]

argumentationis processus, quia sine eo non potest deveniri ad conclusionem judicii. Non excluditur etiam rationis judicium, quia sine eo argumentationis pondus non potest agnosci. Non insuper ipsa ratio humana, quin concurrat ad judicium fidei et theologiam tanquam ad judicium fidei et theologiam tanquam ad divinam obsecutura pro modulo virtutis suae, sive ex similitudinibus creaturarum, sive ex principiis naturalibus, faciendo manifestum objectum veritatis, et ostendendo non impossibile esse quod fidelibus credendum ostenditur. ('Due to the arguments brought forward in the statement of the opposition, it should be noted here that this rule does not exclude the process of argumentation from the judgement of faith; since without it, one could not proceed to the conclusion of the judgement. Rational judgement is also not excluded, since the weight of an argumentation could not be acknowledged without it. In addition, human rationality itself, as long as it concurs with the judgement of faith and with theology as the judgement of faith, and as long as it follows theology as a divine thing as much as it can, [is not excluded from] making manifest the objects of truth, be it through similarities of creatures or through natural principles, and also not from showing that what the believers are taught to believe is not impossible.')

[60] Torquemada 1869, p. 8b: *Sed solum per istam regulam datur intelligi, quod in judicio fidei diffinitivo, in quo determinari habet quam partem quaestionis populus credendam suspicere debeat, auctoritas Sacrae Scripturae sit principaliter consideranda et ponderanda, et secundum eam metienda et pronuncianda sententia. Quare, cum apud omnem catholicum doctorem indubitatum hoc esse debeat, sequitur quod suppositio prima, quam collega meus venerabilis, scilicet magister Joannes de Monte Nigro provincialis Lombardiae, in sua relatione posuit, videlicet quod sacrum concilium in discussione praesentis materiae fidei, magis inniti debeat auctoritatibus quam rationibus, vera sit* ('The given rule should just be understood in such a way that in a definitive judgement of faith, where one has to decide which part of a controversial question the people has to accept as a belief, the authority of Holy Scripture has to be considered and weighed first, and the judgement has to be made and pronounced according to it. Therefore, since this has to be an irrevocable fact for all catholic doctors, it follows that the first proposition, which my venerable colleague, Magister John of Montenero from the Lombardian province, has put forward in his statement, namely, that the Sacred Council should rely more on authorities than on rational reasonings in the current matter of faith, is true.')

[61] See Torquemada 1869, p. 5ab: *tum tertio, quia, quod in relatione ex adverso superioribus diebus facta circa hanc materiam, aliqua dicta sunt contra quaedam*

The question of permissible arguments is at the heart of another issue that divided the two parties. The affirmative statements contain miracles as a part of their argument while the opposing side does not appeal to miracles at all. In Porcher's and Rouvroy's individual and joint statements, miracles are presented as an integral part of the argument. In Segovia's work, they are included as an appendix. The emphasis on miracles has puzzled some researchers on this topic. While he was still entertaining the thought that John of Segovia might have written the initial sermon, Aquilin Emmen saw them as 'a weak side' of the argument and as the result of the 'childish belief of a Spaniard that, as we well know, is very keen on miracle stories.'[62]

An ambivalent attitude is also apparent from the way in which miracles are presented in Segovia's *Allegationes*. Segovia stresses at first the usefulness of miracles, namely, that they can didactically inform the youth.[63] Hyacinth Ameri has inferred from this statement that these miracles *only* served a didactic purpose.[64] Yet Segovia also states that, technically speaking, this kind of divine

---

bene dicta per collegam meum in sua relatione, ad quae per me respondendum venit. ('and third, because in the statement on this matter by the opposition, which was made on previous days, some things have been said against what was well said by my colleague in his statement, it is therefore up to me to respond.') In the finale of his speech, Torquemada apologizes for having spoken so extensively, but still maintains that he left out a number of issues brought up by the opposing party. See Torquemada 1869, p. 779ab.

[62] Emmen 1956, p. 82–83: 'Hier müssen wir vorausschicken, dass Johannes von Segovia als Kind seiner Zeit und, wie wir vielleicht hinzufügen dürfen, mit dem kindlichen Glauben eines Spaniers, bekanntlich auf Wunderberichte einen besonderen Wert legte. [...] Nun ist es schon eine auffällige Tatsache, dass der "Sermo Basiliensis", genauso wie die *Allegationes*, nebst erhabenen und sachkundigen Betrachtungen über die Unbefleckte Empfängnis diese schwache Seite hat, dass ein ganzer Teil der Rede der Aufführung von acht durchaus unkritischen Wunderberichten gewidmet wird.' Concerning the importance of the Immaculate Conception in Spain and its different proponents, cf. Hernandéz 2019.

[63] Segovia, 535a: *Et quia determinatione Ecclesiae subsecuta super hac materia quamplures institerunt, quod ad instructionem parvulorum, servandamque omnium Fidem in scriptis redigerentur Miracula, quae magis authentica essent ad hanc rem pertinentia* ('And after the determination of the Church, many insisted that concerning this matter, in order to instruct the youth and to protect the faith of all, the miracles that are most authentic and most pertinent to this matter should be committed to script').

[64] See Ameri 1954, p. 20.

revelation should trump all other forms of deliberation.[65] But for several reasons it was necessary to leave them out. First, one had to beat back the assailants with the same weapons they used themselves. Second, the opposing side could conclude that one does not have sufficient *ratio* and *auctoritas*. And third, which was the main argument from the opposing side, nothing can be a miracle that is contrary to good Christian doctrine.[66] While miracles might be an expression of God's will, one can, paradoxically, only recognize God's will in them if one has deduced the import of that will beforehand.

In a very courteous manner, John of Segovia claimed that he was eager to meet his opponents on equal terms.[67] One would have to consider, however, the effect the miracles might have had. If one takes a look at the contents of these miracles, they can roughly be divided into those with positive and those with negative consequences. On the negative side, a frequent character in the narrative is a preacher — three times from the Dominican order — who plans to speak against the Immaculate Conception and then suffers some misfortune. The mildest of these is that he forgets his objections and preaches the contrary, while in the harsher case one *lector* of the Dominican order supposedly had his throat ripped out by a wild wolf while sitting in the choir.[68] Juan de Torquemada says that he tried to fact-check these stories. He asked the eldest members of his order if they could remember such a thing. According to him, they just laughed, and nobody could remember any such story.[69] Torquemada also said that he

---

[65] John of Segovia 1664, 535a: *Hoc autem genus probationis licet sit praepotentissimum, superetque omnium argumenta rationum, de ipso in praedictis tribus libris non fuit facta probatio, tum quia adversarii doctrinae hujus gloriabantur assertionem suam fundari in Sacra Scriptura, doctrinaque Sanctorum Doctorum, sic fuit necesse eisdem armis eos repercutere.* ('Although this kind of proof is most potent and would overcome all rational arguments, no proof was gathered from it in our aforementioned three books. Rather, since the adversaries of this doctrine boasted that their assertion was based on Sacred Scripture and the teaching of the Holy Doctors, it was thus necessary to strike back at them with the same weapons.')

[66] See Torquemada 1869, p. xiii, 4, 748b–749a. He also addresses three miracles specifically at ibid., p. 760–762.

[67] He also states that he limited himself to a few miracles and that many more were recounted at the council; see John of Segovia 1664, p. 539a.

[68] See John of Segovia 1664, p. 540 and p. 539, respectively.

[69] Torquemada 1869, p. 749ab.

could name a number of counter examples at will.[70] Yet it was the miracles in favor that dominated the conversation and that were reported and attested by members of the council itself.[71]

Through these stories, it is made clear that accepting or rejecting the Immaculate Conception has actual consequences. Segovia even suggests this for the Council of Basel. In the appendix to his *Avisamenta*, which was obviously finished after the council, he recounts that an outbreak of the plague in Basel immediately ceased as soon as the council had defined the Immaculate Conception as a doctrine of the Church.[72] When Cluny received the message about the proceedings, the plague there also stopped.[73] The other suggestion, made by both Jean de Rouvroy and John of Segovia, was that the work of the council itself would be greatly aided by accepting the doctrine of the Immaculate Conception.[74] As the other positive miracles suggest, the Virgin aids those who stand by her. Thus, the success of the council's three main purposes — fighting heresy, creating peace, and reforming the Church — were directly linked to the dogma of the Immacu-

---

[70] Torquemada 1869, p. 749.

[71] John of Segovia 1664, 381a, again mentions that he avoids using miracles but that many were told by the congregation: *Et in hac deductione non fit mentio principaliter de illa celebri differentia hujus doctrinae ad assertionem contrariam, videlicet, de miraculorum attestatione pro hac parte; nempe ultra illa tria contenta in epistola Anselmi, quae in quam plurimis Ecclesiis pro lectionibus ad matutinas de Festivitate hujus Sanctae Conceptionis solemniter decantatur anniversaria revolutione, coram hoc in Sancto concilio in sermonibus, et alias in ipsius praesentia multa enarrata fuerunt per quosdam ex Patribus, quibus credi merito posset. Reperiuntur etiam scripta in libris editis jam a plurimis annis. Verum circa hoc, prout a principio fuit dictum, non insistitur.* ('And in this argumentation, there was no great mention of the celebrated difference between this doctrine and the contrary assertion, namely, of the attestation of miracles for this side. To be sure, besides those three which are contained in the letter of Anselm, which are sung solemnly in rather numerous churches at the Matins of the festivity of this Holy Conception in the course of the year, [and that were recounted] in front of this Holy Council in sermons, many others were narrated in its presence by some of the fathers, whom one should rightfully believe. They can also be found written in books that have already been published for many years. But on this, as was said in the beginning, I will not insist.')

[72] John of Segovia 1664, p. 539ab. It is peculiar that the edition of Alva has the year 1436, since it was only declared a doctrine of the Church in 1439. Therefore, the text should be checked against the manuscripts, and one can suppose that John of Segovia added these miracles later.

[73] John of Segovia 1664, p. 539b.

[74] See the references in Lamy 2000, p. 595.

late Conception. Despite all attempts to balance the scales, this tactic of leaning on miracles and political prophecy was unacceptable to the opponents of the doctrine.

6. Respect and Disrespect: Stances taken towards the Opposition

As a final point, I want to examine one of the interactions between the two parties, in which the battle lines become especially prominent. While Giovanni di Montenero certainly also refers to his opponent, and John of Segovia mentions Montenero, the antagonism between John of Segovia and Juan de Torquemada is most striking. Torquemada's refutations can easily be mapped to Segovia's work. Torquemada's detailed treatment of his opponent's views makes it clear that he had a copy at his disposal and was perusing it carefully.

Since the number of references that Torquemada made to his opponent is quite large, I will focus on an exchange that occurs near the end of both their treatises. After nearly completing his *Allegationes*, John of Segovia offers something like a summary, which in today's language could be labelled a take-home message. Considering the length of his treatise, the council fathers had probably sat through several full days of argument, so offering a condensed version was undoubtedly useful. I refer to the section that bears the following title: 'Twelve differences between the two doctrines concerning the Holy and Unblemished Conception. And there are many things explained that serve to magnify this doctrine.'[75] Torquemada accepted this challenge and raised the number of *differentiae* to a total of twenty.[76] Here, as Ulrich Horst has noted with some understatement, 'polemic is now afoot.'[77] I first give a short summary of Segovia's theses and then consider some of Torquemada's replies.

---

[75] John of Segovia 1664, p. 371b: *De duodecim differentiis istarum doctrinarum de Sancta et Immunda Conceptione ad invicem: et exponuntur multa, quae pertinent ad magnificationem hujus doctrinae.*

[76] Torquemada 1869, p. xiii, 14–15, 769–773.

[77] Horst 1994, p. 184: 'Nun regt sich, herausgefordert duch Segovias Position, Polemik.'

Segovia's presentation, which can be divided into three individual arguments and two groups, is bookended by arguments 1 and 12, and these two have fundamental implications for his position. Arguments 2–7 could be classified as regular theological arguments. Arguments 8–10 invoke the perspective of the faithful, bringing the customs of the Church into the discussion. Argument 11 defends the antiquity of the doctrine of the Immaculate Conception versus its detractors' attempts to mark it as a novelty.

Segovia further attempts to make his arguments memorable by giving them a shorthand description that indicates the source of the differences that he points out. The first difference originates 'in the root' (*in radice*),[78] the second 'in the measure of time' (*in mensura temporis*),[79] the third 'in conformity to the faith' (*in conformitate Fidei*),[80] and so on, finishing with 'by way of demonstration, in regard to two items' (*in modo probandi quantum ad duo*).[81] He also continually repeats the designations *haec* (*doctrina*), meaning his own, and *illa*, the mistaken, opposing one.

As I have observed, arguments 2–7 can be regarded as fairly standard. Argument 2, for example, points out the seeming inconsistency in the opposing view that Mary was affected by original sin from the moment of her conception, but was sanctified very soon after. If God had the power to preserve her from that (here a version of *potuit, decuit, fecit* appears to be in the background), why maintain the ridiculous notion of considering Mary 'fully worthy of blame and stained' (*plene culpabilis et maculata*)[82] for such a short amount of time?

The remaining arguments all bring something special to the table. The argument 1 is a highly emotionalized juxtaposition of the two standpoints. Arguments 8 to 10 all refer to customs of the Church that were established in the previous centuries and to the sentiments of the faithful. Argument 12, finally, points out two stark methodological differences between the two views.

---

[78] John of Segovia 1664, p. 371b.
[79] John of Segovia 1664, p. 372a.
[80] John of Segovia 1664, p. 372b.
[81] John of Segovia 1664, p. 376b.
[82] John of Segovia 1664, p. 372b.

The first of these differences is that the pro side uses both rationality *and* authority, while the contra view avoids rationality. The second difference concerns something like a logical fallacy. Segovia claims that his view adopts premises that are particular to the Virgin, while the opposing view adopts 'universal premises that could be applied to all sorts of matters and for all humans',[83] and thereby fails to make proper distinctions.

The *differentiae* mentioned, numbers 1 and 8–10, can help us to perceive how deep the divide between the parties was. *Differentia* 1 appeals to the emotional value of the Immaculate Conception, which mirrors its spiritual importance for believers. As the umbrella term *differentia in radice* suggests, the issue at stake is truly fundamental. Segovia casts the choice between the two doctrines as a choice between attributing 'singular grace' to Mary or 'general guilt'.[84] The issue comes down to the question of whether to treat Mary in a special, reverential way or like other humans.[85] Segovia then conjures a true hailstorm of negative attributes that the opposing doctrine supposedly predicates of Mary:

> And this is the central cause of dispute. Since that doctrine about her impure Conception affirms from its heart that the Most Blessed Virgin and Mother of God, Mary, at first would have been odious to God rather than pleasing; detested instead of loved; guilty of offense instead of full of grace; unknowing instead of wise; infected with malice instead of perfected with goodness; shameful, instead of beautiful; reeking horribly instead of smelling pleasantly; damned instead of blessed; most deserving of all censure instead of the highest praise; a slave instead of a free woman; a handmaid instead of a mis-

---

[83] John of Segovia 1664, 376b: *haec probat suum intentum per auctoritates singulares Virgini proprie, vel appropriate competentes; illa per universales, quae ad plures materias, et in omnibus hominibus possent competere.* ('this [position] proves its intended conclusion through special authorities that are specific to the Virgin, or that apply to her properly; the other one does it through universal premises that could be applied to all sorts of matters and to all humans.')

[84] John of Segovia 1664, p. 371b: *Haec [...] doctrina [...] innititur gratiae singulari: alia [...] innititur generali culpae.*

[85] John of Segovia 1664, p. 372a: *illa vero asserit nullam esse differentiam Virginis in sua Conceptione, sed aequaliter esse considerandam cum hominibus universis. Et haec est causa disceptationis.* ('that doctrine, however, asserts that there is no difference in the conception of the Virgin, but that it ought to be regarded in the same manner as all humans. And this is the central cause of the dispute.')

tress; a subject instead of a Queen; related to Demons instead of the mistress of Angels. Satan's daughter instead of God's.[86]

On the contrary, his doctrine (*haec doctrina*) would grant Mary all the positive attributes in full. This very first *differentia* listed by John of Segovia reads like a damning accusation that paints the opposing side as violent aggressors against Mary's honor. While the previous sections exhibited respect towards the speakers of the opposing side, this respect is discarded when the doctrines themselves are compared. In the next chapter, Segovia also compares the opponents of the Immaculate Conception to the ignorant friends of Job, who could not believe that his misfortune was not his fault. It is no wonder if the opposing side felt wrongly accused and insulted.

How does Juan de Torquemada respond to these challenges? To start with, Torquemada claims numerical superiority. In response to Segovia's twelve differences, he lists a total of twenty differences.[87] Second, he attempts to draw the debate back to a controversy of opinions. Segovia had begun his differences with an emotionalized list of accusations and followed up by comparing the proponents of the opposing position to Job's incredulous friends. Torquemada, on the other hand, emphasizes his institutional role and thereby depersonalizes the dispute. He calls himself a 'speaker for the doctrine of the Doctors'.[88] Replying to Segovia's arguments and accusations was not a personal issue but necessary 'for the integrity of the office that has been entrusted to me and for the fidelity that I owe to this doctrine, by command of this Holy Synod, in order to explain the truth.'[89] When finish-

---

[86] John of Segovia 1664, p. 372a: *Et haec est causa disceptationis. Quia illa doctrina de sua immunda Conceptione ex corde asserit, quod Beatissima Virgo Dei Genitrix Maria prius fuerit Deo odiosa quam grata; exosa quam dilecta; rea culpae, quam plena gratiae; ignorans quam sapiens; infecta malitia, quam bonitate refecta; turpis quam pulchra; faetore abominabilis quam odore suavis; maledicta quam benedicta; dignissima omni vituperio, quam laudis praeconio; serva quam libera; ancilla quam Domina; subdita, quam Regina; Daemonis vernacula quam Angelorum Domina; et filia Diaboli, quam Dei.*

[87] Torquemada 1869, p. 768a–778b.

[88] Torquemada 1869, p. 768a: [...] *doctrinam doctorum, quorum relator sum, affirmantem Beatissimam Virginem in conceptione originali peccato obnoxiam fuisse.*

[89] Torquemada 1869, p. 768a: *pro integritate officii mihi crediti, et fidelitate quam ex jussu hujus sanctae synodi huic doctrinae pro illucidatione veritatis debeo.*

ing his speech, he refers to having 'completed the task that was given' by the council.[90] He acknowledges having spoken at length, and lists the seventh cause for this prolixity as the vastness of the opposing argumentation, which he was still unable — or unwilling — to tackle in full.[91] For this decision he gives several reasons, one of them being that some of the opposing arguments were rather insulting. Stooping to that level would have meant departing from the office Torquemada had been given by the council.[92]

Even as he claimed to merely fulfil an assigned task, Torquemada was challenged to respond to Segovia's 12 *differentiae*. The first three of Torquemada's differences hold a similarly eminent position as Segovia's first. Segovia had started by accusing the opposing side of besmirching Mary's honor. Torquemada counters with the functional equivalent claim on his side. Granting Mary's Immaculate Conception would mean detracting from *Christ's* honor: 'The first difference is that this doctrine asserts it to be only Christ's privilege and singular prerogative to be conceived without original sin.'[93] Taking up the first two pairs of contradictory predicates that Segovia used, Torquemada states that if one said that Mary was 'more odious to God than pleasing, and detested instead of loved' that would be 'completely false' if it were taken in its simple or absolute sense, and if it were to imply

---

[90] Torquemada 1869, p. 778a: *Ecce, sacratissima synode, opus consummavi quod dedisti mihi.*

[91] Torquemada 1869, p. 778a: *Septimo, profusio sermonis facti in favorem doctrinae ex adverso, cujus amplitudini non poterat bene sub tractatu satisfieri brevi. Abstinui nihilominus respondere multis ex adverso dictis propter multa.* ('[The] seventh [reason being] the breadth of the statement made in favor of the doctrine from the opposition, the detail of which could not be satisfactorily covered within a short treatise. Nevertheless I abstained from responding to many things said by the opposition concerning many things.')

[92] Torquemada 1869, p. 779b: *Tum, quia quaedam eorum videbantur injuriosa quibus respondere honestatis gratia supersedi, volens sic meum adimplere ministerium, defendendo veritatem horum doctorum ut integra charitas permaneat* ('Then, [I did not address all the opposing arguments], since some of them appeared insulting, and, honestly speaking, I avoided responding to them, as I wanted to fulfil my given task, which is to defend the truth of these doctors, so that charity might remain whole.')

[93] Torquemada 1869, p. 769b: *Prima differentia est quod haec doctrina asserit solius Christi privilegium esse et praerogativam singularem, absque originali peccato conceptum esse.* Note that from Torquemada's perspective, his point of view is *haec doctrina* and Segovia's *illa*, whereas Segovia naturally had it the other way around.

that any personal depravity was imputed to Mary.[94] Torquemada then goes on to say, however, that if one went beyond the surface level and took the statement to imply that Mary, by virtue of her origin in a carnal act, had 'for some time contracted something that is displeasing or odious to God, he would be right'.[95]

Thus Torquemada responds to Segovia's outrage by using the classical scholastic method of drawing distinctions, of separating a superficial sense from a more accurate, deeper one. He continues this train of thought by claiming that 'having something that is displeasing or odious to God does not merit reproach or blame for the person that is conceived in original sin'.[96] On the second difference, Torquemada goes on the counter-offensive, claiming that the ascription of an Immaculate Conception to Mary would detract from Christ's pre-eminence: 'The opposition's doctrine affirming that Mary was immune from original sin at her conception seems to detract from the integrity of both the prerogatives and privileges of Christ.'[97] Torquemada's third difference turns the argument towards the affirmative side: the doctrine he defends would positively put Christ in front of all

---

[94] Torquemada 1869, p. 769b–770a: *Quod vero dicitur ex adverso in assignatione primae differentiae harum doctrinarum, quod haec doctrina asserat quod B. Virgo fuit Deo magis odiosa quam grata, exosa quam dilecta, falsissimum est, intelligendo, sicut dicta illa simpliciter et absolute sumpta sonare videtur, videlicet per deordinationem aut pravitatem alicujus actus personalitatis.* ('However, what is said by the opposition in the assignation of the first difference between these doctrines, that this doctrine asserts that "the Blessed Virgin was more odious to God than pleasing, and detested instead of loved", is completely false, if their words are understood as they sound in a simple or absolute sense, that is, [that she was detested] through a fault or a depravity of some personally attributable act.')

[95] Torquemada 1869, p. 770a: *Si vero intelligat proponens ex adverso quod haec doctrina asserat Virginem gloriosam in conceptione sua, antequam gratia sanctificationis fuisset infusa, habuisse aliquid pro aliquo tempore aut momento contractum per originem, quod Deo displicibile esset et odiosum, verum dicit.* ('If, however, the proponent of the opposite view meant by this that this doctrine asserts that in her conception the Glorious Virgin had, before she was infused by the gift of sanctification, contracted something by her origin for some time or for a moment, something that is displeasing or odious to God, he would be right.')

[96] Torquemada 1869, p. 770ab: *[...] habere aliquid displicibile et odiosum Deo, non est opprobriosum aut vituperosum personae sic in originali peccato conceptae.*

[97] Torquemada 1869, p. 770b: *Doctrina vero ex adverso asserens B. Virginem immunem fuisse in conceptu suo ab originali peccato derogare videtur integritati et praerogativarum et privilegiorum Christi.*

the other saints, in the same way that the head is superior to the members of the body.[98]

By answering Segovia's first *differentia* in this way, Torquemada uses a multipronged approach. First, he stylizes himself as a *relator* of the commonly held opinion of the doctors of the Church. Then he accuses Segovia of understanding matters in a superficial way and finally makes clear that he wants to maintain the privileges of Christ, which would be diminished if Mary's Immaculate Conception were to become a dogma. Torquemada's strategy remains more or less the same throughout his responses to the other seventeen *differentiae*; in these responses he sticks closely to Segovia's *differentiae*, replying to nearly all of them. In the fifth *differentia*, for example, Torquemada again claims that his view is 'more consonant with the pious faith of the Holy Fathers'.[99] In the sixth, like Montenero before him, Torquemada claims that his view relies on the literal exposition of Scripture, while the opposition would introduce unfounded mystical readings. In the eighth, he addresses the objection that his doctrine proceeds according to general principles only, while in the eleventh he claims that 'the evidence of reason', contrary to the message of the opposition, is indeed a central part of his position as well.[100] When answering the arguments drawn from the sentiments of the faithful and the customs of the Church, Torquemada again claims the intellectual high ground. If arguments against the Immaculate Conception were explained properly to the faithful, opposing that doctrine would actually be most gratifying to the Christian people. If, however, some less educated Christians were still to take offence, their recalcitrance would resemble sick eyes sensitive to light, which is otherwise good and helpful, or it would be the result of harmful propaganda.[101]

---

[98] Torquemada 1869, p. 771a: *Tertia differentia est quod haec doctrina confitetur Christum superiorem et excellentiorem incomparabiliter omnibus Sanctis, utpote caput ceteris membris.* ('The third difference is that this doctrine heralds Christ as incomparably superior and more excellent than all the saints, in the same way as the head is above the other [body] parts.')

[99] Torquemada 1869, p. 772a: *Quinta differentia est quod haec doctrina est magis consona pietati fidei sanctorum patrum.*

[100] Torquemada 1869, p. 773b and 774b.

[101] Torquemada 1869, p. 775b: *Doctrina enim haec, cum explicatur et declaratur debito modo assignando rationes et fundamenta ejus et necessitatem, populis illis*

All in all, Torquemada diligently responds to all the *differentiae* that Segovia set forth. As seen in the first three differences, which respond to Segovia's first, Torquemada sometimes uses several *differentiae* to combat a single *differentia* from the other side, bringing his count up to twenty. He tries to confront emotional piety and a higher valuation of rationality by playing the role of a cool messenger who wields the sharper intellectual tools. Yet the impression arises that the two sides argued on different planes of thought, without a chance of ever meeting each other.

7. Conclusions

At the Council of Basel, the debate about Immaculate Conception constituted an act of coordinated intellectual warfare. Even the texts themselves make use of these metaphors, with Segovia talking about beating back the opponent with similar weapons. As we saw at the beginning of this article, the twentieth-century historian Ameri framed the whole debate as an armed battle and he introduced Pierre Porcher through the trope of a knight in shining armor who defended the honor of a lady.[102]

While the individual points of view have been studied in some detail, the unique structure of this exchange allows for a special kind of study. While the aim of this article was not to display the arguments in every detail, I sought to lay the groundwork for future analysis by showing that the exchange *could* be tracked blow by blow as two parties trying to outsmart and outargue each other. Some of these connections between argument and coun-

---

Christiani est gratissima, quibus sapit Christianae religionis doctrina. Quod vero aliquibus minus eruditis exosa sit et minus grata, plane hoc evenit, aut, quia oculis aegris odiosa est lux, quae puris est amabilis, ut ait Augustinus, aut propter sinistras informationes et relationes scandalosas, quae frequenter factae sunt per eos qui doctrinam ex adverso prosecuti sunt. ('This doctrine, however, if it is explicated and declared appropriately by giving its reasons, its fundamentals, and its necessity, would be most gratifying to these Christian people, who appreciate the teachings of the Christian religion. That it is offensive and less pleasing to some lesser educated persons clearly comes from one of two reasons: either because light that is pleasing to clear eyes is odious to sick ones, as Augustine says, or because of shady information and scandalous reports, which were often spread by those who pursued the opposing doctrine.').

[102] See the description of Pierre Porcher in Ameri 1954, p. 10, cited above in n. 34.

terargument are explicit, e.g. when a later speaker answers points raised by previous speakers, such as when Montenero reacts to Pierre Porcher, Segovia to Montenero, and Torquemada spends long hours refuting Segovia. But there also seems to be a tendency to hand over the manuscripts too late, so that the other party would not have them before making a public presentation. The first presentations were shorter and, in Pierre Porcher's case, even lacked detailed argumentation. The second presentations, then, were made by more experienced theologians and were much more expansive. This approach might be likened to sending in light skirmishers first to draw out the opponent, while keeping the heavier troops in reserve. The final statement of the debate, as far as the Council of Basel is concerned, was Segovia's *Avisamenta*. With this statement, a kind of intellectual warfare emerges that separates it, despite all metaphorical congruence, from real war. After all the points have been made, it is possible to synthesize a debate and even to acknowledge the merits of opposing points of view, something that is hard to imagine on a real battlefield.

The format of the debate seems to have aimed at fairness and equity. A shared knowledge base was — supposedly — provided; each side had two speakers and ample time for presentation; and the written statements were — again supposedly — provided to the opposite party. Yet considering the overall circumstances, some doubts can be cast on this impression of fairness. First of all, the Franciscan convent was hardly neutral ground. And despite all efforts to provide balance, some weapons were unattainable for one side. Arguments that called upon experiential resources such as miracles and customs of the Church and its faithful heavily favored the Immaculist side. Torquemada claimed that he could offer counter-narratives, but, tellingly, he ultimately did not list any. The correlation between accepting the doctrine of the Immaculate Conception and the success of the council might have proved decisive. Refusing to accept the doctrine could mean dooming the work of the council, and who would risk that? In that sense, parity was unavailable, and what was set up to look like a fair contest might have simply been an exhibition bout with an inevitable conclusion.

While we see the debaters generally treating each other with respect, some of this respect is abandoned when discussing the opposite position in general. This was especially the case in the twelve and twenty *differentiae* that John of Segovia and Juan de Torquemada listed at the end of their works. Segovia sets the tone here with the emotionally charged accusation that the opposition assigned guilt to Mary and with his likening them to Job's friends; neither attack would, I assume, have been received lightly. Torquemada's response tries to elicit cool rationality and superior thinking, but thereby reinforces the impression that between the hyper-rational and the emotionally faithful there was little common ground.

One purpose of this article has been to show that studying the scholastic techniques employed in this debate about the Immaculate Conception is a worthwhile endeavor. I proposed a dynamic reading of the events, instead of assuming that the two sides were stable and fully formed before the debate began, and traced some of their interactions. In regard to the arguments used, I would suggest that the status and the problem of experiential arguments such as *miracula* and *consuetudines* deserve further study. Given the overall complexity of the debate, one could finally wonder if metaphors of warfare — which are certainly abundant in this literature — are wholly adequate for grasping these complex and interwoven processes.

Bibliography

Primary Sources

CUP = *Chartularium Universitatis Parisiensis*, ed. E. Chatelain & H. Denifle, 4 vols, Paris 1889–1897.

Eadmer of Canterbury, *Eadmeri monachi Cantuariensis Tractatus de Conceptione Sanctae Mariae. Olim sancto Anselmo attributus, nunc primum integer ad codicum fidem editus, adiectis quibusdam documentis coaetaneis a P. Herb. Thurston et P. Th. Slater*, ed. H. Thurston, Freiburg im Breisgau: Herder, 1904.

Jean de Rouvroy (1664), 'Relatio "Tota pulchra es"', in Pedro de Alva y Astorga (ed.), *Monumenta antiqua immaculatae conceptionis sacratissimae virginis Mariae*, Lovanii: Ex Typographia Immaculatae Conceptionis, p. 356–376.

John of Segovia, *Septem Allegationes et totidem Avisamenta pro informatione patrum concilii Basiliensis* [...] *circa sacratissimae virginis*

Mariae immaculatam conceptionem [...], Bruxellis: Typis & Sumptibus Balthasarius Vivien, 1664.

MC = *Monumenta conciliorum generalium seculi decimi quinti* (1857–1935), 4 vols, Vienna: [s.n.]

Scotus, John Duns et al. (1904), *Quaestiones disputatae de immaculata conceptione beatae Mariae Virginis.* Vol. 3. Quaracchi: Typ. Colleg. S. Bonaventurae.

Scotus, John Duns, *Ordinatio, liber 3: A distinctione prima ad decimam septimam*, ed. J. Rodríguez Carballo, Civitas Vaticana: Typis Vaticanis, 2006 (Doctoris Subtilis ac Mariani B. Ioannis Duns Scoti Ordinis Fratrum Minorum Opera omnia, IX).

Thomas Aquinas, *Tertia pars Summae theologiae*, Romae: Ex Typographia Polyglotta S. C. de Propaganda Fide, 1903–1906 (Opera omnia iussu impensaque Leonis XIII P. M. edita, t. 11–12).

Torquemada, Juan de, *Tractatus de veritate conceptionis Beatissimae Virginis: Pro facienda relatione coram patribus Concilii Basileae, Anno Domini MCCCCXXXVII, mense julio*, Oxford and London: Jacob Parker, 1869.

Secondary Sources

Ameri, H. (1954), *Doctrina theologorum de immaculata B. V. Mariae conceptione tempore concilii Basileensis*, Romae: Academia Mariana internationalis (Bibliotheca immaculatae conceptionis, 4–5).

Binder, K. (1955), 'Kardinal Juan de Torquemada und die feierliche Verkündigung der Lehre von der Unbefleckten Empfängnis auf dem Konzil von Basel', in *Virgo Immaculata*. Vol. 6. Romae: Academia Mariana Internationalis, p. 146–153.

Boss, S. J. (2000), *Empress and Handmaid: On Nature and Gender in the Cult of the Virgin Mary*. London: Cassell.

Emmen, A. (1956), '"Mutter der schönen Liebe". Ein unveröffentlichter "Sermo de Immaculata Conceptione", gehalten auf dem Baseler Konzil um 1436', in *Wissenschaft und Weisheit*, 19, p. 81–99.

Emmen, A. (1957), 'Joannes de Romiroy sollicitator causae Immaculatae Conceptionis in Concilio Basiliensi', in *Antonianum*, 32, p. 335–368.

Helmrath, J. (1987), *Das Basler Konzil 1431–1449: Forschungsstand und Probleme*, Köln: Böhlau (Kölner historische Abhandlungen, 32).

Hernández, R. (2019), *Immaculate Conceptions: The Power of the Religious Imagination in Early Modern Spain*, Toronto: University of Toronto Press (Toronto Iberic, 42).

Horst, U. (1987), *Die Diskussion um die immaculata conceptio im Dominikanerorden: Ein Beitrag zur Geschichte der theologischen Methode*, Paderborn et al.: Schöningh (Veröffentlichungen des Grabmann-Institutes zur Erforschung der mittelalterlichen Theologie und Philosophie N.F., 34).

Horst, U. (1994), 'Nova Opinio und Novelli Doctores: Johannes de Montenigro, Johannes Torquemada und Raphael de Pornassio als Gegner der Immaculata Conceptio', in H. Müller & J. Helmrath (eds), *Studien zum 15. Jahrhundert*, Berlin: De Gruyter Oldenbourg, p. 169–191.

Horst, U. (2009), *Dogma und Theologie: Dominikanertheologen in den Kontroversen um die Immaculata Conceptio*, Berlin: Akademie-Verlag (Quellen und Forschungen zur Geschichte des Dominikanerordens N.F., 16).

Ingham, M. B. (2019), '"Fired France for Mary without Spot": John Duns Scotus and the Immaculate Conception', in Steven J. McMichael (ed.), *Medieval Franciscan approaches to the Virgin Mary. Mater Misericordiae Sanctissima, Misericordia, et Dolorosa*, Leiden: Brill (The Medieval Franciscans, 16), p. 174–195.

Izbicki, T. M. (2005), 'The Immaculate Conception and Ecclesiastical Politics from the Council of Basel to the Council of Trent. Dominicans and Their Foes', in *Archiv für Reformationsgeschichte*, 96, p. 145–170.

Kappes, C. W. (2014), *The Immaculate Conception: Why Thomas Aquinas Denied, While John Duns Scotus, Gregory Palamas, and Mark Eugenicus Professed the Absolute Immaculate Existence of Mary*, New Bedford, MA: Academy of the Immaculate (Mariological studies in honor of Our Lady of Guadalupe, 2).

Lamy, M. (2000), *L'immaculée conception: Étapes et enjeux d'une controverse au moyen-âge (XIIe – XVe siècles)*, Paris: Inst. d'Études Augustiniennes (Collection des études augustiniennes: Série moyen âge et temps modernes, 35).

Reynolds, B. K. (2012), *Gateway to Heaven: Marian Doctrine and Devotion, Image and Typology in the Patristic and Medieval Periods*. Volume 1: *Doctrine and Devotion*, Hyde Park, NY: New City Press.

Ricossa, L. B. (1994), *Jean de Ségovie: Son office de la conception (1439): Étude historique, théologique, littéraire et musicale*, Bern: Peter Lang (Europäische Hochschulschriften: Reihe 36, Musikwissenschaft, 113).

Santoni, P. (1979), 'Jean de Rouvroy, traducteur de Frontin et théologien de l'Immaculée Conception', in *Bibliothèque de l'école des chartes*, 137/1, p. 19–58.

Abstract

On 17 September 1439, at its thirty-sixth session, the Council of Basel (1431–1449) declared that Mary, the mother of God, 'had always been free from original or actual sin' and was therefore 'holy' and 'immaculate'. Because the council was considered schismatic at the time, the decree was not accepted and the question of the Immaculate Conception remained unresolved until Pius IX's doctrinal definition in 1854. Despite doubts with regard to the doctrine's legitimacy, the conciliar debates about the doctrine were extensive and original. Given this background, this article takes a closer look at how scholastic argument was performed at the council.

In early 1436, two teams of two theologians were asked to present the case for and against the doctrine. This article reconstructs the order of speakers, identifies the sources that have survived, and considers whether they were available to the opposing parties at the council. Thereafter the article focuses on several main themes of the debate. One central question was which arguments were permissible and which were to be regarded as decisive. While everyone agreed on the use of *rationes* and *auctoritates*, if not on the way they ought to be weighed against each other, it was a matter of some debate whether miracles, the customs of the Church, and practices of the faithful should be admitted as evidence.

The deep rifts between the parties crystallized in a terse exchange between the two main opponents, John of Segovia and Juan de Torquemada. At this point, Segovia seems to have discarded the general respect that had been maintained between the parties, with Torquemada appearing irked in response. By analysing this exchange in detail, I highlight how different the two opponents' ways of thinking were.

Ultimately, what emerges is, on the one hand, a dynamic debate that yields insights into scholastic practices of argumentation. On the other hand, the analysis shows how the two parties, who were meant to debate the same topic, could be extremely far apart.

YELENA MAZOUR-MATUSEVICH
University of Alaska-Fairbanks

AN INTELLECTUAL WARRIOR AND HIS HERO: JOHANNES WESSEL GANSFORT (1420–1489) AND JEAN GERSON (1363–1429)

'For the late Middle Ages, the towering figure of Jean Gerson commands attention'.[1]

Dutch theologian Johannes Wessel Gansfort (1420–1489)[2] — a brilliant academic, intellectual, and one of the most famous members of the Brethren of the Common Life — was at the center of his century's theological polemics, rivalry, and dissent.[3] An active participant in '25 years of scholarly disputations in Heidelberg, Paris, Rome, Cologne and Louvain',[4] this 'tireless and preeminent'[5] theologian began as a champion of 'Cologne neo-Thomism', then became a Scotist, and after that, with an equal passion, a nominalist. Nicknamed by contemporaries *magister contradictionum* (which was 'not an honorific title'[6]), 'he took up all the schools of the existing universities and learned to scorn them all altogether'.[7] He also came into conflict with the Inquisition because of his position on indulgences, 'was investigated for potential heresy by twice rector of the University of Paris and

---

[1] Newman 2013, p. 2.
[2] Both names Wessel and Gansfort have been used.
[3] This article is an updated, reorganized, and extended reworking of a small segment of my book *Le père du siècle. The Early Modern Reception of Jean Gerson (1363–1429): Theological Authority Between Middle Ages and Early Modern*.
[4] Ritchey 2013, p. 154.
[5] Ritchey 2013, p. 153.
[6] Oberman 1981, p. 97.
[7] Iserloh 1980, section 4, chapter 59, p. 598.

twice prior of the Sorbonne' Jacobus Hoeck,[8] and yet was never tried for heresy (unlike his unlucky contemporary, John of Wesel, who died in prison in 1481). The present study sheds light on one aspect of Gansfort's career as an intellectual warrior: the place and role of Jean Gerson (1363–1429) — chancellor of the University of Paris and the most significant intellectual figure of the late medieval period[9] — in the Dutch theologian's polemical letters.

Existing scholarship on Gansfort traditionally places his connection to Gerson in two theological contexts: the *devotio moderna*, and Lutheran historiography. After briefly presenting these two prevailing perspectives, this inquiry examines Gansfort's understanding and use of Gerson's opera and persona. Staying away from ideological bias and 'une construction théorique ouvertement confessionnelle',[10] the paper investigates a multitude of concrete textual links between the Parisian theologian and his Dutch admirer, so far gone unexamined by scholars.

Gerson had a special connection to the *devotio moderna*. He came into direct contact with this movement during his sojourn in Bruges in 1399 and later defended it at the Council of Constance (1414–1418).[11] This defense earned him the gratitude of the devotees, who subsequently elevated the Parisian chancellor to the status of a Father of the Church.[12] His writings circulated among the *devotio* communities during his lifetime,[13] and several early translations of his works came from their houses.[14] His *Opus tripartitum* — with the first part on the Ten Commandments, the second on the art of confession, and the third on ministry to the dying — was the first product of the only printing press owned by the Brethren of the Common Life in the city

---

[8] Oberman 2008, p. 33 & 35.

[9] McGuire 2005; Hobbins 2009; Mazour-Matusevich 2006; Christianson 2008; Rollo-Koster, Izbicki 2009; Mazour-Matusevich 2010; Schüssler 2011; Oakley 2015; Tyler 2017; Denis 2018; Sère 2016; Sère 2018.

[10] Büttgen 2011, p. 78.

[11] Oberman 1981, p. 62. On Gerson's defense of the *devotio moderna*, see Debongnie 1928; Staubach 1997.

[12] Oberman 2008, p. 29.

[13] See Hobbins 2006; Mazour-Matusevich 2006.

[14] Kraume 1980, p. 50.

of Brussels.[15] The reading list of the Martinsal *devotio moderna* monastery in the city of Leuven included all the printed works by Gerson.[16] By the late fifteenth century, the chancellor of the University of Paris was perceived as the principal oracle of the modern devotion[17] and, according to some researchers, as the father of 'la *devotio moderna* toute entière'.[18]

Gerson held particular importance for three prominent members of the Brethren of the Common Life: German theologian and philosopher Gabriel Biel (1425–1495), rector of the University of Tübingen (1485–1489) and 'the last of the scholastics'; Jean (Jan) Standonck (1453–1504), a Parisian preacher, administrator, and principal of the famous College of Montaigu; and the mystical writer and monastic reformer Johannes Mombaer (Mauburnus or John of Brussels, 1460–1501). From the University of Tübingen and from his pulpit at the Cathedral of Mainz, Gabriel Biel, whose twofold identity as an academic and a Brother of the Common Life closely resembles Gansfort's spiritual trajectory — from *devotio moderna* monasteries to professor and back — honored and quoted the French theologian as the first-ranked 'systematic and mystical authority'.[19] Biel's dependence on Gerson is so pronounced that he often almost 'disappoints us by merely referring back to the mystical opus of Gerson',[20] instead of offering original thoughts on a given subject.[21] John Standonck is best known as an educational reformer who conscientiously followed Gerson's ideal of *bonus pastor* by offering the best instructional opportunities to economically disadvantaged students.[22] John Mombaer, whose connection to Gerson lies in sophisticated attempts at systematiz-

---

[15] Habsburg 2002, p. 78.
[16] Debongnie 1928, p. 255.
[17] Martinstal list, Brussels MS K.B. II 1038, f. 91v–94v, cited in Staubach, 1997, p. 429.
[18] Combes 1963, vol. 2, p. 668.
[19] Oberman 1981, p. 331–332.
[20] Oberman 1963, p. 341.
[21] Biel drew from Gerson's *Monotessaron, Super Magnificat, De simplicitate cordis*, and especially from the generally less widespread and less appreciated *De mystica theologia speculativa* (Oberman 1963, p. 330).
[22] On this subject, see Godet 1912; Debongnie 1927, p. 392–402; Debongnie 1928; Combes 1963, vol. 2; Rapp 1994, vol. VII, p. 215–308; Giraud 2016, p. 265–279.

ing contemplative practices, including music, had no university affiliation. He is known as the author of *Rosetum exercitiorum spiritualium et sacrarum meditationum* ('Rose Garden of Spiritual Exercise and Sacred Meditation'), for which Gerson was 'la source des méditations les plus inexorablement méthodiques'.[23] All three of these figures considered themselves Gerson's spiritual children.

Gansfort's reception of Gerson, however, differs from that of Mombaer, Biel, and Standonck. It is less systematic than Biel's, less mystical than Mombaer's, and less pastoral that Standonck's, but more personal and self-reflective than any of them. The reception is traceable in Wessel's letters, which were published as a collection only posthumously in Zwolle in 1521 and in Wittenberg in 1522 under the title *Farrago rerum theologicarum*. Gansfort's writings received attention thanks to the efforts of Martin Luther, who was very fond of the Dutch theologian.[24] It is indeed the Wittenberg reformer himself (although not he alone [25]) who is responsible for the traditional association of Gansfort's name with the Reformation. In his *Preface to the 1522 edition of Gansfort's writings*, Luther famously declared:

> *Prodijt en Vvesselus (quem Basilium dicunt) Phrisius Groningensis, vir admirabilis ingenij, rari et magni spiritus, quem et ipsum apparet esse vere Theodidactum, quales prophetauit fore Christianos Esaias, neque enim hominibus accepisse iudicari potest, sicut nec ego. Hic si mihi antea fuisset lectus, poterat hostibus meis uideri Lutherus omnia ex Vveselo hausisse, adeo spiritus utriusque conspirat in unum.*[26]

---

[23] Combes 1963, vol. 2, p. 668. Mombaer used a great assortment of Gerson's of texts in the *Rosetum*: *Monotessaron, Mystica theologia practica, Monochordum Jesu Christi* (also called *Solatium peregrini*), *Figura scacordi musicalis simul et militaris* and Gerson's letters to his sisters. On Gerson and Mombaer, see Debongnie 1928; Combes 1963, vol. 2; Habsburg 2002; Giraud 2016.

[24] 'Wessel [ist] für Luther ein Inspirator gewesen' (Obermann & Caspers 1999, p. 82).

[25] 'Georg Maior (1502–1574) [...] In eine Reihe mit Patriarchen, Aposteln und Bischöfen der alten Kirche traten Repurgatoren (Reiniger) wie Johannes Tauler (um 1300–1361) und Johannes Wessel Gansfort (1419–1489)' (Bollbuck 2017).

[26] Wesseli epistolae (1522), WA 10/II, 317, 13–18. 'For behold! A Wessel has appeared whom they call Basil, a Frisian from Groningen, a man of remarkable ability and of rare and great spirit; and it is evident that he has been truly taught by the Lord, even as Esaias prophesied the Christians would be. For no one could think that he received these doctrines from men, any more than I have. Had

Given Luther's incentive to root his theology in the past, thereby securing historical precedent for his views, this declaration should be taken with caution. Already during his 1519 Leipzig Disputation with Johannes Eck (1486–1543), Luther designated history as the 'mother of truth',[27] signaling the appearance of a new political strategy. Since Rome had excommunicated him, forcing him out of the Catholic Church and its centuries-long continuum, Luther felt justified in reclaiming his legacy from history itself. This take on history was first endorsed by Luther's right hand, Philip Melanchthon (1497–1560), and later adopted, enriched, and fully developed by Matthias Flacius Illyricus (1520–1575) in his 1556 *Catalogus testium veritatis*. The Lutheran method, based on the model of historical writing first developed by Eusebius (AD 314), had two objectives. The first consisted in demonstrating that all events formed a single pattern, beginning with the creation of the world and leading up to the moment of the triumph of true Christianity, namely, the Lutheran Reformation. The second objective was to present history as a long period of darkness, corruption, and apostasy, in which, before the luminous appearance of the Wittenberg prophet, there had happened to be a few witnesses to God's truth.[28] Gansfort's election as such a witness became a major factor in the Dutch theologian's 'Rise in Celebrity'[29] in the Lutheran camp and then throughout Protestantism.[30] Gansfort's special status as a forerunner and predecessor is affirmed by the Wittenberg reformer himself:

> [...] *iamque nihil dubito me recta docuisse, quando tam constanti sensu peneque eisdem verbis, tam diverso tempore, alijs coelo et terra, alioque casu, sic ille mihi per omnia consentit.*[31]

I read his works earlier, my enemies might think that Luther has absorbed everything from Wessel, his spirit is so in accordance with mine' (Miller 1917, p. 239). Miller based his translation on several editions of Gansfort's works, which he combined into one book.

[27] WA 2, 289: [...], *sed historie que est mater veritatis*, [...].
[28] Augustijn 1997, p. 15.
[29] Augustijn 1997, p. 14.
[30] According to Caspers, Wessel also influenced Zwingli (Obermann & Caspers 1999, p. 82–83).
[31] *Wesseli epistolae* (1522), WA 10/II, 317, 13–18. '[...] I have not the slightest doubt that I have been teaching the truth, since he [Gansfort], living at so different a time, under another sky, in another land and under such diverse circum-

In relation to Gerson, the immediate reason for Gansfort's interest in the French theologian was the latter's criticism of indulgences — *Gerson mult in abusu indulgentiarum reprobat*.[32] This criticism also attracted attention and praise from Martin Luther, whose revolt against the Church of Rome began from his revulsion against this practice:

> *Inde Joannes Gerson damnare audet indulgentias titulo multorum milium annorum donatas, ut mihi miraculum sit, quidnam acciderit haereticae pravitatis inquisitoribus, ut hunc vel mortuum non combusserint, qui contra morem omnium stationum urbis, tum maxime contra usum effusoris illius indulgentiarum, Sixti quarti, tanta fiducia pronunciat, ut etiam moneat prelatos officia sua in hiis corrigendis atque providendis fatuas et supersticiosas appellans titulationes talium indulgentiarum, etc.*[33]

Indeed, Flacius introduces Gerson as a proto-Lutheran, who wrote *longa epistola* against indulgences, plainly proving that he disapproved of them: *eos indulgentia plane abrogandas sinserit*.[34] Following Luther's enthusiastic assessment, Protestant scholars (to whom we owe practically all studies of Gansfort[35]) have continuously portrayed Gansfort's theology as a 'reformatory way of thinking',[36] in the specific sense of a reformer before the Reformation. In fact, since Ullmann called Wessel 'a Reformer before the Reformation' in 1841, this assumption has continued

---

stances, is so consistently in accord with me in all things, not only as to substance, but in the use of almost the same words' (Miller 1917, p. 239).

[32] Wessel, Groningen 1522, p. 107.

[33] WA 1, 545–546. 'Gerson dared to condemn indulgences, which were bestowed as being valid for many thousand years. And I cannot help wondering what happened to the inquisitors of heresy that they have not burned this heretic even after his death, for he condemned indulgences which entitled recipients to many thousand years and he spoke out confidently against the custom of every pilgrimage station in the city [Rome]. He spoke out also against the practice of that squanderer of indulgences, Sixtus IV, as a result of which the latter warned his prelates that it was their duty to correct and give careful attention to these indulgence practices. He referred to the claims of these indulgences as foolish and superstitious, etc.' (*LW* 31. 116).

[34] Flacius 1556, p. 931.

[35] Rupp 1972, p. 155–170; Obermann & Caspers 1999; de Kroon 2009.

[36] Ullmann 1855, p. 556.

uninterrupted, repeated both in academic publications[37] and in popular sources, such as contemporary websites created by various Protestant denominations,[38] where Gansfort has been routinely labelled one of the 'trailblazers for Martin Luther.'[39]

Yet the connection between Gansfort and the French theologian, whose impact on posterity 'has been eclipsed almost completely',[40] exceeds both the general context of *devotio moderna* and the traditional presentation of the Dutch thinker as a transitory figure, filling up 'the interval between Gerson and Luther'.[41] Complex and ambivalent, this connection was formed during Gansfort's studies at the University of Cologne (1449–1455?) and his professional life as university faculty first at Heidelberg (1456–1457) and then in Paris (1458–1473). Both places were two nuclei of Gerson's influence and distribution centers for his works in fifteenth-century Europe. Heidelberg University, the most ancient institution of higher learning in Germany proper, was Gerson's hub. Host to the Heidelberg learned society *Sodalitas litteraria*, the university played an important role in the empire's reception of the chancellor's legacy.[42] As for Paris, its intellectual and pastoral scene was permeated by Gerson's spirit. At the Sorbonne, the chancellor had a celebrity status. His alma mater, the College of Navarre, kept his memory thanks to the efforts of his younger colleague and friend Nicolas Clamanges (1360–1437),

---

[37] Philipp Schaff (1819–1893), in his highly influential *History of Christian Church* (1858–1890), asserts that 'John of Goch, John of Wesel and Wessel of Gansfort have been properly classed with Wyclif and Huss as Reformers before the Reformation' (Schaff 1858–1890). So do other researchers. See Walker 1919, p. 381–383; Krahn 1968; Mansch, Peters 2016.

[38] Needham, 'Seeds of Reformation'. Another example is Amazon's presentation of the reprint of Gansfort's Works: 'The four-hundredth anniversary of the beginning of the Reformation may well revive interest in the precursors of the Reformers', https://www.amazon.com/Wessel-Gansfort-Vol-Writings-Principal/dp/0265250552, last accessed 05.07.2022.

[39] Woods, 'Trailblazers for Martin Luther: 5 Great Reformers'.

[40] 'One should not underestimate the impact of the ideology of laïcité that spread along with the Code Napoléon and the repression of the ancien régime, not only on the actual, battered relationship between State and Church, but inevitably also on historical scholarship, where the contribution by the theologians has been eclipsed almost completely' (Decock 2012, p. 12–13).

[41] Ullmann 1855, p. 382.

[42] On Heidelberg's *Sodalitas litteraria* and Gerson, see Mazour-Matusevich 2006a.

who taught there from 1425 until his death.[43] Academia was not the only consumer of Gerson's works, however. In the city itself, Gerson's pastoral program, as formulated in the aforementioned *Opus tripartitum*, was disseminated in local parishes through popular sermons, or theological 'assemblages', according to the expression of Hervé Martin.[44]

The education that Gansfort received at these universities not only met his intellectual needs, but also stayed with him for the rest of his life. A true intellectual, he famously enjoyed the art of scholarly disputation, which he missed during his stays at monasteries:

> *Supplico, si sanatum uelitis, uos de monte Agnetis crebro mecum contendite, neque desistatis, nisi uel uictores, uel uicti, ueritatis confessionem omnia lauantem extorqueatis.*[45]

Indeed, while the Dutchman was 'in harmony with moral and religious ideas of the *devotio moderna*',[46] he did not necessarily share all its opinions, especially with reference to scholastic methods, learned disputations, and the merit of studying logic and mathematics. 'All historians who have dealt with Gansfort are aware of his thirst for knowledge which carried him far from the environment of the Brethren'.[47] In sharp contrast with *devotio*'s sensibility and in agreement with the chancellor's opinion that without logic men can hardly claim to be human,[48] Gansfort

---

[43] Ouy 1998, p. xlvii: 'On sait que, nommé en 1418 secrétaire du nouveau pape Martin V, Nicolas de Clamanges, au lieu de le suivre à Rome, choisit de s'installer à Paris occupée par les Anglais, de s'inscrire à la Faculté de Théologie et de reprendre son activité d'enseignement depuis longtemps interrompue'.

[44] Martin 2011.

[45] Gansfort 1522, p. 98. 'I beg you, who dwell in Mount St Agnes, if you wish me to be cured, to battle often with me, and not to desist, until — conquering or conquered — you extort a confession of the truth that shall clear away all doubts' (Miller 1917, p. 251).

[46] Jacob 1953, p. 130.

[47] Rogahn 1974, p. 147.

[48] *Collectorium Super Magnificat*, OC 8, p. 182: *Hanc opinor esse causam erroris hominum devotioni se dare putantium, sine logica et metaphysica, sint homines* [...] 'I think this to be the cause of error of the devout men to give themselves an idea that, without logic and metaphysics, they are people [...].' Richard J. Oosterhoff, on the contrary, argues that Gerson 'played a central role in the demise of the 14th century mathematics' (Oosterhoff 2018, p. 45).

affirmed that theologians 'need logic, and in large doses, as proved by the example of Gerson who prevailed thanks to training in logical argumentation'.[49] The Parisian master's broad spiritual profile — which united devotional piety, scholarly learning, and sincere zeal for 'pastoral counter-conduct'[50] in one person — afforded Gansfort the intellectual flexibility and mental independence he craved. Indeed, Gansfort's relation to Gerson is found at the center of Wessel's differences with the Brethren.[51]

Gansfort's motivation in exploring Gerson's legacy was theoretical in the sense that he turned to the late medieval master in order to validate certain contended points of his own theological arguments. But the Dutchman needed *auctoritas venerabilis doctoris et theologi* on a more personal level too, in order to deal with his own spiritual and social challenges. Gerson was for him an *auctoritas* of exceptional weight, representing a sum of qualities that commanded respect for Gerson's opinions, achievements, talents, as well as his person. Indeed, if the nickname *Magister contradictionum* applies to the Dutch scholar in three main respects — '1) as contradiction to untested knowledge; 2) as contradiction against unauthentic authority; 3) as contradiction against his own inner confusion (which lends his work its highly personal and even psycho-therapeutic dimension)'[52] — all three aspects are found in his

---

[49] Oberman 1981, p. 39. *Opus igitur theologis logicam inferre. Et Gerson ipse que tandem tantus ipse theologus, nisi per accuratissimam illam magistri Petri logicam euasit?* (Gansfort 1522, p. 114). 'Theologians must have recourse to logic. And pray how could Gerson himself have become so great a theologian without the aid of the most accurate logic of his Master Peter?' (Miller 1917, p. 309). Yet, being a man of his time, Gansfort strongly discourages female monastics from learning logic: *De studio logicae non inficior, quando ad scholasticam exercitationem conferat, sed ad monasticae solitudinis, ac celsitudine consolationem, quid asserat non video praesertim virginibus tui similibus. Datum vere toti sexui vestro magis desiderio flagrare que arbitrio, ac iudicio ferri* (Gansfort 1522, p. 124). 'With regard to the study of logic, I do not deny that it contributes to scholastic discipline. But I do not see what it adds to monastic solitude and spiritual exaltation, especially in the case of maidens like yourself. As a rule it has been given to your entire sex to glow with eager longing rather than to be distinguished for judgment or discernment' (Letter to Gertrude Reyniers, Miller 1917, p. 241).

[50] Depew 2016, p. 31.

[51] Post 1968, p. 541: 'He retained his own personal views on very essential Christian doctrines, opinions which we do not encounter at all among the Brothers and the Canons'.

[52] Oberman 1981, p. 98.

relation to Gerson's legacy. Gansfort's conscious choice to present the Parisian master as his model for both thought and behavior is theologically and personally motivated.

Gansfort's kinship with the chancellor was based on a close knowledge of Gerson's writings. The Dutch theologian relies, albeit implicitly and mostly without listing them by title, on the following Latin works by Gerson: *De consiliis evangelicis, De potestate ecclesiastica, Collectorium Super Magnificat, Contra Matthaeum de Fussa, De indulgentiis*[53] and, most likely, *Contra Sectam Flagellantium*. Gansfort also cites the vernacular treatise *The Mountain of Contemplation* and a number of sermons. There is little basis to dispute that 'Wessel war ein Rezipient des Werkes von Gerson'.[54] Gansfort's writings abound with explicit references to the chancellor, whom he extols for having single-handedly ended the Western Schism.[55] Gansfort's *Letter concerning indulgences by the venerable master Wessel of Groningen in reply to master Jacob Hoeck, Dean of Naeldwick*, known as *Contra Iacobum Hoeck* and comprising eight chapters, is all about Gerson. Although the question of indulgences is central to the *Letter*[56] Gansfort also cites the chancellor in relation to other specific issues such as papal jurisdiction[57] and

---

[53] Gerson, *De indulgentiis*, OC 9.

[54] Obermann & Caspers 1999, p. 92.

[55] '[...] The entire community of the faithful has to adhere to the wise man [...] as it was done during the Council of Constance, when the community of believers disagreed with pope John XXIII and consented with the theologian Jean Gerson' (Weiler 1999, p. 313).

[56] Wessel Gansfort 1522, p. 107: *Venerabilem illum Gersonem alleges donum allegatu, dignum considerate. Qui multa valde in abusu indulgentiarum reprobat.* 'You cite the distinguished and venerable Gerson, who is worthy to be cited and to be considered, for he strongly condemns many things in the abuse of indulgences' (Miller 1917, p. 289). See Shaffern 1988, p. 643–661.

[57] Letter to Jacob Hoeck, Gansfort 1522, p. 114: *Sic puto sensisse venerabilem illum Gersonem, quia scio de mente sua esse universam autoritatem Apostolicae fedis ex canonicarum scripturarum veritate pendentem, debere moderatis aestimari, non scripturae veritatem ex papali voluntate aut autoritate, etiam si non deliret aut erret.* 'For I know that it was his [Gerson's] understanding that the universal authority of the apostolic see ought to be regulated by and be regarded as depending on the truth of the Canonical Scriptures; and by no means that the truth of the Scriptures depends on the will or authority of the pope, even if he is not deranged or mistaken' (Miller 1917, p. 308).

purgatory.[58] The letter also repeatedly praises the chancellor's personality and his theological approach.

One theme, however, is clearly prevalent in Gansfort's dealings with Gerson's legacy. The Dutchman refers to this theme as the chancellor's tendency to 'moderation', be it in relation to his theological opinions, his personality, or his choices as an ecclesiastical leader. Although generally full of praise *Ad venerabilis Gersonis moderationem* ('With regard of the moderation of the venerable Gerson'),[59] Gansfort seems to both admire and be puzzled by that moderation. When this quality seems appropriate to him, he fully supports it, as in the case of Gerson's advocating for moderation against extreme asceticism and self-imposed suffering in order to commend oneself to God. The chancellor was consistently wary and suspicious of extreme forms of devotion, such as flagellation, sleep deprivation, and severe fasting, and he strictly opposed self-mutilation, castration, and 'baptism by fire' with hot iron, arguing against them in his Latin works such as *Contra Sectam Flagellantium*,[60] as well as in vernacular sermons such as *De la*

---

[58] Letter to Jacob Hoeck, Wessel Gansfort 1522, p. 114: *Quia timor habet, ideo timor not est in perfecta charitate. Purgandi in purgatorio habent poenam & timorem, ergo non sunt perfecti in charitate. Sic puto sensisse venerabilem illum Gersonem* [...]. 'Those who need to be cleansed in purgatory have punishment and fear; hence they are not perfect in love. I think the venerable Gerson was also of this opinion' (Miller 1917, p. 308). Gansfort probably refers to this passage in *De consolatione theologiae*, OC 9, p. 229: *Noli propterea mirari, Monice, si tales inter recordationes positus paveat et extimescat, praesertim cum perfectam charitatem quae foras mittit timorem, non se praesumet adeptum*, 'So do not wonder, Monicus, if he trembles and is fearful in the midst of his recollections, especially since he does not presume that he has acquired that perfect charity [love] which casts out fear' (Miller 1998, p. 225).

[59] Gansfort 1522, p. 113. Miller 1917, p. 306.

[60] OC 10, p. 50: *Immo sicut non licet hominem seipsum propria auctoritate mutilare vel castrare nisi pro sanitate totius corporis consequenda, sic non licet, ut videtur, quod a seipso quis sanguinem violenter ejiciat nisi causa medicinae corporalis; alioquin simili ratione posset se homo cauterizare per ignitum ferrum, quod adhuc nemo posuit vel concessit, nisi forsitan idolatrae vel falsi christiani, quales reperiuntur in India, qui se putant baptizari debere per ignem*. 'Indeed, it is not lawful for a man to mutilate or to castrate himself of his own authority, unless it is for the sake of health of the whole body. So it is not lawful, as it seems, for any man to violently extract blood by himself except for the medical reason. Otherwise, for the similar reason he can brand himself with hot iron, which thus far no one would order or grant, except perhaps idolaters or false Christians, such as are found in India who think they ought to be baptized by fire'. My translation.

chasteté conjugale.[61] Gansfort's strong dislike of bodily severities is very similar.[62]

Like Gerson's German enthusiasts, Johannes Geiler von Kaysersberg (1445–1510) and Gabriel Biel, Gansfort also espoused the middle way in theology, and followed the chancellor's choice of *theologia media* — the middle ground between presumption of merits and quietism. *Theologia media* encourages the Christian soul to call, beg, and cry loudly to God[63] while, at the same time, opening up to accept the divine initiative. In explicit agreement with the French theologian, and in complete disagreement with Luther's future views, Gansfort relies on the idea of 'cooperation with God', which he develops in chapter 1 of the *Farrago*, which is titled *De providentia Dei*:

> *Omnis autem creatura a summo vertice usque ad imum & ultimum, opus est artis divinae. [...] Adeo haec ut caeterae [secundae] causae, non tam causae quam occasiones [...] ut verae cooperationes deo sumus, & in illa cooperatione, deus facit nos cooperari [...] velle est, & perficere, in illa cooperatione nostra,*

---

[61] OC 7: 1, p. 861: 'Ou les abstinances sont legieres et sans grande singularite; et lors elle se peuent faire'. See Mazour-Matusevich 2000.

[62] '[T]here is no necessity for severe fasts or the wearing of a rough goat's-hair garment. The worthy fruit of repentance requires no bodily severities, but only that which is necessary for us all, the piety that avails for all things. Be regular in the observance of your duties [...] and that will suffice for bodily discipline'. (Letter to a Nameless Nun, Miller 1917, p. 245). I could not locate the original Latin text. As Miller states in his Introduction, 'no two editions of the Farrago contain exactly the same letters, nor is there any explanation offered as to the basis of their selection' (Miller 1917, p. 167). For Gerson's opinions on this subject, see *Contra Sectam Flagellantium* (OC 10, p. 46–51) and vernacular works such as *De la chasteté conjugale* (OC 7: 2, p. 861).

[63] Gerson, *Sermon pour la Pentecote*, OC 7: 2, p. 688: 'Appelle maintenant, je te prie, ô ame crestienne, appelle et huche a haulte voix [...]' The theology of spiritual seeking is omnipresent in Gerson's works. For example, see *Pour le mercredi des Cendres*, OC 7: 2, p. 577: 'Pourtant se nous ne donnons nostre consentement a sa grace et misericorde que ainsy nous promet, et se nous ne l'ensuyons, se nous ne nous donnons nous meismes se nous ne metons la main a nous aidier comme il soit ainsy que il veut [...]'. In *De consolatione theologiae*, OC 9, p. 197: *Quamvis enim omnes accedentes ad Deum oporteret credere quod Deus est. Et quod inquirentibus se renumerator sit. [...] Fides itaque rursus dicit ei [...] Quod omnia nostra sunt conformiter ad Christum: Primum querere regnum Dei, et omnia haec adjicientur vobis*, 'Yes, "all those who come to God must believe that he exists, and is a rewarder to them that seek him" (Heb 11:6). Faith says that everything of ours is in conformity to Christ — "seek you first the kingdom of God, and all these things shall be added unto you" (Mt 6:33)' (Miller 1998, p. 87).

> *nostrum peccatum vel nostra pietas. [...] in illa clara die finalis iudicij, quando clare sententiabunt omnes iudicandi, & iudicantes iudicia dei vera iustificata in semetipsis.*[64]

Gansfort not only affirms that *Et ad haec tria minister Christi quantum cooperator [...] quia scilicet verbo vel ministerio concurrit.*[65] He also believes that we humans *consentimus enim operanti deo.*[66] Gansfort is careful, however, to make sure not to embrace the other extreme, human self-sufficiency, and is mindful to leave the initiative to God:

> *Vult Gerson expresse que in peccatorii remissio naturaliter prior sit gratiae infusio, quia culpae remissio, quia nihil aliud est culpae remissio quia gratiae infusio.*[67]

Yet the same wise moderation that Gansfort admired 'as opposed to blind subservience to the letter of the law',[68] seems to baffle him when it clashed with his own strong opinions. In his letter to Dean of Naeldwick Jacob Hoeck, Wessel claims that every time the chancellor's position is *mitius aliquando quam theologica pura veritas habeat, puto pietati magis tacentem condescendere, quo non veritas malicia quorundam pusillis scandalum pariat.*[69] Obviously, what the Dutch theologian calls *theologica pura veritas* (the plain theological truth) corresponds to his own point of view, which

---

[64] This section is based on Gansfort's folios 1 and 2 in *Farrago* (Gansfort 1522). 'Every creature expresses the thought of the divine artist. Though not dependent upon them, God ordinarily works through secondary causes, which are little more than occasions for man to cooperate with him. In this cooperation with God lies the opportunity for godliness or sin. Because of this conscious cooperation or its failure, we shall at the last judgment approve God's verdict upon our lives' (Miller 1917, p. 209).

[65] Gansfort 1522, p. 113. 'According to him [Gerson] [I]n so far as the minister of Christ cooperates with Christ [...] of course he concurs with him in word or ministry' (Miller 1917, p. 306).

[66] Gansfort 1522, folio 2.

[67] Gansfort 1522, p. 113. 'Now Gerson is clearly of the opinion that in the remission of sins the bestowment of grace necessarily precedes the remission of guilt, because the remission of guilt is nothing else than the bestowment of grace' (Miller 1917, p. 306).

[68] de Kroon 2009, p. 28.

[69] Gansfort 1522, p. 114. '[...] milder than what accords with the plain, theological truth, he [Gerson] is silently making a concession in the interest of piety, in order that the truth may not become a barrier for the unprepared "little ones" through the malice of certain men' (Miller 1917, p. 308).

Gerson chooses, on political, spiritual, or pedagogical grounds, not to formulate as bluntly as Gansfort would:

> *Puto igitur prudentem illum virum postque diligentibus lectoribus oculos per eas propositiones quae indubitatam veritatem continent aperuit, consulte remissius rigorosam abditam veritatem, pro tardioribus, propter contentiosos tacuisse. Quomodo enim aliter tam discrepantes, venerabilis illius viri sententias concordabimus? Cum sint quaedam earum tam evidenter pro me, ut in eis meam ego intentionem fundare putem. Sed id interim apud te. Quaedae vero tam remisse atque quiete pro populare assertione, quo tu in eis contra me neque id ab re, quia parite & illum studio communis pietatis allegare puto quo illum scripsisse, cum utrosque par procella iactauerit. Et ego consilium tuum laudo si ita facias doceas & praedicas.*[70]

The quote above exudes a certain degree of frustration, which reflects Gansfort's ambivalent attitude toward what he perceived as the chancellor's intentional strategy. On the one hand, he valued the chancellor's restraint, which allowed him to act in wisdom and *studio communis pietatis* (for the sake of piety).[71] On the other hand, the Dutch theologian found the same moderation somewhat upsetting, difficult to comprehend, and especially hard for himself to emulate, due to differences in his and the chancellor's respective temperaments. Indeed, his description of Gerson's character almost sounds condescending:

> *Nosti studiosam & officiosam viri illius pietatem, quam saepe suam opinionem alijs contra sentientibus deferat. In quo tamen*

---

[70] Gansfort 1522, p. 115. 'I think, therefore, that the prudent Gerson, after opening the eyes of careful readers by propositions which contain undoubted truth, purposely relaxed his strictness somewhat on account of contentious men, and was silent respecting the exact truth hidden within, for the sake of those who were of slower apprehension. Indeed, how shall we otherwise reconcile the great discrepancies we find in the opinions of this venerable man? For certain of these opinions so clearly support me that I think of basing my premise upon them. Yet sometimes he agrees with you. Indeed, in statements intended for the people he expresses his opinions so mildly and gently that you can build on them opposing me. Nor is this without value. For I think that you, after experiencing a storm just as he did, cite him in the same zeal for piety that he displayed in his writings. And if you act, teach, and preach in that spirit, I praise your wisdom' (Miller 1917, p. 310).

[71] Gansfort 1522, p. 115. Miller 1917, p. 310.

valde mirandum videtur tam diversum a vero & recto consilium.[72]

Taken out of context, this description would imply that Gerson was moderate in his opinions due to a weakness of character and lack of solid principles. That, however, is clearly not the case. In an interesting display of self-reflection, and admitting to regretting his own lack of Gerson-like prudence during his own tenure in Paris, Gansfort expresses the wish that he ought to be more circumspect himself: *Unde crebro & illum ac te beatos iudico, quibus officiosior in talibus moderatio est.*[73] A master of contradictions indeed.

Gansfort's seemingly conflicted attitude toward Gerson may be explained by his own unusual situation. Halfway between cloister and academia, spending his last years alternately in several monasteries while still remaining a layman, and controversial without falling into heresy, Gansfort based his ability to stay out of trouble (without sacrificing his ability to negotiate his dissent) on his reliance on Gerson as the main theological authority of the time, as his personal hero, and, very importantly, as a precedent. By endorsing and contextualizing the chancellor's positions, the Dutch theologian justified and defended his own. Thus, his praise of the Frenchman's efforts to avoid, in dealing with complex theological questions, a 'widespread scandal' among 'those who were of slower apprehension', closely follows Gerson's own argument in *Contra Matthaeum de Fussa*:

> [...] *talis assertio non est deducanda ad populum, similiter nec opposita tamquam declarando vel elucidando; sic capiendo enim habet vel non habet veritatem cujus [quoniam] populus non est capax, nec inde aedificationem sumeret sed scandalum.*[74]

---

[72] Gansfort 1522, p. 114. 'You know the devotion and deep piety of this man, and how often he abandons his own opinion when others disagree with him. Nevertheless, in this it seems very strange that this judgment is so different from what is true and correct'. Here the translation is mine. Miller's translation of this fragment seems a little too liberal: 'You know how kindly and complaisant and good he is, and how often he abandons his own opinion when others disagree with him' (Miller 1917, p. 308).

[73] Gansfort 1522, p. 115. 'I often consider you and those persons to be happy, who possess a more complaisant moderation in such questions' (Miller 1917, p. 309).

[74] OC 10, p. 138–139. '[...] Such an assertion should not be intended for the people, and similarly it should be neither opposed, nor professed nor elucidated

Consequently, whenever Gerson's position appears to differ from Gansfort's, it is not due to substantial differences of opinion or even temperament between the mentor and the mentee, but to the chancellor's superior ability to adjust his message to his audience and for a specific purpose. As a learned theologian and a fine psychological observer, the great chancellor knew not only how to condescend to the general imperfection of people, but also how to take into consideration specific circumstances of a given situation. *In disputationibus dico ubi discussionis dente opus est. Non in sermonibus ad populum. Neque in contemplatione ad deum.*[75] Truly, to use the approach adopted during 'the disputations, where there is need of the sharp tooth of discussion', in 'sermons to the people', and in 'meditations Godward' would be both ineffective and inappropriate. Therefore, Gerson's seemingly milder statements must always be interpreted 'in the light of this purpose'[76] and not in the light of their relationship to an essential theological truth as Gansfort understood it.

> *Puto igitur illu studiosum pietatis & aedificationis latissimi in Ecclesia dei scandala ex pertinaci scholasticorum contentione expertum, elegisse magis errorem sustinere veritatis in pusillis, que scissura & scandala charitatis. Et hinc mitiora sua dicta in hanc partem accipienda, uti videmus consilium naufragi suas & caras merces in tempestate iactantis, quo vitam & animam salute, natura duce & lucent, quanon intrunsque quod minis malum subimis, quo maius declinemus. Unde & ergo saepius Parisius & hodie quandoque meipsum reprehendo, que aliquando cum non capacibus materiam istam confero, atque utinam solum sine fructu.*[77]

[to them]; for to have or not to have the truth that the people are not capable of grasping, creates no edification but scandal'. My translation.

[75] Gansfort 1522, p. 114. 'I am speaking of disputations, where there is need of the sharp tooth of discussion; not of sermons to the people, nor of meditation Godward' (Miller 1917, p. 308).

[76] Miller 1917, p. 309. Gansfort 1522, p. 115, see the next note.

[77] Letter to Jacob Hoeck, Gansfort 1522, p. 115. 'I think, therefore, that Gerson in his zeal for piety and edification, knowing by experience what widespread scandal arose throughout the Church of God from the obstinate contentions of Scholastics, preferred to maintain a perversion of truth among the "little ones" rather than cause a schism or any stumbling block to love in the Church. And therefore his milder statements must be interpreted in the light of this purpose; just as we see the wisdom of a shipwrecked man in throwing his precious

It is also clear that through a close association with the universally recognized authority of *saepius Parisius* Gansfort sought to avoid crossing the red line in his criticism of the Church and thus protect himself from potential accusations of heresy. Fearful of the Inquisition, Wessel reproached his superior and former friend, Jacob Hoeck, for writing about his potential theological errors to Cologne's authorities instead of keeping his disapproval 'between you and me alone':

> *Accepi ex ore tuo nonnullis meis doctrinis te scandalisatum, & ea re per motum, scripsisse de super Coloniam. Neque reprehendo, commodious tamen, & ad normam evangelicae rectitudinis vicinius puto, ut me peccantem in te fratrem tuum, primo inter te & me corripuisses.*[78]

Hoeck's stern warning clearly demonstrates why Gansfort, who seems to have had little to none of Gerson's famous discretion, had indeed a great need for the latter's theological support:

> *At unum duntaxat ex literis tuis colligo, quod virum grandem, mea opinione, vehementer dedecet. Id est, quod dura te jactas cervice, qua cunctis in dictis tuis quandam niteris inveniri singularitatem, adeò ut plurimorum judicio Magister contradictionis meritò valeas appellari. Et, ne dubites, tua doctissimi viri singularitas plerosque, scandalisat.*[79]

---

wares overboard in a storm, in order that he may save his life. In so doing he is evidently led by nature, since we do not at any rate suffer both evils, when we undergo the lesser in order to avoid the greater. Hence also I sometimes blame myself today, as I used to more often in Paris, for discussing this subject at all with those who are not fitted for it, and I only hope that at any rate it did no harm [had no effect]' (Miller 1917, p. 309).

[78] Gansfort 1522, p. 98. 'I learned from your own lips [mouth] that you had been displeased at some teachings of mine and that you in alarm had written about the matter to Cologne. For this I do not find fault with you. And yet I think it would have been more obliging and — by the standard of gospel rectitude — more neighborly, if, when I, your brother, sinned against you, you had shown me my fault, between you and me alone' (Miller 1917, p. 266).

[79] *Epistola M. Jacobi Hoeck ad M. Wesselum*, Gansfort 1614, p. 871. 'From your letters, however, I gather that you have one characteristic which in my opinion is extremely [vehemently] unsuited to a great man. This is that you pride yourself on your obstinacy [literally 'stiff neck'] and are bent upon having men find a certain singularity in all your statements, so that in the judgment of many persons you are rightly called "The Master of Contradiction". And unquestionably, in view of your being a most learned man, your singularity gives offense [scandal-

Reprimands of 'obstinacy' and 'singularity,' repeated by Hoeck twice in one paragraph, are alarming, since 'singularity is not a virtue but a vice.'[80] Thereupon Gansfort, who admits that he is often suspected of being 'singular',[81] fiercely defends himself in his answer to Hoeck:[82]

> *Numquam pertinax sui, etiam in certaminibos vanitatis. Circumivi multas universitates, & certamina quaerens, multos reperi contradictores, verum numquam in scandalis dimissos; quia rationibus meis auditis, & perspicaciter consideratis vel consentientes, vel saltem non irrationabiles confitentes, quietos redditi, ut nemo finaliter de me conquereretur.*[83]

At the end of this letter of self-defense, Gansfort takes out and wields, like a shield, *Gerson ipse*, that is, the irrefutable argument of the French theologian's authority:

> *Sed nunquid igitur Gerson haereticus quitam graviter & fundamentalibus verbis hodiernun cursum inussit. Video quorsum*

---

izes] to many' (Miller 1917, p. 267). This letter is not included in the 1522 Basel edition cited here.

[80] Oberman 1981, p. 97.

[81] Gansfort 1522, p. 98: *Fateor, in multis assertionibus meis et crebro singularis invenior, & valde mihi de singularitate suspectus, non parum errare formido.* 'I admit that I am found to be singular in many of my assertions; indeed being very suspicious myself of my unusual views, I dread not a little that I may sometimes be mistaken' (translation based on Miller 1917, p. 267). Miller himself offers a competing translation of this fragment: 'I acknowledge that in some of the assertions that I make I am looked upon as singular. I often suspect myself of singularity, and therefore fear that I frequently fall into error'. (Miller 1917, p. 125).

[82] Hoeck also uses Gerson as a weapon: 'Really, my dear [Gansfort], you ought to regard as a strong reason, nay as stronger than any reason — the authority, not only of the pope, but also of all the prelates and Doctors, who either grant indulgences of all kinds, or write and teach that they ought to be granted. [...] Do not most of the chapters in the body of the law approved by the Church also speak of indulgences? Does not the venerable Gerson seem to be of the same opinion, when he says that the granting of indulgences ought not to be lightly esteemed, but rather ought to be devoutly considered in the faith, hope and love of Christ, who gave such authority to men?' (Miller 1917, p. 279).

[83] Gansfort 1522, p. 98–99. 'I have never been stubborn, even in idle discussions. I have been to many universities, seeking discussion, and I have found many opponents. Sometimes, too, they have been offended by my belief. But never have they parted with me in offense. For when my reasons had been heard and carefully considered, I left them quieted, either agreeing with me, or at least admitting that my statements were not unreasonable; so that in the end no one made complaint concerning me'. (Miller 1917, p. 267).

> *ista tendent, quia si verum illi dicerent, omnis qui contradiceret in regulam fidei, quia contra traditionem apostolorum impingeret & si pertinaciter insisteret, hereticus esset.*[84]

Even though Gansfort's affinity with Gerson might be qualified as 'pre-ideological' — in the sense that it does not express the agenda of any particular denomination or party — it is not disinterested for two main reasons. The first is the need for personal protection, illustrated above, for which Gansfort relied on Gerson's authority as a safeguard. The second has to do with the fact that Gansfort, like Gerson and other fifteenth-century luminaries — such as Nicolas of Cusa (1401–1464), Johannes Geiler von Kaysersberg, and Nicolas Kempf (1414–1497) — belonged to the *reforma perpetua* movement that attempted to improve the Church from within, without undermining its sacramental authority. Even if he afforded Gansfort 'extraordinary latitude to the individual conscience in determining the limits of civil and ecclesiastical authority',[85] Gerson did so in a way opposite to what we understand as individual conscience today. Via Gerson, Gansfort affirmed his ability to remain within the *reforma perpetua* movement, which sought, through criticism no matter how severe, to amend, recover, and uphold traditional Catholic values, among which love for the Church reigned supreme. Although 'caustic and extreme, often shocking his listeners with paradox and violent opinion',[86] Gansfort never denied the value of traditions, church sacraments, or the freedom of will, and defended his right to remain in the Church, not to break with it. It worked. He suffered no personal persecution by the Inquisition and died peacefully as a good Catholic. 'He actually proved how much latitude there was in the fifteenth century'.[87] The fact that his writings were placed on the *Index of Prohibited Books* in 1529, forty years after his death and twelve years after the beginning of Luther's revolt, is more a comment on the change of the times than on

---

[84] Gansfort 1522, p. 111. 'But is Gerson who so forcibly and fundamentally branded the present system on this account [of indulgences] a heretic? [...] then everyone [...] who persists [in it] must be a heretic' (Miller 1917, p. 299–300).

[85] Oakley 2015, p. 206.

[86] Jacob 1953, p. 130.

[87] Iserloh 1980, p. 599.

his actual theology. What Luther said about Gerson in the winter of 1542–1543 fully applies to Johannes Wessel Gansfort: 'Gerson ist der beste; der fieng an, wiewol er nicht gar gewiß war, wo er darin war [...] Er duffte sich nicht derwegen, das er den riß hett gar her durch gethan.[88] Indeed.

Bibliography

Primary Sources

Matthias Flacius Illiricus, *Catalogus testium ueritatis, qui ante nostrum aetatem reclamarunt Papae*, Basel: Perna, 1556.

Johannes Wessel Gansfort, *Farrago rerum theologicarum*, Basel: Adamus Petri, 1522.

Wessel Gansfort, *Opera*, ed. Petrus Pappus à Tratzberg, Groningen: Iohannes Sassius, 1614.

Johannes Wessel Gansfort, *Wessel Gansfort: Life and Writings. Principal Works*, trans. J. W. Scudder, ed. E. W. Miller, New York, NY: Knickerbocker, 1917 (Papers of the American Society of Church History, Special volume, 1–2).

Jean Gerson, *Ioannis Carlerii de Gerson de Mystica Theologia*, ed. A. Combes, Lugano, Switzerland: Thesaurus Mundi, 1958.

Jean Gerson, *Jean Gerson: Early Works*, ed. & trans. B. P. McGuire, New York, NY: Paulist Press, 1998 (Classics of Western Spirituality, 92).

Jean Gerson, *Œuvres complètes de Jean Gerson*, éd. P. Glorieux, 10 vols, Paris: Desclée 1960–1973.

Martin Luther, *Luthers Werke*, Kritische Gesamtausgabe, Schriften, gen. ed. U. Köpf, 73 vols, Weimar: Herman Böhlaus Nachfolger, 1883–2009.

Martin Luther, *Luther's Works*, ed. J. Pelikan & H. T. Lehmann, American Edition, 55 vols, Philadelphia, PA: Muehlenberg and Fortress; St Louis, MO: Concordia, 1955–1986.

---

[88] WA, Tischreden 5, 213, 15–29 [Nr. 5523]. '[...] Gerson was the best; he began [to attack papacy], although he was not altogether sure what he was about. [...] He could not make up his mind to make the break [with the pope] complete'. (*LW 54, 442*).

Secondary Sources

Augustijn, C. (1999), 'Wessel Gansfort's Rise in Celebrity', in F. Akkerma, G. C. Huisman & A. Vanderjagt (eds), *Wessel Gansfort (1419–1489) and Northern Humanism*, Leiden: Brill (Brill's Studies in Intellectual History, 40), p. 1–22.

Bollbuck, H. (2017), *Martin Luther in der Geschichtsschreibung zwischen Reformation und Aufklärung*, in *Luthermania – Ansichten einer Kultfigur*, Virtuelle Ausstellung der Herzog August Bibliothek im Rahmen des Forschungsverbundes Marbach Weimar Wolfenbüttel, http://www.luthermania.de/exhibits/show/harald-bollbuck-martin-luther-in-der-geschichtsschreibung (accessed 07.07.2022).

Christianson, G., T. M. Izbicki & C. Bellitto (eds) (2008), *The Church, the Councils, and Reform: The Legacy of the Fifteenth Century*, Washington, DC: The Catholic University of America Press.

Combes, A. (1963–1965), *La théologie mystique de Gerson: profil de son évolution*, 2 vols, Rome: Desclée et Libraria Editrix Pontificiae Universitatis Lateranensis (Spiritualitas, 1–2).

Debongnie, P. (1927), 'Une œuvre oubliée de Mauburnus: *Le Rosarum Hortulus*', in *Revue d'Ascétique et de mystique*, 8, p. 392–402.

Debongnie, P. (1928), *Jean Mombaer de Bruxelles, abbé de Livry: ses écrits et ses réformes*, Louvain: Librairie universitaire (Recueil de travaux, Sér. 2, 11).

Decock, W. (2012), *Theologians and Contract Law: The Moral Transformation of the Ius Commune (ca. 1500–1650)*, Leiden: Martinus Nijnoff (Studies in the History of Private Law, 4; Legal History Library, 9).

Denis, P. (2014), *Edmond Richer et le renouveau du conciliarisme au XVIIe siècle*, Paris: Cerf.

Denis, P. (2018), 'Edmond Richer, la Sorbonne et les métamorphoses du conciliarisme', in *Dix-septième Siècle*, Paris: PUF, p. 105–120.

Depew, J. F. (2016), 'Foucault Among the Stoics: *Oikeiosis* and Counter-Conduct', in *Foucault Studies*, 21, p. 22–51.

Giraud, C. (2016), *Spiritualité et histoire des textes entre Moyen Âge et époque moderne: genèse et fortune d'un corpus pseudépigraphe de méditations*, Paris: Institut d'Études Augustiniennes (Études augustiniennes, Moyen-Âge et Temps Modernes, 52).

Godet, M. (1912), *La congrégation de Montaigu (1490–1580)*, Paris: Librairie Ancienne Honoré Champion (Bibliothèque de l'École des Hautes-Études, Sciences historiques et philologiques, 198).

Hobbins, D. (2006), 'Gerson on Lay Devotion', in B. P. McGuire (ed.), *A Companion to Jean Gerson*, Leiden: Brill (Brill's Companions to the Christian Tradition, 3), p. 41–78.

Hobbins, D. (2009), *Authorship and Publicity Before Print. Jean Gerson and the Transformation of Late Medieval Learning*, Philadelphia, PA: University of Pennsylvania Press.

Iserloh, E. (1980), 'From the Middle Ages to the Reformation', chapters 58–61, in H. Jedin & J. P. Dolan (eds), *History of the Church*, 10 vols, London: Burns & Oates, 1965–1980, IV: *From the High Middle Ages to the Eve of the Reformation*, ed. H.-G. Beck et al. (1970) p. 566–624.

Krahn, C. (1968), "The Evangelical Sacramentarian Reformation', in C. Krahn, *Dutch Anabaptism: Origin, Spread, Life and Thought (1450–1600)*, The Hague: Martinus Nijhoff, p. 44–79.

Kroon, M. de (2009), *We Believe in God and in Christ, Not in the Church: The Influence of Wessel Gansfort on Martin Bucer*, trans. M. Sherwood-Smith, London: John Knox Press.

Habsburg, M. von, 'The Devotional Life: Catholic and Protestant Translations of Thomas À Kempis, *Imitatio Christi*, c. 1420– c. 1620', (unpublished doctoral thesis, University of St Andrews, 2002). http://hdl.handle.net/10023/2696.

Habsburg, M. von (2011), *Catholic and Protestant Translations of the 'Imitatio Christi' 1425–1650: From Late Medieval Classic to Early Modern Bestseller*, Farham, UK: Ashgate Publishing.

Fraser, J. E. (1953), *Essays in the Conciliar Epoch*. Second edition, Manchester: Manchester University Press.

Kraume, H. (1980), *Die Gerson-Übersetzungen Geilers von Kaysersberg: Studien zur deutschsprachigen Gerson-Rezeption*, Zürich: Artemis (Münchener Texte und Untersuchungen zur deutschen Literatur des Mittelalters, 71).

Mansch, L. D. & C. H. Peters (2016), *Martin Luther: The Life and Lessons*, Jefferson, NC: McFarland.

Martin, H. (2011), 'Les sermons du dominicain Jean Clérée (1450– 1507), jalon parmi d'autres, entre les jeux de mystère et la comédie de mœurs', conference presentation at *Prédication et performance, Fondation Singer-Polignac*, Paris, 23 June 2011, https://www.dailymotion.com/video/xjkp6q (accessed 07.07.2022).

Mazour-Matusevich, Y. (2000), 'From Monastic to Individual Spirituality: Another Perspective on Jean Gerson's Attitude Toward Women', in *Magistra*, 6, p. 61–88.

Mazour-Matusevich, Y. (2006), 'Gerson's Legacy', in B. P. McGuire (ed.), *A Companion to Jean Gerson*, Leiden: Brill (Brill's Companions to the Christian Tradition, 3), p. 357–399.

Mazour-Matusevich, Y. (2006a), 'Jean Gerson (1363–1429) and the Formation of German National Identity', in *Revue d'histoire ecclésiastique*, 101/3–4, p. 963–987.

Mazour-Matusevich, Y. (2010), 'Jean Gerson and the Creation of German Protestant Identity', in *Revue d'histoire ecclesiastique*, 105/3–4, p. 632–651.

Mazour-Matusevich, Y. (2023), *Le père du siècle. The Early Modern Reception of Jean Gerson (1363–1429): Theological Authority Between Middle Ages and Early Modern*, Turnhout: Brepols.

McGuire, B. P. (2005), *Jean Gerson and the Last Medieval Reformation*, University Park, PA: Penn State Press.

Needham, N. 'Seeds of Reformation', Metropolitan Tabernacle, Elephant & Castle, London, https://www.metropolitantabernacle.org/Seeds-of-the-Reformation (accessed 07.07.2022).

Oakley, F. (2015), *The Watershed of Modern Politics: Law, Virtue, Kingship and Consent (1300–1650)*, New Haven, CT: Yale University Press (Emergence of Western Political Thought in the Latin Middle Ages, 3).

Oberman, H. A. (1963), *Harvest of Medieval Theology, Gabriel Biel and Late Medieval Nominalism*, Cambridge, MA: Harvard University Press.

Oberman, H. A. (1981), *Masters of the Reformation: The Emergence of a New Intellectual Climate in Europe*, Cambridge: Cambridge University Press.

Oberman, H. A. (2008), *The Two Reformations: The Journey from the Last Days to the New World*, New Haven, CT: Yale University Press.

Oberman, H. A. & C. Caspers (1999), 'Magister Consensus Wessel Gansfort (1419–1489) und die Geistliche Kommunion', in F. Akkerma, G. C. Huisman & A. Vanderjagt (eds), *Wessel Gansfort (1419–1489) and Northern Humanism*, Leiden: Brill (Brill's Studies in Intellectual History, 40), p. 82–98.

Oosterhoff, R. J. (2018), *Making Mathematical Culture: University and Print in the Circle of Lefèvre d'Etaples*, Oxford: Oxford University Press (Oxford-Warburg Studies).

Ouy, G. (1998), *Gerson bilingue: les deux rédactions, latine et française, de quelques œuvres du chancelier parisien*, Paris: Honoré Champion (Études christiniennes, 2).

Post, R. R. (1968), *The Modern Devotion; Confrontation with Reformation and Humanism*, Leiden: Brill (Studies in Medieval and Reformation Thought, 3).

Rapp, F. (1994), 'Les caractères communs de la vie religieuse,' in J.-M. Mayeur, Ch. & L. Pietri, A. Vauchez & M. Venard (dir.), *Histoire du christianisme*, vol. 7, Paris: Desclée, p. 215–308.

Ritchey, S. (2013), 'Wessel Gansfort, John Mombaer, and Medieval Technologies of the Self: Affective Meditation in a Fifteenth-Century Emotional Community', in E. E. DuBruck, B. Gusick & R. Gasse (eds), *Fifteenth-Century Studies 38*, Rochester, NY: Boydell & Brewer, p. 153–174.

Rogahn, R. H. 'Johan Wessel Gansfort: His Role in the Ecclesiastical and Intellectual Currents of the Fifteenth Century' (unpublished doctoral thesis, University of Southern California, 1974). http://doi.org/10.25549/usctheses-c18-726047.

Rollo-Koster, J. & T. M. Izbicki (eds) (2009), *A Companion to the Great Western Schism* (1378–1417), Leiden: Brill (Brill's Companions to the Christian Tradition, 17).

Rupp, G. (1972), 'Protestant Spirituality in the First Age of the Reformation', in *Studies in Church History*, 8, p. 155–170.

Schaff, Ph. (1997), *History of the Christian Church, vol. VII. Modern Christianity. The German Reformation, § 64. Melanchthon's Theology*, Oak Harbor, WA: Logos Research Systems, Inc.

Sère, B. (2018), *Les régimes de polémicité au Moyen Âge*, Rennes: PUR.

Sère, B. (2016), *Les débats d'opinion à l'heure du Grande Schisme. Ecclésiologie et politique*, Turnhout: Brepols (Ecclesia militans, 6).

Shaffern, R. W. (1988), 'Indulgences and Saintly Devotionalisms in the Middle Ages', in *The Catholic Historical Review*, 84/4, p. 643–661.

Schüssler, R. (2011), 'Jean Gerson, Moral Certainty and the Renaissance of Ancient Scepticism', in H. E. Braun & E. Vallance (eds), *The Renaissance Conscience,* London: Wiley-Blackwell, p. 11–28.

Staubach, N. (1997), '*Memores priscae perfectionis*. The Importance of the Church Fathers for *Devotio moderna*', in I. Backus (ed.), *The Reception of the Church Fathers in the West: From the Carolingians to the Maurists*, 2 vols, Leiden: Brill, p. 405–474.

Tyler, P. M. (2017), 'Mystical Affinities: St Teresa and Jean Gerson', in E. Howells & P. M. Tyler (eds), *Teresa of Avila: Mystical Theology and Spirituality in the Carmelite Tradition*, London: Routledge, p. 36–50.

Ullmann, C. (1855), *Reformers before the Reformation: Principally in Germany and the Netherlands*, 2 vols, trans. R. Menzies, Edinburgh: T&T Clark (Clark's Foreign Theological Library, New Series, 6, 8).

Walker, H. H. (1919), 'A Reformer Before the Reformation', in *The American Journal of Theology*, 23/3, p. 381–383.

Weiler, A. G. (1999), 'The Dutch Brethren of the Common Life, Critical Theology', in F. Akkerman, A. Vanderjagt & A. Laan (eds), *Northern Humanism in European Context, 1469–1625: From the 'Adwert Academy' to Ubbo Emmius*, Leiden: Brill, (Brill's Studies in Intellectual History, 94) p. 307–332.

Woods, M., 'Trailblazers for Martin Luther: 5 Great Reformers' in *Christian Today*, 31 October 2016; https://www.christiantoday.com/article/trailblazers-for-martin-luther-5-great-reformers/99005.htm (accessed 07.07.2022).

Abstract

Existing scholarship on Johannes Wessel Gansfort (1420–1489) traditionally places his connection to Gerson (1363–1429) — chancellor at the University of Paris and the most significant intellectual figure of the late medieval period — in two theological contexts: the *devotio moderna*, and Lutheran historiography. After briefly presenting these two prevailing perspectives, this inquiry examines Gansfort's understanding and use of Gerson's opera and persona. Staying away from ideological bias and 'une construction théorique ouvertement confessionnelle',[89] the paper investigates a multitude of concrete textual links between the Parisian theologian and his Dutch admirer which have so far gone unexamined by scholars of either figure.

---

[89] Büttgen 2011, p. 78.

MARTA CELATI
Università di Pisa

CONDEMNING POLITICAL DISSENT AND ANTI-PRINCELY VIEWS IN FIFTEENTH-CENTURY MILANESE LITERATURE

Introduction

The consolidation of centralized governments in Renaissance Italy is a process that underwent major development during the second half of the fifteenth century, although, in some areas, one-man rulership had already been established during the preceding century. This historical phenomenon characterized the whole peninsula, with different specificities, and was interlaced with the growth of princely ideologies in the realm of political theorization.[1] One of the centres where the affirmation of signorial power was most evident and solid, also in its cultural expressions, is Milan. There, after the Visconti domination from the late thirteenth century to 1447, Francesco Sforza's takeover in 1450 (which followed the brief intermezzo of the Ambrosian Republic, 1447–1450) marked the beginning of a new phase of princely rule. This new regime found its sovereignty mainly by tracing a connection with the government of Filippo Maria Visconti, who died in 1447 and whose daughter, Bianca Maria, married the *condottiero* in 1441.[2] More generally, the Sforza, in direct

---

[1] On fifteenth-century political thought in Italy, see in particular Rubinstein 1991; Skinner 1978, I; Skinner 2002, II; Pastore Stocchi 2014; Hankins 1996, p. 118–141; Hankins 2019. On princely theories, see Gilbert 1977; Baker et al. 2016; Stacey 2007; Canfora 2005; and on political humanism, with a specific focus on Naples, see Cappelli 2016.

[2] Among the numerous contributions on the history of Milan in the fifteenth century, see the fundamental volumes of Cognasso 1955; Catalano 1956; and Chittolini 1990. On the Sforza's rule in particular, see Catalano 1985; *Gli Sforza* 1982; Santoro 1968; Lubkin 1994.

continuity with previous propagandistic practices, strengthened their ducal authority with the collaboration of intellectuals and *literati*, who were actively engaged in the creation of a sophisticated system of cultural politics in support of ducal power.[3] This multifaceted operation in the realm of literature celebrated the leaders in government and was aimed at their legitimization, but the literary operation also affected the authors' approach to the issues of political dissent and anti-princely views, which (despite the autocratic tendency of this territory) emerged during a few phases in the Milanese context and materialized in the opposition to signorial regimes.

A telling example of the fruitful cooperation between rulers and intellectuals in Milan appears in a substantial strand of official historiography: a literary genre that enjoyed exceptional expansion in the second half of the Quattrocento. In many cases, historiographers were appointed directly by ducal government, in particular under Francesco Sforza and Ludovico il Moro. This long-lasting cultural project led to the composition of works devoted to various periods of the city's history, but always with a specific outlook intended to uphold contemporary rulers; the project involved illustrious humanists and historians, such as Lodrisio Crivelli and Giovanni Simonetta, and later Giorgio Merula, Bernardino Corio, and others.[4] While scholars have paid more attention to the strategies of legitimizing signorial power through historical narrative,[5] considering how princely ideologies were built, shaped, and supported by the productive interplay of manifold literary genres is a field of research that still needs

---

[3] On the production of Milanese historiography as part of the system of cultural politics organized by the Sforza rule see Ianziti 1988; and, more generally, on the literary activity see Garin 1956; Tissoni Benvenuti, 1990.

[4] Studies on these historiographical works are still to be expanded: the main contributions are Ianziti 1988; Soldi Rondini 1983. Most texts have yet to be published in a modern edition: Lodrisio Crivelli's *De vita rebusque gestis Francisci Sfortiae*, composed between 1461 and 1463, is published in Crivelli 1731; Giovanni Simonetta's *Commentarii* on Francesco Sforza's deeds (a work devoted to the years 1444–1466 and which was probably finished by 1479) is published in Simonetta 1932. Giorgio Merula's unfinished *De antiquitate Vicecomitum*, a history of Milan from its origin to 1339, which was composed between *c.* 1485 and the author's death in 1494, is published only in the incunable: Merula 1499–1500; a modern edition of Corio's *Historia patria* may be found in Corio 1978.

[5] The most pivotal study in this field is still Ianziti 1988; see also footnote 3.

to be comprehensively investigated. The present article contributes to this area of study by going beyond conventional illustration of the literary praise of princes, and in particular by focusing on intellectuals' attitudes toward political dissent as that matter arises in different kinds of texts. As we shall see, the various works analysed here, though with distinctive undertones, prove to be consistently oriented towards the consolidation of central sovereignty, and sometimes even towards its unspoken definition, through the depiction of models of political conduct, both positive and negative, drawn from contemporary history. Looking at different sources can allow us to better understand how princely ideologies were elaborated and conveyed during this crucial age in Italy, particularly in Milan: a centre that influenced the development of political theory in the following centuries (although the city's variegated literary production still needs to be fully explored from this angle).[6]

My analysis concentrates on the representation of political dissent, and in particular anti-princely views, in fifteenth-century Milanese literature; the argument proceeds via an examination of multiple literary forms in which the topic of political *discordia*, and its decisive censure, was put forward by various writers. If critics have traditionally looked at the notion of *concordia* as the cornerstone of political systems in this age, the present investigation shifts the focus to the opposite, but related, concept of *discordia*, and to how it was portrayed, discussed, and condemned in literature.[7] This concept, and the whole semantic field pertaining to it,

---

[6] More attention has been paid to the development of princely political thought in the Kingdom of Naples, in part due to the more substantial production of 'mirrors for princes' in this area during the Quattrocento: see in particular, Delle Donne-Cappelli 2021; Cappelli 2016; Delle Donne 2015; Bentley 1987. In both Naples and Milan, however, during the same period, the theory of princely statecraft was elaborated not only in treatises but also in other literary works, especially in the form of 'official historiography': the political contribution of this output still needs to be explored comprehensively, but for the identification of the possible influence that Aragonese monarchical historiography might have had on the production of historical works in Milan under the Sforza see Ianziti 1988, p. 5–6. On Neapolitan historiography see Ferraù 2001; Albanese 2009.

[7] An extensive analysis of the pivotal role played by the concept of *concordia* in fourteenth- and fifteenth-century political culture may be found in Pedullà 2018, p. 10-26. The author claims that 'despite the fact that political factions are a classic theme of historiography on the Italian city-states, Renaissance reflections

is usually seen in relation to its antithesis: the opposite and positive pole consisting in social cohesion and political unity, which in this age were regarded as essential for any state to flourish.

In mid-Quattrocento Milan, opposition to centralized power found expression in two main phases. After Filippo Maria Visconti's death, in August 1447, a republican government was established: the so-called Ambrosian Republic, which lasted until Francesco Sforza's takeover in February 1450.[8] Almost thirty years later, in a new historical situation, political dissent against the Sforza resulted in a conspiracy against Galeazzo Maria, who was killed on 26 December 1476 in front of the church of Santo Stefano by three noblemen, Giovanni Andrea Lampugnani, Gerolamo Olgiati, and Carlo Visconti (and other fellow conspirators).[9] These noblemen were driven by a deeply rooted hostility against Galeazzo Maria's autocratic rule and by classical anti-tyrannical tenets:[10] Lampugnani and Olgiati, in particular, had been inspired by Nicola Capponi, called Cola Montano, who was a humanist active in Milan between 1458 and 1475 and a professor of rhetoric in Bologna in 1476–1477. Capponi used to associate the figure of the duke with Tarquinius Superbus, the last despotic Roman king, and praised the most famous tyrannicides of the classical tradition (especially Caesar's killing by Brutus and Cassius).[11] This attempted revolt was thwarted since the rebels were killed or captured. After the duke's murder by the group of plotters, Lampugnani, who was the first to stab Galeazzo on the threshold of the church of Santo Stefano, tried to flee, exploiting the tumult that arose in the church, but he tripped over a woman's dress and was immediately killed by a loyal guard (a *staffiere*) of Galeazzo, called

---

on the evils of discord have not attracted much attention in scholarship' (p. 12, n. 3), and he mentions a few exceptions: Hyde 1972; Bruni 2003. On concord in the classical tradition, see Amit 1962; Loraux 2002; Rocchi 2007.

[8] On the Ambrosian Republic see in particular Cognasso 1955, p. 385–448.

[9] On Galeazzo Maria Sforza, see Lubkin 1994; on the conspiracy and the figures involved in it, see Belotti 1965; Fubini 1994, p. 107–135, 220–252, 327–350; Ilardi 1986; Orvieto 1976; Vaglienti 2002; Vaglienti 2004.

[10] On Galeazzo Maria Sforza's government and his maladministration, see in particular Ilardi 1986, p. 76–80.

[11] On the issue of tyranny in the late Middle Ages and the Renaissance see Hankins 2019, p. 103–152; Quaglioni 1983; Schadee 2018a. On tyrannicide see Turchetti 2013, p. 291–318, 335–365; Villard 2008; Piccolomini 1991.

Moro (because of his dark complexion).[12] The other main conspirators, Olgiati and Visconti, who managed to escape in the first instance, were arrested and jailed. Despite its failure, this plot was a crucial event in the history of the fifteenth century and showed the weaknesses of the Milanese *Signoria* and a general repressed discontent against the duke's maladministration; nevertheless, the Sforza family reacted firmly and maintained power with the regent Bona of Savoy, the widow of the assassinated ruler and mother of the young heir Gian Galeazzo Maria.

From a broader perspective, the issues of political dissent and social upheavals in fifteenth-century Italy were mainly addressed through depicting the danger of political disunity in the state. Especially in the realm of literature, this depiction reinforced the disapproval of popular regimes and of any attempt to overturn established powers (including subversive attempts by noblemen). Indeed, humanists and literati in their works, besides deploring internecine division and factions, often narrate how seditious practices were suppressed by centralized rule, which was seen as the sole guarantor of the common good and the security of society. The condemnation of rebellion and political division characterized almost all Italian states in this age. This phenomenon also applies to Florence,[13] the cultural centre that has been traditionally associated with the growth of republican ideology and the celebration of *libertas* in the early Quattrocento, and that was identified (in direct contrast with Milan) as the home of 'civic humanism', as theorized by Hans Baron.[14] In recent decades, however, this theory has been reconsidered, together with the rigid distinction between republican and princely ideologies in this age.[15] The very relevance of this contrast to the Quattrocento context has been challenged, and the distinction itself is no longer regarded as suitable for providing a comprehensive definition of the complex and multifaceted character of humanist political

---

[12] This figure (identified as 'Gallo Mauro') is mentioned in Corio 1978, II, p. 1401; and in Paolo Giovio's reconstruction of the event in his *Elogia*: Giovio 2006, p. 647.

[13] See in particular Najemy 2000, where specific attention is paid to these topics in the analysis of political works in early fifteenth-century Florence.

[14] Baron 1955.

[15] Hankins 1995; Hankins 2000; Hankins 2010; Witt 1996; Cappelli 2009.

thought, especially if we consider the oligarchic and imperialistic nature of a republican government like Florence (and its evolution under the Medici rule).[16] In particular, while it is true that an antithesis between these two political forms was often put forward in humanist works, especially with regard to the conflict between Florence and Milan in the early fifteenth century,[17] nonetheless, the celebration of republican governments was not always based on authentic institutional elements and was mainly oriented to the affirmation of elitist regimes. This approach characterizes, for example, the political stance of Leonardo Bruni, the humanist who is traditionally regarded as the chief representative of Florentine civic humanism. Also his linguistic views concerning the nature and domain of Latin in comparison with that of the Florentine vernacular have been recognized as an expression of his political position in support of rule by the upper classes and humanist elites. Such rule would naturally exclude the lower parts of society and suppress their claims (for example those of the Ciompi, whose revolt in 1378 had already been decisively condemned by one of most influential figures of Florentine culture during those years, Coluccio Salutati).[18] From a more general perspective, we see that the denunciation of social conflict and the corresponding praise of political unity informed the majority of historical and political literature throughout Italy in the early Quattrocento and even more prominently during the second half of the century (both in princely states and in an oligarchic republic such as Florence).[19]

As for Milan, the issues of political dissent, insubordination, and anti-signorial government found extensive treatment in lit-

---

[16] On these aspects of the Florentine Republic, see Najemy 2000; Hankins 1995; Schadee 2018b. On the evolution of the government in Florence under the Medici, see Rubinstein 1966; Jones 1965; Black-Law 2015.

[17] For example, one of the most famous pieces of this literature is the controversy between Poggio Bracciolini and Guarino Veronese (1435) regarding Scipio and Caesar. See the critical edition in Canfora 2001.

[18] On Bruni, see Schadee 2018b (with a specific focus on his political and linguistic views) and, more generally, Ianziti 2012; and Najemy 2000. For Salutati's position on popular uprisings (with reference, either directly or indirectly, to the Ciompi revolt), see De Rosa 1980, p. 156–157; Salutati 1893, p. 84–86 (cf. also Schadee 2018b, p. 42). On the revolt of the Ciompi, see in particular Stella 1993.

[19] See Celati 2021, p. 16–20.

erature, especially in relation to two historical landmarks, namely, the Ambrosian Republic and the plot against the Sforza. The sources examined in the present article as significant case studies belong to different genres (such as epistles, orations, histories, poems) and were written either in Latin or the vernacular (languages that prove to be employed to convey the same political views, thought they correspond to specific, but also often interrelated, channels of communication). The works in questions either were produced by important intellectuals close to Milanese power, such as Francesco Filelfo, Antonio Cornazzano, and Bernardino Corio, or targeted a more popular audience, as did the *Lamento del duca Galeazzo Maria*, which enjoyed widespread diffusion especially in the sixteenth century.[20] The analysis of these sources (which have never been examined from this point of view, and in some cases have never been published in modern editions yet) reveals how both the historical phase of the Ambrosian Republic and the conspiracy against the Sforza Duke were reconstructed in literature. The reconstruction is imbued with a specific ideological perspective oriented towards the suppression of internal conflict and supporting the principle of political cohesion in a verticalized state. These outcomes are primarily achieved by overturning the main tenets that inspired the dissidents and by condemning their actions through a studied portrayal of anti-princely forces as driven by corrupt, immoral, and even criminal intentions. As we shall see, the aims and principles that were at the foundations of these political enterprises in Milan (similar to comparable attempts in the rest of Italy) were rarely taken into account in coeval historiographical and literary texts;[21] conversely, dissident political tenets were objected to, and in the end defeated, mainly by adopting and imposing a propagandistic view that links them with the notion of civic *discordia*. This was commonly regarded in the Renaissance as an important but totally negative concept: discord was seen as the most dangerous threat to any state and the

---

[20] Bibliography on these authors and their works is provided in the footnotes on the individual texts.

[21] On other conspiracies in the fifteenth century (a period that has been defined as an 'age of conspiracies'), see Fubini 1994, p. 220–252; Martines 1968; and on the production of a substantial corpus of literary works about political plots in early Renaissance Italy, see Celati 2021.

opposite to its essential ingredient, concord, which is instead the core of an ideal political system seen as a hierarchical and harmonious organism.[22]

This political perspective was not new and had a long tradition, from classical antiquity through the Middle Ages. As early as the thirteenth century, the ideas of civic accord and the common good were at the heart of political theorization, and their importance was reflected in the general rejection of rebellion and factionalism as detrimental to any social community. Such an ideological position was often put forward in literary and historical works and was even emphasized in fifteenth-century political thought, thanks to the substantial recovery of classical sources that were adapted to the contemporary historical situation. One of the most emblematic models is Sallust and the political view epitomized in the very famous passage from the *Bellum Iugurthinum* (10, 6): *concordia parvae res crescunt, discordia maximae dilabuntur* ('in concord small things grow, in discord even the greatest things ruin'). This quotation enjoyed remarkable diffusion in the Middle Age and was regularly re-employed in humanist texts:[23] although the sentiment was in its origin more directly correlated with a republican background, now the quotation was re-elaborated in a more flexible way and in different contexts, regardless of the form of government relevant to the particular discussion.[24] More generally, similar classical principles were often deployed to amplify the celebration of the *concordia civium*, which was turned into a goal in itself. Especially in signorial centres like Milan, ideas deriving from classical political thought, even from the republican tradition, were evoked in literary works principally to denounce the danger arising from sedition and the prospect of popular governments.

---

[22] On the idea of the state as an organic system, and more generally on the notion of body politic, see Kantorowicz 1957 (chapter V); for this concept in the Italian Renaissance, see Cappelli 2012; Najemy 1995.

[23] On the reuse of this quotation in the medieval and humanist tradition, see Pedullà 2018, p. 15 (where the author provides references of the texts which cite this passage); Skinner 2002, II, p. 23–24; Witt 2012, p. 258. More generally, on the reception of Sallust in the Middle Ages and the Renaissance, see La Penna 1968; Skinner 1995; Osmond 1995; Osmond 2000; and Celati 2021.

[24] For a reconsideration of the distinction between republican and monarchic ideologies in Italian Humanism, see again Hankins 1995; Hankins 2000; Hankins 2010; Cappelli 2009.

Any attempt at subverting the political *status quo* of centralized power was presented as provoked by the corruption and amorality of the rebels and dissidents, who, when involved in conspiracies, were usually described with the traits of Sallust's Catiline.[25]

The Ambrosian Republic

The brief phase of the Ambrosian Republic occupies a central position in several literary works produced in Milan. Such is the case with the literary output of Francesco Filelfo, one of the most illustrious intellectuals active in Milan already under Filippo Maria Visconti, from 1439, and very close to signorial power. Filelfo repeatedly reserved his bitterest criticism for popular government, a standpoint that informed the whole of his elitist political views and emerged with particular vigour in his remarks and reflections on this turbulent period of Milanese history.[26] His disapproving comments and gloomy descriptions are embedded in a number of his works: letters, orations, and poetry (i.e. both his odes and satires concerning those years).[27] In his literary representations, the inner conflict that enervated the Milanese government and the situation of civic disorder under republican rule were emphasized by a radically anti-popular stance, which would remain central to Filelfo's ideology throughout his life, revealing the persistent influence that this experience had in the evolution of his political thought.[28]

Significantly, during the Ambrosian Republic he was also actively involved in the city's political life, as proved by three

---

[25] On this issue: Celati 2021.

[26] The most complete study of Filelfo's biography is still Rosmini 1808 (on the phase of the Ambrosian Republic, II, p. 38–52); on his multifaceted literary output, see also De Keyser 2019. On Filelfo's activity under the Sforza's rule see Robin 1991; and Adam 1974.

[27] The *Odes* are published in a new critical edition in Filelfo 2020; and with an English translation in Filelfo 2009. For the *Odes* concerning the period of the Ambrosian Republic and their vigorous anti-republican perspective see Celati 2017; and Robin 1991, p. 88–97. Filelfo's epistolary collection is published in the edition Filelfo 2015. On Filelfo's political thought see Hankins 2019, p. 351–363. Filelfo's main works devoted to the figure of Francesco Sforza (the poem *Sphortias* and the *Oratio parentalis*) are published in De Keyser 2015; on the *Sphortias* see De Keyser 2016; Bottari 1986.

[28] On Filelfo's political ideology see in particular Hankins 2019, p. 351–363.

official speeches that he wrote on the occasion of some formal changes in the leading administration. The most significant of these orations, entitled *Oratio ad principes senatum et populum Mediolanensem de laudibus illustris Karoli Gonzagae populi praesidis et praefecti* ('Oration to the princes, senate and the people of Milan in praise of the illustrious guardian and captain of the people Carlo Gonzaga'), was written to celebrate the reconfirmation of Carlo Gonzaga as *Capitano del popolo* on 8 July 1449,[29] an appointment that had already been assigned to Gonzaga on 4 November 1448 and that elevated the Mantuan *condottiero* to the role of leader of the republican institutions.[30] This was a turning point that marked the transition from a more popular government, which was led by the so called 'triumvirate' of Giovanni Ossona, Giovanni Appiani and Gabriele Taverna, to a more oligarchic rule.[31] The new administration, however, lasted only until 11 September 1449, when Gonzaga rejoined Francesco Sforza's forces (Gonzaga had already fought alongside Sforza, but defected before being appointed *Capitano del popolo*) and was finally given the role of ruler *pro tempore* by Sforza after the latter's final takeover at the beginning of 1450.[32] Filelfo was a direct witness of all these sudden political shifts.

The humanist's first-hand experience of this unstable political scenario leaves traces in several literary writings, particularly in the aforementioned epideictic oration to Gonzaga, composed as an official work, and in Filelfo's letters to various interlocu-

---

[29] Only one copy of this oration is still extant; the codex, which is kept in the Biblioteca Ambrosiana in Milan, is ms. F 55 sup. (f. 13r–17v). The other two official orations composed by Filelfo are included in the same manuscript: *Oratio ad Mediolanenses principes de administratione reipublicae* (f. 31r–33v) can be dated to 1 July 1449; *Oratio in creatione domini Capitaneorum et defensione libertatis Mediolani* (c. 37r–38v) was delivered on 1 November 1448. These works have been almost totally neglected by critics; on the oration to Carlo Gonzaga, see Celati 2017.

[30] On Carlo Gonzaga see Lazzarini 2001; and on his military activity in the context of the Ambrosian Republic see also Cognasso 1955, p. 422–423. On the relationship between Filelfo and the Gonzaga family see Luzio-Renier 1890; and Celati 2017.

[31] In his oration to Carlo Gonzaga, Filelfo defines this phase of the Milanese republican government as *diri atque impii triumviratus* ('cruel and evil triumvirate'): Milan, Biblioteca Ambrosiana, ms. F 55 sup., f. 13v.

[32] See again Cognasso 1955, p. 422–423.

tors in those years. This correspondence, despite belonging to the realm of personal writing, acquires a public dimension (as is often the case with epistolography), as evidenced by the author's lifelong project of creating his own epistolary collection.[33] In these diverse but ideologically interconnected literary strands, epistolography and oratory, Filelfo manifests his concern for the chaotic political situation in Milan under the Republic, underlining two main ideological points that would remain fixed in his political thought. First, he expresses hostility to any popular government or dominion by the *vulgus*, which is seen as the chief menace to social cohesion and to the activity of intellectuals. Furthermore, he criticises any kind of sedition or internal political conflict, which Filelfo regards as typical of rule by the people. In particular, he describes the republican regime in Milan as marked by incessant violent fights between opposed factions and by brutal political actions carried out by popular forces, including confiscations and murders perpetrated against the aristocratic class. Such an elitist political view results in a decisive censure of any 'anti-princely ideology', which Filelfo recognizes as emerging in the Milanese context immediately after Filippo Maria Visconti's death, as the humanist openly states in a letter to Giovanni Feruffini, written on 15 August 1447 and, a few days later, on 1 September, in an epistle addressed to Giovanni Aurispa. Filelfo declares his deep apprehension at the growing political dissent against ducal power and underlines the condition of instability, violence, and anarchy that accompanied the establishment of the republican government:

> *Tumultuaria sunt omnia.* [...] *In hac tamen rerum omnium perturbatione videntur omnes publicam libertatem appetere* [...]. *Vaehementissimae mihi videntur procellae tempestatesque impendere* [...]. *Ni Deus ipse providerit, maximi fluctus naufragiaque sequentur.*
>
> (Everything is in a tumultuous state. [...] In this general turmoil, it seems that everyone yearns for public liberty [...].

---

[33] Filelfo's epistles were collected around the 1470s in a manuscript that was put together under the supervision of the humanist himself: this important manuscript is now in Milan, Biblioteca Trivulziana, ms. 873. See now the edition: Filelfo 2015.

It seems to me that the most violent storms loom over us [...].
If God himself will not intervene, the most dangerous waves
and shipwrecks will be the consequence.) [34]

*Nam hic omnia sunt turbulenta. Post obitum illius nobilissimi
principis, Philippi Mariae, qui unus iure meritoque potuit cum
omni hominum memoria de gloria certare, mira hic facta est
mutatio in animis huius populi. [...] ita sunt omnes ad laxam
quandam et dissolutam libertatem incensi atque inflamati, ut
nihil magis oderint quam unius Philippi illius nomen.*[35]

(Indeed here everything is in turmoil. After the death of the
illustrious prince, Filippo Maria Visconti, who is the only
one who can rightly and deservedly compete with the memory of glory of any other man, it is remarkable to see to what
extent the common people changed their mind. [...] all are
inflamed by an unregulated and dissolute liberty and everyone hates nothing more than the distinguished name
of Filippo.)

Significantly Filelfo's pro-signorial outlook is intertwined with a
bitter denunciation of the thoughtlessness of any popular opposition to princely authority. Such opposition is seen as an inconsiderate position and the ultimate cause of the condition of misery
and decadence in which the whole Milanese community has fallen
under the new rule. This same point of view is stressed in an even
more emphatic passage in a letter to Bornio Sala (dated 25 July
1449), where, with a sarcastic and caustic remark, Filelfo mocks
the common people's opposition to signorial domination:

*Atque mirabilis tamen est civitatis huius constantia, ut emori
omnes malint quam dominum quenquam admittere.*[36]

(It is striking to see the constancy of this civic community:
they all prefer to die rather than accept any leader.)

But what is most noteworthy is that in the aforementioned letters to Feruffini and Aurispa, which deal with the situation after

---

[34] Letter to Giovanni Feruffini, 15 August 1447: Filelfo 2015, I, p. 340 (PhE.06.25). All translations in this article are mine.

[35] Letter to Giovanni Aurispa, 1 September 1447: Filelfo 2015, I, p. 340 (PhE.06.26).

[36] Filelfo 2015, I, p. 359 (PhE.06.60).

Visconti's death, Filelfo's disapproval of the common people's position is framed by placing the focus on two elements (one mainly rhetorical, the other more conceptual), which both occur regularly in the humanist's literary output in these years. First, in the epistle to Feruffini, Filelfo represents the situation of disorder and brutal conflict surrounding the Ambrosian Republic through the image of a stormy sea and shipwreck; second, in both letters, Filelfo places the concept of *libertas* in a negative light, describing the popular struggle for freedom as inspired by a degenerate and perilous form of liberty.

The symbolic depiction of the Milanese milieu as a tempestuous sea recurs in Filelfo's correspondence and is also employed in his oration in praise of Carlo Gonzaga.[37] This metaphor becomes an actual rhetorical *topos* in the humanist's output, and its purpose is to convey the author's political views in an effective and sophisticated manner, through a literary frame that enhances his ideological message by means of a powerful poetic and visual image. More generally, the symbolic representation of adversity as a windy sea, against which the human soul resists like a rock beaten by the waves of fortune, was already present in the classical tradition; one of the image's most evocative manifestations can be found in Cicero's *Ad familiares*, 9, 16.[38] In Filelfo's work, an analogous image acquires specific political overtones as a symbol of the unrestrained forces of the masses (not just of the general uncontrolled power of fortune) and becomes a vehicle of elitist political ideology, condensing in itself the ideas of civil *discordia* and insubordination, which are seen as the main obstacles to social tranquillity. In particular, in a letter to Alberto Zancani of 1 February 1448, Filelfo, adopting a personal stance, describes himself as victim of a shipwreck, hit by the waves of civic turmoil,

---

[37] A similar image opens the *Oratio ad Mediolanenses principes de administratione reipublicae*: Milan, Biblioteca Ambrosiana, ms. F 55 sup, f. 31v.

[38] *Ita fit ut et consiliorum superiorum conscientia et praesentis temporis moderatione me consoler et illam Acci similitudinem non modo iam ad invidiam sed ad fortunam transferam, quam existimo levem et imbecillam ab animo firmo et gravi tamquam fluctum a saxo frangi oportere*. Significantly a similar metaphorical representation can be also found in the very famous descriptions of fortune in Leon Battista Alberti's *Libri della famiglia* (I, *Prologo*) and Machiavelli's *Il principe*, 25 (where the action of fortune is symbolically associated to the force of waves or a river, respectively).

and he claims to find shelter only in the 'harbour' provided by his reading, an image that adds a further layer to the symbolism of the storm:

> *Omnis mea consuetudo hoc tempore est cum libris. Itaque semotus a popularibus fluctibus, ne peream naufragio, institui tandiu in huiusmodi portu me continere, donec alicunde secundus aliquis ventus aspiret* [...] [39]
>
> (In this time, books are my only company. Removing myself from the common people's waves, I decided to shelter in such a harbour, in order not to die in a shipwreck, and I will wait for a favourable wind to blow from somewhere.)

In another epistle to Aurispa, dated 27 July 1449, Filelfo explicitly links the image of sailing in unsafe waters to the denunciation of the general peril brought about by civil sedition:

> *Ego, mi Aurispa, in Syrtibus navigo, unde sine maximo periculo erumprere non licet* [...]. *Ubique gentium hoc tempore quam Mediolani esse mallem; ubi neque sine maximo periculo esse possum propter civilis seditiones.*[40]
>
> (My Aurispa, I am sailing in the shallows of Syrtes, where it is impossible to escape without the most dangerous risk [...]. In this time I would prefer to be anywhere except in Milan, where I cannot live if not in the most serious danger on account of civil sedition.)

In addition, Filelfo opens his *oratio* to Gonzaga with the same political symbolism of the storm. This image functions as the introduction to a colourful and detailed description of the internecine conflict and viciousness in the city during the early phase of the Ambrosian Republic, a situation that is put to an end by the new administration (welcomed by Filelfo in his speech):

> *Cum superiores totos sex menses mecum ipse cogitarem, patres conscripti, quam in gravi atque periculosa rerum perturbatione ac procella nostra civitas fluctuaret, dolebam equidem maiorem in modum et quam acerbissime animi cruciabar.* [...]

---

[39] Filelfo 2015, I, p. 345 (PhE.06.37).
[40] Filelfo 2015, I, p. 359 (PhE.06.61).

> *Nam in agro Mediolanensi diripiebantur villae ac villici [...]. At Mediolani, consternatis omnium animis, opulentissimae omnes familiae per omnem ludibrii foeditatem vertebantur in praedam. Cives omnes innocentissimi, qui aut pecunia aut animi magnitudine pollere putarentur, continuo confictis falsisque criminibus aut relegati aut proscripti aut atrocissime necati Ossonam et Aplanam rabiem ne explere quidem suo sanguine poterant. Omnis sacratissimorum templorum ornatus, omnis christiana relligio, omnis divinus cultus cogebatur truculentissimarum libidini belvarum immanitatique parere.*[41]

> (When over the last six months I considered, fathers and counsellors, the terrible and dangerous adversity and storms through which our city was sailing, I grieved more and more, and was most bitterly distraught in my heart. [...]

> For in Milanese territory the country houses and villas were plundered [...]. But in Milan itself all the richest families, to their great consternation, were treated disgustingly and turned into prey. All the most innocent citizens, who were regarded as authoritative in virtue of their money or their nobility of heart, were immediately accused of false crimes and exiled or proscribed or killed in an atrocious manner, and could not even appease Ossona's and Appiani's anger with their blood. Every ornament of the most sacred temples, the whole of the Christian religion, and all aspects of divine worship were forced to obey the lust and barbarity of very ferocious beasts.)

According to this vivid representation of the cruel misdeeds that the popular government perpetrated against the aristocracy, that government was guilty of abusing power and especially of creating a condition of chaos and reprisal against the oligarchic and intellectual classes. This portrayal reveals once more Filelfo's elitist political and cultural views. The dark and unsettling picture of this government, and in particular of its leaders, who are described

---

[41] The text of the oration is quoted from the manuscript in Milan, Biblioteca Ambrosiana, F 55 sup. (f. 13r–v). Original spelling has been maintained, with the exception of the distinction between *v*/*u*, which have been normalized according to modern criteria; diphthongs are introduced according to classical criteria and Filelfo's habits (on the humanist's orthographical uses, see Filelfo 2005, p. cxlvii–cli); punctuation and capitalization have been modernized, and obvious mistakes have been corrected.

as 'ferocious beasts',[42] is reinforced in a subsequent passage that equates this regime with tyranny: the 'triumvirorum impia tyrannis' ('the evil tyranny of the triumviri').[43] These words define a degenerate form of authority, which is in the hands of despots who maintain the state in a perpetual condition of discord and are driven by personal interests. The contrast between the search for the common good and for the pursuit of private benefit is the main factor that distinguished rightful rule from the tyrannical regimes from antiquity, as in the very famous discussion of tyranny in Aristotle's *Politics* (V).

The representation of the republic in Milan as tyrannical is taken a step further by Filelfo by when he introduces an additional parallel: the popular faction, as we have seen, is portrayed as led not merely by authoritarian figures, but by actual criminals. This denunciation of their offences is framed by a moral perspective that overlaps with a political judgment. Moreover, the studied employment of the definition of *tyrannis* as a label for the anti-signorial forces in government is directly connected to another ideological point that is central to Filelfo's works in these years: the use of the concept of *libertas* seen from a princely perspective and interpreted through the lens of criticism of counter-monarchical principles. Significantly, as previously observed, the notion of liberty (which is traditionally considered at the basis of republican movements) is described by Filelfo in his letter to Aurispa (of 1 September 1447) as *dissoluta* and *laxa* ('dissolute and unrestrained'). These two adjectives underline specific negative implications and deplore political dissent against ducal power as inspired by the search for a degenerate form of liberty. In the humanist's view, this corrupted and inauthentic liberty would result in the condition of chaos, excess, and lack of order (encapsulated in the definition of *dissoluta* and *laxa*) that is understood as typical of republican rule in Milan.

It is striking that this very idea of liberty also appears in the narrative devoted to the Ambrosian Republic in one of the most

---

[42] Giovanni Appiani, Giovanni Ossona, Gabriele Taverna; the last one, together with Giorgio Bizzozzero (another member of the popular faction) is evoked only obliquely by Filelfo and is never openly mentioned. Taverna and Bizzozero are victims of *damnatio memoriae*: see Celati 2017, p. 131–132.

[43] Milan, Biblioteca Ambrosiana, ms. F 55 sup., f. 13v.

important histories of Milan in the Renaissance: Bernardino Corio's *Historia patria*. This vernacular history of the city, from its origin to the beginning of the sixteenth century, was composed between 1485 and 1503 by the historian officially appointed by Ludovico il Moro.[44] Although Corio's historical reconstruction is somehow more balanced and not as biased as that of other historians and *literati* of this age (who generally show a more apparent propagandistic attitude in favour of established leaders), the *Historia patria* displays an approach similar to Filelfo's outlook in the portraying the government led by anti-signorial factions. This approach is also parallel to that of Giovanni Simonetta in his *Commentarii* on Francesco Sforza's *gesta*, a fundamental source for Corio's work, together with Cristoforo Landino's vernacular translation of Simonetta's *Commentarii*, which was commissioned by Ludovico il Moro himself, finished around 1485, and published in Milan in 1490: this *volgarizzamento* is often literally quoted by Corio, especially as far as the narrative of the Ambrosian Republic is concerned.[45] This republican rule is significantly defined as 'tyranny' and is described as a time of disorder and uncontrolled violence:

> *A Milano in questo tempo crescevano le discordie e dissensione et ogni cosa era in summa perturbatione, e quegli che sotto colorato studio occupavano la tiramnia già più non erano né reveriti né temuti, il perché in tutta la città in varii luochi molti tumulti se excitavano, per tutto se sentevano querelle, pianti e strida.*[46]
>
> (In this time, discord and dissent grew in Milan and everything was in the greatest turmoil; and those who, with a studied operation, established tyranny were not revered and

---

[44] The text is published in Corio 1978; on Bernardino Corio and his *Historia* see Petrucci 1983; and Meschini 1995.

[45] On Corio's use of these sources see Ianziti 2005, p. 466; Petruccci 1983; Bongrani 1986; Annoni 1874. On Landino's translation of Simonetta's work, which was published in its *editio princeps* in Milan in 1490 by Antonio Zarotto, see also Comanducci 1992. The *editio princeps* of Simonetta's *Commentarii* itself was also published by Zarotto, between 1481 and 1483, after the emission of the official ducal *privilegio*: see in particular Ianziti 1982 (now in Ianziti 1988).

[46] Corio 1978, II, p. 1327. A very similar description in Giovanni Simonetta's work: Simonetta 1932, p. 337. However, Corio's most direct source (here and in other passages) is Landino's translation of Simonetta's text: see Bongrani 1986, p. 43–44.

feared anymore, because tumult was triggered in the whole city in various places, and everywhere you could hear fights, cries and screams.)

This picture highlights the state of *discordia* and uproar distinctive of this political moment, which originated from the affirmation of dissent against signorial power and generated division and violent tensions in the social body. This reading of the political situation is stressed by the frequent use in a few lines of terms that evokes political chaos: *discordie, dissensione, perturbatione, tumulti, querelle*. Moreover, another telling passage alludes to the degeneration that the genuine concept of liberty underwent. This degeneration is condensed in the emblematic expression *ficta libertate* ('fake liberty'), which is adopted to refer to the principles that were at the foundations of anti-princely movements and popular rule:

> [...] *ogni cosa era piena di pianti, ululi, stride e di lamenti, e nientedimeno a niuno era licito parlare se non de la ficta libertate* [...] [47]
>
> ([...] everything was full of tears, howls, cries, and laments, and no one was allowed to talk about anything but 'false' liberty.)

In a subsequent pivotal section, the concept of *libertà* is again portrayed negatively, in order to prove that centralized authority is preferable to any government based on an illusory ideal of liberty, which keeps the whole civic community in poverty:

> [...] *nisuna magiore commodità se poteva fare a la città che ritenere dentro il conte Franscesco Sforza et il primo fu* [scil. Gaspare da Vimercate] *che monstrò de la libertà non se puoteva fare stima alchuna, sì per le molte discordie civile, sì anchora perché era tanto voto il populo de pecunie e tanto oppresso da la fame che più non se puoteva defendere.*[48]
>
> (...nobody could do anything better for the city than welcome the count Francesco Sforza; and he [Gaspare da Vimercate]

---

[47] Corio 1978, II, p. 1326.
[48] Corio 1978, II, p. 1330. For the close correspondence between this passage in Corio's work and Landino's translation of Simonetta's *Commentarii*, see Bongrani 1986, p. 44–45.

was the first who showed that liberty could not be prized and taken in any account, because of the numerous civil conflicts, and also because the common people were so poor and troubled by hunger that they could not defend themselves.)

This disenchanted but unblinkered political judgment coincides with the thought of Gaspare da Vimercate (a military man who fought in Sforza's army and had a political role in the republican institutions too), but is presented as shared by the historian himself. This passage anticipates the section of the text devoted to Sforza's triumphal entry into Milan as the new *princeps*, where Corio emphasizes the general favour of the Milanese people for the *condottiero* and celebrates his takeover as a fundamental turning point in the history of Milan.[49] Sforza's advent is regarded as a decisive landmark: it finally put an end to the condition of internecine conflict that afflicted the whole state and that was misinterpreted by the people as a counterpart of liberty. Indeed, this *libertas* was actually a delusional ideal and only a feigned freedom. It is true that Corio was definitely a partisan of ducal sovereignty, since his work was commissioned by one of the successors of Francesco Sforza, namely his son Ludovico il Moro (who aimed to legitimize his own power by glorifying his father's rule and establishing a connection with it): therefore it is not surprising that the historian supported this ideological standpoint, which also informs the sources he uses and often quotes (in particular Landino's translation of Simonetta's *Commentarii*).[50] Notably this reconstruction views the idea of liberty from a princely angle and overturns some of its traditional nuances: such a perspective was already present in the texts that Filelfo wrote during the republican period. In the aforementioned key passage, it is openly claimed that freedom is not a fundamental political principle in comparison with the common good and *concordia*. Thus the new signorial government was prized because it eradicated discord and subdued the political dissent that had been the cause of misery and decadence for the city. From a broader point of view, such a conception, which was characteristic of traditional monarchical theories, was enhanced

---

[49] See Colombo 1905.
[50] See footnote 45.

in the fifteenth century, when the conventional political tenets of unity and safeguarding the state were placed at the forefront of developing princely ideologies and functioned as justifying ideals for the autocratic policies of newly established leaders.

The Plot against the Sforza

Another crucial watershed in the political history of fifteenth-century Milan is the 1476 conspiracy against Galeazzo Maria, Francesco Sforza's heir. Most works (or sections of works) dedicated to this episode reveal a similar ideological stance in their presentation of the two main factors in the political system: princely authority and, as its negative complementary pole, the opposition to it. Princely authority guarantees social cohesion and prosperity, while opposition to it causes political disintegration in the state, and is, once again, based on an illusory and detrimental idea of liberty. Among the numerous sources for this event, a not very well-known poetic work is particularly noteworthy for its original thematic and rhetorical structure: Antonio Cornazzano's *Capitolo sulla morte di Galeazzo Maria Sforza* (1477). This work is a short poem in the vernacular written by a humanist who was very close to Francesco Sforza: Cornazzano had been active in Milan from around 1454, but, after the duke's death in 1466, he lived mainly in Venice and Malpaga, and in 1475 moved to Ferrara and put his literary talent at the service of the Este family; however, his bond with Milan remained tight, as the literary work on Galeazzo Maria's murder shows.[51] In a sophisticated poetic transposition in *terzine*, the *Capitolo* portrays the emblem of the best Milanese ruler, Francesco Sforza, in the afterlife, where he meets his son after the assassination. Here the father describes how an ideal *princeps* should behave, and his words contain an implicit criticism of his heir's rule, which was almost unanimously perceived as autocratic, maladministered, and distant from a fair regime. In particular, the

---

[51] The text is published in the edition printed in Venice in 1571: *Opera Nova*, f. Dvi[v]–Eiii[v] (with the heading: *Miser Antonio Cornazano per lo illustrissimo Ducha Galeazzo de Milano*). On Cornazzano's biography and his literary output, see Fahy 1964; Bruni-Zancani 1992; Farenga 1983; Dionisotti 1980, p. 352–362; on his main political work, the poem *Del modo di regere e di regnare*, see Musso 1999; Zancani 2000.

main protection for any state is considered to be the subjects' love for their ruler, in accordance with the traditional political theory which prescribes that a prince must be loved rather than feared.[52] In this highly propagandistic work, however, Cornazzano ensures that he also provides enough justification for Galeazzo Maria's despotic behaviour. Thus the murdered prince himself replies to his father, explaining that his young age was the principal cause of his mistakes, together with his bad advisors, the envy of the courtiers around him, and his excessive liberality (which was misjudged for ostentation and waste of resources).[53]

Significantly, Cornazzano also introduces into his *Capitolo* a long section in which Francesco Sforza addresses in a direct speech the main conspirator, Giovanni Andrea Lampugnani, and censures him and his political act as a threat to the whole fatherland (and not as an attack against a despotic ruler). Sforza also stresses, once again, the misleading and feigned idea of liberty that is at the basis of the plotters' inconsiderate enterprise. In general, the conspirators were unanimously condemned in literary sources devoted to this event. Olgiati and Visconti were captured and jailed, and the former gave a lengthy confession detailing the plan of the assassination and the rebels' motives: this document is included in Corio's *Historia patria* and can be read as an admission of guilt.[54] But it is Lampugnani who became the actual scapegoat after the plot, due in part to his immediate demise after the prince's assassination. Lampugnani was recognized as the foremost leader of the conspiracy and became the principal target of pro-Sforza propaganda: he was described as a modern Catiline, corrupted by vices and driven by personal interests and despotic ambitions. This interpretation reversed and removed the anti-tyrannical beliefs that actually animated the plotters. Significantly, Cornazzano's poem effectively conveys this political message, thanks to the studied rhetorical construc-

[52] On this concept of *mutua caritas* in humanist political thought see in particular Cappelli 2003, p. lxxxi–lxxxvii.

[53] Cornazzano's slight criticism of Galeazzo Maria Sforza may be also due to the fact that the poet lost his protection in Milan under Galeazzo's rule and had to move to other cities. On Galeazzo Maria Sforza's excessive expenditures and his intention to establish a splendid and sumptuous court, see Ilardi 1986, p. 77–78.

[54] Corio 1978, II, p. 1401–1407. On Olgiati, see also Ilardi 1986, p. 74–75.

tion of the whole work, in which the symbol of the most perfect *princeps*, Francesco Sforza, condemns in a caustic verbal harangue the main figure responsible for the conspiracy and depicts him as a vicious criminal and evil traitor of the fatherland. The disapproval of Lampugnani's action is encapsulated in the emphatic description of his amoral and unfaithful nature. He is described with terms from the semantic field of treason and dishonesty, e.g. *traditor* and *Iuda* (the traitor par excellence) and by sarcastically evoking Cassius and Brutus ('Ben venga Cassio e ben ne venga Bruto'; 'Welcome Cassius and Brutus').[55] A particularly colourful passage in the text condenses this image of Lampugnani as a corrupt man who is stained by every sort of vice:

> *Di casa Lampognan falso bastardo,*
> *Zoppo da Dio segnato e cervel secco,*
> *De vitii maculato come pardo* [...] [56]

> (False bastard of the lineage of Lampugnani,
> Crippled, scarred by God and of arid mind,
> Stained by vices like a leopard)

But Cornazzano's most cogent representation of the leader of the plot as a wicked enemy of the fatherland is based on the illustration of the key notion of liberty as a twofold principle (positive or negative), seen from a highly princely-oriented perspective (similar to that in the texts concerning the republican period). On the one hand, liberty is presented as a false ideal misinterpreted by the plotter, who exploited a feigned concept of *libertade* in order to justify his selfish action; on the other hand, Cornazzano alludes to the authentic condition of freedom that was gained by Milan, and in particular by the aristocracy, thanks to Francesco Sforza's takeover, after the chaotic political phase of the Ambrosian Republic:

> *Ma dime hai tu più legittima scusa*
> *Di vitii toi che a dir la mia citade*
> *Libera far volea ch'era confusa?*
> *Che gusto havesti mai de libertade*
> *Che tu non eri nato al tempo ch'io*

---

[55] *Opera Nova*, f. E[r]. In all quotations, original spelling has been maintained; punctuation and capitalization have been modernized.

[56] *Opera Nova*, f. E[r].

Strinsi Milan con iustissime spade?
[...]
Il mio prender Milan de stato vile
Trassello a gentilezza e li potenti
Liberi feci d'habito servile.[57]

(But tell me do you have any more legitimate justification for your vices, except to say that you want to free my city, which was in turmoil? What do you think you know of liberty, you, who were not born in the age when I conquered Milan with the most just swords? [...] My takeover in Milan freed the city from misery and brought kindness, and I liberated powerful people from a condition of slavery.)

In the poet's view, the conspirator did not even know the true meaning of *libertade* and just pretended to free the city from civic *discordia* and injustice; however, with a shrewd move, the actual condition of desolation that tormented Milan is recognized by Cornazzano in the situation that proceeded Sforza's rule. Hence it was Sforza who re-established the right social order in the civic community by giving new freedom to the noble and upper classes that had been marginalized and oppressed by the popular party. This portrayal of the political situation in Milan, parallel to that in Filelfo's works (although with distinctive elements), is based on, and at the same time promotes, an organic and highly hierarchical conception of the state. This political model was becoming predominant in those decades in the Italian states through a complex process that was characterized by the interaction of historical, political and cultural factors. The process had one of its major expressions in literature, in the composition of not only political treatises but also histories, orations, and poems, informed by these political ideals.[58]

In Cornazzano's *Capitolo*, censure of the conspiratorial action, and more generally of dissent against established authorities, is also expressed through the image of the revenge and punishment carried out against the plotters, in particular against Lampugnani. After the assassination of the duke, Lampugnani tried to escape

---

[57] *Opera Nova*, f. E^v.

[58] On this ideal of the verticalized and organic state, with specific relation to political theories in Neapolitan humanism, see Cappelli 2016.

from the church but was stabbed by one of Galeazzo's personal soldiers. Then Lampugnani's dead body was dragged around the city by a group of young boys. This act of desecration would be repeated also two years later in Florence after the failure of the Pazzi conspiracy, in 1478, when Iacopo Pazzi's dead body was disinterred, subjected to the same violation, and finally thrown into the river Arno.[59] The representation of the vengeance against Lampugnani is foregrounded in several sources, often in colourful tones that underscore the violence of the reprisal, presenting it as the just counterpart to the brutality of the conspiracy and, symbolically, as a means to reunify the state and overcome disintegrating tendencies. In the *Capitolo*, most remarkably, Cornazzano dwells on the macabre picture of the traitors' infernal punishment, which evokes a symbolic and powerful image of *contrappasso*.[60] Besides, Cornazzano opens the whole section of the poem dedicated to Lampugnani's murder by alluding to the plotter's violent death. Indeed the poet introduces the nobleman in the underworld with a description of his body as it appeared after his brutal killing, providing this particular: 'Mille ferite havea tra i nervi e l'osse' ('He had thousands of wounds in his nerves and bones').[61] In a further passage, Cornazzano implicitly justifies the harsh retaliation against Lampugnani by saying that no traitor who committed such a hideous crime would ever be able to find shelter:

> *Qual tecto amico in terra in mar qual via*
> *Te potea assicurar cervel di matto*
> *Commesso havendo tanta alta follia?*[62]
>
> (What roof on the earth and what way in the sea could ever protect you, crazy man, after you committed such an evil and inconsiderate action?)

The representation of the revenge against the culprits has an even more crucial political bearing in sources that openly mention the

---

[59] On the Pazzi conspiracy, see Fubini 1994, p. 87–106, 253–327; Martines 2005; this episode is vividly narrated in Angelo Poliziano's *Coniurationis commentarium* (1478): see Poliziano 2015, p. 66–69.

[60] *Opera Nova*, f. Eiii^r.

[61] *Opera Nova*, f. E^r.

[62] *Opera Nova*, f. Eii^r.

role of the common people in the reprisal, and in so doing stress that the conservation of the signorial government was achieved thanks to the contribution of the whole social community, in an image that in turn reinforces the idea of re-established cohesion. For example, Bernardino Corio includes in his narrative two explicit references, in two different passages, to the murder of Lampugnani and the violation of his body by the group of young men:

> *Giovanne Andrea, lo quale di subito volse fugire tra le donne che ivi erano per la celebratione dil sancto, da Gallo Mauro, staphero dil Sforcesco, fu morto puoi da fanciulli trasinato per la cità e disperso il suo cadavere* [...] [63]

> (Giovanni Andrea, who immediately tried to flee among the ladies who were in the church for the holy celebration, was killed by Gallo Mauro, a guard of the Sforza, and was dragged throughout the city by some young boys, who scattered the remains of his dead body.)

> *Morto Galeazzo Maria Sforza nel modo dimostrato, lo cadavero dil Lampugnano da fanciulli per la città fu traxinato e vilmente disperse le osse sue e li quarteri de li altri furono posti a le porte de la città li capi sopra il campanile* [...] [64]

> (Since Galeazzo Maria Sforza was assassinated in the way that was showed, Lampugnani's dead body was dragged by some young boys who disgracefully scattered his bones, and parts of the corpses of the others [plotters] were placed at the city's gates and their heads were placed on the bell tower.)

This twofold parallel description, which results in a repetition in the text, puts an unspoken accent on this episode and on the political message that it is supposed to communicate. This image implicitly shows that the entire social body disapproved the prince's assassination, since even some young boys from the plebs were permitted to torture the dead body of the main conspirator, and the corpses of other plotters were dismembered and exhibited in the city. More generally, this kind of reaction was presented by Sforza propaganda as evidence of the consensus around the ducal

---

[63] Corio 1978, II, p. 1401.
[64] Corio 1978, II, p. 1408.

family, whose sovereignty, in such difficult circumstances, was preserved by all subjects united against the rebels.[65]

A similar representation informs a minor poetic work entitled *Questo è il lamento del Duca Galeazo Duca di Milano quando fu morto in Sancto Stephano da Giovanadrea da Lampognano*. This work circulated mainly as an anonymous text, but in some sixteenth-century editions it is attributed to a Florentine author identified as Lorenzo Rota.[66] This short poem in the vernacular was probably composed soon after the conspiracy and definitely before 1482, since it refers to Roberto Malatesta as still living. The poem was disseminated in the last decade of the Quattrocento, and in the 1500s and 1600s in various printed editions (which contains some textual variants).[67] In an edition printed in Florence in 1505, the poem is introduced by a woodcut that offers a lively depiction of the attack against the duke of Milan.[68] This artistic illustration intensifies through visual means the idea of violence and chaos that underlies the literary description of the murder. The image portrays the brutal scene of bloodshed that took place in the church, immortalizing the moment immediately following Galeazzo Maria Sforza's assassination (and not the assassination itself) and documenting some details given in poem: the general turmoil, the people flying in every direction, and, most importantly, the killing of Lampugnani by a 'moorish' guard of the duke. The woodcut depicts the guard in the act of stabbing the conspirator to death. This brave reaction is put into the foreground, though on

---

[65] See in particular the document written by Bona of Savoy to the castellans of Masserano and Crevalcuore, in which she mentions the brutal revenge exacted on Lampugnani and stresses the *devotione* ('devotion') and *fedeltà* ('loyalty') to the Sforza of all cities of the state: Vaglienti 2004, p. 274.

[66] For example, this attribution appears in the edition: *Lamento de l'illustrissimo sig. Galeazzo duca di Milano. Composto per Lorenzo dalla Rota fiorentino*, Venetia: in Frezzaria alla Regina, 1585.

[67] The *editio princeps* is an incunable printed in Venice by Manfredo Bonelli in 1493; on the tradition of the text, see Fadini 2018, p. 210–212.

[68] *Questo è il lamento del Duca Galeazo Duca di Milano quando fu morto in Sancto Stephano da Gionanandrea da rampognano* [sic], Firenze: maestro Bernardo Zucchetta: ad instantia di ser Piero Pacini da Pescia, 1505. I have examined the copy in Milan, Archivio Storico Civico e Biblioteca Trivulziana, Rari Triv. H 314/1. This is the first edition to include this image, which would appear in some reprints (for example in two versions published in Venice), while other editions contain different woodcuts that evoke the plot only obliquely. See Fadini 2018.

the left side of the woodcut: the guard, who is represented as the revenger of the *signore* of Milan, is highlighted by his depiction as a black man, who stands out from the rest of the picture and is easily recognizable.[69] More generally, the woodcut portrays the scenario of brutal violence produced by both the duke's murder and the immediate reprisal against the plotters. Vengeance mirrors the ferocity of the conspiracy and, through this symmetrical correspondence, justifies the revenge. Such a lively portrayal, specifically produced for this cheap pamphlet published in Florence, proves that this political reading of the event had spread outside the Milanese territory, overlapping with political ideologies now dominant across Italy. The woodcut ends up conveying even more effectively the political message encapsulated in the narration of the text. Indeed, it visually intensifies the poet's words that describe the reprisal against the plotter, who, once again, is portrayed as an evil, cruel, and ruthless man: 'col cor tristo, spietato et feroce'. Moreover, in the poem, the narration of the attack ends with the image of Lampugnani's dead body dragged throughout the city: 'Finalmente quel fu tucto tagliato [...] et morto per Milan fu strascinato' ('that man was all dismembered, and his dead body was dragged throughout Milan').[70] This detail, which, as we have seen, recurs in different sources, epitomises a cluster of complementary propagandistic points: the idea of the fair counteroffensive by ducal power, the reunification of the state under that power, and the futility of any violent seditious action.

Conclusion

As the analysis of these different sources has demonstrated, the representation of anti-signorial attempts in Milan and, more generally, of insubordination against ducal domination, played a considerable part in a variety of texts. Through literary trans-

---

[69] On this image see R. Salzberg & M. Rospocher 2017, p. 169–173. This artistic portrayal of the *staffiere*'s action corresponds to the reconstruction of the event provided in other sources, such as Corio 1978, II, p. 1401; and Giovio 2006, p. 647.

[70] *Questo è il lamento*, f. 1v (original spelling has been maintained; punctuation and capitalization have been modernized, and obvious mistakes have been corrected).

position, such representation ended up acquiring specific pro-princely nuances that reversed and obliterated the position of the opponents of one-man governments. Such interpretation is particularly evident in the case of the sources on the Ambrosian Republic analysed here (the only time when Milan was not ruled by signorial authorities) and of the narratives of the conspiracy against Galeazzo Maria Sforza: an attempt that was probably aimed at establishing a government similar to the short-lived rule of the republic (1447–1450).[71] As we have seen, the condemnation of centrifugal forces in the state characterizes, with distinctive specificities, various kinds of works by different intellectuals: Filelfo's orations and epistles, Cornazzano's poem, Corio's history, and even a lament in the vernacular targeted at a popular audience. In all these works, especially in the sections dedicated to the conspiracy, the representation of the events totally overturns the antityrannical intentions of the plotters, subverting their ideological principles and cancelling them from the historical reconstruction that builds the shared memory of the episode. The conspiracy is stigmatized as performed by vicious and corrupt men and is assimilated to an actual crime, rather than to a political (though still violent) act. The dissent against Galeazzo Maria Sforza that spread in the city during his autocratic rule had been present in Milan almost thirty years earlier in the form of the anti-signorial positions that resulted in the Ambrosian Republic. The opposition to Sforza, however, was subdued after the plot by disseminating an image of *concordia* in the state and the picture of a unanimous community reunified under Sforza power by the revenge against the plotters. This propagandistic depiction was not only shaped and promoted by literary sources, but, as we have seen, in the emblematic case of the edition of the *Lamento*, it was conveyed even more effectively through the interplay with artistic channels.

In an age when centralized rule was being strengthened in almost all Italian states, the diffusion of this highly ideological reading of specific historical episodes of insubordination against established authorities reveals the concrete contribution of literature, in its different forms (and sometimes in synergy with visual imagery), to the affirmation of princely theories in the early

---

[71] See in particular Ilardi 1986, p. 74.

Renaissance. Such a phenomenon goes together with the recovery of traditional monarchical doctrines that foster the interpretation of key political notions, such as *libertas* and *concordia*, through specific ideological lenses. In particular, the idea of liberty is regarded as relevant only if adapted to a pro-signorial political perspective and is devoid of its more general connotation. This shift in the concept of *libertas* is evident in the reference to 'fictitious liberty', which appears in different texts and which circumscribes the authentic sense of the term to what is understood as 'true liberty'. True liberty can be guaranteed only by highly hierarchical and verticalized governments, which thwart internal conflict and provide social tranquillity. Consequently, liberty is seen as only functional to the promotion of the principles of unity, *pax* and *securitas*: values that are traditionally prerogatives of monarchical theories. Such values are integrated with the broader tenet of *concordia*, which is now interpreted analogously and placed at the heart of princely ideologies. However, if it is true that concord was considered the conceptual keystone in political systems, the idea of dissent was not erased from the political discourse of this age. Dissent is a pivotal theme in a variety of literary and historical works and, thanks to these cultural vehicles, it was exorcized and brought to reconciliation. Thus, the specific focus placed on discord and on its condemnation in this literary output played a considerable role in the suppression of opposition and the consolidation of centralized political views: a function complementary to that played by the symmetrical eulogy of obedience and social cohesion in signorial states.

Bibliography

Primary Sources

Bernardino Corio, *Storia di Milano*, ed. A. Morisi Guerra, 2 vols, Torino: UTET, 1978 (Classici della storiografia, 4).

Lodrisio Crivelli, *De vita rebusque gestis Sfortiae bellicosissimi ducis et initiis fili eius Francisci Sfortiae Vicecomitis Mediolanensium Ducis Commentarius*, in *Rerum Italicarum Scriptores*, XIX, coll. 627–732, Milano: Società Palatina, 1731.

Francesco Filelfo, *Carminum libri*, ed. V. Dadà, Alessandria: Edizioni dell'Orso, 2020 (Hellenica, 85).

Francesco Filelfo, *Collected Letters (Epistolarium libri XVLIII)*, ed. J. De Keyser, 4 vols, Alessandria: Edizioni dell'Orso, 2015 (Hellenica, 54).

Francesco Filelfo, *Odes*, ed. and tr. D. Robin, Cambridge, MA; London, UK: Harvard University Press, 2009 (I Tatti Renaissance library).

Francesco Filelfo, *Satyrae I* (decadi I–V), ed. S. Fiaschi, Roma: Edizioni di Storia e Letteratura, 2005 (Studi e testi del Rinascimento europeo, 26).

Paolo Giovio, *Elogi degli uomini illustri*, ed. F. Minonzio, trans. A. Gasparri, F. Minonzio, Torino: Einaudi, 2006.

Lamento de l'illustrissimo sig. Galeazzo duca di Milano. Composto per Lorenzo dalla Rota fiorentino, Venetia: in Frezzaria alla Regina, 1585.

Questo è il lamento del Duca Galeazo Duca di Milano quando fu morto in Sancto Stephano da Gioanandrea da Lampognano, Firenze: maestro Bernardo Zucchetta: ad instantia di ser Piero Pacini da Pescia, 1505.

Opera Nova de Miser Antonio Cornazano in terza rima, Venetia: Zorzi di Rusconi, ad instantia de Nicolo dicto Zopino et Vincentio compagni, 1517.

Georgius Merula, *De antiquitate Vicecomitum* [Milano: Alexander Minutianus, 1499–1500].

Angelo Poliziano, *Coniurationis commentarium*, con introduzione, traduzione e commento, ed. M. Celati, Alessandria: Edizioni dell'Orso, 2015 (Ciceronianus, 5).

Coluccio Salutati, *Epistolario*, ed. F. Novati, Roma: Forzani e C. tipografi del Senato, vol. 2, 1893 (Fonti per la storia d'Italia, 16).

Giovanni Simonetta, *Rerum gestarum Francisci Sfortiae Mediolanensium ducis commentarii*, ed. G. Soranzo, *Rereum Italicarum Scriptores*, XXI, 2, Bologna: Zanichelli, 1932.

Secondary Sources

Adam, R. G., 'Francesco Filelfo at the Court of Milan (1439–1481). A contribution to the Study of Humanism in Northen Italy' (unpublished doctoral thesis, University of Oxford, 1974).

Albanese, G. (2009), 'A redescoberta dos historiadores antigos no Humanismo e o nascimento da historiografia moderna: Valla, Facio e Pontano na corte napolitana dos reis de Aragao', in F. Murari Pires (ed.), *Atti del Convegno Internazionale Antigos e Modernos:*

diálogos sobre a (escrita da) história (Universidade de Sao Paulo do Brazil, 2-7 settembre 2007), São Paulo: Alameda Casa Editorial, p. 277-329.

Amit, M. (1962), '*Concordia. Idéal politique et instrument de propagande*', in *Iura*, 13, p. 133-169.

Annoni, C. P. (1874), 'Un plagio dello storico Bernardino Corio', in *Rivista italiana di scienze, lettere ed arti*, 1/2, p. 57-89.

Baker, P., et al. (eds) (2016), *Portraying the Prince in the Renaissance: The Humanist Depiction of Rulers in Historiographical and Biographical Texts*, Berlin: De Gruyter (Transformationen der Antike, 44).

Baron, H. (1955), *The Crisis of the Early Italian Renaissance: Civic Humanism and Republican Liberty in an Age of Classicism and Tyranny*, Princeton, NJ: Princeton University Press.

Belotti, B. (1965), *Storia di una congiura (Olgiati)*, Milano: Dall'Oglio (I corvi. Collana universale moderna, 37; Sezione verde, 6).

Bentley, J. H. (1987), *Politics and Culture in Renaissance Naples*, Princeton, NJ: Princeton University Press.

Black, R. & J. E. Law (eds) (2015), *The Medici: Citizens and Masters*, Firenze: Villa I Tatti, the Harvard University Center for Italian Renaissance Studies (Villa I Tatti, 32).

Bongrani, P. (1986), 'Gli storici sforzeschi e il volgarizzamento landiniano dei *Commentarii* del Simonetta', in *Lingua Nostra*, 47, p. 40-50.

Bottari, G. (1986), 'La Sphortias', in *Francesco Filelfo nel quinto centenario della morte: atti del XVII Convegno di studi maceratesi (Tolentino, 27-30 settembre 1981)*, Padova: Antenore (Medioevo e umanesimo, 58; Studi maceratesi, 17), p. 459-493.

Bruni F. (2003), *La città divisa. Le parti e il bene comune da Dante a Guicciardini*, Bologna: Il Mulino (Collezione di testi e di studi, Filologia e critica letteraria).

Bruni, R. & L. Zancani (1992), *Antonio Cornazzano: la traduzione testuale*, Firenze: L.S. Olschki.

Canfora, D. (2001), *La controversia di Poggio Bracciolini e Guarino Veronese*, Firenze: Olschki (Studi e testi, 15).

Canfora, D. (2005), *Prima di Machiavelli: Politica e cultura in età umanistica*, Milano: Laterza (Biblioteca Universale Laterza, 580).

Cappelli, G. (2003), 'Introduzione', in Giovanni Pontano, *De principe*, ed. G. Cappelli, Roma: Salerno Editrice (Testi e documenti di letteratura e di lingua, 22), p. xi-cxxi.

Cappelli, G. (2009), 'Conceptos transversales: República y monarquía en el Humanismo político', in *Res publica*, 21, p. 51-69.

Cappelli, G. (2012), '*Corpus est res publica*. La struttura della comunità secondo l'umanesimo politico', in L. Geri (ed.) *Principi prima del Principe*, Roma: Bulzoni editore (Studi [e Testi] Italiani 29), p. 117-131.

Cappelli, G. (2016), *Maiestas: politica e pensiero politico nella Napoli aragonese (1443-1503)*, Roma: Carocci Editore (Biblioteca di testi e studi, 1097).

Catalano, F. (ed.) (1956), *L'età sforzesca dal 1450 al 1500*, vol. II, in *Storia di Milano*, Milano: Fondazione Treccani degli Alfieri per la storia di Milano.

Catalano, F. (1985), *Francesco Sforza*, Milano: Dall'Oglio.

Celati, M. (2017), 'Filelfo e Carlo Gonzaga: l'*Oratio de laudibus illustris Karoli Gonzagae*, tra storia, oratoria e teoria politica', in Francesco Filelfo, *Opere storiche e politiche. I. Filelfo e la storia*, ed. G. Albanese & P. Pontari, Firenze: SISMEL – Edizioni del Galluzzo (Ritorno dei classici nell'Umanesimo, 4; Edizione nazionale dei testi della storiografia umanistica, 11), p. 127-144.

Celati, M. (2021), *Conspiracy Literature in Early Renaissance Italy: Historiography and Princely Ideology,* Oxford: Oxford University Press.

Chittolini, G. (1990), 'Di alcuni aspetti della crisi dello stato sforzesco', in J. M. Cauchies & G. Chittolini (eds), *Milano e Borgogna. Due stati principeschi tra medioevo e Rinascimento*, Roma: Bulzoni (Biblioteca del Cinquecento, 47), p. 31-44

Cognasso, F. (1955), *Il ducato visconteo e la Repubblica ambrosiana (1392-1450)*, vol. VI, in *Storia di Milano*, Milano: Fondazione Treccani degli Alfieri per la storia di Milano.

Colombo, A. (1905), 'L'ingresso di Francesco Sforza a Milano', in *Archivio storico lombardo*, 32/7, p. 80-101.

Comanducci, R. M. (1992), 'Nota sulla versione landiniana della *Sforziade* di Giovanni Simonetta', in *Interpres*, 12, p. 309-316.

De Keyser, J. (2015), *Francesco Filelfo and Francesco Sforza. Critical Edition of Filelfo's 'Sphortias', 'De Genuensium deditione', 'Oratio parentalis' and His Polemical Exchange with Galeotto Marzio*, Hildesheim: Georg Olms Verlag (Noctes Neolatinae, 22).

De Keyser, J. (2016), 'Picturing the Perfect Patron? Francesco Filelfo's Image of Francesco Sforza', in P. Baker et al. (eds), *Portraying the Prince in the Renaissance: The Humanist Depiction of Rulers in Historiographical and Biographical Texts,* Berlin: De Gruyter (Transformationen der Antike, 44), p. 391-414.

De Keyser, J. (ed.) (2019), *Francesco Filelfo, Man of Letters*, Leiden: Brill (Brill's Studies in Intellectual History, 289).

De Rosa, D. (1980), *Coluccio Salutati: il cancelliere e il pensatore politico*, Firenze: La Nuova Italia (Pubblicazioni del Seminario di storia medioevale della Facoltà di lettere dell'Università di Firenze, 3; Biblioteca di storia, 28).

Delle Donne, F. (2015), *Alfonso il Magnanimo e l'invenzione dell'Umanesimo monarchico. Ideologia e strategie di legittimazione alla corte aragonese di Napoli*, Roma: Istituto storico italiano per il Medio Evo (Quaderni della Scuola nazionale di studi medievali. Fonti, studi e sussidi, 7).

Delle Donne, F. – Cappelli, G. (2021), *Nel Regno delle lettere. Umanesimo e politica nel Mezzogiorno aragonese*, Roma: Carocci.

Dionisotti, C. (1980), *Machiavellerie*, Torino: Einaudi (Einaudi paperbacks, 113).

Dizionario biografico degli Italiani, ed. Alberto M. Ghisalberti et al., Roma: Istituto della Enciclopedia Italiana, 1960–.

Fadini, M. (2018), 'Cinque edizioni sine notis di letteratura popolare in copia unica: attribuzione agli stampatori ed edizione dei testi poetici', in *Tricontre. Teoria, testo, traduzione*, 10, p. 205-238.

Fahy, C. (1964), 'Per la vita di Antonio Cornazzano. I. Documenti d'archivio', in *Bolettino storico piacentino*, 59, p. 57-91.

Farenga, P. (1983), 'Antonio Cornazzano', in *Dizionario biografico*, 29, p. 123-132.

Ferraù, G. (2001), *Il tessitore di Antequera. Storiografia umanistica meridionale*, Roma: Istituto storico italiano per il Medio Evo (Nuovi studi storici, 53).

Fubini, R. (1994), *Italia quattrocentesca: politica e diplomazia nell'età di Lorenzo de' Medici*, Milano: Franco Angeli (Studi e ricerche storiche, 181).

Garin, E. (1956), 'La cultura milanese nella seconda metà del XV secolo', in Catalano (ed.), p. 539-597.

Gilbert, F. (1977), 'The Humanist Concept of the Prince and *The Prince* of Machiavelli', in F. Gilbert, *History: Choice and Commitment*, Cambridge, MA: Belknap Press; Harvard University Press, p. 91-114.

Hankins, J. (1995), 'The "Baron Thesis" after Forty Years and Some Recent Studies of Leonardo Bruni', in *Journal of the History of Ideas*, 56/2, p. 309-338.

Hankins, J. (1996), 'Humanism and the Origins of Modern Political Thought', in Jill Kraye (ed.), *The Cambridge Companion to*

Renaissance Humanism, Cambridge: Cambridge University Press, p. 118-141.

Hankins, J. (2000), 'Rhetoric, History and Ideology: The Civic Panegyrics of Leonardo Bruni', in J. Hankins (ed.), *Renaissance Civic Humanism: Reappraisals and Reflections*, Cambridge: Cambridge University Press (Ideas in Context, 57), p. 143-178.

Hankins, J. (2010), 'Exclusivist Republicanism and the Non-Monarchical Republic', in *Political Theory* 38/4, p. 452-482.

Hankins, J. (2019), *Virtue Politics. Soulcraft and Statecraft in Renaissance Italy*, Cambridge, MA: The Belknap Press of Harvard University Press.

Hyde, J. K. (1972), 'Contemporary Views on Factions and Civil Strife in Thirteenth- and Fourteenth-Century Italy', in L. Martines (ed.), *Violence and Civil Disorder in Italian Cities, 1200-1500*, Berkeley, CA: University of California Press (Contributions of the UCLA Center for Medieval and Renaissance Studies, 5), p. 273-307.

Kantorowicz, E. H. (1975), *The King's Two Bodies: A Study in Mediaeval Political Theology*, Princeton, NJ: Princeton University Press.

Ianziti, G. (1988), *Humanistic Historiography under the Sforzas. Politics and Propaganda in 15th Century Milan*, Oxford: Clarendon Press.

Ianziti, G. (2005), 'Storici, mandanti, materiali nella Milano sforzesca, 1450-1480', in T. Matarrese & C. Montagnani (eds), *Il principe e la storia*. Atti del Convegno, Scandiano, 18-20 settembre 2003, Novara: Interlinea edizioni (Studi boiardeschi, 4; Studi, 44), p. 465-485.

Ianziti, G. (2012), *Writing History in Renaissance Italy: Leonardo Bruni and the Uses of the Past*, Cambridge, MA: Harvard University Press (I Tatti studies in Italian Renaissance history).

Ilardi, V. (1986), 'The Assassination of Galeazzo Maria Sforza and the Reaction of Italian Diplomacy', in V. Ilardi, *Studies in Italian Renaissance diplomatic history*, London: Variorum Reprints (Collected Studies Series, 239), p. 72-103.

Jones, P. J. (1965), 'Communes and Despots: The City-State in Late Medieval Italy', in *Transactions of the Royal Historical Society*, 15, p. 71-96.

La Penna, A. (1968), 'Brevi note sul tema della congiura nella storiografia moderna', in A. La Penna, *Sallustio e la 'rivoluzione' romana*, Milano: Feltrinelli (Fatti e le idee, saggi e biografie, 181), p. 432-452.

Lazzarini, I. (2001), 'Carlo Gonzaga', in *Dizionario biografico*, 57, p. 693-696.

Loraux, N. (2002), *The Divided City: On Memory and Forgetting in Ancient Athens*, New York, NY: Zone Books.

Lubkin, G. (1994), *A Renaissance Court: Milan under Galeazzo Maria Sforza*, Berkeley, CA: University of California Press.

Luzio, A., Renier, R. (1890), 'Filelfo e l'umanesimo alla corte dei Gonzaga', in *Giornale Storico della Letteratura Italiana*, 16, p. 119–217.

Martines, L. (1968), 'Political Conflict in the Italian City States', *Government and Opposition*, 3/1, p. 69–91.

Martines, L. (2005), *La congiura dei Pazzi: Intrighi politici, sangue e vendetta nella Firenze dei Medici*. Trans. N. Cannata. Milano: Mondadori (Oscar Storia, 389).

Meschini, S. (1995), *Uno storico umanista alla corte sforzesca: biografia di Bernardino Corio,* Milano: Vita e pensiero (Biblioteca di storia moderna e contemporanea, 8; Scienze storiche, 58).

Musso, A. (1999), '*Del modo di regere e di regnare* di Antonio Cornazzano: una *institutio principis* al femminile', in *Schifanoia*, 19, p. 67–69.

Najemy, J. M. (1995), 'The Republic's Two Bodies: Body Metaphors in Italian Renaissance Political Thought', in A. Brown (ed.), *Language and Images of Renaissance Italy*, Oxford: Clarendon Press, p. 237–262.

Najemy, J. M. (2000), '"Civic Humanism" and Florentine Politics', in J. Hankins (ed.), *Renaissance Civic Humanism: Reappraisals and Reflections*, Cambridge: Cambridge University Press (Ideas in Context, 57), p. 75–104.

Orvieto, P. (1976), 'Nicola Capponi detto Cola Montano', *Dizionario biografico*, 19, p. 83–86.

Osmond, P. J. (1995), '"Princeps Historiae Romanae": Sallust in Renaissance Political Thought', in *Memoirs of the American Academy in Rome*, 40, p. 101–143.

Osmond, P. J. (2000), 'Catiline in Fiesole and Florence: The After-Life of a Roman Conspirator', in *International Journal of the Classical Tradition*, 7/1, p. 3–38.

Pastore Stocchi, M. (2014), 'Il pensiero politico degli umanisti', in M. Pastore Stocchi, *Pagine di storia dell'Umanesimo italiano*, Milano: Franco Angeli (Letteratura italiana. Saggi e strumenti, 19), p. 26–84.

Pedullà, G. (2018), *Machiavelli in Tumult: The Discourses on Livy and the Origins of political conflictualism*, Cambridge: Cambridge University Press [Italian edition: G. Pedullà, *Machiavelli in tumulto: conquista, cittadinanza e conflitto nei 'Discorsi sopra la prima deca di Tito Livio'*, Roma: Bulzoni, 2011 (Biblioteca del Cinquecento, 151)].

Petrucci, F. (1983), 'Bernardino Corio', in *Dizionario biografico*, 29, p. 75–78.

Piccolomini, M. (1991), *The Brutus Revival: Parricide and Tyrannicide during the Renaissance,* Carbondale, IL: Southern Illinois University Press.

Quaglioni, D. (1983), *Politica e diritto nel Trecento italiano. Il 'De tyranno' di Bartolo da Sassoferrato (1314–1357)*, Firenze: Olschki (Il Pensiero politico, Biblioteca, 11).

Robin, D. (1991), *Filelfo in Milan: Writings, 1451–1477*, Princeton, NJ: Princeton University Press.

Rocchi, G. D. (ed.) (2007), *Tra concordia e pace: parole e valori della Grecia antica. Giornata di studio, Milano, 21 ottobre 2005, Università degli Studi di Milano, Dipartimento di Scienze dell'Antichità*, Milano: Cisalpino (Quaderni di Acme, 92).

Rosmini, C. de' (1808), *Vita di Francesco Filelfo da Tolentino*, 3 vols, Milano: Mussi.

Rubinstein, N. (1966), *The Government of Florence under the Medici (1434 to 1494)*, Oxford: Clarendon Press.

Rubinstein, N. (1991), 'Italian Political Thought, 1450–1539', in J. Henderson Burns (ed.), *The Cambridge History of Political Thought 1450–1700*, Cambridge: Cambridge University Press, p. 30–65.

Salzberg, R. & M. Rospocher, (2017), 'Murder Ballads. Singing, Hearing, Writing and Reading about Murder in Renaissance Italy', in T. Dean & K. J. P. Lowe (eds), *Murder in Renaissance Italy*, Cambridge: Cambridge University Press, p. 164–185.

Santoro, C. (1968), *Gli Sforza*, Milano: Dall'Oglio.

Schadee, H. (2018a), '"I Don't Know Who You Call Tyrants". Debating Evil Lords in Quattrocento Humanism', in N. Panou & H. Schadee (eds), *Evil Lords: Theories and Representations of Tyranny from Antiquity to the Renaissance*, Oxford: Oxford University Press, p. 172–190.

Schadee, H. (2018b), 'A Tale of Two Languages: Latin, the Vernacular, and Leonardo Bruni's *Civic Humanism*', in *Humanistica Lovaniensia*, 67/1, p. 11–46.

Gli Sforza a Milano e in Lombardia e i loro rapporti con gli stati italiani ed europei (1450–1535). Atti del Convegno internazionale, Milano, 18–21 maggio 1981, Milano: Cisalpino-Goliardica, 1982.

Skinner, Q. (1978), *The Foundations of Modern Political Thought*, 2 vols, Cambridge: Cambridge University Press, I: *The Renaissance*.

Skinner, Q. (1995), 'The Vocabulary of Renaissance Republicanism: A Cultural longue durée?', in A. Brown (ed.), *Language and Images of Renaissance Italy*, Oxford: Clarendon, p. 87-110.

Skinner, Q. (2002), *Visions of Politics,* 3 vols, Cambridge: Cambridge University Press, II: *Renaissance Virtues.*

Soldi Rondini, G. (1983), 'Ludovico il Moro nella storiografia coeva', in *Milano nell'età di Ludovico il Moro: Atti del Convegno internazionale, 28 febbraio-4 marzo 1983*, 2 vols, Milano: Comune di Milano, Archivio storico civico e Biblioteca trivulziana, p. 29-56.

Stacey, P. (2007), *Roman Monarchy and the Renaissance Prince*, Cambridge: Cambridge University Press (Ideas in Context, 79).

Stella, A. (1993), *La Révolte des Ciompi. Les hommes, les lieux, le travail*, Paris: École des Hautes Études en Sciences Sociales (Recherches d'histoire et de sciences sociales, 57).

Tissoni Benvenuti, A. (1990), 'Letteratura dinastico-encomiastica a Milano nell'età degli Sforza', in J. M. Cauchies & G. Chittolini (eds), *Milano e Borgogna. Due stati principeschi tra medioevo e Rinascimento*, Roma: Bulzoni (Biblioteca del cinquecento, 47), p. 195-205.

Turchetti, M. (2013), *Tyrannie et tyrannicide de l'Antiquité à nos jours*, Paris: Classiques Garnier (Bibliothèque de la Renaissance, 11).

Vaglienti, F. M. (2002), 'Anatomia di una congiura. Sulle tracce dell'assassinio del duca Galeazzo Maria Sforza tra scienza e storia', in *Atti dell'Istituto lombardo. Accademia di scienze e lettere di Milano* 136/2, p. 237-273.

Vaglienti, F. M. (2004), 'Giovanni Andrea Lampugnani', in *Dizionario biografico*, 63, p. 272-275.

Villard, R. (2008), *Du bien commun au mal nécessaire: tyrannies, assassinats politiques et souveraineté en Italie, vers 1470-vers 1600*, Roma: École française de Rome (Bibliothèque des Écoles françaises d'Athènes et de Rome, 338).

Witt, R. G. (1996), "The Crisis After Forty Years", in *The American Historical Review*, 101/1, p. 110-118.

Witt, R. G. (2012), *The Two Latin Cultures and the Foundation of Renaissance Humanism in Medieval Italy*, Cambridge: Cambridge University Press.

Zancani, D. (2000), 'Writing for Women Rulers in Quattrocento Italy: Antonio Cornazzano', in L. Panizza (ed.), *Women in Italian Renaissance Culture and Society*, Oxford: European Humanities Research Centre (Legenda), p. 57-74.

Abstract

This contribution investigates the representation of political dissent in fifteenth-century Milanese literature and the multiple literary forms in which the topic of political *discordia*, and its decisive condemnation, was put forward in this context. Around mid-Quattrocento, political opposition to centralized princely power in Milan had its main expression in the brief government of the Ambrosiana Republic (August 1447–February 1450) and, after the takeover by the Sforza in 1450, in the conspiracy against Galeazzo Maria Sforza in 1476. The issue of political conflict also occupied a central position in literary works, where it was mainly addressed by depicting the danger of political disunity and by the disapproval of popular forms of government or any attempts at overturning princely power. The texts examined in this article as significant case studies belong to different genres (epistles, orations, histories, poems) and were produced in the cultural circles close to Milanese power by important intellectuals, such as Francesco Filelfo, Antonio Cornazzano, and Bernardino Corio, but in other cases, in particular the anonymous *Lamento del duca Galeazzo Maria*, the texts targeted a more popular audience. The present contribution analyses how both the Ambrosiana Republic and the conspiracy against the Sforza Duke were presented in these sources through a specific ideological perspective that aimed to contain dissent and support the principle of unity in the state.

PART 2
EARLY MODERN PERIOD (16ᵀᴴ – 18ᵀᴴ CENTURIES)

ANTONIO GERACE
FSciRe / KU Leuven

THOMAS STAPLETON ED ELISABETTA I: UNA RELAZIONE IMPOSSIBILE [*]

Introduzione

Thomas Stapleton (1535–1598) nacque solo un anno dopo che Enrico VIII di Inghilterra, per mezzo dell'*Act of Supremacy*, divenisse *Supreme Head of the Church of England*, arrogandosi un potere che fino a quel momento era stato appannaggio del papa e anticipando di circa vent'anni il principio del *cuius regio eius religio*, definito con la pace di Augusta (1555) per regolare le prerogative dei principi protestanti e cattolici nel Sacro Romano Impero, in termini di politica religiosa. All'*Act of Supremacy* seguirono le prime requisizioni dei monasteri a partire dal 1536, assistendo peraltro a episodi di iconoclastia, di chiara derivazione calvinista, già negli anni '30,[1] rendendo più difficile la vita di coloro che volevano rimanere fedeli alla Chiesa di Roma. Con l'avvento di Edoardo VI nel 1547, l'anglicanesimo ebbe una prima importante svolta, con l'*Act of Uniformity* e la pubblicazione del *Book of Common Prayer* (1549), promulgato dal re, ma elaborato da Thomas Cranmer (1489–1556) e teso a dare un'uniformità dottrinale alla Chiesa d'Inghilterra.[2] Specie nella revisione del 1552, il testo si avvicinava alla teologia calvinista, aggregandosi al *Consensus Tigurinus* nella formulazione del concetto di eucaristia che

---

[*] In questo saggio si riprende e si amplia quanto brevemente affrontato in Gerace 2019, p. 225–229. Nel riprodurre i testi latini si è usato -u- in luogo di –v- (con lettera maiuscola -V-), e -i- in luogo di -j-. Inoltre, & è sempre stato sciolto in *et*.

[1] Heal 2017, p. 186.

[2] Shagan 2017, p. 41. Spink 2017, p. 152–157.

bilanciava le visioni ginevrine e zurighesi.[3] Il *Book of Common Prayer* determinò una prima reazione della popolazione cattolica, repressa nel sangue, specie nel Devon e in Cornovaglia. La situazione si complicò ulteriormente dopo la breve e violenta restaurazione cattolica di Maria I Tudor, durante la quale i sudditi protestanti furono perseguitati, valendole il titolo di *Bloody Mary*.[4] Con il regno di Elisabetta I e il nuovo *Act of Supremacy*, i cattolici subirono lo stesso trattamento che era stato riservato ai loro compatrioti protestanti e, per tal motivo, molti inglesi fedeli al papa decisero di abbandonare la propria patria, in cui la regina aveva diffuso il calvinismo, come dichiarato da Pio V nella bolla di scomunica *Regnans in excelsis* (1570).[5]

I Paesi Bassi si presentavano come la scelta più ovvia per l'esilio: baluardo della cattolicissima Spagna nel nord Europa, erano anche la terra più vicina da raggiungere. Qui Stapleton si rifugiò nel 1558,[6] recandosi dapprima a Lovanio e poi a Douai (1568), dove prese parte alla realizzazione dell'*English College*, insegnandovi teologia dal 1571 al 1582. Proprio in questo periodo, Stapleton incontrò il gesuita brabantino Leonard Lessius e, nel 1582, iniziò il suo noviziato presso la Compagnia di Gesù. Tuttavia, dopo appena due anni fu costretto a lasciare il suo percorso spirituale, a causa delle asperità incontrate.[7] In ogni caso, la breve formazione gesuitica aveva attecchito nella mente del teologo inglese, soprattutto per l'importanza attribuita al libero arbitrio nell'economia della salvezza. Nello specifico, le parole di Luis de Molina lo avevano particolarmente entusiasmato; lo spagnolo, infatti, aveva dimostrato nella sua *Concordia* (1588) che era possibile conciliare la libertà

---

[3] MacCulloch 2017, p. 324.

[4] Ridley 2001.

[5] Muller 2020; Janssen 2012, p. 671–692, McCoog 1996, Salmon 1991, Edwards 1981, Lecler 1955, II, p. 303–325, Pio V 1570: *Libros manifestam haeresim continentes toto regno proponi, impia mysteria et instituta ad Caluini praescriptum a se suscepta et obseruata, etiam a subditis seruari mandauit.*

[6] Albion 1946, p. 901.

[7] Stapleton 1620, I, p. iii. La data è ancora oggetto di discussione. Secondo Albion, Stapleton inzia il suo noviziato nel 1582, si veda Albion 1946, p. 904. Tuttavia, secondo O'Connell, Stapleton 'presented himself to the Jesuits at Douay' nel 1585, si veda O'Connell 1964, p. 41. François segue Albion, dal momento che Stapleton lo avrebbe iniziato quando William Estius lo sostituì alla cattedra di teologia all'Università di Douai, si veda François 2013, p. 50, n. 45.

dell'uomo con l'eterna predestinazione di Dio. La relazione fra due concetti ritenuti in opposizione si rendeva possibile attraverso la *scientia media*, 'una specie di divinazione misteriosa'[8] per mezzo della quale l'Onnisciente preconosceva, ma non vincolava, le azioni dell'uomo, il quale era libero di scegliere nel tempo quello che Egli aveva previsto nell'eternità. La predestinazione rimaneva quindi nelle mani della libertà divina, ma i meriti dell'uomo trovavano comunque il loro spazio, contribuendo alla salvezza.[9]

Il molinismo divenne, agli occhi di Stapleton, il miglior 'antidoto' contro il 'veleno' del calvinismo. Le idee di alcuni esponenti della Compagnia di Gesù, tuttavia, si erano dimostrate fin troppo radicali; in particolare nel 1586 scoppia la disputa fra Lessius, che proponeva una *praedestinatio ex meritis praeuisis* nelle sue *Theses theologicae*, giudicate 'semipelagiane' dall'entourage agostinista presente sia a Lovanio sia a Douai, il cui più importante esponente era certamente Michel de Bay o Baio (1513–1589). Questi reggeva saldamente la cattedra di Scritture Sacre presso l'ateneo lovaniense, professando una teologia particolarmente influenzata da Agostino.[10] In questa disputa, il teologo inglese si schierò con Lessius e, per questo motivo, venne allontanato dalla vita accademica, fino al 1590, quando proprio Stapleton prese il posto di Baio, morto l'anno precedente. Proprio in questo periodo, Stapleton iniziò a pubblicare le sue opere più fortunate, gli *Antidota* e i *Promptuaria*. Dei primi ci si era già occupati in un precedente contributo,[11] dove si era ampiamente dimostrato quanto quest'opera fosse debitrice della *scientia media* di Molina, un'importanza che viene poi riflessa anche nei *Promptuaria*, in particolare nella sesta edizione del *Catholicum*: rispetto alle precedenti, il commento al passo evangelico letto durante la messa del 26 dicembre viene ulteriormente sviluppato, ponendo a margine un chiaro riferimento a Molina e alla sua *Concordia*.[12] Questo contributo si concentrerà proprio sui *Promptuaria*, offerti in due forme, *morale*

---

[8] Martinetti 1928, p. 48.

[9] Sulla questione e per ulteriore bibliografia, si vedano Gerace 2016, Cruz Cruz 2013, Le Bachelet 1931.

[10] Sulla questione si veda Rai 2020, Gerace 2019, p. 150–154, e Rai 2016 e François 2012, p. 255–262.

[11] Gerace 2016, si veda lì per ulteriore bibliografia.

[12] Gerace 2019, p. 223.

e *catholicum*, analizzando specifici brani in cui Stapleton descrive la situazione religiosa del proprio Paese, in mano agli *Anglocaluinistae* e all'*infamis foemina*, ovvero la regina Elisabetta I. Tuttavia, prima di procedere all'analisi della fonte, si valuterà brevemente la fortuna editoriale e l'impatto nel mercato librario del Cinque-Seicento, mostrando inoltre la struttura dei due *Promptuaria*, in modo da comprenderne meglio la differenza.

I Promptuaria *e il loro successo editoriale*

Stapleton offrì ai suoi lettori due *Promptuaria*, uno *catholicum* e un altro *morale*: entrambi si rivolgevano ai *concionatores*, perché potessero costruire le proprie prediche in modo appropriato, rifuggendo qualsiasi possibilità di cadere in deviazioni eretical. I due testi hanno importanti differenze, che Stapleton rimarca sin dai titoli. Il *Catholicum* è pensato *ad instructionem concionatorum contra haereticos nostri temporis, super omnia euangelia totius anni, tam dominicalia quam de festis*.[13] Gli eretici *nostri temporis* sono in particolare i calvinisti, bersaglio polemico anche degli *Antidota*, ed è proprio per istruire i predicatori cattolici contro i loro insegnamenti eterodossi che il testo è studiato, in modo da fornire quelle nozioni fondamentali sulla fede per mezzo delle quali fosse possibile arginare il contagio eretical che aveva investito l'Inghilterra e che stava procurando non pochi problemi al controllo spagnolo dei Paesi Bassi. Quello *Morale*, invece, era pensato per dare al *concionator* uno strumento che avesse un impatto più immediato sul popolo di Dio, essendo teso alla *reformatio peccatorum* e alla *consolatio piorum*.[14] Entrambi i *Promptuaria* erano dunque necessari per chiunque avesse cura d'anime e si rivolgesse direttamente ai fedeli della Chiesa Romana.

Il *Catholicum* apparve per la prima volta sul mercato librario nel 1589, con l'*editio princeps* parigina curata da Michel Sonnius, viziata da alcune incomprensioni fra l'autore e lo stampatore; il *Morale*, invece, fu per la prima volta stampato ad Anversa dal successore di Plantin, Jan Moretus, non senza ulteriori attriti fra l'autore e il nuovo editore, mostrando l'energico carattere del

---

[13] Stapleton 1589.
[14] Stapleton 1591.

teologo inglese.[15] In ogni caso, i *Promptuaria* si rivelarono fin da subito un importante successo editoriale, capace di durare fino al XVIII secolo, come testimoniato dalle edizioni stampate a Lione nel 1707 da Nicolas De Ville e ad Augusta nel 1730 da Mathias Wolff. È notevole in ogni caso notare che nel solo arco temporale che va dal 1589 al 1657, vi sono più di cento edizioni in latino, di cui 22 a Parigi e Venezia, 19 a Lione, 17 ad Anversa, 17 a Colonia, 11 a Brescia, 3 a Magonza e 2 a Aschaffenburg; inoltre, vi sono tre edizioni in tedesco stampate a Ingolstadt.[16] A queste si devono poi aggiungere gli *Opera Omnia*, curati dallo stampatore parigino Robert Foüet nel 1620, e usati in questo contributo come edizione di riferimento attraverso la *Digital Library of the Catholic Reformation*.[17] Il successo editoriale dell'inglese fra la fine del XVI e la metà del XVII secolo deve essere messo inoltre in relazione a un altro dato: 'In 1610, the Antwerp Synod instructed that all parish priests should obtain his *Promptuarium catholicum* and *Promptuarium morale* either in Latin or in translation'.[18] I due *Promptuaria* non erano le uniche opere che il vescovo Jean Le Mire (1560–1611) consigliava caldamente al proprio clero, ma ciò che si può cogliere dalla lista proposta è che la maggior parte dei testi di cui si richiede la lettura sono scritti da gesuiti. Per esempio, vengono indicati i *Catholijcke Sermoonen* e il *Libellus Sodalitatis* di Frans de Costere (1531–1619), il *Directorium* di Juan Alonso de Polanco (1517–1576) o ancora il *Quae fides et religio sit capessenda, consultatio* di Leonard Lessius (1554–1623), così come la *Summa doctrinae Christianae* di Pietro Canisio (1521–1597),[19]

---

[15] Si veda Machielsen 2010.

[16] Tutti i dati relativi alle edizioni delle fonti del XVI e XVII secolo citate in questo contributo sono state desunte dalla consultazione dello *Universal Short Title Catalogue*.

[17] In ogni caso, i *Promptuaria* continuano a essere stampati anche in pieno XVIII secolo.

[18] Machielsen 2010, p. 101.

[19] *Quae omnia ut debit praestari possint, quilibet Pastor solicite et curiose curet ut bibliothecam instructam habet: in qua ut minimum sint Biblia sacra, Catechismus Romanus, Summa doctrinae Christianae per Canisium, Concilium Tridentinum, Synodus Prouincialis Mechiliensis, utraque Antuerpiensis sub piae memoriae Reuerendissimo Francisco Somnio celebrata atque haec nostra, Homiliastae aliqui, Promptuarium Catholicum Stapletoni, Sermones Costeri, eiusque libellus Solidatis, et de controuersiis horum temporum, Lessii Consultatio nuper quae religio sit capessenda, Directorium Polanci, eiusque libellus de frequenti communione et modo*

segno che la teologia della Compagnia di Gesù era considerata uno strumento efficace per controbattere le tesi calviniste e motivo per il quale anche Stapleton era stato scelto, essendo particolarmente influenzato dal molinismo. È evidente, dunque, che l'offerta proposta dal teologo inglese rispondeva a pieno all'esigenza di fornire al clero dei compendi che non solo permettessero di trasmettere al popolo i contenuti della fede cattolica, ma anche di contrastare efficacemente il calvinismo che si stava imponendo nei Paesi Bassi, contro cui Stapleton scriveva esplicitamente e che considerava causa scatenante dell'eresia nella propria madrepatria oltre che nella sua nuova terra in esilio. Stapleton metteva dunque a disposizione la propria esperienza di rifugiato per motivi confessionali da un regno molto vicino, l'Inghilterra, 'inquinato' dal calvinismo — non a caso egli parlava di 'anglocalvinisti' —, per preservare i seguaci della 'vera' fede, in modo da non farli cadere negli stessi errori compiuti al di là della Manica, un pericolo drammaticamente presente ai suoi occhi. Proprio la furia iconoclasta calvinista aveva infatti dato avvio nel 1566 alla ribellione delle provincie olandesi contro la Spagna: i frutti di quell'iniziale rivolta si sarebbero in parte concretizzati con il Trattato di Anversa (1609), per mezzo del quale l'impero cattolico riconobbe infine l'autonomia delle calviniste Sette Provincie Unite.[20]

Il *Catholicum* e il *Morale*, inoltre, mostrano importanti differenze nella struttura, benché in entrambi i casi venissero analizzati i passi evangelici letti durante le messe domenicali e dei giorni festivi. Il primo appare meno elaborato, con un numero minore di citazioni dai Padri della Chiesa rispetto al *Morale*, in cui vi sono peraltro riferimenti a filosofi greci e romani. Si ha l'impressione, in effetti, di avere nel *Catholicum* delle omelie pronte per essere lette o pronunciate di fronte ai fedeli: il passo evangelico non viene citato, ma vi è solo la sua spiegazione. Il *Morale*, invece, vede un'analisi più serrata della pericope, citata per esteso e da cui l'inglese trae una sorta di indice degli argomenti dai singoli versi del brano, fornendone una brevissima spiegazione. Segue poi la

iuuandi morientes, aliique simile pro singulorum capacitate et facultatibus. Rudiores vero et minus instructi in Theologia (quos hactenus ob sacerdotum raritatem et inopiam tolerare cogimur) numquam aliquid dicant pro concione quod ex probato auctore aliquo demonstrare non possit, Miraeus 1610 p. 46–47.

[20] Si veda Soen 2016 e il volume a cura di Lesaffer 2014.

disamina accurata di ogni verso, rendendo la trattazione particolarmente prolissa e anche molto varia nell'estensione. Il fine dunque non era di mettere a disposizione un testo pronto per essere usato come omelia, piuttosto si era prodotta un'opera simile a un commentario esegetico, ma più puntuale nell'analisi delle letture domenicali e con cui il *concionator* avrebbe potuto sciogliere i passi di più difficile interpretazione, indirizzando solo in seguito la predica secondo gli elementi che gli premeva sottolineare di fronte al suo pubblico, riducendone o ampliandone la spiegazione.[21]

Un'eretica sul trono d'Inghilterra

All'interno della propria opera, l'autore fa non pochi riferimenti alla situazione geopolitica e religiosa del suo tempo; in particolare, il bersaglio polemico più importante contro il quale Stapleton dimostra la propria avversione è la regina d'Inghilterra, Elisabetta I, per la quale aveva dovuto lasciare la sua patria circa 30 anni prima. Quando pubblicò il *Catholicum*, Stapleton aveva ormai vissuto più tempo in esilio che nella sua terra natia, essendo fuggito poco più che ventenne. Elisabetta anzitutto compare nel *Morale* nell'analisi della II domenica di Avvento, il cui passo evangelico è Mt. 3. 1–12. In particolare, Stapleton afferma che il versetto 9 *Arundinem uento agitatam?*, tratta *de fortitudine animi, libertate spiritus, et constantia seruanda* nelle avversità e soprattutto nella difesa della verità.[22] Proprio su questo secondo principio, il teologo inglese analizza diversi esempi concreti tratti dalla storia del cristianesimo antico e altri invece a lui contemporanei, ma forse

---

[21] *Hoc ergo nobis in hoc Promptuario Morali propositum est, in singulis per annum Euangeliis, tam de Dominicis quam de Festis, si uita, ualetudo, et negotia caetera permittent, loca seu textus singulos obseruare et annotare, unde aliquid ad bonos mores, et pietatis studium promouendum depromi documentum queat: moxque documentum inde depromptum, et locum inuentum, materia et supellectile morali, quantum possumus copiosa, ex aliis Scripturis ad eam rem facientibus, ex sanctis Patribus, et optimis quibusque Authoribus petita, locupletare: et Exemplis ac Similibus crebro exornare: non sane aut uerbis superfluis rem eandem dicendo, aut sermone accurato quicquam amplificando; sed res ipsas simpliciter proferendo, et accumulando (non tamen absque certo ordine ac methodo, ubi partitio loci id feret) et materiam uberem subministrando (in qua tamen delectum magis quam copiam affectauimus) planeque praeter materiam nihil: quam postea Concionator quisque, prout uolet disponet, exornabit, amplificabit, atque etiam locupletabit*, Stapleton 1591, *proemium*.

[22] Stapleton 1620, p. 15.

il più interessante è l'intreccio che Stapleton crea fra due personaggi, Valente ed Elisabetta, in una sorta di doppio ritratto plutarcheo. Riguardo all'imperatore ariano, Stapleton cita un episodio occorso dopo la vittoriosa campagna armena del 370, condotta dal *dux Terentius*; per ringraziarlo, Valente lo avrebbe invitato a chiedere qualsiasi cosa e il *dux*, devoto cristiano niceno, avrebbe domandato la costruzione di una chiesa ortodossa in Antiochia, con conseguente forte irritazione di Valente, che avrebbe stracciato di fronte a lui la *schedula* della richiesta.[23] L'episodio, tratto dalla *Historia Ecclesiastica* (IV, 32) di Teodoreto di Cirro (*c*. 393–458), serviva al teologo inglese per dimostrare quanto fosse radicata l'eresia in Valente; tuttavia, lo era maggiormente in Elisabetta I. La monarca inglese, infatti, a seguito di una bella esibizione curata da Sebastian Westcott (*c*. 1524–1582), definito *ludimagister* essendo il *Master* della celebre compagnia teatrale *Children of Paul's*, gli avrebbe domandato cosa potesse fare per ringraziarlo, similmente a quanto aveva fatto Valente con Terenzio. Il commediografo rispose di voler professare liberamente il proprio credo cattolico: la regina non solo non glielo avrebbe permesso, ma lo avrebbe fatto anche imprigionare.[24] L'episodio non doveva essere molto noto fuori dall'Inghilterra e, in effetti,

---

[23] *Sed et fortis illa erat confessio fidei quam fecit Terentius dux Valenti Ariano imperatori. Reuersus ille ex Armenia cum magna uictoria, quum eum Imperator petere quam uellet mercedem iuberet, id tantum petiit, ut una Antiochiae Ecclesia Catholicis daretur. Iratus, Imperator petitionis schedulam lacerauit et ut aliud aliquid peteret iussit. Terentius fragmenta schedulae recolligit: "et hoc", inquit, "de tua Maiestate totius mercedis loco accipiam, nec aliud petam"*, Stapleton 1620, p. 17. Su Terenzio, si veda Lenski 2007, p. 104–105.

[24] *Barbare quidem Valens iste, sed magis barbare Elizabetha Angliae regina haeretica, quae Sebastianum Londinensem ludimagistrum, quum insignem comoediam reginae exhibuisset, quae illi egregie placuerat, et mercedem quam uellet petere iussisset, illeque nihil aliud quam suae conscientiae libertatem peteret, ut sine ulla uexatione Catholico more uiuere permitteretur, indignata muliercula, astantibus nobilibus dixit: "Videre, obsecro, bonus iste uir conscientiam habet, sed in carcerem abeat, donec inanes hos conscientiae scrupulos deponere discat moxque pro omni mercede carcerem reportat". Non Christianam, etsi haereticam, sed ethnicam aliquam, aut atheam te audire existimes. Eadem Elizabetha apud D. Geffordum nobilem Catholicum Anglum splendide excepta, post omnes easdemque maximas impensas, captiuum illum secum, sola religionis causa, abduxit. Sed et Richardum Sheileium, uirum nobilem hac sola causa, quod Catholicorum nobilium nomine libellum supplicem pro aliqua religionis Catholicae toleratione, et barbari cuiusdam staturi mitigatione, Reginae porrigere ausus esset, immanissimis primum contumeliis exceptum in carcerem retrusit, ubi non multo post squalore confectus interiit*, Stapleton 1620, p. 17.

Stapleton non si cura di riportarlo correttamente, probabilmente per risaltare la crudeltà della regina nei confronti dei cattolici. In realtà, i fatti si erano svolti ben diversamente: Westcott era sì stato condotto in carcere, in quello londinese di Marshalsea per undici settimane, dal 30 dicembre 1577 al 19 marzo 1578, con l'accusa di essere un papista, ma proprio grazie al favore della regina era stato infine scarcerato.[25] Stapleton fa poi riferimento a Gilbert Gifford (*c.* 1560–1590), che doveva aver certamente conosciuto a Douai, essendo stato accolto nel *English College* nel 1577. Dopo un periodo burrascoso diviso fra Roma, la Francia e l'Inghilterra, Gifford ricevette infine il diaconato nel 1585 e il presbiterato nel 1587. In realtà, anche le vicende di Gifford non sono molto chiare: Stapleton afferma che era stato condotto in prigione *sola religionis causa*, ma omette di dire che era stato arrestato in Francia nel 1587 perché scoperto mentre frequentava un postribolo.[26] Infine, Stapleton ricorda anche Richard Shelley (*c.* 1513–1589), che nel 1585 aveva presentato una petizione alla regina *pro aliqua religionis Catholicae toleratione*: il risultato fu l'incarcerazione e la conseguente morte nel 1586 nel Marshalsea.[27]

Nel *Morale* Stapleton continua la sua invettiva contro Elisabetta I analizzando la lettura della XIX domenica di Pentecoste, dove paragona la regina ai celebri sovrani del passato che avevano perseguitato la 'vera' fede. In particolare, il passo in questione è Mt. 22.1–14 e commentando sul versetto 6, *Reliqui uero tenuerunt seruos eius, et contumeliis affectos occiderunt*, Stapleton afferma che queste parole descrivono la crudeltà dei persecutori dell'ortodossia, a partire dagli imperatori romani dei primi tre secoli e, dopo che il Cristianesimo aveva ormai preso il sopravvento sulle altre religioni, altrettanto persecutori erano stati gli ariani Costanzo II e Valente, i re goti in Italia, i sovrani vandali in Africa e, infine, gli imperatori bizantini iconoclasti: Leone III Isaurico, Costantino V

---

[25] Lennam 1975, p. x.

[26] Inoltre, ma Stapleton non ne era probabilmente al corrente, Gifford era un agente in incognito, doppiogiochista, implicato nel *Barbington Plot* (1586) per l'assassinio di Elisabetta I, per mettere sul trono Maria Stuart — motivo per il quale la regina di Scozia fu infine giustiziata. Tuttavia, la sua fedeltà alla causa cattolica non era indubbia, sembra anzi che avesse lavorato per conto, e non contro, Elisabetta I. Si veda Plowden 2004.

[27] Manning 1962.

Copronimo, Filippico Bardane e Leone V l'Armeno.[28] *Talis est hodie*, afferma Stapleton, che elenca i paesi in cui il protestantesimo si era ormai diffuso: il Sacro Romano Impero, il regno di Danimarca-Norvegia, la Confederazione Elvetica, ma soprattutto il reame inglese, l'unico di cui viene nominato sovrano, appunto Elisabetta I, definita *impotens et infamis foemina*. La persecuzione a cui i cattolici erano soggetti nel suo regno, inoltre, era duplice, in quanto si manifestava non solo come repressione dei 'papisti', ma anche con il tentativo di conversione perpetrato da *magistri seductores*.[29] Stapleton cita anche quattro volumi pubblicati non troppo tempo prima che denunciavano le violenze patite dai cattolici inglesi, in particolare il *De persecutione Anglicana* del gesuita Robert Parsons (1546–1610), pubblicato in latino nel 1582 a Roma, Parigi e Ingolstadt, l'*Ad persecutores Anglos pro Christianis responsio* del cardinale William Allen (1532–1594), stampato nel 1584 a Douai e Rouen, dove era stato già pubblicato in inglese, con il titolo *A True Sincere and Modest Defence of English Catholiques*. Inoltre, Stapleton fa riferimento a un lavoro di un altro gesuita, John Gibbons (1544–1589), la *Concertatio ecclesiae catholicae*

---

[28] *Locus moralis de impietate et crudelitate persecutorum fidei, pietatis, Ecclesiae. Isti enim omnium deterrimi, non contenti non uelle ad nuptias caelestes uenire, negligere et recusare, etiam ipsos Dei seruos ac ministros, tantaeque faelicitatis nuncios, tenuerunt, libertate priuantes: contumeliis affecerunt, honorem uiolantes; ac demum occiderunt, uita spoliantes. Ad hanc impietatem nihil accedere potuisse uidetur. Tales erant in primis trecentis post Christum annis plerique totius mundi imperatores Romani ethnici, etsi decem tantum persecutiones illorum temporum notari soleant, quia illae praecipuae erant, omniumque acerbissimae. Tales postea fuerunt omnium aetatum haeretici principes, Arriani maxime, Constantius, Valens, aliique Gotthorum in Italia, et Vandalorum in Africa reges. Post illos autem in Oriente Iconomachi imperatores multi: Leo Isauricus, Constantinus Copronymus, Philippicus, Leo Armenius, aliique nonnulli*, Stapleton 1620, p. 481–482. Sulle persecuzioni in epoca romana, si rimanda a de Ste. Croix 2006.

[29] *Talis hodie (etsi in Germania, Dania, Heluetia principes ac dominici haeretici multi sint) sola tamen quae religionem orthodoxam cruentis legibus, et omni crudelitatis genere persequitur, in Anglia est Elizabetha impotens et infamis foemina. Illa enim et uinctos tenuit omnes ad unum Catholicos Angliae episcopos, multosque praeterea ecclesiarum illic pastores et doctores, quam primum ad regni gubernacula sedere coepit; et a decem iam circiter annis, omnis ordinis Catholicos, sacerdotes, nobiles, ciues, non tenuit tantum diris carceribus mancipatos, sed et omni praeterea contumelia affectos (sacerdotes maxime, qui ad nuptias caelestes, ad Ecclesiae et sponsae filii Dei unionem, errantes oues reuocabant) immanibus prius tormentis confectos, acerbissimo mortis genere interfecit. De qua afflictissimi illius regni persecutione duplici, una per haereticos magistros seductores, altera per potestates huius saeculi percussores (quae huic loco propria est) ea dici aptissime possunt*, Stapleton 1620, p. 482.

in Anglia, aduersus caluinopapistas et puritanos, edita a Treviri nel 1583. Infine, il quarto autore è il gesuita inglese Edmund Campion (1540–1581), che aveva scritto le *Rationes decem*, pubblicate per la prima volta nel 1581 — anno della sua esecuzione — a Henley-on-Thames da Stephen Brinkley, ma a cui seguirono ben diciannove edizioni fino al 1648, in quattordici città europee.[30] Le *Rationes decem* ebbero in effetti un'eco molto importante: il testo venne confutato dal teologo anglicano William Whitaker (1548–1595) con la sua *Responsio*, stampata a Londra nel 1581 e a cui Campion non poté chiaramente ribattere. A prendere le difese del proprio confratello fu lo scozzese John Dury o Durie (*c.* 1544–1588) con la sua *Confutatio*, pubblicata a Ingolstadt nel 1585. Whitaker, inoltre, nel 1588, quindi poco prima che Stapleton pubblicasse i suoi *Promptuaria*, aveva dato alle stampe forse la sua opera più celebre, la *Disputatio de sacra scriptura*, un testo dichiaratamente controversialista, che reca già nel titolo il nome dei suoi due bersagli polemici: Roberto Bellarmino (1542–1621) e proprio Thomas Stapleton.[31] Per quest'ultimo, dunque, ricostruire la disputa Campion-Whitaker-Dury aveva un duplice scopo: sia ribattere Whitaker sul piano teologico sia denunciare la violenta repressione subita in Inghilterra dai cattolici, la cui posizione risultava compromessa non solo a livello religioso, ma anche dal punto di vista politico, dal momento che l'essere 'papista'

---

[30] *Huius persecutionis Anglicanae, qua seruos Dei ad ipsos ab Ecclesia missos, contumeliis affectos, occiderunt, crudelissima exempla uidere licet in libello de persecutione Anglicana, in altero ad persecutores Anglos libro ac potissimum in illo magno uolumine, Treueris anno superiore edito, cui titulus est 'Concertatio Ecclesiae Catholicae in Anglia, aduersus Caluino-papistas et Puritanos, sub Elizabetha regina, quorundam hominum doctrina et sanctitate illustrium, renouata'. Certe presbyteros plus quam quinquaginta infra hos paucos annos, exquisitis prius tormentis probatos, neci dederunt: inter caeteros uirum eruditione, pietate, eloquentia, morum candore praestantissimum, Edmundum Campianum, Societatis Iesu presbyterum; qui quum decem propositis rationibus (libello insigni) ad nuptias caelestes homines Anglos, et maxime Academicos uocasset, paulo post captus, post contumelias per totam urbem Londinensem acceptas, post equuleos in carcere tertio toleratos, barbaro supplicio per plateas tractus, fune strangulatus, exenteratus, et euisceratus, cum aliis compresbyteris, et gloriosi martyrii sociis occiditur*, Stapleton 1620, p. 482. In particolare, le *Rationes decem* sono state stampate ad Anversa (1581; 1582, 1632), Colonia (1594; 1600), Caen (1616), Cracovia (1605), Graz (1588), Ingolstadt (1583; 1584), Lich (1601), Milano (1582), Munster (1613), Paris (1649), Roma (1582; 1584), Vilnius (1583), Vienna (1594) e Würzburg (1589).

[31] Whitaker 1588.

implicava anche il delitto di lesa maestà.[32] Tale accusa comportava la pena capitale secondo la terribile procedura dell'*hanged, drawn and quartered*, a cui Campion era stato sottoposto e che veniva del tutto legittimata dai quadri dirigenti della monarchia inglese, per esempio da William Cecil (1520-1598), lord di Burghley, nel *The Execution of Justice in England* e nella *Declaration of Favourable Dealing of Her Majesty's Commissioners*.[33] La ragione dell'accusa di alto tradimento seguiva, nell'ottica anglicana, la bolla di scomunica della regina emanata da Pio V *Regnans in excelsis* (1570), in cui si intimava ai cattolici inglesi di non obbedire alle leggi dell'eretica Elisabetta I.[34] Proprio per tale motivo, i cattolici divenivano potenzialmente pericolosi in quanto 'al servizio di un altro principe', come ancora affermato da John Locke (1632-1704) un secolo dopo nella sua *Letter concerning Toleration* (1689).[35]

Alla crudeltà dei persecutori, tuttavia, seguiva la *certa et infallibilis iustitia ac uindicta Dei*, come risulta evidente dal verso

---

[32] *Hodie in Anglia, non solum ipsi serui Dei uocantes ad nuptias, sed etiam qui aliquem presbyterum Catholicum in domum suam recipit; qui in priuato colloquio, ut aliquem ab haeresi ad fidem Catholicam reducat, uel minimum sermonem miscet; qui huiusmodi aliquid, ab alio quopiam praestitum ultra 24. horas celat, laesae Maiestatis crimen committere, et capitali supplicio (quale supra posuimus) afficiendus, publico regni decreto iudicatur. Hoc est: 'Conuertere in absynthium iudicium', etc. Quod de Iudaeorum duritia Deus per Oseam dixit, in hoc persecutionis genere, maxime hodie Anglicanae, locum habet: 'Quid faciam tibi Ephraim, quid faciam tibi Iuda', etc. Propter hoc dolaui in Prophetis meis*, Stapleton 1620, p. 482. Sulla persecuzione dei cattolici durante il regno di Elisabetta I, si veda il capitolo 'La restauration du Protestantism sous Élisabeth et la persecution des catholique (1558-1603)', in Lecler 1955, II, p. 303-325. Sui martiri inglesi, si veda Houliston & Muller 2019.

[33] Anderson 2014, p. 3.

[34] [D]*eclaramus praedictam Elizabetham haereticam, et haereticorum fautricem [...] Praecipimusque et interdicimus uniuersis et singulis proceribus, subditis, populis, et aliis praedictis, ne illi eiusue monitis, mandatis et legibus audeant obedire*, Pius V 1570.

[35] 'That church can have no right to be tolerated by the magistrate which is constituted upon such a bottom that all those who enter into it do thereby ipso facto deliver themselves up to the protection and service of another prince. For by this means the magistrate would give way to the settling of a foreign jurisdiction in his own country, and suffer his own people to be listed, as it were, for soldiers against his own government', Locke 1963, p. 93. Sul concetto di tolleranza di John Locke sono stati realizzati molteplici studi, fra cui Lorenzo 2003 e Lucci 2018 a cui si rimanda per ulteriore bibliografia. È doveroso tuttavia ricordare anche la recente scoperta di un manoscritto di Locke che sembra mitigare la sua iniziale posizione sulla tolleranza — da non applicare — nei confronti dei cattolici, cf. Walmsley & Waldmann 2019.

Mt. 22. 7 *Rex autem cum audisset, iratus est; et missis exercitibus suis, perdidit homicidas illos, et ciuitatem illorum succendit*. Gli esempi storici, per Stapleton, non mancano: gli assiri avevano devastato Gerusalemme quando i suoi re si erano allontanati da Dio — il riferimento è alla distruzione del Tempio di Salomone a opera di Nabucodonosor II (587 a.C.) —, Costanzo II era morto per febbre, Valente era caduto ad Adrianopoli nella celebre battaglia contro i Goti (378). Anche l'ariano Unnerico re dei Vandali era stato un violento persecutore e per questo colpito *a uermibus*, come riportato da Vittore di Vita nella sua *Historia persecutionis* (V, c. 21). L'ortodosso Giustiniano, invece, grazie a Belisario, aveva ripreso il controllo dell'Africa sotto il giogo dei Vandali ariani e, quando l'Impero Romano d'Oriente si era a sua volta allontanato dalla vera fede, Dio aveva punito gli scismatici con l'arrivo dei musulmani. Anche gli imperatori bizantini avevano subito una sorte simile a quella dei loro predecessori: il monofisita Anastasio era stato colpito da un fulmine. La morte aveva colto anche gli autocrati iconoclasti: Costantino V di febbre e Leone V assassinato.[36] Il teologo inglese, tuttavia, non è sempre accurato nel riportare gli eventi storici, difficilmente per ignoranza, più probabilmente per rinforzare il proprio argomento, dimostrando che i persecutori della 'vera' fede muoiono di morte violenta, secondo il disegno della giustizia divina. Per esempio, la morte del monofisita Anastasio è ripotata nella *Historia miscella* di Landolfo Sagace, cronista del X secolo, fonte pubblicata per la prima volta nel 1532 e da cui è possibile che Stapleton abbia tratto la notizia; tuttavia, lo stesso Landolfo descrive l'evento più come un detto che come un fatto.[37]

---

[36] *Sic Iudaeorum Hierosolyma ab Assyriis uastata est. Sic Vandalorum Arrianorum Carthago a Belisario Iustiniani duce direpta est. Sic schismaticorum et contra sancti Spiritus maiestatem haereticorum Orientalium Constantinopolis a Mahumetanis occupata est. Et ut personas ipsas atque homicidas uerae fidei persecutores perstringamus, sic Constantius Arrianus, maerore confectus, cum contra Iulianum proficisceretur, obscure interiit. Sic Valens Arrianus, persecutor grauis, in bello contra Gothos, in casula succensus, obiit. Sic Anastasius, Chalcedonensis concilii hostis fulmine de caelo percussus occubuit. Sic Constantinus Copronymus, Iconomachus, et acerbissimus persecutor, calidis febribus uehementissime agitatus, se uiuentem in ignem coniectum esse uociferatur, et moritur. Sic Leo Armenius Iconomachus quoque in ipsa Ecclesia a conspiratis ipso natalis Dominici die interficitur*. Stapleton 1620, p. 483.

[37] *Quidam autem aiunt, quod diuino fulmine Anastasius a fulgore perierit*. Landulfus 1532, l. 15, p. 193.

Stapleton, inoltre, afferma che il monotelita Filippico Bardane era stato ucciso dai senatori; in realtà, era stato acciecato, morendo poi diversi mesi dopo la congiura. Allo stesso modo, l'inglese sostiene che Valentiniano II, di fede ariana e in contrasto con Ambrogio, era morto per mano di Magno Massimo, benché in effetti non si conoscano perfettamente le circostanze della sua morte. Fra gli imperatori che maggiormente avevano perseguitato i cristiani nei primi secoli dell'era volgare, Stapleton ricorda *Nero, Domitianus, Seuerus, Adrianus, Decius, Valerianus, Maximinanus, Maximinus* affermando che tutti avevano subito una morte violenta: Domiziano era stato ucciso in una congiura di palazzo (96), Adriano di malattia (138), un Severo era stato ucciso dall'esercito, Decio era caduto nella cocente sconfitta presso Abrittus (251), Valeriano era stato catturato dai sasanidi dopo la sua disastrosa campagna contro Sapore I (260), Massimiano si era impiccato (310) e un Massimino aveva trovato la morte per mano dei propri soldati. A questa lunga lista si aggiungono Licinio, giustiziato (325), e l'apostata Giuliano, deceduto durante la campagna sasanide (363); tuttavia, alcune precisazioni sono necessarie. Adriano e Giuliano non sono stati dei persecutori; Stapleton, inoltre, afferma che *Seuerus et Iulius Maximinus filius eius ab exercitu interfecti sunt*. Il riferimento probabile è a Flavio Valerio Severo e Massimino Daia, ma il primo non era padre del secondo e non si hanno notizie di sue persecuzioni. In effetti, *Iulius* fa parte dei *nomina* di Massimino il Trace; tuttavia, Alessandro Severo, suo predecessore, non fu né suo padre né un persecutore. Infine, probabilmente, il Severo citato insieme a Domiziano e Adriano è Settimio, che tuttavia morì di malattia.[38]

---

[38] *Sic Philippicus imperator, tum Iconomachus, tum Monothelita, et ipse quoque Catholicos persequens, a Senatoribus suis in conuiuio occiditur. Sic Valentinianus iunior diuum Ambrosium uexans, et Catholicos persequi studens, a Maximo tyranno trucidatur. Sic Hunericus Arrianus, saeuissimus in Africa persecutor, a uermibus corrosus interiit. Sic denique primi illi Christianae religionis persecutores Nero, Domitianus, Seuerus, Adrianus, Decius, Valerianus, Maximinanus, Maximinus uiolenta morte omnes, uel acerbissima, uel ignominiosa ualde perierunt. Nero, tum sua, tum alterius manu adiutus, ferro peremptus est. Domitianus suorum conspiratione confessus occubuit. Adrianus miserabili fato consumptus est, ut in seipsum saeuire uoluerit, si per domesticos licuisset. Seuerus et Iulius Maximinus filius eius ab exercitu interfecti sunt. Decius cum toto suo exercitu a Gothis caeditur, corpusque paludis uoragine absumptum, nusquam inuentum. Valerianus a Persis captus, miserabili captiuitate conficitur, Persarum Regi subsellii uice seruiens, quum equum consecenderet, et micas*

L'inglese in effetti non è accurato nel riportare le informazioni tratte dalla sua fonte, che appare a margine in corrispondenza di questo passaggio, vale a dire il *De Caesaribus libri III* di Giovanni Battista Cipelli (1478-1553), altrimenti conosciuto come Egnazio. In particolare, questi afferma che sotto Nerone si ha lo spargimento del primo sangue cristiano [39] e che Decio è stato un buon imperatore, pur avendo ucciso papa Fabiano e papa Cornelio.[40] Cipelli, nel riportare quanto avvenuto sotto *Seuerus et Maximinus* — senza indicare alcun rapporto di parentela — afferma che Massimiano 'Christiani sanguinis usque ad insaniam pridem effusi incassum poenitens'.[41] Licino viene definito 'Christianis infestissimus',[42] ma nulla viene detto riguardo al rapporto degli altri imperatori — Domiziano, Settimio Severo, Adriano, e Giuliano —, con i cristiani, pur riportandone la morte violenta laddove avvenuta.

Nella sua disamina della storia romana imperiale dei primi tre secoli, Stapleton riprende nella sostanza le argomentazioni del *De mortibus persecutorum* di Lattanzio, una fonte conosciuta e citata nei *Promptuaria*, anche se non nei brani presi in considerazione.

---

panum sub mensa eius comedere coactus. Maximinianus, Massiliae captus, iussu Constantii necatur. Maximinus Christiani sanguinis appetentissimus, putrescentibus genitalibus, uitae taedio, uim sibi gladio intulit. Sed et praeter istos, Maximianus alter, a Maximino adoptatus ac Caesar renunciatus, Christiano sanguine usque ad insaniam effuso, ulcere inguinibus innato, uermibus undique erumpentibus, obiit. Lycinius quoque tyrannus, Constantini clementia abusus, Christianis infestissimus, Thessalonicae captus, interficitur. In hos omnes iusta ira Dei desaeuit. Iulianus demum Apostata, Christianis molestissimus, in Persia, exercitum ducens, incerto ictu percussus, blasphemans moritur. Qui horum hodie facta imitantur, horum exitus perhorrescant, Stapleton 1620, p. 483-484. Si veda Gerace 2019, 226-228. La letteratura ha ormai ridimensionato molto la portata delle persecuzioni romane così come sono state presentate dagli autori cristiani, si rimanda a González Salinero 2005, de Ste. Croix 2006, Moss 2013, Corke-Webster 2020. Sul presunto editto di Settimio Severo, Schwarte 1963, su Massimino Daia, Mitchell 1988 e Marcos 2013; su Mssimino il Trace, Clarke 1966. In particolare su Giuliano, Bouffartigue 2007 e Marcos 2008, su Nerone Shaw 2015.

[39] Egnazio 1516, [p. 10v]. Non è improbabile che Stapleton avesse a disposizione anche l'*Historiae Ecclesiasticae Scriptores Graeci* (1581) realizzata dal suo compatriota John Christopherson, vescovo di Chichester (m. 1558), in cui vengono raccolte le 'Storia Ecclesiastica' di Eusebio di Cesarea, Socrate Scolastico, Teodorico di Cirro, Sozomeno, Evagrio Scolastico.

[40] Egnazio 1516, [p. 18r-v].
[41] Egnazio 1516 [p. 22v].
[42] Egnazio 1516 [p. 23r].

Questi esempi avevano un comune denominatore – la morte violenta appunto – e dovevano fungere da monito per tutti i regnanti: *In hos omnes iusta ira Dei desaeuit [...] Qui horum hodie facta imitantur, horum exitus perhorrescant*. Fra i sovrani che avrebbero dovuto fare tesoro di questi insegnamenti del passato, vi era in primo luogo il re di Francia Enrico III di Valois, reo di aver prima tollerato i protestanti nel proprio regno e poi di aver osteggiato i difensori del cattolicesimo. Nel 1588, infatti, il monarca francese aveva richiesto e ottenuto l'uccisione sia di Enrico duca di Guisa (1550–1588), colui che aveva costituito la Lega santa con lo scopo di eliminare gli eretici dal regno, sia di suo fratello, il cardinale Luigi di Guisa (1555–1588). Il giudizio divino, tuttavia, non aveva tardato a raggiungere il re, trucidato a sua volta da un membro della Lega, il domenicano Jacques Clément (1567–1589), ucciso poi dalle guardie reali.[43]

L'altra grande persecutrice è chiaramente Elisabetta I, così come lo sono, più in generale, gli anglocalvinisti, che ormai veneravano la regina al pari di una dea a causa del suo regno trentennale, due volte all'anno, il 7 settembre, giorno del suo compleanno, e il 17 novembre, anniversario della sua incoronazione.[44] Anche lei, tuttavia, avrebbe subito l'ira Dio; in particolare, l'intensità della pena sarebbe stata direttamente proporzionale al tempo che Egli avrebbe atteso per applicare la sua giusta vendetta. In effetti — afferma Stapleton — il lungo regno di un persecutore non era stato un caso isolato nella storia del cristianesimo. Fra i tanti, Stapleton ricorda in primo luogo i sasanidi e più in particolare Yazdgard I, che dopo aver garantito per molto tempo la tolleranza ai cristiani, aveva in effetti avviato una politica repressiva alla fine del proprio regno,

---

[43] *Nam et dum haec scribimus, Henricus tertius, Francorum rex, grauis Ecclesiae Dei persecutor, primum tetra hypocrisi, et haereticos tolerando, postea aperta perfidia et catholicos principes, duos fratres Guisianos, cardinalem et ducem, barbare trucidando, iusto demum Dei iudicio trucidatur*, Stapleton 1620, p. 484.

[44] *Similia hodie pleno ore iactant Anglocaluinistae, quorum et eadem pene uerba uidere licet in libro ad persecutores Anglos, pag. 209 et 210, quia uidelicet triginta totis annis regnauit ibi haeretica princeps, prospera semper fortuna usa, quam etiam ob causam, illam pene ut deam colunt, diem natiuitatis eius Septemb. 7 et diem quo ad regni solium peruenit, 17. Nouembris, maxima cum solemnitate toto regno festum celebrantes, eamque in publicum prodeuntem, genu in terram flexo, et manu eleuata acclamantes adorant, idque tanta religione, ut qui hoc studiose non praestat, hostis regni iudicetur*, Stapleton 1620, p. 484.

continuata poi dal suo successore Bahram V Gor.[45] Stapleton cita anche un altro re persiano, *Gararanes*, che avrebbe guidato a lungo la Persia attorno al 480: in base a questa datazione, dovrebbe trattarsi di Perooz I, in carica dal 459 al 484, ma più probabilmente si tratta di Yazdgard II, successore di Bahram V.[46] In effetti, una fonte coeva al *Promptuarium*, la *Cronologia* di Rodrigo Zamorano (1542–1620) del 1594 fa proprio riferimento a *Gararanes*, collocandolo nel pontificato di Leone I e asserendone una politica di persecuzione durata 30 anni.[47] Fra i regnanti eretici, vengono citati nuovamente Valente e Costanzo II, ma la dimostrazione che la giustizia divina prima o poi si sarebbe abbattuta sui governanti che mettevano in pericolo la 'vera' fede si manifesta anche nelle Scritture. Stapleton infatti ricorda Manasse e Zedechia, i quali avevano perseguitato Isaia e Geremia rispettivamente, ed erano conseguentemente caduti entrambi prigionieri di potenze straniere, nelle mani degli assiri il primo e in quelle dei babilonesi il secondo.[48]

Anche nella predica della XX domenica di Pentecoste (Io. 4.46–54) Stapleton dedica ampio spazio alla regina, la cui prossima fine viene prevista attraverso vari segni del cielo. Il più 'evidente' era stato il fulmine che nel giugno del 1561 aveva distrutto la guglia della cattedrale di San Paolo a Londra: il resto del tempio era rimasto illeso.[49] L'evento in ogni caso aveva turbato molto le coscienze

---

[45] Dignas & Winter, p. 35.

[46] Sull'evoluzione dell'impero sasanide, in particolare sotto gli imperatori indicati e sulle relative politiche si rimanda a Frye 1983, p. 143–149.

[47] Zamorano 1594, p. 358.

[48] *Veniet Rex iratus, qui missis exercitibus suis, perdet homicidas istos, sanguinarios Anglocaluinistas, et quosuis alios ueritatis Euangelicae persecutores, et ciuitatem eorum succendet. Non est abbreuiata manus Domini, nec ueritas Euangelii extincta. Cum tempus acceperit, ille iustitias iudicabit, et tarditatem uindictae grauitate pensabit. Fuerunt et alii haeretici principes, qui totis triginta annis Catholicos persecuti sunt, ut in Perside circa annum salutis 400. Isdigertes rex, et ibidem circa annum 480. Gararanes rex; Valens quoque et Constantius Imperatores Ariani in Oriente; ne de suae Elizabethae regno trigesimali glorientur Anglocaluinistae. Impii reges Iudae, qui sanctos prophetas persequebantur, Manasses Esaiam, Sedechias, Ieremiam, et alii alios, longa satis impunitate ac fortuna prospera usi sunt, sed uterque in miseram captiuitatem cum toto tandem populo abducti sunt,* Stapleton 1620, p. 484.

[49] *Sic hodie nihil Elizabetham haereticam Angliae reginam mouerunt uaria de caelo signa. Nobilissimae pyramidis templi diui Pauli Londinensis, toto regno celeberrimi, e caelo media die tactae ad cineres usque adustio, templo ipso saluo, sola excepta mensa ministeriali, quam altaris Catholici loco de nouo (ut suum fecit altare Ieroboam) extruxerant, in cineres quoque redacta: quod totum in ipsa uigilia Vene-*

inglesi di entrambe le confessioni; il primo a essere intervenuto era stato il vescovo anglicano James Pilkington (1520-1576), che aveva ascritto l'evento all'ira divina,[50] come riportato in alcuni suoi brevi libretti.[51] Tuttavia, i cattolici avevano ribattuto che tale ira era dovuta proprio al fatto che gli inglesi avevano abbandonato la vera fede. Il ricorso al passato per interpretare il presente è costante nella trattazione del teologo inglese e si rinnova anche nel sermone per il vangelo della XXII domenica di Pentecoste (Mt. 22. 15-21), specie nell'analizzare l'espressione *Reddite quae sunt Caesaris Caesari et quae sunt Dei Deo*. Se nell'antichità i primi cristiani erano perseguitati dagli imperatori pagani, al suo tempo i cattolici erano soggetti allo stesso trattamento da parte degli eretici; ancora una volta, Stapleton insiste sul fatto che in Inghilterra si assisteva a una duplice condanna, non solo religiosa, ma anche politica, visto che l'essere cattolico determinava *ipso facto* la lesa maestà. Questa sovrapposizione fra l'ambito politico e quello religioso era un'ulteriore dimostrazione dell'empietà anglicana. La regina, infatti, si sarebbe arrogata un diritto non suo: avendo sostituito il papa come capo della Chiesa d'Inghilterra, a lei tutti dovevano prestare un giuramento che Stapleton definisce 'barbaro', 'empio', 'assurdo' e 'sacrilego'. Per un suddito inglese, il voler permanere nel cattolicesimo romano poteva avere quindi solo quattro esiti: 'il carcere, la confisca dei beni, l'esilio o la morte.'[52]

---

rabilis Sacramenti (quem illi nunc diem pro prophano habent) fieri Deus uoluit. Terrae quoque aliquot iugera loco mota, cum arboribus in diuersum actis, uiaque publica adiacente ita conuersa, ut quod Orientem prius spectabat, nunc Occidentem solem aspiciat, et e diuerso, uasto interim et horrendo hiatu relicto. Vna quoque ex pedissequis eius nobilibus, ipsa audiente et uidente, horrendis spectris conterrita, se propter haeresim et impudicitiam certo damnatam horribiliter eiulans, et animam eiulando exhalans, Stapleton 1620, p. 501.

[50] Morrissey 2011, p. 3.

[51] *The true report of the burnyng of the steple and church of Poules in London* (1561), *Exemplum literarum amici cuiusdam ad amicum quendam suum, de uera origine conflagrationis pyramidis, et templi Paulini Londinensis* (1561) e infine *The burnynge of Paules church in London in the yeare of oure Lord 1561* (1563).

[52] *Caesari non solum quod Caesaris est, sed etiam quod Dei maxime proprium est, impie, sacrilege, et barbare tribuunt. Totam doctrinae ueritatem totam cultus ac religionis Christianae rationem a regia auctoritate, a decretis regiis dependere, fluere, et promanare docent, iurant, et omnes iurare compellunt. Sic apud eos non haeresis, non schismatis, non uiolatae religionis, non cultus et obsequii diuini negati, sed rebellionis crimen est, a uera religione (quam scilicet illi ueram esse uolunt) recedere. Sic iuxta eos frustra adiecit Christus: 'Et quae sunt Dei, Deo'. Satis erat dixisse, 'Reddite*

Fra questi, il teologo inglese e molti altri suoi colleghi avevano scelto il terzo, come testimoniato dall'istituzione di vari *English College* nel continente, non solo a Douai (1561), dove si era rifugiato Stapleton, ma anche a Roma (1579), Valladolid (1589), Siviglia (1592) e Lisbona (1628). A questi, si devono però aggiungere anche i vari *Irish College* e *Scots College*, fondati fra XVI e XVII secolo per riunire i sudditi cattolici dei regni d'Irlanda e di Scozia che volevano sfuggire alle misure prese dai monarchi anglicani in madrepatria.[53] Concludendo la sua analisi del passo domenicale, il teologo inglese ricorda che *plura hac de re in altero Promptuario Catholico dicta sunt*. In effetti, la sua analisi dello stesso verso nel *Catholicum* aggiunge altri aspetti, nuovamente associando la situazione del IV secolo con quella del suo tempo: le vite parallele sono ora quelle di Costanzo II ed Elisabetta I, entrambi eretici. Come noto, Atanasio era stato il maggior difensore dell'ortodossia nicena durante il regno dell'imperatore ariano, descritto dal vescovo alessandrino come precursore dell'Anticristo, un elemento che Stapleton mette in risalto citando l'*Epistola ad solitariam uitam agentes*, in cui Atanasio leggeva lo stato in cui versava la Chiesa del suo tempo attraverso la profezia di Daniele 7. Tale interpretazione, tuttavia, poteva essere applicata non solo nei confronti di Costanzo II, ma anche di Elisabetta I, che perseguitava i cattolici attraverso i suoi vescovi, da meglio definirsi *exploratores et uastatores*.[54] La stessa argomentazione, con la stessa citazione,

---

quae sunt Caesaris, Caesari', quandoquidem iuxta eos omnia uni Caesari debentur. Vnus Caesar, unus rex, uel una regina, unus puer, una mulier (tales enim in Anglia, ut suprema ecclesiae Anglicanae capita, regnauerunt) 'caput est, ac suprema gubernacula tenet, non secus in omnibus causis Ecclesiasticis, quam in causis ciuilibus'. Sic enim conceptis uerbis iurant. Et propter hoc unum iuramentum, non minus barbarum quam impium, nec secus absurdum quam sacrilegum, recusatum, omnes illic episcopi, pastores, canonici, doctores, nobiles, ciues, qui catholici esse et persistere uoluerunt, carcerem, rapinam bonorum, exilium, mortem acerbam respectiue passi sunt. Plura hac de re in altero Promptuario Catholico dicta sunt, Stapleton 1620, p. 520.

[53] Sull'istituzione dei *Colleges*, in particolare quelli irlandesi, sia in Spagna sia nei Paesi Bassi, si veda Downey 2017.

[54] *Certe Athanasius maximus ille Arianorum antagonista, tam indigne tulit Constantii Ariani imperatoris arrogantiam de causis Episcoporum cognoscere uolentis, ut eum hoc nomine Antichristum uocet. 'Quid hic* (ait) *quod Antichristi sit omisit? Siquidem iam denuo in locum Ecclesiasticae cognitionis suum Palatium tribunal earum causarum constituit, seque earum litium summum principem et authorem facit'. Et paulo post: 'Quis uidens eum in discernendo principem se facere Episcoporum, et praesidere*

comparirà pochi anni dopo nella *Defensio fidei catholicae et apostolicae aduersus Anglicanae sectae errores* di Francisco Suárez (1548–1617), pubblicato nel 1613 a Coimbra, segno di una probabile dipendenza del gesuita spagnolo dalla lettura del teologo inglese.[55]

Infine, la regina compare un'ultima volta nel *Catholicum*, nell'analisi della *feria IV* della settimana santa, il mercoledì santo. Il brano del vangelo era Lc. 22.39–71; 23.1–53 e in particolare l'attenzione di Stapleton si concentra sul versetto Lc. 22.42 *Quod pro et, Pater, si uis, transfer a me calicem istum*. La rappresentazione della sofferenza di Cristo, manifestata attraverso la passione e crocifissione, si accosta a quella a cui erano soggetti i cattolici inglesi. La persecuzione perpetrata dagli anglicani poneva ovviamente in contrapposizione i familiari di confessione diversa: la più alta dimostrazione di tale empietà era stata l'esecuzione di Maria Stuart, cugina di secondo grado di Elisabetta I, nel 1587.[56] È chiaro dunque che la morte della regina di Scozia era da assimilarsi a un martirio, come lei stessa lo aveva considerato rivelando la veste color cremisi di fronte al patibolo.[57]

---

iudiciis Ecclesiasticis, non merito dicat illum eam ipsam abominationem desolationis esse, quae a Daniele praedicta est? Nam quum circumamictus sit Christianismo, et in loca sancta penetret, et inibi consistens deuastet Ecclesias, abrogans Canones, ut cogens ut sua obtineant: quis, inquam, audebit dicere, hoc tempus Christianis paratum esse, et non potius persecutionem esse a Daniele praedictam?' Si haec tunc temporis Athanasius, quanto hodie plura et acerbiora diceret, si Angliae persecutionem et gubernantem in Ecclesia feminam per suos κατασκόπους hoc est exploratores et uastatores potius quam Episcopos uideret, Stapleton 1620, p. 665–666.

[55] Suárez 1613, lib. V, c. 17, 9, p. 653D–654A. Su Suárez si veda Maryks et Senent de Frutos 2019, in specie i contributi di Robert Fastiggi (p. 115–127), Aaron Pidel (p. 128–153) e Pilar Pena Búa (p. 272–299).

[56] *Christus quum esset persona nobilissima pariterque innocentissima, et qui genti illum ad mortem traditurae innumera beneficia contulisset, tam ignominiosam et crudelem et a tam ingratis hominibus inferendam mortem naturaliter debuit refugere, expauescere et deprecari, uolens eam semel ante oculos suos in sua simplici natura considerandam proponere. Regem aut Reginam uel a suis subditis, uel ab alienis, qui nullam in eos potestatem habent, mortem ignominiosam pati, (cuius barbarum admodum et truculentum exemplum haec aetas uidit, quum Maria Stuarta Scotiae Regina, filia, coniunx, et mater Regis, Princeps innocentissima, ab Elizabetha Angliae Regina, cognata, et hospite, per publici carnificis manum obtruncata fuit) parentem a propriis liberis, aut amicum ab amico interfici, grauiorem haud dubie doloris acerbitatem adfert, quam sola communis mors in seipsa considerata*, Stapleton 1620, p. 809.

[57] Warnicke 2006, p. 250–251.

Conclusione

Stapleton dimostra una profonda avversione nei confronti di Elisabetta I, anche a causa della propria condizione di esiliato politico, oltre che religioso, per le ragioni che egli stesso ha spiegato nei suoi due prontuari omiletici. Tuttavia, la propria esperienza personale o la narrazione di vicende altrui, accostate a esempi più o meno celebri del passato per i fedeli che avrebbero ascoltato il sermone, celano la forte avversione non solo per l'eresia in sé, ma anche per l'idea che un potere temporale potesse prendere decisioni su quello spirituale, così come era successo ai tempi di Costanzo II — che avrebbe voluto sostituire l'ortodossia nicena con l'arianesimo — e nell'Inghilterra del XVI secolo — dove Enrico VIII prima ed Elisabetta I poi avevano imposto l'anglicanesimo. In tal maniera, il potere politico si ergeva sulla 'verità di fede', quella del cattolicesimo romano agli occhi del teologo inglese, una verità oltremondana che in quanto tale non poteva né doveva essere messa in discussione da nessuna autorità terrena. Proprio quella verità era infatti per Stapleton il sostrato ontologico su cui la società si reggeva e senza la cui base era destinata inevitabilmente a crollare sotto i colpi della vendetta divina. Ciò che il teologo inglese osteggia, dunque, è la nuova antropologia politica che si era manifestata con Niccolò Machiavelli (1469-1527), contro cui il teologo inglese si scaglia apertamente nel *Morale*, nelle stesse pagine in cui critica aspramente la regina, ricordandole la *certa et infallibilis iustitia ac uindicta Dei* contro i persecutori della fede. Il pensatore italiano è solo l'esponente di spicco dei *politici* che avevano affermato la maggiore importanza della conservazione dello Stato su tutto, anche sulla religione e, di conseguenza, la superiorità dello Stato sulla Chiesa.[58] In virtù di ciò, i *politici* ritenevano che tutte le

---

[58] *Quae uerba, ut et tota praecedens oratio, contra execrabile hodie Christianorum genus, qui Politici uocantur, et ueri Christiani non sunt, utpote in quibus ethnicorum reuixit spiritus, magisque in impii Machiauelli, quam in Christi schola edocti sunt, plurimum ualent. Isti enim hanc uestem nuptialem adeo non habent, adeo sine illa in nuptiis filii Dei accumbunt, adeo illam prorsus negligunt, ut cum Christianos et Catholicos se dicant, nihil minus quam huiusmodi sint; pacem uidelicet Reipubl. principum libidines, ac iniquas leges, rerum temporalium affluentiam, conseruationem, incrementa, toti penitus Christianae religioni anteponant. Illorum enim axiomata haec sunt: Reipublicae statum et conseruationem priorem et anti-*

confessioni dovessero essere ugualmente tollerate e riconosciute, in modo da mantenere la pace all'interno dello Stato, portando quindi a un relativismo che implicava un ateismo di fondo.[59] In una sorta di scala dell'*impietas*, Stapleton pone al vertice proprio i *politici*, rei di seguire il pensiero pagano — anche se non citato, in particolare quello di Tacito — e peggiori dei musulmani e degli eretici, perché sotto le mentite spoglie di un cattolicesimo superficiale miravano alla conservazione dello Stato sopra ogni altro aspetto della società,[60] non comprendendo che proprio quel relativismo confessionale che proponevano ne avrebbe determinato la disgregazione. Ai *politici*, seguono poi gli eretici, perché si considerano cristiani pur non essendolo realmente e solo dopo di loro si possono annoverare i turchi, gli infedeli per eccellenza nel periodo in cui scriveva Stapleton. In quegli anni, la Spagna di Filippo II stava combattendo contro l'Inghilterra di Elisabetta I, uno sfondo che deve aver sicuramente condizionato la stesura dei due *Promptuaria*, leggendo gli eventi storici con la lente della fede e sperando nella vicina vittoria finale del re cattolico sulla regina eretica. È evidente dunque in Stapleton il rifiuto totale del principio *cuius regio, eius religio*; il suo auspicio, invece, è il ritorno di una *Res Publica Christiana*, guidata da un sovrano come Filippo II che mettesse al centro della vita pubblica il cattolicesimo romano, garantendo così la stabilità dello stato grazie alla benevolenza di Dio.

---

quiorem habere oportet, quam religionis causam. Status ciuilis et politicus, Ecclesiae statum antecellit. Regum decreta ac placita plurimum auctoritatis locum tenent, Stapleton 1620, p. 488.

[59] *Sic enim isti Politici omnes religiones ac sectas, Lutheranorum, Caluinistarum, Puritanorum, atque adeo Catholicam alicubi deuotionem tolerandas, et recipiendas, atque a Regibus permittendas arbitrantur [...] Perinde illis est de qualibet religione, ad quam neminem ulla necessitate adigi posse affirmant, modo pax Reipub. et rerum omnium affluentia in tuto sit. Nulla unquam acerbior pestis orbem Christianum inuasit, quae eo tendit, ut nulla amplius colatur religio, Deus credatur nullus*, Stapleton 1620, p. 488.

[60] *Pseudochristiani, et maxime politici, grauiora infidelibus patientur, quia deteriores illis sunt. Haereticus deterior et perniciosior hostis est quam Turca, aut quilibet infidelis, quia Christianum se dicit, et non est [...] Politicus et haeretico et Turca sceleratior est, quia Christianum et Catholicum se dicit, quum neuter sit, sed in utroque dissimulet, nec Christum, nec Ecclesiam diligens, sed temporalis suae pacis ac faelicitatis bonum utrique praeponens*, Stapleton 1620, p. 489.

Bibliografia

Fonti

Giovanni Battista Egnazio, *De Caesaribus libri III*, Venice: in aedibus haer. Aldo I Manuzio & Andrea I Torresano, 1516.

John Christopherson, *Historiae ecclesiasticae scriptores graeci, nempe: Eusebius, cognomento Pamphilus, Caesareae Palaestinae episcopus. Socrates Scholasticus, Costantinopolitanus. Theodoritus, Cyrenensis episcopus. Heremias Sozomenus. Euagrius Scholasticus, Epiphanensis*, Köln: Birckmann, 1581.

John Locke, *A Letter Concerning Toleration*, ed. M. Montuori, The Hague: Nijhoff, 1963.

Johannes Miraeus, *Decreta synodi dioecesanae Antuerpiensis mense Maio anni MDCX celebratae*, Antwerp: ex officina Plantiniana, apud Ioannem Moretum, 1610.

Luis de Molina, *De liberi arbitrii cum gratiae donis, diuina praescientia, prouidentia praedestinatione et reprobatione Concordia*, Lisbon: apud António Ribeiro expensis João de Espanha et Miguel de Arenas, 1588.

Pius V, 'Damnatio et Excommunicatio. Elisabeth Reginae Angliae. Eiusque Adhaerentium (1570)', in *Magnum bullarium Romanum: bullarum privilegiorum ac diplomatum Romanorum Pontificum amplissima collectio*, 15 vols, Graz: Akademische Druck- u. Verlagsanstalt, 1964–1967, IV/3, p. 98–99.

Thomas Stapleton, *Promptuarium catholicum ad instructionem concionatorum contra haereticos nostri temporis, super omnia evangelia totius anni, tam dominicalia quam de festis*, Paris: apud Michaelem Sonnium, 1589.

Thomas Stapleton, *Promptuarium morale super evangelia dominicalia totius anni ad instructionem concionatorum, ad reformationem peccatorum, ad consolationem piorum*, Antwerp: ex officina Plantiniana apud vid. & Joannem Moretum, 1591.

Thomas Stapleton, *Opera Omnia*, Paris: [Robert Fouet et Nicolas Buon et Sébastien Cramoisy], 1620.

Francisco Suárez, *Defensio fidei catholicae et apostolicae aduersus Anglicanae sectae errores, cum responsione ad apologiam pro iuramento fidelitatis et praefationem monitoriam serenissimi Iacobi Angliae regis*, Coimbra: apud Diego Gomez Loureyro, 1613.

William Whitaker, *Disputatio de sacra scriptura contra huius temporis papistas, inprimis Robertum Bellarminum Jesuitam, pontificium in Collegio Romano, et Thomam Stapletonum, regium in Schola Duacena controuersiarum professorem*, Cambridge, 1581.

Rodrigo Zamorano, *Cronologia y reportorio de la razon de los tiempos: el mas copioso que hasta hoy se à vista*, Sevilla: Rodrigo de Cabrera,1594.

Letteratura

Albion, G. (1946), 'An English Professor at Louvain: Thomas Stapleton (1535–1598)', in *Miscellanea historica in honorem Alberti De Meyer: Universitatis Catholicae in Oppido Lovaniensi iam annos XXV professoris*, Leuven: University Press.

Anderson, D. K. (2014), *Martyrs and Players in Early Modern England. Tragedy, Religion and Violence on Stage*, Farnham: Ashgate.

Bouffartigue, J. (2007), 'L'empereur Julien était-il intolérant?', in *Revue d'études Augustiniennes et Patristiques*, 53, p. 1–14.

Clarke, G. W. (1966). 'Some Victims of the Persecution of Maximinus Thrax.' in *Historia: Zeitschrift für Alte Geschichte*, 15, p. 445–453.

Corke-Webster, J. (2020). 'The Roman Persecutions', in P. Middleton (ed.), *The Wiley Blackwell Companion to Christian Martyrdom*, Hoboken, NJ: Wiley-Blackwell, p. 33–50.

Cruz Cruz, J. (2013), 'Predestination as Transcendent Theology: Molina and the first Molinism', in A. Aichele & M. Kaufmann (ed.), *A Companion to Luis de Molina*, Leiden: Brill.

de Ste. Croix, G. E. M. (2006), *Christian Persecution, Martyrdom and Orthodoxy*, Oxford: Oxford University Press.

Dignas, B. & E. Winter (2007), *Rome and Persia in Late Antiquity*, Cambridge: Cambridge University Press.

Downey, D. M. (2017). '*Pietas Austriaca* and "Dispensers of Royal Authority": The Early Irish Colleges and Habsburg Cultural Strategies', in L. Chambers & T. O'Connor (ed.), *Forming Catholic Communities. Irish, Scots and English College Networks in Europe, 1568–1918*, Leiden: Brill, p. 62–90.

Edwards, F. (1981), *The Elizabethan Jesuits:* Historia Missionis Anglicanae Societatis Jesu *(1660) of Henry More*, London: Phillimore and Co.

Fradkin, J., (2017), 'Protestant Unity and Anti-Catholicism: The Irenicism and Philo-Semitism of John Dury in Context', in *Journal of British Studies*, 56, p. 273–294.

François, W. (2009), '*Augustinus sanior interpres Apostoli*: Thomas Stapleton and the Louvain Augustinian School's Reception of Paul', in R. Ward Holder (ed.), *A Companion to Paul in the Reformation*, Leiden: Brill, p. 363–386.

François, W. (2010), 'Thomas Stapleton (1535–1598) sobre la caída de Adán y las consecuencias de ella para su descendencia. ¿Exégesis agustiniana o cripto-jesuítica?', in *Augustinus*, 55, p. 129–140.

François, W. (2012), 'Augustine and the Golden Age of Biblical Scholarship in Louvain (1550-1650)', in B. Gordon & M. McLean (ed.), *Shaping the Bible in the Reformation: Books, Scholars and Their Readers in the Sixteenth Century*, Leiden: Brill, p. 235-289.

François, W. (2013), 'Thomas Stapleton, controversetheoloog tussen Engeland en de Nederlanden', in V. Soen & P. Knevel (ed.), *Religie, hervorming en controverse in de zestiende-eeuwse Nederlanden*, Herzogenrath: Shaker Publishing, p. 37-64.

Frye, R. N. (1983), 'The Political History of Iran under the Sasanians', in E. Yarshater (ed.), *The Cambridge History of Iran*, III, Cambridge: Cambridge University Press, p. 116-180.

Gerace, A. (2016), 'Luis de Molina's "Middle Knowledge" Thomas Stapleton's 'Antidote' to John Calvin', in *Reformation and Renaissance Review*, 18, p. 105-122.

Gerace, A. (2019). *Biblical Scholarship in Louvain in the 'Golden' Sixteenth Century*, Göttingen: Vandenhoeck & Ruprecht.

González Salinero, R. (2005), *Las persecuciones contra los cristianos en el Imperio romano. Una aproximación crítica*, Madrid: Signifer Libros.

Heal, F. (2017), 'Art and Iconoclasm', in A. Milton (ed.), *The Oxford History of Anglicanism, Volume I: Reformation and Identity, c. 1520-1662*, Oxford: Oxford University Press, p. 186-209.

Houliston, V. & A. Muller (2020), 'The Elizabethan Martyrs', in P. Middelton (ed.), *Wiley Blackwell Companion to Christian Martyrdom*, Hoboken, NJ: Wiley-Blackwell, p. 322-337.

Janssen, G. H. (2012), 'The Counter-Reformation of the Refugee: Exile and the Shaping of Catholic Militancy in the Dutch Revolt', in *Journal of Ecclesiastical History*, 63, p. 671-692.

Le Bachelet, X.-M. (1931), *Prédestination et grâce efficace: controverses dans la Compagnie de Jésus au temps d'Aquaviva 1610-1613: histoire et documents inédit*, Leuven: Louvain Museum Lessianum.

Lecler, J. (1955), *Histoire de la tolérance au siècle de la Réforme*, Lyon: Aubier.

Lennam, T. N. S. (1975), *Sebastian Westcott, the Children of Paul's, and the Marriage of Wit and Science*, Toronto: University of Toronto Press.

Lenski, N. (2007), 'The Chronology of Valens' Dealings with Persia and Armenia, 364-378 CE', in J. den Boeft et al. (ed.), *Ammianus after Julian: The Reign of Valentinian and Valens in Books 26-31 of the Res Gestae*, Leiden: Brill, p. 95-127.

Lesaffer, R. (2014), *The Twelve Years' Truce (1609): Peace, Truce, War, and Law in the Low Countries at the Turn of the 17th Century*, Leiden: Brill.

Lorenzo, D. J. (2003), 'Tradition and Prudence in Locke's Exceptions to Toleration', *American Journal of Political Science*, 47, p. 248-258.

Lucci, D. (2018), 'John Locke on Atheism, Catholicism, Antinomianism, and Deism', *Ethica & Politica*, 20, p. 201-246.

MacCulloch, D. (2017), 'The Church of England and International Protestantism, 1530-1570', A. Milton (ed.), *The Oxford History of Anglicanism, Volume I: Reformation and Identity, c. 1520-1662*, Oxford: Oxford University Press, p. 316-332.

Machielsen, J. (2010), 'How (not) to Get Published: The Plantin Press in the Early 1590s', in *Dutch Crossing*, 34, p. 99-114.

Manning, R. (1962), 'Richard Shelley of Warminghurst and the English Catholic Petition for Toleration of 1585', in *Recusant History*, 6, p. 265-274.

Marcos, M. (2008), '*He forced with Gentlenss*. Emperor Julian's attitude to Religion Coercion', in *Antiquité Tardive*, 16, p. 7-20.

Marcos, M. (2013), 'Portrait of a Persecutor: The Defeat and Death of Maximinus Daia in Christian Historiography', in G. Vespignani (ed.), *Politoro. Studi offerti ad Antonio Carile*, Spoleto: Fondazione CISAM, p. 13-36.

Martinetti, P. (1928), *La libertà*, Milano: Libreria Editrice Lombarda.

Maryks, R. A. & J. A. Senent de Frutos (2019), *Francisco Suárez (1548-1617): Jesuits and the Complexities of Modernity*, Leiden: Brill.

McCoog, T. M. (1996), *The Society of Jesus in Ireland, Scotland, and England 1541-1588: Our Way of Proceedings*, Leiden: Brill.

Mitchell, S. (1988), 'Maximinus and the Christians in AD 312: A New Latin Inscription', in *Journal of Roman Studies*, 78, p. 105-124.

Morrissey, M. (2011), *Politics and the Paul's Cross Sermons, 1558-1642*, Oxford: Oxford University Press.

Moss, C. (2013), *The Myth of Persecution: How Early Christians Invented a Story of Martyrdom*, New York, NY: Harper Collins.

Muller, A. (2020), *The Excommunication of Elizabeth I. Faith, Politics, and Resistance in Post-Reformation England, 1570-1603*, Leiden: Brill.

O'Connell, M. (1964), *Thomas Stapleton and the Counter Reformation*, New Haven-London, CT: Yale University Press.

Plowden, A. (2004), 'Gifford, Gilbert (1560-1590), Spy', in *Oxford Dictionary of National Biography*; https://doi.org/10.1093/ref:odnb/10660 (accessed 10.05.2022).

Rai, E. (2016), 'Between Augustine and Pelagius: Leonard Lessius in the Leuven Controversies, from 1587 to the 20th Century', in *Journal of Baroque Studies*, 4, p. 79–106.

Rai, E. (2020), '*Ex Meritis Praeuisis*: Predestination, Grace, and Free Will in Intra-Jesuit Controversies (1587–1613)', in *Journal of Early Modern Christianity*, 7, p. 111–150.

Ridley, J. (2001), *Bloody Mary's Martyrs: The Story of England's Terror*, New York, NY: Carroll et Graf.

Salmon, J. H. M. (1991), 'Catholic Resistance Theory, Ultramontanism, and the Royalist Response, 1580–1620', in J. H. Burns & M. Goldie (ed.), *The Cambridge History of Political Thought 1450–1700*, Cambridge: Cambridge University Press, p. 219–253.

Schwarte, K. H. (1963), 'Das angebliche Christengesetz des Sep. Sev.', in *Historia*, 12, p. 185–208.

Shagan, E. H. (2017), 'The Emergence of the Church of England, c. 1520–1553', in A. Milton (ed.), *The Oxford History of Anglicanism, Volume I: Reformation and Identity, c. 1520–1662*, Oxford: Oxford University Press, p. 29–44.

Shaw, B. (2015), 'The Myth of the Neronian Persecution', in *Journal of Roman Studies*, 105, p. 73–100.

Soen, V. (2016), 'The Beeldenstorm and the Spanish Habsburg Response (1566–1570)', in *Bijdragen en Mededelingen van de Geschiedenis der Nederlanden – Low Countries Historical Review*, 131, p. 99–120.

Spink, B. D. (2017), 'Liturgy and Worship', in Milton, A., *The Oxford History of Anglicanism, Volume I: Reformation and Identity, c. 1520–1662*, Oxford: Oxford University Press, p. 148–167.

Walmsley J. C. & F. Waldman (2019), 'John Locke and the Toleration of Catholics. A New Manuscript', in *The Historical Journal*, 62, p. 1093–1115.

Warnicke, R. (2006), *Mary Queen of Scots*, New York, NY: Routledge.

Abstract

The English Catholic theologian Thomas Stapleton left his homeland in 1558, finding a safe refuge in the Spanish Low Countries. His condition of both religious and political exiled had of-course a strong impact on his life, as testified by his writings. In particular, his resentment for Elisabeth I comes out in both the *Promptuarium catholicum* and the *Promptuarium morale*, works intended to provide the preachers with a manual for the preparation of mass homilies. Thanks to a careful analysis of selected sermons, the contribution will shed light on the theological and political elements upon which Stapleton builds his arguments against the Queen, hoping for God's vindictive justice against her conduct towards her Catholic subjects. In particular, Stapleton compares Elisabeth I with the Arian emperors Constant II and Valens, prototypes of the heretic rule, who eventually violently died because of their persecution of the 'true' faith. However, the English theologian identifies other enemies of the faith, worse than heretics and infidels, because they have put religion into the foreground respect to other aspects of social life: the *politici*. Indeed, their relativistic approach to the Christian confessions would have given a philosophical dignity to the 'heresies' — hence also Anglicanism — a relativism that would inevitably lead to atheism and to the disintegration of society. Indeed, according to Stapleton, without the 'true' faith, any state is destined to fall because of God's wrath.

Riassunto

Il teologo cattolico inglese Thomas Stapleton lascia la sua madrepatria nel 1558, trovando un rifugio sicuro nei Paesi Bassi spagnoli. La sua condizione di esiliato sia religioso sia politico ha avuto un forte impatto sulla sua vita, come testimoniato nei suoi scritti. In particolare, il suo risentimento nei confronti di Elisabetta I si manifesta sia nel *Promptuarium catholicum* sia nel *Promptuarium morale*, opere intese per fornire ai predicatori un manuale per la preparazione delle omelie. Grazie a un'attenta analisi di alcuni sermoni, il contributo mostrerà gli elementi teologici e politici sui quali Stapleton costruisce le sue argomentazioni contro la regina, nella speranza della vendicativa giustizia divina contro la sua condotta nei confronti dei suoi sudditi cattolici. Nello specifico, Stapleton fa un paragone tra Elisabetta I e gli imperatori ariani Costanzo II e Valente, prototipi del sovrano eretico, morti violentemente a causa della loro persecuzione della 'vera' fede. Tuttavia, il teologo inglese identifica altri nemici della fede, peggiori degli eretici e degli infedeli, dal momento che hanno messo in secondo piano la religione rispetto ad altri aspetti della vita sociale, i *politici*. Il loro approccio relativista alle confessioni cristiane avrebbe fornito, infatti, una dignità filosofica alle eresie — quindi anche all'anglicanesimo — un relativismo che inevitabilmente avrebbe condotto all'ateismo e alla distruzione della società. Infatti, per Stapleton, senza la 'vera' fede, qualsiasi stato è destinato a crollare a causa dell'ira divina.

GIOVANNI MINNUCCI
Università di Siena

*SILEANT THEOLOGI: NEC ALIENAM TEMNANT TEMERE DISCIPLINAM**
LA CONTROVERSIA FRA GIURISTI E TEOLOGI NEL I LIBRO DEL *DE NUPTIIS* DI ALBERICO GENTILI: NUOVE INDAGINI

1. Alla scienza dello *ius publicum Europaeum* è stato rivendicato il *Silete theologi in munere alieno* vergato da Alberico Gentili (1552–1608) al termine del capitolo XII del I libro del *De iure belli*.[1] Si sarebbe così ottenuta la separazione della scienza del diritto dalla teologia, e la creazione dello Stato moderno come luogo di neutralizzazione del conflitto religioso che aveva sconvolto l'Europa:[2] sconvolgimenti che, per lungo tempo, avrebbero continuato a caratterizzarne la storia.

L'apostrofe di Gentili, spesse volte riutilizzata e commentata da parte di alcuni studiosi delle più diverse vocazioni, li ha indotti ad approfondire il pensiero gentiliano sul rapporto tra diritto civile, diritto canonico, teologia e religione e, ancorché sommariamente, le opinioni di quei giuristi e teologi suoi predecessori, ai quali il sanginesino fa spesso riferimento, anche per ampliare l'oggetto della sua indagine ai rapporti tra foro della coscienza e foro esterno;[3] temi e problemi inizialmente e parzialmente affrontati nel 1585, con la scrittura del *De legationibus*, ed approfonditi negli anni seguenti, per giungere alla pubblicazione dei *Disputationum*

---

* Gentilis 1601, p. 25. Preciso che i testi qui utilizzati sono stati fedelmente riprodotti, ad eccezione delle normalizzazioni u/v, e senza intervenire nelle interpunzioni. Nel testo, inoltre, si fa rinvio all'epistolario manoscritto Gentili-Rainolds (cf. *infra*, n. 15) del quale, al momento della consegna dell'elaborato, era in fase di avanzata predisposizione l'edizione critica. Un'edizione successivamente da me data alle stampe in Minnucci 2021b.

[1] Gentilis 1598.
[2] Schmitt 1991.
[3] Cf., da ultimo, Minnucci 2016, Minnucci 2021a; ivi ampia bibliografia.

de nuptiis libri VII dove, nel I libro, il tema viene fatto oggetto di un'ampia riflessione conclusiva:[4] opera, quest'ultima, apparsa nel 1601, e quindi di tre anni successiva alla pubblicazione del *De iure belli* (1598).

Il I libro del *De nuptiis*, al quale il Gentili dette il titolo *Qui est de interprete*, già oggetto di alcuni studi,[5] appare meritevole di ulteriori indagini. Esso, infatti, non contiene esclusivamente una trattazione introduttiva al diritto matrimoniale — tema al quale, anche in questa prima parte dell'opera, si fa più di una volta rinvio — ma una vera e propria elaborazione teorica dell'autore che coglie l'occasione per disegnare quella che potremmo definire una sorta di teoria generale del diritto, avuto particolare riguardo, alle fonti, al metodo, al ruolo del giurista — l'*interpres iuris* — in relazione alle altre scienze e discipline, con uno specifico riferimento alla teologia che, almeno da un punto di vista teorico, avrebbe potuto rivendicare una sua specifica competenza non solo sull'istituto matrimoniale, ma anche su altre relazioni umane.[6]

Muovendo dalla consolidata e secolare competenza dell'autorità ecclesiastica sull'istituto del matrimonio, attestata non solo dalla storia, ma anche da un cospicua letteratura antica e recente, e dalle fonti giuridiche canonistiche (cap. I. *Ius aliud extra civile proponitur*) — fonti cui l'autore dedicherà anche la parte finale del I libro[7] — il discorso gentiliano prosegue — e qui è evidente l'uso del classico metodo della *disputatio* — con un'ampia ed argomentata *defensio* dello *ius civile* e dei suoi interpreti (cap. II. *Defenditur ius civile*), finalizzata a dimostrare la competenza dell'autorità secolare e del giurista civilista, non solo sulla materia matrimo-

---

[4] Per tutto questo percorso gentiliano cf. Minnucci 2018, p. 993–1018.

[5] Gentilis 1601, p. 1–113. Sul I Libro cf. Minnucci 2011a, p. 19–60; Minnucci 2016, p. 191–221; Minnucci 2019, p. 12–19, con rinvii a precedenti contributi; per una prima riflessione generale sull'opera si veda Wijffels 2019, p. 497–512.

[6] Cf. *supra*, n. 4. I temi trattati nel I Libro del *De nuptiis* sono inizialmente desumibili dai titoli dei capitoli del I Libro (cf. *infra*, nn. 7, 8, 13). Su alcuni di essi ci si soffermerà nelle pagine seguenti.

[7] Il capitolo XIX ed ultimo del I Libro del *De nuptiis*, p. 109–113, è intitolato *Peroratio in ius canonicum*; tema, quello del diritto canonico e del suo rapporto con lo *ius civile* affrontato da Gentili anche nei due capitoli immediatamente precedenti: *Quae magistratui relinquantur iure canonico*, Cap. XVII. (p. 95–99); *Quid ius canonicum relinquit civili*, Cap. XVIII. (p. 100–109). Sull'ultimo capitolo dell'opera si veda Minnucci 2019, p. 22–23, e la letteratura ivi citata.

niale che, nella prima parte del primo Libro, ha un ruolo centrale,[8] ma anche su molte altre relazioni umane. Ne è un esempio il reato di omicidio: tema sul quale il giurista si sofferma attraverso un dibattito a distanza soprattutto con i Padri della Chiesa più autorevoli già fatto oggetto di alcune risalenti riflessioni.[9] Emergono, da questa prima parte del testo, il ruolo centrale — l'*auctoritas* per utilizzare la terminologia gentiliana — dello *ius civile* e dei suoi interpreti, e l'affermazione conclusiva del capitolo VII (*De iuris civilis auctoritate*),[10] ove il convincimento che la materia matrimoniale sia da attribuire alla potestà delle autorità laiche e alla *interpretatio iurisconsultorum*, viene fondato in conclusione su due passaggi tratti dalle *Recitationes solemnes* di Jacques Cujas al IV Libro delle Decretali di Gregorio IX:[11]

> At absolvam cum caussis nostris nuptiarum ex Cuiacio: *Quum de nuptiis quaeritur, licitae sint, necne, eius rei cognitionem, quae olim erat principum, vel populi, pontifices suam fecerunt, conniventibus principibus. Sic pontificum maxima evasit iurisdictio, quae nulla fuit*. Sic vero piissimi hodie, et sapientissimi principes recte recipiunt haec rapta sibi. Et sic ab ingenuis iurisconsultis[12] haec iurisdictio omnis asseritur principibus adversum ecclesiasticos. Age, et iurisconsultis interpretationem huius iuris vindicemus nos a theologis.

2. La *vindicatio* della competenza sull'istituto del matrimonio agli interpreti del diritto, con la corrispondente esclusione di quella teologica, posta a chiusura del settimo capitolo del I libro del *De nuptiis*, non costituisce un'affermazione apodittica. È infatti nei capitoli successivi che si assiste ad un'ampia elaborazione dottrinale sul rapporto, spesso controverso, fra diritto e

---

[8] Oltreché nei capitoli I. e II. del I Libro del *De nuptiis* (p. 1–5, 6–11), cui si è fatto riferimento nel testo, la materia matrimoniale viene ampiamente trattata anche nelle parti immediatamente seguenti: I.III. *De nuptiis nobilium cum plebeis* (p. 11–17); I. IV. *De concubinatu* (p. 17–20); I. V. *Omnis improbata libido iure civili* (p. 21–27).

[9] Minnucci 2011b, p. 55–86.

[10] Gentilis 1601, p. 31–37.

[11] Gentilis 1601, p. 36–37, *in marg.*: *Cuia. rub. de consa.* (Cuiacius, ad *X* 4.14, col. 1653) *et c. 4. qui fi. si. le.* (Cuiacius, ad *X* 4.17.4, coll. 1674–1677).

[12] Gentilis 1601, p. 37, *in marg.*: *Germ. ma. cons. 27.* (Ruckerus, cons. XXVII, p. 144–151).

teologia e, soprattutto fra coloro che quelle discipline professano.[13] Una riflessione che risente del dibattito, sviluppato con una notevole vis polemica da entrambe le parti, con il teologo puritano John Rainolds (1549–1607):[14] un dissenso che aveva avuto il suo culmine nella corrispondenza intercorsa fra i due professori oxoniensi fra il 1593 e il 1594[15] e che, come vedremo, si perpetuerà ancora a lungo.

---

[13] Cf. i capitoli seguenti della citata edizione del *De nuptiis*: *Distinguuntur ius divinum et humanum*, Cap. VIII. (p. 37–41); *De theologia, et religione*, Cap. VIIII. (p. 41–49); *Peritiores in secunda tabula iurisconsulti*, Cap. X. (p. 49–54); *Absurde tolli secundam tabulam iurisperitis*, Cap. XI. (p. 55–59); *De lege ultima secundae tabulae*, Cap. XII. (p. 59–63); *De Levitis, et Apostolis*, Cap. XIII. (p. 64–70); *De episcopali audientia*, Cap. XIV. (p. 70–81); *De theologicis quaestionibus*, Cap. XV. (p. 80–88); *De auctoritate theologorum*, Cap. XVI. (p. 88–95).

[14] Cf. Binns 1974, p. 95–120, e Panizza 1981, p. 57–87, che illustrano le posizioni assunte da Rainolds e Gentili nel corso della controversia; cf., inoltre, Minnucci 2022 e, da ultimo, Colavecchia 2018, p. 83–96; Blank 2017, p. 513–547, Leo 2019, p. 119–165; Ragni 2020, p. 119–187.

[15] Del carteggio fra Alberico Gentili e John Rainolds si conoscono complessivamente otto lettere. Le prime quattro, risalenti al 1593, sono conservate in Oxford, Corpus Christi College, MS *352* (= MS) p. 183–184 (Gentili a Rainolds, 7 luglio 1593); p. 185–187 (Rainolds a Gentili, 10 luglio 1593); p. 191–193 (Gentili a Rainolds, 15 luglio 1593); p. 195–208 (Rainolds a Gentili, 5 agosto 1593), e sono state edite per la prima volta da Rainolds 1599, p. 164–190. Queste quattro lettere sono state riprodotte, con traduzione in lingua inglese, in Markowicz 1977, p. 16–135. Le altre quattro, conservate nel medesimo MS, p. 213–307, non sono mai state edite: 1) p. 213–219, *s.d.* ma del 22 novembre 1593, Alberico Gentili a John Rainolds (epistola non autografa, ma copia a più mani). Nella sua lettera del 25 gennaio successivo John Rainolds fa riferimento, più volte, a due epistole che Gentili gli avrebbe scritto (cf. MS, p. 228: *XV. Calend. Novemb.* = 18 ottobre, *et X. Cal. Decembr.* = 22 novembre; nonché p. 270, ove il rinvio a due *literae tuae priores*, con annotazione in margine dei riferimenti temporali: *Dat. Octobr.; Dat. Novembr.*). La certezza che l'epistola conservata alle p. 213–219 sia quella del 22 novembre e non quella del 18 ottobre, la fornisce ancora una volta il Rainolds che, nella sua lettera del 25 gennaio (MS, p. 245 *ca.fi.*) riproduce un passaggio delle due epistole che Gentili gli aveva scritto, per sottolinearne le differenze. Il testo riprodotto dal Rainolds, e da lui identificato come appartenente alla seconda epistola in ordine temporale, è identico a quello che si legge nella lettera di Gentili conservata nel MS, a p. 218. Ne consegue che quella vergata nelle p. 213–219 — l'unica delle due lettere conservate nel MS oxoniense — è del 22 novembre 1593. Che la lettera fosse del mese di novembre era già stato affermato da Binns 1974, p. 110 nt. 45–46, che però non aveva individuato il giorno della sua redazione; 2) p. 221–272, 25 gennaio 1594, Rainolds a Gentili; 3) p. 273–290 + 292, 8 febbraio 1594, Gentili a Rainolds (autografa); 4) p. 295–307, 12 marzo 1594, Rainolds a Gentili. L'epistolario si può ora integralmente leggere in edizione critica in Minnucci 2021b.

I dissensi del Gentili con gli ambienti teologici erano risalenti alla metà degli anni Ottanta del XVI secolo.[16] Apparentemente sopiti, forse in seguito al trasferimento di Gentili in Germania (1586–1587), erano però destinati a riemergere in tutta la loro complessità con il suo ritorno in Inghilterra dopo la nomina a *regius professor* di *civil law* a Oxford (8 giugno 1587). Sembra attestarlo, fra l'altro, la mancata pubblicazione del *De papatu romano Antichristo*: testo — oggi criticamente edito [17] — risalente nella sua redazione originaria al primo quinquennio degli anni Ottanta del XVI secolo, che Gentili ampiamente corresse, rivide e integrò almeno fino al 1591, e che molto probabilmente decise di non dare alle stampe, sia per la necessità di doverlo riscrivere alla luce delle numerosissime correzioni ed aggiunte, sia per i contrasti con la teologia puritana ed in particolare con John Rainolds.[18] Una controversia, quella con l'autorevole teologo, sulla quale appare opportuno spendere qualche breve riflessione.

Come attesta la documentazione conservata in Inghilterra, e come numerose ricerche hanno potuto dimostrare, risale ai primi anni Novanta del '500 la polemica sugli spettacoli teatrali fra William Gager e John Rainolds relativa non solo alla legittimità, da parte degli attori, di assumere ruoli e vesti femminili (si ricordi che alle donne era proibito calcare le scene), in violazione delle disposizioni del Deuteronomio (*Deut.* 22.5) ma, più in generale, alla liceità delle rappresentazioni teatrali: un genere di spettacolo che il Rainolds recisamente condannava.[19] Un contrasto che raggiungerà il suo culmine pubblico nel 1592, allorquando Elisabetta I visiterà l'Università di Oxford. Proprio per l'occasione il giurista di San Ginesio aveva composto un *Sonetto* in italiano

---

[16] Cf. l'epistola di Gentili a Rainolds dell'8 febbraio 1594, MS, p. 277–278: *Et italica tamen, italica levitate tantum peccavi isthic, ut indignissimus fuerim hoc loco, quem apud vos teneo, imo quem apud vos occupo, ut tu clarius vis semper. Et tu de illis fuisti, qui humanissimae genti vestrae labem illam aspersam voluerunt inhumanitatis, dum, extero homini patere locum apud vos, indignum esse vociferabantur.* Sul punto cf. Panizza 1981, p. 51 n. 74, 73 n. 38.

[17] Gentilis 2018.

[18] Gentilis 2018, p. cxxvii–clxi.

[19] Cf. Binns 1974, p. 95–120, anche per i riferimenti bibliografici; Di Simone 2010 e, da ultimo, Ragni 2020, p. 139–153. Questo il testo della Scrittura, *Deut.* 22.5: *Non induetur mulier veste virili, nec vir utetur veste feminea: abominabilis enim apud Deum est qui facit haec.*

dedicato a colei che considerava la sua grande ed autorevolissima protettrice.[20] In occasione della visita, la Regina aveva assistito alle rappresentazioni delle opere di William Gager (1555-1622), con cui John Rainolds aveva polemizzato in relazione agli spettacoli teatrali; a quest'ultimo, il 28 settembre, per questa ragione, la Regina si rivolgeva con fermissime parole di riprovazione: 'Elizabeth schooled Dr John Rainolds for his obstinate preciseness, willing him to follow her laws, and not run before them'.[21]

Malgrado ciò la controversia sul teatro, apparentemente sopita per alcuni mesi, riprenderà vigore nel 1593-1594, e vedrà contrapporsi al Rainolds proprio Alberico Gentili che, nel giugno 1593, aveva pubblicato la *Commentatio ad legem III. Codicis de professoribus et medicis*.[22] E chissà che il dono del Sonetto alla Regina, e la reprimenda pubblica subita nove mesi prima dal Rainolds da parte di Elisabetta I,[23] non abbiano contribuito a far aumentare i sentimenti di avversione, ai quali si è già fatto cenno,[24] che il teologo puritano nutriva nei confronti del giurista di San Ginesio. Una pubblicazione, quella costituita dalla *Commentatio*, nella quale Alberico aveva affrontato, tra le altre, le problematiche che erano state al centro della polemica Gager – Rainolds. In essa egli non solo aveva implicitamente difeso la posizione del Gager, ma aveva messo in discussione la possibilità che i teologi potessero occuparsi legittimamente della questione oggetto di dibattito, giungendo fino al punto di sostenere che, mentre da un lato riconosceva senza dubbio l'influenza che l'elaborazione teologica avrebbe potuto esercitare sul suo pensiero in materia religiosa, una analoga importanza non avrebbe potuto attribuirgli *in re morali et politica*.[25] Ma anche nelle pubblicazioni precedenti, ad iniziare dal *De legationibus* (1585) per finire alla *De iure belli Commentatio*

---

[20] Minnucci 2015b, p. 10-11, 17 n. 35.

[21] Boas 1914, p. 266-267. Il discorso della Regina Elisabetta si legge in Plummer 1887, p. 271-273; parzialmente riprodotto in Minnucci 2015b, p. 5 n. 13: *Moneo ego, ut non praeeatis leges; sequamini. Ne disputetis, non meliora possint praescribi; sed observetis, quae lex Divina iubet, et nostra cogit.*

[22] Testo criticamente annotato con traduzione in lingua inglese in Binns 1972, p. 224-272.

[23] Cf. *supra*, n. 21.

[24] Per i dissensi risalenti alla metà degli anni Ottanta cf. *supra*, n. 16.

[25] *Nam qui histrioniam omnem sublatam esse volunt, hi auctoritate theologorum magis moventur. Ego vero ut theologorum auctoritate in re religionis valde*

prima (1588), era apparso evidente che il Gentili distinguesse nettamente lo *ius religionis* dallo *ius humanum* individuando il discrimine fra i due diritti nei soggetti fra i quali si sarebbe instaurato il rapporto.[26] Lo *ius religionis*, dal suo punto di vista, avrebbe regolato unicamente le relazioni degli uomini con Dio e non quelle fra gli uomini per le quali occorreva far ricorso allo *ius humanum*. Il fatto che Gentili esprimesse da lungo tempo le sue opinioni sui rapporti fra diritto, teologia e religione non era passato inosservato agli occhi attentissimi del Rainolds il quale, peraltro, aveva ben presente la precedente produzione scientifica del giurista di San Ginesio perché anche ad essa, nel corso della polemica, farà più volte riferimento.[27] Il fuoco, che stava covando da tempo sotto la cenere, non aspettava che di essere nuovamente ravvivato, e la polemica fra Gager e Rainolds, cui si aggiungeva subito dopo

---

moveor, ita in re morali, aut politica non valde (Cf. *Commentatio ad l. III Codicis de professoribus* [...], in Binns 1972, p. 247, 269).

[26] Gentilis 1585, II. XI, p. 63: *Secundum argumentum, quo ego in istam definitionem inclino, illud est: quia religionis ius hominibus cum hominibus non est, sed cum Deo. Cum Deo enim communio nobis religione intercedit: nam haec est inter homines, et Deum ratio: quia est religio scientia divini cultus, et habitus observantiae eius, quo habitu nos cum Deo devincimur et religamur.* Identici concetti Alberico esprimerà tre anni dopo allorquando scriverà la *De iure belli Commentatio prima* (Gentilis 1589, p. D3i, *Caussa religionis*) con espresso rinvio al testo del *De legationibus*: *Iuvat porro repetere rationem hic ex undecimo capite libri secundi de legationibus, quod religionis ius hominibus cum hominibus non est. Itaque nec ius laeditur hominum ob diversam religionem. Itaque nec bellum movendum caussa religionis est* e, ancora più avanti, nel *De iure belli*: *Sed haec alia quaestio est de defensione. Quam postea examinabo. Nunc illa est, si uno religionis obtentu bellum inferre possit. Et hoc nego. Et addo rationem: quia religionis ius hominibus cum hominibus proprie non est: itaque nec ius lęditur hominum ob diversam religionem: itaque nec bellum caussa religionis. Religio erga Deum est. Ius est divinum, id est, inter Deum et hominem: non est ius humanum, id est, inter hominem et hominem. Nihil igitur quaeritat homo violatum sibi ob aliam religionem* (Gentilis 1598, I.IX, p. 64–65).

[27] Cf., ad es., l'epistola di Rainolds a Gentili del 10 luglio 1593, con rinvii alla *De iure belli Commentatio secunda* (cf. Markowicz 1977, p. 26 n. 18, 28 n. 21); quella del 5 agosto 1593, con rinvio ai *De iuris interpretibus Dialogi sex* e alle *De iure belli Commentationes prima, secunda et tertia* (ivi, p. 60, n. 42; p. 64, n. 48, p. 68 n. 57–59; p. 72, n. 70; p. 78, n. 81; p. 82, n. 91; p. 90, n. 102; p. 92, n. 106; p. 94, n. 108; p. 116, n. 150; p. 124, n. 167); quella del 25 gennaio 1594, con rinvii alla *De iure belli Commentatio secunda*, ai *De iuris interpretibus Dialogi sex*, alla *Comm. ad l. III Cod. de professoribus et medicis*, al *De legationibus*, alla *Ad tit. Cod. de malef. et mathem.* (cf. MS, p. 221, 222, 226, 228, 231, 234, 236, 238, 239, 246, 250, 255, 259, 261, 267, 269, 270); e infine quella del 12 marzo 1594 con rinvii alla *Comm. ad l. III Cod. de professoribus et medicis* e alla *De iure belli Commentatio secunda* (cf. MS, p. 296, 299, 300, 302, 304).

Alberico Gentili, aveva contribuito, e non poco, a far sviluppare definitivamente l'incendio dando vita ad un vero e proprio scontro, condotto in punta di penna, fra il giurista italiano esule in Inghilterra e il teologo puritano, attraverso la corrispondenza privata cui si è già fatto cenno,[28] che prenderà avvio con un'epistola di Gentili a Rainolds del 7 luglio 1593, e che si chiuderà, almeno sotto questo profilo, con una missiva del 12 marzo 1594 del teologo puritano al giurista italiano.

La controversia in forma epistolare fra Gentili e Rainolds, già parzialmente oggetto di studio, pur prendendo le mosse da temi e problemi relativi alle rappresentazioni teatrali e dalla possibilità per gli attori di assumere vesti e ruoli femminili,[29] è relativa anche al *mendacium*: argomento che era già stato oggetto di riflessione da parte del giurista di San Ginesio il quale lo aveva affrontato nelle *De iure belli Commentationes* (1588-1589) in relazione all'uso degli stratagemmi e degli inganni finalizzati a vincere il nemico, il che evidentemente non solo comportava la violazione dei patti, ma soprattutto l'uso della menzogna: un tema sul quale proprio il Rainolds, in ampie parti delle sue epistole esprimeva una posizione molto critica.[30] In quella sede, Alberico Gentili e John Rainolds si scontravano molto duramente: entrambi, peraltro, nel rivendicare la rispettiva competenza professionale ad occuparsi degli argomenti oggetto di discussione, tendevano, nelle rispettive epistole, ad escludere o a limitare quella dell'altro. Il progressivo ed articolato sviluppo della corrispondenza, ancorché verificatosi nello spazio di nove mesi, si era talmente ampliato da condurli a confrontarsi, attraverso un dibattito sempre più aspro, sul terreno difficile e impervio che costituiva il fondamento delle loro divergenze: quello di determinare cioè, come aveva efficacemente scritto Alberico Gentili nella sua ultima epistola al Rainolds (8 febbraio 1594), chi fosse competente, come teologo e come giu-

---

[28] Cf. *supra*, n. 15.

[29] Cf. *supra*, n. 19.

[30] Non è possibile, in questa sede, evidenziare quali e quante parti dell'epistolario sono dedicate da entrambi gli Autori a questo tema. Rinvio, pertanto, all'edizione critica delle epistole attualmente in fase di predisposizione. Posso solo aggiungere che non pochi passaggi delle lettere di Gentili sono stati da lui riutilizzati cinque anni dopo nel *De abusu mendacii* (per alcuni primi esempi cf. Minnucci 2020). Il tema, alla luce dell'opera gentiliana, data alle stampe nel 1599, è stato studiato di recente dal Lavenia 2015 (cf. *infra*, n. 43).

rista, ad occuparsi dei precetti divini relativi alle relazioni umane contenuti nella seconda parte delle Tavole della Legge: *Supradictae quaestiones, ut dixi, traxerunt ad alias, et illam gravissimam, si secunda tabula legum divinarum ad nos iurisconsultos pertineat magis, quam ad vos theologos*.[31] Tema, quest'ultimo, nel quale si manifestava un contrasto pressoché insanabile.

Basterà qui ricordare, per il momento, che Alberico Gentili riteneva che i teologi non fossero gli unici interpreti della Sacra Scrittura, e che la stessa — come affermava nella corrispondenza col teologo inglese risalente al luglio 1593 — potesse essere ritenuta, del tutto legittimamente, oggetto di studio anche da parte dei giuristi. I testi sacri, pertanto, dovevano essere ritenuti comuni ad entrambe le categorie di studiosi, con la precisazione che ai giuristi doveva essere riconosciuta una maggiore competenza in relazione ai precetti regolatori dei rapporti fra gli uomini.[32] Un punto di vista che il giurista di San Ginesio confermerà, restando pienamente convinto delle sue ragioni, attraverso nuove argomentazioni che illustrerà nel prosieguo della corrispondenza col Rainolds. Muovendo dalla bipartizione delle Tavole della Legge contenenti, la prima, i precetti divini relativi ai rapporti fra Dio e l'uomo (diritto divino) e, la seconda, quelli relativi ai rapporti fra gli uomini (diritto umano),[33] giungerà alla conclusione che ai teologi, sommi interpreti della Sacra Scrittura, deve essere riconosciuta la competenza a studiare ed interpretare i precetti divini regolatori dei rapporti fra l'uomo e Dio, mentre ai giuristi che,

---

[31] Cf. *infra*, n. 33.

[32] Cf. le epistole di Gentili a Rainolds del 7 luglio 1593 e del 15 luglio 1593, in Markowicz 1977, p. 18, 38: *at moralia, et politica sacrorum librorum aut nostra existimavi, aut certe communia nobis, et theologis; Communes sunt sacri libri; et in his, quae spectant ad secundam tabulam, nostri magis, quam vestri.*

[33] MS, p. 283–284, epistola di Gentili a Rainolds dell'8 febbraio 1594: *Supradictae quaestiones, ut dixi, traxerunt ad alias, et illam gravissimam, si secunda tabula legum divinarum ad nos iurisconsultos pertineat magis, quam ad vos theologos. Aio ego, negas tu. Et quaestio est non de simplici, et catechistica interpretatione, instructione, inculcatione; sed de gravioribus, subtilioribus, difficilioribus, excellentioribus. Et licet tu meum paradoxon absurdum dicas, meo tamen nondum respondes argumento: quod hoc fuit, humanum ius tractant sic iurisconsulti, non theologi. Se<d> secunda tabula est ius humanum: ergo secundam tabulam sic tractant iurisconsulti, non theologi. Atque assumptionem ita confirmabam, quod est ius inter hominem et hominem, humanum est: sed secunda tabula hoc ius est inter hominem, et hominem: ergo secunda tabula ius humanum est.*

ratione subiecti (l'uomo e le sue azioni) e *ratione finis* (il diritto umano), sono ritenuti competenti ad interpretare le norme regolatrici delle relazioni umane,[34] resterà il compito, anche alla luce dei precetti della Scrittura, di definire quelle stesse problematiche sotto il profilo del diritto.

Una posizione questa che il Rainolds, recisamente, non condivideva. Il teologo puritano, infatti, che aveva accusato il giurista di San Ginesio di *immodestia* e di *impietas* — accusa quest'ultima rivolta anche a Niccolò Machiavelli e non condivisa da Gentili[35] — affermava che l'interpretazione delle Scritture doveva restare di esclusiva competenza della teologia, l'unica disciplina da considerare *fidei et vitae magistra*.[36] Fra i testi trasmessi dai Libri sacri era ovviamente annoverato il *Decalogo*, per il quale il Rainolds continuava a ritenere fondamentale l'elaborazione teologica: per volontà divina i teologi, *praecipui interpretes*, avrebbero avuto il compito di spiegare alla Chiesa e al Popolo, attraverso la loro funzione interpretativa, i precetti contenuti non solo nella *prima*, ma anche nella *secunda tabula*.[37]

La corrispondenza fra Gentili e Rainolds, però, non era rimasta racchiusa in un semplice scambio epistolare: gli *academici Oxonienses* ne erano venuti a conoscenza. Lo si può dedurre dalla

---

[34] MS, p. 284: *Si ars, uel scientia theologorum distinguitur ab arte iurisconsultorum, fine distinguitur, subiecto distinguitur. Sed hoc iurisconsultorum est ius humanum, divinum theologorum: finis iurisconsultorum homini hominem, finis theologorum deo hominem coniungere. Ergo extra subiectum, et finem vestrum, et in nostris miscetis vos si in iure humano miscetis*. Analoghi concetti nel *De nuptiis*: Quod *si distinguuntur scientię per subiectum, et artes per finem: ut ita distingui docent viri doctissimi: duae utique istae, theologia, et iurisprudentia, sive scientiae, sive artes, per subiectum, aut per finem distinguuntur. Atque quod erit subiectum, aut finis unius, id non erit subiectum, aut finis alterius. Sed theologiae subiectum Deus est: finis ius divinum. Iurisprudentię subiectum homo, sive actiones humanae: finis ius humanum. Et ius hoc humanum in secunda tabula continetur. Ergo est iurisprudentis secunda tabula. Eius scilicet est secunda tabula, cuius est subiectum, et finis secundae tabulae. Subiectum autem, et finis eius tabulae spectare dicetur ad iurisconsultum. quoniam ius aliquod iurisconsulto dare oportet: et itaque vel divinum, vel humanum* (Gentilis 1601, p. 37).

[35] Cf. l'epistola di Rainolds a Gentili del 10 luglio 1593, in Markowicz 1977, p. 24. Cf. Minnucci 2016, p. 139–140.

[36] Cf. Minnucci 2016, p. 139–143.

[37] Epistola di Rainolds a Gentili del 12 marzo 1594, MS, p. 305: *Ac ego theologorum potius sententiae credendum esse confirmavi, quod hi sint praecipui secundae tabulae interpretes. Praecipui quippe sunt, quos Deus instituit, ut eam ecclesiae populoque suo publice explicarent*.

conclusione dell'epistola che Gentili aveva indirizzato al Rainolds l'8 febbraio 1594. In essa il giurista di San Ginesio aveva contestato al teologo di Oxford di aver reso parzialmente noto il loro rapporto epistolare, mostrando in pubblico il testo delle lettere che quest'ultimo gli aveva inviato [38] — il che costituiva, com'è evidente, una rappresentazione di parte del dibattito in atto — e di aver tentato di metterlo in cattiva luce con un personaggio autorevolissimo come Toby Matthew (1546–1628), destinato a diventare di lì a poco vescovo di Durham — col quale Gentili, sin dal suo arrivo in Inghilterra, aveva stretto una forte amicizia — recapitandogli direttamente, o facendogli pervenire, copia delle stesse *epistolae*.[39] Una presunta scorrettezza alla quale Gentili risponderà con un discorso in difesa della *iurisprudentia* rivolto agli *academici Oxonienses*: testo nel quale, oltre a rivendicare i meriti, storicamente attestati, del ceto dei giuristi, rimarcherà, con forza, la funzione del diritto: *Cedunt, cedunt omnia huic nostrae arti. Cessit omnis hodie philosophia, subiecit muta medicina caput, tacita applaudit theologia.*[40]

Una difesa del ruolo della giurisprudenza e di chi quella disciplina professava, avviato da Gentili dalla seconda metà degli anni Ottanta fino agli inizi degli anni Novanta del secolo XVI, e coe-

---

[38] Così scrive Gentili a Rainolds l'8 febbraio 1594: *Tu scis, an promeritus sis, qui per academiam triumphabundus de me absente incedebas cum tuis litteris. quas et ad D. Matthaeum miseras. Testes habeo, qui eas viderunt Oxonii in manibus tabellarii. Quis misisset, nisi tu? Quid voluisti? virum illum mihi alienum facere, quem unum supra omnes colo, et cupio mihi benevolentem?* (MS, p. 288). Né va dimenticato che le precedenti epistole del Rainolds, come riferisce Gentili, erano piene di contumelie nei suoi confronti: motivo di più, per il giurista di San Ginesio, di elevare una vibrata protesta per averle rese pubbliche: *Tu me immodestum, confidentem, irreligiosum, architectum nequitiae et impietatis, Academici dedecoris autorem, impurissimo similem principi dicis: et ego respondere non possum, horum nihil verum esse?* (MS, p. 213; 22 *novembre* 1593).

[39] Lo si legge nell'epistola di Gentili di cui ho riprodotto uno stralcio *supra*, n. 38. Nella risposta, scritta il 12 marzo 1594, il Rainolds negherà la sua responsabilità diretta: *"Testes", inquis, "habeo, qui eas viderunt Oxonii in manibus tabellarii: quis misisset nisi tu"? Itane vero? Et opinaris virum tam insignem, tam bene, de tam multis in Academia nostra meritum, tam paucos benevolos et ei gratificandi cupidos habere, ut exemplar literarum quas libenter eum lecturum suspicentur, a nemine accepturus sit, nisi ego mittam? At descripsit eas amanuensis meus: nam eius manus illa ad D. Matthaeum, cujus haec ad te. Demonstratio certior ex fide instrumentorum: nisi in Academia nostra multi scirent (ut ab amico mihi significatum est ex quo accepi tuas) cuius illae manu, non mei librarii, sint descriptae* (MS, p. 307).

[40] Minnucci 2015a, p. 251.

rentemente completato, almeno dal suo punto di vista, all'aprirsi del nuovo secolo nel I libro del *De nuptiis* (1601) dove — come avremo modo di sottolineare — verranno sviluppate le opinioni espresse nelle opere precedenti e le posizioni assunte nelle lettere inviate al Rainolds.

3. La polemica con il teologo puritano, che aveva preso avvio in relazione al *mendacium*, al teatro e all'uso delle vesti femminili da parte degli attori, si sviluppava, come abbiamo visto, per giungere alla definizione del ruolo e delle competenze del teologo e del giurista.[41] Nel 1599 il Rainolds, quasi a conferma del suo netto dissenso con le tesi gentiliane, darà alle stampe una parte dell'epistolario intercorso con il giurista di San Ginesio, vale a dire le quattro lettere che i due si erano scambiati fra il 7 luglio e il 5 agosto 1593.[42] Pressoché contestualmente il Gentili pubblicava un'opera nella quale sviluppava i suoi convincimenti in relazione ai primi due argomenti sui quali si era accesa la controversia: le *Disputationes duae: I. De actoribus et spectatoribus fabularum non notandis. II. De abusu mendacii*[43] — entrambe dedicate proprio a Toby Matthew che a suo parere era il principale destinatario del presunto tentativo di disinformazione messo in piedi dal Rainolds, cui si è fatto cenno poc'anzi.[44] Leggendo l'epistola dedicatoria premessa alla

---

[41] Cf., ad es., l'ultima epistola di Rainolds a Gentili del 12 marzo 1594, MS p. 296: *Principio igitur, in capite de mendacio, praecipua et primaria nobis quaestio fuit*; p. 299: *Sequitur secundum de histrionia*; p. 304: *Restat caput tertium: quod tanto paucioribus expediri potest, quanto tu in eo similior es tui. Hunc enim facis nostrae quaestionis statum, an secunda tabula legum divinarum ad vos iurisconsultos magis pertineat, quam ad nos theologos*; p. 306: *Quae cum in his tribus capitibus de mendacio, de histrionia, de theologorum autoritate, sic se habeant*.

[42] Rainolds; cf. *supra*, n. 15.

[43] Sulle due *Disputationes* si vedano, da ultimo: per il *De actoribus*, Di Simone 2010, p. 379–410; per il *De abusu mendacii* Lavenia 2015, p. 27–46.

[44] Cf. *supra*, n. 38–39. Sempre al Matthew il Gentili dedicherà la *Ad primum Macbaeorum disputatio*, riconoscendo, all'amico anglicano e Vicecancelliere dell'Università di Oxford, da lui conosciuto subito dopo l'arrivo Oltremanica e col quale aveva sempre intrattenuto ottimi rapporti, il merito di averlo indotto ad applicarsi agli *studia litterarum* che in precedenza aveva fermamente disprezzato e trascurato: *debentur certe ea tibi, et alia a me pluria, quae suo tempore consequentur. Debeo me tibi plurimum, atque plurimum, qui per favorem tuum fundamenta haec quantulęcunque eruditionis ponere potui non penitus incelebris, et illaudatae. Tua humanitas singularis, tua per omne genus officiorum liberalitas, tua amicitia nobilissima fovit peregrinum me et in Anglia novum; protexit infirmum; erexit, et animavit afflictum exulem; fecit in ea studia litterarum incumbere, quas ferme*

prima di esse — *De actoribus* [...] (*Idib. Octobr. 1597* = 15 ottobre 1597) — si apprende che il giurista aveva in animo di dedicare alla terza questione una ulteriore opera dal titolo *De potiore interprete decalogi in secunda tabula*: *sed sequentur illae, alia de abusu mendacii legitimo, alia de potiore interprete Decalogi in secunda tabula. Sequentur, volente Deo, sequentur.*[45] Testo mai pubblicato, al quale il Nostro rinvia anche nell'*Epistola apologetica ad lectorem* che si legge al termine del *De nuptiis* (1601): *tracto quaestionem in primo libro de potiore interprete secundae tabulae, controversam mihi cum viro magno*.[46] Il Maclean, che alle opere gentiliane ha dedicato uno studio assai pregevole, formulava alcune ipotesi circa le ragioni per le quali la *De potiore interprete* non fosse stata pubblicata: per un rifiuto dello stampatore; perché Alberico non aveva consegnato il testo; e, infine, per altri presumibili motivi individuati nella sua natura controversistica, nel costo, o per il fatto che il *De nuptiis* contenesse già gran parte del materiale.[47] Quest'ultima sembra l'ipotesi più plausibile perché è lo stesso Gentili che vi fa un cenno specifico nel passaggio finale della dedicatoria premessa al *De abusu mendacii*: *Porro autem, quae superest disputatio tertia, et quam fortasse simul desideras, de potiore interprete secundae tabulae, ea in maius coniecta opus Disputationum de nuptiis prodire non potest ante, quam illi septem (tot sunt de nuptiis) prodeant libri, qui eam detinent [...] Oxoniæ, Kal. Ianuar. Ann.* MDXCIX.[48]

Ma chi era il *vir magnus* con cui Gentili aveva controvertito ed al quale faceva riferimento nell'*Epistola apologetica ad lectorem* del *De nuptiis*? E quale poteva essere il materiale rifluito nell'opera, mai pubblicata, dal titolo *De potiore interprete Decalogi in secunda tabula*? Il personaggio era sicuramente il Rainolds, e la fonte da cui attingere non poteva non essere costituita dalle *epistolae* che il giurista gli aveva scritto alcuni anni prima.[49] Lo si può

---

abieceram, et deploraram (corpo tondo mio); *in hunc me propemodum evexit splendidissimi locum antecessoris, quem licet potuissem desiderare, sperare non potuissem* (Gentilis 1600, p. 5).

[45] Gentilis 1599, p. 3–4.
[46] Gentilis 1601, p. 687 *ca. fi.*; Maclean 2009, p. 337, no. 39.
[47] Maclean 2009, p. 331, no. 14.
[48] Gentilis 1599, p. 126.
[49] Che il *vir magnus* dovesse essere identificato in John Rainolds lo avevano già intuito sia il Binns e, con maggiore prudenza, il Maclean (cf. Binns 1974, p. 118, n. 75; Maclean 2009, p. 337, no. 39).

intuire dalle affermazioni contenute nella dedicatoria anteposta al *De abusu mendacii* sfuggite sino ad ora, se non vado errato, agli studiosi, e dal passaggio dell'*Epistola apologetica ad lectorem* cui si è fatto sopra riferimento,[50] ma lo si desume con certezza da una prima ineludibile lettura delle epistole inedite, ancor oggi conservate presso il *Corpus Christi College* di Oxford, alla cui edizione critica sto attendendo da qualche tempo, rispettivamente risalenti al 22 novembre 1593[51] e all'8 febbraio 1594.[52] I due testi epistolari gentiliani costituiscono, infatti, come fra poco dimostrerò, un vero e proprio serbatoio di idee dal quale il giurista di San Ginesio estrae alcuni passaggi, corredandoli dei necessari riferimenti normativi e dottrinali, per inserirli e svilupparli proprio nel I libro del *De nuptiis*. Una parte dell'opera, quest'ultima, che conserva tali e tanti riferimenti impliciti alla controversia col teologo puritano,[53] da aver indotto il Nostro a procrastinare nel tempo, ancorché l'avesse preannunciata, la pubblicazione di una *tertia disputatio* alla quale egli stesso aveva attribuito il nome *De potiore interprete decalogi in secunda tabula*: una pubblicazione che, però, non vedrà mai la luce.

4. Dalla lettura della prima parte dell'opera gentiliana dedicata al matrimonio, e delle epistole indirizzate alcuni anni prima al Rainolds, emergono indiscutibili e marcate correlazioni. Mi limito, in questa sede, a pochi esempi, di per sé già sufficienti, riservandomi di approfondire la questione non appena avrò completato l'edizione critica dell'epistolario.

Per dimostrare la competenza del giurista circa le relazioni umane, nella lettera al teologo puritano del novembre 1593 Gentili si esprime sulle partizioni generali del diritto:[54]

---

[50] Cf. *supra*, n. 46–48, nel testo.
[51] MS, p. 213–219 (cf. *supra*, n. 15).
[52] MS, p. 273–290 + 292.
[53] Occorre sottolineare, peraltro, che vi sono un paio di passaggi del I Libro del *De nuptiis*, nei quali Alberico fa riferimento a dispute avute con un teologo: *Theologus aliquando nec apte disputabat contra me hic, quod professor iuris civilis non possit recte isthaec exponere, quae sunt secundae tabulae legum Mosaycarum*; *Qui mecum aliquando contendebat theologus, is contra me asserebat*. (Gentilis 1601, p. 21, 91). Malgrado non ne faccia mai il nome è indiscutibilmente certo, proprio in ragione dei temi trattati e per le connessioni che evidenzierò nel paragrafo seguente, che facesse riferimento a John Rainolds.
[54] MS, p. 214.

> Nam ius diuinum ab humano non adeo distinguitur, quod illud deus ipse, istud per homines tulerit: quam quod diuinum inter deum et hominem, humanum inter homines ipsos est. Et sic tota lex dei, quae utrumque continet ius distribuitur in cultum dei, et dilectionem proximi. Et sic a communione inter gentes, ius gentium, a communione inter cives ius civile, et a communione quadam inter omnia ius naturale definiunt nostri: quia ius communio est.

Si tratta di concetti che riprenderà nell'epistola dell'8 febbraio 1594, per approfondirli nell'VIII capitolo del I libro del *De nuptiis* 'Distinguuntur ius divinum et humanum' (1601), nel quale le sue affermazioni – che dipendono pressoché alla lettera da quelle contenute nell'epistola – vengono corredate dalle necessarie allegazioni normative e dottrinali: [55]

MS, p. 284	*Disputationum de nuptiis libri VII...*, p. 38
Atque assumptionem ita confirmabam, quod est ius inter hominem et hominem, humanum est. Sed secunda tabula hoc ius est inter hominem, et hominem: ergo secunda tabula ius humanum est. Enunciatum uero hic, ita *si ius distinguitur a iure respectu eorum inter quos est*, ius humanum est, quod inter homines est, sed eo modo ius a iure distinguitur. *Sic enim ius civile dicitur, quod civitas sibi constituit.*	Ut *ius a iure distinguitur respectu eorum, inter quos est.* Sic *ius dicitur civile, quod civitas constituit sibi*, quod constitutum iis est, qui sunt eiusdem ciuitatis.[56]
Ius gentium, quod naturalis ratio inter omnes gentes constituit. Ut ita loquuntur iurisconsulti, non ut recitas tu.	*Ius gentium dicitur, quod naturalis ratio inter omnes gentes constituit*: quod hominibus inter se commune est.[57] Hoc appellat ius hominum, aiuntque situm in generis humani societate.[58]

---

[55] Evidenzio in corsivo le parti identiche.
[56] *in marg.*: Cic. Top. (Cicero, *Top.* 9); Inst. tit. 2. (*Inst.* 1.2.1).
[57] *in marg.*: l. i. de inst. (*Inst.* 1.2.1).
[58] *in marg.*: et i. Tusc. (Cicero, *Tusculanae Disputationes*, I.XXVI.64).

> et sic ingeniosissimus Hotomanus, *dum non videt*, brutis et hominibus, *inter bruta et homines* ius esse, aut legem ullam, disputat contra illam definitionem iuris naturalis, ius naturale est, quod natura omnia animalia docuit, *quia ius non sit, ubi communio non est, et nobis cum brutis nulla communio est.*

> Et itaque[59] *dum alii non vident, ius esse inter bruta, et homines etiam negant, ius aliquod esse naturale, quod homines teneat, et animalia.*[60]
>
> *Quia ius non sit, ubi communio non est. Et nobis cum brutis nulla communio est.*

Ma torniamo alla lettera del 22 novembre 1593. Soffermandosi, più specificamente, sullo *ius divinum* — da lui identificato nello *ius religionis* perché regola i rapporti fra Dio e l'uomo (la *communio hominum cum Deo*)[61] — il giurista asserisce che questo è l'unico diritto per il quale i teologi hanno piena competenza, restando loro preclusi tutti gli ulteriori ambiti nei quali lo *ius* esplica la sua efficacia:[62]

> Ius diuinum sic est religio, per quam nobis communio cum deo intercedit: et quae definitur, 'scientia divini cultus, et habitus observantiae eius quo nos habitu cum deo revincimur, et religamur'.[63] Et hoc igitur de iure vestrum est dicere, et docere. Caetera non ad vos pertinent: ut aiunt legislatores in Codice Theodosiano, titulo de religione. Sed et religionem sic circumscribunt Plato, Aristoteles, Cicero, Plutarchus, alii philosophi, et Lactantius, et nostri interpretes, cum alibi, tum ad titulum Codicis Iustinianei de summa trinitate. De quorum uno Azone tibi pro spurca tua de officiosis repono nitidam hic aptam distinctionem. 'Officium' (ait iste) ad titulum Codicis de inofficioso testamento, 'inter patrem et filium pietas dicitur, inter patronum et libertum, obsequium: inter

---

[59] *in marg.*: *Duar. c. 8. de iust.* (Duarenus 1765, ad I.I.V. *De iure naturali, gentium et civili*, p. 5–7).

[60] *in marg.*: *Don. i. con. 6.* (Donellus 1596, I.I.VI., p. 12–13); *Hot. pri. par. iu.* (Hotmanus 1599a, *De iustitia et iure. Titulus primus*, col. 4, no. 9), *et. Inst. tit. 2.* (Hotmanus 1599b, I. II. *De iure naturali, gentium et civili*, coll. 17–42).

[61] Gentili usa talvolta, indifferentemente, le espressioni *ius religionis* e *ius divinum* per indicare i precetti che regolano i rapporti fra Dio e gli uomini e non quelli *inter homines* che, pur essendo stati oggetto di disposizioni divine, costituiscono lo *ius humanum*. Lo attestano, ad esempio, oltre che il *De nuptiis*, il *De legationibus*, le *Commentationes De iure belli* e i *De iure belli libri tres* (cf. *supra*, n. 26).

[62] MS, p. 214. Indico con gli apici i testi estratti dalle opere di altri autori.

[63] Cf. *infra*, n. 67.

hominem et hominem generali vocabulo officium, inter deum et hominem religio'.[64] Et sic etiam Lactantius 'officium', quo 'cum deo coniungimur', 'religionem' appellat.[65]

A tal fine il giurista utilizza, pur senza rinviarvi appositamente, un'espressione già presente nel *De legationibus*:[66] lo *ius religionis* viene definito come *scientia divini cultus, et habitus observantiae eius quo nos habitu cum deo revincimur, et religamur*. Un testo identico lo si rinviene anche nel cap. IX del I libro del *De nuptiis* corredato, questa volta, da un rinvio alla *Universa philosophia de moribus* di Francesco Piccolomini.[67] Ed anche la serie di autori e le fonti normative su cui si sorregge il suo assunto, citate appena di passata nell'epistola al Rainolds, vengono rese esplicite, questa volta, con i pertinenti rinvii, nello stesso capitolo del *De nuptiis*[68] dove, peraltro, si assiste ad un ampliamento di quelle fonti: accanto a Platone,[69] Cicerone[70]

---

[64] Cf. *infra*, n. 73.

[65] Cf. *infra*, n. 71.

[66] Per il testo del *De legationibus*, ove lo stesso identico passaggio (*quia est religio scientia divini cultus, et habitus observantiae eius, quo habitu nos cum Deo devincimur et religamur*), cf. *supra*, n. 26.

[67] Cf. Gentilis 1601, p. 43: *Sed philosophi omnes religionem ita definierunt, esse "scientiam divini cultus, et habitum observantiae eius, quo nos habitu cum Deo revincimur, et religamur"* (*in marg.*: Picc. 4. ci. Ph. 35. = Piccolomineus, 1594, *Philosophiae De moribus Gradus quartus. De virtute morali.* cap. XXXV: *De pietate, Sanctitate et Religione*, p. 182 A: *Religio usurpatur apud Platonem, cum pro scientia divini cultus, tum pro habitu observantię eius, quo habitu nos cum Deo devincimus ac religamus*).

[68] Indico nelle note seguenti i passi del *De nuptiis* che rendono maggiormente esplicito il testo dell'epistola di Gentili al Rainolds.

[69] Cf. Gentilis 1601, p. 42: *Nunc de religione haec cape Platonis. Iusti pars religio in divino cultu versatur: reliqua pars ad homines spectat. Iustitiae tria genera, circa Deum, circa homines, circa defunctos. Illa religio, etc.* (*in marg.*: Pla. Eutyphr. = Plato, p. 12).

[70] Cf. Gentilis 1601, p. 42–43: *Haec Ciceronis. Iuris omnis ratio dividitur in duas partes primas, naturam, atque legem. Et utriusque generis vis in diuinum, humanum. quorum aequitatis est unum, alterum religionis, etc.* (*in marg.*: Cic. part. = Cicero, *De partitione Oratoria*, 129). *Omnis populi Romani religio in sacra, et auspicia divisa est.* (*in marg.*: et 2. de nat. Deo. = Cicero, *De natura deorum ad M. Brutum*, III.5). *"Ius religionis" Cicero distinguit a "iure reipublicae": et ponit in "rebus divinis, sacris, caeremoniis".* (*in marg.*: Cic. pro. do. su. = Cicero, *De domo sua ad Pontifices Oratio*, 32–33). *Caussam religionis ait caussam iurisiurandi. Et itaque religionem a iudice, a teste posci propter iusiurandum.* (*in marg.*: et lib. 1. act. 2. ubi Ascon. Mana. = Asconius Pedianus, V.I., p. 297).

e Lattanzio,[71] al Codice Teodosiano,[72] ad Azzone[73] e alla glossa ordinaria al *Codex* di Giustiniano,[74] nel *De nuptiis* Gentili allega, ad esempio, anche giuristi autorevoli del XIV–XV secolo, come Baldo degli Ubaldi (1327–1400) e Paolo di Castro (1360/62– 1441)[75] nonché, fra i suoi contemporanei, Ugo Donello (1527– 1591) e, fra i teologi, il *praeceptor Germaniae* Filippo Melantone (1497–1560).[76] Una prima evidente dimostrazione che l'epistolario costituisce la fonte alla quale Gentili attinge per la redazione del I libro (*Qui est de interprete*) delle sue *Disputationes* sul matrimonio.

Ma anche la materia matrimoniale risulta oggetto di discussione col Rainolds. Ne sono un esempio palpabile le righe dedicate al concubinato, vergate dal Gentili nell'epistola successiva (8 febbraio 1594):[77] questioni alle quali dedicherà i capitoli IV e V del I libro del *De nuptiis* per rivendicare la competenza del giurista sulla materia. Anche in questo caso egli cita, nella sua lettera,

---

[71] Cf. Gentilis 1601, p. 44: *Audi Lactantium: Primum officium iustitiae est coniungi cum Deo, secundum cum homine. Illud primum religio dicitur, secundum misericordia, vel humanitas appellatur.* atque antea: *Sumus vinculo pietatis obstricti Deo, et religati, unde ipsa religio nomen accepit*, etc (*in marg.*: *Lact. 4. Inst. 28., et lib. 6. cap. 10.* = Lactantius, IV.28, col. 536 A; VI.10, col. 666 B).

[72] Cf. Gentilis 1601, p. 45: *Et sic a me olim notata lex: Quoties de religione agitur, episcopos convenit agitare: ceteras vero caussas, quae ad ordinarios cognitores, vel ad usum publici iuris pertinent, legibus oportet audiri* (*CTh.* 16.11.1).

[73] Cf. Gentilis 1601, p. 43: *Atque eleganter Azo: Officium inter patrem, et filium pietas dicitur: inter patronum et libertum, obsequium: inter hominem et hominem, generali nomine officium: inter Deum et hominem, religio* (*in marg.*: *Azo C. de inoff. te.* = Azo, ad *Cod.* 3.28, rubr., f. 53*rb*, no. 1).

[74] Cf. Gentilis 1601, p. 43 (*in marg.*: *Acc.* = Glossa ordinaria ad *Cod.* 1.1.: *De iustitia tractaturus, de eius parte praecipua quidem tractat, id est, de religione*).

[75] Cf. Gentilis 1601, p. 43 (*in marg.*: *Castr. rubr. C. de su. tri.* = Paulus Castrensis, ad rubr. *Cod.* 1.1., f. 3*rb*, no. 1c: *Item quero, quando religio sit potior pars iustitiae? Respondeo, religio (prout hic sumitur) nihil aliud est, quam cultus diuinus, et iste cultus debetur Deo: quia ad nihil aliud fecit homines, nisi ut ipsum colerent, et suis meritis acquirerent regnum Dei. Sed iustitiae precipuum preceptum est, unicuique tribuere quod suum est: et sic non solum hominibus sed Deo. Sed ista religio et cultus debetur Deo: ergo est pars precipua iustitiae*); (*in marg.*: *Bal. l. 10 de iusti.* = Baldus de Ubaldis 1577, ad *Dig.* 1.1.10, f. 15*v*–16*r*).

[76] Cf. Gentilis 1601, p. 43, 45: *Et religionem definiunt "cultum numinis"* (*in marg.*: *Don. 4. com. 1.* = Donellus, p. 226,53); *Unus item Melanthon quam suggerit multa in Ethicis? Religio duo comprehendit: timorem Dei, et fiduciam misericordiae propter Christum. Religio, hoc est, reuerentia erga Deum. Prima tabula constituit religionem*, etc. (Melanchthon, cap. VI., col. 321).

[77] MS, p. 273–290 + 292.

una serie di fonti normative — costituite soprattutto dal *Corpus iuris civilis* — e dottrinali — quali quelle rappresentate dalle opere giuridiche civilistiche e canonistiche del Duareno (1509–1559), dell'Abate Panormitano (Niccolò de' Tedeschi, 1386–1445), di Francesco Accolti da Arezzo (1416/17–1488) e, ancora una volta, di Baldo degli Ubaldi — per riutilizzarle successivamente nella sua opera sul diritto matrimoniale: [78]

> Concubinatum, scortationem non esse ex legibus nostris peccatum inquis; contra quam lex Dei, et vos exponitis. Ego de concubinatu exposu<i> integra commentatione ad titulum *de sponsalibus*: de qua cape duo haec, Legislatores secutos videri in eo ecclesiae illius temporis iudicium. Ut hoc censuit Duarenus.[79] Itaque si errarunt illi, et vos errastis. Alterum, quod etsi in libris Digestorum vestigia quaedam superesse tibi videatur gentilitatis, in Novellis tamen, quod ius sequimur prae ceteris, et alias deletas esse labes, et hanc de concubinatu. Adi de tuis canonistis principem, Panormitanum ad c. tanta. qui fi. si. leg.[80] Sed ea tamen melior est sententia, ut concubinatus iure civili tantum non puniatur. Quod dixit Bal. ad l. i. de ri. nup.[81] et Aret. ad l. 3. de testa.[82] quicquid alii interpretes, et forte plures definiant. Ego tamen non te onero pluribus. De scortatione immensum falleris. audi l. XLI. de ri. nup. *probrum intelligitur etiam in his mulieribus, quae turpiter viverent, vulgoque*

---

[78] MS, p. 285. Indico in nota i passi del *De nuptiis* che dipendono dal testo dell'epistola di Gentili al Rainolds.

[79] Cf. Gentilis 1601, p. 24, ove il riferimento al Duareno. Cf. Duarenus 1598, ad *Dig.* 24.3, *Quæ sint nuptiae*, p. 244 *ca. me.*: *Atque hinc satis apparet quid inter matrimonium et concubinatum (qui iure civili permittitur) intersit. titul. de concu. infra l. Massutius. de verb. signif.*

[80] Cf. Gentilis 1601, p. 17 (*in marg.*: *Pan. c. 6. fi. qui si. le.* = Nicolaus de Tudeschis, *ad X* 4.17.6, f. 42va, no. 14 del *Summarium*: *Concubinatus de iure canonico est omnino damnatus, et magis prohibetur, quam simplex fornicatio*'; inoltre f. 43va, no. 14, *ca.me.*: *Et ex contraria opin. sequeretur, quod magis faveretur peccato diuturno, et continuo, quam momentaneo*).

[81] Baldus 1599, ad *Dig.* 23.2.1, f. 184rb, no. 2. Cf. Gentilis 1601, p. 17 (ove però il rinvio *in marg.* è a: *Bar. l. I. de ri. nup.* = Bartolus 1602, ad *Dig.* 23.2.1, f. 146vb, ove però nessuna affermazione riferibile al testo gentiliano. Probabile che nell'edizione del *De nuptiis* sia stato scritto per errore 'Bar.' in luogo di 'Bal.').

[82] Cf. Gentilis 1601, p. 17 (*in marg.*: *Aret. l. 3. de testa.* = Franciscus de Accoltis 1589, ad *Dig.* 28.1.3, f. 32vb–34ra, in part. f. 33va *ca. fi.*, no. 5: *Et probat quia de iure civili concubinatus erat peccatum, licet non puniretur poena aliqua in foro contentioso*).

quaestum facerent, etiam si non palam.[83] Audi Iustinianum, *etiam stupri flagitium punitur, cum quis sine vi vel virginem, vel viduam honeste viventem stupraverit?* Inst. tit. ult.[84] *cum meretrice sane non punitur. Sed ea de puniendo alia quaestio est. Et punitur stuprum etiam cum serva tamen.* l. 6. D. de adult.[85]

Ma un elemento ulteriore vorrei qui sottolineare. La perseguibilità di colui che intrattiene una relazione carnale con una schiava prevista dal diritto romano — ancorché non potesse configurarsi come reato di *stuprum* — cui Gentili fa espressamente rinvio nell'epistola,[86] verrà fatta oggetto di approfondimenti nel *Commentario Ad legem Juliam de adulteriis*. Qui il giurista, per contrastare il pensiero di San Girolamo — il quale lamentava che il rapporto sessuale con le *ancillulae* non venisse giuridicamente sanzionato[87] — allega lo stesso passo di Papiniano conservato nel Digesto cui aveva fatto rinvio nell'epistolario (*Dig.* 48.5.6): testo dal quale si desumeva che alcune *actiones* potevano invece essere esperite.[88] Di tutto ciò il Gentili farà tesoro nel I libro del *De nuptiis* nel quale il testo verrà completato, subito dopo, allegando la stessa fonte (Papiniano) citata nella corrispondenza col Rainolds, ed attraverso l'utilizzo di una formulazione pressoché identica a quella del *Commentario* sul *crimen adulterii*:[89]

---

[83] Cf. Gentilis 1601, p. 24 (*in marg.*: l. 41. *de ri. nup.* = *Dig.* 23.2.41).

[84] Cf. Gentilis 1601, p. 24 (*in marg.*: *Inst. tit. ult.* = *Inst.* 4.18.4).

[85] Cf. Gentilis 1601, p. 24 (*in marg.*: l. 6. *de adult.* = *Dig.* 48.5.6).

[86] Cf. *supra*, nel testo, n. 85: *et punitur stuprum etiam cum serva tamen.* l. 6. D. *de adult.* (*Dig.* 48.5.6). Ancorché il rapporto carnale con una schiava non fosse configurabile come *stuprum*, era possibile esperire, infatti, secondo Papiniano, l'*actio legis Aquiliae*, l'*actio iniuriarum*, e l'*actio servi corrupti*. Per un commento di *Dig.* 48.5.6 cf., da ultimo, Perry, p. 24.

[87] Cf. Minnucci 2002, p. 54, 136-137, 179.

[88] Cf. *supra*, n. 85-86.

[89] Cf. Gentilis 1601, p. 25 (in marg.: *Hier. ep. ad Ocea.* = S. Hieronymi ep. LXXVII no. 3, PL 22, coll. 691–992, no. 2); mentre il testo del *Commentario* si legge in Minnucci 2002, p. 179. Evidenzio in corsivo le parti identiche. Sottolineo che, nel testo del *Commentario*, Gentili afferma di aver approfondito la questione in altra sede: *At non permittitur, Hieronyme, non permittitur: etsi quasi adulterium, aut stuprum non punitur. Quod alibi explicaui* (cf., nel testo, la col. di destra). È probabile che faccia riferimento ad un suo *Commentario* sul titolo *De sponsalibus* (un'opera inedita della quale non ho trovato traccia fra i manoscritti gentiliani conservati a Oxford), cui rinvia sia nell'epistola al Rainolds (MS, p. 285: *Ego de concubinatu expos<ui> integra commentatione ad titulum de sponsalibus*), sia

Disputationum de nuptiis libri VII	*Comm. ad l. Juliam de adulteriis*
Sileant theologi: nec alienam temnant temere disciplinam. '*Aliae sunt leges Cæsaris, aliae Christi. Aliud Papinianus, aliud Paulus noster praecipit apud illos impudicitiae frena laxantur: et solo stupro, atque adulterio condemnato, passim per lupanaria, et ancillulas libido permittitur'*. Non permittitur, Hieronyme: ut audire de ipsoque potuisti Papiniano (*Dig.* 48.5.6).	In quincta clamat Hieronymus: '*Aliae sunt leges Caesarum, aliae Christi. Aliud Papinianus, aliud Paulus noster praecipit. Apud illos impudicitiae frena laxantur; et solo stupro, atque adulterio condemnato, passim per lupanaria, et ancillulas libido permittitur*'. At *non permittitur, Hieronyme, non permittitur*: etsi quasi adulterium, aut stuprum non punitur. Quod alibi explicaui. Pluribus tenetur iste actionibus, l. 6 de adult. (*Dig.* 48.5.6).

Ma quel che più rileva è che le espressioni rivolte nel *De nuptiis* a Girolamo — di cui viene riprodotto un passaggio tratto dall'*Epistola ad Oceanum* — sono precedute da un'apostrofe molto simile al *Silete theologi in munere alieno* del *De iure belli*: *Sileant theologi: nec alienam temnant temere disciplinam*.[90] Un'asserzione recisa che fa da contraltare ad un'altra espressione che si rinviene ancora una volta nell'epistola al Rainolds dell'8 febbraio 1594: *Alienam disciplinam temere ne contemnito*.[91]

Affermazioni nette e risolute, quelle di Gentili. Egli — pur dichiarandosi rispettoso delle altre scienze e discipline — continua a rivendicare al giurista la competenza circa le questioni emergenti dalle relazioni umane, escludendo contestualmente, sugli stessi

---

nel *Commentario* alla *lex Julia de adulteriis* (cf. Minnucci 2002, p. 171). Sul passo di Girolamo cf., da ultimo, Agnati, p. 101.

[90] Cf. Gentilis 1601, p. 25.

[91] MS, p. 286: Alienam disciplinam temere ne contemnito (corpo tondo mio). *Repete, non ab efficienti, sed a fine artes distingui oportere: et senties tenuitatem argumenti tui magis. Nunc redeo tecum ad mea. "Religio" (dixi ego) "ius est inter deum et hominem"* (qui Gentili rinvia alla sua epistola del 22 novembre 1593, MS, p. 215–216): *Atque religionem solam docent theologi: ergo theologi ius solum docent inter deum et hominem. Et religionem ego accipio in sua propria natura, et significatione propria: quae habetur ex definitione. Tu mihi rursus de laxa acceptione obiectas aliquot exempla* (qui Gentili rinvia all'epistola di Rainolds del 25 gennaio 1594, MS, p. 256ss). *Quod facis in docta disputatione non docte*.

temi, quella dei teologi: essi, a suo parere, evidentemente irrispettosi delle altrui prerogative, e spesso sostanzialmente incompetenti nella materia giuridica (il *munus alienum*, l'*alienam disciplinam*), avrebbero fatto meglio a tacere![92]

Ai teologi, però, secondo il giurista, occorre continuare a riconoscere non solo la funzione di studiare ed approfondire il testo sacro, ma anche il compito di occuparsi dei rapporti fra gli uomini, col fine esclusivo di illuminarne la coscienza perché, nell'ottica gentiliana, foro esterno e foro interno, reato e peccato, debbono essere tenuti nettamente distinti. Lo si deduce, ancora una volta, dalla lettura del I libro del *De nuptiis* nel quale Alberico riprende il tema, già presente nell'epistolario, relativo all'ultimo precetto della *secunda tabula* del Decalogo, che per brevità era stato racchiuso nell'espressione *Non concupisces*[93] e che, nella sua opera sul diritto matrimoniale. il giurista svilupperà nel capitolo intitolato *De lege ultima secundae tabulae*:[94]

> Ut humana dirigit lex scilicet ad actus externos, ad internos diuina. Ut iurisprudentia est manifesti vindex, theologia etiam occulti. Quae Alciatus noster. Lex nostra non scrutatur conscientiam. Conscientia interior non pertinet ad legem humanam temporalem, nec ad ecclesiasticam. Nemo enim de ea iudicat, nisi solus Deus. Quae Baldus noster.

---

[92] Proprio perché rispettoso della loro competenza, nella lettura dei passi della Scrittura Gentili farà spesso ricorso ai testi della Patristica e della teologia riformata: lo attestano i numerosissimi rinvii alla letteratura teologica rinvenibili nel *De nuptiis*. Fra questi, come ha recentemente sottolineato Alain Wijffels, si deve ricordare che il capitolo VI del Libro IV, dedicato al rapporto genitori-figli circa l'espressione del consenso a celebrare il matrimonio — tema che, essendo relativo alle relazioni umane, alla luce dei convincimenti gentiliani dovrebbe essere di pertinenza più (*magis*) giuridica che teologica — è intitolato *Audiuntur theologi*. Sebbene il suo contenuto richieda uno studio specifico ed approfondito, si può rilevare che, in apertura, subito dopo aver ricordato di aver utilizzato nella stesura del testo le opere teologiche e i passi scritturistici, il nostro giurista rinvia, condividendone il pensiero, ad Ambrogio e Tertulliano — dei quali sottolinea la competenza giuridica (*theologos* [...] *etiam et legum peritos*) — nonché alla legislazione giustinianea, alla letteratura classica, ad una vasta dottrina legale. Sul punto cf., da ultimo, Wijffels 2019, p. 497–512; Minnucci 2019, p. 15–19.

[93] Il riferimento è a *Exo.* 20.17; *Deut.* 20.5; *Rm.* 7.7; cf. le epistole di Rainolds a Gentili del 5 agosto 1593, e del 25 gennaio 1594; la risposta di Gentili a Rainolds dell'8 febbraio 1594; ed infine la lettera di Rainolds a Gentili del 12 marzo successivo, MS, p. 197, 252, 284–285, 305.

[94] Gentilis 1601, p. 59–63.

Tutto ciò che attiene alla coscienza — il cui unico giudice è Dio — essendo racchiuso nel segreto dell'animo, non può essere oggetto di sanzione umana, indipendentemente dal fatto che quest'ultima sia prevista dalla legislazione secolare o ecclesiastica. Entrambe, di per sé, debbono regolare, ed eventualmente punire, gli atti dell'uomo e gli effetti che ne derivano, ma non possono penetrare la *conscientia pura et interior*: un ambito quest'ultimo, quello del foro interno, che non riguarda la legge e il giurista, ma che deve essere riservato alla teologia.[95]

Bibliografia

Bibliografia primaria

Franciscus de Accoltis (1589), *In primam et secundam Infortiati partem commentaria*, Venetiis: apud Iuntas.

Andreas Alciatus (1546), *Oratio in laudem iuris civilis principio studii habita cum Avenione profiteretur*, in *Lucubrationum in Ius ciuile tomus secundus, habet autem* [...] *orationes tres*, Basileae: per Mich. Insigrinium.

Asconius Pedianus (1815), *In Ciceronis Actionis secundae in Verrem seu accusationis liber primum*, in M. T. Ciceronis *Opera*, adiecit C. G. Schütz, Lipsiae: apud Gerhardum Fleischerum iun.

Azo (1564), *In ius civile Summa*, Lugduni: s.n.

Baldus de Ubaldis (1577), *Commentaria in primam Digesti Veteris partem*, Venetiis: apud Iuntas.

Baldus de Ubaldis (1599), *In secundam Digesti Veteris partem commentaria*, Venetiis: apud Iuntas.

---

[95] Gentilis 1601, p. 63, con rinvio in margine: *Alc. orat. Auen.* (Alciatus 1546, p. 509: *Sic legis prudentia, Theologiaque eandem ob causam fuerunt introductae, ut scilicet obuiam iretur delinquentibus: alteraque secreti mali, altera manifesti uindex esset*); nonché a: *Bal. l. 3. C. de fur.* (Baldus de Ubaldis 1585, ad *Cod.* 6.2.3, f. 11ra: *Solutio: tribus modis fit dedicatio: corde tantum et ista nihil operatur quo ad legem fori iudicialis: quia non scrutatur conscientiam, sed actum*); *l. ult. C. de her. inst.* (Baldus de Ubaldis 1585, ad *Cod.* 6.24.14, f. 80va: *Est enim quaedam negatiua contra quam affirmativa non potest probari ut negativa, quae inest in metu: quia sub facto quaedam etiam voluntas includitur: unde affirmativa habet pregnantem negativam, quae si probatur per actum exteriorem, actus interior redditur impossibilis probari. Quia nemo iudicat de ipso, nec per ipsum nisi solus Deus. Et ideo conscientia pura et interior non pertinet ad legem humanam temporalem, nec ecclesiasticam*). Sul punto, più ampiamente, Minnucci 2019, p. 17–19.

Baldus de Ubaldis (1585), *Commentaria in Sextum Codicis librum*, Lugduni: s.n.

Bartolus a Saxoferrato (1602), *Commentaria*, II, *In secundam Digesti Veteris partem*, Venetiis: apud Iuntas.

Paulus Castrensis (1583), *In primam Codicis partem commentaria*, Lugduni: s.n.

Jacobus Cuiacius (1840), *Ad librum quartum Decretalium recitationes solemnes*, in *Opera ad Parisiensem Fabrotianam editionem diligentissime exacta in tomos XIII distributa*, X, Prati: ex Officina Giachetti.

Hugo Donellus (1596), *Commentariorum de iure ciuili Libri viginti octo*, Francofurti: apud Andreae Wecheli heredes, Claudium Marnium, et Ioan. Aubrium.

Franciscus Duarenus (1598), *In lib. XXIIII Digestorum Commentarius. in tit. soluto matrimonio dos quemadmodum petatur, De nuptiis, I. Quae sint nuptiae*, in *Opera*, Francofurti: apud heredes Andreae Wecheli, Claudium Marnium et Ioan. Aubrium.

Franciscus Duarenus (1765), *In primam partem Pandectarum sive Digestorum Methodica Enarratio*, in *Opera omnia*, I, Lucae: typis Josephi Rocchii.

Albericus Gentilis (1585), *De legationibus libri tres*, Londini: excudebat Thomas Vautrollerius.

Albericus Gentilis (1589), *De iure belli Commentationes duae*, Lugduni Batavorum: apud Iohannem de la Croy (ma Londini: John Wolfe).

Albericus Gentilis (1598), *De iure belli libri III*, Hanoviae: excudebat Guilielmus Antonius.

Albericus Gentilis (1599), *Disputationes Duae; I. De actoribus et spectatoribus fabularum non notandis. II. De abusu mendacii*, Hanoviae: apud Guilielmum Antonium.

Albericus Gentilis (1600), *Ad primum Macbaeorum disputatio, ad illustrem d. Tobiam Matthaeus episcopum Dunelmensem*, Franekerae: apud Aegidium Radaeum.

Albericus Gentilis (1601), *Disputationum de nuptiis libri VII*, Hanoviae: apud Guilielmum Antonium.

Albericus Gentilis (2018), *De Papatu Romano Antichristo recognovit e codice autographo Bodleiano D'Orville 607*, a cura di G. Minnucci, Milano: Monduzzi editoriale (Archivio per la Storia del diritto medievale e moderno; Studi e Testi, 17).

Franciscus Hotmanus (1599a), *Epitomatorum in Pandectas. Libri XXII*, in *Opera iuridica*, I, Geneva: excudebant haeredes Eustathii Vignon, et Iacobus Stoer.

Franciscus Hotmanus (1599b), *In quatuor Institutionum iuris civilis libros*, in *Opera iuridica*, II, Geneva: excudebant haeredes Eustathii Vignon et Iacobus Stoer.

Lactantius L. C. F., *Divinarum Institutionum Libri septem*, in PL 6.

Philippus Melanchthon (1850), *Scripta ad Ethicen et Politicen Spectantia et dissertationes iis annexae. In secundum librum Ethicorum Aristotelis enarrationes*, in *Opera quae supersunt omnia*, ed. H. E. Bindseil, Halis Saxonum (Corpus Reformatorum XVI).

Franciscus Piccolomineus (1594), *Universa philosophia de Moribus in Academia Patavina philosopho primo in Gradus decem redacta*, Venetiis: apud Franciscum de Franciscis Senensem.

Plato (1578), *Euthyphro vel De sancto, explorandi causa institutus*, in *Opera quae extant omnia, ex nova Ioannis Serrani interpretatione*, s.l.: excudebat Henr. Stephanus.

Rainolds J. (1599), *Th' Overthrow of Stage-Playes, By the Way of Controversie Betwixt D. Gager and D. Rainoldes […] Whereunto are Added […] Certaine Latine Letters Betwixt the Saed Maister Rainoldes and Doct. Gentiles […] Concerning the Same Matter*, Middleburg: R. Schilders (2 ed. Oxford 1629: printed by John Lichfield), p. 164-190.

Nicolaus Ruckerus (1580), *Matrimonialium consiliorum tomus secundus*, Francoforti ad Moenum: impensis Sigis. Feyerabendii.

Nicolaus de Tudeschis Abbas Panormitanus (1617), *Commentaria in quartum et quintum Decretalium libros*, Venetiis: apud Iuntas.

Bibliografia secondaria

Agnati U. (2015), 'Costantino e le donne della locanda (CTh.9.7.1 = Cod. 9.9.28)', in *Teoria e storia del diritto privato*, 8, p. 1-109.

Binns J. W. (1972), 'Alberico Gentili in Defense of Poetry and Acting', in *Studies in the Renaissance*, 19, p. 224-272.

Binns J. W. (1974), 'Women or Transvestites on the Elizabethan Stage? An Oxford Controversy', in *Sixteenth Century Journal*, 5/2, p. 95-120.

Blank D. (2017), 'Actors, Orators, and the Boundaries of Drama in Elizabethan Universities', in *Renaissance Quarterly*, 70, p. 513-547.

Boas F. S. (1914), *University Drama in the Tudor Age*, Oxford: Clarendon Press.

Colavecchia S. (2018), *Alberico Gentili e l'Europa. Storia ed eredità di un esule italiano nella prima età moderna*, Macerata: EUM. (Centro Internazionale di Studi Gentiliani, San Ginesio; Studi Gentiliani, 3).

Di Simone M. R. (2010), 'Alberico Gentili e la controversia sul teatro nell'Inghilterra elisabettiana', in *Alberico Gentili (San Ginesio 1552 – Londra 1608). Atti dei Convegni nel quarto Centenario della morte*. II. (San Ginesio, 11–12–13 settembre 2008; Oxford e Londra, 5–6 giugno 2008; Napoli "L'Orientale", 6 novembre 2007; Centro Internazionale di Studi Gentiliani), Milano: Giuffrè, p. 379–410.

Lavenia V. (2015), '"Mendacium officiosum": Alberico Gentili's Ways of Lying', in *Dissimulation and Deceit in Early Modern Europe*, ed. M. Eliav-Feldon & T. Herzig, New York, NY: Palgrave Macmillan, p. 27–46.

Leo R. (2019), *Tragedy as Philosophy in the Reformation World*, Oxford: University Press.

Maclean I. (2009), 'Alberico Gentili. His Publishers and the Vagaries of the Book Trade between England and Germany', in *Learning and the Market Place. Essays in the History of the Early Modern Book*, Leiden: Brill, p. 291–337.

Markowicz L. (1977), *Latin Correspondence by Alberico Gentili and John Rainolds on Academic Drama* (Institut für Englische Sprache und Literatur, Universität Salzburg), p. 16–135.

Minnucci G. (2002), *Alberico Gentili tra mos italicus e mos gallicus. L'inedito Commentario Ad legem Juliam de adulteriis*, Bologna: Monduzzi editore (Archivio per la Storia del diritto medioevale e moderno, Studi e Testi, 6).

Minnucci G. (2011a), *Alberico Gentili iuris interpres della prima età moderna*, Bologna: Monduzzi editore (Archivio per la Storia del diritto medioevale e moderno, Studi e Testi, 16).

Minnucci G. (2011b), 'Foro della coscienza e foro esterno nel pensiero giuridico della prima Età moderna', in *Gli inizi del diritto pubblico europeo, 3. Verso la costruzione della modernità. Die Anfänge des öffentlichen Rechts, 3. Auf dem Wege zur Etablierung des öffentlichen Rechts zwischen Mittelalter und Moderne*, a cura di/hrsg. von G. Dilcher & D. Quaglioni, Bologna: Il Mulino/Berlin: Duncker & Humblot (Annali dell'istituto storico italo-germanico in Trento, Contributi 25), p. 55–86.

Minnucci G. (2015a), 'Un discorso inedito di Alberico Gentili in difesa della *iurisprudentia*', in *Quaderni Fiorentini*, 44, p. 211–251.

Minnucci G. (2015b), 'Una lettera inedita su questioni teologiche di Alberico Gentili al padre Matteo con un Sonetto inedito dedicato alla Regina Elisabetta I d'Inghilterra (18 settembre [1592?]', in *Historia et Ius*, 8, paper 11.

Minnucci G. (2016), *"Silete theologi in munere alieno". Alberico Gentili tra diritto, teologia e religione*, Milano: Monduzzi editoriale.

Minnucci G. (2018), '"Bella religionis causa mouenda non sunt". La libertas religionis nel pensiero di Alberico Gentili', in *Nuova Rivista Storica*, CII/3, p. 993–1018.

Minnucci G. (2019), 'La riforma, il diritto canonico e i giuristi protestanti: qualche spunto di riflessione', in *Historia et Ius*, 15, paper 1.

Minnucci G. (2020), 'Il giurista e il teologo: Alberico Gentili contro John Rainolds. Nuove indagini sulle fonti inedite', in *Historia et Ius*, 17, paper 10.

Minnucci G. (2021a), 'Alberico Gentili (1552–1608)', in *Law and the Christian Tradition in Italy: The Legacy of the Great Jurists*, ed. O. Condorelli & R. Domingo Osle, Abingdon – New York, NY: Routledge, p. 281–296.

Minnucci, G. (2021b), *Diritto e teologia nell'Inghilterra elisabettiana. L'epistolario Gentili – Rainolds (1593–1594)*, Napoli: ESI (Collana di Studi "Pietro Rossi", 5).

Minnucci G. (2022), 'Diritto e teologia nell'Inghilterra elisabettiana. La polemica oxoniense fra Alberico Gentili e John Rainolds sulle competenze del giurista e del teologo', in *XV International Congress of Medieval Canon Law* (Paris, July 17–23, 2016), Città del Vaticano, p. 1303-1317.

Panizza D. (1981), *Alberico Gentili, giurista ideologo nell'Inghilterra elisabettiana*, Padova: Tipografia La Garangola.

Perry M. J. (2014) *Gender, Manumission and the Roman Freedwoman*, Cambridge: University Press.

Plummer C. (1887), *Elizabethan Oxford. Reprints of Rare Tracts*, Oxford: Clarendon Press.

Ragni C. (2020), *La nazione e il teatro. Alberico Gentili, Shakespeare e l'Inghilterra elisabettiana*, Perugia: Aguaplano (Scritture e Linguaggi; Collana di Lingue e Letterature, 3).

Schmitt C. (1991), *Il Nomos della terra nel diritto internazionale dello jus publicum Europaeum*, trad. e postfazione a cura di E. Castrucci, cura editoriale di F. Volpi, Milano: Adelphi (= Id., *Der nomos der Erde in Völkerrecht des Jus Publicum Europaeum*, Köln 1950).

Wijffels A. (2019), '*Audiuntur theologi*. Legal Scholarship's claim on the "Second Table" in Alberico Gentili's *De Nuptiis* (1601)', in *De rebus divinis et humanis: Essays in Honour of Jan Hallebeek*, ed. H. Dondorp, M. Schermaier & B. Sirks, Göttingen: Vandenhoeck & Ruprecht, p. 497–512.

Abstract

Alberico Gentili (1552–1608) arrives from Italy in England in 1580, where he fled for his adherence to the Reformation. In 1587 he becomes *Regius professor* of *civil law* at Oxford. Some years later (1593–1594), he is involved in an epistolary controversy with the Puritan theologian John Rainolds in relation to the role of the jurist and theologian. The manuscript letters, still preserved in the *Corpus Christi College* of Oxford, heralds the final Gentili's position in the dispute, which will be completely expressed in the Book I of *Disputationum de nuptiis libri VII* (1601), in which he reproduces — as shown in this essay — parts of the text of his previous unpublished epistles. The author aims to discuss the thought that the Italian jurist expressed in the epistles, and in the First Book of *De nuptiis* where we can read the sentence used as title of this contribution: '*Sileant theologi: nec alienam temnant temere disciplinam*'. Very similar words, though much more known, can be read in *De iure belli libri tres* (I.12): '*Silete theologi in munere alieno*'!

Riassunto

Alberico Gentili (1552–1608) giunge in Inghilterra nel 1580, dopo essere fuggito dall'Italia per la sua adesione alla Riforma. Nel 1587 diventa *Regius professor* di *civil law* a Oxford. Alcuni anni dopo (1593–1594), è coinvolto in una controversia epistolare con il teologo puritano John Rainolds circa le competenze del giurista e del teologo. Le lettere manoscritte, ancora conservate nel *Corpus Christi College* di Oxford, preannunciano i convincimenti che Gentili esporrà alcuni anni dopo nel I libro dei *Disputationum de nuptiis libri VII* (1601), in cui riproduce — come si dimostra in questo saggio — parti del testo delle sue precedenti epistole inedite. L'autore mira a discutere il pensiero che il giurista italiano ha espresso sul tema nella corrispondenza con Rainolds e nel primo libro del *De nuptiis*, dove si può leggere l'espressione utilizzata come titolo di questo contributo: '*Sileant theologi: nec alienam temnant temere disciplinam*'. Parole molto simili, sebbene assai più note, si leggono nei *De iure belli libri tres* (I.12): '*Silete theologi in munere alieno*'!

LEEN SPRUIT
Radboud University, Nijmegen

STRATEGIES AND AGENCY IN THE CENSORSHIP OF MODERN SCIENCE AND NATURAL PHILOSOPHY: SOME CASE STUDIES

This contribution addresses two aspects of the Catholic censorship of early modern science and natural philosophy, namely, the criteria for assessing books and views, and the interaction between the institutions (the Roman Congregations of the Holy Office and of the Index) and the persons involved (defendants, authors). As to the latter, the possibility of negotiation has often been neglected by scholars discussing the praxis of censorship. Such interaction clearly had a social dimension, since members of the higher social classes clearly had better opportunities than other defendants.

The first two sections outline the factors that made early modern science and natural philosophy liable to theological censure, as well as the procedures followed by the Inquisition and the Index. Then I examine several remarkable cases that illustrate the efforts of authors to avoid or to lift the ban on their books, and the defense strategies employed at Inquisition trials. The cases of Francesco Patrizi, Raimondo di Sangro, and the Neapolitan 'atheists' have been selected as significant *exempla*, because the respective archive files of the trials provide extensive documentation of the defense strategies adopted by the defendants. Thus, the article sheds light on which strategies were developed by either side to settle the questions, and on the effects of censorship on intellectual and broader socio-cultural history.

1. *Heterodoxy and Science: Disciplinary Fields and Points of Friction*

Until recently it was a commonplace to regard the activity of the Roman Congregations of the Inquisition and of the Index as the principal reason for the downturn of modern science and innovative philosophical culture in Italy from the second half of the sixteenth century until the end of the nineteenth century. The trials of Giordano Bruno and Galileo Galilei have been labelled time and again as highly emblematic for this process of intellectual decay, at least from the period of the so-called Risorgimento, which eventually led to the unitary Italian state in 1860–1870. For both trials, Copernican astronomy and the new worldview have usually been seen as elements of a typical clash between the Catholic Church on the one hand and modern science and philosophy on the other. Yet in the period from the rise of the Congregations to the end of the eighteenth century, the points of friction were numerous and surely not limited to cosmology.

From the sixteenth to the eighteenth centuries, the ecclesiastical assessment and censure of science underwent remarkable changes. A few examples may clarify this issue. First, many authors of works that can be viewed as scientific in a modern sense were prohibited (or prosecuted) not for specific scientific or philosophical views, but rather for their religious beliefs or for their involvement in disciplines now regarded as pseudo-scientific, such as astrology and magic. Second, as a rule ecclesiastical censorship did not ban technical scientific works, but rather popularizations and philosophical extrapolations. Newton's *Principia* was not placed on the Index, while expositions of his ideas, such as Voltaire's *Éléments de la philosophie de Newton mis à la portée de tout le monde* (Amsterdam 1738) and Algarotti's *Newtonianismo per le dame* (Napoli 1737), were promptly contested or immediately forbidden. Third, the criteria for condemnations were not unchanging.[1] By the middle of the eighteenth century, exponents of the Roman Curia started to realize that traditional geocentrism had become groundless. The influential consultor Pietro Lazzeri proposed to remove the condemnation of heliocentrism from the Index.

---

[1] Baldini & Spruit 2009, 'Introduction', p. 62–69.

His view was adopted by the Index issued under Benedict XIV in 1758, which tacitly removed the general condemnation, but not that of the individual works banned in 1616. Finally, many (scientific and philosophical) works were not condemned tout court, but with the *donec corrigatur* or *expurgetur* proviso. Such provisos meant that the works in question could be permitted either in an emended edition or else that reading permits could be granted for current editions on the condition that they were corrected according to expurgatory *censurae* approved by the central bodies of doctrinal control.

Philosophical and scientific views became liable to theological censure when they contradicted or questioned Holy Scripture, conciliar decrees, papal bulls, and the authority of the Fathers and schoolmen. This reality meant that some disciplinary fields and doctrinal issues were more sensitive than others. A provisional list includes the following: cosmology (Neoplatonic and post-Copernican views contradicting the traditional world picture); psychology (materialism; deviations from Aristotelian hylemorphism; the denial of the organic hierarchy of souls or of the substantial nature of the intellect; assumption of universal principles, including the world soul or a unique intellect; metempsychosis); medicine (non-Galenic theories; medicine's connection to astrology and, in recipes and cures, to magic); chronology (the extension of traditional chronology on the basis of scientific and philological arguments); physics (the rejection of the distinction between substance and phenomenal appearance; the denial of secondary qualities and final causality; atomism).

2. *Procedures of the Inquisition and the Index*

2.1 Inquisitorial Trials

The tribunal of the modern Roman Inquisition did not proceed *ad instantiam partis*, but *ex officio*, though its proceedings were usually triggered by a charge or a denunciation. Consequently, the burden of proof lay with the prosecutor, and guilt had to be demonstrated by formal evidence. Only heresy or suspected heresy justified the arrest of the person under investigation. House arrest was the penalty for lesser forms of heterodoxy, such as blasphemy or entertaining propositions that were *male sonantes*. Although the tribunal's procedures were inspired mainly by contemporary penal courts and hence by criminal law as it had developed since the thirteenth century, the Roman Inquisition introduced new elements into juridical practice, such as the defense attorney, testimony under oath, appeals to a higher court, the adoption of the principle *unus testis, nullus testis*, a sentence to 'life imprisonment' usually being tantamount to a few years of incarceration, and a public defender for the indigent.[2]

It was the task of the Holy Office to establish whether the crime of heresy was committed and, if such should be the case, to proceed against the defendant. An inquisitorial trial proceeded according to a determinate number of steps. The *inquisitio* (usually triggered by a charge brought against an individual) amounted to the collection of circumstantial evidence, which enabled the court to set up the case. After the case was initiated, there was a session in which a decision was about whether the accused should be arrested. Next came an investigation, which included the interrogation of witnesses and of the defendant. This first part of the process concluded with the formalization of the charges, which were communicated to the defendant, together with a copy of the testimonies. At this point the lawyers were admitted. Both the time allowed for the defense and the list of witnesses called by the defendant were established. During this phase of the trial, the witnesses as well as the defendant could be interrogated (again). Then, the so-called *expeditio causae*, that is, a legal sentence was reached.[3]

Finally, during a public session the *sententia* was read, which also synthesized the essential elements of the trial. Once the charge of heresy had been formally proven and confessed, the conviction generally consisted of an *abiura de formali* and a prison term, which as a rule was not established with any exactness. In the frequent cases of suspected heresy, various courses of action were available. Whenever the suspicion was 'light', the defendant

---

[2] For a reconstruction of an inquisitorial trial, see Beretta 1998, chs 1–4; Errera 2000, ch. 1; Mayer 2013, ch. 5.

[3] Baldini & Spruit 2009, p. 48–53.

was sentenced to an *abiura de levi*, while in the case of a strong suspicion an *abiura de vehementi* was required.

Many trials, however, ended without a sentence. A sentence, after all, presupposes a juridical determination — i.e., established on the basis of sound indications — that the defendant was lightly or strongly suspected of heresy. Frequently, the defendant was released on bail and obliged to present himself whenever the inquisitors ordered (the so-called *toties quoties*). As a rule, the defendant in these cases was given house arrest, or if he belonged to the regular clergy he was confined to a house of his order and given minor penalties.

2.2 Book Censorship

Censurae were of two kinds; critical assessments of a view or the content of a work on the one hand, and expurgations, that is, proposals for correction on the other. Expurgation was a remarkable innovation of the Tridentine Index (1564) and concerned books *quorum principale argumentum bonum est, in quibus obiter aliqua inserta sunt, quae ad haeresim seu impietatem, divinationem aut superstitionem spectant* ('whose principal subject is good, in which occasionally are inserted some things that regard heresy or impiety, divination or superstition').[4] Works prohibited with the proviso *donec corrigatur* could be reprinted in an emended edition, or else local bishops or inquisitors could grant reading permits on the condition that the work was corrected according to the instructions of the Congregation of the Index. Italian libraries contain many works that bear the signs of several kinds of intervention, including the cancellation of names and lines, and the covering or physical elimination of individual passages or entire pages and sections. Forbidden books that were not corrected, either officially or privately, were destined for a clandestine circulation.

The reasons motivating correction were multifarious: obscenity, mixing the profane and the holy, derision of rites and devotion, irreverence towards clergy, attribution of divine characteristics to common people, etc.[5] The fundamental problem in expurga-

[4] ILI, VIII, p. 817.
[5] ILI, VIII, p. 803–808.

tion regarded the criteria for an adequate correction. Rule VIII of the Tridentine Index concerned printed heretical or suspect statements which occurred occasionally (*obiter*), and this designation suggested that such statements could be easily isolated. And indeed, when only names or clearly distinct passages were to be eliminated, things were relatively simple. The situation got quite complicated when the book was placed on the Index due to the author putting forth views that were in open or veiled conflict with Catholic doctrine, and in particular when the censor had to tackle erroneous propositions that were woven into complex theoretical systems. Cases in point are the works by Francesco Giorgio and Francesco Patrizi, which did not directly contradict Catholic doctrine, but which contained many views with heterodox potential.

3. *Interaction in Book Censorship*

3.1 Participation in Correction: The Case of Francesco Patrizi

Francesco Patrizi (1529–1597), of Croatian descent, was a Neoplatonic philosopher and a scientist from the Republic of Venice. He is generally known as an opponent of Aristotelianism. In *Discussiones peripateticae libri XV* (1581), he critically assessed Peripatetic philosophy, comparing it with the Presocratic and Platonic traditions. In *Nova de universis philosophia* (Basel, 1591), he developed the view that, whereas Aristotle's teaching was in direct opposition to Christianity, Plato foreshadowed Christian revelation and prepared the way for its acceptance.

On 8 October 1592, the Congregation of the Index began to discuss whether to place Patrizi's *Nova philosophia* on the Index of Forbidden Books. The phrases used in summoning Patrizi to appear, on 7 November 1592, before the cardinals of the Congregation of the Index (*ut sui operis rationem redderet, paratus retractare errata*) reveal that the summons was prompted by a previous assessment of his work, more precisely the assessment written by Pedro Juan Saragoza, fellow of the Master of the Sacred Palace.[6]

---

[6] For the full text of this *censura*, see Baldini & Spruit 2009, p. 2202–2223.

Patrizi first responded to Saragoza's assessment with the *Apologia*[7] and the *Emendatio in libros suae novae philosophiae*,[8] and subsequently with his *Declarationes*.[9] The composition of these works dates to the period between the end of 1592 and 22 April 1594. It seems likely, as Gregory suggested, that the *Apologia* was the first reaction to Saragozza's *censura*.[10] Remarkably, Patrizi had permission to read this assessment, as follows from, among other things, the classification of charges he presented in his defense.[11] In November of 1592, the Congregation judged Patrizi's proposals for emendation to be insufficient.[12]

On 4 December 1592, Patrizi wrote to the Congregation:

> Mi è stato detto, che non ostante, la mia correttione data [the Apologia] a Vostra Signoria illustrissima e Rerendissima e offertomi di emendare tutto il libro mio, si persiste di volerlo mettere nell'Indice *donec expurgetur*. Non mi pare ciò credibile, poiché io tuttavia lo vo espurgando. E la settimana che viene lo darò espurgato tutto. Pero la supplico, a non volere darmi questa perpetua infamia di metterlo in su l'indice, sendo io prontissimo ad obedire a quel Santissimo Tribunale. Sarei venuto io stesso a supplicarla, ma questo mal tempo me ne spaventa. Le bacio humilmente le mani e me le raccomando in Gratia.[13]

And yet the Congregation of the Index did not deem a conditional prohibition defamatory:

---

[7] In Città del Vaticano, Biblioteca Apostolica Vaticana (BAV), *Barb. Lat.* 318; for a partial edition, see Gregory 1953.
[8] Published in Kristeller 1973.
[9] Gregory 1955.
[10] Gregory 1955, p. 392–393.
[11] Gregory 1955, p. 412–413. See also *Declarationes*, in Baldini & Spruit 2009, p. 2245–2259.
[12] Baldini & Spruit 2009, p. 2224.
[13] Baldini & Spruit 2009, p. 2225: 'I have been told, that notwithstanding my correction [the *Apologia*] given to your most illustrious and most reverend Lordship and my offer to emend my entire book, you persist in wanting to put it on the Index *donec expurgetur*. This does not seem credible, however, since I am expurgating it. And in the week that is coming, I will hand it over completely corrected. But I beg you do not give me this perpetual infamy of putting it on the Index, since I am very ready to obey that Blessed Tribunal. I would have come myself to beg, but this stormy weather scares me. I humbly kiss your hands and recommend them in grace.' (this and following translations are by the author).

> M'è stato detto, che non ostante, la mia correttione data a Vostra Signoria illustrissima e Reverendissima e offertomi di emendare tutto il libro mio, si persiste di volerlo mettere nell'Indice *donec expurgetur*.[14]

Thus it was decided, in spite of Patrizi's protests, to place *Nova philosophia* on the Index.[15] The work was prohibited with the stipulation *nisi fuerit ab auctore correcta*,[16] and subsequently Patrizi was listed among a number of living authors who would, if need be, correct their own works.[17] The *Emendatio*, probably written before Christmas 1592 — as follows from Patrizi's letters of 4 December 1592 and 23 March 1593 — did not have the desired effect, and on 23 March Patrizi asked again for expurgation and permission to print an emended edition.[18]

Shortly afterwards the Congregation commissioned a new assessment, by the Jesuit Benedetto Giustiniani, which was handed over by the general of the Society of Jesus to Paolo Pico, secretary of the Congregation. Patrizi also asked to read this assessment, and on 3 July the Congregation granted this permission. Subsequently, Patrizi discussed this *censura* with Pope Clement VIII, who ordered the philosopher to clarify 'detti luoghi opposti et altri piu oscuri'. Thus, Patrizi composed the *Declarationes* after the *censurae*, and not just with the object, as suggested by the author at the outset, of dissipating doubts among his friends and readers.[19]

The *Declarationes* exists in three redactions. The composition of a fourth redaction, which is incomplete, seems to have been interrupted by Patrizi's plans to start yet another one.[20] These plans, however, had no tangible result. On 2 July of the same year,

---

[14] Baldini & Spruit 2009, p. 2225: 'The Congregation has judged that there is no wrong to the petitioner, considering that more illustrious [men] have been put on the Index with the note of purification.'

[15] Baldini & Spruit 2009, p. 2226. The work was prohibited by the Roman Index of 1593 (which was not ultimately promulgated), and then by the Clementine Index (1596); see ILI, IX, p. 876 and 945.

[16] See Baldini & Spruit 2009, p. 2264.

[17] Baldini & Spruit 2009, p. 375, 382; cf. p. 269, 274.

[18] Baldini & Spruit 2009, p. 2227–2233.

[19] This is confirmed by frequent protestations of submissiveness to the ecclesiastical authorities and, moreover, by a letter from Patrizi to the pope, as reported by Gregory 1955, p. 394–395.

[20] See Gregory 1955, p. 397.

apparently on the basis of Cardinal Francisco Toledo's advice, the Congregation decided upon a downright (*omnino*) prohibition of *Nova philosophia*. Possibly due to confusion among some of the consultors, the work was placed in the Clementine Index (1596), as well as in the successive Indexes, with a specific expurgatory proviso, which reveals Patrizi's ample (but insufficient) protection: *nisi fuerit ab Auctore correcta, et Romae cum approbatione R. Magistri Sacri Palatii impressa*.[21]

Patrizi developed an articulate defense strategy. He argued that some statements by pre-Christian authors should not be understood literally and that some philosophical issues were unresolvable. He claimed that various statements of his and some taken from ancient authors, which had been found theologically objectionable by his accuser, in fact referred to the physical world and not to theological matters. Patrizi also argued that his accuser had misquoted him and had taken statements out of context. Throughout Patrizi affirmed the importance of his philosophical synthesis of Plato, the early Neoplatonists, Presocratics, Hermetic authors, and Church Fathers and argued that this synthesis was compatible with Catholic Christianity. At the same time, Patrizi reiterated that Aristotle, who denied divine creation, held the world to be eternal, and denied the immortality of the human soul, was the real corruptor of Christianity.[22]

A brief overview of the most salient points of the *censurae*, in particular those concerning scientific-philosophical issues, explains the reasons for the ban of Patrizi's book. Saragoza first analyzed and condemned the attack on scholastic philosophy, which had charged with substituting *Aristotelis impietates pro fidei fundamentis*; subsequently Saragoza worked out a serial, thematic *censura*, concentrating on the concept of God and Patrizi's interpretation of the Trinity. He regarded Patrizi's use of negative theology in the definition of God (*non est corpus, non natura, non anima, non Intellectus, non vita, non ens*) as contrary to the faith and to Holy Writ. Moreover, seeing God as *unum principium: neque est, neque fuit, neque erit* was qualified as *prava doctrina*. Saragoza condemned Patrizi's interpretation of the procession

---

[21] ILI, IX, p. 945.
[22] For the text, see Baldini & Spruit 2009, p. 2245–2259.

of the Holy Spirit as contradicting the Apostles' Creed, and he described Patrizi's similar teaching about the procession of the Son as *falsa et improprie dicta*. As to the chapter *De rerum productione*, Saragoza challenged the idea of the simultaneous creation of all things as well as the view of a *productio Dei ex necessitate*. Other accusations concerned the existence of an empty space before creation, Patrizi's denial that the world had been created in time, and the uniqueness of heaven, that is, the negation of a hierarchical world of spheres. The censor paid particular attention to Patrizi's Copernicanism: the motion of the earth contradicts Holy Scripture, and it is a fact, according to Saragoza, that the *suprema astra* move as well. Other charges dealt with the animation of celestial bodies, which contradicted *sententiam communem receptam apud patres*, and the accidental nature of form, which Saragoza regarded as an error. Finally, the definition of the agent intellect as *verbum creatum, proximum Deo*, which was proposed in the *Mystica philosophia*, was considered completely absurd.[23]

Of an altogether different tenor is the *censura* by Giustiniani, who at the beginning of his text recalled that central views of Platonism were praised by the Fathers of the Church as *religionis ac fidei nostrae dogmata illustrari, et confirmari possent*.[24] It is surprising that Giustiniani, reviewing the charges formulated by Saragoza, did not immediately take up the charges concerned with the core of Christian dogma, but preferred to discuss first the challenges to Aristotelian philosophy. His overall evaluation contrasts with Saragoza's *censura* on essential points. In Giustiniani's opinion, the uniqueness of heaven and the motion of the earth are purely philosophical issues, which do not affect the Christian faith. With regard to several other views, Patrizi was merely expounding Plato's thinking and that of his followers. Cases in point include the animation of celestial bodies, the existence of an empty space, and the allegedly necessary production of the world. The doctrine *De Deo*, by contrast, refers to the negative theology of Dionysius the

---

[23] For the text, see Baldini & Spruit 2009, p. 2202–2223.

[24] For a similar open-mindedness towards Plato on the part of a contemporary Jesuit, see the long chapter on Plato in Antonio Possevino's *Bibliotheca selecta* (Possevino 1593).

Areopagite. Moreover, one should not misunderstand the author, as if he intended to deprive God of ideas and intellect. Although Giustiniani confirmed the author's obscurity, not only in the distinction between the three persons of the Trinity but also in the treatment of *De rerum productione*, nevertheless — Giustiniani added — *non tamen aberrat à vero*.[25] Giustiniani acknowledged that Patrizi's theory of substance impeded an adequate interpretation of the Eucharist, but Giustiniani recommended keeping in mind that the author was versed in philosophy, rather than theology. In brief, it seemed sufficient to Giustiniani to keep to these few observations in order to avoid error.

In the end, the extremely intricate conceptual framework of Patrizi's philosophy, which merged Neoplatonism, Mosaic teachings, Hermetic philosophy, and anti-Peripateticism, made it virtually impossible to distinguish between acceptable and unacceptable, between orthodox and heterodox, since the components of Patrizi's philosophy were intimately linked.

3.2 An Appeal to the Pope: The Case of Raimondo di Sangro

Raimondo di Sangro, the seventh prince of Sansevero (30 January 1710–1722 March 1771), was a Neapolitan nobleman, inventor, military commander, writer, scientist, alchemist, and freemason. He is best remembered for his reconstruction of the funeral monument of his family, the Chapel of Sansevero in Naples. He was also the author of some remarkably erudite works, especially the *Lettera apologetica dell'Esercitato Accademico della Crusca contenente la difesa del libro intitolato Lettere d'una Peruana per rispetto alla supposizione de' Quipu scritta alla duchessa di S**** e dalla medesima fatta pubblicare* ('Apologetic letter of Esercitato, member of the Academy of the Crusca, containing the defense of the book entitled *Lettres d'une péruvienne* with respect to the supposition of Quipu written to the Duchess of S **** and published by the same').[26] With this *Apologetic Letter*, written and printed in 1750, Raimondo di Sangro aimed to convince a mysterious female interlocutor of the communicative and literary potential of the

---

[25] See Baldini & Spruit 2009, p. 2234–2244.
[26] See my critical edition: Sangro 2002.

quipu, that is, the notation system based on nodes and colors that was used by the Incas in pre-Columbian Peru.[27] The thesis of the *quipus* as a writing system had already been supported in *Lettres d'une Péruvienne* (Paris 1747) by Madame de Graffigny. In presenting a reconstruction of this system, however, di Sangro discussed notoriously thorny issues, such as the relationship between sacred and profane history, the exegesis of Genesis (in particular the mark of Cain), the antiquity of language, and the origin of humankind. Quoting abundantly forbidden and suspect authors with great ease and provocation, he publicized opinions that were difficult to reconcile with the Holy Scriptures and with Catholic dogma. This challenge to the magisterium of the Church, in combination with the biographical digressions and the long, technical, and erudite analyses, allow us to identify the *Lettera apologetica* as a text reflecting the anti-traditional and innovative culture of the Kingdom of Naples. That culture had its roots in libertinism and the radical wing of the Enlightenment, as well as in the peculiar reception of early modern scientific research in southern Italy.[28] Aimed at a broad audience, the book aroused immediate and vehement reaction in ecclesiastical circles.

Between 1751 and 1752, Raimondo's *Lettera* was attacked by two Jesuits. Pasquale De Mattei noted that di Sangro 'advances and promotes issues, perhaps against his intention, which are certainly the basis of atheism'.[29] Focusing on the central part of the *Lettera*, De Mattei identified a series of suspicious positions in which the author had deviated from the teaching of the Church: the preference for secular history; the implicit adhesion to the theory of the pre-Adamites; the esteem for authors such as John Toland, Pierre Bayle, and Anthony Collins; the quotations from works by the Marquis d'Argens and from Montfaucon's *Comte de Gabalis*; the doubts about the authority of the Pentateuch and about miracles; and finally the credit assigned to rabbinic exegesis.[30]

---

[27] For discussion, see Ascher & Ascher 1969, 1972, and 1981.
[28] See Ferrone 1982 and 2000; cf. Sangro 2002, 'Introduction'.
[29] De Mattei 1751.
[30] De Mattei 1751, p. 5–29.

The harsh condemnation of the *Lettera* by another Jesuit father, Innocenzo Molinari, was based primarily on the belief that it was a 'cabalistic' work, that is, a work written in code. Molinari claimed that the *Lettera*, ostensibly dealing with a harmless topic, in fact sent messages that were contrary to the Catholic religion.[31] In his critical assessment of the *Lettera*, Molinari distinguished four groups of topics: (1) the origin of the world; (2) the conception of the *Archea* as the soul or life of the world,[32] in connection with the origin of human souls, the origin of animal souls, and the generation of humankind; (3) the Catholic Church, Christian morality, Holy Scripture, and the Fathers; and (4) the *quipu*. In the last chapter of his virulent pamphlet, Molinari identified the theoretical foundations 'to which the doctrine of the Apologist can be reduced' as the eternity of the world and the Archea. From these two theses derive all the other pernicious propositions, namely, religious indifferentism (putting Sacred Scripture and the Koran, the Fathers of the Church and the rabbis on the same level), the conception of the pre-Adamites, pantheism or Spinozism, and doubts about revelation and miracles. Due to its rare vehemence, Molinari's treatise was declared libelous in a session of the Neapolitan Real Jurisdiction (29 November 1752) and therefore prohibited.[33]

Equally severe was the judgment expressed by the Augustinian father Agostino Giorgi, appointed by the secretary of the Congregation of the Index, Agostino Ricchini, to examine the *Lettera apologetica*.[34] In large part, Giorgi's *censura* touches on predictable arguments: it indicates the prince's affinity with heretical conceptions such as those concerning the pre-Adamites and the eternity of the world; and it denounces his doubts about the authority of Moses as the first author ever, as well as Raimondo's esteem, or rather his preference, for pagan historians against biblical authors. Giorgi also bitterly criticized not only Raimondo's claim to be able to replicate the San Gennaro miracle by natural means, but

---

[31] Molinari 1752, p. 3–4.
[32] The origin of this concept is in Helmont 1648, p. 144–145; for discussion, see Giglioni 2000, p. 54–58.
[33] Cf. Schipa 1901, p. 158.
[34] Sangro 2002, p. 235–236.

also the casual references to heretical or suspicious authors such as Bayle, Locke, Collins, as well as the *Telliamed*. In short, the prince advocated the worst sort of materialism, as is apparent from the juxtaposition that he suggests between God and Christ, on the one hand, and the Peruvian mythological figures of Pachamac and Viracocha, on the other, which entails a downright derision of the incarnation.[35] Thus it came as no surprise that Sansevero's book was placed on the Index on 29 February 1752, being — as this censor declared — a work 'scandalous, audacious, offensive to the pious ears, that favors heresy and materialism.'[36]

Although this prohibition left little room for maneuver, Raimondo di Sangro nonetheless attempted to change the course of events. In the autumn of 1753, he published a *Supplica a Benedetto XIV* ('*Petition to Benedict XIV*').

This petition is an articulate harangue formulated to obtain the removal of the *Lettera apologetica* from the Index of Prohibited Books. Starting from the firm conviction that the work contained no real errors — which would otherwise have been explicitly indicated by the Congregation of the Index[37] — di Sangro elaborates on the groundlessness of the accusation launched by Molinari against the use of 'malicious jargon'. The central point of the defense is the essentially ironic character of the *Lettera*, in addition to a declaration by di Sangro that he never explicitly endorsed the incriminating theses, cited from forbidden or suspect authors, and that, on the contrary, he detested and blamed such ideas.[38]

With this petition Raimondo di Sangro tried to convince the pope and subsequently the Congregation of the Index, to which the pope passed the matter via a letter of 12 February 1754, to remove the *Lettera apologetica* from the Index. Di Sangro's cause was advocated by the Neapolitan plenipotentiary to the Holy See, Geronimo Sersale, duke of Cerisano, who wrote a letter to Benedict XIV. The pope addressed Agostino Ricchini, secretary of the Congregation, asking him to read and examine the *Supplica*. After

---

[35] Sangro 2002, p. 236–255.
[36] For a reconstruction of the events, see Sangro 2002, p. 52–59, 223–226.
[37] Sangro 2006, p. 34–35.
[38] See, for example, Sangro 1753, p. 66, 70–71, and 78. Actually, most of these declarations had been explicitly requested by the ecclesiastical authorities; see the preliminary *censura* published in Sangro 2006, 'Appendix', doc. 45.

a few days, Ricchini concluded that the request had to be rejected for a series of reasons, the final one being the dangerous precedent of removing forbidden books from the Index on the basis of a simple afterthought by the author:

> Finalmente è da riflettersi, che accordandosi all'oratore il decreto rilassativo che implora, ei certamente vorrà pubblicarlo. Ed allora oltre l'esempio inaudito, e l'ansa che prenderanno altri scrittori viventi di chiedere simile rilassazione alle loro opere proibite con esibirne unitamente l'Apologia, o dichiarazione, potrà credersi, o sospettarsi, che La Sagra Congregazione nel proibire il libro accennato (e così discorrasi in casi simili) non abbia maturamente usato tutte le opportune considerazioni, né abbia ben inteso la mente, ed il senso dell'autore posto in chiaro nell'Apologia del libro, e che perciò permettendone la lettura unitamente à quella dell'Apologia, venga à ritrattare il suo primiero giudizio, il che altamente ridonderebbe in disdoro, e pregiudizio della Congregazione medesima e della Santa Sede, etc.[39]

In other words, by accepting the delayed repentance of forbidden authors, the Congregation would admit to not having accurately and adequately considered the prohibition decree, and by consequence the Congregation might as well stop its work altogether.

4. Conflicts and Agency: Atomism and the Social, Political, and Cultural Implications of the Atheism Trial in Naples (1688–1697)

In November 1673, ten years after the prohibition of Descartes by the Index,[40] the Holy Office decided to send a circular letter to

---

[39] Sangro 2002, 'Appendix', doc. 10, p. 262: 'Finally, one should reflect that by agreeing with the speaker to the withdrawal of the decree that he begs, he will certainly want to publish it. And then, beyond the unheard-of example, and the cravings that other living writers will take to ask for similar relief for their forbidden works by exhibiting an apology or declaration, it may be believed or suspected that the Sacred Congregation in prohibiting the aforementioned book (and proceeding thus in similar cases) has not entertained all the appropriate considerations, nor understood the mind and the intention of the author, which is made clear in the book's Apology, and therefore by allowing its reading together with that of the Apology, come to retract its first judgment, which might lead to disdain and prejudice of the Congregation itself and of the Holy See.'

[40] ILI, XI, p. 281–282; for discussion, see Armogathe & Carraud 2001.

all local inquisitors in Italy commanding them not to permit the printing of any work containing atomistic lore, that is, any work 'in which it is held that (material) substances are not composed of matter and form, but of corpuscles or atoms'.[41]

Despite this prohibition issued by the Roman Holy Office, atomistic notions continued to spread in Catholic lands. They also reached southern Italy, where they quickly assumed broader cultural and political dimensions. From 1688 to 1697, Naples, capital of the Spanish kingdom in southern Italy, provided the stage for a large-scale inquisitorial trial against a great number of people accused of embracing atomism and therefore of subscribing to atheism.[42]

In the early 1670s, Naples' ecclesiastical authorities had begun to warn against the spread of mechanical philosophy and atomism. Notably the members of the Accademia degli Investiganti (1663–1670) had been much taken with these new ideas. After the official closure of the academy, this circle enlarged and began to meet in less secluded places and to discuss its ideas more openly, thereby attracting a new generation of intellectuals to the new philosophy. A series of books and manuscripts testifies to the ever broader appeal of corpuscular theories.[43]

The Church responded to this situation with hitherto unseen determination. Prominent Church leaders delivered fiery sermons condemning a doctrine that, according to them, denied the existence of God, the immortality of the soul, and the possibility of miracles, including the liquefaction of the blood of San Gennaro.

In March 1688, a certain Francesco Paolo Manuzzi managed to trigger a drawn-out, high-profile court case. Manuzzi presented himself 'spontaneously' to the representative of the Holy Office

---

[41] The decree is in Archivio della Congregazione per la Dottrina della Fede, Sanctum Officium, *Decreta*, 1673, f. 395r: *Eminentissimi mandarunt, ut scribantur litterae circulares omnibus Inquisitoribus, quod non permittant impressionem librorum, in quibus continetur, composita substantialia non componi ex materia, et forma, sed ex opusculis, seu atomis.* It should be kept in mind that the Cardinals Inquisitors did not grasp that atoms and corpuscles are quite different things.

[42] Discussed in Osbat 1974.

[43] Di Capua 1681, Cornelio 1683, and Francesco D'Andrea's widely circulating manuscript *Apologia in difesa degli atomisti* (c. 1685), published in Borrelli 1995.

in Naples in order to denounce a group of people in Naples who endorsed the 'philosophy of the atoms' and who had lost their faith.

From his depositions, it can be discerned that Manuzzi denounced the idea that before Adam the world had been inhabited by men and animals which were composed of atoms. Men started to build houses, castles, and cities; because they developed a political organization and a social hierarchy, the most judicious among them were viewed as sons of a deity. A similar hierarchy triggered veneration, and by consequence the exercise and expansion of power. It is in this context that we should interpret the message and life of Jesus Christ, who was ambitious and declared to be the Son of God. Since Christ was not in fact the Son of God, the authority of St Peter and his successors in the Catholic Church lacked any foundation, and thus the popes could not excommunicate dissidents, issue edicts, or require obedience in matters temporal or spiritual. Sacraments or dogmas simply did not exist, while the entire New Testament was senseless. In sum, atomism led to denying creation, the existence of God, hell, purgatory, paradise, and miracles. In fact, however, none of these claims is found in any other early modern atomistic or corpuscular philosophy.[44]

4.1 One City — Two Inquisitions

It should be kept in mind that the war on heresy in Naples was quite particular. Upon several occasions, the Neapolitan population fiercely protested against the introduction of the Spanish or Roman Inquisition (1509–1510, 1547, 1564–1565, 1661). As a result, there was no official local delegate inquisitor, as there was in northern and central Italian cities, but only a representative, first described as a 'commissioner', and then as a 'minister' of the Roman Holy Office. In trials regarding the faith, this minister was supposed to cooperate with the archbishop, but this imposed cooperation did not always run smoothly and led to the well-known situation of one city and two inquisitions. Then the 1661 revolt against the Holy Office triggered in Naples a permanent

---

[44] Osbat 1974, p. 255–257.

Deputation for the Holy Office, whose members were delegated by the several *piazze nobiliari* and the *piazza del popolo* (the representative organs for the nobility and the rising bourgeoisie, respectively). Their main aim was to eliminate the Inquisition, or at least to limit its activities and authority as much as possible. The result was a rather unique situation for a Catholic kingdom and its 'most faithful city' (*città fedelissima*).[45]

Other factors also turned the Neapolitan situation into a wasps' nest. The minister and the archbishop corresponded with the Holy Office in Rome, but heterodox phenomena were also reported by the apostolic nuncio to the Vatican's Secretary of State. The nuncio also maintained diplomatic relations with the viceroy, who in turn corresponded with the court in Spain and the Consiglio d'Italia, the commission for Italian affairs in Madrid. Finally, in Rome the Neapolitan affairs were handled and discussed with the Spanish ambassador and with the nuncio in Madrid. Thus, in a most peculiar reverse Bermuda triangle — in which nothing disappeared — between Naples, Madrid, and Rome the arrest of some young lawyers was the prelude to an intricate joust between ecclesiastical and political forces.

As it is impossible to reconstruct the trial in any detail, I dwell on some significant moments, and then turn to de Cristofaro's defense strategy.

4.2 Naples in Uproar: 1691–1693

After the deposition and abjuration of Manuzzi in June 1688, proceedings slowed down, and it was not until the summer of 1691 that events started to gain momentum again. In August of that year the new minister arrested Giacinto de Cristofaro in the rooms of the Vicaria tribunal, triggering violent protests against the Holy Office in the city. In autumn several other suspects were arrested. De Cristofaro rapidly became the principal defendant in the trial. He was accused of being the source of the heresies referred to in the deposition by Manuzzi: existence of pre-Adamite humans made of atoms; errors and abuses committed by Christ and the pope; and the non-existence of God, hell, purgatory, paradise, and

---

[45] Romeo 1988.

the sacraments. Moreover, with Filippo Belli, de Cristofaro had attempted to convince Manuzzi and his friend Basilio Giannelli of the truth of these heretical ideas.[46]

In November 1692 the new minister arrested another group of suspects, including Giovanni De Magistris (scribe in the Banco dell'Annunziata, later a physician), and Carlo Rosito (*speziale*, that is, an apothecary). After only three months, De Magistris and Rosito were sentenced by the archbishop, who had taken the office of minister, to a formal abjuration, which was conducted on 15 February 1693 before a large audience in the local cathedral.

In the following week, the Deputation for the Holy Office started to discuss a proceeding directed personally against the archbishop, protesting the violation of the principles of law in trials regarding the faith. On April 16, the Deputation met again and decided to appeal to the pope for the abolition of the inquisitorial tribunal in Naples. After meetings of the six noble seats (*piazze* or *seggi*) and the civil class (*piazza popolare*), the Deputation decided on May 26 to delegate Pietro Di Fusco and Mario Loffredo, marquis of Monteforte, to present its requests to Rome.[47]

4.3 Giacinto de Cristofaro's Defense

How did Giacinto De Cristofaro react to his arrest, and how did he defend himself? First, in the extensive series of interrogations that took place in 1692, he systematically and firmly denied all accusations. Second, during his captivity he submitted a huge number of petitions to the local Holy Office and bishop in Naples, to the cardinals of the Congregation in Rome, and to the assessor of the Holy Office in Rome. In some of these petitions, he asked to be 'habilitated', that is, to be transferred to a more comfortable prison or cell, or even to be granted house arrest. The latter request he did not obtain, but one month after his arrest he was moved from the

---

[46] The major part of the documentation of the trial is in two codices: one is in Archivio Storico Diocesano di Napoli (ASDN), ms. 761, which contains the documents kept in the file of the trial by the minister of the local Holy Office; another is in Biblioteca Nazionale di Napoli, ms. I.AA.32, which contains many copies of documents from the Diocesan codex as well as materials from the defense of Giacinto De Cristofaro.

[47] Osbat 1974, ch. 5.

inquisitorial prison in the convent of San Domenico to that of the archiepiscopal palace, and when he complained about 'humid and dark' rooms, he was moved to more comfortable lodgings.

In November 1692, when the interrogation of the witnesses were finished, de Cristofaro received a copy of their depositions and subsequently prepared, with the aid of his lawyer Michelangelo Baccalà, a counter questionnaire for all testimonies that had previously been heard, about thirty-five in number. Their questionnaire consisted of sixty-three questions, which can be divided into three parts.[48]

The first part contained the following sections: personal information and reliability (1–5); duty (7–10); acquaintance or friendship with heretics (6, 12, 43); education and memory of past events (11, 16, 18, 22–23); relationship with other persons linked to the trial (14–15, 19, 44–45); knowledge of or friendship with atheists (17, 21–21); acquaintance with sinful people (24–30); knowledge of atomism or atomists (31–32). The second part starts with questions that regard: the faith and piety of Giacinto (33–42, 61); his friends and his reputation (46–50); the proposition *remota fide ac remota veritate* (51); de Cristofaro's relationship with the neighborhood (52–55, 59). In the questions of the third part, the witness is asked whether his or her deposition has been correctly verbalized, whether he or she had been threatened or put under pressure, and other issues related to the trial (56–58, 62–63).

For number 31, De Cristofaro and Baccalà formulated the following questions regarding atomism:

> Item s'interroghi se esso testimonio sappia che cosa sia atomo, o scienza d'atomi, chi siano l'autori che di quella trattano, se detti Autori siano cattolici o heretici o Athei, se sia stata dannata detta scienza, da chi sia stata dannata, perché sia stata dannata, quando sia stata dannata, se vi siano in Napoli o fuori Persone che seguitano detta scienza, se siano cattolici o heretici o Athei, se siano stati o siano amici, et come le conosca et se li libri che trattano detta scienza siano prohibiti.[49]

---

[48] There are several drafts and copies of this questionnaire; the most complete and apparently final version is in ASDN, ms. 761, f. 194r–200v.

[49] ASDN, ms. 761, f. 197v: 'Ask whether the witness knows what an atom is, or the science of atoms, who the authors are who treat it, if said authors are Catholics or heretics or atheists; if this science has been condemned, by whom

The issue of atomism was a central charge in Manuzzi's accusation in 1688, and thus it is worthwhile to examine the answers of the some of the major witnesses and accusers involved in the trial. Basilio Giannelli answered:

> Ho procurato di sapere prima, che cosa sia Atomismo e la dottrina degli Atomisti, ma doppo, che la mia causa, che fu sbrigata in Spagna, hò procurato di abolire della mia mente sifatta dottrina, e di non saperne niente più, come occasione del mio errore: *in reliquis dixit se nescire*.[50]

Francesco Paolo Manuzzi, the first and main accuser in this trial, formulated the most detailed answer:

> Mentre stavo in Napoli ho studiato qualche cosa di questa filosofia naturale, [...] intesi, che cosa sia Atomo, o scienza d'Atomi, consistente in questo, che sincome l'Aristotelici dicono ogni cosa esser composta di materia e forma, così la scienza dell'Atomi insegna, che il principio d'ogni cosa siano detti Atomi di specie differenti, chi quadri, chi tondi, chi uncinati, e che questi poi facciano il composto d'ogni cosa. L'autori che trattano di quella scienza, secondo che citava nelli scritti di Nicolò Galitio nostro lettore erano Gassendo, e Cartesio, quali stimo che siano Cattolici, perche non sono libri proibiti. Io non so se detta scienza sia stata dannata, e stimo che nò, perché detto Nicolò Galitio la leggeva publicamente, et in Napoli si leggeva, come hò detto publica, e stimo, che si seguiti da molti, perché era una quantità di sudetti, che veniva là ad impararla e li conosco tutti per Cattolici quelli, che venivano con me a sentire detta filosofia. Io però non mi strinsi con essi in amicitia, perché com'ho detto poco ci attesi pochi mesi e poi lasciavo detto studio, perché conobbi che mi distoglieva da studij legali.[51]

---

was it condemned, why it was condemned, when it was condemned, if there are in Naples or elsewhere people who endorse that science, whether they are Catholics or heretics or atheists, whether they were or are friends, and how the witness knows them, and whether the books treating that science are prohibited.'

[50] ASDN, ms. 761, f. 204r: 'At first I tried to find out what atomism is and the doctrine of the atomists, but afterwards, when my cause was dealt with in Spain, I tried to abolish such doctrine from my mind, and to know nothing more, being an occasion for my mistake.'

[51] ASDN, ms. 761, f. 217rv: 'While I was in Naples, I studied something of this natural philosophy [...] [and] I understood what an atom is, or the science

Paolo d'Acunto, whose deposition was aggravating in particular for de Cristofaro, replied as follows:

> Io so che l'atomi sono quelli punti indivisibili de' quali si compongono tutte le cose, e che siano principio costitutivo di tutte le cose, come dicono diversi Autori, sia gentili, come cattolici, quali cattolici impugnano detta scienza per essere quella contra la nostra santa fede cattolica, del quale io professo, et in reliquis ut in eius depositione.[52]

Finally, Angelo Barone:

> Io so che gl'atomi sono alcune particelle quantitative ma indivisibili, e l'autori che trattano di esse sono diversi, et in particolare Pietro Cassenno, Beradino Telesio, il P. Magnan dell'Ordine de Minimi di S. Francesco, Errico Regio, Renato des Cartes, et altri, li quali sono tutti Cattolici; e la detta scienza come tale non e stata dannata, et in Napol quelli che sono professori di detta scienza, quali io conosco, sono cattolici e molti sono miei amici, e so che Renato des Cartes sia proibito, *donec corrigatur*.[53]

Many witnesses, however, did not answer at all, denied knowing about atomism, or had a fairly limited idea of what atomism was.

---

of atoms, consisting in this: now while the Aristotelians say that everything is composed of matter and form, the science of the atoms teaches that the beginning of everything should be called atoms of different species, those which are square, those which are round, those which are hooked, and that they make up the compound of everything. The authors dealing with that science were Gassendi, and Descartes, whom I estimate to be Catholics, because their books are not forbidden. I do not know if this science has been condemned, and I do not think so, because Nicolò Galitio read it publicly, and in Naples it was followed by many, who came there to learn it, and I know them all as Catholics. However, I did not cling to them in friendship, because I knew that it distracted me from legal studies.'

[52] ASDN, ms. 761, f. 305v: 'I know that atoms are those indivisible points of which all things are composed, and that they are constitutive principle of all things, as several authors say, whether they are gentile or Catholics; the Catholics challenge such science as being against our holy Catholic faith, which I profess; and as to other issues, see his deposition.'

[53] ASDN, ms. 761, f. 308r: 'I know that atoms are some quantitative but indivisible particles, and the authors who deal with them are different, and in particular Pietro Cassenno [*sic*, for Gassendi], Beradino [*sic*, for Bernardino] Telesio, father Maignan of the Order of Minims of St Francis, Enrico Regio, Renato des Cartes, and others, who are all Catholics. And the said science as such has not been condemned, and in Naples those who are professors of this science, as I know, are Catholics, and many are my friends, and I know that Renato des Cartes is forbidden, *donec corrigatur*.'

Giuseppe de Domenico, for example, simply stated that 'atom means an indivisible particle'. Enigmatically, Nicola de Domenico held that 'in the opinion of Renato and Cassendo, atoms are a combination of particles'.[54] And most surprisingly, the main defendant, De Cristofaro, systematically avoided answering the question in his numerous depositions.

It is worth highlighting that from these replies one gathers that the defenders of the 'philosophy of the atoms' in Naples were defending a quite eclectic approach and — conflating Descartes and Gassendi — that their opponents were not especially subtle in their condemnations.

De Cristofaro remained incarcerated in the archiepiscopal palace, because all his requests to be released had been rejected. In the period between his arrest and the spring of 1697, he wrote over twenty petitions to the archbishop Cantelmo, the Deputation for the Holy Office, the cardinals of the Holy Office, and the assessor of the Congregation, but with the exception of his being transferred to more comfortable lodgings, these petitions were of no avail. That he declared himself innocent made little impression, and his request to be released, or at least to be transferred to and judged in Rome, was therefore judged inadmissible. On 15 March 1697, he was asked to present his defense, in order to conclude his cause. In vain, he asked again to be judged by the Congregation in Rome, and on 16 April he was summoned to hear the verdict and to pronounce his abjuration. He thus came to know that the views for which he had been denounced and was now being condemned included the following: the denial that Christ was God's Son; the existence of pre-Adamites composed of atoms; the rejection of the pope's power; the denial of paradise, hell and purgatory, of miracles and providence; the uselessness of the invocation of saints and the veneration of images; the mortality of the soul; and the denial of the real presence of Christ in the sacrament of the Eucharist. De Cristofaro was placed under house arrest and obliged to confess, receive communion once a month, practice spiritual exercises, and attend liturgical ceremonies on major holidays.[55]

---

[54] See ASDN, ms. 761, f. 285r and 327r, respectively.
[55] See ASDN, ms. 761, f. 536rv, 539r (sentence), and f. 537rv (abjuration).

Concluding Remarks

It is a commonplace that the effectiveness of book censorship was seriously compromised by the many possibilities of avoiding it, e.g. by hiding books and manuscripts as well as through self censorship and dissimulation. Moreover, censorship in the Roman bodies of doctrinal control was not a rigid application of rules, because censorial practice frequently had a pragmatic, situational character. The ('generous') grant for reading permits is a case in point.

During the sixteenth and seventeenth centuries, many professionals in Italy and abroad, including physicians and jurists, complained to local ecclesiastical officials that the prohibitions interfered with their work. Many of these professionals became involved in negotiations with the Church for the availability of texts they deemed necessary for their profession. Thus Catholic censorship succeeded in repressing the circulation of some texts while simultaneously creating a platform for discussing scientific knowledge. To be sure, the Catholic bodies of doctrinal control sought to delineate and delimit the reading of banned books, establishing conditions for reading permits, in addition to keeping such books out of the hands of large portions of European society. And yet the practice of censorship led to a paradoxical situation: while the Roman Congregations of the Holy Office and of the Index, and the Master of the Sacred Palace, all worked to detect and disrupt the circulation of prohibited books, they also simultaneously issued thousands of licenses to readers, permitting them to 'keep and read' books that were banned.[56]

The system of reading permits shows that in the pre-modern period both censor and author were active in the same social and cultural environment, and they were part of the same system of communication, that is, the learned society of clergymen, scientists, poets, historians, and the leading figures of the academic world. This situation entailed the possibility of negotiation. Authors of forbidden books were not completely helpless

---

[56] For the case of medical books, see Marcus 2020; on reading permits for scientific books, see Baldini & Spruit 2009, p. 2567–2779; and the extensive chapter 'Licences' in Baldini & Spruit 2024 (in preparation).

victims, since the jurisdiction and guarantees of inquisitorial law offered them some space to maneuver, though often with minimal results, at least compared to people who asked to read forbidden books.

Indeed, the apologies of Patrizi and di Sangro, though divided by more than one hundred and fifty years, show that authors were taken seriously by the Congregation of the Index, but also that it was not sufficient to make minor revisions if the heterodoxy was an integral part of the conceptual framework and did not appear in the text merely *obiter*. Under several guises authors apologized or appealed to the conscience of the members of the Congregation of the Index. But neither Patrizi's plea to avoid the defamatory mark of prohibition nor Raimondo di Sangro's direct appeal to the pope caused the minds of the cardinals of the Index, or of its secretary, to relent.

The situation was different with regard to inquisitorial processes, not least because of the threat posed by an arrest and the possible consequences of a conviction for heresy (prison fines, confiscation of property, forced exile). To be sure, the exchange between inquisitors and defendants cannot be defined as a *herschaftsfreie Diskussion*, since the relationship between the censors and the accused author was asymmetric. And yet, neither did the Holy Office in Rome and the peripheral seats represent a purely repressive organization. De Cristofaro's case shows that defendants were able to write numerous petitions, which, though often without tangible success, led in some cases to surprising results. The cross-interrogation of over thirty-five witnesses, according to the scheme established by de Cristofaro and his lawyer, is a clear example of the significant guarantees that were allowed to defendants. Nevertheless, the broader cultural and political context should be considered. Indeed, as in book censorship, the phenomenon of a corporate society of censors and the censored also emerges from the huge difference between the Inquisition's treatment of the learned and the lower levels of the population.

De Cristofaro was an educated lawyer, and he came from an important family of jurists. He was acquainted with the ins and outs of legal procedure, and he knew on what grounds he could plead his case. Other defendants, such as the pharmacist Carlo Rosito and the bank employee Giovanni De Magistris, did not have these options. They were arrested in November 1692, and their case was concluded in a few months; in February 1693, they were forced to hear their verdict read out before a large audience in the Neapolitan cathedral. In his monograph on the atheism trial in Naples, Luciano Osbat argued that the danger of the atomistic philosophy lay not so much in the atheism to which it could give rise, but rather in the sense of loss and mistrust that the philosophy might generate towards an organic body of traditional truths and beliefs, and especially towards the Church, which administered this tradition. Such danger was much more concrete when the penetration of those ideas had reached the humble layers of the population. This danger explains why Archbishop Cantelmo organized the recantation and condemnation of minor poets such as Rosito and de Magistris, in a choreographed procedure that was supposed to frighten the middle class, thereby rendering it immune to any influence that was not of its clergy.

Bibliography

Primary Sources

Tommaso Cornelio (1663), *Progymnasmata physica*, Venetiis: Typis haeredum Francisci Baba.

Pasquale de Mattei (1751), *Lettera dell'Accademico tra gli'Incogniti il Ponderante, al Signor ****** Contenente alcune Riflessioni sulla Lettera Apologetica dell'Accademico Esercitato*, Venezia: Presso Simone Occhi.

Leonardo Di Capua (1681), *Parere del signor Lionardo di Capoa divisato in otto Ragionamenti, ne' quali partitamente narrandosi l'origine, e 'l progresso della medicina, chiaramente l'incertezza della medesima si fa manifesta*, In Napoli: Per Antonio Bulifon.

Jan Baptista van Helmont (1648), *Ortus medicinae, idest initia physicae inaudita, Progressus medicinae novus, in morborum ultionem, ad vitam longam. ... Edente authoris filio, Francisco Mercurio van Helmont, cum eius praefatione ex belgico traslata*, Amsterodami: apud Ludovicum Elzevirium.

Innocenzo Molinari (1752), *Parere intorno alla Vera Idea contenuta nella Lettera Apologetica composta dal Signor' Accademico Esercitato Per rispetto alla supposizione de' Quipu &c. Dell'Abbate **** Inviato ad un suo amico in Napoli*, [Napoli: s.i.].

Antonio Possevino (1593), *Bibliotheca selecta qua agitur de ratione studiorum in historia, in disciplinis, in salute omnium procuranda*, 2 vols, Romae: Ex Typographia Apostolica Vaticana.

Raimondo di Sangro (2002), *Lettera apologetica dell'Esercitato Accademico della Crusca contenente la difesa del libro intitolato Lettere d'una Peruana per rispetto alla supposizione de' Quipu scritta alla duchessa di S**** e dalla medesima fatta pubblicare*, ed. L. Spruit, Napoli: Alòs.

Raimondo di Sangro (2006), *Supplica a Benedetto XIV*, ed. L. Spruit, Napoli: Alòs.

Secondary Sources

Armogathe, J.-R. & V. Carraud (2001), 'La première condamnation des Œuvres de Descartes, d'après des documents inédits aux Archives du Saint-Office', in *Nouvelles de la République des Lettres*, 21, p. 103–137.

Ascher, M. & R. Ascher (1969), 'Code of ancient Peruvian knotted cords (*quipus*)', in *Nature*, 222, p. 529–533.

Ascher, M. & R. Ascher (1972), 'Numbers and relations from ancient Andean Quipus', in *Archive for History of Exact Sciences*, 8, p. 288–320.

Ascher, M. & R. Ascher (1981), *Code of the Quipu: A Study in Media, Mathematics, and Culture*, Ann Arbor, MI: University of Michigan Press.

Baldini, U. & L. Spruit (eds) (2009), *Catholic Church and Modern Science: Documents from the Roman Archives of the Holy Office and the Index*, vol. I: *Sixteenth-Century Documents*, 4 tomes, Roma: Libreria Editrice Vaticana (Fontes Archivi Sancti Officii Romani, 5).

Baldini, U. & L. Spruit (eds) (2024), *Catholic Church and Modern Science: Documents from the Roman Archives of the Holy Office and the Index*, vol. II: *Seventeenth-Century Documents*, 5 tomes, Roma: Libreria Editrice Vaticana (in preparation).

Beretta, F. (1998), *Galilée devant le Tribunal de l'Inquisition. Une relecture des sources*, ThD thesis, Universitè de Fribourg.

Borrelli, A. (1995), *D'Andrea atomista. L' 'Apologia' e altri inediti nella polemica filosofica della Napoli di fine Seicento*, Napoli: Liguori Editore (Quaderni del Dipartimento di filosofia e politica, Istituto universitario orientale, 14).

Errera, A. (2000), *Processus in causa fidei. L'evoluzione dei manuali inquisitoriali nei secoli XVI–XVIII e il manuale inedito di un inquisitore perugino*, Bologna: Monduzzi Editore (Archivio per la storia del diritto medioevale e moderno, 4).

Ferrone, V. (1982), *Scienza, natura, religione. Mondo newtoniano e cultura italiana nel primo Settecento*, Napoli: Jovene (Storia e diritto, 9).

Ferrone, V. (2000), *I profeti dell'Illuminismo. Le metamorfosi della ragione nel tardo Settecento italiano*. New enlarged edition, Bari: Laterza.

Giglioni, G. (2000), *Immaginazione e malattia. Saggio su Jan Baptiste van Helmont*, Milano: Angeli (Filosofia e scienza nel Cinquecento e nel Seicento. Serie 1, Studi 53).

Gregory, T. (1953), 'L'*Apologia ad Censuram* di Francesco Patrizi', in *Rinascimento*, 4, p. 89–104.

Gregory, T. (1955), 'L'*Apologia* e le *Declarationes* di Francesco Patrizi', in *Medioevo e Rinascimento. Studi in onore di B. Nardi*, vol. I, Firenze: Sansoni (Pubblicazioni dell'Istituto di Filosofia dell'Università di Roma, 1–2), p. 385–424.

Index des livres interdits, ed. J. M. De Bujanda et al., 11 vols, Sherbrooke (Québec): Éditions de l'Université de Sherbrooke; Genève: Librairie Droz, 1980–2002 [= ILI].

Kristeller, P. O. (1973), 'Francesco Patrizi da Cherso, *Emendatio in libros suos novae philosophiae*', in *Rinascimento*, 10, p. 215–218.

Marcus, H. (2020), *Forbidden Knowledge. Medicine, Science, and Censorship in Early Modern Italy*, Chicago, IL-London: University of Chicago Press.

Mayer, Th. F. (2013), *The Roman Inquisition: A Papal Bureaucracy and Its Laws in the Age of Galileo*, Philadelphia, PA: University of Pennsylvania Press.

Osbat, L. (1974), *L'Inquisizione a Napoli. Il processo agli ateisti 1688–1697*, Roma: Edizioni di storia e letteratura (Politica e storia, 32).

Romeo, G. (1988), 'Una città, due inquisizioni: l'anomalia del Sant'Ufficio a Napoli nel tardo '500', in *Rivista di storia e letteratura religiosa*, 24, p. 42–67.

Schipa, M. (1901), 'Raimondo di Sangro castigato nel 1752 dal Consiglio comunale di Napoli', in *Napoli nobilissima* 10, p. 157–158.

Abstract

From their foundation in the sixteenth century, the Roman Congregations of the Inquisition and the Index, as bodies of doctrinal control, have generally been associated with the repression of heresy and other forms of heterodoxy. In actuality, authors and defendants under investigation were not deprived of agency, and several forms of interaction between the machinery of orthodox normativity and heterodox challenges were developed in the early modern period to secure a socially determined space for negotiation. This essay identifies a range of practices emerging from the dynamic coexistence or network of censorship and heterodoxy. I focus on two cases of book censorship in which the authors (Francesco Patrizi and Raimondo di Sangro) negotiated with the Congregation of the Index, and on the remarkable Inquisition trial in Naples against the so-called atheists (1688–1697).

MATHILDE ALBISSON
Université Autonome de Barcelone

L'INQUISITION ESPAGNOLE, ARBITRE DES CONTROVERSES ENTRE LES ORDRES RELIGIEUX (XVIIe SIÈCLE)*

Introduction

L'objet de ce chapitre est d'étudier le rôle joué par le tribunal de l'Inquisition espagnole dans les controverses théologiques et ecclésiastiques qui opposèrent plusieurs ordres religieux après le concile de Trente. De fait, à partir de la fin du XVIe siècle, les divergences qui existaient entre les différentes écoles théologiques se creusèrent et donnèrent lieu à de virulentes querelles. Certaines d'entre elles réavivèrent d'anciennes disputes médiévales, que l'apparition des mouvements réformés avait momentanément dissipées, car, face au protestantisme émergent, l'Église catholique cherchait avant tout à apparaître comme un front uni sur le plan ecclésiastique et unanime en matière doctrinale.[1] Une fois la menace de la Réforme estompée, les discussions reprirent de plus belle, dynamisées par le renouveau théologique post-tridentin.[2] L'esprit de Contre-Réforme constitua un vivier propice aux disputes doctrinales entre les ordres, qui s'opposèrent dans le but de se rendre maître de la vérité théologique et d'occuper une place dominante sur la scène religieuse post-conciliaire.[3] Cette lutte pour le prestige et la supériorité spirituelle généra d'importantes rivalités entre les

---

* Ce chapitre s'inscrit dans le cadre du projet I+D *Los límites del disenso. La política expurgatoria de la monarquía hispánica* (PGC2018-096610), dirigé par María José Vega Ramos et financé par le Ministerio de Ciencia, Investigación y Universidades (Espagne).

[1] Alabrús Iglesia 2012, p. 170.
[2] Vázquez 1979, p. 419.
[3] Martínez Ruiz (éd.) 2004, p. 481.

religieux, qui s'accusaient mutuellement de transgresser les doctrines de l'Église.[4] La Compagnie de Jésus, ordre récemment créé, aspirait à s'imposer face à des communautés implantées de longue date, comme les Dominicains, qui contrôlaient depuis l'époque médiévale l'appareil inquisitorial, théologique et universitaire espagnol.[5] En outre, les universités ainsi que les chaires et centres d'enseignement de la théologie se multiplièrent dans l'Europe moderne, favorisant l'apparition de courants doctrinaux divergents, qui donnèrent lieu à des controverses.[6] Ces dernières furent essentiellement des guerre de plumes, dès lors que leurs protagonistes s'affrontaient à coup de traités, de conclusions théologiques (imprimées et défendues publiquement), de mémoriaux, de textes polémiques et parfois même d'écrits satiriques, dans lesquels les considérations théologico-doctrinales se trouvaient mêlées à des appréciations plus subjectives, voire à des insultes et des railleries. Souvent, le point de départ de ces querelles coïncidait avec la publication d'un livre par un membre d'un ordre religieux, qui suscitait aussitôt une virulente réaction de la part de la communauté adverse.

L'objectif de la présente étude est d'examiner le rôle de l'Inquisition espagnole et plus particulièrement de la censure exercée par celle-ci dans ces querelles post-tridentines. Pour comprendre la particularité que revêt l'intervention inquisitoriale dans de telles disputes, il faut commencer par rappeler brièvement les circonstances de la création de cette institution et les missions qui lui étaient assignées. Fondée en 1478, l'Inquisition était à la fois un tribunal ecclésiastique, qui tenait sa juridiction de la papauté, et une institution intégrée au système polysynodal de la monarchie hispanique. La finalité première qui lui fut attribuée à sa création consistait à consolider l'unité politique de l'Espagne sur la base d'une uniformité spirituelle, en poursuivant les judaïsants (les juifs convertis au catholicisme mais restés fidèles en secret aux prescriptions de la Loi judaïque) ainsi que les mahométans (les musulmans ayant officiellement embrassé le catholicisme mais qui continuaient à pratiquer secrètement la religion islamique).

---

[4] Egido 2015, p. 49.
[5] Martínez 2011, p. 140.
[6] Vázquez 1979, p. 429–430.

L'Inquisition était une institution très malléable, qui sut s'adapter à la gestion de nouvelles dissensions perçues comme un danger pour la préservation de la foi des fidèles et de la pureté du dogme.[7] L'émergence de nouveaux courants idéologiques et spirituels dans le premier quart du XVIe siècle fut à l'origine de plusieurs aménagements juridictionnels de l'institution inquisitoriale.[8] C'est ainsi qu'à partir des années 1520, elle s'attaqua à l'hérésie protestante et aux écrits des réformés. La mission censoriale du Saint-Office espagnol comportait plusieurs facettes : publication d'Index de livres interdits, examen doctrinal de textes suspects et, le cas échéant, le décret de leur interdiction ou expurgation. Le tribunal contrôlait aussi la circulation des livres dans les royaumes d'Espagne et entre l'Espagne et l'extérieur, dans le but d'empêcher l'importation de publications jugées hétérodoxes. À cet effet, les frontières maritimes et terrestres, de même que les librairies et les bibliothèques privées, étaient soumises à un règlement strict et à des inspections fréquentes.

Le concile de Trente influença significativement l'évolution de la politique de l'institution inquisitoriale et en particulier les critères et cibles de la censure. À partir de la seconde moitié du XVIe siècle, le tribunal de l'Inquisition devint le bras exécuteur de la Contre-Réforme en Espagne. Il se transforma alors en un outil de contrôle destiné à encadrer strictement les croyances, les pratiques religieuses, les discours et les comportements individuels et collectifs des catholiques, en accord avec les principes tridentins.[9] À partir de la fin du XVIe siècle, le Saint-Office hispanique, qui n'avait en principe pas vocation à intervenir dans des débats intra-religieux, s'immisça, suite à plusieurs dénonciations, dans ces controverses qui opposaient différents ordres religieux et courants théologiques. Le tribunal ne prit pas parti pour une tendance ou pour un ordre en particulier ; il endossa au contraire un rôle de médiateur. Son but était avant tout d'arbitrer au mieux les affrontements entre religieux afin d'éviter les déchirements

---

[7] Pour une approche diachronique de l'activité inquisitoriale, voir Dedieu 1979, p. 15–42.

[8] Escandell Bonet 1996, p. 253–266.

[9] Escandell Bonet 1996, p. 264 ; Bœglin 2003, p. 27 ; Pardo Tomás 2009, p. 76. Sur l'évolution de la censure inquisitoriale dans l'Espagne post-tridentine, voir Albisson 2020.

au sein de la communauté catholique. Il s'efforça de tempérer les excès auxquels ces débats passionnés pouvaient parfois conduire, car il redoutait que ces luttes intestines ne fragilisent et discréditent l'image de l'Église aussi bien aux yeux des fidèles qu'à ceux des hérétiques.

Dans sa tentative pour réguler les querelles, le tribunal de l'Inquisition se heurta à bien des difficultés. En premier lieu, il faut rappeler que sa mission était avant tout de combattre l'hétérodoxie, et non de trancher sur des questions proprement doctrinales ou théologiques, c'est-à-dire, internes à la religion, dont la délibération revenait au Saint-Siège. L'Inquisition dépendait donc des résolutions de la papauté pour interdire ou autoriser la circulation de certaines thèses. L'indétermination de la Curie sur plusieurs sujets doctrinaux constitua une difficulté majeure pour l'arbitrage des conflits. Le deuxième obstacle auquel se heurta l'Inquisition était que ses experts théologiques, les qualificateurs, qui étaient chargés d'examiner les livres suspects, appartenaient, pour la plupart, à des communautés religieuses acteurs de ces controverses. Dès lors, les divergences d'opinions théologiques et les solidarités entre les ordres compromettaient la réalisation de censures impartiales dans la mesure où les qualificateurs étaient parfois amenés à expertiser des textes de polémistes qui appartenaient soit à leur propre communauté soit à un ordre adverse. De plus, les examens doctrinaux n'étaient pas réalisés à l'aveugle, par conséquent, les censeurs connaissaient parfaitement l'identité des auteurs dont ils jugeaient les livres. Une telle situation fut inévitablement source d'irrégularités et de conflits d'intérêt.[10] Le troisième obstacle auquel firent face les inquisiteurs était la forte politisation de ces confrontations religieuses. Celles-ci se doublaient parfois de tensions diplomatiques entre la papauté et la monarchie espagnole, ce qui embarrassait considérablement leur résolution.

Les polémiques entre ordres religieux dans lesquelles intervint l'Inquisition peuvent être divisées en deux groupes : les contro-

---

[10] Dans une consultation adressée en 1646 au roi Philippe IV, l'inquisiteur général de l'époque, Diego de Arce y Reinoso, fit part au monarque des difficultés du tribunal à trouver des censeurs impartiaux, car ils étaient si attachés à leur communauté qu'ils tenaient systématiquement pour vraies les thèses défendues par leur ordre et pour téméraires ou erronées les opinions contraires (López Vela 2006, p. 53).

verses théologiques et les controverses ecclésiastiques. Les premières avaient pour objet un désaccord à propos d'une question d'ordre doctrinal. Dans ces querelles, les ordres religieux revendiquaient l'inscription de leurs thèses dans la tradition de l'Église et accusaient l'opinion adverse d'"innover', c'est-à-dire, d'élaborer des doctrines contraires à ce qui faisait autorité et était communément admis. La nouveauté constituait, par définition, une réalité suspecte, car non approuvée par les Docteurs et Pères de l'Église. Les disputes ecclésiastiques, quant à elles, opposaient les religieux autour de questions relatives à leur communauté (récit de leur fondation, miracles associés à leurs membres, prérogatives particulières, etc.).

Dans ce chapitre, nous nous proposons d'examiner deux des grandes polémiques dans lesquelles interféra l'Inquisition espagnole, notamment, au moyen de son dispositif censorial : la controverse d'ordre théologique portant sur les aides de la grâce, qui opposa les Jésuites aux Dominicains, et la querelle ecclésiastique relative à l'origine prophétique de l'ordre du Carmel, dans laquelle s'affrontèrent les Carmes et le reste du clergé régulier, et plus particulièrement la Compagnie de Jésus. La finalité de ces pages n'est pas de reconstruire l'intégralité du déroulement de ces deux polémiques ni d'analyser dans le détail les questionnements doctrinaux et ecclésiastiques en jeu.[11] Notre objectif consiste à analyser le rôle de la censure inquisitoriale dans ces disputes ainsi que les raisons et les modalités de son intervention dans un champ intellectuel qui était jusqu'alors réservé aux milieux académiques.

La controverse sur les aides de la grâce

1. Origines et enjeux de la polémique

La controverse sur les aides de la grâce, dite controverse *de auxiliis*, qui éclate en Espagne dans les années 1580, est un débat extrême-

---

[11] Sur les aspects théologiques de la controverse sur les aides de la grâce, qui a pour objet la doctrine de la justification, voir, entre autres travaux, McGrath 2005 ; Broggio 2006, p. 53–86 ; Quilliet 2007 ; Matava 2016, p. 417–446 ; Matava 2020 ; François & Gerace 2019, p. 15–44 ; Rai 2020, p. 111–150. Pour un récit du déroulé de la polémique sur l'origine prophétique de l'ordre du Carmel, voir Santa María 1940.

ment complexe, tant sur le plan doctrinal que dans son déroulé. L'objet de cette polémique sont les secours accordés par la grâce divine (*auxilia*) à l'homme (autrement dit, les secours divins) pour qu'il puisse parvenir au salut éternel. La problématique sur laquelle repose ce débat peut être formulée de la manière suivante : Comment concilier la prescience (ou l'omniscience) et l'initiative salvatrice de Dieu avec la liberté humaine ? Comment rendre compatible la prédestination (le fait que Dieu ait déterminé le destin de l'humanité et de l'univers) avec le libre arbitre (le pouvoir de décider de réaliser ou non tel ou tel acte, en l'occurrence, la possibilité de choisir entre le bien et le mal) ? Quelle est la part assignée à la grâce et celle attribuée à l'homme dans le chemin vers son salut ? L'enjeu de ce débat était loin d'être négligeable pour l'époque dès lors qu'il concernait des thèmes clefs de la religiosité moderne, à savoir, la prédestination, la grâce et le libre arbitre. Il touchait aussi l'un des principaux fondements de la chrétienté : le salut de l'âme après la mort.[12]

Le débat post-tridentin sur les aides de la grâce n'était pas inédit. La querelle remonte au Ve siècle, avec la condamnation par l'Église des thèses du moine Pélage, qui considérait que l'homme assurait son salut au moyen de ses seules bonnes actions, sans les secours de la grâce.[13] Entre le XVe et le XVIe siècle, les discussions autour de la grâce divine et de la liberté revinrent sur le devant de la scène théologique. La controverse qui émerge alors est fondée sur des interprétations divergentes de la doctrine de la grâce, formulée par des Pères de l'Église et notamment saint Augustin.[14] Cette divergence d'interprétation fut l'un des points de désaccord entre réformés et catholiques : face aux doctrines fatalistes de Luther et Calvin, qui radicalisèrent la conception augustinienne en conférant à la grâce un rôle exclusif dans la salvation,[15] les Pères du concile de Trente réaffirmèrent, à l'inverse, l'existence de la liberté humaine tout en maintenant la priorité des secours divins pour réaliser une œuvre méritoire.[16] Cependant, ils ne se pronon-

---

[12] Sur ces enjeux, voir Caro Baroja 1978, p. 223–245 ; Broggio 2009, p. 50–51. Pour une approche anthropologique de ce débat, voir Delemestre 2018, p. 67–105.

[13] Lecuit 2014, p. 108–109.

[14] Rai 2020, p. 115.

[15] Chantraine 1981, p. 187–190.

[16] Cf. Décret *De iustificatione*, session VI, 13 janvier 1547.

cèrent pas sur la manière dont la grâce pouvait agir sur la volonté de l'homme tout en respectant sa liberté. L'indéfinition dogmatique de cette articulation entre grâce et libre arbitre donna lieu, à l'issue du concile, à la polémique *de auxiliis*, qui éclata au sein du monde catholique à l'université de Louvain, avec Michel De Bay et le jésuite Léonard Lessius,[17] et s'approfondit ensuite avec l'antagonisme des Dominicains et des Jésuites, plus particulièrement dans la péninsule ibérique. Tandis que les premiers soutenaient que la grâce disposait d'une antériorité causale sur les actions humaines ('prémotion physique') ; les seconds défendaient une conception qui laissait une place bien plus importante à la liberté. Les Jésuites considéraient que réaliser ou non un acte dépendait de l'existence de 'possibilités alternatives', dont Dieu avait la connaissance. En clair, ce dernier savait ce que chacun pouvait faire dans telle ou telle situation, si telle ou telle condition était réalisée.[18]

2. Affrontements entre Dominicains et Jésuites

Le point de départ du conflit postconciliaire dans la péninsule ibérique fut le débat théologique célébré en 1582 à l'université de Salamanque sous la direction du mercédaire Francisco Zumel. Au cours de cette discussion publique, le jésuite Prudencio de Montemayor argumenta en faveur de la thèse suivante : si Dieu avait donné au Christ l'obligation de mourir, ce dernier ne se serait pas sacrifié librement et cet acte n'aurait, par conséquent, aucun mérite.[19] Le dominicain Domingo Báñez dénonça cette proposition au Conseil de l'Inquisition, au motif qu'elle constituait une doctrine 'téméraire' (c'est-à-dire, nouvelle, inusitée, non défendue par les Pères et Docteurs de l'Église), au relent de pélagianisme. À la suite de cette accusation, Montemayor fut suspendu de sa charge d'enseignement de la théologie. Quelques années plus tard, le jésuite Luis de Molina publia à Lisbonne une œuvre intitulée *Concordia liberi arbitrii cum gratiae donis* (1588), dans laquelle il exposait les idées principales de la thèse qui serait

---

[17] Van Eijl 1994, p. 207–282 ; Broggio 2009, p. 50–61 ; Matava 2020, p. 421–422 ; Rai 2020, p. 115–118.
[18] Grossi & Sesboüé 1995, p. 360.
[19] Sales Souza 2010, p. 496.

dorénavant défendue par la Compagnie de Jésus sur l'articulation entre la providence divine et la liberté humaine. La théorie de Molina constituait une proposition intermédiaire entre les positions les plus radicales concernant le libre arbitre et la providence divine. La thèse du jésuite reposait sur le concept de 'science moyenne' (*scientia media*), selon laquelle Dieu sait ce que chaque personne, pourvue de la grâce divine, ferait ou ne ferait pas dans telle ou telle circonstance hypothétique mais possible (*i. e.* les futurs contingents). Dans le monde que Dieu a décidé de créer, ce dernier donne à tous la 'grâce suffisante' pour être sauvé mais celle-ci s'avère 'efficace' si et seulement si la volonté humaine donne son libre consentement au bien. Cette théorie laissait ainsi à l'homme sa part de liberté et de responsabilité dans l'accès au salut, sans porter atteinte à la souveraineté de Dieu de créer un certain ordre ni à la forme de prédestination que cela implique pour les hommes.[20]

La publication de l'œuvre de Molina suscita la réaction immédiate des Dominicains. En 1590, Domingo Báñez publia à Salamanque un ouvrage intitulé *Relectio de merito et augmento charitatis*, dans lequel il décriait la doctrine moliniste. Quant à Francisco de Zumel, fervent opposant aux thèses de la Compagnie sur les secours de la grâce, il dénonça le livre de Molina à l'Inquisition.[21] Entre 1590 et 1594, des théologiens des universités de Salamanque et d'Alcalá se réunirent dans le but de déterminer quels livres dérogeaient au décret du concile de Trente sur le libre arbitre et devraient, par conséquent, être prohibés ou expurgés.[22] De fait, malgré l'interdiction de critiquer l'opinion adverse sur les *auxilia*, l'œuvre de Molina continuait d'être la cible de critiques de la part des Frères Prêcheurs.

3. Intervention de la papauté et médiation inquisitoriale

Face à l'hostilité dominicaine, la Compagnie de Jésus, très liée à la papauté, chercha à obtenir l'appui du souverain pontife et

---

[20] Sur la thèse de Molina, voir, entre autres travaux, Dekker 2000, Quilliet 2007, p. 335–352 et Gerace 2016, p. 105–122.

[21] Archivo Histórico National (désormais, AHN), Inquisition, liasse 4437, dossier 6 : lettre de Francisco de Zumel, 20 juin 1592.

[22] Broggio 2009, p. 80.

demanda à ce que le sort de la *Concordia* soit décidé directement par le Saint-Siège et non par l'Inquisition,[23] afin que l'opinion soutenue par les Jésuites puisse être reconnue comme orthodoxe et cesse d'être attaquée par les Frères Prêcheurs. En 1597, le pape Clément VIII réunit à cet effet une commission de dix théologiens, la *Congregatio de auxiliis divinae gratiae*, chargée d'examiner le livre de Molina. Le nonce en Espagne, Camillo Caetani, communiqua aux supérieurs dominicains et jésuites que l'examen de la *Concordia* était désormais entre les mains de la papauté (et non plus de l'Inquisition) ; les membres des deux communautés furent invités à faire parvenir à Rome les informations qu'ils jugeaient nécessaires pour aider à la résolution du débat.[24] Pendant ce temps, les religieux avaient l'obligation de s'abstenir d'alimenter la controverse : en clair, ils ne pouvaient ni publier ni exposer publiquement leur opinion sur la question des aides de la grâce.[25]

L'intromission de la papauté dans ce conflit espagnol suscita le mécontentement de la royauté. En 1594, Philippe III adressa une lettre sentie à son ambassadeur, le duc de Sessa, dans laquelle il insistait sur le préjudice intellectuel que représentait l'interdiction radicale, dictée par la papauté, de publier sur un sujet aussi important pour la théologie.[26] Par ailleurs, le monarque désapprouvait que le nonce en Espagne ait pris la liberté d'intervenir dans une affaire qui était déjà traitée par le tribunal de l'Inquisition. Il souhaitait que les décisions du Saint-Siège relatives à cette dispute soient dorénavant prises par les inquisiteurs et non plus par le nonce. Le roi faisait savoir à la papauté que les universités et théologiens espagnols continueraient les travaux amorcés sur les *auxilia*, malgré que la Curie ait décidé de prendre en main cette affaire. Toutefois, peu de temps après, le Conseil de l'Inquisition informa le monarque qu'il avait résolu de se ranger sur la décision papale et d'interdire aux ordres religieux de traiter des aides de la grâce, quand bien même ils ne brocarderaient pas l'opinion

---

[23] Broggio 2009, p. 83.
[24] Vázquez 1979, p. 439.
[25] AHN, Inquisition, livre 1232 : circulaire datée de 1594.
[26] AHN, Inquisition, livre 251, f. 135r–137v : lettre datée du 26 septembre 1594.

adverse.[27] Les inquisiteurs avaient aussi convenu d'envoyer à Rome les résultats des rapports des théologiens, prélats et universités concernant cette question. Ainsi, tandis que le roi semblait vouloir préserver les prérogatives censoriales du tribunal inquisitorial face à la Curie, ledit tribunal, quant à lui, paraissait désirer se débarrasser de la résolution délicate de cette mésentente doctrinale.

En 1597, à l'issue de onze réunions, la commission romaine finit par émettre un vote négatif sur l'œuvre de Molina, cependant celui-ci fut par la suite révisé et remis en question à l'aune des rapports adressés par l'Espagne. Au vu de cette impasse, le pape Clément VIII décida de réunir un deuxième comité afin de soumettre la *Concordia* à un nouvel examen.[28] L'objectif du souverain pontife était d'arriver à un compromis entre les deux doctrines mais cette tentative de conciliation se solda par un échec. Le pape décida alors de prendre les choses en main et réunit des congrégations papales, qui furent présidées d'abord par lui-même puis par Paul V.

Dans l'attente de la résolution du conflit par Rome, l'Inquisition espagnole s'efforça, tant bien que mal, d'apaiser les esprits échauffés des Jésuites et des Dominicains, qui défiaient les directives du Saint-Siège, en défendant leurs thèses publiquement, dans les chaires et dans les presses. Le 22 février 1602, le tribunal rappela aux religieux qu'il leur était défendu de donner leur avis sur la question des *auxilia* sans autorisation préalable de la papauté et du Conseil inquisitorial.[29] Le 17 mai, l'Inquisition ajouta que les réguliers n'étaient pas autorisés à exposer leur opinion lors de la défense de conclusions théologiques publiques.[30] Malgré ces différentes interdictions, les inquisiteurs continuaient de recevoir des dénonciations de la part de religieux, qui signalaient la parution de livres de l'ordre adverse qui désobéissaient à l'interdiction papale.

---

[27] AHN, Inquisition, liasse 4437, dossier 1 : lettre du Conseil de l'Inquisition à Philippe II, 22 septembre 1594.
[28] Vázquez 1979, p. 440.
[29] AHN, Inquisition, liasse 4426, dossier 31 : circulaire du 22 février 1602.
[30] *Ibid.*

4. Insolubilité du débat et perpétuation des oppositions

Le 28 août 1607, soit vingt ans après l'émergence de la controverse et treize ans après le début des discussions au sein de la Curie, Paul V mit fin aux travaux des congrégations sans pour autant se prononcer en faveur de l'une ou l'autre des thèses (jésuite ou dominicaine), ni formuler une doctrine intermédiaire. Pas plus que son prédécesseur, le souverain pontife n'avait voulu trouver une issue au désaccord en se positionnant pour l'une des deux doctrines, probablement par crainte de la réaction de l'ordre lésé. Paul V se limita en effet à affirmer l'orthodoxie des deux opinions : il déclara que la prémotion physique, défendue par les Dominicains, n'avait pas de lien avec le calvinisme et que la doctrine jésuite ne pouvait être qualifiée de pélagianiste.[31] Dès lors, il autorisait les communautés religieuses à défendre leurs idées, à la condition qu'elles ne discréditent pas la thèse contraire. Pour éviter que la controverse ne gagne le grand public, le pape interdit de traiter des *auxilia* dans des sermons ; seul le cadre de l'enseignement et des écrits théologiques était autorisé.[32] Quant à la résolution doctrinale définitive, elle fut repoussée *sine die* par la papauté. En 1608, le secrétariat d'État du Saint-Siège écrivit à Decio Carafa, nonce apostolique en Espagne, pour l'informer que le différend entre les Dominicains et les Jésuites devrait désormais être réglé par l'Inquisition.[33] En d'autres termes, Rome se déchargeait de la responsabilité d'une affaire qu'elle ne voulait vraisemblablement pas trancher, pour laisser à l'Inquisition le soin d'assumer la médiation entre les deux partis. De fait, la décision de Paul V — ou mieux dit, son indécision — ne parvint pas à étouffer la polémique, qui fut sans cesse réactivée au cours du XVIIe siècle, notamment avec l'apparition du jansénisme, qui minimisait le rôle de la liberté humaine dans l'obtention du salut.

La papauté et l'Inquisition se virent donc contraintes de réitérer plusieurs fois les différentes interdictions. Les inquisiteurs espagnols continuèrent en outre de recevoir fréquemment des délations de la part de religieux, qui demandaient au tribunal d'in-

---

[31] Renault 1998, p. 135.
[32] AHN, Inquisition, liasse 4438, dossier 2.
[33] Archivum Apostolicum Vaticanum, Secrétariat d'État – Espagne (désormais, AAV, SS), livre 35, 140/141 : lettre du 22 avril 1608.

terdire des publications de l'ordre adverse. En 1611, par exemple, des jésuites dénoncèrent *In tertiam partem Sancti Thomae commentariorum et disputationum* (1602), du hiéronymite Pedro de Cabrera, au motif que ce dernier réprouvait l'opinion de la Compagnie sur les aides de la grâce et faisait allusion aux auteurs de l'ordre de saint Ignace en des termes injurieux et offensants.[34] En 1624, l'Inquisition procéda à l'examen des *Responsionum ad obiectationes adversus Concordiam liberi arbitrii* (1622), du dominicain Diego Álvarez, l'un des principaux défenseurs de la position thomiste, qui prit part aux Congrégations romaines sur les *auxilia*.[35] Les censeurs se penchèrent aussi sur *Operis conciliatorii gratia et liberi arbitrii* (1622), du franciscain Francisco Arriba, qui y exposait le point de vue de son ordre. Les qualificateurs Antonio Pérez, Jerónimo Salcedo et Juan de San Agustín, qui n'appartenaient à aucun des ordres en conflit, jugèrent que les deux livres ne comportaient rien qui mérite véritablement d'être censuré. Cependant, ces derniers n'arboraient pas la licence inquisitoriale requise pour pouvoir publier sur les *auxilia*. Juan de San Agustín faisait remarquer que ne pas sanctionner ces écrits donnerait le mauvais exemple et ouvrirait la porte à des publications semblables, ce qui ne ferait que réaviver la querelle. L'interdiction de ces ouvrages ne fut donc pas motivée par une question doctrinale mais par le fait qu'ils s'opposaient aux décrets régulant l'impression de textes relatifs à la controverse. C'est en effet au nom de ce manquement formel et non de leur contenu que le tribunal se résolut à les confisquer.

La plupart des publications sur la grâce interdites par l'Inquisition au cours du XVIIe siècle ne furent pas inscrites à l'Index,[36] sort qui attendait en principe tout livre interdit en Espagne. Le tribunal craignait probablement d'attiser la polémique en inscrivant ces œuvres dans le catalogue des livres proscrits, car la mise à

---

[34] Real Academia de la Historia, Jésuites, 9/3742 (5).
[35] AHN, Inquisition, liasse 4521, dossier 21.
[36] Par exemple : Paolo Beni, *Qua tandem ratione dirimi possit controversia quae in praesens de efficaci Dei auxilio et libero arbitrio inter nonnullos Catholicos agitatur* ... (1603), saisi le 7 août 1604 (AHN, Inquisition, liasse 4426, dossier 31) ; Francisco Dávila, *De auxiliis divinae gratiae ac eorum efficacia* (1599), saisi le 7 août 1604 (*ibid.*) ; Vicente Ferrer, *Sacrae Theologiae placita in solenni S. Catharinae Virginis et martyris festo publice disputanda* (1609), AHN, Inquisition, liasse 4438, dossier 4.

l'Index d'un écrit était vécue comme un affront pour un auteur et, le cas échéant, pour l'ensemble de sa communauté, sur laquelle rejaillissait le discrédit de l'interdiction.

En résumé, le rôle joué par l'Inquisition espagnole dans la controverse *de auxiliis* fut moins un rôle doctrinal qu'un rôle d'arbitre. L'institution inquisitoriale s'efforça à grand-peine d'empêcher les débordements d'une violente querelle qui opposait deux ordres religieux influents, en interdisant les publications qui ne respectaient pas les régulations imposées. Les inquisiteurs durent aussi composer avec la papauté, dont les décisions n'allaient pas toujours dans le sens de la pacification. L'indécision du Saint-Siège fut probablement l'une des causes de la perpétuation du litige. Au début du XVIIe siècle, sous le règne de Philippe III, la diplomatie espagnole se saisit de l'affaire et tâcha de faire pression sur la papauté afin qu'elle s'empresse de se positionner sur la question. Pour le monarque, l'enjeu de la résolution de cette dispute était moins une question doctrinale qu'un moyen de maintenir la réputation des ordres religieux et de garantir la tranquillité de ses territoires.[37] De son côté, l'Inquisition employa elle aussi, sans plus de succès, les armes de la diplomatie, en faisant intervenir son agent à Rome, afin qu'il lui fasse part des discussions officieuses du Saint-Siège. Le tribunal essaya par tous les moyens d'obtenir la prise de position de la papauté sur le sujet, mais en vain.

La querelle autour de l'origine prophétique de l'ordre du Carmel

Un autre des motifs de frictions entre les ordres dans l'Espagne moderne fut lié aux débats autour de la fondation et l'ancienneté des communautés de religieux réguliers. La société de l'Espagne moderne accordait une grande importance à cette ancienneté car tout ce qui relevait de la tradition était perçu de manière positive, à l'inverse de la nouveauté.[38] De ce point de vue, la controverse sur

---

[37] Dès la fin du XVIe siècle, le nonce d'Espagne Camillo Caetani communiqua au Saint-Siège le souhait du nouveau monarque d'en finir avec cette dispute (AAV, SS, livre 49, 388/389 : lettre du 14 novembre 1598).

[38] Egido 2015, p. 50.

les origines prophétiques de l'ordre du Carmel fut sans doute l'un des débats les plus passionnés. La polémique, qui s'étendit sur plusieurs dizaines d'années, connut de multiples rebondissements. Elle prit forme aussi bien dans les chaires d'églises et d'universités que dans les presses.

Le Carmel, ordre mendiant contemplatif, fut fondé au XIIe siècle, mais ses membres faisaient remonter sa création à l'époque de l'Ancien Testament et soutenaient que leur communauté avait été instituée sur le mont Carmel, situé sur la baie de Haïfa, par le prophète Élie et des ermites. Les Carmes considéraient ce dernier, qui se serait auto-déclaré moine, comme le fondateur du monachisme. Il s'agissait là d'une thèse paradoxale d'un point de vue ecclésiastique, car, par définition, le monachisme désigne un mode de vie et de spiritualité créé après la venue du Christ, dont il est le modèle. Les Carmes soutenaient par ailleurs que le prophète Élie aurait précédé la Vierge dans son vœu de virginité, une affirmation qui allait, encore une fois, au rebours de la tradition ecclésiastique, qui attribue généralement l'initiative de ce chaste engagement à Marie. En donnant la préséance à l'ordre du Carmel sur tous les autres, du fait de son ancienneté et de sa dimension prophétique et miraculeuse, ces thèses suscitaient la jalousie et la réprobation des autres ordres, et notamment de la jeune Compagnie de Jésus, qui décriait de telles origines légendaires, qu'elle qualifiait de fantaisistes.[39]

1. La censure de l'*Histoire prophétique* de Francisco de Santa María (1630)

L'œuvre du chroniqueur carmélite Francisco de Santa María intitulée *Historia general profética de la Orden de Nuestra Señora del Carmen* (en français, *Histoire générale prophétique de l'ordre de Notre-Dame-du-Carmel*), publiée à Madrid en 1630, vint cristalliser la polémique. L'auteur y défendait avec verve les origines vétéro-testamentaires de son ordre. Il proclamait qu'un véritable monachisme avait existé dans la Loi ancienne, c'est-à-dire, un mode de vie et de spiritualité fondé sur le respect des trois vœux

---

[39] Egido 2015, p. 52.

religieux établis à partir des principes évangéliques : obéissance, chasteté et pauvreté.[40] Le caractère audacieux des thèses défendues par ce livre suscita l'indignation de religieux, et en particulier des Jésuites, qui le dénoncèrent à l'Inquisition.

Le Saint-Office espagnol était conscient qu'il se trouvait face à un sujet épineux, dès lors que ce dernier opposait deux ordres religieux influents. C'est pourquoi il fit appel à de nombreux qualificateurs, afin d'éviter tout jugement partial, et prit également soin qu'aucun d'eux n'appartienne à l'ordre du Carmel, car un censeur carmélite aurait inévitablement pris la défense du chroniqueur. Suite à ce premier examen et en dépit des protestations de l'auteur, l'*Histoire prophétique* fut condamnée à être expurgée de plusieurs passages.[41] L'œuvre fut inscrite par la suite dans le nouvel Index de livres interdits et expurgés publié par l'Inquisition en 1632. Au lieu de marquer un terme à la dispute, cette censure déclencha une véritable guerre de papier entre, d'une part, les Carmes, qui défendaient le caractère prophético-miraculeux de leur ordre, promu par Francisco de Santa María, et de l'autre, les Jésuites, qui considéraient ces épisodes prétendument historiques comme de pures inventions.

2. Généralisation de la controverse : affrontements entre Carmes et Jésuites

Suite à l'expurgation de son livre, Santa María chercha à rassembler des soutiens auprès des milieux académiques, en vue de la publication d'un plaidoyer dans lequel il défendrait les propositions expurgées par l'Index. Les Carmes espagnols ne demeurèrent pas en reste et s'associèrent par la plume au combat mené par le chroniqueur. Plusieurs religieux présentèrent ainsi à l'Inquisition, au nom du procureur général de leur ordre, différents plaidoyers en faveur de l'*Histoire prophétique*, comme celui que, le 9 octobre 1632, Tomás de San Vicente remit au Conseil de l'Inquisition, dans lequel il répondait aux objections des Jésuites à l'encontre de l'*Histoire prophétique* : *Respuesta a las objeciones contra la defensa de las proposiciones, que mandó borrar el nuevo Expurgatorio, en la*

---

[40] Santa María 1940, p. 99.
[41] AHN, Inquisition, liasse 4444, dossier 19.

Historia profética de la Orden de Nuestra Señora del Carmen.[42] La même année parut à Madrid la *Defensa de las proposiciones quitadas por el nuevo Expurgatorio en el tomo primero de la Historia profética de la Orden de Nuestra Señora del Carmen*, de Martín de Jesús María, lecteur de théologie au collège des carmes déchaussés de Salamanque, qui contestait les censures infligées à l'œuvre de Santa María.

Tandis que l'ordre du Carmel défendait vigoureusement les thèses de ce dernier, les Jésuites s'offusquèrent de l''indulgence' de l'Index, qui, selon eux, n'avait pas censuré assez de passages. Ce positionnement ne manqua pas de faire réagir les religieux de l'ordre adverse, comme Pedro de la Concepción, carme déchaussé, qui publia en 1634 un mémorial dans lequel il répondait aux critiques formulées par le qualificateur jésuite Luis Torres dans ses *Selectarum disputationum in Theologiam Scholasticam* (1634) à propos de l'*Histoire prophétique* et des écrits rédigés en sa faveur.[43] Face à cette levée de boucliers, l'Inquisition se résolut à faire réexaminer l'œuvre du carme, dans le but d'apaiser le mécontentement général.

3. Nouvelle censure de l'*Histoire prophétique* et poursuite du conflit

Encore une fois, le grand nombre de censeurs mobilisés pour réexaminer l'*Histoire prophétique* (une vingtaine) montre le caractère hautement polémique de la controverse. La commission d'experts qui élaborait alors le nouvel Index inquisitorial fut elle aussi chargée d'examiner le livre de Santa María. Le jugement qu'elle formula à propos de ce dernier ne fut guère élogieux.[44] La commission estimait que cet écrit non seulement ne présentait aucune utilité mais introduisait des doctrines nouvelles, contraires à celles défendues jusqu'alors par l'Église. Il constituait, de surcroît, un motif de sédition entre les ordres religieux, puisqu'il conférait une

---

[42] AHN, Inquisition, liasse 4515, dossier 3.

[43] Pedro de la Concepción, *Respuesta a los lugares del padre Luis de Torres de la Compañía de Jesús, en que se censura las opiniones de la Historia Profética y de los Defensorios hechos acerca de ella en el libro … Disputaciones selectas … impreso en León año 1634 … y especialmente se trata del insigne … Santo Profeta Elías*, s. a. [1634 ?].

[44] AHN, Inquisition, liasse 4515, dossier 1.

supériorité au Carmel sur tous les autres ordres, dans la mesure où il faisait remonter sa création à l'Ancien Testament. Le président de la commission, Juan Dionisio Portocarrero, rappelait que l'institution des communautés religieuses était un sujet qui devait être traité avec rigueur, afin d'éviter que les hérétiques ne se servent des négligences des catholiques pour discréditer l'Église. Il estimait qu'on ne pouvait introduire dans l'histoire ecclésiastique des variantes remettant en question ce qui avait toujours été soutenu, et, qui plus est, si ces thèses alternatives n'étaient pas fondées sur des arguments solides. En l'occurrence, il jugeait que ceux avancés par les Carmes ne l'étaient pas assez. Il soulignait, par ailleurs, que s'il avait existé un ordre religieux pré-christique fondé sur les trois vœux monastiques — chasteté, pauvreté et obéissance — il ne serait pas passé inaperçu aux Pères et Docteurs de l'Église, qui auraient, tout au moins, relevé l'existence du vœu de chasteté, 'le plus difficile à respecter', selon l'inquisiteur, en raison de la 'résistance naturelle' de l'homme à cette condition. Il signalait en outre que, dans l'Ancien Testament, la chasteté ne constituait pas autre chose qu'une vertu ou qu'une 'mortification volontaire' mais non un vœu monastique, car c'est Jésus-Christ qui avait été l'inspirateur de ces vœux. Portocarrero rappelait à ce propos que l'ordre du Carmel avait été fondé au XIIe siècle par la bulle d'Alexandre III et la règle de l'ordre, donnée en 1171 par Albert de Jérusalem ; or, ni la bulle ni la règle ne faisaient mention d'Élie ni d'une quelconque fondation monastique dans la Loi ancienne.

En 1635, soit deux ans après avoir pris la décision de faire réexaminer l'*Histoire prophétique*, le tribunal inquisitorial ne s'était toujours pas prononcé, probablement en raison de nombreux désaccords en son sein. L'ordre du Carmel commençait à s'impatienter car l'enjeu était de taille ; il en allait de son crédit et de son prestige aux yeux de l'Église. Le Conseil de la Suprême Inquisition, qui renonça vraisemblablement à se fier à ses qualificateurs, trop impliqués dans cette querelle, décida de confier le soin de résoudre cette affaire à l'inquisiteur général, Antonio de Sotomayor. Ce dernier nomma plusieurs conseillers afin qu'ils expertisent l'ouvrage et les différents plaidoyers en sa faveur. Assez maladroitement, il fit appel à un jésuite, Hernando Chirino de Salazar, ce qui suscita une vive réaction de l'ordre du Carmel. En dépit des protestations, les conseillers du tribunal remirent leur rapport en 1636. Les héritiers d'Élie espéraient que celui-ci serait plus favorable que le jugement rendu quatre ans plus tôt mais ils déchantèrent rapidement et pour cause, l'Inquisition les autorisait à publier une nouvelle édition de l'*Histoire prophétique*, qui devrait être expurgée de plusieurs passages, encore plus nombreux que ceux mentionnés dans l'Index de 1632. Quant à l'édition de 1630, elle demeurait intégralement interdite. Révoltés, les Carmes accusèrent immédiatement le conseiller jésuite de parti pris[45] et s'organisèrent pour préparer une nouvelle défense. Ils s'adressèrent cette fois-ci directement au monarque pour solliciter la réunion d'une commission composée de qualificateurs reconnus pour leur qualité et leur impartialité. Le roi prit au sérieux leur requête et convoqua en plus de trois archevêques pas moins de douze censeurs, dont aucun n'appartenait à la Compagnie ni à l'ordre du Carmel. En 1639, suite aux travaux réalisés par cette commission, les inquisiteurs décrétèrent de nouvelles expurgations, dont tint compte Santa María dans la nouvelle version de son œuvre, qu'il publia en 1641, après avoir obtenu l'approbation de l'Inquisition.[46] Si l'*Histoire prophétique* pouvait désormais circuler, les plaidoyers demeuraient quant à eux interdits, vraisemblablement parce qu'ils défendaient des propositions censurées dans l'œuvre de Santa María et qu'ils risquaient d'attiser la polémique. Avec la parution de cette édition amendée, la controverse semblait résolue, mais les Jésuites n'avaient pas dit leur dernier mot et la controverse reprit de plus belle.

4. Les émules de Francisco de Santa María et les détracteurs jésuites

Bien que l'œuvre du chroniqueur carmélite constitue le pivot autour duquel tournait la controverse entre le Carmel et la Compagnie, d'autres textes vinrent alimenter la querelle, et ce, même après la parution de la seconde édition de l'*Histoire prophétique*. Outre les apologies déjà mentionnées et d'autres parues

---

[45] Santa María 1940, p. 111–112.
[46] Francisco de Santa María, *Historia profética de la Orden de Nuestra Señora del Carmen … corregido de nuevo y enmendado por su autor en esta segunda impresión*, Madrid : Diego Díaz de la Carrera, 1641.

postérieurement, plusieurs écrits relatifs aux origines du Carmel passèrent entre les mains des censeurs du tribunal inquisitorial. Parmi les livres examinés, on compte *Paradisus carmelitici decoris* (1639), de Marco Alegre de Casanate, qui fut expurgé des passages allant à l'encontre des décrets inquisitoriaux de 1636 et 1639,[47] de même que *Vinae Carmeli seu Historia Eliani* (1662) et *Magni Prophetae Eliae sacri ordinis Carmelitarum fundatoris*, de François Crespin (1665),[48] qui furent dénoncés par le qualificateur Antonio Dávila en 1666[49] avant d'être expurgés. Certains écrits antérieurs à l'*Histoire prophétique*, qui avaient circulé jusqu'alors sans difficulté, furent soumis à une relecture sévère. Par exemple, en 1633, Alonso de la Mota y Aranda dénonça le *Libro de la antigüedad y santos de la Orden de Nuestra Señora del Carmen y de los especiales privilegios de su cofradía* (1599), du carme Tomás de Jesús,[50] alléguant qu'il contenait des propositions peu fiables d'un point de vue historique. Quand bien même certaines thèses n'étaient pas censurables en soi, il estimait que l'accumulation de tant de 'fabulations' au sujet de l'histoire ecclésiastique méritait une sanction.

L'Inquisition ne se préoccupa pas uniquement des publications carmélites, elle se montra aussi attentive aux écrits jésuites qui contredisaient les propositions considérées comme licites par les décrets de 1636 et 1639 ou qui s'avéraient offensants envers les héritiers d'Élie. En 1652, par exemple, Silvestre de la Asumpción, procureur général de l'ordre du Carmel, dénonça les *Commentaria in libros Machabaeorum canonicos* du jésuite Petrus Redanus.[51] Le délateur accusait l'auteur de ne pas respecter les décrets inquisitoriaux et d'outrager l'Inquisition, le Carmel, ses traditions et les doctrines approuvées par les inquisiteurs. Les qualificateurs du tribunal estimèrent que l'œuvre en question devait être expurgée mais la décision des inquisiteurs fut vraisemblablement plus sévère car les *Commentaria* apparaissent intégralement interdits dans l'Index.

---

[47] AHN, Inquisition, liasse 4444, dossier 37.
[48] AHN, Inquisition, liasse 4442, dossier 58.
[49] AHN, Inquisition, liasse 4442, dossier 57.
[50] AHN, Inquisition, liasse 4450, dossier 6.
[51] AHN, Inquisition, liasse 4442, dossier 60.

5. Les objections des Bollandistes : la critique historique face aux légendes

La discorde entre les deux ordres se perpétua jusqu'à la fin du XVIIe siècle. Dans les années 1690, le débat fut réavivé à la suite des critiques formulées par une société savante intégrée par des jésuites érudits qui, dans la lignée des hagiographes néerlandais de la Compagnie de Jésus Héribert Rosweyde (1569–1629) et Jean Bolland (1596–1665), se consacraient à la publication et à la critique de la vie des saints, dans le but d'offrir des versions les plus fiables possible. À partir de 1643, ces jésuites, à commencer par Bolland, qui donna son nom à la société, entreprirent la publication d'une collection hagiographique monumentale, les *Acta sanctorum*, dans laquelle, l'un des auteurs, Daniel van Papenbroeck (1628–1714), s'attaquait aux origines vétéro-testamentaires de l'ordre du Carmel. La critique du jésuite anversois suscita une vive réaction du côté carmélite. En 1691, Juan Gómez Barrientos et José de Jesús María dénoncèrent à l'Inquisition quatorze tomes des *Acta sanctorum*,[52] dans lesquels l'origine prophétique et miraculeuse de leur ordre était mise à mal. En raison de la prolixité de la délation, les qualificateurs du tribunal de la Suprême Inquisition n'eurent pas la possibilité de l'examiner dans le cadre de leurs réunions. Afin qu'ils aient le temps nécessaire pour l'étudier, ils se répartirent des copies de la dénonciation, qui avait été imprimée en plusieurs exemplaires au frais de l'ordre du Carmel, désireux que le tribunal se positionne au plus vite sur cette œuvre qui leur portait préjudice.[53] Cependant, l'Inquisition ne prit aucune décision avant 1694, date à laquelle les carmes Juan Gómez Barrientos, Pedro de la Concepción et Ángel de la Purificación publièrent un mémorial[54] dans lequel ils réclamaient que les *Acta sanctorum* soient promptement examinés par le tribunal.[55] Une commission inquisitoriale composée de six qualificateurs fut alors réunie dans

---

[52] Santiago Medina 2011, p. 79.

[53] Santiago Medina 2011, p. 79–80.

[54] *Expostulación que en nombre de su religión y de toda la Iglesia hacen al … Supremo Tribunal de la Fe contra el Padre Daniel Papebrochio de la… Compañía de Jesús y contra las doctrinas de sus libros intitulados Acta Sanctorum totius anni*, Madrid : s. n., 1694.

[55] Santiago Medina 2011, p. 81–82.

le but de statuer sur les deux délations présentées par l'ordre du Carmel contre l'œuvre des Bollandistes (celle de 1691 soumise par Juan Gómez Barrientos et celle que ce dernier ainsi que Pedro de la Concepción et Ángel de la Purificación firent imprimer en 1694).[56] L'examen de la première délation dura de longs mois. Lors de la dernière séance, qui se tint en 1695, la commission émit un jugement sévère. Elle déclara que l'auteur des *Acta sanctorum* alléguait de nombreuses propositions téméraires, c'est-à-dire, insuffisamment fondées, et d'autres injurieuses envers l'ordre du Carmel et la papauté, dès lors qu'elles mettaient en doute l'authenticité de certaines bulles. Papenbroeck fut lui-même considéré comme 'suspect' et 'ami des nouveautés'. En conséquence, le Conseil inquisitorial décida de prohiber les quatorze tomes des *Actes des saints*.[57]

Une fois encore, le Compagnie de Jésus ne tarda pas à riposter. Le différend se régla de nouveau dans les presses. Du côté carmélite, les principaux écrits contraires à Papenbroeck et à ses méthodes de travail furent *Exhibitio errorum* (1693) et *Motivum iuris* (1693), de Sebastián de San Pablo, professeur de théologie à l'université de Louvain et provincial des Flandres.[58] En 1696, Daniel de San Pedro fit imprimer à Séville une adaptation en castillan des œuvres de San Pablo, sous le titre *Memorial que en defensa de la verdad y en prueba de la inocencia se presenta al Tribunal de la Recta Razón*. Du côté jésuite, le bollandiste Conrad Janninck apporta son soutien à Papenbroeck dans *Epistola familiaris* (1693). Papenbroeck se défendit à son tour des accusations de San Pablo dans le *Responsio… ad Exhibitionem Errorum per ad N. R. P. Sebastianum a S. Paulo* (1696-1698). Ces joutes textuelles donnèrent lieu, en parallèle, à la parution de virulents libelles, souvent anonymes, qui cherchaient à discréditer l'ordre adverse.

L'intervention du pape Innocent XII en 1698, soit près de soixante-dix ans après le début des hostilités, contribua à calmer les opposants mais elle ne suffit pas à étouffer définitivement la querelle.[59] De fait, en 1706, l'historien jésuite José Casani solli-

---

[56] Santiago Medina 2011, p. 81–82.
[57] AHN, Inquisition, liasse 2334, dossier 7.
[58] Santiago Medina 2011, p. 85.
[59] Santa María 1940, p. 119.

cita la révision des censures des *Acta Sanctorum*.[60] L'inquisiteur général accéda à sa demande et réunit l'année suivante seize qualificateurs afin qu'ils soumettent à un nouvel examen l'œuvre de l'hagiographe néerlandais. Les Carmes manifestèrent alors leur mécontentement car ils jugeaient que la plupart des censeurs convoqués étaient favorables à la Compagnie. Une fois encore, la résolution de l'affaire s'éternisa et pendant plus de trois ans aucune décision ne fut prise. Mécontent, Casani finit par s'adresser directement au roi Philippe V pour lui demander d'intervenir. Le monarque, surpris par l'inertie du tribunal, demanda aux inquisiteurs de résoudre cette affaire promptement.[61] Mais il fallut encore attendre plusieurs années avant qu'ils ne se prononcent car ce n'est qu'en 1715 que l'Inquisition finit par lever l'interdiction générale des *Actes des Saints*, dans lesquels il ne fallait plus réaliser qu'une expurgation minime. Cette décision, qui supposait un renversement total de la position du Saint-Office au sujet de l'œuvre de Papenbroeck, s'explique probablement par l'influence croissante de la Compagnie de Jésus sur le tribunal inquisitorial et la censure de livres. La résolution papale, relativement pacificatrice, et la mort des principaux protagonistes de la querelle finirent par éteindre les braises d'une discorde ecclésiastique qui avait duré près d'un siècle.

Conclusions

Dans la controverse *de auxiliis* comme dans la querelle sur les origines prophétiques du Carmel, l'Inquisition se trouva dans une situation délicate, d'une part, en raison de l'implication de ses censeurs dans des polémiques dont ils étaient à la fois les acteurs et les juges et, d'autre part, à cause de la pression d'ordres religieux influents. La durée des procédures inquisitoriales menées contre les livres qui alimentaient ces débats et la multiplication des instances censoriales disent bien la difficulté de l'Inquisition à se prononcer sur des sujets aussi sensibles, qui mettaient en jeu non seulement le crédit d'un ordre religieux mais aussi la vérité dogmatique, dans le cas de la controverse sur les aides de la grâce,

---

[60] AHN, Inquisition, liasse 4457, dossier 1.
[61] AHN, Inquisition, liasse 4457, dossier 1.

et la véracité d'un épisode de l'histoire ecclésiastique, dans celui du débat autour de la fondation de l'ordre carmélite. De fait, dans ces deux polémiques, l'Inquisition s'efforça avant tout de réguler les conflits et de sanctionner les excès des antagonistes, faute de se positionner sur l'orthodoxie des doctrines débattues, soit parce que leur délibération revenait au Saint-Siège, dans le cas de la querelle sur les aides de la grâce, soit parce qu'elle ne parvenait pas à un consensus, dans celui de la controverse sur l'origine de l'ordre du Carmel.

L'implication du Saint-Office espagnol dans ces disputes intra-religieuses témoigne du déplacement de l'activité censoriale inquisitoriale qui se produit après le concile de Trente, ou plus exactement, de l'élargissement de ses compétences aux problématiques internes à l'Église. En censurant les écrits excessivement critiques ou qui dérogeaient aux interdictions prescrites, l'Inquisition prétendait sauvegarder l'image d'une communauté catholique unie et unanime et préserver l'unité doctrinale de l'Église, qu'elle considérait menacée par des innovations théologiques, qui, à l'instar de l'hérésie, risquaient de mettre en péril son intégrité. Les deux controverses étudiées, comme bien d'autres débats de l'époque, reposaient, de fait, sur une opposition entre tradition et nouveauté. Dans l'Espagne moderne, la tradition désignait ce qui faisait autorité et le communément admis ; la nouveauté, en revanche, était regardée avec suspicion, dès lors qu'elle n'avait pas l'appui des autorités théologiques et bouleversait les croyances établies. Dans ces querelles, les ordres religieux défendirent leurs thèses en alléguant leur ancienneté et cherchèrent à discréditer celles des ordres adverses en les taxant de 'nouvelles' : en d'autres termes, les religieux prétendaient que leur propre doctrine s'inscrivait dans la tradition ecclésiastique ou dogmatique de l'Église et accusaient l'opinion adverse 'd'innover', c'est-à-dire, d'introduire des opinions et des doctrines inédites, non reconnues par les autorités.

L'intervention censoriale de l'Inquisition visa à protéger l'intégrité institutionnelle de l'Église, menacée par les hostilités entre les ordres religieux, qui faisaient planer la menace d'un schisme, ou pour le moins, de graves dissensions, qui entachaient l'image de l'institution ecclésiastique catholique.

Bibliographie

Manuscrits et sources d'archives

Città del Vaticano, Archivio Apostolico Vaticano, Secrétariat d'État – Espagne, livre 35, 140/141 ; livre 49, 388/389.

Madrid, Archivo Histórico Nacional, Inquisition, livres 251 et 1232 ; liasse 2234, dossier 7 ; liasse 4426 (dossier 31) ; liasse 4437 (dossiers 1 et 6) ; liasse 4438 (dossiers 2 et 4) ; liasse 4442 (dossiers 57, 58 et 60) ; liasse 4444 (dossiers 19 et 37) ; liasse 4450 (dossier 6) ; liasse 4457 (dossier 1) ; liasse 4515 (dossiers 1 et 3) ; liasse 4521 (dossier 21).

Madrid, Real Academia de la Historia, Jésuites, 9/3742 (5).

Imprimés

Alabrús Iglesia, R. M. (2012), 'Las relaciones de dominicos y jesuitas en la Cataluña moderna', dans Á. Atienza López (éd.), *Iglesia memorable: crónicas, historias, escritos ... a mayor gloria. Siglos XVI-XVIII*, Madrid : Sílex Ediciones, p. 169-186.

Albisson, M., *Le livre en procès : les nouveaux enjeux de la censure inquisitoriale dans l'Espagne du XVIIe siècle* (thèse de doctorat inédite, Université Sorbonne Nouvelle, 2020).

Bœglin, M. (2003), *L'inquisition espagnole au lendemain du concile de Trente : le tribunal du Saint-Office de Séville (1560-1700)*, Montpellier : Presses de l'Université Montpelier III.

Broggio, P. (2006), 'Ordini religiosi tra cattedra e dispute teologiche: note per una lettura socio-politica della controversia *"de auxiliis"* (1582-1614)', dans *Cheiron*, 43-44, p. 53-86.

Broggio, P. (2009), *La teologia e la politica: controversie dottrinali, Curia romana e Monarchia spagnola tra Cinque e Seicento*, Firenze : Leo S. Olschki Editore.

Caro Baroja, J. (1978), *Formas complejas de la vida religiosa*, Madrid : Akal.

Chantraine, G. (1981), *Érasme et Luther. Libre et serf arbitre. Étude historique et théologique*, Paris : Lethielleux & Presses Universitaires de Namur.

Dedieu, J.-P. (1979), 'Les quatre temps de l'Inquisition', dans B. Bennassar (éd.), *L'Inquisition espagnole (XVe-XIXe siècles)*, Paris : Hachette, p. 15-42.

Dekker, E. (2000), *Middle Knowledge*, Leuven : Peeters.

Delemestre, G. (2018), 'Enjeux anthropologique et juridique de la controverse *de auxiliis* entre Luis de Molina et Domingo Bañes', dans *Réforme, Humanisme, Renaissance*, 87, p. 67-105.

Egido, T. (2015), 'Jesuitas, Carmelitas, Palafox y José Antonio Butrón', dans M. D. Gimeno Puyol & E. Viamonte Lucientes (éds), *Los viajes de la Razón: estudios dieciochistas en homenaje a María-Dolores Albiac Blanco*, Saragosse : Institución Fernando el Católico, p. 49-64.

Escandell Bonet, B. (1996), 'Sobre las adaptaciones de la Inquisición al contexto ideológico del siglo XVI', dans P. Fernández Albaladejo et al. (éds), *Política, religión e Inquisición en la España moderna: homenaje a Joaquín Pérez Villanueva*, Madrid : Ediciones de la Universidad Autónoma de Madrid, p. 253-266.

François, W. & A. Gerace (2019), 'The Doctrine of Justification and the rise of pluralism in the Post-Tridentine Catholic Church', dans K. Boersma & H. J. Selderhuis (éds), *More than Luther: The Reformation and the rise of pluralism in Europe*, Göttingen : Vandenhoeck & Ruprecht, p. 15-44.

Gerace, A. (2016), 'Luis de Molina's "middle knowledge": Thomas Stapleton's "antidote" to John Calvin', dans *Reformation and Renaissance Review*, 18 (2), p. 105-122.

Grossi, V. & B. Sesboüé (1995), 'Grâce et justification : du concile de Trente à l'époque contemporaine', dans B. Sesboüé et al. (éd.), *L'homme et son salut : anthropologie chrétienne : création, péché originel, justification et grâce, fins dernières ; l'éthique chrétienne : des autorités au magistère*, Paris : Desclée (Histoire des dogmes, 2), p. 325-373.

Lecuit, J.-B. (2014), 'Grâce et liberté : énigme résolue ou mystère insondable ?', dans *Recherches de Science Religieuse*, 102 (1), p. 107-127.

López Vela, R. (2006), 'Los Dominicos y el gobierno de la Inquisición en el siglo XVII. El dominio de una doctrina "muy fuerte contra los herejes"', dans A. Palacio Bernal (éd.), *Praedicatores, inquisidores, Volumen II: La Orden dominicana y la Inquisición en el mundo ibérico e hispanoamericano. Actas del II Seminario Internacional sobre los Dominicos y la Inquisición (Sevilla, 3-6 de marzo de 2004)*, Rome : Istituto Storico Domenicano, p. 27-57.

Martínez, F. J. (2011), 'Poder y teología en la escolástica barroca: las claves del debate sobre la gracia (el pensamiento de san Agustín en la polémica *de auxiliis*)', dans *Criticón*, 111-112, p. 137-151.

Martínez Ruiz, E. (éd., 2004), *El peso de la Iglesia: cuatro siglos de órdenes religiosas en España*, Madrid : Actas.

Matava, R. J. (2016), *Divine Causality and Human Free Choice: Domingo Báñez, Physical Premotion and the Controversy* de auxiliis *Revisited,* Leiden : Brill.

Matava, R. J. (2020), 'A Sketch of the Controversy *de auxiliis*', dans *Journal of Jesuit Studies,* 7/3, p. 417-446.

McGrath, A. E. (2005), *Iustitia Dei: A History of the Christian Doctrine of Justification,* Cambridge : Cambridge University Press.

Pardo Tomás, J. (2009), 'Palabra de hereje: ciencia y ortodoxia religiosa en controversias médicas cortesanas (1665-1724)', dans M. P. Díaz (éd.), *Las Españas que (no) pudieron ser: herejías, exilios y otras conciencias (s. XVI-XX),* Huelva : Universidad de Huelva, p. 75-92.

Quilliet, B. (2007), *L'acharnement théologique. Histoire de la grâce en Occident (IIIe-XXIe siècle),* Paris : Fayard.

Rai, E. (2020), 'Ex Meritis Praevisis: Predestination, Grace, and Free Will in intra-Jesuit Controversies (1587-1613)', dans *Journal of Early Modern Christianity,* 7/1, p. 111-150.

Renault, L. (1998), 'Bañezianisme – Molinisme – Baianisme', dans J.-Y. Lacoste (éd.), *Dictionnaire critique de théologie,* Paris : Presses Universitaires de France, p. 133-136.

Sales Souza, E. (2010), 'Disputa *De auxiliis*', dans A. Prosperi (éd.), *Dizionario storico dell'Inquisizione,* 4 tomes, Pise : Edizioni della Normale, II, p. 496-497.

Santa María, S. de (1940), *Historia del Carmen Descalzo en España, Portugal y América, Volumen IX: Los estudios en la Reforma – Vida de venerables nuevas fundaciones (1619-1650),* Burgos : Imprenta El Monte Carmelo.

Santiago Medina, B. (2011), '¿Herejía o difamación?: los Bolandistas ante el Santo Oficio (1691-1715)', dans *Documenta & Instrumenta,* 9, p. 75-97.

van Eijl, E. J. M. (1994), 'La controverse louvaniste autour de la grâce et du libre arbitre à la fin du XVIe siècle', dans M. Lamberigts & L. Kenis (éds), *L'augustinisme à l'ancienne Faculté de théologie de Louvain,* Leuven : Peeters & Leuven University Press, p. 207-282.

Vázquez, I. (1979), 'Las controversias doctrinales postridentinas hasta finales del siglo XVII', dans R. García-Villoslada (éd.), *Historia de la Iglesia en España, Volumen IV: La Iglesia en la España de los siglos XVII y XVIII,* Madrid : Biblioteca de Autores Cristianos, p. 419-474.

Résumé

Cet article étudie le rôle joué par l'Inquisition espagnole dans les controverses qui opposèrent à l'époque post-tridentine plusieurs écoles théologiques incarnées par différents ordres religieux. Au XVIIe siècle, les divergences entre ces dernières se creusèrent et donnèrent lieu à de virulentes polémiques. Les différends intellectuels se traduisirent par des 'guerres de plumes' entre les ordres religieux, qui s'affrontèrent par l'intermédiaire de textes dans lesquels la diatribe se mêlait souvent à la théologie. À partir du XVIIe siècle, l'Inquisition, dont la mission originelle était de lutter contre l'hérésie, s'immisça dans ces querelles intra-religieuses, par le biais de la censure. Son but était avant tout d'éviter les déchirements au sein de l'Église catholique, en arbitrant ou interdisant ces débats. Dans les Index de livres interdits et expurgés élaborés par l'Inquisition espagnole au cours du XVIIe siècle, on rencontre de nombreux ouvrages publiés par des membres du clergé régulier, qui alimentèrent les polémiques théologiques du moment. Dans sa tentative de réguler les disputes intra-religieuses, le tribunal de l'Inquisition se heurta à une difficulté majeure, à savoir, le profil de ses censeurs (les qualificateurs), qui, pour la plupart, appartenaient à des ordres religieux variés. Dès lors, les divergences d'opinion théologiques et les solidarités entre les ordres compromettaient la réalisation de censures impartiales. Cette situation généra plusieurs irrégularités et des conflits d'intérêt ainsi que de vifs débats au sein de l'Inquisition. Cet article étudie le rôle joué par l'Inquisition espagnole dans ces controverses théologiques et ecclésiastiques, un rôle conditionné à la fois par un corps de censeurs eux-mêmes impliqués dans ces polémiques et par des enjeux politiques, liés aussi bien à la monarchie espagnole qu'à la papauté. Cette étude prend comme exemple deux des principales controverses religieuses qui agitèrent l'Espagne du XVIIe siècle : la polémique *de auxiliis* et la querelle relative à l'origine prophétique du Carmel.

Abstract

This paper studies the role played by the Spanish Inquisition in the controversies which opposed in the post-Tridentine era several theological schools of thought, represented by different religious orders. In the seventeenth century, their divergences increased and led to violent polemics. These intellectual disagreements manifested as 'wars of quills' between religious orders, which clashed through some texts that mixed theology with diatribe. Although its original mission was to combat heresy, from the seventeenth century onwards, the Inquisition intervened in these intra-religious controversies, by means of censorship. Its aim was to avoid divisions within the Catholic Church by arbitrating or forbidding those debates. The Index of forbidden and expurgated books published by the Spanish Inquisition in the seventeenth century includes many works written by members of the regular clergy. These works fuelled the theological polemics of the time. In its attempt to regulate the intra-religious disputes, the Inquisitorial Court faced a major difficulty, which was that most of the censors belonged to various religious orders. In this way, the divergences of theological opinions and the solidarity within and between the orders compromised the impartiality of the censures. This situation gave rise to some irregularities and conflicts of interest, and sparked off lively debates within the Inquisition. This paper studies the role played by the Spanish Inquisition in the theological and ecclesiastical controversies, which was conditioned both by a corps of censors involved in these polemics and by political concerns related to the Spanish Monarchy and the Papacy. This paper focuses on two of the main controversies in seventeenth-century Spain : the *de auxiliis* polemics and the dispute about the prophetic origins of the Carmelite order.

MAGDALENA RYSZKA-KURCZAB
Pedagogical University of Krakow, Poland, ORCID 0000-0002-4175-9414

VERNACULAR RELIGIOUS DISPUTES IN THE POLISH-LITHUANIAN COMMONWEALTH DURING THE LATER SIXTEENTH AND EARLY SEVENTEENTH CENTURIES

The rising tide of the Reformation in the Polish-Lithuanian Commonwealth, which had been gathering strength since the mid sixteenth century, contributed to the development of considerable religious tolerance, which was guaranteed in law by the Warsaw Confederation Act, signed on 28 January 1573.[1] After Sigismund Augustus, the last king of Poland and grand duke of Lithuania from the Jagiellonian dynasty, had died heirless in Knyszyn on 7 July 1572, the threat of civil war loomed over the Commonwealth. Faced with the need to elect a new ruler, and the fact that the two most serious candidates for the throne — Ernest II von Habsburg and Henry Valois III — were ardent Catholics, the threat of civil war seemed real to contemporaries.[2] The dissident segment of the nobility strove to guarantee themselves freedom of confession, and this was secured by the Warsaw Confederation Act, which became part of the *pacta conventa*, a set of legal acts signed by each king-elect before his coronation. In this way, the principle of religious tolerance and freedom of confession for individuals as well as communities (*pax inter dissidentes in religione*) was elevated to something of a constitutional norm.[3]

In this atmosphere of allowing individual churches to proclaim their own theology, public religious disputations became one form

---

[1] On the Warsaw Confederation, see Korolko 1974, Salomonowicz 1974, Maciuszko 1973. On religious tolerance in the Commonwealth in the sixteenth century, see Tazbir 1967, Tazbir 1973, Zarzycki 2010, p. 25–28.

[2] Maciuszko 1984, p. 129–135.

[3] Zarzycki 2010, p. 26–27.

of religious canvassing (alongside the publication of theological works or apologetic and polemical religious writings). Since there were no legal consequences for participating in them, disputations were never subject to such strict control in the Polish-Lithuanian Commonwealth as in England, France, or Germany.[4] Moreover, one of the local characteristics of public religious disputations in the Commonwealth was that even representatives of the most radical wing of the Reformation in the Polish Crown and the Grand Duchy of Lithuania, namely, the Polish Brethren (*fratres Poloni*, or Unitarians, who were derisively called 'Arians' by their religious opponents),[5] were allowed to participate in the disputations.

In the Commonwealth, as in other European countries, religious disputes and debates took many forms.[6] This paper will look only at those disputes that were open to the public and conducted in the vernacular, as opposed to meetings held during sessions of the Diet (Sejm), such as those in 1562/3 and 1565, or at synods (e.g. in Sandomierz in 1570) or during religious colloquies (e.g. that in Thorn in 1645).

Little research into public religious disputations in the Commonwealth has been carried out to date.[7] This article sets out to

---

[4] Tazbir 1980, p. 296–297.

[5] International scholarship uses various names for this denomination. The 'Polish Brethren' is probably the most appropriate. The term 'Arians' is widely accepted by scholars, though it is not neutral, since it echoes the disparaging attitudes of their opponents towards the Polish Brethren themselves and their doctrine by naming them after Arius (256–336), the anti-Trinitarian theologian and 'heretic' condemned by the First Council of Nicaea. The terms 'Unitarians' and 'Anti-Trinitarians' reflect the salient points of their doctrine. I will use all these terms interchangeably.

[6] Fuchs 1995, p. 1–16; Scheib 2009, I–II.

[7] Among the few relevant publications, the following should be mentioned: an article by Stanisław Tworek about the Lewartów disputation of 13 and 14 January 1592 (Tworek 1960); articles by Janusz Tazbir and Katarzyna Meller devoted to the unsuccessful attempts to organise a Calvinist-Catholic dispute in Poznań at the turn of 1575 (Tazbir 1965; Meller 2014); an article by Kazimierz Drzymała about the disputation at Vilnius on 2 June 1599 (Drzymała 1979); and Jan Kamieniecki's paper about the principles of religious discourse in old Polish polemical texts (Kamieniecki 2009). Isolated incidental mentions of particular disputations or general remarks about disputations can be found, for example, in Scheib 2009, II, p. 432–441, 552–557, and in studies on anti-Jesuitical religious polemics (Stec 1988, p. 113–146), controversial polemical theology in the sixteenth through the eighteenth centuries (Natoński 2003), tolerance in the Polish-

review the rules for public vernacular religious disputes in Poland and Lithuania during the later sixteenth and early seventeenth centuries. The article considers elements that were new to the rules of the *disputatio* as observed in schools and universities; such elements include the organisers of disputations, the duration and venue of the events, use of the national language and the consequent broadening and diversification of the audience, and the controversies that grew up around this disputation method.

It is important to stress that in every case, the accounts of the disputes that are the basis of scholarly analysis, whether they are in manuscript or printed form, were written from one or another denominational perspective, and thus cannot be considered unbiased renderings of historical truth. This consideration applies in particular to the opinions and judgments the accounts convey, and to a lesser extent to facts independent of the religious standpoint, such as empirical details of a meeting (e.g. duration, venue, or participants).

The Denominational Situation in the Polish-Lithuanian Commonwealth during the Later Sixteenth Century

During the second half of the sixteenth century, the Reformation in the Polish-Lithuanian Commonwealth moved into the confessionalisation phase.[8] Calvinism was one of the new Christian churches that were slowly gaining adherents. Under the influence of the Italian 'heretics' (e.g. Francesco Stancaro and Giovanni Giorgio Biandrata), anti-Trinitarian views came increasingly to the fore in the Calvinist community, leading in 1562–1565 to a split, and the division of the community into the Calvinist *Ecclesia Maior* and the *Ecclesia Minor* — the Arian Church. The dogmatic stance[9] of the Polish Brethren was far

---

Lithuanian Commonwealth (Tazbir 1980), and individual figures embroiled in battles over the Reformation in Poland and Lithuania. These studies, however, do not take into account the specificity of the disputation or its characteristic method of formulating arguments and counterarguments, and they ignore the important context of the school *disputatio*.

[8] Maciuszko 1997, p. 17–19.

[9] Because they are irrelevant to the subject of dogmatic disputations, I leave to the side social and ethical aspects of the Arians' ideology and religion, such as

from clear and coherent.[10] The central dogma of the Arian doctrine was anti-Trinitarianism. In time, a theological Unitarianism began to dominate: the belief that the only God is God the Father, while Christ was born a man, was subsequently raised to the messianic role, attained the dignity of God only after his death and resurrection, and therefore was not an eternal God. The Unitarians denied the pre-existence of Christ and subordinated Jesus to God the Father, but still considered Jesus worthy of adoration. The doctrine of the Polish Brethren, combined with the call for a return to the Scriptures, earned this new religious community implacable adversaries. The other Protestant confessions in the Polish-Lithuanian Commonwealth — the Lutherans, the Calvinists, and the refugee Church of the Bohemian Brethren — passed over the Arians when undertaking any joint initiatives. They were excluded, for instance, from the coalition concluded between the other Protestant denominations in the Commonwealth on 12 April 1570 at Sandomierz (known as the Union of Sandomierz), whose purpose was to create a common Reformation front in order to oppose the Catholic Church more effectively.[11]

The Polish Brethren were, however, covered by the provisions of the Warsaw Confederation (1573), which ensured religious peace in the Commonwealth and protected anyone from persecution for proclaiming any, even the most radical, religious views.[12] The atmosphere of free religious expression encouraged the shift of dogmatic church discussions, which had previously been strictly internal, into the public sphere. During the 1570s and 1580s, religious disputations were organised with increasing frequency, and for the new churches these disputations became an attractive tool for religious canvassing.

---

strong opposition to any kind of violence, including armed service and carrying weapons. On the social and ethical ideology of the Polish Brethren, see Kot 1932.

[10] Wajsblum 1927; Drzymała 1963; Ogonowski 1960.

[11] On the Union of Sandomierz, see *Akta synodów różnowierczych* 1972, vol. 2, p. 251–304.

[12] In her recent book, Magdalena Luszczynska states that the Arians were the only denomination excluded from the Warsaw Confederation (Luszczynska 2018, p. 12). In fact they were covered by the provisions of the Confederation act just like all the other Protestant confessions in the Commonwealth. The Arians were only excluded from the Warsaw Confederation in 1632 (Korolko 1974, p. 133–134).

The Unitarians also took advantage of this opportunity to spread their doctrine through public disputations, but not all the other churches permitted disputation with them. The Calvinists blamed the Unitarians for destroying the unity of their church and, consequently, for weakening their community and ruining the Protestants' chances of constituting an effective counterweight to the Catholic Church. Moreover, Calvin's own intransigence with respect to the anti-Trinitarian heresy affected the attitude of Polish Calvinists towards the Arians. Leading Calvinist activists consistently tried to force successive rulers to take the radical legal action of banning the Polish Brethren from the Commonwealth.[13] Calvinist polemicists such as Andrzej Wolan or Stanisław Sarnicki spared no effort in fighting the Arian heresy in writing. Even so, the Calvinists consistently refused to engage in dogmatic disputations with the Unitarians.[14]

The Catholics, especially the Jesuits, took a different approach to public disputations with the Unitarians. This approach consisted in allowing the Polish Brethren to speak, in order to then demonstrate publicly the falsity of their doctrine and discredit them. It was public disputations between Catholics (usually Jesuits) and Arians that were most frequent type of disputation during the later sixteenth and early seventeenth centuries.

In addition to vernacular Catholic-Unitarian disputations, there were also disputes between Catholics and Calvinists. Some public disputations were planned as two-day, trilateral events (e.g. there would be a *disputatio* between a Catholic and a Unitarian one day, and between a Catholic and a Calvinist the second day).

---

[13] Tazbir 1956, p. 168–175.

[14] This attitude is exemplified in the position taken by the General Synod of Kraków on 29 September 1573: '[...] until they have abandoned their convictions, let us have no business with them [the Polish Brethren]. Let us not enter into any disputes with them, and, as the Holy Spirit tells us, let us beware of them and their writings, so that we do not allow ourselves to be brought into any doubt or to be moved from the foundation of Christian devotion or the invincible faith in God (in whose name we are baptised).' ('[...] żadnej więcej z nimi [Braćmi Polskimi] zabawy (dokąd przedsięwzięcia swego bronią) nie miejmy. W żadne dysputacje z nimi się nie wdawajmy, ale i osób i ksiąg ich, według rozkazania Ducha Świętego się strzeżmy, żebyśmy snadź fundamentu nabożeństwa krześcijańskiego i niezwyciężonej wiary o Bogu (w którego imieniuśmy krzczeni) pod sobą wzruszyć a w wątpliwość przywodzić się nie zdali.', *Akta synodów różnowierczych* 1983, vol. 3, p. 11).

The theses concerned specific dogmatic controversies. The repertoire of issues was in fact limited and was usually repeated in disputation after disputation. In the case of the Unitarians, the central issue was most often related to the Trinitarian dogma and the preexistence of Jesus Christ (e.g. 'Jesus Christ was not only a man, but is also the eternal God, who created everything and became man for us' [thesis disputation in Navahrudak, 24–25 January 1594]; 'That the Holy Spirit is a person and God' [disputation in Śmigiel on 2 July 1592]). In Catholic-Calvinist disputations, the theses concerned the primacy of the pope or sacramentology, i.e. the Lord's Supper (e.g. 'That the Lord Christ established in His Church one visible head and supreme Shepherd in His place' [the Vilnius disputation, 2 June 1599]; 'That Jesus Christ left us the sacrament of His body and His blood, in which is His true body and true blood in the form of bread and wine' [issue disputation in Lewartów, 13–14 January 1592]).

Alongside religious disputations in Polish, disputations in Latin were also organised. These covered a broader denominational spectrum than those held in the vernacular. In addition to Catholic-Unitarian and Catholic-Calvinist disputations, there were also Catholic-Lutheran and even Calvinist-Lutheran and Catholic-Orthodox events. In this paper, religious disputations in Latin will not be covered, as noted in the introduction.

General Terms of the Dispute

In the Polish-Lithuanian Commonwealth, public religious disputations were initiated either by secular protectors of the Reformation or Counter-Reformation movements, or by Catholic priests, monks, or congregational ministers. Disputes also differed significantly in prestige, numbers of participants, and repercussions. The widespread knowledge of the disputation method, which was learned in schools and universities, and what was often a truly ardent commitment to doctrinal issues, reveal how useful disputes were during the Reformation as a tool for confronting confessional controversies and propagating the faith.

Ex promptu (unprepared) debates were sporadic. Only one of the sixteen Catholic-Unitarian disputations in the years 1579–1616, recorded in the two manuscript lists of Unitarian disputations published by Stanisław Kot,[15] ensued without prior announcement and formulation of theses. The author of this 'Kolozsvar manuscript', who was most probably Andrzej Lubieniecki the Elder (1551–1623), recalls that in 1594, on the occasion of the Synod of the Polish Brethren in Śmigiel, 'a great many pious people and scholars came to the town from Greater Poland, Lesser Poland, and Lithuania'. The abbot of Przemęt (in Greater Poland), Stanisław Ostrowski, accompanied by a dozen or so noblemen, relatives, and neighbours, also went there. He inquired about the names of the foremost Unitarian ministers, whom he apparently did not know personally. He then declared that he had come to dispute with Piotr Statorius (the Younger), who was then minister of the Unitarian Church in Lucławice in Lesser Poland and one of the best Arian disputants. Ostrowski apparently formulated a thesis on the spot about the 'Divinity of the Son of God, about which they also had a moment's discussion'. Statorius allegedly defeated him easily (though the disputation was mentioned only briefly, without details of the disputants' arguments). The author of the manuscript also notes that 'the abbot was then drawn into a disputation about the Trinity'.[16]

The second example of a spontaneous disputation of which I am aware is the Navahrudak disputation, which took place on 9 January 1616. Benedict Brivilius, a Jesuit, had come to Navahrudak from nearby Nesvizh and attended a service in the Calvinist church, where a sermon was preached on a passage from the Book of Isaiah (Is. 60.1–10) by Jan Zygrovius, a theologian and Calvinist polemicist, then minister in Navahrudak. After the service, Brivilius entered into a conversation with Zygrovius, which set the stage for a disputation that was held that same day, in the evening.[17]

Usually, however, disputations were arranged much further in advance and with great care. Mutual agreement on the terms of the disputation was mandatory, especially regarding language, venue,

---

[15] These are *Dysputacje arjan polskich*, 1935, ed. S. Kot, and *Dysputacyj braci polskich katalog*, 1939, ed. S. Kot.

[16] *Dysputacje arjan* 1935, p. 352.

[17] Wądłowski 1616, f. A2r.–A2v. There are two accounts of the disputation in Navahrudak (9 January 1616), one from the Catholic perspective (Gradowski 1616) and one from the Calvinist perspective (Wądłowski [Jan Zygrovius] 1616).

duration, method, and acceptable sources of argumentation. This manner of proceeding allowed for more thorough preparation for the confrontation, and also made it possible to announce the disputation in advance, which in turn enabled everyone interested to attend and take part in the disputation as a member of the audience. Many mentions of disputations include the information that they took place in the presence of important guests, senators, or deputies. One strategy that ensured a large and prestigious audience was to organise interdenominational disputations when members of the nobility gathered for sessions of parliament and tribunals, or in connection with synods or chapters. The Jesuits especially had a reputation for organising disputations with heretics 'wherever there was a convention of nobles'.[18]

Submission of Theses

The theses for disputation were sent to the adversaries in advance. There was evidently some flexibility in this regard. Such theses were usually delivered a week ahead of the debate, as Jakub Wujek proposed in *Dialysis*.[19] We know that Hieronim Powodowski (a Catholic priest and polemicist) sent his assertions exactly a week before the disputation of 2 July 1592, to which he challenged the Unitarians from Śmigiel.[20] In the case of the Lewartów disputation, which was planned as a trilateral event (Catholic-Unitarian and Catholic-Calvinist) and organised on 13–14 January 1592, Stanisław Tworek reports that the theses were sent to both the Polish Brethren and the Calvinists on 26 December 1591, i.e. almost three weeks in advance.[21] On occasion, however, the theses were not delivered to the adversaries very far ahead of time; for one disputation organised in Lublin in 1586, the Jesuits sent the Unitarian community in Lublin the printed *Theses de Ecclesia et Primatu Papae* (*Theses on the Church and the Primacy of the Pope*) 'only five days before the appointed

---

[18] Jocher 1842, II, p. 652.
[19] Wujek 1580, f. A3v.
[20] [Powodowski] 1592, f. A7v.
[21] Tworek 1960, p. 56.

day of the disputation'.[22] And in the case of the 1591 disputation in Śmigiel, Stanisław Ostrowski, a Catholic polemicist and the abbot of Przemęt, sent his opponent, a Unitarian minister and most probably the author of the 'Kolozsvar manuscript', namely, Andrzej Lubieniecki, a handwritten verse from the Gospel of St John (8.58) only three days before the disputation; what is more, as the author of the manuscript points out, the verse was incorrectly translated into Polish.[23] As it was unusual to send only one verse as the basis for a disputation, Lubieniecki tried to persuade Ostrowski to move on to other subjects after this verse had been debated, so that all the main points of Catholic and Unitarian contention could be addressed. The abbot, however, declined: 'it is not customary to dispute what is not in the theses, and I sent you this verse *loco thesium*, so I will not discuss anything more than this'.[24]

Duration and Venue

In some cases the duration of a disputation was precisely defined and accepted in advance by both parties as part of the *leges disputationis* ('the terms of the dispute').[25] For the Lublin dispute of 22 and 23 May 1592, for instance, 'it was agreed that the disputation would be conducted from ten o'clock in the morning until eight o'clock in the evening, for as many days as proved necessary'.[26] Disputations usually lasted several hours. Sometimes we have the precise information that the disputation lasted, say, seven hours (as in the case of the disputation between Hieronim Powodowski and Jan Niemojewski in 1579), or six hours (the Vilnius disputation on 2 June 1599). Time was kept by moderators, two of whom were usually selected by each party. It was they who officially announced the end of the disputation. The course and duration of less prestigious disputations was approached more

---

[22] *Dysputacje arjan* 1935, p. 343.
[23] In 1594 the same Stanisław Ostrowski took part in a disputation in Śmigiel with the Unitarian Piotr Statorius (the Younger).
[24] *Dysputacje arjan* 1935, p. 345.
[25] *Leges disputationis* also appear in the sources as *kondycyje*, from the Latin *conditio* ('condition'); or as *kautie*, from the Latin *cautio* ('caution').
[26] *Dysputacje arjan* 1935, p. 351.

freely. Such was the case, for example, in a disputation about church services that was held in Gaj on 20 July 1592 between the Jesuits from Poznań and the Unitarians from Śmigiel (Krzysztof Lubieniecki and Krzysztof Ostorodt). According to the anti-Trinitarian author of the manuscript describing the event, who was clearly averse to the Jesuits, the latter, allegedly perceiving the Unitarian disputants to have the advantage, addressed the dispute only briefly, before exclaiming: 'It is noon, time to eat, let us give peace to the disputation', and 'after lunch they talked about their important duties, and immediately afterwards they left'.[27]

When the initiators of disputations were powerful and influential figures, the venue for the event was usually the residence of one or the other of them. For instance, Duke Krzysztof Radziwiłł ('Piorun', or 'the Thunderbolt'), the voivode of Vilnius, was the host of a disputation between Marcin Śmiglecki, a Jesuit and professor at the University of Vilnius, and Daniel Mikołajewski, an elder of the Calvinist congregations in Cuiavia, which was held on 2 June 1599 in the great hall of the Radziwiłł Palace in Vilnius.[28] The idea to stage the disputation was conceived ten days earlier, during deliberations between Orthodox, Calvinist, Lutheran, and Bohemian Brethren theologians in Vilnius on 24 May 1599 initiated with the aim of presenting a more united front against the Catholic Church.[29] The disputation was to be held with an audience of more than two thousand people, and in the presence of five voivodes.[30]

Disputations might also be staged in private homes, even when the hosts were of lower social standing than the aforementioned Duke Radziwiłł. Of the sixteen Catholic-Arian disputations on

---

[27] *Dysputacje arjan* 1935, p. 350–351.

[28] Drzymała 1981, p. 34; Kempa 2016, p. 240. There are two detailed accounts of the Vilnius disputation (2 June 1599): one from the Catholic perspective (Śmiglecki 1599), and one from the Calvinist perspective (Mikołajewski 1599). For other details, see Drzymała 1979; Niedźwiedź 2012, p. 278–283; Kempa 2016, p. 240–241.

[29] Kempa 2016, p. 238.

[30] Namely, Krzysztof Radziwiłł ('Piorun'), voivode of Vilnius; Konstanty Ostrogski, voivode of Kiev; Krzysztof Ziemowicz, voivode of Brest-Litovsk; Jan Abramowicz, voivode of Smolensk; and Andrzej Leszczyński, voivode of Brześć Kujawski.

record, four took place in private homes: [31] in Lublin 'at [the home of] Mr Chycki', deputy of Sandomierz; in the Kraków townhouse of Prospero Provano, who was an Italian, a crown leaseholder, and the manager of the salt mine in Wieliczka; in Gaj, in the manor that had belonged to the nobleman Szczęsny Jaktorowski; and in Śmigiel at the home of Elżbieta Zborowska, widow of Andrzej Dudycz, excommunicated bishop and co-proprietor of Śmigiel. It was undoubtedly a question of being able to guarantee a spacious venue that could accommodate all those wishing to attend. The manuscript that documents the debate in Gaj, Greater Poland, mentions that the guardians of Jaktorowski's minor orphans — the guardians being people of 'various denominations, Unitarians, Calvinists, and Papists' [32] — together inaugurated a disputation between four Jesuits from Poznań and two Arian ministers from Śmigiel (Krzysztof Lubieniecki and Krzysztof Ostorodt). It took place in the manor house that had belonged to Jaktorowski, where there was a 'big chamber in which many people could fit'. And as the news of the disputation spread, on the appointed day 'many worthy people of various denominations, not summoned, and unexpectedly, desirous of listening to the conversation, converged on the manor'.[33]

Nevertheless, the vast majority of vernacular disputations were organised in churches, and less often in Unitarian meeting houses. Ten of the sixteen Arian disputations described in the Lubieniecki manuscript took place in churches, and only two in meeting houses. It is important to remember that in the sixteenth-century Polish-Lithuanian Commonwealth, churches served as venues for *sejmiks* (local parliaments, district noble conventions), so they were already recognised spaces which served non-sacral social functions, since they could accommodate many people.

The vast majority of churches remained in Catholic hands; only on private estates could they serve denominations other than Catholicism. Some of the churches belonged to religious orders. This is why the Jesuits, for example, had the status of hosts of dis-

---

[31] These were disputes nos 1, 2, 7, and 10 in *Dysputacje arjan* 1935, p. 341–342, 350, 352.

[32] *Dysputacyje arjan* 1935, p. 350.

[33] *Dysputacje arjan* 1935, p. 350.

putations that were held in their churches. Sometimes they tried to take advantage of this fact for their own benefit. In 1592, during a disputation with Arian Jan Niemojewski, one of the leaders of the Arian community in Lublin, the Jesuits manipulated the positions of the disputants so as to give their own disputant an advantage. The Jesuit Justus Raabe occupied a raised pulpit, so he could be heard perfectly in the whole church, while the Unitarians were seated on chairs below, making it much harder for them to be heard and understood. This kind of manipulation was a calculated move to disadvantage the opponents:

> gdy z Justem jezuitą naszy dysputowali, a jezuita z kazalnice disputował, y wszyscy go mowiącego słyszeć mogli, a naszy na dole na krzesłach siedzieli, ktorych mało ludzi słyszeć mogło, choć dźwięk mowi słyszeli, ale słów nie rozumieli.[34]
>
> (when our people were disputing with the Jesuit Justus, and the Jesuit was disputing from the pulpit and all could hear him speaking, but ours sat below on chairs, and few people could hear them, and though they heard the sound of speech, yet they did not understand the words.)

The sources also cite other examples of the Jesuits' manipulation of space and the way in which the disputants presented themselves during the confrontation. For example, on the first day of the disputation in Lewartów (13 January 1592), the Jesuit Adrian Radzymiński apparently sat on a high, ornamented chair — 'he sat in a lofty place, on a green senator's chair (on which there was also a velvet headrest), and that chair was covered with red cloth' — while the rector of the Unitarian school in Lewartów, Wojciech of Kalisz, who was representing the Arians, was ordered to leave his seat and stand before the Jesuit. In the Unitarian description of this disputation, this fact caused justified complaint and resentment:

> Toć w prawdzie tak było, że mu [Rektorowi] ks. Radzymiński miejsce odjął, które mu było naznaczone i przed sobą mu stać na ławce kazał jako żakowi, który tekst recytuje i chłopu jakiemu swemu, co też i Rektor uczynił. [...] Miejsce [mu] odjęto,

---

[34] *Dysputacje arjan* 1935, p. 351–352.

przed jezuitą stać kazano, spotwarzano i zelżono i do ludzi w pośmiech podano i zhukano i wyszydzono.[35]

(It was in truth that Father Radzymiński denied him [the Rector] the place that had been ascribed him, and told him to stand on the bench in front of him like a pupil who recites a text in front of the teacher, like his peasant; this the Rector did [...] He was denied his place, told to stand before the Jesuit, was calumniated and vilified, he was made a laughing stock in front of the gathered people, he was shouted at and mocked.)

After these instances of unequal positioning of disputants during debates, the Unitarians issued an open demand for equal treatment, which is also recorded in Catholic sources. Jan Przylepski, describing the dispute organised in Lublin on 22–23 May 1592, noted that the Unitarian minister Piotr Statorius (the Younger) was seated on a high chair because he did not want to be lower than the Jesuit disputant Adrian Radzymiński. Przylepski mentioned that Statorius was seated as he wished so that the Unitarians could not later 'rightly complain'.[36]

During the 1560s and 1570s the Jesuits were forbidden to conduct disputations outside of their colleges, so it was a challenge for the parties to agree on a mutually acceptable venue, especially in the 1570s. This lack of consent to disputations outside the colleges was one of the reasons why the meeting sought by Jakub Niemojewski in 1575 (the influential leader of the Calvinists of Greater Poland) was not held. Niemojewski challenged the Jesuits of Poznań to a disputation, proposing a venue 'where the most listeners could be accommodated, thus, either at the weigh house, or in the parish church'.[37] It was for the same reason that the Catholic priest Hieronim Powodowski went to Śmigiel in 1581, as a substitute for the Jesuits of Poznań, for a dispute with the minister Jan Krotowski of Śmigiel.[38]

As we know, Catholic churches were not enthusiastically accepted by Protestants as venues for public disputes. Aside from

[35] [Wojciech z Kalisza] 1592, f. A3v.–A4r.
[36] Przylepski 1592, f. B2v.
[37] Niemojewski 1579, f. A6v.
[38] Szamotulski 1581, f. A5r.

the fears surrounding the unfair, manipulative positioning of the disputants described above, accounts by the Polish Brethren also mention explicit concerns for their attendees' health and even lives.[39] The reason for this concern was that disputations often raised emotions among the excited crowd to such an extent that riots broke out against the dissenters, especially the hated Arians. And although disputants on both sides often explicitly declared their intention to conduct a peaceful and Christian conversation, in fact the threat of riots was almost always real. In 1581, for instance, following a dispute in Lublin with the Jesuits Stanisław Warszewicki and Justus Raabe, Jan Niemojewski 'was hit in the back by a stone',[40] and during a disputation with the Catholic priest Hieronim Powodowski in 1596, Niemojewski was severely assaulted.[41]

The choice of a congregation meeting house rather than a church as venue for the disputation was no guarantee of a calm event. In 1596 there was turmoil during a dispute organised in the meeting house of the Polish Brethren in Lublin. Catholics came to the church in large numbers. The Unitarians gave up places for them in the building, and positioned themselves on the porch so as to be able to save themselves by escaping in case of trouble. Only Jan Niemojewski and six other Arians remained inside the building:

> Dla tego aby więcey ludzi obcych we Zborze zmieścić się mogło, bo było y Mnichów i Xiężej rozmaitych y pospolstawa barzo wiele, chyba Jezuitowie nie byli, tedy za oknami na ganku Bracia Zborowi byli, więc y dla tego, żeśmy się bali,

---

[39] Although this information about the Unitarians' fears for their life and health during disputes figures in their own, i.e. Unitarian, sources, there is no reason to treat such reports as 'solely coloured by doctrinal differences'. Although religious relations in the Commonwealth were much better than in other European countries, this does not mean that there were no conflicts between Catholics and non-Catholics. Incited by the Catholic clergy, which had been intensifying its religious canvassing since the 1570s, religious 'tumults' took place in cities, during which fanaticised mobs destroyed Protestant churches and more than once threatened the lives and health of people who professed a religion other than Catholicism. Those most vulnerable to attack were precisely the 'Arians', who were considered blasphemers and the most heinous of heretics (Ogonowski 2015, p. 139–143).

[40] *Dysputacyj braci polskich* 1939, p. 459.

[41] Szczucki, Tazbir 1978, XXIII, p. 15.

> aby na nas nie uderzyli adwersarze, bo był wielkim dworem Cardinał przyjechał y było tam przy tey disputaciey Paniąt niemało zuchwałych z Comityvy iego, y woleliśmy tam bracią mieć za okny w zamknieniu osobnym, dla ich snadnieyszego ustąpienia, sami się na śmierć resolvowawszy.[42]

> (So that more of the outsiders could fit into the church — because there were monks and priests of all kinds, and many common people, but likely no Jesuits — the brethren from the congregation were outside the windows on the porch, and [this was] also because we were afraid that the adversaries would strike at us, because the cardinal had come with his great court, and there were also several bold nobles of his acquaintance there, and so we preferred to have our brethren outside the windows, in a separate room, for their easier retreat, we ourselves being reconciled with death).

When in the course of this confrontation the argument turned to the verse John 8. 28, Hermolaus Ligęza, then a courtier of Cardinal Jerzy Radziwiłł, and later grand treasurer of the Crown,[43] who was present at the dispute, called the Unitarians 'Turks and Jews'. To this, Krzysztof Lubieniecki retorted that it was the 'Trójczacy' (a disparaging name for the Trinitarians), like the Jews and the Turks, who wanted to believe in one God, and ignore Jesus Christ, and therefore they resembled Turks and Jews more than the Unitarians. Ligęza was incensed at these words and began to threaten the Unitarians. Duke Jerzy Radziwiłł, who as cardinal had come to Lublin to inspect the local monasteries and churches, was rapidly informed of the tense situation. Many of the Catholic participants in this disputation were members of his court. Cardinal Radziwiłł decided to intervene immediately, and he sent to Lord [Jan] Ostroróg, the voivode of Poznań and marshal of the tribunal, asking him to go to the church to keep the peace. The marshal did so forthwith, arriving at the meeting house with the assistance of hundreds of men, and ordered all those present, of all confessions, to leave the meeting house and the courtyard.

The anti-Trinitarians often tried to use the *leges disputationis* to guarantee their safety. One such attempt was made by Jan Kro-

---

[42] *Dysputacje arjan* 1935, p. 353.
[43] Kowalska 1972, XVII, p. 315–316.

towski, an Arian minister from Śmigiel, who was scheduled to go to Poznań in 1581 to conduct a disputation with the Jesuits there. Out of fear for his life and health, he went to the grand marshal of the Crown and prefect (*starosta*) of Poznań, Andrzej Opaliński — despite the fact that Opaliński was a Catholic, and an ardent protector of the Jesuits[44] — to request protection. Opaliński indeed accompanied Krotowski to the disputation 'to monitor his security and lead him away from the Jesuits whole'.[45] Five years later, before the dispute in Lublin, the stipulation was also made that the event take place 'in a quiet place and in the Polish language, and with the maintenance of the peace by the castle and city authorities'.[46]

Permitting the participation of laypeople and uneducated listeners in disputations made the *disputatio* into a kind of spectacle, a popular entertainment.[47] Evaluation of doctrinal nuances or the correctness of the syllogisms formulated by the disputants exceeded the capabilities of simple audiences. During one disputation in Lublin in 1616, the church was 'filled with simple and drunken people' who loudly mocked and challenged the Calvinists who were disputing with the Jesuits that day. On the following day, therefore, when the Unitarians were to conduct their disputation, 'vulgar people were not permitted to enter the church', which helped to prevent turmoil. Security was overseen by the voivode of Podolia, Stanisław Lanckoroński, who placed several of his servants and fifty *hajduks* ('private bodyguards') in front of the entrance to prevent drunken, simple people and 'peasants' from entering, allowing in only the 'reasonable and serious'. With the strengthening of the position of the Catholic religion in the Commonwealth (from the reign of the pro-Catholic Sigismund III Vasa, 1587–1632), anti-Protestant moods intensified, especially with regard to the despised Arians, who were often subjected to intimidation campaigns.

---

[44] Dworzaczek 1979, XXIV, p. 72–78.
[45] *Dysputacje arjan* 1935, p. 342.
[46] *Dysputacje arjan* 1935, p. 343.
[47] Stec 1988, p. 114, 119.

Language

While Latin was the language of the school disputation,[48] the choice of language for religious disputations was not so obvious. Throughout the sixteenth century and beyond, public religious disputations in the Polish-Lithuanian Commonwealth were also organised in Latin. The Protestants, however, evidently pushed for *in vulgari* disputations. The choice of language was a source of controversy, especially in the first years when disputes were held in Poland-Lithuania. During the 1570s the Jesuits refused to conduct religious disputations in Polish. Testimony to the divergent expectations regarding the language of the *disputatio*, and consequently the intended objectives of the proceedings and the expected competence of the audience, may be found in the history of the attempts to organise a Jesuit-Calvinist disputation in Poznań at the beginning of 1575. In 1579, the Calvinist Jakub Niemojewski published a printed work entitled *Diatrybe albo kolacyja przyjacielska z ks[iężmi] jezuitami poznańskiemi* (*Diatribe, or a friendly Collatio with Jesuit Priests from Poznań*), in which he described the circumstances surrounding the confrontation, which ultimately never took place. He included the answer he received from Jakub Wujek, the rector of the Jesuit college in Poznań; in the letter Wujek explains why he considered Latin to be the only possible language for public debate on issues of the faith:

> My się nie wymawiamy, żebyśmy *publice* dysputować nie mieli [...] a ktemu po łacinie, nie tylko iż między nami są niektórzy, co i słowa po polsku nie umieją, ale i dla tumultu pospólstwa. A to że nie chcemy mieć *vulgum iudicem controversiarum* [pospólstwa sędzią naszych sporów], ale *eruditos* [ludzi uczonych]. Ktemu iż *disputare non convenit, nisi linguarum peritis, Latinae praesertim, Graecae ac Hebraicae* [nie można dysputować bez biegłej znajomości języków, zwłaszcza łaciny, greki i hebrajskiego].[49]
>
> (We are not declining to conduct a public disputation [...] We want to dispute in Latin, not only because there are some

---

[48] Chang 2004, p. 137–138.
[49] Niemojewski, 1579, f. A3v.–A4r.

among us who cannot speak a word of Polish, but also because of the commotion of the crowd. And we do not wish to have *vulgum iudicem controversiarum* ['a commoner as the judge of our controversies'], but people of learning. Because *disputare non convenit, nisi linguarum peritis, Latinae praesertim, Graecae ac Hebraicae* ['it is not possible to dispute without fluency in languages, chiefly Latin, Greek, and Hebrew'].)

Niemojewski considered such a response an unworthy evasion of the disputation and an attempt to prevent simple pious people from understanding issues of faith:

> słowa tej ceduły świadczą, że mi rozmowy polskiej nie pozwolili, o jaką ludzi zacnych i pobożnych wiele prosiło, ani czasu do tego żadnego złożyli, ani pospolitego człowieka kr[ześcijańskiego] do tego przypuścić chcieli ku rozsądkowi, jedno te, co by po łacinie, po grecku i po żydowsku umieli. [...] Tak mi tu Ich M[ości] Panowie Jezuitowie napisali: nie chcemy mieć *vulgum*, to jest pospolitego człowieka sędziem naszej rozmowy. Iż dysputować nie należy, jedno uczonym, a języków łacińskiego, greckiego i żydowskiego umiejętnym i przetoż o wierze po polsku ze mną mówić nie chcieli.[50]

> (The words of this letter prove that they would not allow me to have the Polish conversation which many worthy and pious people had requested, nor would they devote time to it, nor did they wish the common Christian man to be admitted to it, but only those who would know the Latin, Greek, and Hebrew tongues. [...] This is what the Most Esteemed Jesuits wrote to me here: we do not wish to have the common man [*vulgus*] judge our conversation. That one should not dispute, but that he be a scholar, and that he be skilled in the Latin, Greek, and Hebrew languages, and so they did not wish to discuss the faith with me in Polish.)

Furthermore, Niemojewski accused the Jesuits of deliberately wanting to use Latin so that ordinary, simple people who did not know that language could not discover the errors of the Catholic faith. He supported his argument with the biblical example of St Paul, who exhorted that the Word of God be preached in a language understood by the listeners, and with the example

---

[50] Niemojewski 1579, f. A4v.–A5r.

of St Augustine, who avoided syllogisms in disputations with his adversaries:

> [jezuici] nie chcą po polsku mówić z nami [...] dlatego nie chcą, aby nie rozumiano, a wyrozumiawszy, aby ludzie nie poczuli ich błędów. Lecz Paweł Św[ięty] rozumny[m] a własnym językiem rozkazuje mówić we zborzech krześcijańskich dla wyrozumienia słuchaczów [...] Bo tak mawiał Augustyn święty z przeciwniki wiary krześcijańskiej wieku swojego, nie szkolnym obyczajem, ani *syllogistice*, chocia to barzo dobrze umiał, aleby to nie było do wyrozumienia człowiekowi pospolitemu.[51]

> ([The Jesuits] do not want to speak with us in Polish lest the common Christian people be able to understand our conversations and in thus understanding learn of their errors. But St Paul commands that we speak in Christian churches in a comprehensible language, their own, that the listeners might understand [...] And thus it was that St Augustine spoke to the opponents of the Christian faith of his own age, not in a scholastic manner, nor using syllogisms, though he was well able to do so, but then it would not have been understandable to the ordinary people.)

A year later, in 1580, Jakub Wujek published in print his response to Niemojewski's *Diatrybe*, titling his work *Dialysis, to jest rozwiązanie albo rozebranie assercyi Pana Jakuba Niemojewskiego z dowodami jego naprzeciw jezuitom poznańskim* (*Dialysis, or a refutation or deconstruction of Jakub Niemojewski's assertions, with his evidence against the Poznań Jesuits*). Wujek, referring there to the circumstances of the cancelled disputation, refutes Niemojewski's charges thus:

> A też Paweł św. nie broni i bronić nie każe mówić inszemi językami, zwłaszcza gdy są którzy je rozumieją, jako ich w Poznaniu jest barzo wiele, którzy *mediocriter* [dostatecznie] umieją po łacinie, których wszystkich na disputacyję przypuszczamy. Przywodzi i Augustyna św., że on nie szkolnym obyczajem dysputowała [...] To jednak za nami, że on po łacinie dysputował. A co się dotyczy obyczaju, wolno jemu było, jako biskupowi [...], ale nam najpodlejszym, a niegod-

---

[51] Niemojewski 1579, f. A5v.–A6r.

nym sługom Kościoła Świętego powszechnego nie godzi się granic nam zamierzonych przestępować.[52]

(But St Paul does also not forbid the speaking of other languages, nor order this forbidden, especially when there are those who understand them, of whom there are so many in Poznań, who can speak mediocre Latin, all of whom we admit into disputations. [Niemojewski] also makes reference to Augustine, that he did not dispute in a syllogistic manner. [...] But this is in our favour, that he disputed in Latin. As for custom, he might do otherwise, as a bishop [...], but it does not befit us, the most despicable and base servants of the Holy Catholic Church, to transgress the boundaries imposed on us.)

During the 1580s the Jesuits were still reluctant to accept Polish in disputations, although Latin was no longer a *sine qua non*. In 1586, the Lublin Jesuits sent their *Theses de Ecclesia et Primatu Papae* (*Theses on the Church and the Primacy of the Pope*) to the local Unitarian community. Yet because the Jesuits would not agree to a disputation outside their own church and college, and refused to entertain the possibility of speaking in Polish, the Unitarians proposed a written polemic instead of a disputation, to be read out publicly in the Jesuit church in Lublin on an agreed date. Jan Niemojewski, a theologian, activist, Unitarian polemicist, and younger brother of the aforementioned Jakub Niemojewski, reportedly 'did not sleep for three nights, but responded'. On the arranged date, however, the Jesuits brought many noble and worthy guests to the church ('ten leading senators and prefects, and very many nobles'), then refused to allow Niemojewski to read out his response, claiming that 'we do not want to listen to the script; anyone who wishes to can read it at home', and finally demanded a dispute in Polish so that their opponents would not use the disagreement over language, either written or spoken, as an excuse to avoid the confrontation. In this case, the Unitarians interpreted the controversy about the language and venue of the disputation as a Jesuit trick designed to ruin their chances of thoroughly preparing for the disputation. In the course of the disputa-

---

[52] Wujek 1580, f. B1r.

tion, Jan Niemojewski addressed his adversary, the Jesuit Justus Raabe, with the ironic words:

> obrachuicie się iakieieście szczerości użyli w tey sprawie, na odpis pozwoliwszy, teraz mu mieysca nie daiecie, z disputaciey wypuściwszy teraz się iey domagacie, tusząc, że się wam nie stawią, abyście z nich triumfować mogli. [...] Kiedy was o disputatią polskiem jezykiem proszono dla tych waszych ludzi pospolitych, y tych mniszek, których tu nie mało widzę, tedyście się zbraniali, a teraz kiedy was nie proszą, pozwalacie.[53]

> (Establish what honesty you have applied in this matter in accepting the copy and now not allowing it; having first refused the disputation, now you demand it, hoping that they [the Polish Brethren] will not attend, so that you can triumph. [...] When you were asked to dispute in Polish for all those ordinary people, and for these nuns, of whom I see some considerable number here, then you refused, and now when they do not ask, you allow it.)

Aside from the problem of audiences lacking the competence to understand complex dogmatic issues and the authority to examine the truths of the faith independently, disputations *in vulgari* ('in the vernacular') also presented the issue of the very method of disputation, especially the method by which syllogisms were formed in the vernacular (i.e. in Polish). Prior to the disputation with the Polish Brethren in Śmigiel on 27 December 1581 regarding the eternal divinity of Christ and the Holy Trinity, the Catholic polemicist and disputant Hieronim Powodowski formulated his expectations regarding the method of disputation as follows:

> To też sobie wymawiam, aby rozmowa krótka a porządna była. A iż polskim językiem syllogismy formować trudno, tedy się odprawujmy *per enthymemata, inductiones et exempla: consequentia ex antecedenti* [za pośrednictwem entymematów, indukcji i przykładów, wyprowadzając wnioski z poprzednika] jako nakrócej, *sine amplificationibus* [bez rozwodzenia się] pokazując, a dla lepszej pamięci, każdej assercyjej krótko powiedzianej, liczbę argumentów albo dowodów zarazem mianując.[54]

---

[53] *Dysputacje arjan* 1935, p. 344.
[54] Szamotulski 1581, f. A7r.

(Thus I postulate that the conversation be kept short but substantive. And since it is difficult to form syllogisms in Polish, let us act *per enthymemata, inductiones et exempla consequentia ex antecedenti* ['through enthymemes, inductions and examples, drawing conclusions from what precedes'] as the briefest form, demonstrating *sine amplificationibus* ['without over-elaboration'], and for better recall, each assertion stated briefly, at the same time citing the number of arguments or proofs).

I am not aware of any research on the relationship between Polish and syllogisms in the sixteenth century, but it would seem to be an interesting issue. The disputants themselves clearly considered Latin to allow much easier formation of syllogisms. Undoubtedly, the school system habituated students to learning logic in Latin, and the skills of constructing correct syllogistic figures and modes were practised in Latin. When the language of *disputatio* shifted to Polish, the lexical and syntactic differences between the two languages were such that problems arose which were difficult to deal with. My preliminary observations of syllogisms in Polish confirm that vernacular syllogisms are often indeed less well structured, as their premises and conclusions frequently deviate from subject-predicate propositions. These issues, however, require systematic research.

Furthermore, the use of the Polish language in religious disputations had significant consequences for the verses of Scripture with which the propositions of syllogisms were justified or were used for counter-argumentation: in disputations in Polish, both *proponens* and *opponens* usually quoted Scripture in Polish, extemporaneously translating the relevant fragments into the vernacular from the Latin or Greek. The correctness of these translations often provoked the reservations of the adversaries in the disputation, thus becoming a part of their refutational strategy.

Method

In the early modern period, the method of disputation was essentially carried over from mediaeval school practice.[55] The basic

---

[55] Weijers 2013, p. 176.

elements of this practice persisted, such as categorisation of the disputants into *proponens* and *opponens*, formulation of proofs refuting the theses in the form of syllogisms, attacking the premises of syllogisms rather than their conclusions, and the conventional terminology.[56] In the early period in particular, during the 1570s and 1580s, the strongly formalistic, syllogistic method of disputation started to provoke reservations or open criticism from representatives of the new churches. The Catholics, however, declared their faithfulness to the dialectic method, holding it to be the only one that ensured the orderly conduct of the disputation and its conclusiveness.

The two main reservations about the method are given above in the context of criticising the use of Latin as the language of the *disputatio*. Jakub Niemojewski in his *Diatribe* reproached the Jesuits, arguing that the scholastic method on which they insisted led only to obscurity and confusion. He accused them of using dialectics to attempt to conceal from people the truth necessary for salvation:

> dla tego, aby nikt nie zrozumiał, jedno żacy, albo ci tylko, którzy się sofistyjej uczyli. A iżby tym snadniej było panom szczyrą naukę wiary krze[ścijańskiej] po prostu od Apostołów podaną zaćmić i przytrzasnąć próżną philosophią i wymysły ludzkimi. Lecz takowe dysputacyje w szkołach dla ćwiczenia ludzi młodych są od filozofów wynalezione. A między ludem krze[ścijańskim] rozkazuje św. Paweł słowo Boże szczerze a prosto powiadać, bez fortelów i bez filozofiej.[57]

> (So that no one should understand it except scholars, or only those who have learned sophistry. And so as to render it the easier to becloud and trap these gentlemen using vain philosophies and human inventions in place of the genuine teaching of the Christian faith left by the Lord's Apostles on paper. But such disputations invented in schools to train young people were invented by philosophers, while St Paul commands that the word of God be spread honestly and simply among the Christian populace, without artifice and without philosophy.)

---

[56] For a description of the post-mediaeval *ars disputandi*, see Felipe 1991.
[57] Niemojewski 1579, f. A5v–A6r.

Niemojewski's second accusation concerned the inaccessibility of the disputation method to the average listener:

> Nad to inaczej niechcąc ze mną mówić, jedno po łacinie i szkolnym obyczajem, czegom już odwykł. A podobno kiedyby się wszytka Wielka Polska na to zjechała, ledwaby ich dziesiąci nalazł, coby takowej rozmowie szkolnej rozumieć mogli, oprócz doktorów i studentów, i z tych nie każdy. Gdzież tedy nas ci panowie chcą podzieć, cośmy się tych szkolnych syllogismów nie uczyli.[58]

> (Moreover, they will not talk with me otherwise than in Latin and according to the scholarly custom, to which I have grown unaccustomed. And it is likely, if the whole of the Great Poland had come together for it, that there would barely have been ten of them who would have understood such a scholarly conversation, excepting doctors and students, and not all of them. Whatever do these gentlemen want to do with us who never learned these scholarly syllogisms.)

Jakub Wujek defended himself against these accusations, explaining that the Jesuits were desirous of conducting a disputation with Niemojewski, but they wanted:

> dysputować *rite ac legitime, more in Academiis servari solito* [należycie i zgodnie z zasadami, podług zwyczaju panującego w Akademiach], to jest porządnie a *dialectice* [według zasad dialektyki], *breviter* [krótko] dla rychlejszej odprawy.[59]

> (to dispute *rite ac legitime, more in Academiis servari solito* ['duly and according to the rules, according to the custom in the Academies'], that is, *dialectice* ['according to the rules of dialectics'], *breviter* ['briefly'] in order to finish the sooner.)

These two accusations, that of concealing the truth and excluding the majority of the listeners, who were not trained in logic and syllogistics, are also the accusations most often repeated in other sources. For instance, when the Unitarian Andrzej Lubieniecki the Elder, minister of a Lublin congregation, met the Jesuit Justus Raabe for a disputation in the Jesuit church in Lublin in 1581, Lubieniecki protested the dialectical method of dispu-

---

[58] Niemojewski 1579, f. A4v.–A5r.
[59] Niemojewski 1579, f. A4r.

tation, describing it as 'scholastic logical traps' (Polish: 'łapaczki szkolne'). The Jesuit seized on this criticism to accuse the Unitarians of 'not wanting to dispute using logic', which in his opinion was tantamount to 'wanting to dispute not properly, but *confuse* [i.e. confusingly] and without conclusion'. Lubieniecki defended himself in these words:

> O co wam idzie o dialektykę, my to wiemy, że jey wam z nieba nie podano, aniście iey z ziemie wykopali, tenże Aristoteles iey was co y nas nauczył, nie srodzyście nam dialektyką, a nie o to nam szło, abyśmy *confuse* y bez concluzyi disputowali, ale o to abyśmy to pospolstwo wasze czego dobrego nauczyli, *de figuris et modis* [o figury i tryby] nie swarząc się po żakowsku.[60]
>
> (What is it about dialectics; we know that it was not given to you from heaven, neither did you dig it out of the earth; Aristotle taught it to you just as to us; you do not frighten us with your dialectics, and it was not our intention to dispute *confuse* ['confusingly'] and without conclusion; we wanted to teach your common people something good, without fighting *de figuris et modis* ['about figures and modes'] like schoolboys.)

Thus for some members of the new churches, dialectics, as training in logic and knowledge of syllogistic modes and figures (*figurae et modi*), became synonymous with 'scholastic logical traps', human inventions, and vain quarrels (which fitted well with the humanist criticism of scholastics). Such people shared the strong belief that an understanding of the basic tenets of faith does not require syllogistic tools. The logic taught at school was contrasted with 'good', 'sincere', 'simple' Bible study. This aversion to and general criticism of syllogistic reasoning was not accompanied by any form of deeper reflection on an alternative method that might supersede it. This deficiency gave Catholic disputants reason to be acerbic. When Jakub Niemojewski, after his unsuccessful attempts to organise a Calvinist-Catholic dispute in Poznań, published his own answers to the theses submitted to the Jesuits for disputation, his adversary, the Jesuit Jakub Wujek, noted ironically that Niemojewski, who had so loudly protested against the use of dialectics in disputation, was now using it himself:

[60] *Dysputacje arjan*, 1935, p. 344.

> potym napisał dziesięć *assertiones* albo artykułów przeciwko nam i nauce naszej jako wszystkiego Kościoła powszechnego [...] a dowodzi tego na nas im najwięcej może, a ktemu syllogismami i dialektyką, na którą sam zezwolić pierwej nie chciał, zowiąc to sofistyką, fortelami i próżną philosophią.[61]
>
> (after which he wrote ten *assertiones* or articles against us and our doctrine, and also the entire Catholic Church [...] and he argues this to us to the utmost — and does so using syllogisms and dialectics, which he himself at first did not want to permit, calling them sophistry, tricks, and vain philosophy.)

In most sources, however, logic (syllogistics), with its overriding aim of distinguishing between truth and falsehood, is held up as an efficacious tool of disputation because it provides an effective means of 'searching for the truth'. For example, the person who wrote the description of the Catholic-Unitarian dispute in Śmigiel (probably Hieronim Powodowski himself), noted that during the disputation the Unitarian minister Jan Krotowski:

> na porządną rozmowę pozwolił, wszakoż iżby filozofijej nie mieszać. A gdy mu ks[iądz] kanonik [Hieronim Powodowski] wywiódł, iż to nie *philosophia*, ale *ex logica* jest to obyczaj jako najprostszy do porządnego prawdy dochodzenia, tedy za tym i on obiecał także krótko i porządnie mówić.[62]
>
> (assented to a decent conversation, as long as philosophy was not involved. And when the canon [Hieronim Powodowski] demonstrated that not philosophy but *ex logica* is the easiest way to seek the decent truth, then he also promised to speak concisely and substantively.)

As in the above passage, the dialectical method was usually identified with conciseness, simplicity, and precision of thought and speech. It was contrasted with what was associated with rhetoric, i.e. 'the multitudinousness and ornamentalism of words', and 'verbosity'. Before the dispute between the Unitarian Jan Stoiński and the Jesuit Mikołaj Łęczycki, Stoiński said 'Wise people speak well: *Simplex est veritatis oratio* ["truthful speech is simple"]'.[63]

---

[61] Wujek 1580, f. A2v.–A3r.
[62] Szamotulski 1581, f. A7v.
[63] *Dysputacje arjan* 1935, p. 355.

And before a disputation with the Jesuits organised in Vilnius (2 June 1599), the Calvinist Daniel Mikołajewski postulated:

> Aby się *praefacyami* [wstępami], *acclamacyami* [aklamacjami] i wielomownością, kazaniom raczej niż dysputacyjom należną, nie bawili, gdyż krótkie argumentacyje i do pojęcia służą i do zbudowania.[64]

> (Would that they did not dabble in introductions, acclamations, and loquacity, which are appropriate rather to sermons than to disputations, since short arguments and short concepts serve understanding and formation.)

And Jakub Wujek perceived in dialectics a certain severity that was opposed to courtly, subtle, and delicate customs:

> To też P[an] Bóg widzi, żebyśmy ani p[ana] Niemojewskiego ani żadnego człowieka w tym pisaniu nieradzi obrazili, przetoż jeślibyśmy dworskich obyczajów abo ceremonij świeckich w czym nie zachowali, używając *terminos artis* (jako w dysputacjach być musi) i zowiąc prawdę prawdą a fałsz fałszem, etc., tedy prosim, aby się nikt obrażać nie raczył a naszę prostotę na lepsza stronę wykładał.[65]

> (The Lord God sees that we did not wish to offend in our writing either Mister Niemojewski or any [other] human being. If we, despite lack of ill-intention, had violated courtly customs or secular ceremonies using [as disputation requires] terms of art, calling truth truth and falsehood falsehood, etc., then we kindly ask you not to be offended, and see our simplicity in a better light.)

The *leges disputationis* usually included comments on the method. These were sometimes very general, as in the case of the dispute in Śmigiel (27 December 1581), when Hieronim Powodowski proposed that 'the conversation be short and substantive' and that the premises of the syllogisms be based on the Old and New Testaments.[66] Before the disputation with Krzysztof Ostorodt (Śmigiel, July 2, 1592), Powodowski exhorted the adversaries to speak 'in an orderly manner, drawing conclusions from proposi-

---

[64] Mikołajewski 1599, f. C3r.
[65] Wujek 1580, f. A8v.–B1r.
[66] Szamotulski 1581, f. A6v.–A7r.

tions already proven, closing with well-defined reasons, and also responding with the use of the same order'.[67] At other times, the most important rules of conduct in a disputation were enumerated in more detail. Before the dispute in Vilnius (2 June 1599), for instance, the 'manner and order of speaking' was publicly read out before the dispute itself by one of the 'designated Moderators', the Chancellor of the Grand Duchy of Lithuania, Leo Sapieha:

> 1. Aby dwa dysputatorowie mówili, a nikt się inszy nie wtrącał bez pozwolenia Ich Mości Panów Moderatorów.
>
> 2. Aby sami Panowie Ministrowie argumentowali, a inszego na swe miejsce nie kładli wedle *pacta* i zezwolenia samych Panów Ministrów.
>
> 3. Niech będą odcięte prefacyje, aklamacyje, kazania i wszelkie długie mowy, ale raczej krótkim argumentem rzecz zawiązać, co służy i do pojęcia i do zbudowania.
>
> 4. Dowody mają bydź z Pisma św. A jeśli Panowie Ministrowie chcą *ex Patribus*, to im wolno, ale mają tez ich *testimonia* przeciwko sobie przyjmować.
>
> 5. Mają Panowie Ministrowie *directe* przeciwko podanym artykułom mówić, a nie inszą rzecz wtrącać, aż to co podano pierwej odprawiwszy.[68]

> (1. That the two disputants speak for themselves, and no one else interfere without the permission of the Gentlemen Moderators.
>
> 2. That the Ministers themselves should argue, and not substitute another in their place, according to the *pacta* and private arrangements of the Ministers themselves.
>
> 3. Let preambles, acclamations, homilies, and all lengthy speeches be cut off; rather, let the matter be tied up with a brief argument, which serves both understanding and formation.
>
> 4. The evidence is to be from the Scriptures. And should the Ministers desire *ex Patribus*, they are allowed, but they also have to accept such *testimonia* against themselves.

---

[67] [Powodowski] 1592, f. A7r.
[68] [Śmiglecki] 1599, f. A2v.

> 5. The Ministers are to speak *directe* against the articles given, and not introduce any other matter until that which was first given is dispatched.)

Issues that invite further systematic research are how the method of disputation was adapted for use in the Polish language and applied to local religious controversies.

Conclusion

In the sixteenth-century Polish-Lithuanian Commonwealth, the *disputatio* was still understood according to the mediaeval tradition, as a tool for seeking and establishing the truth.[69] The heuristic aims of the disputation seem to have served religious controversies and the testing of dogmatic differences well. At the same time, the advent of the Reformation forced the dispute to function in circumstances that had changed since the Middle Ages: now disputes could take place outside academies and have other than strictly academic objectives. The religious freedom in the Commonwealth guaranteed by the Warsaw Confederation (28 January 1573) encouraged the quest for a new formula, or set of rules, for the *disputatio*. The transformation of the *disputatio* did not happen without controversy, which reflected the conflicting expectations that the different parties had regarding the aims of the disputation in its new, vernacular form. The need for mutual agreement regarding the terms of each planned disputation reveals the participants' hopes and concerns about admitting to the *disputatio* simple people (including women), who may have been unfamiliar with either dogmatic issues or with a strongly formalised, dialectic method. The risk of riots and mob violence against the disputants became a real problem. As we know, controversy also grew up around the adequacy of the syllogistic method for disputes about faith and for use with the Polish language, which was different in its syntax and lexis from Latin. In the new conditions, there was also no master (*magister*) who had in scholastic contexts provided an authoritative resolution to the dispute in the form of a *determinatio magistri*. It was the audi-

---

[69] Ryszka-Kurczab 2018, p. 124–127.

ences, listening to vernacular disputations in churches, congregational meeting houses, or private homes, who in a sense became the arbiters of the disputations. The decision to recast the *disputatio* as a tool available to a wider audience means that the aims of conducting disputations as reported in the sources — 'seeking the truth of salvation', and 'showing listeners who speaks the truth' — begin in this period to coexist with the aims of religious propaganda.

Bibliography

Primary Sources

Dysputacje arjan polskich, ed. S. Kot (1935), in *Reformacja w Polsce*, 7, p. 341–370.

Dysputacyj braci polskich katalog, ed. S. Kot (1939), in *Reformacja w Polsce*, 9–10, p. 456–464.

Marcin Gradowski, *Relacyja prawdziwa dysputacyjej nowogrodzkiej*, Wilno: Józef Karcan, 1616.

Daniel Mikołajewski, *Dysputacyja wileńska, którą miał ks. Marcin Śmiglecki Soc[ietatis] Jesu z ks. Danielem Mikołajewskim, sługą Słowa Bożego de prymatu Petri*, Toruń: Andrzej Koteniusz, 1599.

Jakub Niemojewski, *Diatribe albo kolacyja przyjacielska z ks. jezuitami poznańskiemi o przedniejsze różnice wiary krzescijańskiej czasu tego*, [Grodzisk: Melchior Nering, 1579].

[Hieronim Powodowski], *Dysputacyja wtóra księdza Hieronima Powodowskiego z śmigielskimi różnobożany. O trzech personach w jednymże Bóstwie i o krzczeniu małych dziatek. Odprawowana w Śmiglu 2. dnia lipca roku 1592*, Poznań: Barbara Wolrab i dziedzice Jana Wolraba, 1592.

Jan Przylepski [Adrian Radzymiński?], *Dysputacyja lubelska ks. Adryjana Radzymińskiego [...] z Statoriuszem ministrem nowokrzczeńskim o przedwieczności Bóstwa Pana i Boga naszego Jezusa Chrystusa dnia 22 i 23 maja roku 1592*, Kraków: Jakub Siebeneicher, 1592.

Piotr Statorius-Stojeński the Younger, *Dysputacyja lubelska Piotra Statoriusa sługi słowa Bożego o przedwiecznym Bóstwie Syna Bożego z ks. Adryjanem Radzimińskim jezuitą*, [Kraków]: Aleksy Rodecki, [1592].

Sebastian Szamotulski [Hieronim Powodowski], *Dysputacyja ks. Hieronima Powodowskiego z ministrem zboru nowoariańskiego śmigielskiego Janem Krotowicjuszem, o niektórych artykułach przed-*

wiecznego Bóstwa Syna Bożego i Trójce Przenaświętszej, tamże w zborze śmigielskim odprawowana [...] *dnia 27. grudnia w roku 1581*, [Poznań: Jan Wolrab, 1581].

Marcin Śmiglecki, *Dysputacyja wileńska, którą miał ks. Marcin Śmiglecki S.J. z ministrami ewangelickimi 2 Junii w r. 1599 o jednej widomej głowie Kościoła Bożego*, Wilno: Paweł Wołłowicz, 1599.

[Marcin Śmiglecki], *Dysputacyja wileńska, którą miał ks. Marcin Śmiglecki Societatis Iesu z ministrami ewangelickimi* [...] *o jednej widomej głowie Kościoła Bożego*, Kraków: Drukarnia Łazarzowa, 1599.

Łukasz Wądłowski [Jan Zygrowiusz?], *Dysputacyja nowogrodzka odprawowana Roku Pańskiego 1616 dnia 9. Stycznia*, Lubcz [Piotr Blastus Kmita], 1616.

[Wojciech z Kalisza], *Krótkie a prawdziwe opisanie dysputacyjej, która była w Lewartowie anno 1592 d. 13 i 14 stycznia, w której ks. Radzymiński theses dał, a Calissius rektor lewartowski i ks. Franciszek minister kurowski i pan Jan Niemojewski opugnowali*, Kraków: Sebastian Sternacki, 1592.

Jakub Wujek, *Dialysis, to jest rozwiązanie albo rozebranie asercyi pana Jakuba Niemojewskiego z dowodami jego naprzeciwko jezuitom poznańskim wydanych*, Poznań: Jan Wolrab, 1580.

Secondary Sources

Angelelli, I. (1970), 'The Techniques of Disputation in the History of Logic', in *Journal of Philosophy* 67, p. 800–815.

Chang, K. (2004), 'From Oral Disputation to Written Text. The Transformation of the Disputation in Early Modern Europe', in *History of Universities* 19/2, p. 129–187.

Drzymała, K. (1963), 'Bracia Polscy zwani arianami', in *Studia Theologica Varsaviensia*, 2, p. 241–306.

Drzymała, K. (1964), 'Marcin Śmiglecki obrońca prymatu św. Piotra i jego następców', in *Ruch Biblijny i Liturgiczny*, XVII/4, p. 215–320.

Drzymała, K. (1979), 'Dysputa wileńska Marcina Śmigleckiego z ewangelikami w r. 1599', in *Studia Historyczne*, 22/3, p. 379–399.

Drzymała, K. (1981), *Ks. Marcin Śmiglecki T. J.*, Kraków: Prowincja Polski Południowej Towarzystwa Jezusowego.

Dworzaczek, W. (1979), 'Andrzej Opaliński', in E. Rostworowski (ed.) *Polski Słownik Biograficzny*, XXIV, Wrocław: Zakład Narodowy im. Ossolińskich, p. 13–16.

Felipe, D. L. (1991), 'The Post-medieval Ars Disputandi' (unpublished doctoral thesis, University of Texas at Austin).

Fuchs, Th. (1995), *Konfession und Gespräch. Typologie und Funktion der Religionsgespräche in der Reformationszeit*, Köln: Böhlau Verlag (Norm und Struktur, 4).

Jocher, A. (1842), *Obraz bibliograficzno-historyczny literatury i nauk w Polsce od wprowadzenia do niej druku po rok 1830 włącznie, z pism Janockiego, Bentkowskiego, Ludwika Sobolewskiego, Ossolińskiego, Juszyńsiego, Jana Winc[enta] i Jerzego Sam. Bandtków*, vol. II., Wilno: Drukarnia Jerzego Zawadzkiego.

Kamieniecki, J. (2009), 'Zasady prowadzenia dyskursu religijnego zawarte w staropolskich tekstach polemicznych', in M. Sarnowski & W. Wysoczański (eds), *Wyraz i zdanie w językach słowiańskich. Opis, konfrontacja, przekład*, 7, Wrocław: Wydawnictwo Uniwersytetu Wrocławskiego (Acta Universitatis Wratislaviensis, 3159; Slavica Wratislaviensia, 150), p. 93–100.

Kempa, T. (2016), *Konflikty wyznaniowe w Wilnie od początku reformacji do końca XVII wieku*, Toruń: Wydawnictwo Naukowe Uniwersytetu Mikołaja Kopernika.

Korolko, M. (1974), *Klejnot swobodnego sumienia: polemika wokół konfederacji warszawskiej w latach 1573–1658*, Warszawa: Instytut Wydawniczy 'Pax'.

Kot, S. (1932) *Ideologia polityczna i społeczna braci polskich zwanych arianami*, Warszawa: Kasa im. Mianowskiego Instytut Popierania Nauki.

Kowalska, H. (1972), 'Hermolaus Ligęza z Bobrku', in E. Rostworowski (ed.) *Polski Słownik Biograficzny*, XVII, Wrocław: Zakład Narodowy im. Ossolińskich, p. 315–316.

Lehmann, J. (1937), *Konfesja sandomierska na tle innych konfesji w Polsce XVI wieku*, Warszawa: skład Księgarnia W. Mietke.

Luszczynska, M. (2018), *Politics of Polemics: Marcin Czechowic on the Jews*, Berlin: De Gruyter Oldenbourg.

Maciuszko, J. T. (1984), *Konfederacja warszawska 1973 roku. Geneza, pierwsze lata obowiązywania*, Warszawa: Chrześcijańska Akademia Teologiczna.

Maciuszko, J. T. (1997), 'Proces konfesjonalizacji w Europie i w Polsce. Kontekst wyznaniowy synodu generalnego toruńskiego w 1595', in *Czasy Nowożytne*, 2, p. 17–26.

Meller, K. (2016), 'Fatalne skutki pewnej "kolacyi" Jakuba Niemojewskiego z jezuitami poznańskimi, czyli poznańska polifonia wydawnicza w XVI wieku', in J. Borowczyk, L. Marzec & Z. Kopeć (eds), *Poznań pisarek i pisarzy*, Poznań: Wydawnictwo 'Poznańskie Studia Polonistyczne', (Biblioteka Literacka 'Poznańskich Studiów Polonistycznych', 70), p. 85–100.

Natoński, B. (2003), *Humanizm jezuicki i teologia pozytywno-kontrowersyjna od XVI do XVIII wieku. Nauczanie i piśmiennictwo*, Kraków: Wydawnictwo WAM (Klasycy jezuickiej historiografii, 2).

Niedźwiedź, J. (2012), *Kultura literacka Wilna (1323–1655). Retoryczna organizacja miasta*, Kraków: TAiWPN (Biblioteka Literatury Pogranicza, 20).

Ogonowski, Z. (1960), *Socynianizm polski*, Warszawa: Wiedza Powszechna (Myśli i Ludzie 2 Filozofia Nowożytna i Współczesna).

Ogonowski, Z. (2015), *Socynianizm. Dzieje, poglądy, oddziaływanie*, Warszawa: Oficyna Wydawnicza Aspra-JR: Instytut Historii Nauki im. Ludwika i Aleksanda Birkenmajerów Polskiej Akademii Nauk.

Rodda, J. (2014), *Public Religious Disputation in England, 1558–1626*, London: Routledge (St Andrews Studies in Reformation History).

Ryszka-Kurczab, M. (2018), '*May every lover of truth find it through reading*. Manners of Authenticating the Message in Sixteenth-Century Accounts of Polish Religious Disputations', in *Terminus*, Special Issue, p. 105–136; https://www.ejournals.eu/Terminus/2018/Terminus-2018-SpecialIsuue/art/13286/ (accessed 20.03.2021).

Salomonowicz, S. (1974), 'Geneza i treść uchwał Konfederacji Warszawskiej', in *Odrodzenie i Reformacja w Polsce*, 19, p. 7–30.

Scheib, O. (2009), *Die innerchristlichen Religionsgespräche im Abendland*, 3 vols, Wiesbaden: Harrassowitz Verlag (Wolfenbütteler Forschungen, 122).

Sipayłło, M. (ed.) (1972), *Akta synodów różnowierczych*, Warszawa: Wydawnictwa Uniwersytetu Warszawskiego, vol. II: 1560–1570.

Sipayłło, M. (ed.) (1983), *Akta synodów różnowierczych*, Warszawa: Państwowe Wydawnictwo Naukowe. vol. III: Małopolska 1571–1632.

Stec, W. (1988), *Literacki kształt polskich polemik antyjezuickich z lat 1578–1625*, Białystok: Dział Wydawnictw Filii UW (Rozprawy Uniwersytetu Warszawskiego, 340).

Szczucki, L. & J. Tazbir (1978), 'Jan Niemojewski', in E. Rostworowski (ed.) *Polski Słownik Biograficzny*, XXIII, Wrocław: Zakład Narodowy im. Ossolińskich, p. 13–16.

Tazbir, J. (1956), 'Walka z Braćmi Polskimi w dobie kontrreformacji', in *Odrodzenie i Reformacja w Polsce*, 1, p. 165–207.

Tazbir, J. (1965), 'Polemika Jakuba Niemojewskiego z Jezuitami poznańskimi', in G. Labuda (ed.) *Munera Poznaniensia. Księga pamiątkowa Uniwersytetu im. Adama Mickiewicza w Poznaniu dla uczczenia 600-lecia założenia Uniwersytetu Jagiellońskiego*, Poznań: Uniwersytet im. Adama Mickiewicza, p. 236–260.

Tazbir, J. (1967), *Państwo bez stosów: szkice z dziejów tolerancji w Polsce XVI i XVII wieku*, Warszawa: Wydawnictwo Iskry.

Tazbir, J. (1973), *Dzieje polskiej tolerancji*, Warszawa: 'Interpress'.

Tazbir, J. (1980), 'Rola żywego słowa w polskiej propagandzie wyznaniowej', in *Kwartalnik historyczny*, 87, p. 291–309.

Tworek, S. (1960), 'Dysputa lewartowska w 1592 roku', in *Rocznik Lubelski*, 3, p. 51–62.

Wajsblum M. (1927), *Dyteiści Małopolscy (Stanisław Farnowski i Farnowianie)*, Kraków: Krakowska Spółka Wydawnicza.

Weijers, O. (2013), *In Search of the Truth: A History of Disputation Techniques from Antiquity to Early Modern Times*, Turnhout: Brepols (Studies on the Faculty of Arts; History and Influence, 1).

Zarzycki, Z. (ed.) (2004), *Historia prawa wyznaniowego. Wybór tekstów źródłowych*, Kraków: Oficyna Wydawnicza AFM (Materiały Dydaktyczne – Krakowska Szkoła Wyższa im. Andrzeja Frycza Modrzewskiego, 7).

Zarzycki, Z. (2010), 'Wolność religijna w pierwszych polskich konstytucjach do połowy XIX wieku', in A. Mazglewski, M. Ordon & P. Stanisz (eds), *Studia z prawa wyznaniowego*, 13, p. 25–44.

Abstract

The atmosphere of religious tolerance in the Polish-Lithuanian Commonwealth, guaranteed by the Warsaw Confederation Act (signed on 28 January 1573), emboldened adherents to proclaim freely their own religious doctrines, even the most radical, such as Unitarianism. Religious disputations, whether they were held in Latin or in a vernacular language, had been increasingly popular since the 1570s and became a useful tool for conducting doctrinal polemics. The rules that governed *disputatio*, which were widely known from schools and universities, were undoubtedly a point of reference for how disputes were organised and conducted, though under the changed conditions of greater religious pluralism many of these rules had to be rethought, and often renegotiated and re-established.

This paper deals with an issue never previously researched: it surveys the rules for public vernacular religious disputations in Poland

and Lithuania during the later sixteenth and early seventeenth centuries. The paper examines new elements of protocol not present in the previous *modus operandi* of the disputation, such as the greater variation in rank and prestige of people initiating disputations, the duration and venue of disputations, controversies concerning the use of the national language for public disputation, doubts about the formalised and syllogistic method of disputation, and the risk of public unrest against dissidents at vernacular disputations.

In Poland and Lithuania during the second half of the sixteenth century and the seventeenth century, declarations that the aim of the disputation was to 'seek the truth' were still widespread; nevertheless the modifications made to the circumstances and rules of vernacular religious disputations went a long way towards transforming them into an efficacious instrument of religious propaganda.

ELENA DAHLBERG

Uppsala University

LATIN VERSUS THE VERNACULAR IN SEVENTEENTH-CENTURY UPPSALA
JOHANNES SCHEFFERUS' LATIN ATTACK ON OLOF RUDBECK'S SWEDISH DISSECTION PROGRAMME

Academia has always been conflictual, and, like today, the disagreements that took place in the early modern university were usually multi-layered.[1] This contribution discusses one such complex dispute that erupted in seventeenth-century Uppsala. It involved two of the city's most established scholars, viz. the polymath Olof Rudbeck the Elder (b. 1630 – d. 1702) and the philologist Johannes Schefferus (b. 1621 – d. 1679). Rudbeck's decision, in May 1677, to use the Swedish language for his invitation to attend a dissection of a human body ran overtly counter to the university's Latinate practices. Johannes Schefferus was the first to react. In a letter to one of the university secretaries, he listed several items in order to demonstrate why Latin was superior to the vernacular in a context like this. There is no doubt that his criticism was fully justified: Latin was the standard language of the sciences. Yet closer inspection reveals that these two academic celebrities employed and tailored their texts to fan the flames of their other quarrels.

The present article approaches the controversies between Rudbeck and Schefferus from three different angles. First, the article examines the background to Schefferus' criticism of Rudbeck's linguistic preferences. Second, the article explores how these two

---

[1] The research presented here has been made possible thanks to a generous research grant from the Åke Wiberg Foundation, to which I am most grateful. I am also grateful to Hans Helander (Uppsala) and Sofia Guthrie (Warwick) for their valuable comments on an earlier draft of this article, including their remarks on my translations from Latin. Special thanks to the anonymous referees, whose comments helped to improve my manuscript.

scholars' disagreements in other fields affected their debate on the role of Latin in academia. Third, the article considers their respective choices of medium. What this contribution adds to the previous surveys of the conflict is a deeper inquiry into the role of Latin in the early modern university and an examination of the quarrel's humanist characteristics.[2]

Rudbeck, Schefferus, and Verelius: The Superstars of Swedish Academia

Olof Rudbeck was born into a learned family.[3] His father Johannes Rudbeckius (b. 1581 – d. 1646) was a bishop, who before assuming his clerical position had held several professorships, first the chair of mathematics, then the chair of Hebrew, and later the professorship of theology, all of them at Uppsala University. In 1613, Rudbeck's father had moreover served as that university's rector. As a child, Olof came to live with his elder brothers, who were students in Uppsala; they would become his first teachers. After absorbing the newest intellectual and scholarly trends during his own time as a student at the university, his international breakthrough came in the summer of 1653 with the publication of his *Noua exercitatio anatomica exhibens ductus hepaticos aquosos et uasa glandarum serosa*. In that work, Rudbeck described his discovery of the lymphatic system and gave a tentative analysis of its function. Even though there were some who questioned the study's primacy, the importance of Rudbeck's observations was widely recognised.[4]

During his long career at Uppsala, Rudbeck held a chair of medicine (appointed in 1660) and for several terms acted as the university's *rector magnificus*. Interested in architecture, he saw to it that the old university building was equipped with a mod-

---

[2] The fullest surveys of this famous dispute at Uppsala are Annerstedt 1908, p. 172–174; Lindroth 1975, p. 311–315.

[3] For Rudbeck's biography, see Eriksson 2002; Eriksson 1994, p. 1–12.

[4] Rudbeck's study appeared right after the publication of Thomas Bartholin's *Vasa Lymphatica*, which led to a feud between the two. Nevertheless, the *Noua exercitatio* was included in the Dutch physician Siboldus Hemsterhuis' *Messis aurea triennalis, exhibens anatomica nouissima et utilissima experimenta* (1654), which was an overview of the key studies of the lymphatic vessels issued between 1651 and 1653. Von Hofsten 1939; Eriksson 2002, p. 57–69.

ern anatomical theatre. This construction would become known across Europe for innovative features such as cleverly designed skylights that provided the dissection room with natural light.

In addition to anatomy, architecture, and engineering, Rudbeck's scholarly interests included mechanics, astronomy, botany, music, and perhaps most famously archaeology. His inquiries in the latter field would result in a four-volume opus entitled *Atlantica*, in which he contended that Atlantis had been situated in Sweden and that Graeco-Roman civilisation was indebted to a Scandinavian precedent. Rudbeck's methodological tools were philological as well as archaeological. Even though some aspects of his approach were dubious, many of them were in line with contemporary practices of antiquarian research carried out on the continent.[5] Relying on earlier historiographers such as Johannes Magnus, who in turn drew on old sources such as Jordanes' *Getica*, Rudbeck explained that the Swedish people originated from the old Scyths and Goths. The first volume of the *Atlantica* would not appear until 1679, but many of its fantastic arguments had been disseminated through Rudbeck's lectures and letters prior to its publication.[6]

Johannes Schefferus grew up in Strasbourg in the family of the German merchant Johan Scheffer.[7] The son Johannes began his university studies in his home city and later pursued a learned peregrination abroad. Upon his return home, he published his first work, *De uarietate nauium* (1643), a study of the ancient rowing galleys. It was immediately recognised as proof of a high scholarly acumen. In 1647, at the age of twenty-seven, Schefferus was invited to Sweden to become professor Skytteanus. The chair was unique. Established in 1622 through a donation by the renowned diplomat Johan Skytte (b. 1577 – d. 1645), the professorship implied training of future government officials and diplomats.[8] On two occasions, in 1658 and 1664, Schefferus also acted as the university's rector. His scholarly production was both prolific and

---

[5] Momigliano 1950. Cf. Eriksson 1994, p. 87–95.

[6] Thus, the Italian diplomat Lorenzo Magalotti knew of the book's content before it was officially released. Eriksson 2002, p. 270.

[7] The first full account of Schefferus' life is Fant 1782. See also Lewin 1985, p. 49–58.

[8] Lewin 1985, p. 9–29; Ingermarsdotter 2011, p. 241–246.

versatile. His 1665 edition of a fragment of Petronius' *Cena Trimalchionis* is considered to have laid the foundation for critical editions of classical texts.[9] When the *Collegium Antiquitatum* — whose task was to document material relating to Sweden's history — received its official instructions in 1677, Schefferus became one of its four assessors. The methodological tools that Schefferus had used for studying classical antiquity were now applied to his study of Sweden's past. His famous *Lapponia* (1673) is an example of his careful antiquarian research. It was in this capacity, as a scholar of Swedish antiquities, that Schefferus published in 1666 a work entitled *Upsalia antiqua*, which contained an extensive discussion of the city's topography. Relying on sources such as Ericus Olai's *Chronica regni Gothorum* from the fifteenth century, Schefferus concluded that the old pagan temple of Uppsala had been situated in the place now occupied by the Trinity Church in downtown Uppsala. This proposed location conflicted with the hypothesis advanced by Rudbeck's teacher and friend Olof Verelius (b. 1618 – d. 1682), who believed that the old Viking temple had been located outside the city proper.[10] While Schefferus' methodology may have been unflawed, in this particular case his proposition turned out to be wrong.

Olof Verelius was a professor of Swedish antiquity, who had recently gained renown for his pioneering studies of Icelandic literature.[11] His 1672 edition of the *Hervarar saga* proved these texts to be an invaluable source for the pre-modern history of the Nordic peoples' language. Verelius had also launched the theory that the Hyperboreans were the Swedes' ancient ancestors. All these theories found an eager supporter in Olof Rudbeck, who adopted them in his *Atlantica*. Moreover, Rudbeck assisted Verelius in his work by producing two maps for his edition of the *Hervarar saga*.

In his comments on the *Hervarar Saga*, Verelius contested the idea that the pagan temple had been situated within Uppsala proper. Even though Schefferus was not mentioned explicitly, it

---

[9] Forssberg Malm 2015; see also Grafton 2001, p. 211–213.

[10] The dispute that evolved around these two theories concerning the pagan temple of Uppsala is delineated in Annerstedt 1891; Schück 1933, p. 322–351.

[11] On Verelius' scholarship, see Lindroth 1975, p. 275–281.

could be understood that Verelius was referring to that scholar's *Upsalia antiqua*. In the following year (1673), Schefferus issued his edition of the chronicle of Uppsala's archbishops, *Chronicon de archiepiscopis [...] ecclesiae Upsaliensis*. There, Schefferus slightly altered his hypothesis concerning the location of the old temple, but still placed it within the city proper and stubbornly disagreed with any opposing view. This edition pushed the debate to a new stage. In 1677, Verelius published additional notes on the *Hervarar saga*. The work was entitled *Auctarium notarum* and this time Verelius openly named Schefferus. These additional remarks must have been composed much earlier than 1677, as they are clearly a response to Schefferus' edition of the *Chronicon de archiepiscopis*, and the date of the composition given in the printed item is said to be 1674. It was during this time that Rudbeck was finalising the first part of his *Atlantica*, where the old temple would be one of his main concerns. It is the more intriguing to see that Verelius' *Auctarium notarum* was dedicated to Rudbeck. Furthermore, it was with Rudbeck's help that Verelius' new work was approved for printing, despite its blatant *ad hominem* attacks on their colleague.

Just months after the publication of Verelius' *Auctarium notarum*, Schefferus released a new treatise, once again addressing the problem of the location of the old temple. Bearing the title *De situ et uocabulo Upsaliae [...] epistola defensoria*, it came out in April 1677. There, Schefferus openly attacked Verelius and implicitly Rudbeck. It was also during the spring of 1677 that another conflict blossomed in Uppsala, and it involved the same three scholars, Rudbeck, Schefferus, and Verelius.

Breaching the Code:
Rudbeck's Swedish Dissection Programme from 1677

On the first of May 1677, the professors and students of Uppsala University encountered something relatively unusual in their otherwise Latinate world: Olof Rudbeck greeted them with an invitation to attend a dissection of a human body, a programme that was composed in Swedish.[12] It was not only the language that

---

[12] Since classical antiquity, the word *programma* had signified a written announcement. In the early modern university, *programmata* were printed to

failed to follow the university's strict norms, but also Rudbeck's drastic formulations: stuffed with frivolous phrasings, it seemed to mock the venerable conventions of that prestigious seat of learning. The programme's tone was set in its first sentence. This is how the initial part of the invitation reads:

> Gunstige Läsare, Jag hade wäl nu, såsom åtskillige gånger tillförenne, ärna budit eder, Gode Herrar, med ett latinskt anslag; men såsom iag uthi inga böcker, ännu har funnit, at Aristoteles eller Cicero hafwa giort det Giötiska eller Skytiska språket, som likwäl är det älsta, den äran, och den studerande ungdomen til några dygdens öfningar derigenom kallat: altså vill jag Aristoteli, Ciceroni och hela des anhang, den vanliga äran, denna gången afbryta. Och såsom de på sitt modersmål, iag nu på goda rena Svenskan vårt moderssmål, eder alla Goda Herrar, sampteligen biuder, att i wilien tillse, huru en Menniskia på det Anatomiska bordet, sin prydna eder till nytta och gagn, i dag klockan 2 afläggia skall.[13]

> (Benevolent readers,
> I would have, like a number of times before, readily invited you, my dear gentlemen, by means of an announcement in the Latin language, but as I have not yet found in any books that Aristotle or Cicero have done the Gothic or Scythian language (which is also the oldest one) the same honour, and that they have thereby invited young students to put their virtue into practice, I want therefore this time to stop the usual credit to Aristotle, Cicero and their whole entourage. And as they did in their mother tongue, I am inviting you all, my dear gentlemen, now in the good, pure Swedish, our mother tongue, to watch how a human being, to be of service and benefit to you, will take off his adornment today at 2 o'clock on the anatomical table.)

Rudbeck's nationalist sentiment is unmistakable: he argues that there is nothing wrong with teaching in Swedish. The reader

---

announce events such as disputations, installations, and the like. The historical development of the *programma* is delineated in Neumann 2005. This is how Neumann describes the early modern programme: 'Aufs Ganze gesehen dienen die ‹programmata› also als öffentliche Bekanntmachungen von Informationen über die akademisch-universitären Organisationsformen oder Veranstaltungen'.

[13] Quoted from Annerstedt 1893, p. 148 f. The original programme is kept in the special collections of Uppsala University Library.

could not fail to note that Rudbeck was referring to the theories recently launched by Verelius. According to these, the Swedish language had Japhethan-Scythian roots and was thus more venerable than any other language in the world. The linguistic theory advanced by Verelius and later embraced by Rudbeck followed the latest trend in early modern studies of language. As a preceptor of two young aristocrats, Verelius had visited, among other seats of learning, Leiden and must have therefore been familiar with the pre-comparative studies that had been carried out by Dutch scholars. Among these early modern 'comparatists' we find Johannes Goropius Becanus (b. 1519 – d. 1573), who believed that Dutch was older than Hebrew.[14] These developments prompted the idea that the vernacular could be used in the areas where Latin was traditionally applied, since the vernacular had the full capacity of expressing any concept or term. For example, the Flemish mathematician Simon Stevin (b. 1548 – d. 1629) had promoted Dutch as the language of the sciences and contended that his mother tongue was perfectly appropriate for the creation of neologisms to accommodate new scholarly developments.[15]

Further, Rudbeck's invitation explained the educational aspect of the dissection that was going to take place in the anatomical theatre. He paraphrased a sentence from Ex. 2.32: 'Strip yourself of your ornament, child of Israel, by mount Horeb', words that were read from the pulpits during public prayers in churches across the country.[16] The passage referred to the Israelites' request that Aaron make them a god out of their jewellery. When given a golden calf made of their ornaments, the Israelites begin to worship the image and thus expose their corruption. Rudbeck clarified his comparison in a way that might seem strained to the modern reader: the inside of the human being is like its exterior. Hence a person mourning a child's death will never put on a colourful garment. Rudbeck was outraged by his own compatriots' way of expressing their sorrow during the hard times suffered by their fatherland as a result of the ongoing war between Sweden

---

[14] For assessments of Becanus as a linguist, see Van Hal 2010, chapter 3; De Clercq, Swiggers & Van Hal 2009, p. 553–554.

[15] Cohen 2015, p. 158–160.

[16] 'Lägg aff tin prydning tu Israels baarn wid Horebs bärg.'

and Denmark. This observation led Rudbeck to ask rhetorically why people put on layers of clothes. He argued: 'We live up to the old saying: *Nitimur in uetitum*'.[17] His point becomes more and more farfetched, as he says that a similar multitude of layers will be found inside our bodies.[18]

After using this rather unconventional metaphor of the human body as a microcosm, Rudbeck compared its various parts to garments. Thus, the omasum and the abomasum are said to have the appearance of sleeves, whereas the mesentery reminds Rudbeck of a jester cap:

> [Ty] kommer alla up, så skola i få see, att de tre och fyrdubbla ärmstrumpor finnas igän i slarfsyltan, som kallas hoos Anatomicos omasus och abomasus: Narrkappan finnes igen uti tarmmalen (mesenterio). Purgationskiortelen finnes igen i isterhinnan (omento). Släpen uti productione mesenterii och omenti ad intenstinum rectum; hwilken när han lös slipper, giör han tarmlop (herniam). Flors-hufwan i hiernhwarfwe, rete mirabili: afhuggna armar eller armkorgar, uti musculo marsupio carnoso.'

(For, if everyone attends, you will see that those threefold and fourfold sleeves are to be found in the stomach [19] that among *Anatomici* are referred to as *omasus* and *abomasus*,[20] that there is a jester cap inside the mesentery, that a purgative skirt [21] can be found in the lace net (*omentum*); that there is a train [22] in *productione mesenterii* and *omenti ad intestinum rectum*,[23] which if it comes off, results in intestinal breakage (*hernia*).

---

[17] Here, Rudbeck reused Ovid's *Amores* 3,4,17.

[18] Eriksson 2002, p. 194–198, provides a thought-provoking analysis of Rudbeck's text by suggesting that any theatre was a potential venue for the teaching of morals and that Olof Rudbeck had adopted this view of the theatre's educational purpose from his father who was a very devout man.

[19] Rudbeck uses the word *slarfsylta* ('mince meat'), which probably refers to the stomach, or perhaps rather to its contents.

[20] *Omasus* and *abomasus* (*omasum* and *abomasum*) normally refer to the third and fourth stomachs of a ruminant.

[21] 'Purgative skirt' seems to refer to the greater omentum that in medicine books is described as a large, apron-like, fold of visceral peritoneum that attaches to the greater curvature of the stomach. Cf. Drake, Wayne Vogl & Mitchell 2014, p. 307–308.

[22] I.e. a train that trails on the ground behind the wearer.

[23] Viz. in the continuation of the mesentery and the omentum to the rectum.

And the fine veil of the brain membrane, the *rete mirabile*. And detached arms or short and wide sleeves [24] will be found in the *musculo marsupio carnoso*.[25])

This imagery heralds the closing part of the invitation, according to which not every person in the audience could be expected to master Latin. In addition, the Swedish language was better suited for a situation like this one:

> Iag wet wäl om iag detta alt, skulle hafwa utfört, på latiniska och anatomiska ordsät, hafwer minsta delen aff den gunstige läsaren förståt. Där till med, så hafwa, den härlige prydnats ord, aff svenskan eij kunnat til latin göras.
>
> (I know well that if I had expressed all this in the Latin and anatomical terminology, then not many of the benevolent readers would have understood. Moreover, to translate the words describing the splendorous ornament from Swedish into Latin has been impossible.)

What was to be exposed at the anatomical theatre, says Rudbeck, was our fragility and pitiful condition. He went on to call upon the Lord to provide humans with a better (i.e. heavenly) garb.[26] At the end of the invitation, Rudbeck announced that the procedure would be performed by his colleague Petrus Hoffwenius and

---

[24] In the SAOB (The Dictionary of the Swedish Academy), the sense of the word *armkorgar* (with the sole occurrence from our text here) is supposed (with a question mark!) to be 'short and wide sleeves'.

[25] The term *musculus carnosus* ('fleshy muscle'), is used by, e.g. Vesalius in reference to a muscle stretching from the neck to the *clauicula*. The term is now obsolete. The sense of *marsupium*, the pouch of marsupial animals, in this context is not clear to me. Did it make sense to the readers of the programme? For further discussion of the analogy of the human body with the cosmos as perceived by Rudbeck, see Dunér 2008, p. 125–126.

[26] 'Kommer derföre flitigt tillstädes, och tilseer, huru denna menniskian, på detta anatomiska bärget, sin prydna aflägga skal: där wij ögonskinligen få se wår underliga tillsammansatte konstige bräckeligheet och älendigheet, och må innerligen där aff lära att sucka til Gudh den högsta, att han nådigst måtte gifwa oss en gång i stellet den oförvanskeliga prydna, som är utan smitto och fläckiar.' (Therefore, take the trouble to attend and watch when this human being, on this anatomical mound, will strip off his adornment: there we will get to see with our own eyes our peculiar and cleverly assembled fragility and wretchedness and will sincerely learn from this to make a sighing appeal to the most sublime God to have the mercy to instead give us that immaculate adornment that is untainted and without blemish.)

excused himself by saying that he could not watch all 'this fresh beef', presumably a reference to the entrails of the dissected body. Rudbeck's text clearly aimed to produce some kind of amusement among his readers, but it also contained a pronounced criticism of the university's formality and its obsession with Latin.

It did not take long for the first critical remark to appear. On the fourth of May 1677, viz. three days after Rudbeck's announcement, Johannes Schefferus dispatched a letter to one of the university secretaries.[27] In it, he listed seven complaints against Rudbeck's Swedish text. Of those, four dealt with its author's choice of language. The letter began in the following way:

> *In multiplice sum aere tuo propter et ad finem curandum opusculum meum et exemplaria huc missa. Ea diuisa sunt statim inter amicos. O. Rudbeckio nolui mittere, ne uiderer id per exprobrationem facere. Et scio accepisse statim a socero meo plus ipsi fauente quam mihi.*

> (I am most grateful to you for helping me with the completion of my little work and for sending the copies here. Accordingly, they have been distributed among my friends. I was not willing to send it to Olof Rudbeck, in order not to seem as if I was doing this to reproach him. And I know that he has received a copy from my father-in-law, who is his supporter rather than mine.)

The work that Schefferus was referring to was his *De situ et uocabulo Upsaliae* [...] *epistola defensoria*, which had just been published and in which he discredited Verelius for his theory concerning the location of the pagan temple. The father-in-law was the professor *honorarius iuris* Johannes Loccenius (b. 1598 – d. 1677), to whose daughter Schefferus was married. Loccenius had held the Skytt ean chair in the years 1628–1648 and was now one of the assessors of the *Collegium Antiquitatum* together with Schefferus and Verelius. It was well known that he was an enthusiastic admirer of Rudbeck, to the obvious disappointment of his son-in-law.[28]

After this introduction, Schefferus moves on to his discussion of Rudbeck's frivolous invitation:

---

[27] For a transcript of the letter, see Annerstedt 1910, p. 194–195. With all probability, it was addressed to the secretary Erik Palmskiöld.

[28] Cf. Lindroth 1975, p. 285.

> *Mitto hic inuicem hoc programma, si forte aliunde ad te nondum peruenit. In quo uelim notes:*
>
> *1. Scriptum sermone Suedico, quod nec Upsaliae nec in ulla alia academia factitatum, non sine dedecore academiae, ex solo praepostero nouitatis studio.*
>
> (In turn, I am hereby sending you this programme, in case it has not yet reached you through someone else. I would like you to notice that
>
> 1. It is written in the Swedish tongue, which is not the practice at Uppsala and not at any other university, an apparent disgrace to our academy, solely [used] because of a preposterous longing for innovation.)

At Uppsala, Latin was the language of every official university domain: lectures, catalogues of lectures, disputations, exams, conferment ceremonies, eulogies, dissertations, speeches, and the so-called programmes all had to be composed in this language. The practice was dictated by the university's statutes and was maintained at least until the end of the eighteenth century.[29] Issued as an official programme, Rudbeck's invitation was supposed to adhere to this standard. Of the 735 *programmata* issued in Uppsala between 1599 and 1678 and listed in Ernst Meyer's *Program utgifna vid Upsala universitet 1599–1700* (1905), only a handful were composed in a language other than Latin and then that other language was Greek.[30] This means that Rudbeck's programme from May 1677 was the first ever at Uppsala to be issued in Swedish. Likewise, 1615 of the 1622 dissertations submitted at Uppsala between 1600 and 1679 were written in Latin, whereas the remaining seven were written either in Greek or in Hebrew.[31]

In fact, Sweden would gain a special status in regard to its scholars' proficiency in Latin. That was how the German humanist Petrus Kalchbrenner described his perception of the Swedes in 1722: 'die Schweden schreiben immer auf Latein als *uersatissimi in humanioribus*'.[32] Even when a more pragmatic attitude towards teaching was taking over, Latin still found its defenders. Thus, we

---

[29] Lindberg 2017, p. 73.
[30] Meyer 1905, p. 1–90.
[31] Örneholm & Östlund 2013, p. 4.
[32] Lindberg 2017, p. 72, n. 170.

have dozens of dissertations submitted in the second half of the eighteenth century in support of Latin as the language of scholars and scientists. For example, under the presidency of Petrus Ekerman (b. 1697 – d. 1783), professor of eloquence and poetry at Uppsala between 1737–1779, we have eighteen dissertations devoted to the merits of Latin.[33] Thus, the 1758 dissertation entitled *De sermone Latino optimo scientiarum interprete Academiaeque Upsaliensi commendatissimo*, submitted with Ekerman as its *praeses*, explained that scholars needed a common language, their own scholarly vernacular:

> *Verum enimuero, si exquisitam eruditionem ac scientias ad fastigium quoddam euectas unquam uidebimus, necesse est, adminicula, rei perficiendae quam maxime inseruitura praesto sint. Vigeat, multa ut paucis complectar, dulcissima pax; crebraque inter eruditos instituantur commercia ad ueritates rite examinandas, in lucemque, quo pluribus innotescant, ope comati et limati sermonis, transfundendas. Prout Respublica literaria monarchici regiminis est impatiens, ita libertas sentiendi ac scribendi unicuique sarta, tecta, praestetur, saltem iis in rebus, ubi nihil detrimenti reformidabit capietque status publicus. Sic ad florem culturamque debitam scientiarum plurimum, sine ulla exceptione, id conducit, quod peculiari utantur lingua eruditi, quae inter illos uicem gerat communis Mercurii, meditatas commentationes tum antiquioris aeui, tum recentioris et placita, et inuenta memorabilia, sic patefacientis, ut, sensim pedetentimque detecta, in medium uenire possint. […] Necessarium proinde est, ut sensa et cogitata animi inter se communicent eruditi, idque lingua ipsis quasi uernacula futura.*[34]

(Indeed, if we one day want to see the knowledge and science that we search for to some extent being reached, then it is necessary that we have special tools that help us achieve this to greatest degree possible. In order to say much in a few words: May the sweetest peace flourish and may there be numerous ways for the learned to communicate the truth that they want to explore in a proper manner and pour out to the world to

---

[33] On Ekerman as a writer and *praeses* of dissertations, see Lindberg 1984, p. 46–64. Lindberg also notes that the dissertations submitted under Ekerman's presidency ought to be viewed against their generic background: they were exercises in eloquence and could have the character of praise. Lindberg 1984, p. 59.

[34] Ekerman (*praeses*) & Suedelius (*respondens*) 1758, p. 1–2.

make it known to as many as possible by means of an elegant and polished language.[35] Just as the Republic of learning is impatient with monarchist rule, so the liberty of thinking and writing should be kept safe and protected for everyone, at least in the matters where the state of public affairs will not need to fear and incur any damage. What thus most of all brings about the necessary blossom and cultivation of science, with no exception, is the fact that the learned use their own language, which will serve the purpose of a shared messenger who can bring to light judicious studies of ancient as well as modern times and also memorable opinions and inventions [bring to light, I say] in such a way that they, once they have been discovered gradually and step by step, may be communicated for the benefit of all. [...] Therefore it is indispensable for the learned [to be able] to exchange their observations and ideas and to do so in a language that would be, as it were, their vernacular.)

Further, the author warned against linguistic diversity and described what this would mean for the community of the learned:

Praeterea, si, e.g. Polonus, Germanus, Gallus, etc. suam adoptaret linguam in scientiis exhibendis, tot diuersas addiscerent necesse est linguas, qui ex eorum scriptis sapere praegestiunt. Sic aliter fieri nequit, quam linguarum multitudo ut potissimam aetatis partem occuparet conficeretque, atque adeo inutilis noster foret labor, uix unquam bonis, quod aiunt, auibus absoluendus. Vitam porro totam et memoriam in linguarum cognitione consumere uelle, ita est stultum, ac si quis omnes horas impenderet reserendae ianuae aedium suarum, ipse licet illas nunquam ingrederetur.[36]

(Moreover, if for example the Poles, the Germans, the Frenchmen, etc. adopted their language to communicate science, then those who wish to taste their writings would need to learn so many different languages. So what would happen is that the great number of languages would occupy and consume the greatest part of our lives, and our work [to learn them] would be so unserviceable that it would hardly ever be

---

[35] The author of the dissertation complains that the ongoing war on the continent — known to history as The Seven Years' War (1756–1763) — is disastrous for scholars who now cannot exchange ideas and findings.

[36] Ekerman (*praeses*) & Suedelius (*respondens*) 1758, p. 4–5.

brought to a close, as they say, under good auspices. Furthermore, to be willing to use all your life and memory to learn languages is so fatuous, as if someone devoted all of his hours to try to open the door of his own house, although he would never enter it.)

This particular argument was an almost *uerbatim* quotation from the preface to the recently published English-Swedish dictionary composed by Jacob Serenius. The author behind this *praefatio* was the Swedish bishop, and later archbishop, Eric Benzelius (b. 1675 – d. 1743), who claimed that learning only a tenth of Europe's languages would require more than one life-time, and the person who is planning on doing this will find himself in a more miserable situation than that of Tantalus.[37] The contemporary academicians who read Ekerman's dissertation could not fail to notice that the reasoning echoed Jean le Rond d'Alembert's *Preliminary Discourse* to Diderot's *Encyclopédie* published in 1751. Thus, d'Alembert is quoted in a 1758 dissertation submitted under the presidency of Erik Sotberg and entitled *De multitudine linguarum ciuitati literariae noxia*:

> Les Savans des autres nations à qui nous avons donné l'exemple, ont crû avec raison qu'ils écriroient encore mieux dans leur Langue que dans la nôtre. L'Angleterre nous a donc imité; l'Allemagne, où le Latin sembloit s'être réfugié, commence insensiblement à en perdre l'usage: je ne doute pas qu'elle ne soit bien-tôt suivie par les Suédois, les Danois, et les Russiens. Ainsi, avant la fin du dix-huitième siècle, un Philosophe qui voudra s'instruire à fond des découvertes de ses prédécesseurs, sera contraint de charger sa mémoire de sept à huit Langues différentes; et après avoir consumé à les apprendre le tems le plus précieux de sa vie, il mourra avant de commencer à s'instruire.
> [...]
> L'usage de la Langue Latine, inquit, dont nous avons fait voir le ridicule dans les matières de goût, ne pourroit être que très-utile dans les Ouvrages de Philosophie, dont la clarté et la précision doivent faire tout le mérite, & qui n'ont besoin que d'une Langue universelle & de convention. Il seroit donc à souhaiter qu'on rétablit cet usage: mais il n'y a pas lieu de

---

[37] Benzelius 1734, p. 5.

> l'espérer. L'abus dont nous osons nous plaindre est trop favorable à la vanité et à la paresse, pour qu'on se flate de le déraciner. Les philosophes, comme les autres écrivains, veulent être lus, et surtout de leur nation. S'ils se servaient d'une langue moins familière, ils auraient moins de bouches pour les célébrer, et on ne pourrait pas se vanter de les entendre. Il est vrai qu'avec moins d'admirateurs, ils auraient de meilleurs juges: mais c'est un avantage qui les touche peu, parce que la réputation tient plus au nombre qu'au mérite de ceux qui la distribuent.[38]

The next item in Rudbeck's invitation that had infuriated Schefferus was the author's derision of the standard ancient authorities:

> *2. Imperitissime nominari Aristotelem et Ciceronem, quasi isti fuerint professores academici et studiosos umquam ad labores academicos inuitauerint.*

> (Aristotle and Cicero are quoted in a most ignorant manner as if they had been university professors and had invited students to attend academic classes.)

A reliance on these classical authors to corroborate findings and arguments was a common humanist practice well into the eighteenth century. In 1764, Ekerman addressed the problem in a new dissertation: *De lingua Latina, scientiarum administra uere commemorabili.* This treatise provided a list of the most important Roman authors, acquisition of whom still happened through Latin. The text emphasised that many of the recent scholarly works were in Latin too:

> *Talis est Lingua Latina, quippe quae diu durauerit multamque non potuerit non colligere doctrinam, collectam propagare, scientias, a gente ad gentem, a saeculo ad saeculum, transferendo. Sic ingens librorum multitudo, qui tam antiquioribus sunt, hac lingua, quam recentioribus etiam temporibus, conscripti, et adhuc perscribuntur, sententiam de administra scientiarum meam adfirmat. Libros, Latini sermonis idiomate exaratos, memoriaque dignissimos, in medium uocare, nec conuenit, nec uacat. Dixisse sufficiat, quod, ex ueteribus, iura interpretetur Iustinianus, Medicinam Celsus, Mathesin Manilius, Historiam Natu-*

---

[38] Sotberg (*praeses*) & Urling (*respondens*) 1758, p. 26–27.

rae Plinius, Geographiam Pomponius Mela; agricolam doceant Cato, Varro, Columella, oratorem Tullius ac Quintilianus, architectum Vitruuius, gentium historiam enarrent Liuius, Sallustius, Curtius, etc.[39]

(Such is the Latin language, due to the fact that it has been in existence for a long time, and hence collected a vast amount of knowledge, and then diffused what it has gathered, thus transferring the sciences from nation to nation and from generation to generation. A great number of books from both ancient and modern times are composed in this language and are still being written in it, which corroborates my observation that it is an assistant to the sciences. It is not serviceable, and there is no time to here call as witnesses books that have been written in Latin and deserve to be handed down to posterity. It will suffice just to state that of the ancient writers Justinian is the interpreter of law, Celsus the interpreter of medicine, Manilius of mathematics, Pliny of natural history, Pomponius Mela of geography. Cato, Varro and Columella are the instructors of the farmer, Tullius and Quintilian of the orator, Vitruvius of the architect. Livy, Sallust and Curtius explain the history of people, etc.)

These names had constituted the cornerstone of earlier Renaissance humanists' educational programmes and would continue to supply the *respublica literaria* of later generations with both vocabulary and argumentation.[40]

The third item in Schefferus' letter against Rudbeck's Swedish invitation concerned the negative impact that teaching in Swedish would have on the image of the university:

3. Praetendi causam Suedicae scriptionis, quod pars maxima studiosorum Latine non intelliget. Quae res si exteris innotescat, putabunt pueros hic esse in schola triuiali, non studentes, summa cum iniuria horum egregiorum iuuenum.

---

[39] Ekerman (*praes*) & Bergström (*respondens*) 1764, p. 5.

[40] On the concept of the *respublica literaria* as a scholarly community, see Lindberg 2014, especially p. 16–19. Cf. Clark 2006, p. 186, where the early modern idea of the republic of letters is defined a little bit differently: Clark sees it as a community of poets and rhetoricians as opposed to university scholars. Lindberg corrects this observation by contending that the educational system of the early modern university stemmed from the first Renaissance humanists' teaching programme. Lindberg 2014, p. 17.

(The reason for composing it in Swedish is said to be that the vast majority of students will not understand Latin. If this were known abroad, they will think that our young men attend a *schola triuialis* and that they are not university students, and this is also a great insult to these distinguished young men.)

The Swedish *trivialskola* was a lower-level school, whose curriculum focused on the subjects of the *triuium*, i.e. Latin grammar, logic, and rhetoric. The level of Latinity there was generally low and only became significantly higher at the gymnasium.[41]

Rudbeck's reference to his students' poor knowledge of Latin seems to have been recognised as a problem at other early modern universities too. Françoise Waquet describes a similar situation at sixteenth-century Oxford, where the teacher in charge of instructing surgeons had to use first Latin and then English due to the fact that many of the students did not understand the former.[42] Rudbeck's own realisation of the necessity to facilitate teaching was tightly connected to the utilitarian ends of his other classes. In addition to anatomy, Rudbeck taught engineering and could clearly see the value of using the vernacular for instruction in practical situations. In 1665, he praised the Leiden scholar Frans van Schooten (1615–1660), who had introduced Dutch as the language of instruction for teaching practical mathematics.[43] We can expect that dissections of human bodies in Rudbeck's *theatrum anatomicum* gave rise to situations of exactly this kind: they might very well have entailed supervision of assistants who had no Latin.

A contemporary parallel from Sweden, another telling example, is offered by the manuscripts of university lectures. Bo Lindberg has been able to show that manuscripts of lectures from Uppsala, Åbo, and Lund were usually a mixture of Latin and Swedish. Professors frequently switched between the languages, with a clear tendency to use Swedish when the topic was very attractive for the audience. The study of human reproduction was such a case: young male students were for obvious reasons particu-

---

[41] Hörstedt 2018, p. 13, n. 1.
[42] Waquet 2002, p. 88.
[43] Lindberg 2017, p. 74.

larly interested in the lectures about human intercourse, especially when the issue was explained in their mother tongue.[44]

There is no doubt that all of these arguments were known to Schefferus, but his words signalled a concern that damage to the university's reputation would have a detrimental impact on opportunities to exchange students and to network. What seats of learning would want to accept Swedish students if they had no Latin?[45] Schefferus himself maintained an impressive correspondence with scholars from abroad, almost entirely conducted in Latin.[46]

The last linguistic point made by Schefferus satirised Rudbeck's poor knowledge of the tongue of the learned:

> *4. Etiam ideo dici hoc factum, quia pleraque, quae sit dicturus, Latine efferri nequeant, quod si de ipso est intelligendum, sine dubio uerissimum, si de linguae Latinae inopia et insufficientia numquam probabitur.*

(It is therefore even indicated that he has done this because most of what he plans to say cannot be expressed in Latin. In respect to that, if this should be understood to refer to himself, then it will without a doubt be demonstrated to be the utmost truth, but if it should be understood to refer to any *inopia* and *insufficientia* of the Latin language, then there will never be such a demonstration.)

It was a common practice among humanists to accuse one's rival of shortcomings in learning and scholarship. The famous feud between Poggio Bracciolini and Francesco Filelfo well illustrates imputations of this kind. When trying to diminish the scholarly achievements of Poggio and Niccolò Niccoli, Filelfo time and again depicted them as unknowledgeable: he portrayed Poggio

---

[44] Lindberg 2017, p. 78. There is an obvious contradiction between the university's statues that required the use of Latin at all times and the fact that the extant manuscript lectures contain a mixture of Latin and Swedish. A further study of the actual practice at Uppsala and other early modern universities is needed in order to understand this inconsistency.

[45] Françoise Waquet uses Uppsala University as a case in point in her discussion of Latin as a means of preserving the university's prestige. Waquet 2015, p. 183–184. Cf. Lindberg 2015, p. 178–181.

[46] For a more or less complete database of Schefferus' correspondence stored at Uppsala University Library, see Klein 2020.

as an ignoramus in Greek literature and accused Niccoli of not knowing Greek and having a poor knowledge of Latin literature.[47] Another example closer in time and space is provided by the English naturalist John Ray, who condemned his adversary as ignorant because he did not write in Latin.[48]

The remaining three items contained in Schefferus' letter dealt with the ethical aspects of Rudbeck's text. First of all, Schefferus did not approve of Rudbeck's choice of forum for his discussion of the corruption of public morals. A dissection of a human body was not the appropriate place to treat such a matter! Schefferus also reproached Rudbeck for his opinion that the right attire automatically equipped one with the right ethics. Last but not least, Schefferus questioned Rudbeck's suitability to teach his students the principles of right and wrong, as his own way of living was a far cry from being exemplary. Once again, what we see is a typically humanist attack. When clashing with each other, early humanists could ascribe to their rivals the most scandalous things, including perversity.[49]

Timing and Media

Rudbeck and Schefferus had conflicting views on several questions that related to their scholarship and professional status. With much at stake, they were keen to make the most of opportunities to communicate their points of view. Hence Rudbeck's Swedish invitation was issued when he was putting the final touches on his *Atlantica*, a work that he himself saw as the pinnacle of his scholarly accomplishments. Schefferus penned his letter just days after publishing his *De situ et uocabulo Upsaliae*, which rejected Rudbeck's and Verelius' hypothesis concerning the old pagan temple of Uppsala. It is interesting to note that at the end of his letter, Schefferus once again brings the secretary's attention to his work. There, he provides a list of the colleagues among whom he wants to distribute his antiquarian treatise and asks the secretary to investigate why the university chancellor Magnus Gabriel de

---

[47] De Keyser 2015, p. 18–20.
[48] Waquet 2002, p. 80.
[49] Cf. De Keyser 2015, p. 13–14; 16–17.

la Gardie has not been willing to gag Verelius. One of the first things that the readers of the *De situ et uocabulo Upsaliae* encountered was Schefferus' complaint that his theory had been exposed to harsh criticism because he was a foreigner.[50] At the end of that work, the reader also found Schefferus' appeal to have the final word in the debate, a request that would eventually be granted.[51]

Besides timing, Rudbeck and Schefferus were aware of the importance of the right forum for propagating their views. Rudbeck's invitation was printed as an official programme that was a public document to be read by everyone who visited the university. Furthermore, the *programma* was a medium for discussing bigger issues that concerned the scholarly community as a whole.[52] A considerable number of the *programmata* from the years in question, apart from various invitations and festive speeches, contain disciplinary regulations for students and relegation warnings to professors.[53] So it is unsurprising that Rudbeck saw this document as an efficient tool for changing the university's established practices.

Schefferus chose a different way to make his voice heard. To ensure the success of his appeal he wrote his text as a letter to one of the university secretaries, whom he knew personally. Ennio Rao, when describing the invective in fifteenth-century Italy, makes the observation that its 'usual means of publication was by distribution among mutual friends and acquaintances, seldom to the adversaries'. He adds that it often took the form of an open letter sent to a third party.[54] It therefore becomes clear that Schef-

---

[50] *De situ et uocabulo Upsaliae* [...] *epistola defensoria*, p. 4: 'Sed res cecidit longe aliter, quam speraueram. Reperti enim paulo post, pauci illi quidem, unus tamen atque alter, qui censerent nefas, si quis peregrinus Sueticis se immisceret negotiis, et de rebus obsoletis antiquorum dicere sententiam auderet.' (But things turned out very different from what I had expected. For, a short time later, there was in fact a number of people, although only one or two persons, who considered it an abomination for a foreigner to interfere in Swedish matters and dare to voice his opinion concerning this ancient people's worn-out affairs.)

[51] Verelius' answer entitled *Notae in epistulam defensoriam Johannis Schefferi Argentoratensis de situ et uocabulo Upsaliae* was not printed in time, and when it was published, all the copies had to be withdrawn. Annerstedt 1891, p. 134–136.

[52] The university *programma* as source material still needs more exploration. A very welcome study in this direction has recently appeared: Lesigang-Bruckmüller 2020.

[53] For a thorough categorisation of the programmes from Uppsala University, see Meyer 1905, p. 3–14.

[54] Rao 1992 (1989), p. 266.

ferus employed the standard strategy used by humanist writers of invectives to belittle their opponent.

What were the ultimate outcomes of this string of disagreements between these two intellectual giants? The debate about the pagan temple was officially closed right after Schefferus' appeal to the university chancellor, which was in Schefferus' favour. Schefferus would also have been pleased to discover that Latin would remain the language of the Uppsala dissertation as the *optimus scientiarum interpres* well into the nineteenth century. As to Rudbeck, just four weeks after publishing his Swedish invitation he issued a new programme in Swedish. This time even those who adhered to the Japhetho-Scythian theory could not tolerate Rudbeck's frivolous way of using the Swedish language and pointed in their pasquins to the grammatical mistakes in his invitation.[55]

Concluding Remarks

In his book on the history of the academic lecture in Sweden, Bo Lindberg lists the pros and cons of the use of Latin in early modern academia. Among the advantages of employing the vernacular he identifies three: patriotism, pragmatism, and the students' poor knowledge of Latin.[56] All of these arguments are found in Rudbeck's Swedish invitation from 1677. To them can be added a fourth, viz. Rudbeck's aversion to the university's inflexibility. His ridicule of it recalls the Swedish humanist Georg Stiernhielm's harsh words written two decades earlier to describe, in an almost Baconian spirit, how the grip of authority can be like tyranny to the republic of letters:

> *Haec (sc. praecepta opinio et uirorum magnorum authoritas) etenim ingeniis quantumuis acribus et ad sublimiora tendentibus, alas praecidunt, eaque cogunt per trita uiarum humi repere. Haec spes, et conatus ad ulteriora infringunt, deiiciunt et exarmant. Haec praecipua sunt, quae tyrannidem exercent in Republica literaria.*[57]

[55] Annerstedt 1908, p. 174. Two of these lampoons are reproduced in *Småsaker til Nöje och Tidsfördrif. Del IV* (1756), p. 46–55.
[56] Lindberg 2017, p. 73–75. Cf. Lindberg 2015, p. 181–182.
[57] Lindberg 2014, p. 18, n. 8.

(They [i.e. the preconceived opinion and the authority of great men] clip the wings of minds that are very sharp and that aim for higher achievements and instead force them to crawl on the ground on a well-trodden path. They weaken aspirations and the quest for what is farther on; they throw them down and disarm them. They are the principal forces that exercise tyranny in the Republic of letters.)

Moreover, it was not the first time that Rudbeck discredited his *alma mater* for its obsolete rules. In 1663, as one of the university's *curatores*, he advocated abolition of the diploma in theology that was mandatory for gaining a magister's degree. Rudbeck also criticised the wages of the professors of theology: they were much higher than the salaries of the professors of all other disciplines and, according to him, undeservedly so.[58] Expectedly, the faculty of theology followed Schefferus' example and wasted no time delivering their critical remarks.[59]

As shown above, the debate delineated here found counterparts in other academic milieus. The struggle to keep Latin as the language of academia was tightly bound to the university's conventions, especially those of its written discourse, which included the use of ancient sources and ready-made formulations. The language of the Romans also gave early modern scholars a sense of continuity by making them a part of the Latinate world.

The tools employed by Rudbeck and Schefferus in their intellectual battle bring to mind the practices of other humanists, both earlier figures and contemporaries. There is no doubt that these two scholarly superstars were aware of their unique role in the republic of letters. As the editors of *The Forms of Conflict and Rivalries in Renaissance Europe* point out, these clashes were a productive force that generated new intellectual activity and helped individual scholars forge their professional identities.[60] Even if the medium and genre varied, the overarching goal was to further a particular discussion. In other words, the Uppsalian dispute seems to represent what the early modern university was all about: the struggle for tradition, a concern for status, and a constant desire to debate.

---

[58] Annerstedt 1908, p. 76–80.
[59] Annerstedt 1908, p. 173, n. 1.
[60] Lines, Laureys & Kraye 2015, p. 8–9.

Bibliography

Annerstedt, C. (1891), *Schefferus och Verelius. En literär fäjd i sjuttonde seklet*, Uppsala: Akademiska Boktryckeriet.

Annerstedt, C. (1893), *Bref af Olof Rudbeck d.ä. rörande Upsala universitet I. 1661–1670*, Uppsala: Akademiska Bokhandeln (Uppsala Universitets Årsskrift = Acta Universitatis Upsaliensis, 1893).

Annerstedt, C. (1908) *Upsala universitets historia II. 1655–1718. Förra avdelningen. Universitetets öden*, Uppsala: Akademiska Bokförlaget.

Annerstedt, C. (1910), *Upsala universitets historia. Bihang II. Handlingar 1655–1694*, Uppsala: Akademiska Bokförlaget.

Benzelius, E. (1734), 'Praefatio', in J. Serenius, *Dictionarium Anglo-Suethico-Latinum*, Hamburg: Apud Rudolphum Beneken.

Clark, W. (2006), *Academic Charisma and the Origins of the Research University*, Chicago, IL: University of Chicago Press.

De Clercq, J., P. Swiggers & T. Van Hal (2009), 'Goropius Becanus, Joannes', in H. Stammerjohann (ed.), *Lexicon Grammaticorum. A Bio-bibliographical Companion to the History of Linguistics*. Second edition, revised and enlarged, Tübingen: Max Niemeyer Verlag, p. 553–554.

Cohen, H. F. (2015), 'From *Philosophia Naturalis* to Science, from Latin to the Vernacular', in J. Bloemendal (ed.), *Bilingual Europe. Latin and Vernacular Cultures, Examples of Bilingualism and Multilingualism, c. 1300–1800*, Leiden: Brill (Brill Studies in Intellectual History, 239), p. 144–160.

Drake, R., A. Wayne Vogl & A. W. M. Mitchell (2014), *Gray's Anatomy for Students*. Third edition, Edinburgh: Churchill Livingstone.

Dunér, D. (2008), 'Maskinen människa', in G. Broberg (ed.), *Til at stwdera läkedom. Tio studier i svensk medicinhistoria*, Lund: Sekel.

Ekerman, P. (*praeses*) & D. Suedelius (*respondens*) (1758), *De sermone Latino optimo scientiarum interprete Academiaeque Upsaliensi commendatissimo*, Uppsala: L. M. Höjer, Reg. Acad. Typogr.

Ekerman, P. (*praeses*) & L. P. Bergström (*respondens*) (1764), *De lingua Latina, scientiarum administra uere commemorabili*, Uppsala.

Eriksson, G. (1994), *The Atlantic Vision. Olaus Rudbeck and Baroque Science*, Canton, MA: Science History Publications (Uppsala Studies in History of Science, 19).

Eriksson, G. (2002) *Rudbeck, 1630–1702. Liv, lärdom, dröm i barockens Sverige*, Stockholm: Atlantis.

Fant, E. M. (1782), *Minne öfver Joh. Schefferus*, Stockholm: J. A. Carlbohm.

Forssberg Malm, L. '*Ex stribliginum tenebris perluxit nitor*. Johannes Schefferus och *Cena Trimalchionis* tidigmoderna text- och tolkningstradition' (unpublished master thesis, Uppsala University, 2015).

Grafton, A. (2001), 'Petronius and the Neo-Latin Satire: The Reception of the *Cena Trimalchionis*', in A. Grafton, *Bring out Your Dead. The Past as Revelation*, Cambridge, MA: Harvard University Press, p. 208–223 (repr. from *Journal of the Warburg and Courtauld Institutes*, 53, p. 237–249).

Van Hal, T. (2010), '*Moedertalen en taalmoeders*'. *Het vroegmoderne taalvergelijkende onderzoek in de Lage Landen*, Brussel: Koninklijke Vlaamse Academie voor Wetenschappen en Kunsten (Verhandelingen van de Koninklijke Vlaamse Academie van België voor Wetenschappen en Kunsten, Nieuwe reeks, 20).

Von Hofsten, N. (1939), 'Upptäckten av bröstgången och lymfkärlssystemet. En kronologisk kommentar', in *Lychnos*, p. 262–288. With a summary in French.

Hörstedt, A., 'Latin Dissertations and Disputations in the Early Modern Swedish Gymnasium. A Study of a Latin School Tradition c. 1620 – c. 1820' (doctoral thesis, University of Gothenburg, 2018). http://hdl.handle.net/2077/55897 (accessed 15.07.2022).

Ingermarsdotter, J. (2011), *Ramism, Rhetoric and Reform. An Intellectual Biography of Johan Skytte (1577–1645)*, Uppsala: Uppsala University (Uppsala Studies in History of Ideas, 42).

De Keyser, J. (2015), 'Francesco Filelfo's Feud with Poggio Bracciolini', in D. A. Lines, M. Laureys & J. Kraye (eds), *Forms of Conflict and Rivalries in Renaissance Europe*, Bonn: Bonn University Press (Super alta perennis. Studien zur Wirkung der Klassischen Antike, 17), p. 13–27.

Klein, A. (2020), 'The Res publica Schefferiana – the correspondence of Johannes Schefferus (1621–1679)', at https://doi.org/10.18710/VDLBWH (accessed 15.07.2022).

Lesigang-Bruckmüller, A. (2020), 'The Programma in Relation to Disputations/Dissertations at the Faculty of Law of Leipzig University around 1750', in M. Friedenthal, H. Marti & R. Seidel (eds), *Early Modern Disputations and Dissertations in an Interdisciplinary and European Context*, Leiden: Brill (Intersections, 71), p. 555–576.

Lewin, B. (1985), *Johan Skytte och de skytteanska professorerna*, Stockholm: Almquist & Wiksell International (Acta Universitatis Upsaliensis. Skrifter utgivna av Statsvetenskapliga föreningen i Uppsala, 100).

Lindberg, B. (1984), *De lärdes modersmål. Latin, humanism och vetenskap i 1700-talets Sverige*, Gothenburg: University of Gothenburg (Gothenburg Studies in the History of Science and Ideas, 5).

Lindberg, B. (2014), 'De lärdes republik. Om statsskicket i vetenskapens värld', in A. Hellerstedt & E. Hagström Molin (eds), *Lärda samtal. En festskrift till Erland Sellberg*, Lund: Ellerströms, p. 15–32.

Lindberg, B. (2015), 'Universitetets språk' in M. Lindström & A. Wickberg Månsson (eds), *Universitet som medium*, Lund: Lund University (Mediehistoriskt arkiv, 27), p. 175–193.

Lindberg, B. (2017), *Den akademiska läxan. Om föreläsningens historia*, Stockholm: Kungl. Vitterhets Historie och Antikvitets Akademien (Historiska serien, 36).

Lindroth, S. (1975), *Svensk lärdomshistoria. Stormaktstiden*. Stockholm: Norstedt.

Lines, D. A., M. Laureys & J. Kraye (2015), 'Foreword', in D. A. Lines, M. Laureys & J. Kraye (eds), *Forms of Conflict and Rivalries in Renaissance Europe*, Bonn: Bonn University Press (Super alta perennis. Studien zur Wirkung der Klassischen Antike, 17), p. 7–11.

Meyer, E. (1905), *Program utgifna vid Upsala universitet 1599–1700. Bibliografi*, Uppsala: Akademiska Boktryckeriet (Uppsala universitets årsskrift, 1905, 3).

Momigliano, A. (1950), 'Ancient History and the Antiquarian', in *Journal of the Warburg and Courtauld Institutes*, 13, p. 285–315.

Neumann, F. (2005), 'Programm', in G. Ueding et al. (eds), *Historisches Wörterbuch der Rhetorik. VII (Pos–Rhet)*, Tübingen: Max Niemeyer Verlag, p. 154–158.

Rao, E. (1992 [1989]), 'The Humanistic Invective as Literary Genre', in G. C. Martín (ed.), *Selected Proceedings of the Pennsylvania Foreign Language Conference. 1988–1990*, Pittsburgh, PA: Duquesne University Department of Modern Languages Publications, p. 261–267.

Schefferus, J. (1677), *De situ et uocabulo Upsaliae […] epistola defensoria*, Stockholm: Excudit Nicolaus Wankiif, Reg. Typ.

Schück, H. (1933), *Kung. Vitterhets historie och antikvitets akademien. Dess förhistoria och historia III. Antikvitetskollegiet II*, Stockholm: Kung. Vitterhets historie och antikvitets akademien.

Små-saker til Nöje och Tidsfördrif. Del IV (1756), Stockholm: Wildiska Tryckeriet.

Sotberg, E. & P. A. Urling (1758), *De multitudine linguarum ciuitati literariae noxia*, Uppsala: L. M. Höjer, Red. Acad. Typogr.

Waquet, F. (2002), *Latin or the Empire of a Sign. From the Sixteenth to the Twentieth Centuries*, trans. J. Howe, London: Verso.

Waquet, F. (2015), 'Latin et Vernaculaires dans l'Université du XVIIIe siècle / Latin and Vernacular Languages in the Eighteenth-Century University', in J. Bloemendal (ed.), *Bilingual Europe. Latin and Vernacular Cultures, Examples of Bilingualism and Multilingualism c. 1300–1800*, Leiden: Brill (Brill's Studies in Intellectual History, 239), p. 176–186.

Örneholm, U. & K. Östlund (2013), *De linguis dissertationum academicarum Suecicarum annis 1600–1855 prelo mandatarum schediasma*, Uppsala; at urn:nbn:se:uu:diva-210356 (accessed 15.07.2022).

Abstract

In May 1677, the scholars and students of Uppsala University witnessed an animated debate regarding what language should be used at their seat of learning. Was it to be Latin, the *lingua franca* of scholars and scientists throughout the Western world, or Swedish, the students' mother tongue? The debate erupted after the professor of medicine Olof Rudbeck had published an invitation — in Swedish — to attend the dissection of a human body in his *Theatrum anatomicum*. Furthermore, the *programma* was formulated in a way that was perceived by some to be frivolous. The first scholar to openly criticise Rudbeck's choice of language and blunt expressions was the renowned philologist Johannes Schefferus. In his denunciation of Rudbeck's linguistic preferences, Schefferus emphasised the role that Latin played in the preservation of the university's prestige. This article studies the Uppsala conflict against a background of the early modern university's traditions and its almost exclusively Latinate milieu. The article also shows how the disagreement between Rudbeck and Schefferus in other scholarly fields contributed to their quarrel. In addition, the present contribution explores the combatants' choices of medium, and how their disagreement fit into the context of the so-called humanist *Streitkultur*, a culture in which figures such as Rudbeck and Schefferus were highly skilled at a range of techniques that could be employed to belittle their adversary's academic achievements.

LAURA BECK VARELA
Universidad Autónoma de Madrid

HISTORIA LITTERARIA IURIS
MAPPING CONTROVERSIES IN EIGHTEENTH-CENTURY JURISPRUDENCE

Introduction

Why do jurists often hold different opinions about the same topic? What are the causes of dissent among jurists? Which controversies in the field of jurisprudence are the most significant? Which controversies occupied Roman jurists, medieval jurists, and modern jurists, and why?

These questions were raised by the law professor Carl Ferdinand Hommel (1722–1781) at the beginning of a long chapter dedicated to the controversies of jurists (*De controuersiis iurisconsultorum*). Hommel's essay on controversies was one of the most detailed chapters of his *Litteratura iuris*, published in Leipzig in 1761 and reprinted in 1779 with significant amendments.[1]

As possible causes for the large number of quarrels in the legal field, even differences in the 'blood pressure' and 'physical shape' of the jurists' bodies had been considered, echoing the old humoral theory.[2] Hommel, however, was not so interested in investigating the causes of the proliferation of controversies in jurisprudence.

---

[1] Hommel 1761, Hommel 1779. Laura Beck Varela is a member of the research project 'La nación traducida. Ecologías de la traducción 1668–1830' (reference code: PGC2018–095007-B-I00).

[2] According to some authors, he argued, if the humors were the same for all, if the blood that ran in everyone's veins were the same for all, then learned men would have shared identical opinions, instead of different ones: *Fuerunt etiam, qui dissensionum causas in corporum constitutione et sanguinis temperatura quaererent, ita existimantes, si humores cunctis iidem forent, si idem sanguis per venas omnium flueret, easdem eruditos, non diversas, sententias habituros esse* (Hommel 1779, 1, XVIII, § 1, p. 202).

Paraphrasing Ulpian, he stated that the jurists' disputes were only another sign of the inevitable human inclination towards dissent (*Naturalis est homini ad dissentiendum facilitas*).[3] Rather than taking an interest in the causes of this phenomenon, Hommel set forth an extensive account of more than thirty illustrious disputes that belonged to jurisprudence as an academic discipline.

Carl Ferdinand Hommel is practically forgotten today, despite the recognition he enjoyed during the eighteenth century as a professor of law at the University of Leipzig and as a magistrate in the Upper Court of the Kingdom of Saxony (*Oberhofgericht Leipzig*).[4] Hommel, a follower of Christian Thomasius, was a prolific author whose writings touched upon all the main legal branches of the time. He was also responsible for the first German translations of the Marquis of Beccaria's works.[5] Some of Hommel's treatises also dealt more directly with forensic praxis, such as his *Teutscher Flavius* (1763), a guide for lawyers,[6] his edition of Johann Georg Bertoch's *Promptuarium iuris practicum* (1777),[7] as well as his alphabetic repertoires for professional and lay audiences, such as the *Pertinenz- und Erbsonderungsregister* (1767), reprinted several times,[8] and the *Catalogus testium* (1780).[9] Other writings were devoted to the critical study of the legal sources, such as the *Corpus iuris civilis cum notis variorum* (1768) (reprinted under the title *Hommel redivivus* as late as 1858),[10] his editions of Georg Beyer's *Notitia autorum* [sic] *iuridicorum*[11] and his edi-

---

[3] The original sentence of the Digest was ...*propter naturalem hominum ad dissentiendum facilitatem* (D. 4.8.17.6). For the quotations of the Digest, I am using Mommsen and Krueger's Latin edition, *Digesta Iustiniani Augusti* (Berlin 1870), vol. 1.

[4] For Hommel's biographical data, see Hof 2017, Lieberwirth 1972, Stintzing & Landsberg 1898, and Teichmann 1881, besides his own autobiography in Hommel 1760.

[5] Rother 2004.

[6] Hommel 1775.

[7] Hommel 1777.

[8] Hommel 1782 (4th reprint).

[9] Hommel 1780. The *Catalogus testium* was translated into German in 1843.

[10] Schimmelpfeng (ed.) 1858. See the critical note in Landsberg 1898, III/1, p. 398.

[11] Hommel worked on some of the volumes of Georg Beyer's *De utili et necessaria autorum iuridicorum et iuris arti inservientium notitia schediasma*, the first volume of which had appeared in 1726.

tion of the celebrated indexes of Abraham Wieling and Jacques Labitte.[12] He was also a very active book reviewer in the various protojournals of the time.[13] His double role as critical reviewer and editor of legal texts inspired his *Litteratura iuris*, whose chapter on controversies guides the present essay. Hommel has fallen into oblivion because, for various reasons, he was excluded from the canon of legal history built by the German Historical School in the nineteenth century.

The aim of this paper is not to rehabilitate another forgotten jurist, but rather to follow Hommel's selection of controversies as a sort of Ariadne's thread through the ways in which jurists conceived and conceptualized dissent and its role in the self-fashioning of jurisprudence as a discipline in the eighteenth century. Hommel's *Litteratura iuris* is the swan song of a certain legal genre, the corpus of works usually known as *historia litteraria iuris*, whose legacy can be seen, for example, in Gustav Hugo's *Lehrbuch der civilistischen Litterair-Geschichte* (1812) and Friedrich Carl von Savigny's *Geschichte des Römischen Rechts im Mittelalter* (1815).[14] The *historia litteraria iuris* was a subset of the *historia litteraria*, a genre (or ensemble of genres) that had flourished from the middle of the seventeenth century to the 1740s, the era of *polyhistorismus*, especially in German and Dutch universities. The authors of this kind of work devoted considerable attention to the identification of the several controversies in the various fields of knowledge. They understood this sort of 'cartography of dissent' as central to any *historia litteraria*.

Therefore, this paper will begin by briefly delineating *polyhistorismus* and *historia litteraria* (I. *Polyhistorismus* and *Historia litteraria*: Mapping the World of Knowledge), before presenting their impact and uses in the field of jurisprudence (II. *Historia litteraria iuris*: Mapping the Legal Discipline). The paper then analyzes how and for which purposes jurists represented contro-

---

[12] Hommel 1767. Abraham Wieling's and Jacques Labitte's were basic reference works for professional jurists. See Labitte 1557, Wieling 1727.

[13] See, for instance, various articles from his pen in the journal directed by J. A. Bach, 1750–1758.

[14] For an overview of *historia litteraria iuris*, see Mohnhaupt 2013. In this article, I transcribe the original spelling of words such as *litteraria*, *auctor* or *feudalis*, among others, which vary considerably in these sources.

versies in the works of *historiae litterariae iuris*, focusing on Carl Ferdinand Hommel's extensive account (III. *Historia litteraria iuris*: Mapping Controversies in Law). Finally, I refer to criticism of the portrayal and selection of juridical controversies during this period, in the framework of a growing dissatisfaction with the early forms of writing *historia litteraria iuris* (IV. *Historia litteraria iuris* in Decline: Reframing Controversies in Law).

I. Polyhistorismus *and* Historia litteraria: *Mapping the World of Knowledge*

In 1687, Daniel Georg Morhof (1639–1691), a scholar from Lübeck, wrote the *Polyhistor siue de notitia auctorum et rerum …* (in later editions, *Polyhistor literarius*). This work became a fundamental reference for the development of the so-called *polyhistorismus*, which thrived, as previously indicated, between the middle of the seventeenth century and the first half of the eighteenth. Morhof was preceded by, among others, the Hamburg scholar Peter Lambeck (1628–1680), whose *Prodromus historiae literariae* was issued in 1659,[15] as well as by Martin Lipenius (1630–1692), who also conceived his various bibliographies as fundamental tools for *historia litteraria*. Lipenius' thesaurus for jurists, the *Bibliotheca realis iuridica*, which was issued in 1679 and was reprinted and enhanced several times up to the beginning of the nineteenth century,[16] inspired other reference works, such as those prepared by the librarian and jurist Burkhard Gotthelf Struve (1671–1738).[17]

In recent decades, as part of the growing body of scholarship dedicated to analyzing erudition as a cultural practice,[18] several investigations of different authors, works, and questions related to the *polyhistors* and *historia litteraria* have appeared,[19] eschewing the anachronistic association between *polyhistorismus* and

---

[15] Lambeck 1659.
[16] Lipenius 1757.
[17] Struve 1756.
[18] Mulsow & Zedelmaier (eds) 2001.
[19] Jaumann 1990, Grafton 1985, Waquet 2000, Grunert & Vollhardt 2007, Gierl 2007.

academic superfluity.[20] The focus has shifted from *historia litteraria* as a pre-history of our contemporary historical understanding of science to an inquiry into the epistemological foundations of *historia litteraria*, its scientific and practical function, and its achievements in its social context.[21] The broad spectrum of *historia litteraria* offers for exploration sources that are rich in different aspects of the history of scholarship, such as the practices and methods of erudition, reading and writing habits, networking efforts, the moral dimension of intellectual activity, and the construction of community standards regarding criticism and polemics. This blooming and insightful scholarship, however, has paid little attention to the world of jurisprudence, despite the jurists' active participation in *historia litteraria* as a scholarly enterprise.

Focusing on Daniel Morhof, including his wide academic networks, his writing and excerpting techniques,[22] as well as his impact on several disciplines and educational levels, scholars have stressed that *historia litteraria* emerged 'not as a discipline, but as a universally applicable method',[23] a sort of 'critical history of human knowledge'.[24] Morhof conceived of his work not as a mere accumulation of data, but as a productive tool of ordering, classifying, and hierarchizing. He played a crucial role in this 'new mapping of the world of learning'.[25] One of the key elements of his eclectic method was the identification of the relevant controversies in every discipline; in natural philosophy, for instance, in a chapter dedicated to *De consensu et dissensu veterum et recentiorum, eorumque conciliatione* (*Polyhistor*, II, 1, XVIII[26]), the idea was 'to sort out the points of consensus and difference between ancient and modern natural philosophers, his task being the reconciliation of the two'.[27] Regarding jurisprudence, in the section

---

[20] This association is omnipresent in the nineteenth-century narratives of the main *polyhistors* and writers of *historiae litterariae*. See, for example, the biographical entry for Gottlieb Stolle: Waldberg 1893.

[21] Zedelmaier 2017, p. 83.

[22] Blair 2004, Décultot, Krämer & Zedelmaier 2020.

[23] Nelles 2000, p. 42.

[24] Waquet 2000, p. 10.

[25] In allusion to Waquet's title (2000).

[26] Morhof 1747, p. 261–266.

[27] Nelles 2000, p. 37.

entitled *De controversiarum et argumentorum specialium scriptoribus* (*Polyhistor*, III, 6, VIII), Morhof attacked certain juridical authors for the improper way in which they had mixed controversies with other issues in their compilations, generating more chaos and confusion.[28]

One of the clear influences on the *polyhistors'* approach was Francis Bacon (1561–1626), whose *On the advancement of learning* (1605) (the expanded version was printed in Latin in 1623) was evoked in Morhof's preface and throughout his work.[29] Another important figure was the lesser-known Gabriel Naudé (1600–1653), with his *Advis pour dresser une bibliothèque* (1627). Bacon's influence is manifest in the application of empirical, experimental tools to the task of ordering the world of knowledge. These tools were combined with Renaissance learning and teaching traditions. The empirical goal of *historia litteraria* was to assemble and order 'all that had been written on a given subject, not as a reductive exercise, but in order to provide a starting point for a fresh investigation'.[30] Knowledge was no longer conceived as an eternal treasure to be 'rediscovered, exhumed and transmitted': it was rather seen as an open work, a task that would be constantly enhanced, corrected, and completed, thanks to the joint effort of many generations of scholars.[31] This was one of the innovations of the *polyhistors'* approach in comparison with other major 'information-storage' bibliographical projects of the sixteenth and early seventeenth centuries, such as Conrad Gesner's *Bibliotheca universalis*.

Morhof's perspective also differed from that of other philosophers such as Gottfried Wilhelm Leibniz (1646–1716), whose *Nova methodus discendae docendaeque iurisprudentiae* (1668) was harshly criticized in the pages of the *Polyhistor literarius*. Analogously to other so-called encyclopedists, Leibniz had departed from abstract, a priori criteria for ordering the mass of knowledge.[32] Leibniz had indeed conceived of *historia litteraria* as one

---

[28] Morhof 1747, p. 593.

[29] Nelles 2000, p. 43; on the legacy of Francis Bacon, see especially Grunert & Vollhardt 2007, p. vii–xi.

[30] Nelles 2000, p. 41–42.

[31] Waquet 2000, p. 8–9.

[32] *Eorum Brocardicorum reformationem promisit Autor Methodi nouae iurisprudentiae Godfr. Guilh. Leibnitius, ad perfectam uniuersalitatem se omnia reduc-*

of the pillars of his mathematical method, linking it to his ideal of scientific progress.[33] Christian Wolff (1679–1754) detached himself from the empirical approach of Bacon as well as from Leibniz's understanding of *historia litteraria* as a transdisciplinary methodological procedure. For Wolff, *historia litteraria* was rather a tool for contextualizing specific scientific problems and thus one of the fundamental elements of his rationalistic logic.[34]

Most compendia of *historia litteraria* exhibit basic common features with regard to their structure, content, and goals, besides having been widely used for propaedeutic purposes.[35] These compendia were often divided into two main parts: a bibliographical one (*notitia librorum*) and a biographical one (*notitia auctorum*). Other important chapters included the method of writing and preparing excerpts, and some compendia have a special chapter on the existing public and private libraries, whose consultation was one of the pillars of the *polyhistors*' empirical procedure.[36] In the very first book of his work (*liber I: Bibliothecarius*), Morhof stated that only the knowledge of libraries (*notitia bibliothecarum*) showed the way to an accomplished knowledge of all things.[37]

The structure of these works also reflects a diachronic perspective, an effort to present a chronological account of learned wisdom, organized by discipline, from the beginning of learning until present times. As Christoph Heumann wrote in his influential *Conspectus Reipublicae Literariae* (1708), *historia litteraria* is the history of letters and of men of letters, or a narrative about the origins and progress of literary studies until our times (*Historia literaria est historia literarum et literatorum, siue narra-*

---

turum sperans, qui ne spe sua excidat, ualde uereor. Quae enim uere uniuersalia sunt, pauca sunt, neque cum tanta turba et apparatu comparent (Morhof 1708, III, 6, 7, p. 93).

[33] Zedelmaier 2007, p. 92.
[34] Zedelmaier 2007, p. 93.
[35] Grunert 2010, Syndikus 2008.
[36] For Morhof's third book, on methods of excerpting, see Zedelmaier 2000.
[37] *Sed steriles fuisse hos labores iamdudum compertum est: sola perfectae omnium rerum cognitioni uiam sternit bibliothecaria notitia; quae quamdiu non est tota exculta, non sperari poterit perfecta et uniuersalis omnium seculorum et artium doctrina. At uero rem infinitam postulas, dixerit aliquis: imo non est infinita, et satis commode finibus suis coercebitur, modo in promptu sint subsidia ad illam rem idonea* (Morhof 1708, I, I, 20, § 3, p. 251).

tio de ortu et progressu studiorum literariorum ad nostram usque aetatem).[38] In other words, the compendia aimed at presenting a succession of the 'literary', or 'scientific genius' of every single period of time.[39] It is noteworthy that both the terms *historia* and *litteraria*, in the early modern context, are hardly translatable into present-day equivalents. *Litteraria* did not refer to fictional writing but rather to the learned written tradition in general, while *historia* evoked a corpus, a collection of experiences, data, facts, statements, and propositions that formed the basis of the sciences and were indisputable.[40] *Historia* was not necessarily an independent discipline: rather, the special fields of knowledge could be themselves defined in terms of *historiae*. The definitions written by Daniel Nettelbladt, one of the most prominent authors of *historiae litterariae iuris*, give us an idea of how eighteenth-century readers attributed to these very same words a completely different meaning than they might be supposed to have today. He defined, for example, *anatomy* as that part of the 'history of the bodies' which contains 'true statements' about their structure (*Anatomia est pars historiae corporum quae continet ueritates de eorum structura*) and *chemistry* as that part of the 'history of the bodies' which contains truths about their substance (*Chymia est pars historiae corporum, quae continet ueritates de eorum materia ex qua constant*), and he gave similar definitions for experimental physics and other sciences.[41] In this sense, *historia iuris* was also a corpus of data and statements (*res litterariae*) that contained the facts from which the laws (*leges*) and their modifications originate.[42]

Grunert and Syndikus have summarized four main programmatic goals associated with *historia litteraria*. The first was to provide a selection of sources and to foster discernment and critical thinking. The second was to promote information storage and to pursue the progress of knowledge (*Wissenspeicherung und geleherter Fortschritt*). These works played an important role

---

[38] Heumann 1763, p. 1.

[39] Waquet, 2000, p. 9.

[40] *Historie*, according to Zedler's *Universal-Lexicon* (1735, 13), was a 'Sammlung von Erfahrungen, auf die alle unsere Wissenschaften gründen'.

[41] Nettelbladt 1747, § 108–110, p. 30.

[42] *Est uero Historia iuris pars historiae ciuilis in specie sic dictae, quae continet facta quibus leges originem et mutationes debent* (Nettelbladt 1747, § 94, p. 27).

in assembling information that circulated in the constant flow of academic dissertations and new learned journals (*Gelehrten Zeitungen*) of the time. Third, *historia litteraria* intended to reinforce moral standards through the selection of books (*die Moral der guten Bücher*). Finally, *historia litteraria* should present an entertaining and aesthetic character, offering readers 'beauty and amusement' (*Schönheit und Vergnügen*).[43] This last aspect is connected with what was known in the learned circles of the time as *micrologia litteraria*.[44]

All these goals were also shared by the jurists who by that time were referring to *notitia auctorum, notitia librorum, bibliothecae iuris*, and *historia litteraria iuris* in the title pages of their writings.

II. Historia litteraria iuris (I): Mapping the Legal Discipline

Historia litteraria, as an approach to the ordering and hierarchizing of knowledge, as a 'bridge between new experimentalism' and 'the older, text-based traditions of the Renaissance',[45] stimulated the publication, in the jurisprudential domain, of a multitude of new titles, academic dissertations and orations, periodical journals (*ephemerides*), and bibliographical repertoires. Equally relevant in this collective enterprise of selecting and reordering of materials to build the canon of the *historia litteraria iuris* were the reprints of old and recent authorities, many of them imported from the Catholic south and undertaken in Leipzig and Frankfurt printing houses. The juridical-literary landscape was enriched through new editions, containing significant notes, preliminary texts, and appendices by German jurists.[46] Old jurisprudential authorities

---

[43] Grunert & Syndikus 2015.
[44] Hummel 2002.
[45] Nelles 2000, p. 42.
[46] Examples include adaptations of the axioms collected by the Portuguese jurist Agostinho Barbosa (1589–1649) (reprinted in Leipzig, 1707); *De claris legum interpretibus* by Guido Panziroli (1523–1599) (reprinted in Lepzig, 1721); *De antiquo iure populi Romani libri XI*, by Carlo Sigonio (1524–1584) (reprinted in Leipzig, 1715); the *Origines iuris ciuilis*, by Gianvincenzo Gravina (1664–1718) (reprinted in Leipzig, 1708); the *Respublica iurisconsultorum* by Giuseppe Aurelio di Gennaro (1701–1761) (reprinted in Leipzig in 1733). We could add

were reactivated and recycled as valuable sources of materials, even if the materials had to fit into a new framework.

During the eighteenth century, several law professors active in the various universities of the Holy Roman Empire issued their incursions into the field of *historia litteraria*. Most of these professors chose the Latin language for their elementary compendia, such as August Bünemann (*Historiae litterariae iuris primae lineae in usum studiosorum iuris: specimen ad excitandas doctiorum acroases*, Hannover, 1750), Johannes Friedrich Eisenhart (*Institutiones historiae iuris litterariae*, Helmstedt, 1752; reprinted 1763), and Johannes Heumann (*Apparatus iurisprudentiae litterarius*, Nuremberg, 1752; 1780²), besides the previously mentioned Daniel Nettelbladt, with his *Initia historiae litterariae iuridicae universalis* (Halle, 1764; 1774²) and Hommel with his *Litteratura iuris* (Leipzig 1761; 1779²).

The multifaceted Gottlieb Stolle (1673–1744) had applied the *historia litteraria* approach to theology, medicine, philosophy, and arts, before the publication of his *Anleitung zur Historie der juristischen Gelahrtheit* in 1745. One of Stolle's discourses, delivered in 1714 as director of the gymnasium in Hildburghausen, *Discours von dem Nutzen der Historiae et Notitiae literariae…*, brings together the genre's main goals and its impact on education. Other works written by *polyhistors* outside the legal field had also been used in the introductory courses of the law schools: this was the case with Christoph Heumann's *Conspectus* or Morhof's third book, *Polyhistor iuridicus*, dedicated to jurisprudence.[47]

The various *ephemerides* functioned as fundamental tools for mapping the legal discipline. Reviews of law books and accounts of university life abounded in general journals (such as Chris-

---

to this list the edition of Gregorio Mayans y Siscar's correspondance, produced by Gottlob August Jenichen in 1737: *Epistolarum libri sex*, also in Leipzig, and the 1753 edition of the *Specimen Bibliothecae Hispano-Majansianae siue idea noui catalogi critici operum scriptorum Hispanorum, quae habet in sua bibliotheca Gregorius Majansius generosus Valentinus* (Hannoverae, Impensis Jo. Guil. Schmidii), produced by the bibliophile David Clement, author of the *Bibliotheque Curieuse* (Göttingen: Schmid, 1750–1760).

[47] Nettelbladt mentions the use of Heumann's *Conspectus* in Carrach's lessons at Halle (Nettelbladt 1758, p. 394, 726), and he also refers to the teaching of *historia litteraria* in the preface to his *Initia* (Nettelbladt 1764).

tian Thomasius' *Monatsgespräche*[48]) and in the newly founded juridical journals, many of them short lived, such as the *Acta iurisconsultorum* (Wittenberg, 1734–1737), *Juristischer Büchersaal, oder gründliche Nachricht von den besten juristischen Büchern, der berühmtesten Rechtsgelehrten Leben und anderen zur Rechtsgelahrtheit dienenden Sachen* (Leipzig, 1737–1739), the *Hallische Beyträge zu der juristischen Gelehrten Historie* (Halle, 1755–1762) edited by Daniel Nettelbladt, or the previously mentioned *Unpartheyische Critik über juristische Schriften inn- und ausserhalb Deutschland*, directed by Johann August Bach (Leipzig, 1750–1758), himself an author of juridical-literary *opuscula*.

Another important source of materials was the regular flow of academic dissertations and orations, oftentimes printed as appendices to major works or in collections of *opuscula*. Examples of the concern with the legitimation and methods of *historiae litterariae* in this genre include Johann Gottlieb Oleari's *Dissertatio de utilitate et necessitate rei litterariae in iurisprudentia* (Königsberg, 1713), Johannes Carrach's *Exercitationes iuridicae de necessario litteraturae iuridicae studio* (Halle, 1751), or the volume compiled by Gerhard Oelrich, *Collectio dissertationum historico-antiquario-iuridicarum in Academiis Germanicis habitarum ...* (Bremen, 1785). The topic was also presented in orations delivered by prestigious law professors, such as Augustin von Balthasar's *Vorbericht von dem Nutzen des studii historiae litterariae, und der Art und Weise dasselbe besonders in der Rechtsgelahrtheit nützlich und ordentlich zu tractiren* (Greifswald, 1752) or Nicolaus Hieronymus Gundling's *Kurtzer Entwurf eines Collegii über die Historiam Literariam vor die Studiosos Juris* (Halle, 1703).

Another corpus of juridical works related to the *historia litteraria* approach emerged during the last decades of the eighteenth century. In this late wave of publications, the use of German was consolidated, and emphasis was placed on the need to systematize the unstoppable growth of the *bibliotheca iuris* in the various legal fields, such as Johann Stephan Pütter's *Litteratur des Teutschen Staatsrechts* (Göttingen 1776–1783), one of the most celebrated legal repertoires. These 'protobibliographies' often evoked the word 'library' in their titles, as a genre or a special branch of *histo-*

---

[48] Thomasius 1690.

ria litteraria: this was the case of August Friedrich Schott's *Bibliothek der neuesten Juristischen Litteratur* (Leipzig, 1783–1790) and of Johann Christian von Selchow's *Juristische Bibliothek von neuen juristischen Büchern und Abhandlungen* (Göttingen, 1765–1782).[49] By the end of the eighteenth century, the term *polyhistor* had acquired a negative connotation and was used with restraint in the legal field.[50] Jurists had always preferred allusions to *historia litteraria* and to other terms (*notitia auctorum*, *bibliotheca*, among others), even if some had flirted with direct references to *polyhistorismus*, possibly in order to attract readers beyond the restricted circle of learned jurists. This appeal to a broader readership was probably behind the changes to the title page of the work by Heinrich Kestner, law professor in Rinteln, in 1699.[51] The very same work, with the very same printed gatherings circulated simultaneously under two different title pages, with two different imprints: one of the versions started with the catchy *Polyhistor* (Frankfurt edition), while the other, *Prudentia studendi iura* (Rinteln edition), sounded more medieval.[52] The typographical result is a rare case of what bibliographers call, technically, a *separate issue*, perhaps a printers' strategy to conquer new markets.[53]

In any case, this episode is emblematic of one of the most idiosyncratic features of the works of *historia litteraria iuris*, which distinguishes them from other genres of juridical writings. While legal literature is typically self-referential and targets its own readers (law students, academic or professional jurists), the attempt to go beyond the usual law books' readership and to communicate

[49] Mohnhaupt 2013, p. 13.

[50] One of the exceptions was Herman Conring, one of the leading figures in German jurisprudence (despite his chair in medicine, at Helmstedt), who was praised as a *polyhistor*: Nettelbladt 1774, I, § 32, p. 25–26; II, § 160, no. 91, p. 128.

[51] See Feige 1969.

[52] The remaining sentences of the title are exactly the same, except for the headings: see Kestner 1699a and 1699b. The word *polyhistor* had already been used by jurists in the sixteenth century, but not associated with the critical empirical approach of the late seventeenth-century *polyhistorismus*. See, for example, Costanus 1598.

[53] A *separate issue* refers to the publication of two editions at the same time with the clear intent on the part of the editors or printers to present each of the editions as a distinct unit. The title of the work and the imprint on the cover are changed, even if the preliminaries remain the same. The category of *separate issue* should be utilized with restrictions, according to Bowers 1949, p. 100–101.

with other members of the republic of letters, is omnipresent in the *historia litteraria iuris*. In terms of style, this peculiarity is visible in various elements.

First, there were adventurous experiments of writing legal works in unusual forms. For instance, the highly praised Neapolitan scholar Giuseppe Aurelio di Gennaro wrote his *Respublica iurisconsultorum*, already mentioned above, in the form of a *fabula*, a fictional narrative.[54] Second, the writers of *historia litteraria iuris* made copious references to the necessity of 'amusing' readers; such references were not found in the usual commentaries on the Digest or in other juridical genres. Hommel provided information that, in his own words, was neither necessary nor useful, but was entertaining (*nec necessarium, nec utilem, at iucundum tamen*).[55] Nettelbladt aimed at the 'recreation of the soul' through delightful juridical-literary studies (*...recreationem animi ex amoenissimo hoc studio capiendam*).[56]

All these elements are connected, via constant allusions and parallels, to the notion of the republic of letters, as a self-representation of a community of scholars.[57] As Nettelbladt stated, jurists had long ago achieved the 'right of citizenship' in the republic of letters (*Dudum etiam ius ciuitatis impetrarunt iurisconsulti in orbe litterato*).[58] This concern of the jurists with their own image, their status, and their belonging to an idealized republic of letters, similar to a concern that Goldgar has highlighted for the scholarly community in general,[59] is also illustrated by the polemic between Denis de Sallo (1626–1669) and the jurist and poet Gilles de Ménage (1613–1692), author of the *Amoenitates iuris civilis* (1664, reprinted in Frankfurt, 1738). According to Hommel,[60] the disagreement arose from the neglect of law books

---

[54] In his *Prolegomena de historia iurisprudentiae litteraria generatim* (1779, § 2, p. 5–6), Hommel compared Ianuario with Jonathan Swift's *Itinera*.

[55] *Bibliotheca Iuris Rabbinica et Saracenorum Arabica, quem librum nec necessarium, nec utilem, at iucundum tamen, raptim et fugiente penna collegi, et 1762 Byruthi in octauo edidi* (Hommel 1779, 1, II, p. 39).

[56] Nettelbladt 1774, § 15, p. 9.

[57] Jaumann 2001, p. 11–19.

[58] Nettelbladt 1774, § 37, p. 30.

[59] Goldgar 1995, p. 6–7.

[60] Hommel 1779, *Prolegomena*, § 7, p. 14; Nettelbladt 1774, § 37, p. 30.

in the famous *Journal des Sçavants*, founded by Sallo in 1655.[61] *Historia litteraria iuris*, therefore, was one of the arenas in which to display the jurists' dignity as scholars in an imaginary republic of letters and to negotiate the disciplinary frontiers of jurisprudence with other emerging fields.

As far as structure is concerned, the works of *historia litteraria iuris* were frequently divided into two main parts, dedicated to the *notitia auctorum* and *notitia librorum*, emulating the usual classifications of *historia litteraria*. The first one, *notitia auctorum*, relied largely on medieval and early modern volumes, prefaces, and other texts about the 'lives' of jurists (*uitae iurisconsultorum*) as well as on recent biographical notes and funeral eulogies that circulated in the periodical journals. One of the first reference works in this regard was Georg Beyer's (1665–1714) *De utili et necessaria autorum iuridicorum et iuris arti inseruientium notitia schediasma*, printed in 1698 and enlarged in subsequent editions during the eighteenth century by Carl Ferdinand Hommel, Gottlob August Jenichen, and others.

The part dedicated to the *notitia librorum* contained four types of sections, or chapters, that integrated virtually all works that belonged to the genre of *historia litteraria iuris*.

The first section aimed at presenting an overview of the most important reference books in the different branches of law: *ius ciuile, ius feudale, ius canonicum, ius publicum, ius naturae et gentium, ius criminale, ius Germanicum*, etc. Through the works of *historia litteraria iuris*, we observe the increasing process of disciplinary fragmentation within the legal field.

A second section or group of chapters was dedicated to what we might broadly, anachronistically refer to as 'legal methodology', oftentimes identified under the label *de ratione discendi docendique iuris*. This methodological, pedagogical chapter frequently included references to the more ambitious efforts at systematizing legal materials in the sixteenth century (Conrad Lagus, Hugues Doneau, Nicolaus Vigelius) as well as more practically ori-

---

[61] According to Birn 1965, Gilles de Ménage responded to Sallo's attacks both orally and in the preface to Malherbe's poems. In the preface, however, there is no explicit complaint about the absence of jurists: 'Et sa dignité, quelque respect que j'aye pour elle, ne m'en auroit pas empêché: *Senatori maledicere non licet; remaledicere jus fasque est*' (Ménage 1666, s.n.).

ented advice about the methods of studying, excerpting, note-taking, and reading habits. Both elements were inseparable, since the acts of reading and writing were not understood as abstract intellectual processes, independent from the concrete ways of appropriating written materials. Those types of advice had circulated during the early modern period through the genre of *methodus studendi in utroque iure*, of which Giovanni Battista Caccialupi's (1420–1496) and Mateo Gribaldi Mofa's (1505–1564) works constituted the most renowned examples. Influenced by Morhof's experimental approach, the topic of libraries was also present in the legal literature of the time. When explaining the method, the *via et ratione* of acquiring *notitiae rei litterariae iuris*, Hommel, for instance, mentioned the pillars of the empirical method, such as the need to visit private and public libraries, the reading of library catalogues and repertoires, *Relationes litterariae* (*Gelehrte Zeitungen*), and the promotion of *itinera*, or *Ausbildungsreisen*.[62] In the same direction, understanding the knowledge of libraries as a constitutive part of the critical method, Burkhard Gotthelf Struve (1671–1738), a jurist and librarian, before publishing his influential *Bibliotheca iuris selecta* in 1703, which was constantly enhanced by other authors during the eighteenth century, had defended his dissertation *De iure bibliothecarum* under the presidency of Samuel Stryk in Halle, 1702.[63]

A third type of chapter commonly found in the *historia litteraria iuris* dealt with controversies and will be examined in the following section. Finally, the *historia litteraria iuris* typically contained one or more chapters (or several dispersed notes throughout the work, as in Stolle's *Anleitung*, mentioned *infra*) on illegitimate forms of authorship, enumerating pseudonyms, anonymous works, and famous plagiarizers in the field of law. Those catalogues of plagiarizers in jurisprudence followed the path inaugurated by Jakob Thomasius in 1673, and were connected with the primary goals of *historia litteraria* in general.[64] The attempt at identifying plagiarizers in all disciplines was one of the pillars of Morhof's *Polyhistor*. Jurisprudence appeared

---

[62] Hommel 1779, *Prolegomena*, p. 14.
[63] Struve 1702, Struve 1703.
[64] On Jakob Thomasius, see Jaumann 2000.

to be one of the fields particularly infected by the plagiarizers' plague: the opening paragraph of the *Polyhistor*'s book on jurisprudence was devoted to the various genres of writings about controversies and the frequency of plagiarism (*Multitudo huius generis scriptorum et plagia frequentia*). The importance of identifying pseudonyms, anonyms, and plagiarizers had become a topos in the *historia litteraria iuris* compendia: *Non frustra laborant, qui eruditis homonymis, pseudonymis, anonymis, plagiariis, impostoribus dignoscendis operam nauant*, stated Johannes Heumann, in his *Apparatus iurisprudentiae literarius*.[65] Giuseppe Aurelio de Gennaro, mentioned above, offered one of the most unmerciful overviews of the abuses committed in the legal literary community in his *Respublica iurisconsultorum*.

As Nettelbladt pointed out, immoderate forms of polemic and plagiarism were both portrayed as serious transgressions for jurists and learned men in general. He condemned as moral vices an excessive love of debate (*nimio disputandi amore abrepti*), disproportionate indulgence in emotion during debate (*in disputando affectibus nimium indulgentes*), and plagiarism (*plagii litterari rei*).[66] The moral dimension of the literary acts was as relevant to explaining cleavages between jurists as were the intellectual differences of opinion: Brunquell, for instance, situated the moral and epistemic motivations for disagreement among twelfth-century glossators at the same level.[67] Hommel shared this opinion, invoking the vices of emulation and envy (*aemulatio*, or *occulta aemulatio*, and *inuidia*) as the sources of controversy, which caused

---

[65] Heumann 1780, § 182, p. 196. For an overview of the *polyhistors*' search for pseudonyms and other illegitimate forms of authorship, see Mulsow 2006.

[66] In the following paragraph, Nettelbladt identified the main vices of the jurists: *Ast cum et in republica literaria dentur ciues male morati, boni ciuis officia non implentes, et inter iurisconsultorum nationem tales proh dolor obueniunt. Sunt enim et inter hos qui, ut alii eruditi: 1) praeiudicio auctoritatis occoecati, 2) nimio disputandi amore abrepti, 3) in disputando affectibus nimium indulgentes, 4) plagii litterarii rei nec non allotrioepiskopoi qui nimirum temere artis suae fines transgrediuntur* (Nettelbladt 1774, § 37, p. 31–32).

[67] *A duobus itaque et quidem celebrioribus Irnerii discipulis nimirum Martino Gosiano et Bulgaro, cum uterque ad docendum se dedisset, et partim ex aemulatione partim ex dissentiendi studio contrarias sententias fuisset, quilibet autem suos sectatores et asseclas inuenisset, duae diuersae iuris interpretum familiae, quae usque ad Franciscum Accursium durarunt, sunt orate ...* (Brunquell 1725, p. 8).

damage to the *respublica litteraria* in general and to the progress of jurisprudence in particular.[68] In the next section, we consider which juridical controversies he had in mind and why he wanted to present them to his readers.

III. Historia litteraria iuris *(II)*: Mapping Controversies in Law

Hommel divided his *Litteratura iuris* into two main parts, dedicated to *notitia librorum* and to *notitia iurisconsultorum*, reflecting the standard structure of *historia litteraria* textbooks.

Hommel's work contains all four types of chapters mentioned above: first, an overview of the most important reference books in the different branches of law, including the usual references to natural law, canon and civil law, public law, feudal law, Germanic and criminal law.[69] In the second revised edition of 1779, besides other small changes in the structure of the book and in some of the chapters' titles, Hommel added new chapters: one of them was dedicated to the laws of Jewish and 'other barbaric nations' (*Litteratura*, 1, II: *Leges Mosaicae aliarumque barbararum gentium*).[70] Another addition was the miscellaneous and heterogeneous chapter entitled *De iuribus pusillis* (literally, 'on the insignificant laws'), or *Libri classici iuris Politiae, Principum priuati, Opificialis, Cambialis, Mercatorii, Maritimi, Naualis, Cameralis, Georgici, Forestalis, Venatorii, Metallici, Militaris, Iudaici*.[71] This addition was clearly a symptom of the proliferation of new legal branches and of the growing relevance of *Kameralistik* and *Polizeiwissenschaften*. Even if he dedicated positive words to

---

[68] Hommel invoked Christian Otto Böckel's opinion, in the sense that the diversity of 'families' of jurists emanated fundamentally from *aemulatio* and envy: *ex sola aemulatione atque inuidia diversas eorum opiniones promanasse* (Hommel 1779, XVIII, § 1, p. 201).

[69] *Libri classici iuris naturalis et gentium, Libri classici iuris ciuilis, Libri classici iuris canonici, Thesauri utriusque iuris* (in the first edition: *Libri classici iuris canonici, ubi de thesauris iuris utriusque*), *Libri classici iuris Germanici, Libri classici iuris Feodalis, Libri classici iuris criminalis, Libri classici iuris publici, Libri classici processus et extraiudicialis practicae* (in the first edition: *Libri classici processus iudicialis*).

[70] Hommel 1779, 1, II, p. 37–41.

[71] Hommel 1779, 1, XI, p. 149–154.

some of the titles reviewed in this chapter, such as Heumann's *Initia iuris politiae* (1758),[72] Hommel acted rather as a guardian of a more traditional order of knowledge. He included the new fields that threatened the centrality of jurisprudence in order to criticize the unnecessary multiplication of legal disciplines and to diminish the role of the emerging ones, expressing his concern about the 'subversion of order and doctrine' of these new 'small' or 'insignificant' laws.[73] If this excessive division of *iuris capita* were to continue, he argued, there would be a risk of producing in the near future commentaries on subjects such as the law of camels, the law of beetles, of dormice, of vampires, or of sphinxes.[74]

Second, the *Litteratura iuris* contained the typical methodological chapter, entitled *De variis ius docendi discendique methodis* (*Litteratura*, I, XVII, in the second edition), where Hommel expressed his negative view of Leibniz's *Nova methodus*, qualified as childish (*puerilis*) and unworthy (*indigna*) of both philosophers and jurists.[75] Hommel also showed his affiliation with Christian Thomasius (1655–1728),[76] as well as the influence of the empirical approach of Morhof and Bacon, despite detaching himself from both of them in certain respects.[77]

Finally, he included the chapters on controversies and on the illegitimate forms of authorship,[78] besides the various miscellaneous, 'micrological' accounts that not only permeated the whole book but also deserved one chapter expressly entitled *Micrologica varia* (2, V). Hommel situated the two chapters dedicated

---

[72] Hommel 1779, 1, XI, § 2, p. 150–151.

[73] Hommel 1779, 1, XI, p. 149. For the criticism of the old scheme based on the four superior disciplines, to which Kant refers in *Der Streit der Fakultäten* (1798), see Füssel 2011, p. 60–61.

[74] *Si in tot frustra artem scindas et in puluerem capita iuris conteras, si praeter necessitatem multiplices doctrinas, quis tandem finis erit? Auertat Deus, ne simili instituto iurisprudentiam Ludimoderatorum, Balneatorum aut Mendicantium scribere, cuiquam in mentem veniat, aut ne quis futuris temporibus de iure Camelorum, Scarabaeorum, Glirium, Vampyrarum aut Sphyngum commentari velit.* (Hommel 1779, 1, XI, § 1 *De iuribus pusillis*, p. 150).

[75] Hommel 1779, 1, XVII, § 11, p. 196.

[76] On Thomasius and *historia litteraria*, see Scattola & Vollhardt 2003.

[77] For his criticism of Morhof, see Hommel 1761, p. 25, 354.

[78] In the 1779 edition, chapter XIX: *De libris sine parente genitis seu de scriptoribus innominatis et pseudonymis* and chapter XX: *De furtis litteraris iureconsultorum aliisque fraudibus*.

to safeguarding authorship and exposing plagiarism immediately after the extensive account on controversies — the three of them placed in the first part of the book (*Liber primus, qui est Bibliographicus, notitiam librorum subministrat*), in its second section, dedicated to miscellaneous aspects (*Varia et promiscua ad librorum notitiam pertinentia in se continens*).

Hommel's extensive list of controversies in chapter XVIII included references to more than thirty scholarly and personal disputes, involving different individuals or schools.

It is a manifold, heterogeneous inventory, offering a short summary of the contents or main thesis under dispute and the main antagonists or schools involved, stretching from Roman times until the first half of the eighteenth century. Hommel did not follow a chronological order nor did he declare an explicit criterion for his selection. His list was capacious enough to include the opposition between Grotius and Selden on the law of the sea, disagreements on usury, hereditary rights, Irnerius's authorship of the notes known as *Authenticae Codicis*, and an account of Filippo Decio (1454–1536) and Giasone del Maino (1435–1519) throwing stones at each other. Hommel's rich catalogue of controversies included what we would call 'scientific' or 'epistemic' matters together with 'political' and 'social' matters of discussion. What was the role of such an account of controversies in the *historia litteraria iuris*? How did jurists — Hommel, in this case — portray the controversies in their discipline? What logic, which criteria, lay behind Hommel's selection of controversies?

Even if he did not announce a clear taxonomy for his extensive inventory, by looking at the content and the various uses of these controversies in Hommel's discourse, they can be divided into five different groups.

1. In this essayistic exercise of examining and classifying Hommel's history of controversies, the first group is the largest one. It comprehends famous disputes concerning different thematic issues: *controuersia* here was understood as a debatable topic, not necessarily engendering long-lasting *sectae*, or opposed schools and factions. We could describe this group as *thematic*, since it includes a long inventory of disagreements about questions of public relevance, such as polygamy, divorce, usury, matters

related to the rights of succession, or polemics about the exercise of power and sovereignty. Hommel used these disputes to declare his own views regarding controversial topics, as well as to present a detailed account of the legal opinions involved.

These disputes involve, for example, various schools of thought related to public law and the exercise of sovereignty (*quod ius imperii publicum attinet...*). This is where Hommel alluded to the *Caesariani*, the *Monarchistae*, the *Monzambanistae*, and the *Fürstenerii*[79] (Severinus de Monzambano was the pseudonym of Samuel Pufendorf, while Caesarini Fürsteneri was Leibniz's pseudonym in *De jure suprematus*). The antagonism between Claude Saumaise (Salmasius) and John Milton regarding the decapitation of Charles Stuart gave Hommel occasion to deal with the binary of *monarchomachos* and *machiavellistas*,[80] and the quarrel between Pufendorf and Valentinus Albertus was an excuse to side with new approaches to natural law against orthodox theologians. The same Claude Saumaise, who was well known for his belligerence, was the protagonist of several other disputes, such as the one against Cyprianus Regnerus ab Oosterga (on the nature of usury), to which I will refer again *infra*.

Other famous disagreements summarized by Hommel are the ones between Hugo Grotius' *Mare liberum*, written against the Catholic monarchy, and Johan Selden's *Mare clausum*.[81] Also related to *dominium* and *imperium* was the debate between Johann Friedrich Horn (1629–1665) and Wilhelm Leyser (1628–1689) about the *dominium supereminens*, that is, whether all goods belonged to the prince or not. Hommel also mentioned controversies regarding polygamy. The discussion of whether polygamy was against natural law had divided Catholic and Protestants and occupied various jurists and reformers (Bernardino Ochino, Johann Friedrich Böckelmann, and Laurentius Beger, among others), especially after the episode of Philipp of Hessen's bigamy in the early years of the Reformation. Hommel also included disagreements about more precise topics, such as the disagreement

---

[79] Hommel 1779, 1, XVIII, § 5, p. 209.
[80] Hommel 1779, 1, XVIII, § 11, p. 216.
[81] Hommel 1779, 1, XVIII, § 10, p. 215.

between Johann Ulrich von Cramer and Senkenberg regarding the hereditary rights of daughters.[82]

All of these disputes were matters of public relevance, and Hommel deliberately presented them as part of the jurisprudential tradition.

2. The second group of controversies identified in Hommel's inventory relates more directly to the *interpretatio legis*, or to different approaches to authoritative texts. These controversies were unique to jurisprudence, distinguishing it from other higher disciplines, such as theology and medicine. To this second group belonged the rivalries between Sabinians and Proculians in classical Rome, between the followers of the twelfth-century glossators Martino Gosia and Bulgaro (*Gosianorum versus Bulgarianorum sectas*), and between Legists and Canonists, as well as the sixteenth-century *Realistarum versus Humanistarum sectae* — other terms for the opposition between *mos Italicus* and *mos Gallicus*, which was also invoked by Hommel in some passages.[83] The lively eighteenth-century antagonism between *Germanists* and *Romanists* (*Germanizantium versus Romanizantium sectas*), about which Hommel expressed a moderate and conciliatory view (*ambidexteros nos esse oportet*),[84] could be also included in this group.

The glossators' controversy, discussed in eighteenth-century academic dissertations and resumed even in early nineteenth-century editions of sources,[85] could be said, as Brunquell wrote in 1725, to replicate the polarization between Sabinians and Proculians in classical Roman jurisprudence.[86] Why this enduring interest in the medieval glossators? Together with the controversy between *Legistarum* and *Decretistarum*, that is, the study of *ius civile* (*leges*) versus *ius canonicum* (*canones*), the rivalry between

---

[82] Hommel 1779, 1, XVIII, § 21, p. 235–236.

[83] ...*non more Italico, sed Gallico, quem scilicet Cuiacius introduxisset*, wrote Hommel, referring to Muretus' and others' criticism of Pierre Loriot (Hommel 1779, 1, XVIII, § 3, p. 205).

[84] Hommel 1779, 1, XVIII, § 4, p. 208.

[85] At the beginning of the nineteenth century, Christian Gottlieb Haubold edited one of the important sources of medieval controversies, the *opusculum* of Roffredo de Beneventano (?–1265): Beneventano 1821. On Haubold and the antiquarian philological approach in this period: Vano 2000, p. 72–73.

[86] Brunquell 1725.

the Bolognese doctors Martino and Bulgaro helped to illustrate some of the favorite topics of Protestant narratives regarding the formation and authority of canon law. When deciding upon the arguments between Martino and Bulgaro, for instance, the pope had converted the errors of the glossators into established law thanks to the authority of canon law (*ut errores Glossatorum per autoritatem iuris canonici ius constituerint*).[87] Decretists, or Canonists, and Legists, supposedly reflected the medieval divisions between Guelphs and Ghibellines, the rival parties that supported the papacy and the Holy Roman emperors, respectively. Hommel used the contest between Legists and Decretists to present the development of canon law and the concession of the university degrees by the pope in terms of 'hate' and 'envy'.[88] This moral assessment was a commonplace in Protestant legal literature, and the authors of *historia litteraria iuris* contributed to its spread. For instance, Johann Friedrich Eisenhart's *Institutiones historiae iuris litterariae* (which has already been mentioned and which circulated together with an appendix containing an oration on the various schools of jurists in Rome by Franz Carl Conrad), alluded to the 'mutual hate' between *Legistae* and *Decretistae* (*se autem inuicem maximo odio et diris prosequebantur*).[89] For Eisenhart, *ius canonicum* was fundamentally born out of envy and hatred towards *ius civile*.[90]

---

[87] This is one of the explanations given by Brunquell, reproducing Justus Henning Böhmer's opinion: *Ita vero saepe factum, ut errores Glossatorum per autoritatem iuris Canonici ius constituerint. In arduis enim quaestionibus glossatores ut plurimum sese aliosque deceperunt, quippe qui haud instructi erant doctrina morali, et antiquitates Romanas ignorabant, inde nubem pro Iunone saepe acceperunt, et ipsos pontifices in eundem deduxerunt errorem, adeo ut inde plures utriusque iuris differentiae ortae sint* (Brunquell 1725, p. 21–22) (see footnote no. 67).

[88] Hommel 1779, 1, XVIII, § 2, p. 203–204; in the final Index, the references are to *Pontifex Romanus ... doctores odit* and *Pontifex Romanus ... eorum machinationes*.

[89] Eisenhart 1763, § XI, p. 351.

[90] [*Legistae* et *Decretistae*] *se autem inuicem maximo odio et diris prosequebantur* [...]. *Supra iam dictum est, Pontifices Romanorum inuidiosis quasi oculis magnam, quam inuenerat iuris Iustinianei studium, auctoritatem prosecutos fuisse. Odium hoc Pontificum ius ciuile inprimis sustentabat iurisconsultorum assentandi studium, qui omnem potestatem imperatoribus tribuebant. Factum inde est, ut Pontifices non solum clericos a studio iuris ciuilis auocarent, et ne Parisiis illud doceretur,*

In other words, two capital sins had motivated the creation of canon law. In this same sense, the Roman jurists' division between Sabinians and Proculians (D.1.2.2.47)[91] was one of the most prolific sources of discussion, being the object of several academic dissertations. The Sabinians and Proculians were appealed to in discussing, among other things, philosophical divisions,[92] the criteria for legal reasoning (whether this should be based on natural reason or equity, *ratio naturalis* or *aequitas*[93]), the value of 'innovation' in law, and even the values of the Roman Republic in opposition to the emperor's power.[94]

The dispute between Sabinians and Proculians was a key controversy for illustrating the 'progress' (*de incrementis*) of *iurisprudentia*, which was one of the primary goals of *historia litteraria*. The search for 'footprints' of the two schools (*uestigia sectarum*), in order to find new clues for solving the antinomies and contradictions between various fragments of the Digest, inspired several writings and dissertations, such as Rebhan and Böckel's *De sectis, seu diuersis ueterum iurisconsultorum familiis* (1666) and Gottfried Mascov's *De sectis Sabinianorum et Proculianorum in iure civili diatribe* (1728).[95]

---

prohiberent; verum etiam decretum a Gratiano collectum in scholas introducerent, Eisenhart 1763, p. 351.

[91] *Post hunc maximae auctoritatis fuerunt Ateius Capito, qui Ofilium secutus est, et Antistius Labeo, qui omnes hos audiuit, institutus est autem a Trebatio. Ex his Ateius consul fuit: Labeo noluit, cum offerretur ei ab Augusto consulatus, quo suffectus fieret, honorem suscipere, sed plurimum studiis operam dedit: et totum annum ita diuiserat, ut Romae sex mensibus cum studiosis esset, sex mensibus secederet et conscribendis libris operam daret. Itaque reliquit quadringenta volumina, ex quibus plurima inter manus versantur. Hi duo primum veluti diuersas sectas fecerunt: nam Ateius Capito in his, quae ei tradita fuerant, perseuerabat, Labeo ingenii qualitate et fiducia doctrinae, qui et ceteris operis sapientiae operam dederat, plurima innovare instituit* (D.1.2.2.47).

[92] Slevogt 1724.

[93] As in one of the dissertations presided over by Hommel in 1750, which was praised in Struve's *Bibliotheca* (Struve 1756, p. 12).

[94] Peter Stein challenged the traditional binary between an innovative view attributed to Labeo, head of the Proculians, one the one side, and a more conservative view associated with Ateius Capito, head of the Sabinians, on the other side: Stein 1972.

[95] See especially the long chapter entitled *Signantur praecipua sectarum vestigia* (Mascov 1728, XI, p. 145–276). This work was an enlarged version of the author's doctoral dissertation: Mascov 1724.

3. A third type of controversy, related to the previous group, directly concerned the authenticity (and hence the authority) of the fundamental juridical texts of classical Roman origin. This was the case for the endless controversy regarding Irnerius' authorship of the *Authenticae* (the marginal glosses to the Codex), a controversy conducted during the previous centuries by various jurists, such as Ulrich Zasius, Charles du Moulin, or Cornelius van Bynkershoek.[96] Henri Brenkman's *Historia Pandectarum*, printed in 1722 after an extensive *iter Italicum* in search of manuscripts, instigated another vivid debate, regarding the authenticity and value of the Florentine codex of the Digest; this debate was narrated in detail by Hommel.[97] Even if this kind of textual discussion seemed self-referential and directed to a readership of specialized jurists and law students; in the context of *historia litteraria iuris*, such discussions also served the self-fashioning purpose of presenting texts that conferred on jurisprudence the identity (and hence dignity) of an academic discipline.

4. A fourth group in this experimental typology of Hommel's controversies, dealt with the social role of jurists. This group encompasses episodes as manifold as the quarrels between the law faculties and the municipal courts or the classical controversy about the superiority of arms or letters. This category exemplifies the double dimension of early modern polemics, which embraced more than debates about knowledge, as Bremer and Spoerhase have emphasized. Besides an epistemic dimension (as confirmation or denial of scientific claims), polemics also had an eminently *social* dimension in which the gain or loss of social recognition was at stake.[98]

Hommel paid special attention to the prohibition of doctors in law in municipal courts and institutions, which generated clashes with the law faculties (*Ortas esse novimus, inter Facultates iuridicas et Scabinatus, quasdam discordias*).[99] The accounts of early modern disputes regarding the presence of jurists in the

---

[96] Hommel 1779, 1, XVIII, § 16, p. 224–225. For an overview of this subject, see Pennington 2011.
[97] Hommel 1779, 1, XVIII, § 19, p. 227–231. See B. H. Stolte, Jr. (2004).
[98] Bremer & Spoerhase 2011, p. 114.
[99] Hommel 1779, 1, XVIII, § 4, p. 206.

administration of justice served a symbolic and self-fashioning cultural purpose.[100] Such accounts aimed at displaying a constructive narrative about the fundamental role of jurists in the social order. The underlying message was that without jurists, any society would fall into chaos. The absence of jurists was typical of primitive societies, such as the antediluvian ones, and the origin of jurists was European — neither Asian nor African.[101] Both the classical debate regarding arms versus letters and the conflicts generated by the prohibition of doctors in law at the municipal courts reflect this need to exhibit a positive public image of jurists and their role in society.

The arms-versus-letters motif (*De Togae et militiae excellentiore dignitate*) became visible in the field of jurisprudence through the antagonistic views of Signorolo de Omodei (Homodeis senior) (1308/1310–c. 1371) on the one side and Ludovico Bolognino (1446–1508) and Francesco de Accoltis (c. 1418–c. 1486) on the other. The *sedes* for this controversy was Ludovico Bolognino's critical annotations to Omodei's argument for the superiority of the *milites* in the latter's *Utrum praeferendus sit doctor an miles*. The topic of the nobility of doctors in law had received its first systematic treatment in Bartolo de Sassoferrato's works, which had focused rather on its social and legal aspects than on the moral ones.[102]

Also related to the categories of the *Ständegesellschaft* was the argument about the origins of chivalry, the lower nobility (*cavallarios siue milites, quos hodie inferiores nobiles appellamus*),[103] and whether chivalry belonged to the nobility (*illa difficilima quaesito, utrum milites seu equites ad nobilium, an vero ad ingeniorum classem relati fuerint?*).[104] Hommel dedicated to this dispute a consid-

---

[100] See the insightful essay by Kirwan 2013.

[101] *I[uris]c[onsul]torum origo apud populos post diluvium ortos quaerenda, inter quos, non Asiae et Africae, sed potius Europae incolae primos produxerunt i[uris]c[onsult]os* — and not even among the Hebrews there had ever been proper jurists (Nettelbladt 1774, § 33, p. 27; this idea is often repeated: see for instance § 201, p. 207).

[102] Signorolo degli Omodei, *Utrum praeferendus sit doctor an miles, cum additionibus domini Ludovici de Bolognini*, in *Tractatus universi iuris*, XVIII, f. 25va, no. 54–56. See Treggiari 2014, p. 39–40.

[103] Hommel 1779, 1, XVIII, § 22, p. 237.

[104] Hommel 1779, 1, XVIII, § 22, p. 236.

erably larger space, relative to the other disputes described in this chapter.[105] He probably did so for two reasons.

First, Hommel had personally engaged in an argument about this matter with Carl Friedrich Pauli, who, in his *Einleitung in die Kenntniß des Deutschen Hohen und Niedern Adels* (1753), had criticized Hommel's dissertation on the particle 'Von' (*De particula 'Von' nostris temporibus nobilitatibus charactere*, 1752). The quarrel about the origins of the lower nobility took shape in the pages of the *Göttingische Anzeige* and in later responses,[106] and Hommel used the pages of the *Litteratura iuris* to make his case and to send readers to his other writings on the same topic collected in his *Rhapsodiae* (*Observationes*, 503, 588). Hence, the works of *historia litteraria iuris* also functioned as a means for the *publicisation d'une querelle*, bringing it to public attention and submitting the matter to the judgement of the learned community.[107]

Second, it is manifest that the definition of nobility played a central role in the hierarchical society of the eighteenth century. Nobility determined privileges, tax exemptions, ceremonial protocols, access to certain offices that required the noble condition, or the exclusion of illegitimate children. The classifications and taxonomies of nobility that circulated in the juridical texts were certainly an important piece in the process of recognition and building social distinction.[108] In this process, the *sedes materiae* were mainly juridical texts such as the *Speculum Saxonicum* (3, 45) and jurists' compilations on *ius feudale*, such as the baron of Senkenberg's *Corpus iuris feudalis Germanici*, quoted by Hommel.

It is meaningful that Hommel penned a rather detailed description of the controversy about nobility and situated it in the final pages of his chapter. Hommel not only gave his final word on a contentious issue in which he had been directly involved, but framed the debate in jurisprudential terms. The cat-

---

[105] Hommel 1779, 1, XVIII, § 22, p. 236–240.

[106] See C. F. Pauli (1753a) and C. F. Pauli (1753b). Hommel also refers to his response entitled *Abhandlung vom Ursprunge des niedern Adels in Teutschland*, inserted in a *Samlung einiger ausgesucheten Stüke der Geselschaft der freyen Künste zu Leipzig* (Leipzig, 1755), which I was unable to consult.

[107] Bodenmann & Rey 2013, p. 242–243.

[108] On the topic of nobility in early modern legal treatises, see A. M. Hespanha 1993.

egories of nobility — the definition of the social actors, their distinctive position, and its consequences in the hierarchical society — belonged mainly to the field of jurisprudence, to its traditional texts, and to its *historia litteraria*.

5. Finally, a fifth group of controversies concerns personal hostilities between individual jurists. Hommel narrated episodes not only of verbal outrage but also of violent physical encounter.

Some of the famous clashes concerned fifteenth- and sixteenth-century jurists, such as Giasone del Maino and Filippo Decio, who threw stones at each other (*se etiam lapidibus inuicem petierunt*),[109] and the conflict between François Ory (Osius Aurelius) and one of his fellow students named Monetus. After defending Cujas' opinion in a certain matter, Ory was insulted and literally punched by Monetus to the point of seeing 'little stars in plain daylight'.[110] Hommel, however, was apparently more interested in commenting on a relatively recent episode. The protagonists were Georg Christian Gebauer and Gottfried Mascov, the author of the aforementioned work on the conflict between the Sabinians and the Proculians. Hommel did not give many details (*Ambos professores, Themidosque e stemmate fratres / Dum leges tractant, publice in arma ruunt*), but it was well known that after a physical fight, in 1739, Mascov lost his chair at the University of Göttingen.[111]

This episode and others gave Hommel the occasion to censor those who shamed the learned community of jurists by violating the basic principles of *honeste uiuere* and *neminem laedere*, crystalized in the authoritative juridical texts (D.1.1.10.1), and to criticize those who spread filthy clamor (*conuicia denique impurissima spargunt*).[112] Two other episodes concerned verbal violence

---

[109] Hommel 1779, 1, XVIII, § 6, p. 210.

[110] *Narrat in Dispuncto (sic) ad Merillium Osius Aurelius [...] se, cum Cuiacii sententiam tuitus a Monetio, et forte ei contumeliosius oblocutus esset, eo rem deuenisse, ut ab eo uapularet et, ob impactum non perfunctorie colaphum, uideretur sibi uidere micantes igniculos stellulasque media luce discurrentes* (Hommel 1779, 1, XVIII, § 6, p. 210).

[111] Hommel 1779, 1, XVIII, § 6, p. 210. On this episode, see Eisenhart 1884.

[112] Hommel 1779, 1, XVIII, § 6, p. 210–211. The celebrated passage by Ulpian is *Iuris praecepta sunt haec: honeste vivere, alterum non laedere, suum cuique tribuere* (D.1.1.10.1).

between jurists, especially the one between Claude Saumaise (Salmasius) and Didier Herault (Desiderius Heraldus). Salmasius was famous for his immoderate insults, and Hommel offered a sample of his copious repertoire (*belluam, magnam bestiam, mulum togatum, animal Arcadicum, imperitiae prostibulum, fungum putridum, mentis febricitantis leguleium, iuris dedoctorem, nugicrepum et nugiuendulum, Lotaringum bubalum, caprimulgum, Anubin foraneum*).[113]

Insults of another level were exchanged between the jurists Johann Wolfgang Trier (1686–1750) and Gottfried Sellius (1704–1767), who excelled also as a naturalist. The dispute concerned the use of Johann Gottlieb Heineccius' axiomatic method in law. Trier, who was according to Hommel a 'resented' rival of Heineccius in Frankfurt an der Oder, had dissimulated his identity under the name 'Schüz' in a critical examination of Heineccius' book. He was later dismissed from his university position and moved to Denmark, where he worked as the secretary of a commercial company.[114]

Nevertheless, Hommel's primary interest seemed to lie in the public development of the quarrel, particularly its poetic form and use of scatological terms, in the 'style of Plautus' (*...in ea controuersia multi Plautini sales et inficeta...*), rather than in the methodological aspects of the dispute. The mutual offenses included scornful ironic comments on the names of both Trier (Schüz) and Sellius. The latter had ridiculed the name Schüz (Trier) by associating it with feces, excrement (*quasi a Schieten siue a cacando traxerim auitum nomen meum...*), while Trier, in a spicy response in verse, invoked Latin synonyms for latrine to refer to Sellius: '*...nominis tui officium imple, sellaeque stercorariae locum subi*'; '*...ire ad latrinam;*' '*Vertendus est culus foras*'; '*Dic, cur iacenti in os cacasti Sellio?*'; '*Non peius est in orbe litterario / Monstrum, nec est usquam latrina spurcior*'.[115]

---

[113] Hommel 1779, 1, XVIII, § 11, p. 217.

[114] *Erat nempe Trier, Heineccii in Viadrina quondam collega, cui insomnes noctes iniiciebat adversarii gloria. Neque tamen palam aggredi ausus, hinc nomen dissimulauit* (Hommel 1779, 1, XVIII, § 20, p. 200). See Landsberg 1894, p. 605–606, and an edition of the polemic texts in Sellius & Trier 1735.

[115] Hommel 1779, 1, XVIII, § 20, p. 234.

What lies behind this apparently anecdotal ensemble of versified gossip? How did the authors of *historia litteraria iuris* make use of these episodes?

On the one hand, such episodes may well have been included for the sake of amusement, for the purposes of entertainment, which was one of the main goals of this kind of juridical literature.[116] The comedic style of the quarrel between Trier and Sellius, so unusual in legal writings, was noteworthy per se. On the other hand, these episodes could also function as a strong pedagogical *Disziplinierung* device, since they offered the opportunity of censoring immoderate conduct and thus of communicating acceptable rules for engaging in academic dispute. As previously mentioned, I believe that, analogously to *historia litteraria* in general, the works of *historia litteraria iuris* intended to reinforce moral patterns and thus served as 'civility guides' for the circles of learned jurists of the time. Civility played a fundamental role as a mode of social cohesion within the scholarly community,[117] even for the most critical authors of *historia litteraria iuris*.

IV. Historia litteraria iuris *in Decline: Reframing Controversies in Law*

Hommel's vast assemblage of controversies, mixing epistemic disagreements with controversies related to the social role of jurists and the identity of jurisprudence as a discipline, along with personal hostilities between individuals, was typical of a certain juridical literary genre that was in visible decline by the end of the century.

Criticism against the works of *historia litteraria iuris* focused, among other aspects, on the exaggerated and unnecessary catalogues of controversies. Within the circle of writers of *historia litteraria iuris*, a prestigious author such as the Halle professor Daniel Nettelbladt presented his *Initia historiae litterariae iuridicae uniuersalis* as a critical counterpart to Hommel's *Litteratura*.[118]

---

[116] Grunert & Syndikus 2015, p. 272.
[117] Goldgar 1995, p. 6–7.
[118] *Praefatio primae editionis* (dated 3 May 1764) in Nettelbladt 1774, s.n.

Nettelbladt, a follower of Christian Wolff's methodical approach, was quite frugal in his account of juridical controversies. In a short chapter titled *De sectis iurisconsultorum*, he was concerned about establishing precise definitions and 'cleaning the field' of the *micrologiae* and excesses of the *morhofian* style in which Hommel had engaged. Not all controversies between jurists, Nettelbladt explained, developed as a result of opposing schools of thought, and in such cases the controversies should not be included in an account of the *historia iurisprudentiae*.[119]

After distinguishing between *controuersiae iuris*, *controuersiae iurisconsultorum*, and *sectae iurisconsultorum*, Nettelbladt narrowed down and reframed the really important controversies to a very brief list of disputes:

> § 42 Sunt itaque potius ad sectas Iurisconsultorum, easque illustriores, referendae *Sabinianorum* et *Proculeianorum*; *Bulgarionorum* et *Gosianorum*; *Realistarum* et *Humanistarum*; *Naturalistarum* seu, si mauis, *Haereticorum* et *Orthodoxorum*; *Methodistarum* seu *Systematicorum* et quos dicere liceat *Textualium*; *Latinistarum*, speciatim *Romanistarum*, et *Germanistarum*, sectae, de quibus singulis suo loco in historia iurisprudentiae agendum.[120]

Moreover, he refused to engage in a thorough discussion about the origins and causes of these schools, which unfortunately infected the whole of the *respublica litteraria*, and not only the *iurisconsultorum natio*. He expressed a negative view of the different 'schools of thought', since they had always 'disturbed' the progress of jurisprudence — and still did. The causes of factions among jurists were the same as among the learned men in general: the 'itch of innovation' (*nouandi et per nouationes inclarescendi pruritus*), the 'prejudice of authority' (*auctoritatis praeiudicium*),

---

[119] *Prout non omnes dissensiones eruditorum, indeque ortae controuersiae, erumpunt in sectas: ita et idem ualet de Iurisconsultorum dissensionibus et disputationibus. Tum enim ex eruditorum, et speciatim Iurisconsultorum, dissensionibus, sectarum semine, nascuntur sectae, si, orto inter Iurisconsultos dissensu, non tam hanc uel illam specialem doctrinam, quam potius uniuersae iurisprudentiae seu partis cuiusdam principia et oeconomiam concernente, contingit, multos, non infimi subsellii, Iurisconsultos, stare ab una, aliosque ab altera parte; licet alii sint medii seu neutrarum partium Iurisconsulti* (Nettelbladt 1774, § 40, p. 33).

[120] Nettelbladt 1774, § 42, p. 35.

financial greed (*lucri bonus odor*), and sometimes, more rarely, even 'love for the truth' (*ueritatis amor*).[121]

The outcome of Nettelbladt's attempt at applying the 'demonstrative-mathematical' method to *historia litteraria*[122] was a short selection of the disputes that might have had relevant consequences or contributed in some way (he used the word *incrementis*) to the progress of jurisprudence.[123] This is not the place, however, to expound the legal thinking of Nettelbladt, who has been better treated than Hommel by later historiography.[124] Suffice it to note that Nettelbladt took a step forward towards understanding law as a science, *Recht als Wissenschaft*. The supposedly scientific nature of jurisprudence squared better with an image of linearity, consensus, and unity among the learned community contributing to the 'progress' of jurisprudence, which was reinforced by the late nineteenth-century positivistic approach. For the self-representation of the juridical community in the last decades of the eighteenth century, the baroque, 'micrological' style of Hommel, exposing the dirty laundry of jurists in terms of dissent, insult, and even physical violence, no longer seemed appropriate.

In spite of his critical approach, or his closeness to an epistemic change in legal writing, Nettelbladt was still deeply committed to the moralizing mission of this kind of literature and still counted the 'recreation of the soul' as one of its main goals.[125] Throughout

---

[121] *Quae sunt in genere sectarum inter eruditos causae, sunt etiam sectarum inter iurisconsultos causae. Sunt itaque nouandi et per nouationes inclarescendi pruritus; auctoritatis praeiudicium; lucri bonus odor ex re qualibet, etc. saepe sectarum inter Iurisconsultos causae; licet et ueritatis amori nonnunquam sectas originem debere, negari nequeat. Unde ortis sectis, vel uni alteriue sectae, quae optima est, adhaerendum, uel media, si datur, eligenda est uia* (Nettelbladt 1774, § 43, p. 35–36).

[122] Mohnhaupt 2013, p. 15.

[123] *...eiusque incrementis obex positus, ostendatur; quippe quae sibi merito uindicat historia iurisprudentiae: sed ita potius ut non nisi generalia quaedam, de hoc malo orbis litterati iuridici necessario, hic praemittantur* (Nettelbladt 1774, § 39, p. 34).

[124] Wieacker attributed to Nettelbladt nothing less than the foundation of the emblematic *Allgemeiner Teil*, later incorporated into the 1900 German Civil Code and one of the landmarks of the *Pandektenwissenschaft* (Wieacker 1967).

[125] *Sic euicta historiae litterariae iuridicae necessitate, de eius utilitate nemo dubitabit, qui perpendit facere eam ad 1) fugienda praeiudicia; 2) euitandos soloecismos litterarios iuridicos; 3) minuendum studii iuridici laborem immensum, quoad*

his *ouevre*, the topic of vices and virtues of the jurists still played a role,[126] even if later historiography tends to neglect this aspect of his work.[127]

At any rate, both Hommel's multifarious ensemble of controversies and Nettelbladt's concise selection show that the production and acquisition of knowledge in early modern polemical discourse were not seen as morally neutral activities.[128]

Concluding Remarks

Recent scholarship has emphasized the significance of scholarly controversy in early modern intellectual life as an often constructive and innovative mechanism, highlighting 'la force productive de la conflictualité comme construction d'un territoire commun de l'échange'.[129] As previously noted, controversies were not only debates about knowledge: besides their epistemic dimension (as confirmation or denial of scientific claims), they also had an eminently social dimension in which the gain or loss of social recognition was at stake.[130]

The works of *historia litteraria iuris*, themselves rich sources for analyzing the forms of interaction in scholarly communication in the field of law, illustrate this double social and epistemic dimension of dissent as well as dissent's potentially constructive aspect. These works show how jurists battled against new emerging disciplines and built narratives to safeguard the prominent social role of jurisprudence, thereby expressing a widespread concern with their own identity as scholars. Academic jurisprudence, like other university disciplines, was constantly negotiating its own frontiers, social position, and place in the ever-changing hier-

---

theoriam tam, quam quoad praxin; 4) recreationem animi ex amoenissimo hoc studio capiendam (Nettelbladt 1774, § 15, p. 9).

[126] Nettelbladt 1774, § 37, p. 31–32 (see footnote no. 66).

[127] According to Repgen, for Nettelbladt the goal of legal education was not a virtuous life, but an abstract and scientific understanding of law (Repgen 2001, p. 467).

[128] Kivistö 2014, p. 259. For the appeal to vices and virtues and their impact on intellectual production, especially in the jurists' polemics concerning authorship and plagiarism in the eighteenth century, see Beck Varela 2013, p. 47–86.

[129] Bodenmann & Rey 2013, p. 247.

[130] Bremer & Spoerhase 2011, p. 114.

archies of knowledge, both in relation to other popular or new forms of legal knowledge (such as the novel field of 'administration sciences' in the eighteenth century) and in relation to other established university disciplines, such as theology. The works of *historia litteraria iuris* also illustrate the need to offer models of civility, in order to domesticate and reprehend immoderate forms of dissent and to propose acceptable rules for engaging in academic disputes.

Hommel's extensive promenade through the millenary history of jurisprudential dissent, from the Roman Sabinians and Proculians to the Middle Ages' glossators and the most recent and manifold polemical issues, mirrored in many aspects the methods, procedures, goals, and styles fostered by the late seventeenth-century *polyhistors*. As Hommel's work illustrates, controversies were a *pratique usuelle du dialogue savant* in all scholarly fields.[131] Controversies and crises were also occasions for mobilizing the past and for inventing disciplinary traditions. For Hommel, civility — but not necessarily consensus — was an ideal. For the later critics of this genre of writing, such as Nettelbladt, the old lists of heterogeneous controversies had to be reduced to a brief list of schools of thought and reframed according to a new scientific approach, despite the fact that the moralizing and even the entertaining dimensions were still present in his work. This new understanding of the scientific nature of law tended to depict the development of jurisprudence in a rather monolithic and harmonious fashion, as a linear succession of schools of thought and their contributions to the history of law. The new understanding cast a long shadow in nineteenth- and twentieth-century narratives about law. This long shadow, however, is beyond the scope of this short essay, whose purpose has been to examine an unexplored legal-literary genre, namely, *historia litteraria iuris*, and to reflect upon the economy of dissent in law, in a diachronic perspective. Studies dedicated to the cultural history of scholarship would gain by integrating the neglected world of jurists into their picture. Jurists and legal historians would also gain by challenging the traditional self-referential history of law as an internal history of legal doctrines and legal science. To investigate such

---

[131] Bodenmann & Rey 2013, p. 240.

forgotten genres of legal literature, focusing on their production, circulation, uses, and social impact as part of a larger cultural, intellectual, and historical process might be one of the pathways to overcoming these deeply rooted disciplinary biases.

Bibliography

Primary Sources

J. A. Bach (dir.), *Unpartheyische Critik über juristische Schriften inn- und ausserhalb Deutschland*, Leipzig: Lankisch, 1750–1758.

R. Beneventano (aut.); C. G. Haubold (ed. lit.), *Rogerii Beneventani de dissensionibus dominorum siue de controuersiis ueterum iuris Romani interpretum, qui glossatores uocantur opusculum. Emendatum edidit et animaduersionibus atque adcessionibus locupletauit ... Christianus Gottlieb Haubold*, Lipsiae: sumtibus I. C. Hinrichsii, 1821.

G. Beyer, *De utili et necessaria autorum iuridicorum et iuris arti inseruientium notitia schediasma. Exhibens indicem autorum, quos recitandos et excerpendos sibi proposuit cum specimine futuri laboris duas autorum decades sistente*, Lipsiae: Grossianus (et al.), 1698.

J. S. Brunquell (1725), *Prolusio academica de sectis et controuersiis iuris Justinianei interpretum, quos glossatores appellamus; uentilationi Compendii Lauterbachiani permissu illustris iurisconsultorum ordinis in Academia Ienensi publice instituendae praemissa ...* Jenae: Ritter.

A. G. Costanus, *Quæstionum iuris memorabilium liber unus. Acceßit seorsum eiusdem auctoris polyhistor, et apologeticon. Omnia nunc primum in Germania in lucem edita. Cum rerum et verborum Indice copiosiss.*, Hanoviæ: apud Guilielmum Antonium, 1598.

J. F. Eisenhart, *Institutiones historiae iuris litterariae in usum auditorii adornatae. Accessit B. Francisci Caroli Conradi ... De fatis scholae iuris civilis Romanae oratio. Editio nova auct. et emendat.* Helmstadii: apud Christ. Frider. Weygand, 1763.

J. A. R. von Eisenhart, 'Mascov: Gottfried M. (auch Mascovius), Rechtsgelehrter', *Allgemeine Deutsche Biographie*, 20, p. 551–554, 1884.

C. A. Heumann, *Conspectus reipublicae literariae, sive Via ad historiam literariam iuuentuti studiosae aperta ... editio septima eademque ultima,* Hanoverae: apud hæredes Nic. Foersteri et filii, 1763.

J. Heumann de Teutschenbrunn, *Apparatus iurisprudentiae literarius. Hac secunda editione novis accessionibus locupletatus a D. Io. Chr. Siebenkees*, Norimbergae: Lochnerus, Grattanauerus, 1780.

J. Heumann de Teutschenbrunn, *Apparatus iurisprudentiae literarius*. Norimbergae: Impensa Ioannis Georgii Lochneri, 1752.

C. F. Hommel, *De principali causa dissensionum inter Labeonem et Capitonem horumque sectatores ... Praeside Carolo Ferdinando Hommelio Iur. utrq. doct d. XVI. Iulii Anno MDCCL Disputabit Guilielmus Keck Lipsiensis ...* Lipsiae: Ex Officina Langenhemiana, 1750.

C. F. Hommel, 'Carl Ferdinand Hommel', in Christoph Weidlich, *Zuverlässige Nachrichten von denen jetzlebenden Rechtsgelehrten*, 4. Theil, Halle: Kümmel, IX, p. 249–280, 1760.

C. F. Hommel, *Litteratura iuris*, Lipsiae: apud Ioannem Wendlerum, 1761.

C. F. Hommel, *Palingenesia librorum iuris ueterum siue Pandectarum loca integra ad modum Indicis Labitti et Wielingi oculis exposita et ab exemplari Taurelli Florentino accuratissime descripta...*, Lipsiae: impensis Theophili Georgi, 1767.

C. F. Hommel, *Teutscher Flavius, das ist: Vollständige Anleitung sowohl bey bürgerlichen als peinlichen Fällen Urthel abzufassen, worinnen zugleich die Advocaten bey rechtlichen Klagen und Vorbringen, die Schlusbitte behörig einzurichten, belehret werden. Dritte Ausgabe, durchgehends stark vermehret*, Bayreuth: bey Johann Andreas Lübeck, 1775.

C. F. Hommel, *Promtuarium iuris Bertochianum ad modum lexici iuris practici siue locorum communium ...* Lipsiae: Fritsch, 1777.

C. F. Hommel, *Litteratura iuris. Editio secunda, adeo reformata ut fere nouum opus uideri possit*, Lipsiae: apud Casparum Fritsch, 1779.

C. F. Hommel, *Pertinenz und Erbsonderungs Register, worinnen alle Zubehörungen eines gekauften oder ererbeten Landguthes, Hauses, Gartens, Schiffes, Weinbergs u. s. w. insonderheit die Lehns Pertinenzen wenn bey Rittergüthern die Töchter mit den Lehnfolgern sich abtheilen, nebst dem, was der Witbe an Mustheile, Morgengabe und Gerade sowohl dem nächsten Schwerdmagen an Heergeräthe als auch wenn ein Pfarherr stirbet seinem Amtsfolger zuständig. Bey Erbtheilungen und Käufen als ein Handbuch zu gebrauchen; Mit vielen Zusäzen und Verbesserungen aus den Handschriften des verstorbenen Herrn Hofraths und mit einer Vorrede herausgegeben von Karl Gottlob Rößig, B. R. B. Vierte verbesserte und stark vermehrte Ausgabe*. Leipzig: Junius, 1782.

C. F. Hommel, *Catalogus Testium Alphabeticus: ex quo cognoscitur, qui testes plane inhabiles, qui semitestes, qui plus quam semitestes, et qui semitestibus fide minores sint...*, Vratislaviae: Korn, 1780.

G. Hugo, *Lehrbuch der civilistischen Litterair-Geschichte*, Berlin: Mylius, 1812.

Justinian (aut.), Theodor Mommsen (ed. lit.), Paul Krueger (ed. lit.), *Digesta Iustiniani Augusti. Recognouit Th. Mommsen adsumpto in operis societatem Paulo Kruegero*, Berolini, apud Weidmannos, 1870.

H. Kestner, *Polyhistor, in quo praeter methodum in singulis iurium partibus observandam, praecipui iuris naturalis, civilis, publici, feudalis, ecclesiastici, et qui in praxi solidi quid scripserunt doctores, quin et ornamenta studii iuridici, adjectis in calce uitae regulis, recensentur*, Francofurti: apud Nicolaum Försterum, 1699.

H. Kestner, *Prudentia Studendi iura, in qua praeter methodum in singulis iurium partibus observandam, praecipui iuris naturalis, civilis, publici, feudalis, ecclesiastici, et qui in praxi solidi quid scripserunt doctores, quin et ornamenta studii iuridici, adiectis in calce uitae regulis, recensentur*, Rintelii: Enax, 1699.

J. Labitte, *Index legum omnium quae in Pandectis continentur: in quo singulae ad singulos iurisconsultorum libros ex quibus desumptae sunt ...* Parisiis: apud Sebastianum Niuellium, 1557.

P. Lambeck, *Liber primus Prodromi Historiae Literariae nec non libri secundi capita quatuor priora, cum appendice, quae sciagraphiam continet, sive primam delineationem praecipuarum personarum ac rerum, de quibus, volente Deo, reliquis triginta duobus eiusdem libri capitibus plenius et accuratius agetur; accedunt insuper tabulae duae chronographiae uniuersalis, quarum priori successio omnium seculorum a creatione mundi usque ad initium uulgaris aerae Christianae, posteriori autem continuatio eorundem ab initio uulgaris aerae Christianae usque ad nostram aetatem exhibetur [S.l.]*: Sumptibus Autoris; Hamburgi: Piperus, 1659.

E. Landsberg, 'Trier, Johann Wolfgang', in *Allgemeine Deutsche Biographie* [ADB] 38, 1894, p. 605–606.

M. Lipenius, *Bibliotheca Realis Juridica post uirorum clarissimorum Friderici Gottlieb Struvii et Gottlob Augusti Jenichenii curas emendate ...*, Lipsiae (et al.): Wendlerus (facs. repr.: Hildesheim/New York: Georg Olms Verlag, 1970), 1757.

G. Mascov, *Exercitatio inauguralis de sectis Sabinianorum et Proculianorum in iure ciuili quam consensu incluti ordinis iuridicis pro obtinendis in utroque iure summis honoribus ad d.XX Iuli 1724 solemni disqisitioni subiiciet Gottfried Mascov*, Altdorfii Noricorum: Typis Iod. Guil. Kohlesii Acad. Typogr, 1724.

G. Mascov, *De sectis Sabinianorum et Proculianorum in iure ciuili diatribe. Inserta est disquisitio de Herciscundis*, Lipsiae: apud Jacobum Schuster, 1728.

G. de Ménage, in F. De Malherbe, *Les poésies de M. de Malherbe avec les observations de Monsieur Ménage*, À Paris: chez Louis Billaine, 1666.

D. G. Morhof, *Polyhistor, in tres tomos, literarium (cuius soli tres libri priores hactenus prodiere, nunc autem quatuor reliqui, a Viro in Acad. Lipsiensi erudito reuisi atque aucti, e MSS. accedunt,) philosophicum et practicum, (nunc demus editos, primoque adjunctos) divisus. Opus posthumum, ut multorum uotis satisfieret, accurate reuisum, emendatum, ex autoris annotationibus ... Accedunt indices necessarii. Cum privilegio Sacrae Caesarae Majestatis*, Lubecae: Sumptibus Petri Böckmanni, 1708.

D. G. Morhof, *Polyhistor, literarius, philosophicus, et practicus ... cum accessionibus virorum clarissimorum Ioannis Frickii et Iohannis Molleri... Editio quarta cui praefationem, notitiamque diariorum litterariorum europea praemisit Io. Albertus Fabricius* ... Lubecae: sumtibus Petri Boeckmanni, 1747.

D. Nettelbladt, *Praecognita uniuersae eruditionis generalia et in specie iurisprudentiae naturalis tam quam positiuae in usum praelectionum publicarum adornata a D. Dan. Nettelbladt Pot. Bor. Regi a Cons. Aul. Iuriumque in Fridericiana Prof. Publ. Ord.,* Halae Magdeburgicae: in officina libraria Rengeriana, 1747.

D. Nettelbladt, 'Hallische Juristische Neuigkeiten', in id. (ed.), *Hallische Beyträge zu der juristischen Gelehrten Historie. Zweyter Band. V. Bis VIII. Stück. Nebst vollständingen Register*, Halle im Magdeburgischen: zu finden in der Rengerischen Buchhandlung, 1758.

D. Nettelbladt (ed.), *Hallische Beyträge zu der juristischen Gelehrten Historie*, Halle im Magdeburgischen: Rengerischen Buchhandlung, 1755–1762.

D. Nettelbladt, *Initia historiae litterariae iuridicae uniuersalis*, Halae Magdeburgicae: prostat in Officina libraria Rengeriana, 1764.

D. Nettelbladt, *Initia historiae litterariae iuridicae uniuersalis. Editio secunda, auctior et emendatior*, Halae Magdeburgicae: prostat in Officina libraria Rengeriana, 1774.

G. Oelrichs (comp.), *Collectio dissertationum historico-antiquario-iuridicarum in Academiis Germanicis habitarum* ... Bremae: s.n., 1785.

C. F. Pauli, *Einleitung in die Kenntniß des Deutschen Hohen und Niedern Adels, entworfen von Carl Friedrich Pauli, d. W. W. u. B. R. D. des Staats-Rechts und der Geschichtskunde Lehrer der Friedrichs hohen Schule*, Halle: Gebauer, 1753.

C. F. Pauli, *Erweis und Rechtfertigung einiger Sätze seiner Einleitung in die Kenntniß des deutschen hohen und niedern Adels, welche in dem*

107 Stück der Göttingischen Anzeigen von gelehrten Sachen dieses Jahres in Zweifel gezogen und verfälscht worden, Halle: bey Johann Justinus Gebauer, 1753.

J. Rebhan (Präses); C. O. Bökel (Resp.), *De sectis, seu diuersis ueterum iurisconsultorum familiis*, Argentorati: Paulli (Straßburg, Jur. Disp. v. Febr.) 1666.

T. Schimmelpfeng (ed.), *Hommel redivivus, oder Nachweisung der bei den vorzüglichsten älteren und neueren Civilisten vorkommenden Erklärungen einzelner Stellen des Corpus iuris civilis*, Kassel: Theodor Fischer, 1858.

Gottfried Sellius, Johann Wolfgang Trier [Gottfried Jacob Schütz], *Examen methodi axiomaticae, qua in Elementis iuris ciuilis usus est... Joh. Gottl. Heineccius. Editio Tertia: accedunt responsiones ad uindicias huius methodi a Gothofredo Sellio editas*, Francofurti/Lipsiae: [s.n.], 1735.

G. Slevogt, *De sectis et philosophia iurisconsultorum opuscula ... collegit recognouit et praefatione de elogiis i[uris]c[onsul]torum Romanorum ac progr. de disputatione fori auxit ...* Jena: Meyer, 1724.

R. Stintzing, E. Landsberg, *Geschichte der deutschen Rechtswissenschaft*, III/1, München/Leipzig, Oldenbourg Verlag (2nd repr. fac., Aalen: Scientia Verlag, 1957), 1898.

G. Stolle, *Discours von dem Nutzen der Historiae et notitiae Literariae, welchen der Verfasser den 19. April. 1714. als damahliger Director des Gymnasii Illustris zu Hildburghausen bey Intimation eines Collegii literarii daselbst ans Licht gestellt*, in *Kurtze Anleitung zur Historie der Gelahrheit, Denen, So den freyen Künsten und der Philosophie obliegen, Zu Nutz in dreyen Theilen ausgefertiget ...* Halle im Magdeburgischen: Neue Buchhandlung, 3, p. 191–221, 1718.

G. Stolle, *Anleitung zur Historie der juristischen Gelahrheit: nebst einer ausführlichen Nachricht von des seel. Verfassers Leben und Schrifften ... mit einer Vorrede ... von Herrn Christian Gottlieb Budern*, Jena: Meyer Erben, 1745.

B. G. Struve, *Bibliotheca iuris selecta. Acessit Bibliotheca selectissima iuris studiosorum ... emendauit et copiose locupletauit Christian. Gottlieb Buder. Editio octava*, Ienae: apud Christian. Henr. Cuno (facs. repr.: Aalen, Scientia Verlag, 1970), 1756.

B. G. Struve, *Bibliotheca iuris selecta, secundum ordinem litterarium disposita atque ad singulas iuris partes directa accessit selectissima bibliotheca iuris ...* Ienæ: Bailliar, 1703.

B. G. Struve, *Dissertatio inauguralis de iure bibliothecarum quam... praeside dn. Samuele Strykio ... pro licentia summos in utroque iure capessendi honores ... publicae disquisitioni* ..., Halae Magdeb.: Henckelius, 1702.

R. Teichmann, 'K. F. Hommel', in *Allgemeine Deutsche Biographie* [ADB] 13, 1881, p. 58–59.

C. Thomasius (dir.), *Freymüthige Lustige und Ernsthaffte jedoch Vernunfft- und Gesetz-mäßige Gedancken Oder Monats-Gespräche, über allerhand, fürnehmlich aber Neue Bücher: Durch alle zwölff Monate des 1688. und 1689. Jahrs* ... Halle (et al.): Salfeld (et al.), 1690.

M. von Waldberg, 'Stolle, Gottlieb', in *Allgemeine Deutsche Biographie* [ADB] 36, 1893, p. 408–409.

A. Wieling, *Jurisprudentia Restituta, siue Index chronologicus in totum iuris Justinianæi corpus, ad modum Iac. Labitti, Ant. Augustini et Wolfg. Freymonii, noua tamen et faciliore methodo collectus: accesserunt Opuscula IV ... in usum auditorum animadversiones passim adjecit Abraham Wieling*, Amstelaedami: Ianssonio-Waesbergios, 1727.

J. H. Zedler, *Großes vollständiges Universal-Lexikon* (repr. Graz: Akad. Dr.- und Verl.-Anst., 1994), 13, 1735.

Secondary Sources

Beck Varela, L. (2013), *Literatura jurídica y censura. Fortuna de Vinnius en España*, Valencia: Tirant lo Blanch (Tirant monografías, 863).

Birn, R. (1965), 'Le Journal des Savants sous l'Ancien Régime' in *Journal des savants*, 1, p. 15–35.

Blair, A. (2004), 'Note Taking as an Art of Transmission', in *Critical Inquiry*, 31/1, p. 85–107.

Bodenmann, S. & A.-L. Rey (2013), 'La guerre en lettres: La controverse scientifique dans les correspondances des Lumières', in *Revue d'histoire des sciences*, 66/2, p. 233–248.

Bowers, F. (1949), *Principles of Bibliographical Description*, Princeton, NJ: Princeton UP.

Bremer, K. & C. Spoerhase (2011), 'Rhetorische Rücklosigkeit. Problemfelder der Erforschung gelehrter Polemik um 1700', in id. (eds), *Gelehrte Polemik: Intellektuelle Konfliktverschärfungen um 1700*, Frankfurt am Main: Vittorio Klostermann, p. 111–122.

Décultot, E., F. Krämer, & H. Zedelmaier (2020), 'Introduction: Towards a History of Excerpting in Modernity', in *Berichte zur Wissenschaftsgeschichte*, 43/2, p. 169–179.

Feige, R. (1969), 'Heinrich Ernst Kestner (1671–1723): ein Beitrag zur Geschichte der Rintelner Juristenfakultät', in *Schaumburg-Lippische Mitteilungen, Schaumburg-Lippischer Heimatverein*, 20, p. 25–35.

Füssel, M. (2011), 'Akademische Aufklärung. Die Universitäten des 18. Jahrhunderts im Spannungsfeld von funktionaler Differenzierung, Ökonomie und Habitus', in W. Hardtwig (ed.), *Die Aufklärung und ihre Weltwirkung*, Göttingen: Vandenhoeck & Ruprecht (Geschichte und Gesellschaft. Sonderhefte, 23), p. 47–75.

Gierl, M. (2007), 'Historia litteraria. Wissenschaft, Wissensordnung und Polemik im 18. Jahrhundert', in F. Grunert, F. Vollhardt (eds), *Historia literaria. Neuordnungen des Wissens im 17. und 18. Jahrhundert*, Berlin: Akademie Verlag, p. 113–127.

Goldgar, A. (1995), *Impolite Learning. Conduct and Community in the Republic of Letters, 1680–1750*, New Haven, CT: Yale University Press.

Grafton, A. (1985), 'The World of the Polyhistors: Humanism and Encyclopedism', in *Central European History*, 18/1, p. 31–47.

Grunert, F. & A. Syndikus (2015), 'Historia literaria: Erschließung, Speicherung und Vermittlung von Wissen', in id. (eds), *Wissensspeicher der Frühen Neuzeit. Formen und Funktionen*, Berlin: De Gruyter, p. 243–293.

Grunert, F. (2010), 'Historia literaria in Helmstedt', in J. Bruning (ed.), *Das Athen der Welfen: Die Reformuniversität Helmstedt 1576–1810*, Wiesbaden: Harrassowitz (Ausstellungskataloge der Herzog-August-Bibliothek, 92), p. 240–245.

Grunert, F. & F. Vollhardt (2007), 'Einleitung', in id. (eds), *Historia literaria. Neuordnungen des Wissens im 17. und 18. Jahrhundert*, Berlin: Akademie Verlag, p. vii–xi.

Grunert, F. (2007), 'Von *guten* Büchern. Zum moralischen Anspruch der Historia literaria', in id., F. Vollhardt (eds), *Historia literaria. Neuordnungen des Wissens im 17. und 18. Jahrhundert*, Berlin: Akademie Verlag, p. 65–88.

Hespanha, A. M. (1993), 'A Nobreza nos Tratados Jurídicos dos séculos XVI a XVIII', in *Penélope*, 12, p. 27–42 (reprinted in *A Política Perdida. Ordem e Governo Antes da Modernidade*, Curitiba: Juruá, 2010, p. 167–183).

Hof, H. (2017), 'K. F. Hommel', in Gerd Kleinheyer, Jan Schröder (eds), *Deutsche und Europäische Juristen aus neun Jahrhunderten. Eine biographische Einführung in die Geschichte der Rechtswissenschaft*. Sixth edition, Tübingen: Mohr Siebeck, p. 206–210.

Hummel, P. (2002), *Mœurs érudites: étude sur la micrologie littéraire (Allemagne, XVIe – XVIIIe siècles)*, Genève: Droz (Histoire des idées et critique littéraire, 395).

Jaumann, H. (2001), 'Respublica litteraria/Republic of letters. Concept and Perspectives of Research', in id. (ed.). *Die europäische Gelehrtenrepublik im Zeitalter des Konfessionalismus*, Wiesbaden: Harrassowitz (Wolfenbütteler Forschungen, 96), p. 11–19.

Jaumann, H. (2000), 'Öffentlichkeit und Verlegenheit. Frühe Spuren eines Konzepts öffentlicher Kritik in der Theorie des *plagium extrajudiciale* von Jakob Thomasius (1673)', in *Scientia Poetica. Jahrbuch für Geschichte der Literatur und der Wissenschaften* 4, p. 62–82.

Jaumann, H. (1990), 'Was ist ein Polyhistor? Gehversuche auf einem verlassenen Terrain', in *Studia Leibnitiana*, 22, p. 76–89.

Kirwan, R. (2013), 'Introduction: Scholarly Self-Fashioning and the Cultural History of Universities', in id. (ed.), *Scholarly Self-Fashioning and Community in the Early Modern University*, Farnham: Ashgate, p. 1–20.

Kivistö, S. (2014), *The Vices of Learning: Morality and Knowledge at Early Modern Universities*, Leiden: Brill (Education and Society in the Middle Ages and Renaissance, 48).

Lieberwirth, R. (1972), 'K. F. Hommel', in *Neue Deutsche Biographie* [NDB] 9, p. 592.

Mohnhaupt, H. (2013), '*Historia literaria iuris*. Beispiele juristischer Literaturgeschichten im 18. Jahrhundert', in *Max Planck Institute for European Legal History Research Paper Series*, 3, p. 1–23.

Mulsow, M. (2006), 'Practices of Unmasking: Polyhistors, Correspondence, and the Birth of Dictionaries of Pseudonimity in Seventeenth-Century Germany', *Journal of the History of Ideas* 67/2, p. 219–250.

Mulsow, M. & H. Zedelmaier (2001) (eds), *Die Praktiken der Gelehrsamkeit in der Frühen Neuzeit*, Tübingen: Niemeyer (Frühe Neuzeit, 64).

Nelles, P. (2000), 'Historia litteraria and Morhof: Private Teaching and Professorial Libraries at the University of Kiel', in F. Waquet (ed.), *Mapping the World of Learning: the Polyhistor of Daniel Georg Morhof,* Wiesbaden: Harrassowitz (Wolfenbütteler Forschungen, 91), p. 31–56.

Pennington, K. (2011), 'The Beginning of Roman Law Jurisprudence and Teaching in the Twelfth Century: The Authenticae', in *Rivista Internazionale di Diritto Comune*, 22, p. 35–53.

Repgen, T. (2001), 'Daniel Nettelbladt', in M. Stolleis (ed.), *Juristen. Ein biographisches Lexikon*, München: Beck, p. 467–468.

Rother, W. (2004), 'Strafrechtsreformdiskussionen in Leipzig: Karl Ferdinand Hommel, *Germanorum Beccaria*', in H. Marti (ed.), *Die Universität Leipzig und ihr gelehrtes Umfeld 1680-1780*, Basel: Schwabe (Texte und Studien, 6), p. 459–486.

Scattola, M. & F. Vollhardt (2003), '*Historia litteraria*, Geschichte und Kritik: Das Projekt der *Cautelen* im literarischen Feld', in M. Beetz (ed.), *Thomasius im literarischen Feld*, Tübingen: Niemeyer (Hallesche Beiträge zur Europäischen Aufklärung, 20), p. 159–186.

Stein, P. (1972), 'The two schools of jurists in the early Roman Principate', in *The Cambridge Law Journal*, 31/1, p. 8–31.

Stolte, Jr., B. H. (2004), 'Preface', in H. Brenkman (1722), *Historia Pandectarum, seu fatum exemplaris Florentini. Accedit gemina dissertatio de Amalphi*, Trajecti ad Rhenum: apud Guilielmum vande Water (repr. Vico-Verlag, Frankfurt am Main, 2004).

Syndikus, A. (2008), 'Historia literaria als Propädeutikum an der Königsberger Universität des 18. Jahrhunderts', in H. Marti (ed.), *Die Universität Königsberg in der Frühen Neuzeit*, Köln: Böhlau, p. 379–422.

Treggiari, F. (2014), '*Doctoratus est dignitas*: la lezione di Bartolo', in id., *Per la storia dell'Università di Perugia: estratto da Annali di Storia delle Università Italiane*, 18, p. 35–46.

Vano, C. (2000), *Il nostro autentico Gaio. Strategie della scuola storica alle origini della romanistica moderna*, Napoli: Editoriale Scientifica (Pubblicazioni del Dipartimento di Diritto romano e estoria della scienza romanistica dell'Università degli studi di Napoli 'Federico II', 16).

Waquet, F. (2000), 'Introduction', in id. (ed.), *Mapping the World of Learning. The Polyhistor of Daniel Georg Morhof*, Wiesbaden: Harrassowitz (Wolfenbütteler Forschungen, 91), p. 7–12.

Wieacker, F. (1967): *Privatrechtsgeschichte der Neuzeit unter besonderer Berücksichtigung der deutschen Entwicklung*. Second edition, Göttingen: Vandenhoek & Ruprecht (Jurisprudenz in Einzeldarstellungen, 7).

Zedelmaier, H. (2017), 'Heumanns *Conspectus Reipublicae Literariae*: Besonderheiten, Kontext, Grenzen', in M. Mulsow, K. R. Eskildsen, H. Zedelmaier (eds), *Christoph August Heumann (1681-1764): gelehrte Praxis zwischen christlichem Humanismus und Aufklärung*, Stuttgart: Franz Steiner Verlag (Gothaer Forschungen zur frühen Neuzeit, 12), p. 71–89.

Zedelmaier, H. (2007), 'Zwischen Fortschrittsgeschichte und Erfindungskunst. Gottfried Wilhelm Leibniz und Christian Wolff über Historia literaria', in F. Grunert, F. Vollhardt (eds), *Historia literaria: Neuordnungen des Wissens im 17. und 18. Jahrhundert*, Berlin: Akademie Verlag, p. 89–99.

Zedelmaier, H. (2000), 'De ratione excerpendi: Daniel Georg Morhof und das Exzerpieren', in F. Waquet (ed.), *Mapping the World of Learning. The Polyhistor of Daniel Georg Morhof*, Wiesbaden: Harrassowitz, (Wolfenbütteler Forschungen, 91), p. 75–92.

Abstract

As in other scholarly fields influenced by *polyhistorismus* and the methods and procedures of *historia litteraria* between the seventeenth and the eighteenth centuries, the authors of *historia litteraria iuris* engaged in a 'cartography of dissent', identifying and discussing the several controversies that belonged to the history of jurisprudence. This paper follows Carl Ferdinand Hommel's selection of controversies in order to explore the ways jurists conceived and conceptualized dissent and its role in the self-fashioning of jurisprudence as an academic discipline in the eighteenth century.

Though often portrayed in negative terms, as inevitable and damaging factors, controversies served multiple purposes in the jurists' narratives, especially in the writings of *historia litteraria iuris*, which aimed at reaching beyond the usual readership of law books. The inventories of controversies not only presented the fundamental topics of public relevance that belonged to the corpus of jurisprudential sources, questions, and references (from the law of the sea to the sovereign's prerogatives): such inventories also helped to display the jurists' dignity as scholars in the republic of letters or to negotiate the boundaries between jurisprudence and other emerging fields. Moreover, the detailed accounts of immoderate forms of verbal and physical violence between jurists worked as 'civility guides', helping to construct community standards for criticism and polemics.

NAME INDEX

Aaron 373
Abelard 27, 109
Abramowicz, Jan 340
Accolti da Arezzo, Francesco 263, 417
Acis 68
Acunto, Paulo d' 294
Adam 289
Adrian IV, pope 73
Aethelwold, bishop of Winchester 71
Ailly, Pierre d' 92–94 *see also* Pierre d'Ailly
Alain de Lille 107
Albert of Jerusalem OCarm 319
Albert the Great 119
Albertus, Valentinus 412
Albion, Gordon 218
Alciatus, Andreas 266
Alcuin 58, 97
Aleman, Louis d', cardinal 124
Alexander III, pope 73–75, 319
Alfonso V, king of Aragon 121
Algarotti, Francesco 274
Allen, William, cardinal 226
Álvarez, Diego 314
Amadís 29, 45–46
Ambrose 230, 266
Ameri, Hyacintus 117, 121, 123–124, 134, 144
Anastasius I Dicorus, emperor 229
Ángel de la Purificación OCarm 322–323

Anselm of Canterbury 119, 136
Appiani, Giovanni 186, 191–192
Aquinas, Thomas 119 *see also* Thomas Aquinas
Arce y Reinoso, Diego de 306
Aristotle 31, 41, 43, 192, 260, 278, 281, 372, 381
Arriba, Francisco 314
Athanasius of Alexandria 235
Augustine 58, 118, 120, 308, 349–350
Aurispa, Giovanni 187–188, 190, 192
Ausonius 71

Baccalà, Michelangelo 292
Bach, Johann August 395, 403
Bacon, Francis 398–399, 410
Badel, Pierre-Yves 93
Baius, Michael 219, 309
Baldus de Ubaldis 262–263, 266
Balthasar, Augustin von 403
Báñez, Dominigo 309–310
Barbosa, Agostinho 401
Bardane, Filippico 226, 230
Baron, Hans 181
Barone, Angelo 294
Bartholin, Thomas 368
Bartolus de Saxoferrato 417
Bateson, Gregory 30
Bayle, Pierre 284, 286
Bayless, Martha 67
Bebel, Heinrich 33

Becanus, Johannes Goropius 373
Beccaria, Cesare 394
Beger, Laurentius 412
Belisarius 229
Belli, Filippo 291
Benedict XIV, pope 19, 275, 286
Benzelius, Eric 380
Bernard of Clairvaux 119
Berry, Jean de 96 see also Jean de Berry
Bertoch, Johann Georg 394
Beyer, Georg 394, 406
Biandrata, Giovanni Giorgio 333
Biel, Gabriel 153–154, 162 see also Gabriel Biel
Binns, J. W. 257
Bizzozzero, Giorgio 192
Bloch, Howard 61, 65
Böckel, Christian Otto 409, 415
Böckelmann, Johann Friedrich 412
Boethius 32
Böhmer, Justus Henning 414
Bolland, Jean 322
Bolognino, Ludovico 417
Bona of Savoy 181, 202
Bonaventure 119
Bonelli, Manfredo 202
Bouvet, Honoré 93
Boyer, Jean-Baptiste de, marquis d'Argens 284
Bracciolini, Poggio 182, 384
Braham V Gor, king of the Sasanian Empire 233
Bremer, Kai 416
Brenkman, Henri 416
Brinkley, Stephen 227
Brivilius, Benedict 337
Bruni, Leonardo 182
Bruno, Giordano 41–42, 274
Brunquell, Johann Salomon 408, 413–414
Brutus, Marcus Junius 13, 180, 198
Bulgarus 413–414
Bünemann, August 402
Buridan, Johannes 41 see also Johannes Buridan
Bynkershoek, Cornelius van 416

Cabrera, Pedro de 314
Caccialupi, Govanni Battista 407
Caesar, Gaius Julius 13, 180, 182
Caetani, Camillo 311, 315
Cain 284
Cajetan (Tommaso de Vio) 10, 29, 38–39
Calvin, John 308, 335
Calvinism, Calvinists 11, 15–16, 217–220, 222, 232, 313, 332–338, 340–341, 343, 346–347, 355, 357
Campeaux, William 27
Campion, Edmund 227–228
Canisius, Petrus 221
Cantelmo, Giacomo, cardinal 295, 298
Capellanus, Andreas 61, 73
Capito, Gaius Ateius 415
Capponi, Nicola 13, 180 see also Montano, Cola
Carafa, Decio, archbishop of Naples 313
Carmelites 20, 307, 315–325
Carrach, Johannes 403
Casanate, Marco Alegre de 321
Casani, José 323–324
Cassius Longinus, Gaius 13, 180, 198
Castel, Jean (de) 97, 99–100, 102, 112
Castro, Paolo di 262
Catiline, Lucius Sergius 185, 197
Cato the Elder 382
Cecil, William, lord of Burghley 228
Celsus 381–382
censor and censorship 18–20, 93–94, 104, 273–274, 277–278, 282, 286, 296–297, 305, 307, 312, 324–325, 419, 421
Charles I, king of England 412
Charles V, emperor of the Holy Roman Empire 29
Charles VI, king of France 99
Charles VII, king of France 122
Chastellain, Georges 100

Chirino de Salazar, Hernando   319
Christine de Pisan   17, 91–97, 99–108, 110–112
Christopherson, John, bishop of Chichester   231
Cicero, Marcus Tullius   58, 105, 189, 260–261, 372, 381–382
Cipelli, Giovanni Battista ('Egnazio')   231
Clamanges, Nicolas de   93, 157–158 *see also* Nicolas de Clamanges
Clark, William   382
Clemens VIII, pope   280, 311–312
Clément, Jacques   232
Clichtove, Josse   37, 43–45
Col, Gontier   92–93, 95, 106
Col, Pierre   93–96, 101, 103–104, 106–108, 110
Collins, Anthony   284, 286
Columella, Lucius Junius Moderatus   382
Conrad, Franz Carl   414
Conring, Herman   404
Constantine V Copronymus, emperor   225–226, 229
Constantius II, emperor   225–226, 229, 233, 235, 237
Corio, Bernardino   178, 181, 183, 193–195, 197, 201, 204
Cornazzano, Antonio   17, 183, 196–200, 204
Cornelius, pope   231
Costere, Frans de   221
councils (church)   11–12, 16, 18, 69, 73, 84
    Basel   12, 16, 18, 20, 117, 121–128, 130–131, 133, 135–137, 141, 144–145
    Constance   121, 152, 160
    Ferrara-Florence   128
    Nicaea   332
    Trent   19, 303, 305, 308–310, 325
council of the State   73–74, 77, 79
Cramer, Johann Ulrich von   413
Cranmer, Thomas   217
Crespin, François   321

Cristofaro, Giacinto de   290–292, 294–295, 297
Crivelli, Lodrisio   178
Croesus, king of Lydia   109
Cujas, Jacques   247, 419
Curtius Rufus, Quintus   382

D'Alembert, Jean le Rond   380
Daniel   235–236
Daniel de San Pedro OCarm   323
Dávila, Antonio   321
Debure, Guillaume-François   98
Decio, Filippo (Decius)   411, 419
Decius, emperor   230–231
Dentith, Simon   67
Descartes, René   287, 293–295
Diderot, Denis   380
Dido   109
Dionysius the Areopagite   282–283
Domenico, Giuseppe de   295
Domenico, Nicola de   295
Dominicans   12, 20, 119, 131, 135, 304, 307, 309–314
Domitianus, emperor   230–231
Doneau, Hugues   406
Donello, Ugo   262
Dorp, Maarten van   42
Drzymała, Kazimierz   332
Duarenus, Franciscus   263
Duby, Georges   27
Dudycz, Andrzej   341
Dulles, Avery   26
Duns Scotus, John   120 *see also* John Duns Scotus
Dury, John or Durie   227

Eadmer   119–120
Eck, Johannes   38, 155
Edward VI, king of England   217
Eisenhart, Johannes Friedrich   402, 414
Ekerman, Petrus   378, 380
Elijah   320–321
Elizabeth I, queen of England   13, 217–218, 220, 223–226, 228, 233, 235–238, 249–250
Emmen, Aquilin   131, 134

Empedocles 109
Erasmus of Rotterdam 42–45
Ernest II von Habsburg, duke of Austria 331
Este (family) 196
Estius, William (Guilielmus) 218
Eugene IV, pope 128
Eusebius of Caesarea 155, 231
Euw, Anton von 95
Evagrius Scholasticus 231

Fabian, pope 231
Feruffini, Giovanni 187–189
Ficino, Marsilio 40 *see also* Marsilio Ficino
Filelfo, Francesco 13, 17, 183, 185–193, 195, 199, 204, 384 *see also* Francesco Filelfo
Filide 109
Flacius Illyricus, Matthias 155–156
Fleming, John Vincent 98, 103
Foüet, Robert 221
Francesco Filelfo 13, 17, 183, 185–193, 195, 199, 204, 384
Francesco Giorgio 278
Francis I, king of France 95
Franciscans 12, 117, 119, 121, 123–125, 131, 145, 314
Francisco de Santa María OCarm 316–318, 320
François, Wim 218
Frederick III, elector of Saxony 39
Fusco, Pietro Di 291

Gabriel Biel 153–154, 162 *see also* Biel, Gabriel
Gager, William 249–251
Galathea 68
Galileo Galilei 274
Gallo Mauro 181, 201
Gansfort, Wessel 12, 20, 151–170
Ganymede 68 *see also* Helen
Gararanes, king of Persia 233
Gardie, Magnus Gabriel de la 385–386
Gassendi, Pierre 293–295
Gasser, Karen 62–63
Gaucourt, Charles de 100

Gebauer, Georg Christian 419
Geiler von Kaysersberg, Johannes 162, 169
Gennaro, Giuseppe Aurelio di 401, 405, 408
Gentili, Alberico 13–14, 17, 20, 245–246, 248–258, 260, 262–266
George of Trebizond 31
Gerson, Jean 12, 18, 92–95, 101, 106–109, 111, 151–154, 156–170
Gesner, Conrad 398
Giannelli, Basilio 291, 293
Giasone del Maino 411, 419
Gibbons, John 226
Gifford, Gilbert 224–225
Gilbert de la Porrée (Gilbert of Poitiers) 32
Giorgi, Agostino 285
Giovanni di Montenero 12, 123–127, 129–133, 137, 143, 145 *see also* Montenero, Giovanni di
Giovio, Paolo 181
Giustiniani, Benedetto 280, 282–283
Goldgar, Anne 405
Gómez Barrientos, Juan 322–323 *see also* Juan Gómez Barrientos OCarm
Gonzaga, Carlo 186, 189–190
Gonzaga, Guido 91
Gosia, Martino 413–414
Graffigny, Françoise de (Madame de Graffigny) 284
Gravina, Gianvincenzo 401
Gregory IX, pope 247
Gregory the Great 76
Gregory, Tullio 279–280
Grosseteste, Robert 38 *see also* Robert Grosseteste
Grotius, Hugo 411–412
Grunert, Frank 400
Gundling, Nicolaus Hieronymus 403

Hadrian, emperor 230–231
Hamel, Christopher de 95

NAME INDEX

Hartmann, Carmen Cardelle de 59–60, 65
Haubold, Christian Gottlieb 413
Hebe 68
Heineccius, Johann Gottlieb 420–421
Helen 68 *see also* Ganymede
Helmrath, Johannes 117
Heloise 109
Hemsterhuis, Siboldus 368
Henry I, duke of Guise 232
Henry II, king of England 75–76
Henry III, king of France 41, 232, 331
Henry VIII, king of England 217, 237
Herault, Didier (Desiderius Heraldus) 420
Heumann, Christoph 399, 402
Heumann, Johannes 402, 408, 410
Hicks, Eric 91, 93
Hoeck, Jacobus 152, 160, 163, 167–168
Hoffwenius, Petrus 375
Hommel, Carl Ferdinand 14, 18, 393–396, 402, 405–413, 415–425
Horn, Johann Friedrich 412
Horst, Ulrich 137
Hrotsvitha 71
Hugh of St Victor 59
Hugo, Gustav 395
Huneric, king of the Vandals 13, 229
Hus, Jan 157

Imbach, Ruedi 32
index
    congregation 19–20, 273–275, 277–279, 285–286, 296–297
    of forbidden books 19, 169, 274–275, 277–281, 286–287, 305, 314–315, 317–318, 320–321
Innocent XII, pope 323
inquisition (general) 151, 167, 169, 289–290, 297
    Spanish 19–20, 289, 303–307, 309–315, 317–322, 324–325
    Roman 19–20, 273–276, 287–291, 295–297
Irenaeus 118
Irnerius 411, 416
Isaiah 154, 233, 337

Jaktorowski, Szczęsny 341
Janninck, Conrad 323
Jean de Berry 96 *see also* Berry, Jean de
Jean de Meun 18, 92–94, 101–104, 106–107, 111–112 *see also* Meun, Jean de
Jean de Rouvroy 12, 121–126, 129–131, 134, 136 *see also* Rouvroy, Jean de
Jenichen, Gottlob August 402, 406
Jeremiah 233
Jeroboam, king of Northern Israel 49
Jerome 264–265
Jesuits 11, 15, 20, 218–219, 221–222, 226–227, 236, 280, 282, 284–285, 304, 307, 309–314, 316–324, 332, 335, 337–338, 340–351, 353–357
Job 140, 146
Johannes Buridan 41 *see also* Buridan, Johannes
John Duns Scotus 120 *see also* Duns Scotus, John
John I the Fearless, duke of Burgundy 92
John of Brussels 153–154 *see also* Mombaer, Johannes (Mauburnus)
John of Goch 157
John of Monzón 121
John of Palomar 121
John of Segovia 117, 119, 123–146
John of Wesel 152, 157
John XXIII, antipope 160
Jordanes 369

441

José de Jesús María OCarm   322
Juan de San Agustín   314
Juan Dionisio Portocarrero   319
Juan Gómez Barrientos OCarm   322–323 *see also* Gómez Barrientos, Juan
Julian the Apostate, emperor   230–231
Justinian I, emperor   14, 260, 262, 299, 381–382

Kalchbrenner, Petrus   377
Kamieniecki, Jan   332
Kant, Immanuel   410
Kappes, Christiaan W.   119
Kasten, Ingrid   60, 63
Kempf, Nicolas   169
Kestner, Heinrich   404
Krotowski, Jan   343, 345–346, 356

Labeo, Marcus Antistius   415
Labitte, Jacques   395
Lactantius   231, 260–262
Lagus, Conrad   406
Lambeck, Peter   396
Lampugnani, Giovanni Andrea   17, 180, 197–203
Lamy, Marielle   121
Lanckoroński, Stanisław   346
Landino, Cristoforo   193–195
Langlois, Ernest   95, 98
Lapidge, Michael   69, 71, 73
Lawn, Brian   33
Lazzeri, Pietro   274
Le Mire, Jean   221
Łęczycki, Mikołaj   356
Lefèvre d'Étaples, Jacques   31, 37, 45
Leibniz, Gottfried Wilhelm (Caesarini Fürsteneri)   398–399, 412
Leo I, pope   233
Leo III the Isaurian, emperor   225–226
Leo V the Armenian, emperor   226, 229
Lessius, Leonardus   218–219, 221, 309
Leszczyński, Andrzej   340

Leyser, Wilhelm   412
Licinius, emperor   230–231
Ligęza, Hermolaus   345
Lindberg, Bo   378, 382–383, 387
Lipenius, Martin   396
Livius, Titus   382
Loccenius, Johannes   376
Locke, John   228, 286
Loffredo, Mario   291
Loriot, Pierre   413
Lorris, Guillaume de   100
Louis II de Lorraine, cardinal of Guise   232
Louis VII, king of France   75
Lubieniecki, Andrzej (the Elder)   337, 339, 354–355
Lubieniecki, Krzysztof   340–341
Lucanus, Marcus Annaeus   70
Ludovico il Moro   178, 193, 195
Lull, Raymond   59
Luszcynska, Magdalena   333
Luther, Martin   29, 38–39, 43, 154–157, 162, 169–170, 308
Lutheranism, Lutherans   44, 152, 155–156, 334, 336, 340

Machiavelli, Niccolo   237, 254
Maclean, Ian   257
Magalotti, Lorenzo   369
Magistris, Giovanni De   291, 297–298
Magnus Maximus, emperor   230
Magnus, Johannes   369
Malatesta, Roberto   202
Malherbe, François de   406
Manasseh, king of Judah   233
Manilius   381–382
Manuzzi, Francesco Paolo   288–291, 293
Marsilio Ficino   40 *see also* Ficino, Marsilio
Martialis, Marcus Valerius   70
Martín de Jesús María OCarm   318
Martin V, pope   158
Martin, Hervé   158
Mary I, queen of England   218
Mary, queen of Scots   225, 236
Mascov, Gottfried   415, 419

Mattei, Pasquale De   284
Matthew, Toby   255–256
Maximianus, emperor   230
Maximinus Daza, emperor   230–231
Maximinus I Thrax   230–231
Mayans y Siscar, Gregorio   402
Mazo Karras, Ruth   28
McLaughlin, Mary   35, 39
Medea   109
Meiss, Millard   96
Melanchthon, Philip   155, 262
Meller, Katarzyna   332
Ménage, Gilles de   405–406
Merton, Robert   41
Merula, Giorgio   178
Meun, Jean de   18, 92–94, 101–104, 106–107, 111–112 see also Jean de Meun
Meyer, Christoph H. F.   37
Meyer, Ernst   377
Mikołajewski, Daniel   340, 357
Miller, Edward W.   155, 162, 165
Milton, John   412
Mofa, Mateo Gribaldi   407
Molina, Luis de   218–219, 309–312
Molinari, Innocenzo   285–286
Molinet, Jean   100
Mombaer, Johannes (Mauburnus)   153–154 see also John of Brussels
Montano, Cola   13, 180 see also Capponi, Nicola
Montemayor, Prudencio de   309
Montenero, Giovanni di   12, 123–127, 129–133, 137, 143, 145 see also Giovanni di Montenero
Montfaucon de Villars, Nicolas-Pierre-Henri   28
Montreuil, Jean de   91, 93–95, 101, 104–105, 110
Moretus, Jan   220
Morhof, Daniel Georg   396–399, 402, 407, 410
Moses   285
Mota y Aranda, Alonso de la   321
Moulin, Charles du   416
Muret, Marc Antoine   413

Naudé, Gabriel   398
Nebuchadnezzar II, king of Babylonia   229
Nero, emperor   230–231
Nettelbladt, Daniel   400, 402–403, 405, 408, 421–425
Neumann, Florian   372
Newton, Isaac   274
Niccoli, Niccolò   384–385
Niccolò de' Tedeschi   263 see also Panormitanus
Nicolas de Clamanges   93, 157–158 see also Clamanges, Nicolas de
Nicolas of Cusa   169
Nicolò Galitio   293–294
Niemojewski, Jakub   343, 347–350, 353–355, 357
Niemojewski, Jan   339, 342, 344, 350–351
Novikoff, Alex   66

O'Connell, Marvin   218
Ochino, Bernardino   412
Oelrich, Gerhard   403
Olai, Ericus   370
Oleari, Johann Gottlieb   403
Olgiati, Gerolamo   180–181, 197
Omodei, Signorolo de   417
Oosterga, Cyprianus Regnerus ab   412
Oosterhoff, Richard J.   158
Opaliński, Andrzej   346
Origenes   109
Ory, François (Osius Aurelius)   419
Osbat, Luciano   298
Ossona, Giovanni   186, 191–192
Ost, Heidrun   109
Ostorodt, Krzysztof   340–341, 357
Ostrogski, Konstanty   340
Ostroróg, Jan   345
Ostrowski, Stanisław   337, 339
Ovidius Naso, Publius   107, 374

Pachamac   286
Palmskiöld, Erik   376
Panormitanus   263 see also Niccolò de' Tedeschi
Panziroli, Guido   401

Papenbroeck, Daniel van   322–324
Papinianus, Aemilius   264–265
Paré, Gérard   99
Parsons, Robert   226
Patrizi, Francesco   19, 273, 278–283, 297
Paul V, pope   312–313
Paul, apostle   265, 348–350, 353
Pauli, Carl Friedrich   418
Pazzi, Iacopo   200
Pedro de la Concepción OCarm   322–323
Pedullà, Gabriele   179
Pelagius   308
Pérez, Antonio   314
Peroz I, king of the Sasanian Empire   233
Peter, apostle   289
Peters, Edward M.   42
Petrarca   91
Petronius Arbiter, Gaius   370
Petrus Hispanus   31
Philip II, king of Spain   29, 238
Philip III, king of Spain   311, 315
Philip IV, king of Spain   306
Philip V, king of Spain   324
Philipp, landgrave of Hesse   412
Piccolomini, Francesco   261
Pico della Mirandola, Giovanni   10, 25–27, 29, 38, 46
Pico, Paolo   280
Pierre d'Ailly   92–94 see also Ailly, Pierre d'
Pilkington, James   234
Pius V, pope   218, 228
Pius IX, pope   122
Plantin, Christopher   220
Plato   58, 260–261, 278, 281–282
Plinius   382
Plotzek, Joachim   95
Plutarch   260
Poel, Marc van der   44
Polanco, Juan Alonso de   221
Polish Brethren / Unitarians   11, 332–346, 350–351, 354–356
Poliziano, Angelo   200
Polyphemus   68

Pomponius Mela   382
Porcher, Pierre   123–125, 130–131, 134, 144–145
Possevino, Antonio   282
Powodowski, Hieronim   338–339, 343–344, 351, 356–357
Premierfait, Laurent de   92
Provano, Prospero   340
Przylepski, Jan   343
Pufendorf, Samuel (Severinus de Monzambano)   412
Pütter, Johann Stephan   403
Pygmalion   111

Quintilian   382

Raabe, Justus   342, 344, 351, 354
Radziwiłł, Jerzy   345
Radziwiłł, Krzysztof   340
Radzymiński, Adrian   342–343
Rainolds, John   13–14, 17, 20, 248–258, 262–266
Ranke, Friedrich   64
Rao, Ennio   386
Ray, John   385
Rebhan, Johann   415
Redanus, Petrus   321
Reed, Thomas   60, 65–66
Regio, Enrico   294
Reiss, Edmund   63
Repgen, Tilman   424
Ricchini, Agostino   285–287
Ricci, Seymour de   98
Riga, Petrus   73
Robert Grosseteste   38 see also Grosseteste, Robert
Roche Fontenilles, Bernard de la   131
Roffredo de Beneventano   413
Rosito, Carlo   291, 297–298
Rosweyde, Heribert   322
Rota, Lorenzo   202
Rouvroy, Jean de   12, 121–126, 129–131, 134, 136 see also Jean de Rouvroy
Rudbeck, Olof (the Elder)   15, 367–377, 381–388

444

Rudbeckius, Johannes 368
Rueil, Jean du 95, 98

Sagax, Landolfus 229
Saint-Amour, Guillaume de 107
Sala, Bornio da 188
Salcedo, Jerónimo 314
Sallo, Denis de 405–406
Sallust 184–185, 382
Salomon 229
Salutati, Coluccio 182
Sangro, Raimondo di 19, 273, 283–286, 297
Sansevero 286
Sapieha, Leo 358
Saragoza, Pedro Juan 278–279, 281–282
Sarnicki, Stanisław 335
Saumaise (Salmasius), Claude 412, 420
Savigny, Friedrich Carl von 395
Schaff, Philipp 157
Scheffer, Johan (father of Johannes Schefferus) 369
Schefferus, Johannes 15, 367, 369–371, 376, 381–382, 384–388
Scheurl, Christoph 38
scholasticism and scholastic 26, 29–32, 35–37, 42–43, 57, 60, 62–67, 83, 85, 132, 142, 146, 153, 158–159, 166, 281, 349, 353, 355, 359
Schooten, Frans van 383
Schott, August Friedrich 404
Schulthess, Peter 32
Scipio 182
Sebastián de San Pablo OCarm 323
Selchow, Johann Christian von 404
Selden, Johan 411–412
Sellius, Gottfried 420
Seneca the Elder 42
Senkenberg, Heinrich Christian von 413, 418
Septimius Severus, emperor 230–231
Serenius, Jacob 380
Sersale, Geronimo 19, 286
Severus Alexander, emperor 230

Severus II, emperor 230
Sforza (family) 177, 179–181, 183, 197, 201–202, 204
Sforza, Bianca Maria 177
Sforza, Francesco 17, 177–178, 180, 185–186, 193–199
Sforza, Galeazzo Maria 13, 180, 200–201, 204
Sforza, Gian Galeazzo Maria 181, 183, 196–197, 202
Shapur I, king of the Sasanian Empire 230
Shelley, Richard 224–225
Sigismund Augustus, king of Poland 331
Sigismund III Vasa, king of Poland 346
Sigismund, emperor 121
Sigonio, Carlo 401
Silber, Eucario 25
Silvestre de la Asumpción OCarm 321
Simonetta, Giovanni 178, 193–195
Sixtus IV, pope 156
Skytte, Johan 369
Śmiglecki, Marcin 340
Socrates Scholasticus 231
Sonnius, Michael 220
Sotberg, Erik 380
Sotomayor, Antonio de 319
Sozomen 231
Spoerhase, Carlos 416
Stancaro, Francesco 333
Standonck, Jean or Jan 153–154
Stapleton, Thomas 13, 16, 20, 217–227, 229–238
Statorius, Piotr (the Younger) 337, 339, 343
Stein, Peter 415
Stevin, Simon 373
Stiernhielm, Georg 387
Stoiński, Jan 356
Stolle, Gottlieb 397, 402, 407
Stotz, Peter 60
Struve, Burkhard Gothelf 396, 407, 415
Stryk, Samuel 407
Suárez, Francisco 236

445

Sutton, Robert B.   42
Swift, Jonathan   405
Symes, Carol   71
Syndikus, Anette   400

Tacitus   238
Tantalus   380
Tarquinius Superbus, king of Rome   13, 180
Taverna, Gabriele   186, 192
Taylor, Andrew   27
Tazbir, Janusz   332
Telesio, Bernardino   294
Tempier, Étienne   40
Teodoret of Cyrus   224, 231
Terence   70–71, 78
Terentius (*dux*)   224
Tertullian   266
Tesnière, Marie-Hélène   96, 109, 111
Theodosius II, emperor   262
Theophrastus   105
Thomas Aquinas   119 *see also* Aquinas, Thomas
Thomasius, Christian   11, 45–46, 394, 403, 410
Thomasius, Jakob   407
Tignonville, Guillaume de   101
Toland, John   284
Toledo, Francisco   281
Tomás de Jesús OCarm   321
Tomás de San Vicente OCarm   317
Torquemada, Juan de   124, 126–130, 132–135, 137, 140–146
Torres, Luis   318
Trier, Johann Wolfgang   420–421
Tworek, Stanisław   332, 338

Ullmann, Carl   156
Ulpian   9, 394
university   10, 27, 30–31, 33–36, 38, 41–43, 46, 154, 304, 312, 316, 367–368, 371, 377, 381–384, 386, 388, 402, 414, 424–425
    Abo   383
    Alcalá   310–311
    Cologne   157
    Douai   218–219, 225, 235

Göttingen   419
Heidelberg   157
Leipzig   394
Louvain / Leuven   218–219, 309, 323
Lund   383
Oxford   249, 256
Paris   40, 121, 151–153
Salamanca   310–311
Tübingen   153
Uppsala   15, 21, 367–369, 371–372, 376–377, 382–388
Vilnius   340
Wittenberg   37

Valens   13, 224–226, 229, 233
Valentini, Andrea   91
Valentinianus II, emperor   230
Valerianus, emperor   230
Varro   382
Venus   110–111
Verelius, Olof   368, 370–371, 373, 376, 385–386
Vergil   70
Veronese, Guarino   182
Vesalius   375
Victor IV, antipope   73–75
Vigelius, Nicolaus   406
Ville, Nicolas De   221
Vimercate, Gaspare da   194–195
Viracocha   286
Visconti, Carlo   180–181, 197
Visconti, Filippo Maria   177, 180, 185, 187–189
Vita, Vittore di   229
Vitruvius   382
Voltaire   274

Waquet, Françoise   383
Warszewicki, Stanisław   344
Weijers, Olga   31
Weiß, Marian   68–69
Westcott, Sebastian   224–225
Whitaker, William   227
Whitman, Jon   64
Wieacker, Franz   423
Wieling, Abraham   395
Wijffels, Alain   266

Winrich of Trier   79
Winterfeld, Paul von   71
Wojciech of Kalisz   342
Wolan, Andrzej   335
Wolff, Christian   399, 422
Wolff, Mathias   221
Wujek, Jakub   338, 347, 349, 354–355, 357
Wyclif, John   157

Yazdgard I, king of the Sasanian Empire   232

Yazdgard II, king of the Sasanian Empire   233

Zamorano, Rodrigo   233
Zancani, Alberto   189
Zasius, Ulrich   416
Zborowska, Elżbieta   341
Zedekiah, king of Judah   233
Ziemowicz, Krzysztof   340
Zumel, Francisco   309–310
Zwingli, Huldrych   155
Zygrovius, Jan   337